Quantitative Methods for Assessing the Effects of Non-Tariff Measures and Trade Facilitation

Quantitative Methods for Assessing the Effects of Non-Tariff Measures and Trade Facilitation

Philippa Dee
Australian National University, Australia

Michael Ferrantino
US International Trade Commission, USA

World Scientific

NEW JERSEY • LONDON • SINGAPORE • BEIJING • SHANGHAI • HONG KONG • TAIPEI • CHENNAI • TOKYO

Published by

APEC Secretariat
35, Heng Mui Keng Terrace
Singapore 119616

and

World Scientific Publishing Co. Pte. Ltd.
5 Toh Tuck Link, Singapore 596224
USA office: 27 Warren Street, Suite 401-402, Hackensack, NJ 07601
UK office: 57 Shelton Street, Covent Garden, London WC2H 9HE

Library of Congress Cataloging-in-Publication Data
Quantitative methods for assessing the effects of non-tariff measures and trade facilitation / [edited by] Philippa Dee, Michael Ferrantino.
p. cm.
"Papers ... originally presented at an APEC capacity-building workshop on quantitative methods for assessing non-tariff measures and trade facilitation, held in Bangkok on 8–10 October 2003"--Ackn.
Includes bibliographical references and index.
ISBN-13 978-981-256-051-3 -- ISBN 981-256-051-3
1. Non-tariff trade barriers--Mathematical models--Congresses. 2. Tariff--Mathematical models--Congresses. 3. Import quotas--Mathematical models--Congresses. 4. Foreign trade regulation--Mathematical models--Congresses. 5. Commercial policy--Mathematical models--Congresses. I. Dee, Philippa S. II. Ferrantino, Michael J.

HF1430.Q36 2005
382'.5'015195--dc22 2004043135

British Library Cataloguing-in-Publication Data
A catalogue record for this book is available from the British Library.

APEC#204-CT-04.1

CONTENTS

ACKNOWLEDGMENTS

The papers themselves were originally presented at an APEC capacity-building workshop on quantitative methods for assessing non-tariff measures and trade facilitation, held in Bangkok on 8–10 October 2003. The workshop was conducted as an Australia-United States joint project, co-organized by the United States International Trade Commission and the Australian Productivity Commission, with financial support from the APEC Trade and Investment Liberalization Fund. The editorial staff at World Scientific have made it possible for us to disseminate the results of this conference to a wider audience. We are especially grateful to both Juliet Lee and Chean Chian. At the USITC, Cecelia N. Allen did the bulk of converting individual papers in preparing the camera-ready copy. Ted Wilson came to the rescue on numerous issues of style and presentation which were essential to make the final product look like a real book.

The workshop organisers would like to acknowledge and thank Mr. Xianguo Tong, and his team at the APEC Secretariat for their extensive logistical assistance and moral support, especially Belinda Chok and Jacqueline Tan. Joining the organizers as Project Overseers who shepherded the project through the APEC process were Arnold Jorge of the Australian Department of Foreign Affairs and Trade (DFAT), who served as chair of the APEC Market Access Group during the time the project was under consideration, and Barbara Norton of the Office of the United States Trade Representative, as well as Chris Brettingham-Moore of DFAT.

We also benefited enormously from the assistance of Bijit Bora (WTO Secretariat), Christopher Findlay (Australian National University), Will Martin (World Bank), Marcus Noland (International Food Policy Research Institute and Institute for International Economics), and Robert Scollay (University of Auckland Business School), who helped us both to identify the community of researchers at whom the conference should be aimed and to determine the final program.

Philippa Dee was Assistant Commissioner at the Australian Productivity Commission when the project was conceived. She is grateful to senior management at the Commission for their moral support, and to Duc Nguyen-Hong for assistance at the workshop. We also benefited greatly from the regional contacts of researchers at the Asia-Pacific School of Economics and Government at Australian National University in obtaining contact details for participants. Pat Thomas of USITC handled an enormous volume of pre-conference communication of all types for us, and Jennifer Jacobson created an attractive Web presence for the conference information and papers.

Mr. Kent Prachumsuk of the Banyan Tree Hotel, Bangkok, and his staff deserve special thanks for making the conference itself particularly enjoyable and successful.

We would like to thank the appropriate parties at the OECD for consenting to the use of Bijit Bora's paper, at the World Bank for the permission to use the paper by Alan Deardorff and Robert Stern, and the Journal of Economic Integration for permission to use the paper by Thomas Hertel, Terrie Walmsley, and Ken Itakura.

The editors would also like to commend to readers the work of Johannes Moenius in quantifying the effects of technical standards. His excellent work in this area was represented at the workshop, but unfortunately could not be included in this conference volume.

The views expressed in these papers are solely those of the authors. In particular, they do not represent the views of the U.S. International Trade Commission, the Australian Productivity Commission, or any of their Commissioners.

INTRODUCTION

Philippa Dee
Australian National University[1]

Michael Ferrantino
U.S. International Trade Commission[2]

Non-tariff measures are pervasive. In the area of merchandise trade, although tariffs have fallen worldwide, there has been no shortage of bureaucratic imagination in conceiving new non-tariff measures, or in turning existing regulatory instruments to protectionist ends. In the area of services trade, there is also a growing realisation that domestic regulatory regimes designed to address legitimate market failures may have incidental but unwarranted effects on services trade.

Non-tariff measures are difficult to quantify. Tariff levels are published in tariff schedules, and while these can be large, cumbersome and difficult to read, the numbers are there. Furthermore, they are there in an economically significant form. Tariff levels give the extent to which import prices have to rise, and if the domestic good and the import are perfect substitutes, they also give the extent to which the price of the domestic good can rise. By contrast, non-tariff measures are often regulatory, with no immediate 'number' attached that captures their economic significance.

Non-tariff measures are politically sensitive. To the extent that such measures may arise through the lobbying activity of vested interests, these interests benefit from a lack of scrutiny. Measures that are difficult to quantify may also be less transparent, which helps to avoid public discussion. When such measures do receive public attention, their direct impact on trade may be less clear to the public than for easily quantified measures such as tariffs. This makes it more likely that ideas such as 'fairness', 'self-sufficiency' or 'legitimate cultural interests,' which do not always have measurable counterparts, will take a

---

[1] Dr. Philippa Dee is currently a visiting Fellow at the Australian-Japan Research Centre, Asia Pacific School of Economics and Government, The Australian National University.

[2] Michael Ferrantino is with the Office of Economics, U.S. International Trade Commission. The views expressed in this article are those of the author. They are not the views of the U.S. International Trade Commission (USITC) as a whole nor any of its individual Commissioners. The author may be contacted *via* email at *michael.ferrantino@usitc.gov*.

relatively large role in the public discussion of such measures, while analysis of their economic effects takes a back seat.

The purpose of this volume is to bring together the 'state of the art' in quantifying non-tariff measures. The aim is to facilitate the hard economic analysis that will help to facilitate public understanding of the effects of these measures. One payoff will be that when costs and benefits are discussed, the interests of consumers as well as producers will be taken into account. Another payoff is that when the liberalisation of non-tariff measures is discussed in domestic or international forums, the discussion can focus on what is important, not just on what is easily measurable.

Most of the chapters of the book show how particular techniques can be used to analyse particular non-tariff barriers or trade facilitation measures. This material includes both results pertaining to the effects of public policies and analytical material. The final section of the book is devoted to 'aids to methodology', and contains more detailed material which goes in-depth into certain of the practical techniques involved in preparing quantitative analyses of trade policy and conveying them to policymakers.

The remainder of this chapter describes how the quantification chapters are organised. In the process, it gives some overall guidance as to which quantification techniques are likely to be fruitful for analysing which sorts of non-tariff or trade facilitation measures.

In his introductory chapter, **Bijit Bora** notes that the key analytical problem is (i) identifying non-tariff measures and (ii) developing a tractable taxonomy that allows for a coherent and robust analysis of their effects. His analytical conclusion is not optimistic – non-tariff measures cannot readily be defined, and existing taxonomies and databases are not helpful. Yet his policy prescription is both pragmatic and pertinent – focus on what is known, choose the appropriate response (*e.g.* lay down principles that encourage transparency and predictability, or ask for higher level obligations), and choose the appropriate forum (*e.g.* multilateral or otherwise).

The approach to selecting the policy content for this volume has been equally pragmatic. The selection has been based on available analysis of the non-tariff policy topics that are currently being negotiated in multilateral and regional forums. The net has been cast widely, and the policy topics include:

- quantitative restrictions;
- trade facilitation;
- anti-dumping;
- rules of origin;

- services trade barriers;
- domestic regulatory regimes; and
- technical measures (*e.g.* standards).

The techniques used to analyse these non-tariff measure range from the descriptive to the highly analytical:

- data sources;
- frequency counts or coverage ratios;
- price gap measures;
- quantity measures (*e.g.* gravity model measures);
- partial equilibrium modelling;
- computable general equilibrium (CGE) modelling.

The geographical focus of the papers is generally, but not exclusively, on the Asia-Pacific region.

In many cases, the most time-intensive part of the analysis is simply obtaining the necessary qualitative information about the non-tariff barriers or trade facilitation measures that apply. However, there are several relatively comprehensive databases of qualitative information about non-tariff measures affecting both goods and services trade, including the National Trade Estimate Report on Foreign Trade Barriers, prepared annually by the Office of the U.S. Trade Representative, the European Union's Market Access Database, and the World Trade Organization's (WTO) Trade Policy Reviews. In part I, the paper by **Diane Manifold** and **William Donnelly** shows how this information can be harvested in a systematic manner into a single database, with a consistent classification of products and trade measures, for use in subsequent economic analysis. The resulting database contains information on formal government regulations (*e.g.* customs regulations, import licensing, quotas and prohibitions) and policies (*e.g.* investment-related measures, services trade barriers), as well as informal barriers and practices (*e.g.* non-transparency, arbitrary enforcement, corruption). The resulting database is text-based, but can be interrogated to produce frequency counts of different types of measures affecting particular goods or services categories. In the section on methodological aids, **Robert Koopman** describes the key principles for successfully using this type of data and its subsequent analysis (including *via* modelling) to inform the policy-making process.

Also in the section on methodological aids, a related presentation by **Vlad Manole** describes the World Integrated Trade Solutions (WITS) software, developed by the World Bank. This software is a user-friendly way of accessing and combining four types of data on merchandise trade – import and export flows, applied tariffs, WTO tariff bindings, and some qualitative information in non-tariff barriers. These underlying data come from the Comtrade database on trade flows developed by the UN Statistics Division, the TRAINS database of trade flows, applied tariffs and non-tariff barriers developed by UNCTAD, the WTO's Integrated Database of applied tariffs and trade, and the WTO Consolidated Tariff Schedules, which contain tariff bindings. The non-tariff measures in the UNCTAD TRAINS database include price and quantity control measures (including export restraint arrangements), automatic licensing measures (including import monitoring), monopolistic measures (*e.g.* a single channel for imports) and technical measures (*e.g.* sanitary and phytosanitary measures, standards). The user must obtain access to the underlying databases independently, but the WITS software for accessing and interrogating the data can be downloaded without charge from *http://wits.worldbank.org*. The presentation shows in detail how to use the software.

Firm-level surveys are another way of obtaining raw qualitative information about non-tariff or trade facilitation measures. The paper by **Ronald Fischer** ably demonstrates some of the strengths and weaknesses of this approach. He surveyed the executives responsible for exports in a representative sample of 15 Chilean agricultural and manufacturing firms. He found that even though the executives had experienced non-tariff barriers, they were unable to compute the effect of those barriers in reducing the margins on their exports – indeed, they were barely able to do an ordinal comparison of the effects of non-tariff barriers in different countries. Nevertheless, the paper yielded some interesting policy insights. One was that administrative procedures are, from the point of view of exporters, one of the most effective barriers to trade. Another is that Chilean exporters found Brazil significantly more protectionist than other Latin American countries, even though Chile is an associate member of Mercosur, a preferential trade area that includes Brazil. These findings suggest that trade facilitation may be even more important than reducing non-tariff barriers, from the perspective of merchandise exporters. They also demonstrate that a preferential trading agreement need not neutralise the non-tariff barriers imposed by a particular member.

Several papers use techniques to quantify the benefits of trade facilitation measures. The paper by **John Wilson**, **Catherine Mann** and **Tsunehiro Otsuki** looks at four different dimensions of trade facilitation – port efficiency (both water and air transport), the customs environment (prevalence of hidden import barriers and bribes), the regulatory environment (transparency and control of corruption), and what they call services sector infrastructure (Internet access and use). Index measures of these policy dimensions of trade facilitation were available from existing studies. The authors entered these index measures into a gravity model of bilateral merchandise trade flows between countries, in order to estimate econometrically the link between trade facilitation and trade flows, holding other factors constant. Consistent with a standard gravity model specification, key other factors were the sizes and per capita income levels of the exporting and importing countries, and the geographic distance between them. The authors also controlled for the effects of preferential trade arrangements, language similarity and adjacency. In a separate presentation, **Tsunehiro Otsuki** explains the methodology in more detail. The results suggest that a country can expand its exports significantly, not just from the trade facilitation efforts of its partner countries, but also from its own trade facilitation efforts. The paper elaborates on the WTO initiatives in place to further these trade facilitation efforts.

The paper by **Peter Walkenhorst** and **Tadashi Yasui** instead uses multiregional computable general equilibrium analysis to quantify the economy-wide gains in various regions from trade facilitation efforts in specific sectors. The authors undertake a wide-ranging and thorough review of the recent literature that reports measures of the size of trade transactions costs (TTCs) in different sectors. This review is of interest in its own right. The size of the estimates are not always linked explicitly to particular policy measures, as was the case in the previous paper. But the size of these overall estimates define the scope of potential trade facilitation efforts (*i.e.*, they define the size of the shocks to the CGE model). Importantly, the authors distinguish two kinds of effects. They argue that indirect trade transactions costs, such as longer border waiting times, are best thought of as resulting in a wasting away of the product being shipped (the so-called 'iceberg' representation of TTCs). But the direct transactions costs, such as form-filling, while being a cost to the exporter or importer, are a source of income for the form fillers. These costs are best modelled as being tax-like, a recognition that they have a large transfer component rather than a wastage component. The distinction is crucial, because costs that lead to wastage will have much larger economy-wide effects than costs with a large transfer component (a point that is also highly relevant to CGE modelling of services trade barriers). Accordingly, they argue that previous CGE results of the effects of trade facilitation may have been overstated. Their distinction also has direct implications for where policy priorities in trade facilitation should lie, namely, in reducing the indirect costs.

The difficulties of obtaining raw qualitative information about non-tariff measures are arguably more acute in services than in goods. The best single database of services trade measures is the WTO's database of services trade commitments made by members under the General Agreement on Trade in Services (GATS). However, the GATS agreement takes a positive list approach to scheduling commitments, which means the database contains useful information about the trade barriers that member countries wish to retain only in those services sectors that the member countries chooses to list. Other services sectors may be rife with barriers, but if they are not listed, then there is no requirement for members to reveal information about them. The paper by **Philippa Dee** describes other useful sources of qualitative information about services trade barriers.

Services also differ from (at least some) goods in another important respect – services are typically highly differentiated, and there can be no presumption that the services produced by domestic firms are perfect substitutes, either for services traded cross-border (whether literally cross-border, or *via* the temporary movement of either the producer or the consumer to the territory of the other), or for services provided domestically by affiliates of foreign firms. Were these services perfect substitutes, price differences between them would reflect artificial barriers to trade. Because they are not perfect substitutes, the domestic-import price comparisons that are sometimes used in goods trade as overall measures of the effects of all trade barriers (tariff and otherwise) cannot be used. Instead, the counterfactual – what the price of domestic services would be in the absence of trade barriers – needs to be constructed from an econometric model of what determines domestic prices. The paper by **Alan Deardorff** and **Robert Stern** shows theoretically what the challenges are in implementing this research strategy. The papers by **Philippa Dee** and **Duc Nguyen-Hong** show, in increasing detail, how the strategy has been implemented in practice. First, qualitative information about services trade barriers and associated domestic regulatory regimes is converted into a quantitative index of trade restrictiveness. Then a sector-specific partial equilibrium model of what determines price (or some other measure of domestic economic performance) is constructed, and used to estimate econometrically the effects that the index of trade restrictions or regulations has on performance, holding all other factors constant. In one sense, this is a generalisation, for a single services sector, of the gravity model approach to quantifying trade impacts for the economy as a whole. The paper by Dee also discusses the extent to which such econometric work can yield information about whether the services trade barriers or regulatory measures create rents (with associated transfers from consumers to producers) or add to real resource costs. This is a similar issue to whether trade transactions costs are transfers or wastage.

As noted, services may be traded in a number of ways, one of which is *via* the services supplier moving temporarily to the territory of the consumer. This mode of services trade poses particular policy challenges, because of its relationship with domestic immigration and employment policies – policies that have traditionally been seen as the sole prerogative of domestic governments, and not the subject of trade negotiation. Yet many in the developing world are convinced that there would be significant 'gains from trade' to be had by the temporary movement of either skilled personnel (*e.g.* computer programmers) or unskilled personnel (*e.g.* agricultural workers, construction workers or maids) from developing to developed countries. The paper by **Soumodip Sarkar** describes the main barriers affecting such trade. These include Economic Needs Tests and labour certification tests, as well as requirements for visas and work permits. The paper employs back-of-the-envelop calculations using estimates of current wage differentials to quantify the gains from an expansion in the temporary movement of workers in the ICT industry. Critical to the estimated size and distribution of such gains is the assumptions made about the productivity levels of the workers before and after they move, and the remittances they make while they are away. In Sarkar's paper, the gains from a relatively small expansion in such trade are very large.

Several papers use techniques to quantify the effects of import or export quotas. The paper by **Ronald Babula**, **Suchada Langley**, **Agapi Somwaru** and **Shiva Makki** examines the effects of a wheat import quota (similar to that applied to imports of certain Canadian wheat into the United States during the year ending 11 September 1995) on the US markets for wheat and wheat products. The authors note that while structural partial equilibrium models are well-equipped to compare the static equilibria before and after a shock, they are not well-equipped to address the speed or direction of the dynamic path from one to the other. Vector autogregression (VAR) methods involve econometrically estimating a reduced form system with a rich dynamic specification. While this does not give direct estimates of the structural supply and demand elasticities that determine the way that shocks are passed down the production chain, it does give a clear picture of the resulting dynamic adjustment. A drawback of traditional VAR methods is that, while they allow for a rich lag structure, they do not allow for contemporaneous correlation among the endogenous variables. The authors combine Bernanke's structural VAR approach, which uses prior notions of causality to impose structure on the contemporaneous correlations, with directed acyclic graph (DAG) analysis, which is a statistical way of choosing among competing alternatives. After estimating the resulting system, the authors find that each percent decline in the quantity of wheat would elicit a 0.7 per cent rise in the wheat price and a 0.3 per cent rise in the flour price, without having much effect on the markets for bread, cookies, mixes or cereals further downstream.

By contrast, the paper by **Joseph Francois** and **Dean Spinanger** takes a structural approach to evaluating the effects of the export quotas on textile and clothing trade that are currently in place under the Agreement on Textiles and Clothing (ATC, the successor to the MultiFibre Arrangement). Beginning with a standard import demand system, and using bilateral trade data on textile and clothing trade, underlying tariffs, and quota coverage under the ATC, the authors develop non-linear least squares estimates of the tax equivalents of ATC quota restrictions on bilateral trade. They compare these estimates to earlier estimates for the years since the inception of the ATC, to gauge the extent to which the ATC has actually led to quota liberalization.

Three papers provide quite different examples of the use of price comparison techniques for quantifying the effects of non-tariff measures. **Mitsuyo Ando** estimates the tariff equivalents of both core and non-core non-tariff measures using price differentials between the CIF price of imported goods and the domestic producer price of the domestic substitute at the 4 digit level. This contrasts with other approaches that make comparisons at other points in the distribution chain (*e.g.* comparing the domestic retail price with an overseas reference price of the same good). Core non-tariff measures are price and quantity control measures, and non-core measures are automatic licensing measures, monopolistic measures and technical measures (based on the UNCTAD classification system). The authors use the price comparisons (net of tariff levels) to estimate overall tariff equivalents of both types of non-tariff measures across a range of commodities and countries. They then econometrically estimate a relationship between these overall tariff equivalents and by-type frequency ratios (with other control variables), and use this estimated relationship to decompose the overall tariff-equivalents into price effects by type of measure. The authors find that both core and non-core measures afford some degree of protection. In particular, developed countries with low general tariffs, or with low preferential tariffs under a number of free trade agreements, tend to use non-core measures significantly to protect domestic producers.

Judith Dean, **Robert Feinberg**, **Michael Ferrantino** and **Rodney Ludema** examine NTMs using city-level retail price data. Thus, their price comparisons take place at a later point in the distribution chain than those in Ando's paper. In their theoretical discussion, these retail prices are considered to be composites of the prices of imported and domestically produced goods. Further, the prices include distribution costs (*e.g.* wholesale and retail margins) and transport costs. A number of simplifying assumptions permit the theoretical model to be estimated using the available data. The model is estimated using a vector of city-specific characteristics that are expected to influence markups, exploiting the fact that markup activities involve labor-intensive services whose price characteristics across countries can be measured. Additional variables include measures of distance (to proxy transport costs), tariffs, country-specific dummy variables to control for the presence of non-tariff measures, and product-specific dummy variables to control for unobservable product-specific effects. The method yields estimates of the tariff-equivalents of non-tariff measures which vary across sectors and regions.

Finally, **Jungho Yoo** shows how price comparisons can be used to calculate nominal and effective rates of protection afforded by tariffs and non-tariff barriers together. The paper gives a good outline of these concepts. The nominal rate of protection is essentially the same as a tariff-equivalent. The effective rate recognises that the protection afforded a domestic industry by a tariff or non-tariff barrier on its output can be eroded by tariffs or non-tariff barriers on its inputs, and corrects the measure of protection accordingly. The author describes a major initiative undertaken within the Korean bureaucracy to estimate nominal and effective rates in a way that captured both tariffs and non-tariff barriers. It involved a survey of producers in 6,547 establishments about the domestic and border prices of 766 products (defined at the 8 digit level) in the mining and manufacturing sectors. Producers were asked to pick three specifications of a product they produced and to supply both the domestic price (before indirect taxes) and a border price (a c.i.f. price for import-competing goods, or an f.o.b. price for export goods). The author reports that the effective rates of protection were found to differ widely across industries, and for some they were negative. The author wonders whether the large protective tax in place at the time was worth the resulting incentive structure, which could have been far from what was intended. The paper demonstrates how a research program can be organised to undertake a comprehensive quantification of tariffs and non-tariff barriers, with major implications for the transparency of domestic policy-making.

The paper by **Antoni Estevadeordal** and **Kati Souminen** addresses an issue that is of increasing importance as preferential trading arrangements proliferate. Rules of origin (RoOs) establish criteria by which a commodity will be treated as 'originating' within the area, and hence eligible for preferential treatment (though RoOs are also required to establish origin in non-preferential trade). If no preferential RoOs were established, there would be an incentive to bring commodities into the area through the country with the lowest external tariff, and then transship them duty-free to other parties as 'originating' products. Preferential RoOs are designed to prevent such trade deflection. If the criteria to be 'originating' are set very tightly, a substantial amount of content from within the area may be required before a product qualifies as 'originating'. This may diminish the trade-enhancing effect of the preferential treatment. It may also distort input choices away from third parties in order to ensure compliance with the rules of origin. Finally, the combination of effects may distort foreign direct investment choices. The paper does not go as far as quantifying these trade- and investment-distorting effects. But it gives a comprehensive discussion of the issues, describes the different RoOs now in common use, and identifies which characteristics of them are likely to reduce their distorting effects. The authors demonstrate that the extent of distortion does not necessarily follow from the complexity or simplicity of the measures. Further, there are important interactions – despite the apparent convergence towards a few ostensibly similar models for preferential RoOs, even slight differences between them can have important implications for firms' outsourcing and investment decisions, and potentially lead to the rise of exclusive trade- and investment-distorting hubs. The authors argue that the current Doha Round of WTO multilateral negotiations presents a timely opportunity to attack the problems, eg through harmonisation of non-preferential RoOs, and commitments to harmonise non-preferential RoOs.

The paper by **Tianshu Chu** and **Thomas Prusa** documents the rise of another form of non-tariff protection, through anti-dumping action. The paper notes that the number of anti-dumping cases targeting China's exports is high both in absolute terms and relative to the value of China's exports, that the cases cover a wide range of sectors, and that many of these cases are associated with high levels of duty. The paper analyses some of the institutional characteristics of these cases. A simple econometric analysis suggests an association between anti-dumping cases filed on Chinese exports and inward FDI flows into China.

The final three papers are CGE studies that use as inputs some of the available estimates of the direct, first round impact of non-tariff measures on prices or other aspects of performance, and quantify the flow-on effects and overall implications for the economic well-being of producers, consumers, and economies as a whole. **Scott Bradford** uses price gap measures as his overall measure of the height of tariff and non-tariff barriers on OECD economies. The discussion in this section of the paper complements that in the above papers on price gaps measures. The work that Bradford draws on uses retail price data, along with direct data on distribution margins, transport costs and indirect taxes from input-output sources, and uses a level of product classification where perfect substitution is more likely to be a reasonable assumption, in order to generate estimates of overall price gaps between goods in different countries. Finally, it corrects for the effects of tariffs in order to have a measure of the tariff equivalent of non-tariff barriers. Bradford concludes this section with a discussion of the strengths and weaknesses of the resulting estimates, a comparison with other studies, and a discussion of the trade policies that are likely to lie behind the price gaps. Finally, Bradford reports on the welfare results from eliminating non-tariff barriers in a CGE model that allows for increasing returns to scale and dynamic adjustment of the capital stock. Bradford assumes that all non-tariff barriers are tax-like, rather than creating waste or adding to the real resource cost of doing business. Accordingly, he treats them in the same way as tariffs. He considers their removal on a unilateral, multilateral and preferential basis. He finds that in most cases, the extra gains from removing non-tariff barriers would outweigh the gains from tariff removal, so that the total gains from including non-tariff barriers are generally more than twice the gains from just removing tariffs. Removing non-tariff barriers generally also bestows significant extra gains on trading partners. Bradford concedes that complete opening may not be an option politically, particularly given the negative impact on the owners of fixed factors (land and natural resources). The analysis is not a recipe for reform, but does show the potential gains from deeper integration.

While Bradford's paper focuses on non-tariff barriers to goods trade, the paper by **Thomas Hertel**, **Terrie Walmsley** and **Ken Itakura** examines some of the 'new age' issues outside of the goods area that were being considered for a preferential trade agreement between Japan and Singapore. The first such element they model is customs automization. They find estimates of the saving in direct costs of reduced paperwork, storage and transit expenses, along with the saving in indirect time costs. A second element is security and harmonisation measures designed to make e-commerce between the two countries safe and acceptable to consumers. They find estimates of the corresponding reductions in wholesale-retail margins from greater penetration of e-commerce. A final element is liberalisation of services trade. They use available estimates of the tariff-equivalent of services trade barriers for business and construction services. Note that, in contrast to the previous paper, all these measures are treated as creating waste and adding to real resource costs, rather than as being tax-like. The authors quantify the welfare effects of these measures, along with conventional preferential tariff cuts, using a dynamic CGE model with capital accumulation and international capital mobility. Not surprisingly, given their treatment of non-tariff measures, they find significant gains from liberalisation.

They also find that the e-commerce and customs automization initiatives do not produce trade diversion in the same way as the preferential tariff cuts do (this is likely also to be a result of their treating the new age measures as reducing waste). Their paper is one of the first CGE studies to tackle these new age issues.

The final paper by **Soamiely Andriamananjara**, **Michael Ferrantino** and **Marinos Tsigas** uses new estimates of the price gaps created by non-tariff measures on merchandise trade, obtained using the procedures documented in the earlier paper by Dean, Feinberg, Ferrantino and Ludema. The authors use these estimates in a conventional multiregional CGE model to quantify the global welfare effects from liberalising the non-tariff barriers. One important contribution of their paper is that the authors model the barriers in three different ways – as import tax wedges (for footwear), as export tax wedges (for apparel), and as what they call 'sand in the wheels', or waste (for processed foods). This does not allow a comparison of the effects of the different treatment on the same commodity, but it is based on careful consideration of the types of non-tariff measures applying in each sector. For each sector, they find that liberalisation of non-tariff measures leads to a substantial jump in world trade, and improved global welfare, though at the expense of global production of the good being protected. And most of the gains accrue to the liberalising region, in the form of lower prices to consumers. Most other regions experience at least some welfare gains due to increased market access. Estimated welfare losses are unusual geographically, and negligible in value when they occur.

Finally, a short summary paper by **Robert Scollay** draws together some of the research and policy implications from this collection of papers.

DIRECTIONS FOR RESEARCH AND POLICY

Robert Scollay

University of Auckland Business School and PECC Trade Forum

A key research theme from the papers in this volume is the extent to which analysis of non-tariff measures is data-driven.

The TRAINS database remains a key source of raw data for non-tariff measures affecting goods trade. This allows frequency counts to be computed, but without further analysis it does not provide an indication of economic impacts, nor an indication of policy priorities. Hence additional techniques are required to draw out these implications.

The TRAINS database records non-tariff measures that have been notified to UNCTAD. By contrast, the database of non-tariff measures compiled by Diane Manifold and William Donnelly is a database of complaints that have been recorded by organisations such as the Office of the U.S. Trade Representative. The two databases need not place the same emphasis on various non-tariff measures, and Judith Dean and co-authors make use of both databases in their subsequent analysis.

The TRAINS database does not cover services. But the analytical problems in measuring services trade barriers are similar to those in goods trade, in that there is no readily identifiable tax-equivalent of these behind-the-border measures. Furthermore, the theoretical analysis of Alan Deardorff and Robert Stern shows that in services trade, the 'tax equivalent' (the vertical shift in supply or demand curves) may not equal the 'price wedge' (the extent to which domestic prices change as a result of the trade barriers). A method is needed to link the two — more on this later.

Overall, the papers in this volume show that going from measures of frequency to measures of economic and policy significance involves a diversity of techniques, all of which require ingenuity, tenacity and sheer hard work. It is an endeavour made more heroic because of the assumptions needed to deal with data problems.

The papers suggest that survey techniques may not be successful in assessing economic significance directly, because firms have difficulty putting a direct monetary cost on non-tariff measures. Yet firms may still be able to provide accurate information about some of the data items from which economic significance can be computed indirectly. The paper by Jungho Yoo is an example of the successful use of survey techniques in this indirect way.

The papers on non-tariff measures affecting goods trade suggest that price comparisons can be a fruitful way to assess economic significance. But there are some practical problems to be dealt with. The paper by Mitsuyo Ando raises the issue of whether to use prices or unit values. The papers by Judith Dean and coauthors and Scott Bradford raise the issue of whether to use actual retail prices or a reference retail price. Further, the price comparison approach can provide an overall measure of the effects of all non-tariff measures, but not the effect of individual measures. However, the paper by Mitsuyo Ando shows how frequency ratios can be used to pro-rate the overall price gap into the components due to individual measures.

An alternative way of assessing the effects of individual measures is to decide in advance which particular measures are most important in any given sector, and to confine the analysis to those measures. This is the approach taken by Soamiely Andriamananjara and coauthors. They also show the importance of a sector-by-sector assessment of how to model the non-tariff measures in a computable general equilibrium context, as different treatments generate different welfare effects.

In the areas of services trade and rules of origin, trade restrictiveness indexes have been constructed to characterise a range of information on non-tariff measures that is not captured in the TRAINS database. In the area of services trade, econometric analysis has then been used to convert the 'first round' information captured by the trade restrictiveness index into a price wedge. In the framework of Alan Deardorff and Robert Stern, the trade restrictiveness index is akin to the 'tax equivalent', while the econometrics produces the 'price wedge'. This is how the two concepts have been linked in practice.

Several of the papers deal with trade facilitation. The papers by Tsunehiro Otsuki and Peter Walkenhorst, each with coauthors, share the view that trade facilitation is affected by non-tariff barriers to trade. The former paper uses secondary sources to construct index indicators of such measures. These papers share with the paper by Terrie Walmsley and coauthors a focus on the quality of customs procedures and the availability of e-commerce as important determinants of the transactions costs of trade. The various papers demonstrate the different uses of econometrics and computable general equilibrium modelling. The gravity model approach identifies effects on trade volumes, while computable general equilibrium modelling identifies the welfare effects.

The paper by Ron Babula and coauthors shows the rewards from looking in detail at a single non-tariff measure, in this case import quotas. The paper by

Jungho Yoo shows the rewards from attention to detail. The paper by Soumodip Sarkar shows the benefits of liberalising the temporary movement of people, benefits that are easily understood in a Heckscher-Ohlin framework.

Some of the papers have more unexpected findings. The use of non-tariff measures can itself reflect the success of liberalisation elsewhere. This is most clearly seen in the observation that as average tariff levels have fallen, the number of anti-dumping cases has risen. The paper by Tianshu Chu and Thomas Prusa documents the rise in the use of anti-dumping cases against China.

Similarly, work in the standards area comes to the surprising conclusion that standards harmonisation is not always beneficial, because standards can provide information about the characteristics of complex goods and can therefore facilitate trade.1 Nevertheless, shared standards are found to be better than non-shared standards. But note that shared standards may also cause trade diversion, in the same way that selective trade facilitation may also be trade diverting. These additional possibilities are not canvassed by the authors.

The selective use of trade facilitation or the selective encouragement of shared standards is increasingly on the agenda in the negotiation of regional trading arrangements. Another important dimension of these arrangements is their rules of origin. The paper by Kati Suominen and Antoni Estevadeordal brings together all the relevant information about these rules, to determine which types are likely to be least trade-restricting.

Finally, the paper by Robert Koopman discusses how to translate information about the economic effects of non-tariff measures and trade facilitation into policy advice to governments. However, there is an additional step. Information about these economic effects should also be used to inform international trade negotiations. For example, the paper by Soamiely Andriamananjara and coauthors suggests how the results of computable general equilibrium analyses can identify adjustment pressures from trade reform, and even be used to design compensation schemes for the losers. But for the analysis to be used in this way, there needs to consensus on the sizes of the relevant tax or price wedges, and consensus on how and where they should be introduced into the models. The price and cost impacts that have been estimated in the area of services trade come closest to what is required to inform trade negotiations.

[1] Editors' note: The paper on standards by Johannes Moenius was presented at the APEC Workshop on Quantitative Methods for Assessing Non-tariff Measures and Trade Facilitation, held in Bangkok on 8–10 October 2003, but could not be included in this volume.

THE QUANTIFICATION AND IMPACT OF NON-TARIFF MEASURES

Bijit Bora

World Trade Organisation[1]

1. Introduction

It is now almost passé to justify the importance of any non-tariff trade measure by appealing to declining tariff levels. The argument is that non-tariff measures (NTMs)[2] should be addressed because they have become relatively more important as trade policy issues. Such an approach necessarily diminishes the absolute importance of NTMs as an impediment to world trade. National governments have always been able to discover and implement new and sometimes ingenious ways to reduce the volume and value of trade. Not surprisingly, the result is a vast array of measures that fit even the narrowest definition of an NTM. Individually, each measure may not be important. However, when all NTMs are taken together as an aggregate they are a significant deterrent to trade.

Recognising the need to address NTMs is not the issue. The problem is identifying them and developing a tractable taxonomy that allows for a coherent and robust analysis of their effects. Even if these two tasks are accomplished the difficult policy issue of the appropriate forum and framework within which to address NTMs still remains.

The objective of this paper is rather modest–to identify the pitfalls and problems in defining NTMs. It surveys previous work on NTMs and shows that the only common thread running through the literature is the impossibility of establishing a unifying framework for the analysis of NTMs. This creates obvious difficulties since an NTM, by definition, may simply be whatever anyone wants to define it to be as long as it isn't a statutory tariff.

---

[1] Bijit Bora is a Counsellor in the Economic Research and Statistics Division of the World Trade Organisation in Geneva, Switzerland. The views expressed in this paper are personal. They should not in anyway be interpreted as those of the World Trade Organisation or its Member states.

[2] The term measure is used in this paper as opposed to barrier. In the literature both terms are used interchangeably. The rationale for using the term measure is that in some cases policies that increase the volume trade, in the short run, such as export subsidies or cross-border predatory pricing could the definition of a non-tariff measure. A barrier is something different. It means the prevention of something – in this case trade. Export subsidies could not be considered a barrier to trade.

The next section examines the issue of identifying an NTM. The overall conclusion is not particularly optimistic given the complex nature of NTMs. This problem then feeds into the question of examining the incidence of NTMs. Without a proper definition and a statistically robust dataset it is difficult to be precise about the degree of protection afforded by NTMs in a particular market. Section D examines the impact of select NTMs and the issue of NTMs and the Doha Development Agenda is taken up in the concluding section.

2. Identifying a Non-Tariff Measure

2.1. *Defining an NTM*

Before negotiations on NTMs can proceed it would be useful to at least have a working definition of an NTM. Baldwin (1970), in his seminal work on NTMs, defines "non-tariff distortion" as "any measure (public or private) that causes internationally traded goods and services, or resources devoted to the production of these goods and services, to be allocated in such a way as to reduce potential real world income." This is a useful definition, but is problematic in the context of defining 'potential' real world income.

An alternative, yet still complementary, approach would be to focus on the effects of a particular measure. For example, negotiations aimed at eliminating non-tariff measures would necessarily result in a situation where price deviations across trading partners would be due solely to tariffs. If tariffs were then to be eliminated all trading nations would be part of a 'single market'. Lloyd (1996), when writing on regional trade agreements, defines a single market as one in which the law of one price prevails. He further clarifies by stating that:

> "This means that in a competitive market, for either a produced commodity or a factor, there is only one price, allowing for transport and other transfer costs which prevent perfect arbitrage. It implies the removal of all border and non-border restrictions on commodity trade, and the harmonisation of commodity taxes and other measures which affect access to markets" (page 44).

Lloyd's insights are used to distinguish between the concepts of regional free trade and regional integration. The removal of border measures will liberalise trade, but may not necessarily result in integration. Hence, he defines the new regional trade agreements (RTAs) which include competition policy and investment as those moving towards regional integration. International integration is, therefore, more than just the removal of tariffs.

Lloyd's definition complements that of Baldwin. Baldwin does not specifically state the "law of one price" argument as succinctly as Lloyd. Nevertheless, the role of prices as a signal to allocate resources and determine the pattern and quantity of goods and services that are traded are implicit in his definition.

Both the Baldwin and Lloyd approaches point to a broad definition of a non-tariff measure. Indeed, the only tangible aspect of both definitions is that an NTM can be defined by what it is not, not by what it is. This means the set of NTMs is very large and encompasses a significant range of measures – both public and private.

2.2. *Developing a Taxonomy of NTMs*

Baldwin (1970) developed the first taxonomy of NTMs. They include:[3]

- Quotas and restrictive state-trading policies
- Export subsidies and taxes
- Discriminatory government and private procurement policies
- Selective indirect taxes
- Selective domestic subsidies
- Restrictive customs procedures
- Antidumping regulations
- Restrictive administrative and technical regulations
- Restrictive business practices
- Controls over foreign investment
- Restrictive immigration policies
- Selective monetary controls and discriminatory exchange-rate policies

Another approach to examining NTMs is provided by Laird and Vossenaar (1991). They classify, NTMs according to intent or immediate impact of the measures (*cf.*, the motives or objectives – see below). Five such categories are identified, of which (iv) has been adapted to cover restrictions as well as subsidies:

(i) *Measures to control the volume of imports*. For example, prohibitions and quantitative restrictions (QRs) on imports as well as export restraint agreements (ERAs). Licenses are often used to administer QRs. ERAs

[3] Baldwin (1970) pages 10-12 as cited in PECC (2001).

consist of voluntary export restraints (VERs) (covering, *inter alia*, measures employed for the administration of bilateral agreements under the Multi-Fibre Arrangement) and Orderly Marketing Agreements (OMAs).

(ii) *Measures to control the price of imported goods*. These include the use of reference or trigger price mechanisms, variable levies, anti-dumping duties, countervailing measures, *etc*. Tariff-type measures such as tariff quotas and seasonal tariffs also are usually intended to increase import prices under given circumstances. Voluntary export price restraints fall under this broad category of intent.

(iii) *Monitoring measures include price and volume investigations and surveillance*. Such practices are often associated with charges by domestic interests of unfair trading practices by exporters, *e.g.*, dumping and subsidization. Licenses are sometimes used as a monitoring instrument. Monitoring measures may be a prelude to other actions, and, if seen as such, may lead to export restraints. They may have a harassment effect.

(iv) *Production and export measures*. Subsidies may be directly applied to output or value added, or they may be indirectly applied, *i.e.*, paid to material or other inputs to the production process. They may arise from payments or the non-collection of taxes that would otherwise be due. Restrictions by mean of taxes or prohibitions may also be imposed on production or exports.

(v) *Technical barriers* imposed at the frontier are used to apply various standards for health and safety reasons to imported products to ensure that imported products conform to the same standards as those required by law for domestically produced goods. They may lead to the prohibition of non-complying imports or oblige cost-increasing production improvements.

Deardorff and Stern (1997) have authored the most recent systematic work on NTMs.[4] Their study covers the various elements of NTMs including their measurement. An interesting aspect of their study is to approach the issue of defining an NTM by using stylised characteristics. The characteristics are:

- *Reduction in quantity of imports*. NTMs are most often imposed with the intent of reducing the quantity of imports.

---

[4] Deardorff and Stern using the term NTB. This has been changed to NTM in this paper. In doing so, however, it should not prejudice their use of their term NTB.

- *Increase in price of imports*. NTMs succeed in reducing the quantity of imports only to the extent that they raise the actual or shadow price of imports to demanders.
- *Change in the elasticity of demand for imports*. NTMs often alter the slope of the demand curve for imports, and thus they alter the responsiveness of imports in a particular sector to price changes. Finally, the elasticity effect of an NTM is also important in assessing, in a general equilibrium context, the role of NTMs in influencing the outcome of other events such as a change in tariffs. An increase in a tariff on a final good, for example, will have its protective effect reduced if there is an elasticity-reducing NTM in place on an important intermediate input.
- *Variability of NTMs*. Unlike tariffs, NTMs often are defined relative to a benchmark quantity or price independently of market conditions. If this benchmark is held fixed when underlying conditions of supply and demand, exchange rates, and other market conditions change, as they inevitably do, then the effectiveness of the NTM will vary. Such variability may constitute a neglected cost that the NTM imposes on society and thus is very important to measure along with its more obvious average price and/or quantity effects.
- *Uncertainty of NTMs*. All government policies are uncertain in their implementation, but this seems to be especially true of some NTMs. Indeed, some practices such as antidumping and countervailing duty investigations have been identified as NTMs almost entirely because of the uncertainties that they impose on international traders. Even those barriers that are clearly restrictive, however, can become more so if their implementation is uncertain.
- *Welfare costs of NTMs*. For this purpose the price and/or quantity measures of the NTM provide sufficient information. Welfare costs are separate because of their importance in the literature on NTMs.
- *Resource Costs of NTMs*. In addition to the traditional welfare costs just noted, there are also certain costs that are associated with the manner in which the NTM is administered. First are the direct administrative costs themselves, that is, the resources used directly in enforcing whatever rules an NTM imposes. It is essential that more careful measurements of them be attempted. Second, and perhaps of much greater importance, are the resources lost to rent seeking and related phenomena. These are the time and other resources that are wasted by individuals and firms in their efforts to secure the profit opportunities and other benefits that are created by an NTM.

While Deardorff and Stern (1997) is predominantly theoretical in nature, the authors provide a number of practical suggestions on how to move towards a better understanding of the implications of NTMs. They propose a classification system, which has at its core price (other than tariffs) and quantity border measures. To these they add the remaining (other) set of measures that may affect trade and then customs and technical barriers as a separate category.

When the proposed framework of Deardorff and Stern (1997) is compared with that of UNCTAD TRAINs some differences emerge (table 1). The most significant difference is the inclusion of a range of measures that affect foreign investment and the environment for trade such as corruption. Another difference is the collapse of all the quantitative measures and what are essentially other duties and charges and trade defence measures into one category. The advantage of this categorisation is that many of the policies included in the two categories are easily identifiable.

Finally, the WTO has an Inventory of Non-Tariff Measures that was first established in 1968 in the context of the work done in the Committee on Trade in Industrial Products. It was based on some 800 notifications which, in the view, of the notifying Contracting Parties constituted non-tariff barriers. Following the Tokyo Round, the Inventory was kept up to date by first the Group on Quantitative Restrictions and Other Non-Tariff Measures (created in 1982) and subsequently the Technical Group on Quantitative Restrictions and Other Non-Tariff Measures (created in 1986).

At the time of the Uruguay Round, and in the context of the work done in the Negotiating Group on Non-Tariff Measures, the classification contained in the Inventory was used to sort out proposals submitted by participants. After the Uruguay Round, a decision by the Council for Trade in Goods taken on 1 December 1995 and entitled "Decision on Reverse Notification of Non-Tariff Measures" (G/L/60) terminated this Inventory of Non-Tariff Measures. A new Inventory of Non-Tariff Measures was open for notification as from the date of the Decision. However, only one reverse notification has been received to date.

3. Incidence of NTMs

Landscaping the incidence of NTMs depends upon the definition and available data. As indicated in the previous section there is no agreed definition as to what constitutes an NTM. Furthermore, UNCTAD hosts the only database on NTMs for public use. The WTO has a database based on notifications, which includes: licenses, quotas, prohibitions, and voluntary export restraints, plus information related to customs surcharges, minimum import prices, additional taxes and charges, and approval processes for imports and exports. This database is limited

Table 1. Comparison of UNCTAD and Deardorff and Stern taxonomies of NTMs

UNCTAD TRAINs	Deardorff and Stern
Price control measures • Administrative pricing • Voluntary export price restraint • Variable charges • Antidumping measures • Countervailing measures **Finance control measures** • Advance payment requirements • Multiple exchange rates • Restrictive official foreign exchange allocation • Regulations concerning terms of payment for imports • Transfer delays **Automatic licensing measures** • Automatic licence • Import monitoring • Surrender requirement **Quantity control measures** • Non-automatic licencing • Quotas • Import prohibitions • Export restraint arrangements • Enterprise specific restrictions **Monopolistic measures** • Single channel for imports • Compulsory national services **Technical measures** • Technical regulations • Pre-shipment formalities • Special customs formalities • Obligation to return used products **Miscellaneous measures for sensitive product categories** • Marketable permits • Public procurement • Voluntary instruments • Product liability • Subsidies	**Quantitative restrictions and similar specific limitations on imports or exports** • Import quotas • Exports limitations • Licensing • Voluntary export restraints • Exchange and other financial controls • Prohibitions • Domestic content and mixing requirements • Discriminatory bilateral agreements • Countertrade **Non-tariff charges and related policies affecting imports** • Variable levies • Advance deposit requirement • Antidumping duties • Countervailing duties • Border tax adjustments **Government participation in trade; restrictive practices; general policy** • Subsidies and other aids • Government procurement policies • State trading, government monopolies, and exclusive franchises • Government industrial policy and regional development measures • Government financed research and development; technology policies • National systems of taxation and social insurance • Macroeconomic policies • Competition policies • Foreign investment policies • Foreign corruption policies • Immigration policies **Customs procedures and administrative practices** • Customs valuation procedures • Customs classification procedures • Customs clearance procedures **Technical barriers to trade** • Health and sanitary regulations and quality standards • Safety and industrial standards and regulations • Packaging and labelling regulations, including trademarks • Advertising and media regulations

compared to the UNCTAD data, which is collected from national sources restricted by infrequent or incomplete notification.

This section examines two techniques with which to identify NTMs: frequency measures and business surveys.

3.1. *Frequency Measures*

UNCTAD's NTM data is frequency data and not measures of impact. They show for cross-market and cross-product analysis the extent to which national tariff lines within a Harmonized System 6-digit classification are affected by certain NTMs.

A core NTM includes the following three major categories of non-tariff measures:

- Quantity control measures, excluding tariff quotas and enterprise-specific restrictions;
- Finance measures, excluding regulations concerning terms of payment and transfer delays;
- Price control measures.

By way of illustration, consider the following hypothetical example to better understand the frequency approach to estimation.[5] Assume an imaginary HS089876 tariff line with four sub-headings that include separate lines for apples and bananas, grapes and melons, oranges and pineapples. An import licence applies to apples and oranges, while an advance import deposit applies to grapes and melons.

In the above example, the NTM incidence is 100 percent for the orange tariff line, since they are subject to licensing, 50 percent as only apples are affected by licensing, 0 percent for pineapples and 100 percent for grapes and melons. Therefore, the percentage term reflects only the incidence and not the impact of the NTM. Furthermore, given the way the number is calculated it is important to note that it is dependent on the number of lines that are affected, not the number of measures.

---

[5] Based on table 1 of Bora *et al.* (2002).

In reality, however, many researchers would want to consider the incidence of NTMs at a higher level. In this case, the calculation at the level of an HS6 line is calculated by taking the simple average of the incidence for each national tariff line. In the above example, the NTM incidence for an HS 089876 is 62.5 percent calculated as the sum of the percentage incidence (250) divided by the number of tariff lines (4).

The above analysis was conducted using simple averages. This gives a good picture, but it also might introduce certain biases in the assessment of the protective effect of an NTM structure. For example, an economy could have many tariff lines where imports are zero or negligible and where the tariff rate is also low. An frequency of 100 percent for an NTM in this case could either be meaningless, due to demand conditions, or significant in the sense that it maybe prohibitive. This would typically bias the assessment of protection downwards. Protection, after all, is implemented to reduce competition in a particular sector. In order to account for this, and bearing in mind that any weighting scheme introduces biases, a weighting vector can be applied to the vector of NTMs. This procedure is quite popular and can have an effect on the final assessment of an economy's trade regime (Bacchetta and Bora, 2001).

Two possible approaches can be adopted to account for some of the biases that exist in the context of simple averages. The first is to calculate an import coverage ratio – the value of imports in a tariff line that are covered by an NTM. In reality, of course, this may not be the case. A second approach is to reverse the analysis of table 2 and examine the pattern of NTMs (or protection for that matter) from the perspective of the exporter.

The results of the second approach are taken from Bacchetta and Bora (2001) and are reported in table 3 for five groups of exporters: least developed economies, major developing country exporters, petroleum exporters, other developing economies and developed economies. The next step was to define the markets for those exports. Ideally, one would like to have the markets selected using a process similar to the one used for products; that is, the markets should be the key markets for each exporter. However, given the diversity of export structures, a much simpler, yet still policy-friendly approach was used. The world was divided into markets according to the World Bank's geographical classification. They comprise South Asia, the Middle East and North Africa, Latin America and the Caribbean, Europe and Central Asia, South Asia and sub-Saharan Africa, plus the developed economies and the rest of the world.[6] It is

[6] The developed economies are also subdivided, generating another region, the Quad (EU, United States, Canada and Japan).

Table 2. WTO/GATT Inventory of non-tariff measures

PARTS AND SECTIONS	DESCRIPTION
Part I	<u>Government Participation in Trade and Restrictive Practices Tolerated by Governments</u>
A	
B	Government aids
C	Countervailing duties
D	Government procurement
E	Restrictive practices tolerated by governments
	State trading, government monopoly practices, *etc.*
Part II	<u>Customs and Administrative Entry Procedures</u>
A	Anti-dumping duties
B	Valuation
C	Customs classification
D	Consular formalities and documentation
E	Samples
F	Rules of origin
G	Customs formalities
Part III	<u>Technical Barriers to Trade</u>
A	General
B	Technical regulations and standards
C	Testing and certification arrangements
Part IV	<u>Specific Limitations</u>
A	Quantitative restrictions and import licensing
B	Embargoes and other restrictions of similar effect
C	Screen-time quotas and other mixing regulations
D	Exchange control
E	Discrimination resulting from bilateral agreements
F	Discriminatory sourcing
G	Export restraints
H	Measures to regulate domestic prices
I	Tariff quotas
J	Export taxes
K	Requirements concerning marking, labelling and packaging
L	Others
Part V	<u>Charges on Import</u>
A	Prior import deposits
B	Surcharges, port taxes, statistical taxes, *etc.*
C	Discriminatory taxes on film, use taxes, *etc.*
D	Discriminatory credit restrictions
E	Border tax adjustments
F	Emergency action

Source: WTO document TN/MA/S5, 11 September 2002.

important to point out that not all members of each one of those geographical regions report their import tariff and NTMs, therefore, this limited the scope of our analysis to those economies that actually provide this information.

Table 3 indicates that for all the exporters in each of the markets, agricultural products is the sector with the highest incidence of NTMs. This is followed by textiles and clothing. In terms of the geographical dispersion of the incidence of NTMs, very little can be said about the overall numbers in view of the dispersion across the product categories.

3.2. *Survey Studies*[7]

An alternative to data collected from national sources is the use of business surveys. Such surveys allow the possibility of prioritising the importance of different types of instruments. For example, under the frequency approach the application of a quota would be counted as an NTM. However, through business surveys the fact that the quota maybe under-filled would imply that it is not important to the exporter.

A number of such surveys exist. The OECD (2002a) in a very useful document has collated the results from a number of different surveys and summarised the results. Not surprisingly, due to the large variance in sampling techniques their conclusions are heavily qualified. Nevertheless, there appears to be strong evidence that technical measures and customs rules and procedures are both frequent and also rank as very important. Where internal taxes or charges and competition-related restrictions on market access are reported they are also ranked quite highly.

The surveys that are analysed also provide detailed data on specific measures that business finds to be most important. With respect to technical measures these are divided into two categories: specifications and standards; and conformity assessment procedures. For both these categories some of the key identified measures and problems are:

- Labeling
- Quality assurance
- Quarantine

[7] This section is based on OECD (2002).

Table 3. Frequency of NTMs by products of export interest to developing economies, selected markets

Description	Developed economies	South Asia	Middle East & North Africa	Latin America & Caribbean	Europe & Central Asia	East Asia & the Pacific	Sub-Saharan Africa	Quad
Agricultural and fishery products	**48.24**	**14.87**	**57.69**	**34.24**	**32.93**	**24.42**	**18.58**	**41.98**
Crustaceans (live)	58.64	8.33	75.00	30.98	43.56	22.22	20.00	50.00
Other fish	64.49	14.07	75.16	30.96	43.85	22.87	20.28	55.43
Edible fruit and nuts	53.95	19.21	54.61	37.09	32.36	24.21	28.20	54.67
Coffee and substitutes with coffee	32.25	17.86	44.64	28.10	20.63	26.19	18.18	21.43
Oil seeds and miscellaneous grain, seeds and fruits	53.93	14.20	68.55	40.75	38.49	28.71	25.12	37.41
Other agricultural and fishery products	43.50	11.11	52.08	35.28	28.59	32.87	17.80	27.50
Minerals and fuels	**6.72**	**3.29**	**5.73**	**6.64**	**6.72**	**4.52**	**0.16**	**6.53**
Ores, slag and ash	1.74	0.98	3.31	9.93	10.03	6.05	0.00	1.47
Crude and refined petroleum oil	26.88	22.73	28.13	14.53	38.01	17.75	4.55	12.19
Other minerals and fuels	4.55	0.00	0.00	18.33	0.00	11.11	0.00	0.00
Manufactures	**10.67**	**7.20**	**10.96**	**11.68**	**7.15**	**5.57**	**1.74**	**16.48**
Automatic data processing machines	14.94	4.17	8.04	6.90	13.69	0.21	0.00	8.93
Cotton products	9.09	16.67	6.25	36.67	0.00	11.11	4.55	25.00
Diamonds	9.09	11.67	12.50	0.67	31.11	11.11	9.09	12.50
Electronic integrated circuits and microassemblies	15.50	0.00	10.23	2.10	0.00	0.00	0.00	6.26
Footwear	19.83	8.60	18.55	14.18	12.45	0.00	4.25	10.97
Furniture, bedding and lamps	2.01	10.59	8.07	5.92	7.16	0.30	4.30	4.05
Iron and steel	12.95	0.27	1.26	2.51	2.68	9.60	0.00	35.42
Knitted or crocheted articles	30.46	16.59	17.43	17.82	18.27	4.78	7.02	68.64

Table 3. Frequency of NTMs by products of export interest to developing economies, selected markets—Continued

Description	Developed economies	South Asia	Middle East & North Africa	Latin America & Caribbean	Europe & Central Asia	East Asia & the Pacific	Sub-Saharan Africa	Quad
Motor vehicles for transporting persons	40.91	51.85	25.69	21.94	39.75	45.95	0.00	50.00
Non-knitted or crocheted articles	30.89	16.53	17.96	18.35	19.02	8.26	2.27	66.15
Other electrical equipment	14.50	4.48	19.67	7.07	5.47	4.22	0.39	6.90
Other manufactured articles	14.34	14.74	18.49	13.01	10.43	3.79	5.99	27.66
Other mechanical parts	11.06	2.64	7.46	6.75	4.09	3.32	0.20	3.87
Other motor vehicle and parts	10.83	16.04	9.31	12.69	16.75	15.17	1.56	24.04
Other office machines	10.61	1.39	0.00	2.96	0.46	0.00	0.00	4.17
Plastics	1.38	3.36	2.76	5.75	3.76	2.49	0.35	2.08
Reception apparatus	23.46	13.73	25.06	7.57	15.85	13.89	0.80	23.35
Rubber and rubber products	5.67	2.11	3.17	4.59	1.34	2.37	1.12	7.44
Ships, boats and floating structures	9.76	13.73	7.72	8.28	4.58	3.98	1.47	25.37
Synthetic yarns and woven fabrics	13.06	9.33	11.38	17.81	5.47	1.44	0.14	35.72
Wood and wood products	17.33	13.82	8.73	18.94	3.23	8.74	2.69	28.76

Note.–Compiled from tables 21-24. Other manufactured products from each of the tables were deleted.

Source: Bacchetta and Bora (2001).

- Lack of transparency
- Discrimination in the application of standards

With respect to customs rules and procedures some of the key measures and problems are:

- Excessive documentation
- Slow customs clearance
- Lack of predictability
- Arbitrary enforcement of rules
- Lack of harmonization and simplification of clearance procedures

4. Impact of NTMs

Studies on the impact of NTMs yields a number of diverse results, which reflect the difficulties in measuring and quantifying NTMs. Not surprisingly the work is more advanced in areas driven by the policy debate. For example, the use of domestic support and export subsidies in agriculture, or trade facilitation measures. This section selectively lists some of the studies that have tried to quantify some NTMs. While tempting, no attempt has been made to sum these estimates and compare them against estimate of tariff liberalisation.

4.1. *Domestic Support and Export Subsidies*

Domestic support and export subsides are the most prevalent in the agricultural sector and, for good reason, are subject to intense scrutiny.[8] Although the precise estimates vary, the gains from the elimination of these measures are almost equal to the gains from the complete elimination of tariffs. The pervasive nature of these measures is underscored by the fact that trade in agricultural products account for just a little more than 10 percent of world merchandise trade.

A common theme of all the studies of the gains from agricultural trade liberalisation is the importance of tariff liberalisation. Nevertheless, domestic support and export subsidies are important, not only for their pernicious effects on trade, but also because of the nature of their impact. Tariffs raise the prices of imported products in a market. Domestic support and export subsidies serve to lower the world prices of products making it difficult for producers in non-

---

[8] Certain types of export subsidies in non-agricultural products are permitted for economies that meet certain criteria, but only for a limited time.

subsidised economies to compete. The total effect, therefore, is ambiguous. The removal of such measures would benefit producers, but not consumers (IMF, 2003, World Bank, 2002).

4.2. *Quantitative Restrictions*

The Uruguay Round achievements did much to eliminate quantitative restrictions. The Agreement on Agriculture mandated the conversion of quantitative restrictions into tariffs, albeit with tariff rate quotas. The Agreement on Textiles and Clothing is a ten-year transition process which was divided into four distinct phases to eliminate quotas in those sectors. To date approximately 80 percent of quotas remain, although they must be eliminated by end December 2004. These include a total of 239 quotas maintained by Canada, 167 quotas maintained by the European Union and 701 quotas maintained by the United States. Estimates of the gains from moving to a tariff-only environment in textiles and clothing range from \$6.5–\$324 billion *per annum*. Furthermore, the provisions of Agreement on Trade Related Investment Measures prohibit the use of local content schemes.

4.3. *Standards*

Regulatory policies designed to achieve social objectives are an important component of the policy environment in all economies. Elimination of such policies would in all likelihood have negative welfare consequences. For example, standard are designed to facilitate information exchange, ensure quality. Therefore, the issue on standards and regulations in the trade context is how to establish a regime that recognises the diversity of economies, their regulations and also their ability to enact and enforce regulation, but at the same time reduce the trade decorative nature of regulations.

The trade decorative element of standards does not arise from the standards themselves, since it can be shown that they can benefit producers and consumers. What is of concern is their discriminatory application to imported products. Discriminatory regulations could be designed to provide a strategic advantage for domestic firms. Or, in some cases, their application could in a non-transparent manner that increases the costs of compliance for foreign firms. In both cases the overall result is a prejudice against imported products.

Even if standards are transparent, compliance costs, especially for developing economies can be quite significant as illustrated in OECD (2002a). The landscape for standards is such that developed economies typically have more stringent standards than developing economies. This will have the effect of favouring intra-developed country trade since producers from these economies will have more experience in meeting the standards. Producers from developing economies, on the other hand, will be at a disadvantage.

4.4. *Trade Facilitation*

The WTO defines trade facilitation as the "simplification and harmonisation of international trade procedures with trade procedures being the activities, practices and formalities involved in collecting, presenting, communicating and processing data required for the movement of goods in international trade. This definition is narrower than that used by other agencies such as APEC. Nevertheless, there is little doubt that it still provides the opportunity to increase the benefits to developing economies from the multilateral trading system.

Estimates of the gains from trade facilitation initiatives vary depending upon the model and the approach used to quantify the costs of inefficient practices. In some cases, estimates are based on the costs of the value of the savings. These estimates range from 4 to 10 percent of the value of trade (table 4). The overall gains are modelled by applying a cost saving value to the costs of transport (Dee, Geisler and Watts, 1997). In these cases, the relative magnitude of gains is estimated to be as high as a third of the gains from total tariff liberalisation.

4.5. *Government Procurement*[9]

The few empirical analyses of the costs and benefits of trade-related procurement reform point to tangible gains. In the case of Korea's accession to the WTO's plurilateral agreement on government procurement in 1994/5, Choi (2001) estimated that the cost savings to the Korean government from goods sourced abroad increased from 18.5 percent to 23.1 percent after accession. The use of limited tending procedures—which tend to reduce the number of potential bidders—fell also (from over 27 percent to 23.1 percent in 1996-1998.) Likewise, Srivastava (2000) estimates that if India joined this WTO agreement the welfare gains would be equivalent of between 0.3 and 1.7 percent of national income.

---

[9] I thank Simon Evennett for his input on this section.

Table 4. Summary of some of the major estimates on trade transaction costs and trade facilitation benefits

Study	Scope	Estimates on costs	Estimate on benefits	Note
US NCITD (1971)	direct costs: documentation costs required by government; finance & insurance; carrier; and forwarder/ broker or their contractual counterpart	average documentation costs are \$375.77 for exports and \$320.58 for imports. Total costs aggregate represents 7.5% of the value of the total US export and import.	(none)	based on business survey
Ernst and Whinney (1988a,b) for Cecchini et al (1988)	(1) direct costs: customs compliance costs. (2) indirect costs: road hauliers; and business foregone	customs compliance costs (7,500 million ECU), road hauliers (415-830 million ECU), and business foregone (4,500-15,000 million ECU). Approximately around 1.5% of total intra-EC trade value for customs compliance; 1-3% for business foregone.	(none)	based on business survey: survey on lost business opportunities and road hauliers had some methodological reservation
SWEPRO (1985)	direct costs: customs compliance costs	customs compliance costs are 4% of the value of import or export; *i.e.*, 8% of the total value of goods traded	(none)	apparently certain figures were obtained from Swedish customs and businesses
EU COST 306 Final Report (1989)	direct costs: documentation costs	documentation costs are 3.5-7% of the value of goods traded; with errors becomes 10-15%	(none)	no information about the methodology

Table 4. Summary of some of the major estimates on trade transaction costs and trade facilitation benefits—Continued

Study	Scope	Estimates on costs	Estimate on benefits	Note
UNCTAD (1994b)	direct and indirect costs - transaction costs include: banking/insurance; customs; business information; transport; telecommunication	transaction costs are US$400 billion (10% of the total world trade value), trade transaction costs are at 7-10% of the world trade value.	one-quarter of transaction costs (US$100 billion) can be saved by "efficiency" by the year 2000, (*i.e.*, one-quarter of US$400 billion): approximately 2-3% of import value	Use UNCITD (1971), EU COST 306 Final report (1989), SITPRO (1991) and some other.
Dee, Geisler and Watts (1996)	APEC trade liberalisation programmes including trade facilitation measures, TBT, competition policy, government procurement, and transparency	used the estimates of Cecchini (1988), and UNCTAD (1994b)	5% of value of value of goods traded (trade facilitation measures only); 10% (if TBT, competition policy, government procurement, and transparency measures are taken into account)	apparently used a secondary reference
APEC (1997)	APEC trade liberalisation programmes including trade facilitation measures, TBT, competition policy, government procurement, and transparency	general reference to Cecchini (1988), UNCTAD (1994b) and Dee, Geisler and Watts (1996)	While assuming that a consensus estimate on direct savings from trade facilitation is around 2-3% of total import value, corrected to 1-2%	apparently used a secondary reference
Staples (1998), *et al*	direct costs: customs compliance costs	customs compliance costs are 7-10% of the value of international trade	(none)	apparently used a secondary reference

Source: OECD (2002).

4.6. *Export Cartels*

A recent survey of empirical work on competition policy highlights the relative magnitudes of cartel enforcement and tariff liberalisation. By of illustration the study shows that, at least for one estimate, agricultural liberalisation would be considerably less than the benefits from deterring international hardcore cartels (WTO, 2003).

5. Doha Development Agenda and NTMs

The picture of NTMs that has been drawn is not a particularly optimistic one. They can't be defined, nor can they be measured. And, in cases where they can the data is not particularly useful. This, of course, makes it difficult to pronounce on the opportunities for improving market access in the context of the Doha Development Agenda (DDA). Nevertheless, a number of comments can be made on the work programme, which focuses on the issue of building on past achievements without duplicating the work in other organisations.

The mandate for NTMs in the DDA is in paragraph 16 and is the responsibility of the Negotiating Group on Market Access (Box 1). It provides virtually no guidance as to what negotiators should be considering as NTMs. As a result the tentative first step on how to deal with NTMs can best be described as cautious. Those NTMs that are being dealt with in other bodies should continue to be dealt with in those bodies. Those which are not, can either be dealt within the NGMA, or passed on to other bodies, or ignored completely. The interesting issue will be how to deal with the NTMs that fall in the first category: those that the Group decides should be dealt with.

Given the premature nature of discussions on NTMs and the need to try to look forward, the rest of this section lays down some basic, hopefully common sense, principles with which to focus the discussions. The previous sections highlighted the complexity and diversity of NTMs and the absence of any workable definition. Therefore, the first principle is to focus on what is known.

5.1. *Focus On What Is Known*

While the universe of NTMs cannot be defined concrete evidence exists on specific NTMs and problems that they cause. For example, in the case of quantitative restrictions there is ample evidence of the incidence and impact of quotas in the textile industry and local content schemes in the automotive industries. Both policies, however, are currently under the jurisdiction of the

Agreement on Textiles and Clothing (ATC) and the Agreement on Trade Related Investment Measures (TRIMs). Local content schemes are also disciplined in some regional trade agreements such as the North American Free Trade Agreement. These agreements supplement the general provision on the elimination of quotas contained in Article XI of GATT 1994.[10]

Evidence was presented in the previous section on the importance of customs procedures and the difficulties in transporting goods. The negotiations and work on trade facilitation in the WTO focuses on the following areas:

- Excessive documentation
- Lack of automation and inadequate use of information technology;
- Lack of transparency, with unclear and unspecified import and export requirements;
- Inadequate procedures, especially a lack of audit based controls and risk-assessment techniques and
- lack of cooperation among customs and other government agencies, which thwarts efforts to deal effectively with increased trade flows.

Practical guidelines to foster transparency, predictability and uniformity that would be consistent with GATT Articles V (freedom of transit), VIII (fees and formalities connected with importations and exportation) and X (publication and administration of trade regulations) would include:

- Harmonisation of laws and regulations;
- Simplification of administrative and commercial formalities, procedures and documents; and
- Standardization of transport means: modal infrastructure (related to sea, road, rail and air) including interfaces between different modes of transport loads and handling equipment commercial practices and services and information technology.

[10] Quotas have not been entirely abolished from the multilateral trading system. They can still be used to enforce safeguard measures. For example, Article XII allows the use of quotas to restrain imports during a balance of payments crisis and Article XIII allows them if they are applied in a non-discriminatory fashion. (Castel, *et al.*, 1997).

BOX 1. NTMS AND THE DRAFT ELEMENTS OF MODALITIES FOR NEGOTIATIONS ON NON-AGRICULTURAL PRODUCTS

13. The following elements are proposed for the modalities on NTBs:

a) It is understood that the NGMA maintains overall responsibility for addressing non-tariff barriers (NTBs) as part of the Doha Declaration;

b) The negotiating group will proceed with the identification and examination of the various types of NTBs; [11]

c) After completing the identification, participants will aim to categorise the NTBs as well as clarify and seek additional information where necessary, and then proceed in the following manner:

Selected NTBs, to be agreed upon by the participants, would be dealt with by the NGMA on the basis of modalities, which could include request/offer, horizontal, or vertical approaches;

NTBs that have a specific negotiating mandate in the Doha Declaration in other areas should continue to be addressed in that body but information on the progress or outcome of those negotiations should be reported to this group for transparency;

Work on NTBs which relate to other areas of the Doha Declaration which currently do not have a specific negotiating mandate would progress in other fora but information on the progress should be reported to this group for transparency; and

NTBs that currently do not have a specific negotiating mandate would, after further clarification and if the group decides there is a need to send them to another WTO body, be reported to the TNC in order to be forwarded to the appropriate WTO body for action and reporting back.

Source: WTO Document TN/MA/35

Two of the most frequently cited NTMs that are also part of the Deardorff and Stern (1997) taxonomy are competition related issues and investment restrictions. Both of these have been under consideration since 1996 when Working Groups[12] were established at the First WTO Ministerial. Both are also due for further consideration at the Fifth Ministerial in Mexico. It should be pointed, however, the importance of the use of the term trade in this context. Any initiative in these two areas that would be supported under the umbrella of an NTM work programme will have to focus on the specific link between those issues and trade flows.

---

[11] In this respect, it is recalled that work has already been initiated with the notification of non-tariff barriers by participants.

[12] They are the Working Group on Trade and Investment and the Working Group on the Interaction between Trade and Competition Policy.

Standards and technical barriers to trade highlighted previously as being of great importance to private sector are covered, respectively, under the Agreement on Sanitary and Phytosanitary Measures and the Agreement on Technical Barriers to Trade. The extent to which these agreement discipline the use of measures that are designed to protect markets is an empirical question. However, it should be noted that the transparency principle is an important component of both agreements.

Contingency measures such as anti-dumping and countervailing duties, and safeguard measures, are also part of the Uruguay Round Agreements.

Therefore, in terms of examining the further gains that would accrue from a more aggressive approach to disciplining NTMs it maybe useful to obtain a better understanding of how existing multilateral agreements cover the set of NTMs. For those that are known, but not dealt with participants in the negotiations will need to weigh carefully the twin issues of the appropriate response and the appropriate forum. For some issues the WTO and DDA may not necessarily be the best place. Conversely, the DDA provides a genuine opportunity to improve market access.

5.2. *Choose the Appropriate Response*

As the reader will note the text so far has been careful not to stray into the issue of precisely which NTMs are not part of the current WTO debate. So far, only one measure that would fit any definition of an NTM reviewed earlier has been discussed – export taxes.[13] They could, arguably, be considered an NTM (OECD, 2002b, c). Similarly, the work programme mandated under the Doha Ministerial Declaration on competition policy, investment, trade facilitation and transparency in government procurement foresees the possibility of negotiations. Each of these four issues has their own strong supporters and some notable developing economies as detractors. Furthermore, the case for their inclusion as part of the set of multilateral trade rules relies to a certain extent on a number of issues beyond those that would be considered as trade restrictions. Therefore, one issue for careful consideration is the appropriate response. Should the response be one of laying down principles that encourage transparency and predictability? Or, is there a case for a higher level of obligation?

[13] Export restrictions are covered under the TRIMs agreement. See Annex paragraph (c).

The current pattern of rules governing NTMs ranges from disciplines under the TRIMs agreements to transparency obligations under the SPS and TBT agreements. Addressing outstanding NTMs will require similar flexible treatment. Some may not be conducive to rigid binding obligations; indeed transparency and cooperation principles could succeed in achieving a certain degree of liberalisation. Other measures, however, especially those that are directly trade distorting may need to be subject to a set of disciplines.

5.3. *Choose the Appropriate Forum*

The diversity of NTMs requires a flexible response in terms of the level of discipline and correspondingly a flexible response as to the appropriate forum. The policy response to NTMs can be at a number of different levels, of which the multilateral level is one. Lessons that have been learned regarding the costs and difficulties associated with implementing some of the agreements should not be lost. Conversely, a related issue is whether or not addressing NTMs at the regional or bilateral level through RTAs is the optimal response. The value in multilateral cooperation, just as it is in the gains from trade, can be eroded if the set of participants is limited or restricted. This is especially the case with issues where the benefits arise from coordination and cooperation.

References

1. Bacchetta, Marc and Bijit Bora (2001), *Post-Uruguay Round Market Access Barriers for Industrial Products*, UNCTAD Policy Issues in International Trade and Commodities, Study Series No. 12 (New York and Geneva: United Nations), UNCTAD/ITCD/TAB/13, Sales No. E.01.II.D.23.
2. Baldwin, R. (1970), Non-Tariff Distortions in International Trade, Brookings Institutions, Washington, D.C.
3. Bora, B., A. Kuwahara and S. Laird (2002) *Quantification of Non-tariff Measures*, UNCTAD Policy Issues in International Trade and Commodities, Study Series No. 12 (New York and Geneva: United Nations), UNCTAD/ITCD/TAB/18, Sales No. E.01.II.D.18.
4. Castel, J., W. Graham, S. Hainsworth, A. de Mestral and M. Warner (1997), *The Canadian Law and Practice of International Trade*, Toronto, Emond Montgomery publications.
5. Choi, I (2000), "The Long and Winding Road to the Government Procurement Agreement: Korea's Accession Experience", presented at the World Bank conference East Asia and Options for WTO 2000, Manila.
6. Deardorff, A. and R. Stern (1997), "Measurement of Non-Tariff Barriers", OECD Economics Department Working Paper No. 179 (Paris: OECD).
7. IMF (2003), *World Economic Outlook*, (Washington: IMF).

8. Laird, Sam and René Vossenaar (1991), "Porqué nos preocupan las bareras no arancelarias?," *Informacion Comercial Española*, Special Issue on Non-tariff Barriers, November, pp. 31-54.
9. Lloyd, P. (1996) "The Changing Nature of RTAs" in B. Bora and C. Findlay (eds.), *Regional Integration and Asia Pacific*, Melbourne, Oxford University Press.
10. OECD (2002a), *Overview of Non-tariff barriers: Findings from Business Surveys* (Paris: OECD).
11. OECD (2002b), Analysis of Non-Tariff Measures: The case of non-automatic import licensing (Paris: OECD).
12. OECD (2002c), *Analysis of Non-Tariff Measures: The case of export duties* (Paris: OECD).
13. OECD (2002d), *Analysis of Non-Tariff Measures: The case of export restrictions* (Paris: OECD).
14. Pacific Economic Cooperation Council (PECC) (2001), *Impediments to Trade and Investment in the APEC Region*, PECC Secretariat, Singapore.
15. Vousden, Neil (1990) *The Economics of Trade Protection*, Cambridge University Press, Cambridge, UK.
16. World Bank (2002), *Global Economic Prospects*, Washington, World Bank.
17. World Trade Organisation (2003), Study on issues relating to a Possible Multilateral Framework on Competition Policy, Geneva, World Trade Organisation. TN/WGTCP/W/228.

A COMPILATION FROM MULTIPLE SOURCES OF REPORTED MEASURES WHICH MAY AFFECT TRADE

Diane Manifold

U.S. International Trade Commission[1]

William Donnelly

U.S. International Trade Commission[2]

1. Overview

The Office of Economics of the U.S. International Trade Commission is currently conducting research with the objective to improve the quantification of the effects of non-tariff measures on trade flows and other economic variables.[3] A central feature of this effort is the generation of a compilation of measures for both goods and services that have been alleged as affecting trade. This preliminary compilation includes information obtained from several primary sources including the Office of the United States Trade Representative's (USTR) National Trade Estimate Report on Foreign Trade Barriers (NTE), the European Union's (EU) Market Access Database, and the World Trade Organization's (WTO) Trade Policy Reviews.[0] The information relates to measures that have been reported for 53 economies (Table 1). Information is also provided on goods and services and on the sectors alleged to be affected by such measures. The compilation includes economies in the Asia Pacific Economic Cooperation forum (APEC) and the

---

[1] Diane Manifold and William Donnelly are affiliated with the Office of Economics, U.S. International Trade Commission. The views expressed in this article are those of the authors. They are not the views of the U.S. International Trade Commission (USITC) as a whole nor any of its individual Commissioners. The authors may be contacted via email at diane.manifold@usitc.gov and william.donnelly@usitc.gov, respectively.

[2] We acknowledge the help of John Giamalva and Saba Zeleke for their assistance in compiling some of the information. In addition, we thank Robert Koopman, Arona Butcher, Michael Ferrantino, and Linda Linkins for their helpful comments on this paper. All remaining errors are those of the authors' alone.

[3] Inclusion of a citation or item in the compilation does not constitute an opinion regarding the WTO-consistency or lack thereof, discriminatory impact or lack thereof, or economic effect of that item. The intended purpose of the compilation is for general research into the economic effects of NTMs in support of USITC's customers.

[4] For access to the USTR database, see http://www.ustr.gov/Document_Library/Reports_Publications/2002/2002_NTE_Report/Section_Index.html; for the EU database, see http://mkaccdb.eu.int/; and for the WTO database, see http://www.wto.org/english/tratop_e/tpr_e/tpr_e.htm.

proposed Free Trade Area of the Americas (FTAA).[5] The various elements of the compilation are discussed in this article, followed by a preliminary overview of the information contained therein.

Table 1. Economies in the compilation

Argentina #	Hungary	Paraguay #
Australia *	Iceland	Philippines *
Azerbaijan	India	Poland
Bangladesh	Indonesia *	Romania
Brazil #	Israel	Russian Federation *
Cameroon	Japan *	Singapore *
Canada * #	Kenya	South Africa
Chile * #	Korea (Republic of) *	Switzerland
China *	Libya	Chinese Taipei *
Colombia #	Malaysia *	Thailand *
Costa Rica #	Mexico * #	Tunisia
Czech Republic	Morocco	Turkey
Ecuador #	New Zealand *	United States * #
Egypt	Nigeria	Uruguay #
European Union	Norway	Venezuela #
Gabon	Pakistan	Vietnam *
Guatemala #	Panama #	Zimbabwe
Hong Kong *	Papua New Guinea *	

* denotes APEC economies; # denotes FTAA economies

Source: Compiled by USITC staff.

There are a number of reference sources that provide information on measures that may affect trade, however, there are strengths and limitations associated with these reference sources. All of the sources generally include some of the same categories of alleged measures as those which appear in this compilation; however, the descriptions of specific measures vary, as does their coverage. For example, the EU's Market Access Database contains information on reported measures for most economies prior to 2001, but includes only a few categories and provides only general information for each category. The WTO reviews economies with varying frequencies and does not assess all of them annually. Therefore, the WTO Trade Policy Reviews do not provide information for every economy under consideration in this compilation. The compilation includes only information from the Trade Policy Reviews conducted from 1998 to 2002. The Trade Policy

---

[5] The compilation contains information for 19 of the 21 APEC economies and 14 of the 34 FTAA economies.

Reviews are most detailed for such categories as import prohibitions, quotas, licensing, and standards. For many economies, the USTR's NTE report provides more in-depth information on measures, than does either the EU Market Access Database or the WTO Trade Policy Review.

This compilation provides information on fifteen categories of measures compared to fewer categories for the other references. The information contained in the NTE reports and the EU database survey of foreign trade measures as reported by government officials and company representatives in the United States and the EU. The WTO Trade Policy Reviews provide information on an economy's trade regime as reported by the WTO Secretariat.

In addition to specific economy and product/sector information, the compilation contains information on both generic and specific reported measures. There is no standard classification scheme for measures. However, several major different classifications have been developed such as those of Robert Baldwin (1970, 1984),[6] UNCTAD (TRAINS, 2000), Deardorff and Stern (1985),[7] and OECD (2002).[8] The main problem with classifying reported measures is that they cover a very broad range of policies and practices, especially if all measures–other than tariffs–that affect trade are included. And, although not all categories of measures are applicable to all economies and sectors/products there are similarities in measures across categories, economies, and sectors/products.

The measures in the compilation include both formal governmental regulations (customs regulations), and policies (investment-related measures), and informal barriers and practices (nontransparency, arbitrary enforcement, corruption). These formal and informal measures affect a large number of sectors and different tariff lines. For example, there may be formal governmental measures that affect only a few sectors or tariff lines or there may be informal practices such as inadequate enforcement of anticompetitive practices or corruption which might affect imports in many sectors. Table 2 lists the 15 categories of measures in the compilation. These categories are to be found in other classification systems.

---

[6] Baldwin, Robert E. (1984), "Trade Policies in Developed Countries," Chapter 12 in Handbook of International Economics Volume 1: International Trade, Jones, Ronald W., and Peter B. Kenen, eds., Elsevier Science Publishers, Amsterdam. Baldwin, Robert E. (1970), Nontariff Distortions of International Trade, The Brookings Institution, Washington, DC.

[7] Deardorff, Alan V., and Robert M. Stern (1997), "Measurement of Non-Tariff Barriers," University of Michigan, OECD/GD(97)129.

[8] Fleiss, Barbara (2002), Trade Directorate, OECD, Paris, "Work at OECD on NTMs," WTO Seminar on Market Access, Geneva, May 30.

Table 2. Categories of measures

Anticompetitive practices / competition policy	Intellectual property rights
Corruption	Investment-related measures
Customs procedures	Sanitary and phytosanitary requirements
Exports	Services
Government procurement	Standards, testing, certification and labeling
Import licensing	State-trading
Import prohibitions	Taxes
Import quotas	

Source: Compiled by USITC staff.

2. Explanation of Terminology and Information in the Compilation

2.1. *Generic and Specific Measures*

There are over 3,300 individual entries currently in the database, including many related to agricultural products and to types of services. Each entry includes information entered regarding: (1) an economy, (2) a category of reported measure; (3) a generic/specific measure, and (4) product/sector. One example of an entry would be: (1) Australia; (2) sanitary and phytosanitary requirements; (3) inspection, and (4) fruit (apples). In some cases the description of the measure is listed as "horizontal" if it is reported to affect many or all products or sectors. The purpose for constructing this compilation is to identify policies that influence industrial and agricultural market access so as to be able to utilize the information in economic modeling of the potential measures.

Many sectors are affected by the same measures and therefore, generic and specific measures appear across the range of categories. These situations arise because the categories of measures do not relate either to particular products or to specific industries. A type of service, such as the services of a foreign-licensed accountant which might be thought to be unique to the "services" category, can actually appear either in that category or in the "standards, testing, certification and labeling" or the "import prohibitions" category or in any of the categories. The generic measure in this example would be "certification." Several other examples of generic measures which cross categories are presented in Table 3. For example, some form of "approval" is reported in the these categories as well: (1) "import licensing;" (2) "sanitary and phytosanitary requirements," (3) "standards, testing, certification and labeling," (4) "services;" (5) "exports;" (6) "investment-related measures," and (7) "customs procedures."

Table 3. Categories of measures

	Number of	Generic	Number of
		approval	
Import licensing	62		
Sanitary and phytosanitary requirements	10		
Services	6		
Exports	5		
Investment-related measures	5		
Customs procedures	3		
Standards, testing, certification and labeling	1		
		approval	92
		certification	
Standards, testing, certification and labeling	58		
Sanitary and phytosanitary requirements	27		
Import licensing	4		
Customs procedures	2		
Exports	2		
Services	1		
		certification	94
		licensing	
Import licensing	81		
Exports	77		
Services	21		
Import prohibitions	5		
Standards, testing, certification and labeling	3		
Customs procedures	1		
		licensing	188
		prohibited	
Import prohibitions	327		
Exports	82		
Investment-related measures	50		
Services	38		
Sanitary and phytosanitary requirements	17		
Import licensing	15		
Customs procedures	3		
Standards, testing, certification and labeling	3		
Anticompetitive practices / competition policy	1		
Intellectual property rights	1		
		prohibited	537

Source: Compiled by USITC staff.

Another aspect of the compilation is the information on the specific products or sectors affected by alleged measures. The compilation contains both industrial sectors such as motor vehicles (automobiles) and pharmaceuticals as well as specific products such as alcoholic beverages (wine) and margarine. It also includes a large number of service sectors such as telecommunications, banking, and legal services. Some sectors or products are affected by more than one measure. For example, a product such as wheat may be affected by import prohibitions as well as state-trading. Many sectors or products are affected by similar measures. For example, imports of cosmetics, medical equipment, and lighting fixtures are each affected by required inspections in some economies.

3. Preliminary Data Summary

3.1. *Categories of measures*

The number of entries in the compilation should be interpreted with caution, since the information relates to large economies, and to more readily identifiable or transparent policies. Potential measures affecting market access in smaller markets or in developing economies may be under-represented, as are less transparent measures. In particular, inferences about the prevalence or severity of particular types of measures should not be made. The information regarding the total numbers of entries is presented here for illustrative purposes only.

It may be noted that some categories of measures are more frequently identified among the 53 economies in the preliminary compilation than are others. According to the following tabulation, the data indicate that 46 economies were cited as having some inadequacy with regard to intellectual property rights protection. The next most widespread categories of measures were "investment-related measures" (40 economies), "standards, testing, certification and labeling" (38), "services" (36), and "import prohibitions" (34). "corruption" was cited least, in only 15 economies.

Table 4. Entries

	All economies		APEC economies	
Categories of measures	**Number of entries**	**Number of Economies**	**Number of entries**	**Number of Economies**
Exports	430	33	187	13
Import licensing	408	30	244	12
Standards, testing, certification and labeling	407	38	250	15
Import prohibitions	334	34	163	16
Services	297	36	166	15
Investment-related measures	280	40	183	15
Intellectual property rights	253	46	109	18

Table 4. Entries—Continued

Categories of measures	All economies		APEC economies	
	Number of entries	Number of Economies	Number of entries	Number of Economies
Customs procedures	213	32	132	11
State-trading	174	29	7	11
Sanitary and phytosanitary requirements	156	25	67	12
Government procurement	109	33	52	11
Import quotas	94	17	64	8
Taxes	68	17	19	7
Anticompetitive practices / competition policy	55	17	35	8
Corruption	33	15	10	4

Source: Compiled by USITC staff.

For the compilation as a whole, the measures which are reported with the greatest number of entries are found in the "exports," "import licensing," and "standards, testing, certification and labeling" categories.[9] The above categories do not necessarily reflect the way in which issues may be raised in trade negotiations. Several of the categories in this compilation refer to topics as referenced in the Doha Declaration under areas other than "industrial market access." Four other categories (intellectual property rights, investment-related measures, government procurement, and competition policy) are referenced under major headings of the Declaration, one (customs procedures) is arguably related to "trade facilitation" by reference to particular GATT articles, and one (sanitary and phytosanitary standards) is referenced in Doha under "trade and environment."

3.2. *Products and Sectors*

The number of entries of products and sectors in the compilation presented in Table 5 is very preliminary. Most of these are goods, however the predominant one "services," which refers to the aggregation of services products wherever in the categories those services appear. In constructing the compilation of measures,

[9] With regard to the latter category, technical regulations, standards, and conformity assessment procedures are covered under the WTO Agreement on Technical Barriers to Trade ("TBT Agreement"). The TBT Agreement provides for certain exceptions to international standards for specific, legitimate objectives such as "to ensure the quality of ... exports, or for the protection of human, animal or plant life or health, of the environment, or for the prevention of deceptive practices" whenever international standards do not exist or are inadequate.WTO, "Agreement on Technical Barriers to Trade, "The Results of the Uruguay Round of Multilateral Trade Negotiations (Geneva: WTO, 1995). See, for example, the Preamble and TBT Article 1 (General Provisions), at Art. 1.6.

Table 5. Products and sectors

Products/sectors	Number of entries
Services	430
Horizontal	389
Agricultural products, fruits, grains, and dairy products	250
Animal products and meat	157
Pharmaceuticals, medicines, etc.	97
Textiles and apparel	90
Motor vehicles and parts	89
Animals	79
Alcoholic beverages	73
Weapons	67
Machinery, equipment, and appliances (except electrical or electronic)	60
Fish	45
Wood and wood products	44
Electrical/electronic equipment and products, including telecom equipment	42
Chemicals	39
Petroleum and petroleum products	39
Computer software	38
Recordings (audio & video)	30
Footwear and parts	20
Toys	14
Tires	14
Medical devices	14
Fertilizers	13
Cosmetics	11

Source: Compiled by USITC staff.

related products and sector were grouped together and an attempt to standardize the nomenclature was made. No attempt has been made to exclude entries referring to policies which may be WTO-consistent, or related to obvious health, safety, or national security concerns.

3.3. *Services Products*

There are a large number of different service sectors affected by these kinds of measures. According to the compilation, there are more than 100 different services products enumerated in this compilation that are affected by these measures.[10] These services range from accounting services to water services and occur across categories of measures. For example, 13 measures reported as affecting services were identified as present in the category "anticompetitive practices / competition policy," 7 in "corruption" (Table 6).

---

[10] Services products are different from the "Services" category, because many services products are entered in other categories.

Table 6. Measures that may affect services products

Category of measures	Total compilation of measures Number of entries	APEC economies Number of entries
Services	229	13
Investment-related measures	72	48
State-trading	43	5
Intellectual property rights	42	22
Government procurement	16	11
Anticompetitive practices / competition policy	13	8
Corruption	7	1
Standards, testing, certification and labeling	4	4
Exports	3	2
Sanitary and phytosanitary requirements	1	0

Source: Compiled by USITC staff.

3.4. *Horizontal Measures*

There are 389 categories of measures classified as horizontal, that is, they are reported as affecting most or all products. This appears to be particularly true of "government procurement," "customs procedures," "investment-related measures," "exports," "intellectual property rights," and "anticompetitive practices/competition policy." "Standards, testing, certification and labeling," while often cited as "horizontal," affects certain specific products or sectors.

Table 7. Horizontal measures

Categories of measures	Compilation of measures Number of entries	APEC economies Number of entries
Government procurement	62	20
Customs procedures	60	20
Investment-related measures	59	25
Exports	58	18
Intellectual property rights	39	9
Standards, testing, certification and labeling	37	13
Anticompetitive practices/competition policy	22	13
Corruption	13	2
Import prohibitions	12	7
Taxes	8	3
Import licensing	7	0
State-trading	6	4
Sanitary and phytosanitary requirements	5	2
Services	1	0

Source: Compiled by USITC staff.

Some additional insights can be gained from looking at multiple citation patterns relating to major categories of measures relating to products, such as was presented in Table 6. For example,

- Motor vehicles and parts are particularly affected by import licensing, import prohibitions (particularly for parts and used vehicles) and import quotas.
- Import licensing also affects chemicals, equipment and machinery, fish, petroleum, and weapons.
- Chemicals, pharmaceuticals, and recordings are particularly affected by intellectual property rights.
- Pharmaceuticals are also affected by product standards in many economies, as are cosmetics, equipment, motor vehicles, and textiles.
- Customs procedures are particularly important for textiles and footwear.
- Sectoral entries for investment-related measures refer primarily to services. Significant references for industrial products include motor vehicles and weapons.

In conclusion, the compilation is in its preliminary stages of development. Therefore, final conclusions cannot be drawn based on its contents at the present time, although a broad summary of the information from the reference sources has been provided here. The most frequently cited category of measures overall is "standards, testing, certification, and labeling," perhaps because this category of measure is very broad and may affect many individual products goods and services products. Finally, the compilation shows that a very large number of services sectors are currently affected by measures. The sectors range from broad areas such as telecommunications and legal services to specific professions such as accountants and journalists.

EFFECTS OF PROTECTIONISM ON CHILEAN EXPORTERS: AN EXPLORATORY SURVEY

Ronald Fischer

Universidad de Chile [1]

1. Introduction

Traditional protectionism consisted in tariffs on imported goods and services. However, it has been widely known, at least since the Tokyo Round of GATT, that successive multilateral reductions in tariffs were being partially neutralized by increases in alternative forms of protectionism. These include contingent protection measures such as safeguards, antidumping and countervailing measures.[2] An additional set of protectionist measures (which we may call non-traditional), include administrative measures, invasive inspection of containers, the misuse of phitosanitary and other standards for protection, *etc.* The object of this paper is to document the failure of a straightforward attempt at measuring the global effect of all forms of non-tariff protection in the case of Chilean firms. As we know, any barriers to trade can be transformed into equivalent tariffs.[3] Therefore, the cumulative effect of all the non-tariff barriers to trade can be described by a tariff equivalent.

Since firms are the subjects of nontariff barriers, it seemed reasonable to assume that firms would be able to compute the effect of these barriers as reduced margin on their exports compared to a situation in which these measures were eliminated. Alternatively, they might be able to compare the relative margins between economies. Thus the aim of the survey was to explore whether the executives that were responsible for exports in a representative sample of Chilean firms were able to estimate these quantitative effect of these barriers, or alternatively, if they were able to estimate the additional affect of trade barriers in one country as compared to another.

Unfortunately, the executives were unable to make these computations, and even though they had all faced non-tariff barriers, they had never considered

---

[1] CEA-DII, Universidad de Chile. Support was provided by Fondecyt project #1010430. The opinions in this paper are personal do not represent those of the government. Asexma, Ricardo Carrasco and Andrés Concha were very kind in helping me obtain the interviews. The author may be contacted *via* e-mail at *rfischer@dii.uchile.cl*.

[2] See Finger (1987). An examination of the impact of these measures appears in Prusa (1997).

[3] This is the basis of the tarification of nontariff barriers during the GATT rounds.

trying to quantify their effects on their own exports. In fact, executives were barely able to do an ordinal comparison of the effects of non-tariff barriers in different economies. This does not mean that the survey results were uninteresting, since there are several details that came out that are important.

First, the firms faced few problems in the developed economies and most of the barriers (especially administrative) were set by Latin American (and in some cases Arab) economies. However, these answers have to be qualified, since there are at least two possible explanations that do not involve higher non-tariff barriers in developing economies. First, it may be that since developed economies are large buyers, exporters adapt their products to their standards and other rules (Fischer and Serra (2001)), and since they do not change often, they are forgotten in their answers. Second, it may that the lack of stability of the rules in developing economies is the root cause of the executives attributing more protectionism to these counties.[4] These are speculative explanations, and have not been tested, so the working hypothesis has to be that developing economies use more nontariff barriers and as we show below, Brazil is the most protectionist economy in Latin America, from the point of view of Chilean exporters.

Antidumping and countervailing subsidy measures are well established and they have been examined from different points of view by a series of authors. These include Ethier (1982), who examines dumping as an equilibrium response to shocks in a world where fixed costs differ among economies, as well as Fischer (1992), Reitzes (1993) and Prusa (1994), who examine the strategic effects of antidumping laws on firm behavior.[5]

The empirics of antidumping and countervailing subsidy appear in Prusa (2003). A complete overview of AD appears in Blonigen and Prusa (forthcoming). There has been far less work on other types of nontariff protection, such as the use of standards, administrative measures and other exceptional protectionist measures.[6] There has been even less work on non-traditional (as opposed to non-tariff) barriers, such as administrative measures, invasive inspection of containers, *etc.* The empirical analysis of these measures is it in its early stages. The papers collected in Maskus and Wilson (2001) and Deardorff and Stern (1998) are some of the few organized attempts at measuring these barriers to trade.

---

[4] The survey documents the executives' perceptions of protection, and not the levels of protection *per se*.

[5] See also Bagwell and Satiger (1990) and Fischer and Osorio (2002).

[6] Among the few theoretical sources are Fischer and Serra (2000) on standards and the collection of articles in Bhagwati and Hudec (1996).

The next section provides a brief description of the Chilean economy. The third section describes the survey and the firms selected, the fourth provides the survey responses and the fifth section concludes.

2. A Brief Description of Chilean Trade

Chile is a developing economy with a GDP of about US$70 billion. It had a period of fast growth during the years 1985-1997, which averaged 6 to 7 percent annually. Since then, growth has been slow, averaging about 3 percent *per* year, though prospects are improving. It is a very open economy, with maximum tariffs of 6 percent (excluding sugar, wheat and oil imports) and average duties of 3.5 percent when we consider all the Trade Agreements the economy has signed.

Chile has signed Free Trade Agreements with most economies in South America: Bolivia, Colombia, Ecuador, Peru and Venezuela and Mercosur.[7] Other agreements include: European Union, Canada, Mexico, the United States, EFTA, Central America, and a recently ratified agreement with South Korea, that economy's first FTA. The fact that Chile has signed all these FTA's imply that in many cases, the only protection exporters face is non-tariff protection.

Trade represents about 55 percent of Chile's GDP. Exports grew fairly rapidly until the Asian crisis of 1997, which led to declines in the prices of many Chilean exports. Exports volumes continued to grow, however, and the recent increase in exports prices means that the value of exports surpassed US$20 billion in 2003.

Chile has few nontariff barriers and few barriers to services, there is national treatment of foreign providers in sales to government, and Chile is generally regarded as one of the most open economies in the hemisphere.

Chilean exports (see table 1) are to a large extent based on natural resources, though in many cases they have been processed. Copper is the main export, with forestry products, wine, fruit, salmon and other seafoods are other important sectors.[8] Around 12 percent of exports go to Central and South America, 24 percent to NAFTA economies, 24 percent to the European Union, and almost 31 percent is exported to the Asian Pacific basin.[9]

---

[7] Mercosur, includes Argentina, Brazil, Paraguay and Uruguay. The agreements with Mercosur and the other South American economies are Acuerdos de Complementación Ecónomica, a slightly more inclusive form of trade agreement, because it includes investment and other measures.

[8] Wine can be thought of as fruit plus capital, and salmon as fishmeal plus capital. So these products belong to a second stage of processing of the underlying natural resource. See Fischer (2001).

[9] The source of the data is Prochile, for January-November 2003.

Figure 1. Chilean trade

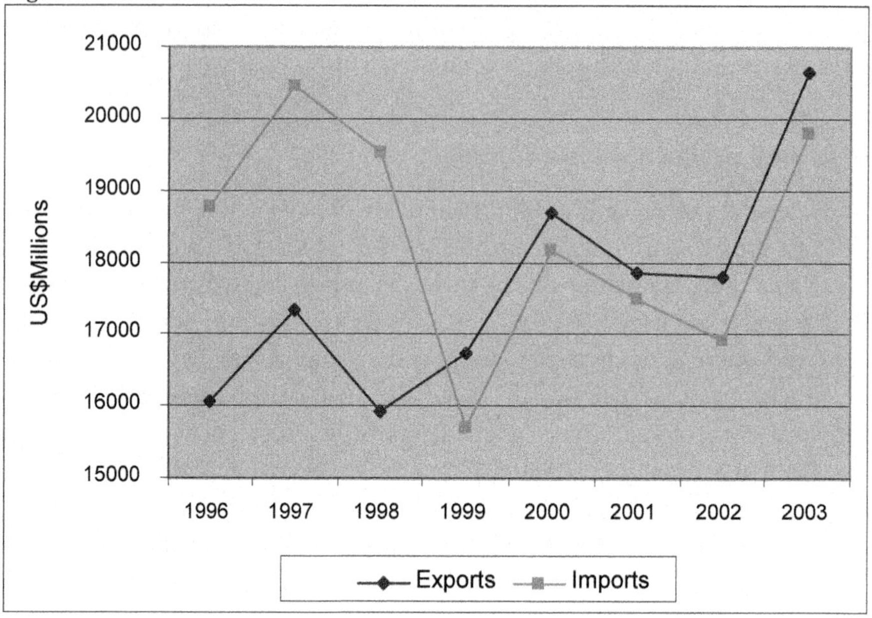

Source: Banco Central de Chile.

Table 1. The main Chilean exports, 2000

Rank	Classif.	Name	Value (US$ thousands)	Exports (Percent)
1	7403	Refined copper	4,662,385	25.3
2	2603	Copper minerals and concentrates	2,383,813	12.9
3	4703	Cellulose	1,111,697	6.0
4	0806	Grapes	693,448	3.8
5	0304	Fish fillets and other fish meat	603,211	3.3
6	2204	Wine	580,231	3.1
7	0303	Frozen fish	490,610	2.7
8	4407	Sawn wood	334,230	1.8
9	2905	Acyclic alcohols	316,911	1.7
10	7108	Gold	291,746	1.6
11	0016	Services for ships	290,571	1.6
12	7402	Unrefined copper	286,085	1.6
13	0808	Apples, pears	256,269	1.4
14	2301	Fish meal	235,345	1.3
15	2710	Petroleum oils	174,070	0.9
16	2613	Molybdenum	170,367	0.9
17	0809	Peaches, apricots, cherries	161,337	0.9
18	2801	Fluorine, chlorine, bromine and iodine	147,085	0.8
19	2601	Iron minerals	141,879	0.8
20	4401	Wood and chips	133,794	0.7
		Total	18,425,000	100.0

Source: Fischer (2001).

3. The Survey

The object of this paper is to provide a preliminary evaluation of the non-traditional barriers to trade affecting Chilean exporters by means of semi-structured interviews with the executives in charge of exports in a sample of Chilean exporters (export specialists in the case of large firms). The ministry of economics already has an inventory (or cadastre) of all trade barriers affecting Chilean exporters.[10] However, this list of barriers makes no effort to compare the importance of the various trade barriers and their impact on exporters. This exploratory survey, on the other hand, is an attempt at evaluating, from the point of view of exporters, the relative importance of the different NTB's. Moreover, it provides a subjective evaluation of measures that are difficult to classify and describe in a cadastre.

Originally, the survey intended to evaluate the quantitative impact of standards and other NTB's on exports by having export executives provide the tariff equivalent impact of these barriers. In an initial pilot survey, it became clear that firms and executives are unable to make these cost computations. Given the results of the pilot survey, the survey changed into an examination of the qualitative effects of protection on firms. In any case, the failure of the pilot study suggests that large exporting firms should begin to study tariff equivalences of the barriers they face in order to make better choices of the markets of destination for their products as well as to know where expend their efforts at eliminating these barriers.

The firms belonged to a wide range of industries, ranging from firms that export hundreds of millions of dollars to others that export less than a million dollars or export only sporadically (table 2). The range of firms includes firms whose main market is exports to those that export only sporadically. Some of the firms export primarily within the western hemisphere (Canada, the United States, and Latin America), while others specialize in the developed economies. The goods that are exported range from abalone to avocado and from medical gloves to gases.

One important conclusion is that most trade within Latin America is protected by free trade agreements that confer an advantage to Chilean exporters. This is a form of trade deviation, since at least some exporters can only export to those markets due to the tariff differential facing their exports as compared to more efficient third country producers.[11]

---

[10] See *http://www.minecon.cl*, catastro.

[11] For a theoretical analysis of trade creation and trade deviation, see Panagariya (2000). The political economy of the agreements is described in The World Bank (2000).

Table 2. Surveyed firms

Company	Exports 2002 (US$ thousands)	Products
1	350,000	Cellulose
2	66,000	Copper manufactures
3	61,000	Paper for newspapers
4	500	Bicycles
5	8,000	Plastic packaging
6	478,000	Cellulose
7	223,000	Lumber cut to shape
8	66,000	Tires
9	6,500	Electrodes and soldering wire
10	400	Latex gloves
11	3,600	Turbot and abalone
12	33,000	Tomato paste, canned fruit, jams, pulp
13	-	Detonators for mining
14	70	Plastic bags
15	38,000	Avocados, lemons, grapes

Source: Prochile web page, processed by the author.

On the other hand, the complaints of the executives surveyed concentrated on the Latin American economies as compared to developed economies.[12] The economy in Latin America that receives the most complaints is Brazil. It imposes non-tariff trade barriers of all types, and in several cases dissuaded exporters from even attempting to enter the market or caused them to cease exporting to its markets. Those firms that export to Brazil usually consider it the most closed market in the Americas. Recall that Chile has had a free trade agreement with Mercosur, and therefore with Brazil, for more than five years.

Some of the important problems affecting Chilean exporters in Latin America consist in bureaucratic and administrative problems on arrival. In many cases, exporters prefer to export FOB, so that they do not face these difficulties directly. The advantage is that the importer, who has the local know-how, is the one that deals with these bureaucratic difficulties, which in many cases may involve payments to these bureaucrats. For other firms, which have their own local distributors in the foreign markets, this is not possible, and they must face the gamut of trade restrictions. As an example consider the case of Mexico, where one problem is the propensity of custom officers to set containers on the ground

---

[12] Very few firms export to African and Saharan economies, but they all complain about the procedures and their lack of transparency, which appear to be worse than those of Europe, Asia and the Americas. Due to the few observations, it is impossible to determine whether this perception is significant.

for some inspections, which adds considerably to total costs.[13] Argentina and Peru have accused some Chilean exporters of dumping. In a few cases these accusations have prospered and the exporters are excluded from those markets.

Moreover, there are some self-inflicted problems for exporters due to Chilean procedures. Those include the rigid schedules of the SAG (Servicio Agrícola y Ganadero, which supervises the quality of exports of agricultural goods) and Sernapesca (which plays a similar role in fishing and aquiculture exports). Similarly, the Foreign Ministry is very slow in performing the signature verifications required for some markets, such as those in Arab economies.

These difficulties imply that there are at least two areas in which the government can have a positive effect on exporters. First, it can improve administrative procedures, increasing the flexibility of the work schedules of the inspectors associated to different services or by increasing the speed of the procedures at the Ministry of Foreign Relations. Second, it might be useful that the same ministry would examine the administrative procedures in the destination markets (perhaps through a program of interviews similar to the present survey) and would act directly with the governments of the importing economies. This should lead to improvements in procedures.

4. Survey Responses

4.1. *Pilot Study*

The first four companies were part of an initial pilot program of surveys, in order to determine whether the survey could be carried out. As has been mentioned, the original objective was to determine a quantitative tariff equivalent of tariff measures.

4.1.1. *Firm 1*

Its exports are mainly cellulose, a homogenous forestry product – a precursor to paper – that is distinguished mainly by the type of production process and particularly by the use of chlorine in it.[14] The firm has a global market and exports to Europe, Asia and Latin America, with similar margins in all markets.

The executives responsible for exports were unable to estimate the cost of nontariff barriers in their destination markets. They are adamant that these

---

[13] The charges for putting containers on the ground and putting them back on carriers are high, and there are costly delays associated to these revisions.

[14] Since protectionism in this product is linked to environmental concerns and chlorine laced effluents contaminate rivers.

restrictions exist and that they are costly. In some cases, they are able to determine the different costs of similar procedures across economies. The executives also questioned the need for physical (in many cases destructive) revisions of container cargo. The main executive was unable to provide even a ranking of protectionism among the various economies.

4.1.2. *Firm 2*

Exports copper tubes, sheets, wires and other copper manufactures. Sixty percent of its exports go to Latin America. According to the firms, exports to the United States and to Latin America face few problems except in Brazil, which imposes many restrictions. Among others there are different measures adding up to a tariff equivalent of 25 to 30 percent.

Since Firm 2 had not obtained the ISO 9000 standards, it had some problems in Europe, but the firm expected them to be temporary, until it obtains the certification. Exports to Australia have faced problems, since the containers have been fumigated and placed under quarantine, which raises the costs of storage as well as increasing the cost of capital. Even though this is an outwards oriented firm, the executives had trouble even understanding the concept of the quantitative cost of a non-tariff measure. They were, however, able to establish an ordering of economies in terms of protectionism. Brazil is the most protectionist economy, followed by Europe and Australia and then Latin America and the United States (which usually includes Canada).

4.1.3. *Firm 3*

This firm exports newsprint paper. Though most economies do not impose restriction on these imports, due to the opposition of the written press, they face restrictions in certain economies.

Some of these problems are due to the existence of monopolies or imperfect competition. An example is provided by the costs of maritime transport to Brazil, which are 66 percent more expensive than shipments for similar distances to other economies. The higher cost is due to a restriction to transport between the two economies to ships of either flag, and the fact that the main Chilean company is the owner of the Brazilian shipper.

The executives were able to order destination economies according to the ease of access to their markets. Brazil is clearly the most protectionist market (and not only due to the higher shipping costs). Mexico is another difficult market due to its high inspections charge and the fact that it inspects all of the cargo originating in South and Central America in search of drugs. In many cases, this damages the cargo. Venezuela is another economy that sets restrictions to the imports of newsprint. In markets such as Peru, Argentina or Ecuador, protection levels are lower.

4.1.4. *Firm 4*

A firm that produces bicycles under license and under its own brand name for the Chilean and Latin American markets. It uses a network of exclusive distributors in its export markets.[15] It exports approximately 30 percent of its production, amounting to approximately US$0.5 million.

The export manager was able to order the different destination markets according to their level of non-standard protectionism, even though he had difficulties in distinguishing between economies with similar levels of protection (the ranking is from more to less protectionist):

1. Brazil: The firm does not export to that market since the 1995-96 season, due to the combination of high tariffs, administrative barriers and the lack of seriousness of local distributors.
2. Colombia: Imposes a complex and cumbersome procedure that involves manually listing serial numbers on the bicycles, which only applies to firms that have serial numbers on their exports, and therefore does not apply to competitors from Asia.
3. Mexico has cumbersome administrative procedures.
4. Peru has a cumbersome pre-embarkation procedure and bill of lading difficulties.
5. Ecuador has relatively few problems and the administrative costs are no more than 1 percent.
6. Bolivia also does not have important restrictions to imports.
7. Venezuela restricts imports using quality standards that favor its own assembly plants, especially since the norms appear not to be totally defined. The country risk is high and imports face many bureaucratic hurdles.
8. Argentina places no restrictions in imports, except for those due to corruption in the administrative apparatus. It is one of the few economies in which the bill of lading does not represent a problem.

---

[15] Apparently, it is able to export due to trade diversion caused by the FTAs signed by Chile with Latin American economies.

4.1.5. *Firm 5*

Produces containers of various types: metal containers for agricultural industry, polypropylene sacks and cloth and raschel nets. It exports approximately US$8.5 million, representing, on average, 45 percent of its production, mostly going to other Latin American economies.

The firm has faced problems in Argentina, where tariffs were raised to 30 percent, excluding it from the market of polypropylene sacks. In an attempt to evade these tariffs, it bought a plant in Argentina so it could export polypropylene cloth for manufacture into sacks. It was then accused of dumping cloth and had to agree to a minimum price that left it out of the market again. Imports of raschle netting face a 32-percent tariff after a recent change in the customs classification.[16]

Brazil is another market that is closed for sacks, because even though exports face only an 8 percent tariff, it imposes a non-tariff barrier by requiring that sacks have batch labeling, which adds significantly to costs and applies only to non-Mercosur sacks. Brazil is also totally closed to imports of metal containers. Both Argentina and Brazil impose costly physical inspections. In general, Mercosur–with the exception of Uruguay–is very protectionist on the market segments covered by this company.

In Peru, there is non-reciprocity, since their sacks are imported under the general tariff (now 6 percent), whereas the company's exports face a 20 percent tariff. Moreover, local sack producers have pressured for a series of non-tariff barriers. Sacks for fishmeal are allowed entry only temporarily, so they can only be used for Peruvian fishmeal exports and not for local consumption. It is difficult to export to Bolivia due to the combination of non-tariff barriers, the high transport costs and the administrative costs.

Colombia, Ecuador, Venezuela and Mexico pose no serious problems.[17] However, in Mexico the firm has been careful to keep no more than 5 percent of the market, so as not to provoke a protectionist response due to a lobby of domestic producers.

Even though Firm 5 does not operate in Europe, it believes it is a relatively closed market. There are no problems with exports to the United States. When asked for a ranking, the most protectionist economy was Brazil, followed by Argentina and Peru, while the other economies pose fewer restrictions.

---

[16] Recall that Argentina is a member of Mercosur, with which Chile has signed an FTA.

[17] Except for the difficulties with letters of credit in Venezuela.

4.1.6. *Firms 6 and 7*

A large producer of paper, cellulose and of wood cut to shape, which is a global exporter. It faces problems in the Middle East, which requires large amounts of documentation, which in turn requires signature verification at the Chilean Foreign Office. This is a cumbersome procedure and the Foreign Office approves at most five signatures *per* day.

The company exports a lot of paper to Asia (Korean Rep., Chinese Taipei and Japan), which require packing lists with special formats. The Popular Republic of China asks for redundant phitosanitary certificates and has incoherent and cumbersome rules, but it is an attractive market.[18]

The firm finds it difficult to export to Brazil due to the need for certificates of origin and because of problems with invoices. Peru, Ecuador (which changes its rules frequently) and Central America require phitosanitary certificates for sawn wood imports. Mexico requires the original bill of lading and generally works though problems subsist.

In developed economies, the firm's exports face no problems, except in the United States, when the quota limit for the tariff exemption under GSP is reached. The economies that are most protectionist are those of the Middle East and Northern Africa. Central America and Ecuador are also difficult. Brazil is not a problem because the company almost does not export to that market, and it is entirely closed to wood exports.

4.1.7 *Firm 8*

This firm specializes in tires, though it has smaller production lines of car batteries and conveyor belts, which represent about 8 to 10 percent of sales. It exports about US$65-70 million a year, of rubber-based products with a price of US$80/100lb. The firm has plants around the world that have specialized and export to each other.

The Chilean plant is quite modern and productive. It exports 1.2 million tires to Mexico, 0.8 million to the United States (racing tires and value line tires sold as generic tires by large department stores). Current production is 2.5 million tires with plans for producing 7.5 million in 2005. Firm 8 exports to all of Latin America, Canada, Europe (including BMW), and US$1 million in tires for Wrangler jeeps in Australia.

---

[18] The manager mentions that the Agriculture and Animal Husbandry Service is efficient in obtaining the certificates.

Table 3. Exports of surveyed firms

(a) Exports of firm 1, 2002

Economy	US$ FOB
Holland	65,528,304
Italy	40,294,060
China	35,126,078
South Korea	30,387,485
Germany	27,803,768
Brazil	19,553,969
France	16,842,870
Japan	15,885,774
Peru	15,391,834
Chinese Taipei	14,111,052
Columbia	13,632,719
Venezuela	12,512,635
Indonesia	10,898,547
Other	37,696,017
Total	352,666,102

(b) Exports of firm 2

Economy	US$ FOB
USA	13,518,510
Brazil	12,533,731
Venezuela	7,210,450
Germany	6,156,665
Austria	6,089,937
Columbia	5,352,288
Ecuador	4,835,632
Peru	2,239,503
Mexico	1,908,635
Argentina	1,779,328
Other	3,913,471
Total	66,138,154

(c) Exports of Firm 3

Economy	US$ FOB
Peru	13,828,272
China	7,320,404
Venezuela	6,386,975
USA	4,881,729
Brazil	3,969,397
India	3,816,193
Dominican Republic	3,309,378
England	2,805,611
Ecuador	2,603,281
Bolivia	2,037,875
Columbia	2,019,870
Vietnam	1,934,546
Paraguay	1,756,320
Uruguay	1,496,041
Other	4,402,063
Total	61,072,214

(d) Exports of firm 4, 2002

Economy	US$ FOB
Peru	208,537
Mexico	125,327
Ecuador	98,587
Colombia	40,348
Bolivia	32,860
Paraguay	29,221
Venezuela	14,868
Uruguay	2,356
Total	552,104

(e) Exports of firm 5, 2002

Economy	US$ FOB
Peru	2,942,008
Argentina	2,891,357
Colombia	1,869,871
Mexico	281,719
USA	206,963
Ecuador	78,943
Portugal	60,829
Uruguay	54,763
Venezuela	40,001
Total	8,426,453

(f) Exports of firm 6, 2002

Economy	US$ FOB
China	161,548,242
Italy	51,329,105
Belgium	46,451,225
Chinese Taipei	45,773,304
Korean Rep.	36,563,615
Thailand	23,496,329
Indonesia	19,000,560
Spain	16,514,775
Japan	13,503,697
Colombia	12,786,839
Venezuela	11,627,715
France	9,738,154
Brazil	5,944,732
Other	23,956,970
Total	478,235,563

Source: Prochile.

Exports to Mexico are fairly simple, except that they require a certificate of origin that takes 3-4 days to obtain. Recall, however, that these tires are exported to another branch of the firm, which reduces the lobbying pressure of domestic competitors. Mexico does impose security restrictions and requires certification of new tire models, a process that can take up to a year.

The bureaucracy in Brazil is worse than in Mexico, with delays of a month to obtain an import license, plus a security certificate from a State laboratory. In general, exports to Brazil face many problems. The other markets in Latin America are smaller and less protectionist and this also occurs in the other markets of the firm. A ranking of protectionism indicates that Brazil is the most protectionist, followed by Mexico (basically due to its bureaucracy), followed by the other economies at similar protection levels. Colombia is a particularly open market.

4.1.8. *Firm 9*

Produces and exports gases such as oxygen, nitrogen, carbon dioxide and argon, as well as soldering electrodes. It sells about US$100 million a year, of which approximately US$7 million are exported.

Normally its markets are Latin America (45 percent to Mexico, 20 percent to Colombia, 20 percent to Venezuela). About 8 to 10 percent of its exports are sent to the United States. One of the major costs the firm faces with its imports is the physical inspections on departure and arrival. Another problem is due to the fact that any problem with the bill of lading means the container will be set on the ground, with the associated costs.

Brazil is an economy to which it is impossible to export. Even though tariffs are low, there is a special tax of 5 percent that applies only to imports, as well as other taxes known as the AFR, which has a cost of US$350 (compared to the equivalent cost of US $30 in Chile). Ecuador is also a complex economy to export to, since it has inspections that cost US$180 + VAT, with the risk that the container is set on the ground, which delays the process by 15-20 days. According to the interviewees, the protectionist ranking would be: 1. Brazil, 2. Ecuador, 3. Peru, 4. Argentina, 5. Colombia-Venezuela, 6. Mexico, 7. Canada and the United States.

4.1.9. *Firm 10*

A small firm that makes latex gloves. It exports about US $400,000 a year, *i.e.*, around 40 percent of annual sales. Its exports are possible due to trade deviation caused by free trade agreements of Chile and other Latin American economies.[19] In general, the firm faces few problems in its export markets: Colombia, Mexico, Peru, Paraguay, Ecuador and Argentina. Brazil asks for a sanitary certificate that requires nine months of processing. The firm has not made efforts to export to

---

[19] Trade deviation also occurs for production destined for local consumption because the main input, latex, is imported from Guatemala, without tariffs.

Brazil, among other things, because of capacity limitations. Most other economies — except for Mexico — have no domestic production, which is the main reason there is no protectionism. The executives at Firm 10 were unable to rank economies according to their protectionism.

4.1.10. *Firm 11*

Two linked companies that produce and exports aquiculture products, specializing in turbot and abalone, two high value species. The company exports most (84 percent) of its production of abalone to Japan and most of the rest to the United States. The export prices are US$9/kg for turbot and US$24/kg for abalone. The company exports mainly to developed markets, so it does not face some of the problems facing firms that export to other markets. It faces competitive pressures in Europe, both due to the higher transport costs as well as the high tariffs in those economies. However, tariffs should fall with the FTA between Chile and the UE, which should increase exports substantially, as their lower production costs will compensate for their higher transportation costs. There have been some lost opportunities due to the fixed schedules of the local SAG inspectors. In general, protection is not a problem for this company.

4.1.11. *Firm 12*

This is an agricultural firm that concentrates in exports of tomato concentrates, fruit juices and pulp, canned peaches, marmalades and other agricultural manufactures. It exports about US$33 million a year.

Apart from Japan, its main export markets lie in Latin America, where it is protected by the Free Trade Agreements signed by Chile. On the other hand, it finds it difficult to compete in Europe or with European exporters due to the subsidies they receive, especially in canned peaches and in tomato paste.[20] It also faces problems in exporting to Brazil, though this seems to be improving in 2003.

4.1.12. *Firm 13*

A firm dedicated to the production of detonators, explosives and other products for mining. It is a subsidiary of a US firm. Though it does export sporadically under special conditions, it has never encountered problems.

[20] In this regard, they are willing to pursue countervailing subsidy procedures against Mexican imports of European provenance.

4.1.13. *Firm 14*

A small firm that produces plastic bags and exports sporadically, when it finds attractive opportunities, and does not consider it an important market. For that reason, it does not have a clear opinion on the problems of protectionism in the export markets.

Table 4. Exports of surveyed firms

(a) Exports of firm 8, 2002

Country	US$ FOB
Mexico	25,822,901
USA	15,980,237
Bolivia	10,534,064
Peru	2,719,369
Argentina	2,511,441
Colombia	1,818,343
Ecuador	1,509,238
Other	4,958,928
Total	66,075,520

(b) Exports of firm 9, 2002

Country	US$ FOB
Mexico	1,413,321
Ecuador	1,265,101
Colombia	838,069
Peru	740,522
Argentina	733,889
Venezuela	620,093
USA	429,259
Other	523,435
Total	6,563,686

(c) Exports of Firm 10 2002

Country	US$ FOB
Colombia	156,370
Argentina	85,360
Mexico	73,604
Ecuador	45,425
Bolivia	19,401
Peru	13,107
Spain	11,111
Paraguay	5,134
Total	409,511

(d) Exports of firm 11, 2002

Country	US$ FOB
Japan	1,431,361
USA	1,156,984
Switzerland	218,495
Italy	221,138
Spain	278,177
Hong Kong	203,918
China	144,997
Germany	140,287
Other	178,223
Total	3971741

(e) Exports of firm 12, 2002

Country	US$ FOB
Mexico	8,860,451
Japan	3,743,758
Ecuador	3,383,046
Venezuela	2,971,996
Dominican Republic	1,461,570
Colombia	1,399,429
Brazil	1,389,452
Argentina	1,202,340
Peru	1,058,426
Thailand	1,013,500
Other	6409974
Total	32894315

(f) Exports of firm 14, 2002

Country	US$ FOB
Peru	34,973
Argentina	27,444
Bolivia	6,754
Total	69,171

Source: Prochile.

4.1.14. *Firm 15*

A firm dedicated to exporting fresh agricultural products such as avocados (its main product representing almost 50 percent of sales), lemons, grapes, nectarines, cherries and other fruits. Exports in 2002 were US$38 million. It exports 98 percent of its production of avocados to the United States. Lemons are exported to Japan and to the United States. In avocados, the firm observes no problems, except for the cumbersome phytosanitary controls, problems with the cooling chain in the USDA, and other minor problems. Another problem is the advantages that trade deviation gives to Mexican avocados (though these will disappear with the FTA between Chile and the United States). There is a marketing board, but this is not a problem as Chilean firms can participate in the mechanisms for fund disbursal. Antiterrorist measures have created some problems for shipments. Japan poses no problems, except those that relate to the special quality requirements. Europe is also not a problem for this exporter.

In Latin America, the firm encounters problems in Mexico due to incorrect manipulation and the typical problems with the bills of lading. According to the company, there are no problems exporting to Brazil. Although they do not export to that market, Saudi Arabia imposes many restrictions: monopoly issuance of import licenses requires special documents and it is impossible to export directly, since it is necessary to go through a local importer. An ordering of protectionism would be: Saudi Arabia, ex-socialist economies, the United States, Mexico (because of problems with the customs legislation), and Japan due to the existence of sporadic marketing orders.[21]

Table 5. Exports of surveyed firms

(a) Exports of firm 15, 2002

Country	US$ FOB
USA	26,396,889
Japan	6,726,026
Mexico	1,684,494
England	678,248
China	427,985
Holland	404,117
Spain	391,562
Saudi Arabia	321,153
Other	1,081,165
Total	38,111,641

[21] Note that in the two cases in which Arab economies are mentioned, there are no exports to Brazil, normally a sign of extreme protectionism.

5. Results of the Survey

This is an exploratory survey, and as such, the results are not conclusive. Nevertheless, there are some conclusions that can be derived from these results. First, the main object of the survey, which was to determine the quantitative effect of non-tariff barriers as exporters perceived them, was a failure. Exporters have a very vague idea about the impact of these types of measures and tend to confuse minor inconveniences with major problems. Moreover, it is possible that exporters do not perceive major markets as protectionist because they have already adapted all their processes to those markets, whereas smaller markets could appear to be more protectionist because the fixed cost of adaptation has to be divided among fewer units, as described in Fischer and Serra (2000). Moreover, it may be that exporters are confused by the constantly changing pattern of protection in Latin America and believe it is more serious than developed country protection, when in fact there may be higher levels of protection in developed economies, but these are fixed.

It appears that there is a need to develop accounting systems within firms that attempt to measure the costs of non-tariff barriers to their exports as a means of basing their export decisions. At most, exporters were able to order economies on an ordinal scale of protectionism. Nevertheless, this allows us to obtain a few results. In general, it appears that rules are more widely respected in developed economies. These economies may have higher quality requirements but once these are satisfied, the problems facing exporters are relatively minor. The Middle East appears to be highly protectionist, but the sample of economies involved and firms that export to them is too limited, so this conclusion must be qualified. In any case, it is not a significant market for Chilean exporters, representing less than 1 percent of exports. Latin America, on the other hand, is an important destination for Chilean exports and they face various problems. Brazil is clearly the most protectionist market in the sample, and this can be tested. Since six interviewees mentioned Brazil as the most protectionist economy, two mentioned the Arab economies and the remainder were unable to decide on which economy is the most protectionist, we can test the null hypothesis that Brazil is no more protectionist than the other Latin American markets, conditional on the fact that the surveyed executive has a protectionist ranking. Considering the average of seven economies to which the typical firm exports, we have that the probability of observing the results, conditional on the ability to rank economies is

$$P = 7/7^6 <<$$

1 percent, implying that the probability that Brazil is no more protectionist than the other markets in Latin America is much smaller than 1 percent.

Latin American protectionism often takes the form of administrative protectionism, even though contingent protection measures are also often used in combination. It is very common for local firms to recur to lobbying for protection. Exports of sacks to Argentina were stopped *via* the use of special tariffs, and when the company started local production, importing the required materials from Chile, these imports were also blocked *via* antidumping regulation. In Colombia, bureaucratic measures such as the revision of serial numbers in bicycles can have significant costs. In Mexico, customs procedures can be complex and may require "greasing" (by local importers) the officers in order not to practice destructive inspections or setting the container on the ground with the attendant costs. Brazil has a host of administrative measures, such as special taxes—not tariffs, even though they mainly fall on imports—and import licenses. There are many exporters that prefer to avoid Brazil altogether, given the difficulties it poses for exporters.

Venezuela is not categorized as very protectionist, but there are many problems with financing imports (letters of credit) under the current conditions. Peru and Ecuador are economies with intermediate degrees of protectionism, and in some sectors protectionism can be important, while in others it poses no problems.

References

1. Bagwell, K. and Staiger, R.W. (1990). A theory of managed trade. *American Economic Review*, **80** (4), 779-795.
2. Bhagawati, J. and Hudec (1996). *Fair Trade and Harmonization.*. MIT Press, , Cambridge, MA.
3. Blonigen, B.A. and Prusa, T.J. (Forthcoming) Antidumping in *Handbook of International Economics.* Basil-*Blackwell.*
4. Deardorff, A.V. and Stern, R.M. (1998). *Measurement of Nontariff Barriers* Michigan University Press.
5. Eithier, W.J. (1982). Dumping. *Journal of Political Economy*, 90(3), 487-505.
6. Finger, M.J. (1987). Antidumping and antisubsidy measures. In M.J. Finger and A. Olechowski, Editors, *The Uruguay Round: A Handbook for Multilateral Trade Negotiations.* The World Bank, Washington, DC.
7. Fischer, R. (2001). Liberalizacion del comercio, desarrollo y politica gubernamental. *Estudios Publicos*, **84**, 324-359
8. Fischer, R. and Osorio, M. (2002). Why do we need antidumping rules? Technical Report 134, Centro de Economia Aplicada

9. Fischer, R.D. (1992). Endogenous probability of protection and firm behavior. *Journal of International Economics*, **32**, 149-163.
10. Fischer, R.D. and Serra, P. (2000). Standards and protection. *Journal of International Economics*, **52,** 377-400.
11. Fischer, R.D. and Serra, P. (2001). Minimum standards: A new source of protection. In R.D. Fischer, editor, *Latin America and the Global Economy: Export Trade and the Threat of Protectionism.* Palgrave, UK
12. Maskus, K.E. and Wilson, John S., E. (2001). *Quantifying the Impact of Technical Barriers to Trade: Can It Be Done*?. Studies in International Economics. The University of Michigan Press.
13. Panagariya, A. (2000). Preferential trade liberalization: The traditional theory and new developments. *Journal of Economic Literature*, **XXXVIII**(2), 287-331.
14. Prusa, T.J. (1994). Pricing behavior in the presence of antidumping law. *Journal of Economic Integration*, **9**(2), 260-289.
15. Prusa, T.J. (1997). The trade effects of U.S. antidumping actions. In R.C. Feenstra, editor, *The Effects of U.S. Trade Protection and Promotion Policies*, pages 191-213. The University of Chicago Press, Chicago.
16. Prusa, T.J. (2001). On the spread and impact of antidumping policy. *Canadian Journal of Economics*, **34**(3), 591-611.
17. Reitzes, J.D. (1993). Antidumping policy. *International Economic Review*, **34**, 745-763.
18. The World Bank (2000). *Trade Blocs*. Oxford University Press, New York.

MEASURING AND MODELLING BARRIERS TO SERVICES TRADE: AUSTRALIA'S EXPERIENCE

Philippa Dee

Australian National University[1]

1. Why Worry?

Why should trade theorists and trade policy practitioners worry about services?

First, 60 percent of the world's GDP is earned there (World Bank 2001). This is not just a rich economy phenomenon – 119 of the 132 economies listed in the World Development Report have a services share of GDP that exceeds their industry share. And 81 have a services share of GDP that exceeds 50 percent – from Bangladesh and Botswana to Zambia and Zimbabwe.

Second, close to a third of world trade is generated there (Karsenty 2000). It is no longer tenable, if it ever was, to regard services as non-traded. Nor is it correct to say that most services trade is via commercial presence and hence not comparable to merchandise trade. Karsenty shows that on the basis of available statistics, 'traditional' trade in services – defined to measure cross-border transactions – is today larger in absolute size than establishment-related trade in services. And some of the economies most dependent (in relative terms) on services trade are also some of the poorest (*e.g.*, Armenia, Lesotho and Kiribati).

Third, barriers to services trade are significant. Because they are primarily regulatory, and differ substantially from traditional tariffs or quotas, there is no simple 'tariff equivalent' with which to compare to merchandise trade barriers. But the effects of removing them can be substantial. As will be shown, Dee and Hanslow (2001) suggest that the global gains from eliminating barriers to trade in services, based on preliminary estimates of those barriers, could be about the same as those from eliminating all remaining barriers to trade in agriculture and industrials. And significant gains would accrue to developing economies.

Fourth, services trade barriers are currently subject to negotiation in both multilateral and regional forums. Under the Doha Development Agenda, the first rounds of services requests and offers have been made. And of the 18 extant preferential trading agreements (PTAs) examined by Adams *et al.* (2003), 12 had significant coverage of services and foreign direct investment – issues that extend

[1] Dr. Philippa Dee is currently a visiting Fellow at the Australian-Japan Research Centre, Asia Pacific School of Economics and Government, The Australian National University.

beyond the boundaries of merchandise trade. Further, the coverage of non-merchandise trade issues increases, the more recent the agreement.

So it is incumbent on both trade theorists and trade policy practitioners to understand the nature of services, trade in services and services trade barriers. The aim should not just be to identify theoretical possibilities. It should also be to identify negotiating priorities, so as to maximise net benefits and reduce unintended consequences in a policy area that is still, sadly, largely unchartered territory empirically. With services sectors being large in most economies, the downside risk from getting it wrong is significant, and the risk is certainly there (*e.g.*, Dee, Hardin and Holmes 2000, Francois and Wooten 2001).

The purpose of this paper is to describe relevant industrial organisation features of services industries, and to outline their implications for the way that services trade barriers need to be measured and modelled.

2. What's Special About Services?

Services are often delivered face to face. This means that trade in services often takes place via the movement of primary factors of production – people or capital.

Firstly, the consumer may move to the producer's economy. This happens most clearly with tourism services, but it also happens with services such as education and health, when the student or patient moves to another economy for education or treatment. In the language of the General Agreement on Trade in Services (GATS) under the WTO, this mode of services trade is called 'consumption abroad'.

Alternatively, the producer may move to the consumer's economy. This also happens in education, where teachers move to another economy to teach short courses. It is also very common for professionals to travel temporarily to the economy into which they are delivering professional services. In the language of the GATS, this mode of service delivery is called the 'movement of natural persons' (to distinguish it from the movement of corporate or other legal entities).

Many other services are delivered to other economies via 'commercial presence'. In banking and telecommunications, for example, it is common for companies to set up a permanent corporate presence in another economy and to make their sales from their foreign affiliate. The GATS also recognises commercial presence as a mode of services delivery. This has policy significance, because it means that the GATS is a vehicle for negotiating foreign direct investment issues in the services area.

Another characteristic of services is that they are intangible. This means that where services are traded in the traditional 'cross-border' fashion, e-commerce is an important vehicle for that cross-border trade.

With services traded via the movement of people or capital, the transaction typically occurs behind the border. Even when cross-border trade takes place via e-commerce, it is not easily observed by customs officials.

So services transactions are not amenable to tariff protection. Instead, services trade barriers are typically behind-the-border, non-price regulatory measures.

Services are also an area where market failures can occur. Natural monopoly characterises a range of network services such as telecommunications and air transport. Almost by definition, asymmetric information characterises professional services, as well as health and education.

Thus trade in services may also be affected by domestic regulatory regimes that are designed to deal with the market failure. While they are not intended to be protective, they may not be the 'least burdensome' necessary to achieve their objectives. An example would be a requirement for foreign health professionals to retrain in a new economy. Here the legitimate domestic objective of ensuring quality could be achieved by the less burdensome requirement to resit a qualifying examination.

3. How to Measure Services Trade Barriers?

If services trade barriers are typically non-tariff measures, does this mean that the same techniques can be used to measure them as are used to measure non-tariff measures affecting merchandise trade? Or is there something special about services trade that means that different measurement techniques need to be used.

It is argued here that services trade barriers cannot be measured by the 'price comparison' techniques that are prevalent in the literature on merchandise trade (as surveyed by Deardorff and Stern 1997, for example), because services are highly differentiated products.

Services are commonly differentiated by economy. A domestic telephone call in the United States is not the same as a domestic telephone call in Australia, because the former is between Washington and Los Angeles whereas the latter is between Sydney and Melbourne. Similarly, the practice of law differs in the two economies, because the legal systems and legal traditions differ. What is more, some of the relevant trade restrictions in legal services are precisely to do with whether foreign legal professionals are able to practice host-economy law, home-economy law or international law in the host economy.

Services are also commonly differentiated by firm. This is because the production of services often involves firm-specific human capital. Microsoft is not the same as any other software firm because Bill Gates is not the same as any other software proprietor. And the development and maintenance of Microsoft required considerable fixed and sunk expenditure in R&D and other 'headquarters services'. Thus the relevant industrial organisation model for services is the same model of firm-level product differentiation and economies of scale that has been used to characterise the multinational manufacturing enterprise (*e.g.*, Markusen 1995).

Not only are services differentiated by economy and firm, they are also differentiated to the needs of individual customers. The legal services that my solicitor provides to me are not precisely the same as the services she provides to any of her other clients, because I have a unique individual situation. This characteristic was noted by Ethier and Horn (1991), and is one level of product differentiation below that now included in most trade models. I am not aware of any subsequent analysis that has included this characteristic explicitly, but it seems to be implicit in the choice of nesting structure of demand for varieties in some more recent models of services trade. This issue is discussed in more detail in Dee (2003a).

So if services are highly differentiated, it is not appropriate to measure services trade barriers using domestic-foreign price comparison techniques or their derivatives (such as the producer and consumer subsidy equivalent measures developed by the OECD for agriculture, or the various non-tariff extensions of the concept of the effective rate of protection). All such price comparison measures assume that the foreign price is a good 'benchmark' measure of what the domestic price would be in the absence of the trade distortion. But this presupposes that the domestic and foreign goods are perfect substitutes. For services, this is not the case.

Instead, for services it is necessary to construct the counterfactual – what the domestic price would be in the absence of the distortion – from an econometric model of what determines domestic prices. While most of the studies to date have used datasets (either cross-sectional or panel) that have a cross-country dimension, this is not because they are measuring domestic-foreign price wedges. Instead, they are exploiting cross-country (or panel) variation in the extent of barriers to trade, and cross-country variation in the domestic price (or some other measure of domestic performance), to quantify a 'cross-country average' relationship between barriers and performance, controlling for all other factors that affect that performance.

These studies tend to be of two types (see tables 1 and 2 for examples).

Sectoral studies quantify the direct impact of services trade barriers on sector-specific measures of performance. These effects on performance can be levels effects (if the performance measures are in levels) or could be growth effects (if the performance measures are in growth rates – though in practice, no sectoral studies have identified growth effects). But the key to these studies is that they are sectoral, and do not add up the effects of services trade barriers for the economy as a whole, as CGE studies do.

Table 1. Sectoral studies of the effects of services trade (and other regulatory) barriers

Sector in which barriers occur	Study	Sectoral performance measure	Growth or level effects	Cross-country or panel
Air passenger transport	Gonenc and Nicoletti (2000)	Airfares Load factors Airline efficiency	Level	Cross-country
	Doove *et al.* (2001)	Airfares	Level	Cross-country
Banking	Kalirajan *et al.* (2000)	Net interest margin	Level	Cross-country
	Claessens, Demirgüç-Kunt and Huizinga (2001)	Net interest margin Non-interest income Overhead expenses	Level	Panel
	Barth, Caprio and Levine (2002)	Bank development[1] Net interest margin Overhead cost Non-performing loans Prob. of bank crisis	Level	Cross-country
	Dee (2003b)	Net interest margin	Level	Cross-country
Business/finance	Francois and Hoekman (1999)	Exports	Level	?
Construction	Francois and Hoekman (1999)	Exports	Level	?
Distribution	Kalirajan (2000)	Cost	Level	Cross-country
Electricity generation	Steiner (2000)	Price Utilisation rates Reserve plant margins	Level	Panel

Table 1. Sectoral studies of the effects of services trade (and other regulatory) barriers–Continued

Sector in which barriers occur	Study	Sectoral performance measure	Growth or level effects	Cross-country or panel
	Doove *et al.* (2001)	Price	Level	Panel
Maritime	Kang (2000)	Price	Level	Cross-country
	Fink, Mattoo and Neagu (2001)	Price	Level	Cross-country
	Clark, Dollar and Micco (2001)	Costs	Level	Panel
Professionals – engineering	Nguyen-Hong (2000)	Price Cost	Level	Cross-country
Telecommunications	Warren (2000b)	Quantity Price	Level	Cross-Country
	Trewin (2000)	Cost	Level	Panel
	Boylaud and Nicoletti (2000)	Price Labour productivity Quantity	Level	Panel
	Doove *et al.* (2001)	Price	Level	Panel
	Dee (2003b)	Quantity Price	Level	Cross-Country
	Fink, Mattoo and Rathindran (2002)	Quantity Productivity	Level	Panel

[1] Bank credit to the private sector as a share of GDP.

Source: See table for references.

Instead, the first round impacts from sectoral econometric studies provide the key inputs into CGE studies, which then trace through the effects of services trade barriers on other sectors of the economy and, where a disaggregated approach is taken, can also add up the effects of services trade barriers across different services sectors. In doing so, the output of CGE models will be in levels terms if the inputs are in levels terms, but could equally be in growth terms if the inputs are in growth terms. There is nothing inherent in CGE models that restricts them to levels effects. Nor is there anything inherent in CGE models that restricts them to looking at a single aggregate services sector, although most CGE studies to date have been of that form. One of the highest priority areas for research is to build models with disaggregated services sectors, to allow for special features of different services and to examine sectoral priorities for liberalisation.

Table 2. Economy-wide studies of the effects of services trade (and other regulatory) barriers

Sector in which barriers occur	Study	Economy-wide performance measure	Growth or level effect	Cross-country or panel
Finance	Francois and Schuknecht (2000)	*Per capita* GDP	Growth	Cross-country
	Eschenbach and Francois (2002)	*Per capita* GDP	Growth	Panel
	Mattoo, Rathindran and Subramanian (2001)	*Per capita* GNP	Growth	Panel
Telecommunications	Mattoo, Rathindran and Subramanian (2001)	*Per capita* GNP	Growth	Panel

Source: See table for references.

Economy-wide studies quantify the *overall* effects of services trade barriers on some *economy-wide* measure of performance. Again, these effects can be levels effects (if the performance measures are in levels – though in practice, no economy-wide studies have identified levels effects) or growth effects (if the performance measures are in growth rates).

These studies are aiming to do the same 'adding up' job as CGE studies. But whereas CGE studies take a structural approach to spelling out how barriers in one sector flow through to other sectors and the economy as a whole, the econometric studies typically take a reduced form approach (although Francois and Schuknecht (2000) and Eschenbach and Francois (2002) have some structural elements).

And so the comparison of these economy-wide econometric approaches with CGE models hinges on the differences between structural and reduced form approaches. CGE approaches have a higher information content, and are less testable. But econometric studies need to control for all other factors affecting performance, and to deal (where necessary) with simultaneity issues. This is easier in a panel than in a pure cross-country context. In addition, economy-wide econometric studies are subject to the Lucas (1976) critique – their estimates of flow-on costs or benefits are appropriate so long as the economy stays with the same structure, but could be highly misleading in the face of structural change. And one of the main effects of reducing or removing barriers to services trade is to induce structural change.

The remainder of this paper discusses sectoral methods for estimating the direct effects of services trade barriers, and the ways in which they can be used as inputs into CGE models to estimate the economy-wide effects of services trade liberalisation.

4. Services Trade Barriers – Some Examples

Before proceeding, it is useful to list some concrete examples of barriers to trade in services. Table 3 gives a broad outline of the main barriers affecting trade in two different services – banking, and legal services.

Table 3. Description of barriers to trade in banking and legal services

Banking	Legal services
Restrictions on:	Restrictions on:
- number of bank licences	- form of establishment (*e.g.*, partnership)
- equity participation	- equity participation
- joint ventures	- nationality or citizenship
- raising funds	- licensing and accreditation
- lending funds	- quotas or needs tests
- other lines of business	- advertising and fee setting
- number of branches	- multidisciplinary practices
- temporary or permanent movement of executives	- activities reserved by law to the profession

Source: McGuire and Schuele (2000), Nguyen-Hong (2000).

The key thing to note about the measures in table 1 is that they do not always discriminate against foreigners.

In banking, the measures that affect only foreign participants are those that restrict equity participation, require it to take the form of a joint venture with a local partner, or restrict the temporary or permanent movement of executives. All other measures can be equally applied to domestic new entrants. These include restrictions on the number of banking licences or number of branches, restrictions on where and how banks can raise funds or lend, and on whether banks can undertake other lines of business (*e.g.*, insurance or securities).

Similarly, for legal services, a few measures affect only foreign practitioners – requirements for nationality or citizenship, and whether quotas or needs tests are applied in order to practice. Other measures can affect domestic practitioners as well. These include restrictions on equity participation, since some economies place restrictions on whether non-lawyers can have an equity stake in a law practice. They also include restrictions on the form of establishment (*e.g.*, whether corporate structures are allowed), licensing and accreditation requirements, restrictions on advertising or fee setting, restrictions on whether other disciplines (*e.g.*, accountancy) can be practiced out of a law firm, and the reservation of certain activities (*e.g.*, conveyancing) to the legal profession.

The GATS agreement similarly recognises that services trade barriers need not be discriminatory against foreigners. It recognises a specific list of (mostly quantitative) restrictions on 'market access' that are not discriminatory. Many analysts have extended the definition of 'market access' to cover all measures that are non-discriminatory. The GATS also recognises 'derogations from national treatment', which is GATS-speak for discriminatory restrictions.

Thus a key feature of services trade barriers is that they often protect incumbent service suppliers from any competition, be it from domestic or foreign new entrants. This is the single most important feature distinguishing services trade barriers. It has implications both for the economic effects of services trade liberalisation, and for the political economy of services trade reform. These implications are drawn out later in the paper.

5. A Measurement Methodology

The methodology used in Australia to quantify the direct effects of services trade barriers is outlined in Findlay and Warren (2000). It is the result of a collaborative research project between the Australian Productivity Commission and Australian National University. There are two key steps.

The *first step* is to quantify the extent of current barriers to services trade. Because the relevant trade barriers are primarily regulatory, this is by no means straightforward. The general approach in Findlay and Warren is to convert qualitative information about regulatory restrictions into a quantitative index, using *a priori* judgements about the relative restrictiveness of different barriers. This is generally less contentious within a given category of barrier than between. For example, it makes sense to score a regime that restricts foreign ownership to 25 percent or less as being twice as restrictive as one that restricts foreign ownership to 50 percent or less. What is less obvious is how to weight the scores on foreign ownership restrictions together with those on licensing requirements, or those on restrictions on lines of business. Nevertheless, some of the inherent arbitrariness of the weighting procedures can be tested empirically at the next stage.

The first step produces an index score for each economy of the form

$$R = R_1 + R_2$$

where R_1 and R_2 are scaled so that their maximum possible values reflect their relative economic significance, and typically sum to unity.

The *second step* is to develop an econometric model and use it to estimate the effect of the services trade restrictiveness index R on some sectoral measure of economic performance Y (typically price, cost, price-cost margin, quantity or productivity), while controlling for all the other factors X that might affect performance in that industry.

$$Y = \alpha + \beta R + \gamma X + \varepsilon$$

The appropriate control variables will obviously vary from one sector to the next.

It is also possible to use the econometric stage to test the weighs that were assigned *a priori* to different categories of restrictions in the first stage, essentially by reestimating them. This is done by entering the index scores for the different categories of restrictions separately into the estimating equation.

$$Y = \alpha + \beta_1 R_1 + \beta_2 R_2 + \gamma X + \varepsilon$$

Often this approach is precluded by one of two econometric problems – multicollinearity, or lack of in-sample variation in one or more of the restrictiveness index components. However, the regulatory work by the OECD (Gonenc and Nicoletti 2000, Boylaud and Nicoletti 2000, Steiner 2000) is suggestive of how factor analysis (of which principal components is an application) could be used to overcome these problems. Prior to any econometric estimation, they used factor analysis to identify a set of orthogonal 'factors' that explained most of the variation in their original data on regulatory restrictions. But as Doove *et al.* (2001) point out, high cross-country variation in restrictions may have little or no relationship with the relative economic importance of particular restriction categories:

> … the use of factor analysis could lead to paradoxical results – in the sense that the more important restrictions, if they were applied widely and consistently across countries, could also have low cross-country variation and thus low factor analysis weights. (p. 17)

If, instead, principal components were used as the method of econometric estimation, then problems of multicollinearity would be overcome and orthogonal linear combinations of individual restrictions could be identified that explained most of the variation in economic outcomes – a truer measure of economic significance.

Once the econometric estimation is completed, the 'on-average, *per* unit' effects of services trade restrictions are given by the estimated coefficients β. If total liberalisation would yield a restrictiveness index score of zero, then βR itself gives an estimate of the 'total, country-specific' effects of current restrictions on economic performance, relative to a free-trade benchmark (equivalent to vertical shifts in supply or demand curves). Mathematical manipulation can convert this into a percentage 'tax equivalent' (the appropriate manipulation depending on the particular measure of performance and the particular functional form for the estimating equation). The base for the tax would be the price, cost or other performance measure chosen.

However, a 'free trade' benchmark need not always coincide with zero regulation. The method is flexible enough to allow that in a free trade situation, it would still be appropriate to have prudential regulation of financial services, safety regulation of air passenger transport services, and so on. Thus, free trade could be associated with an alternative value R' of the restrictiveness index, and the value of β(R – R') would then be converted into a regulatory tax equivalent.

The first thing to note about the methodology is that it can be generalised fairly easily to include additional economies or additional time periods. Once a coefficient estimate for β has been obtained from a particular sample, all that is required for additional economies or time periods is to produce an index score R to characterise the services trade restrictions at that point in time, and the new 'tax equivalents' can be calculated from the existing coefficient and the new index score without redoing the econometrics. Obviously, the original sample needs to be fairly representative for such 'out-of-sample forecasting' to be appropriate. Many of the studies on Table 1 include, at minimum, the APEC economies, the members of the European Union, and often key economies from the rest of the world (*e.g.*, Switzerland, Turkey, India, and South Africa).

A second advantage of the methodology is that it produces estimates of the effects of trade barriers that are explicitly linked to characterisations of the restrictions themselves, rather than being generated as an 'unexplained residual'.

While it would be desirable to use information about every conceivable barrier affecting trade in a particular service in these exercises, this is not always possible. Where the index measures of services trade barriers are to be used in an econometric model, issues of comparability also arise. It would be inappropriate to use a dataset that showed a particular economy to be very liberal (or very illiberal), simply because information on some barriers to services trade was unavailable for that economy. Hence, the trade restrictiveness indexes used in econometric exercises may not be fully comprehensive, but they generally measure a broad range of barriers for which comparable data are available for all the economies in the sample.

In this respect, it is important that the information on restrictions be more comprehensive than that provided in the GATS schedules of WTO Members. Other sources have proved fruitful, including material produced by the Asia Pacific Economic Cooperation (APEC) forum, the OECD, the WTO and the United States Trade Representative.

A final issue is how to interpret the 'tax equivalent' measures. There are two related issues:

- what is the appropriate measure of performance Y; and
- what does each measure tell us about whether the restrictions are rent-creating or cost-escalating.

Take the second issue first. Restrictions could either create pure rents for incumbent firms, and should therefore be modelled as tax or tariff equivalents, in the same way as the MultiFibre Arrangement. Liberalisation would therefore be modelled as the elimination of those tax or tariff equivalents, yielding 'triangle gains' associated with improvements in allocative efficiency, along with redistributive effects associated with the elimination of rents to incumbents. As Dee and Hanslow (2001) demonstrate, the former effects would not be trivial, but the latter effects could also be significant. Alternatively, restrictions could increase the real resource cost of doing business. Liberalisation should therefore be modelled as a productivity improvement (saving in real resources), and yield 'rectangle gains' in terms of freeing resources for use elsewhere.

The distinction is critical, for two reasons. First, in a unilateral or multilateral setting, rectangle gains are likely to exceed triangle gains by a significant margin, especially given the importance of the services sectors in most economies. Secondly, in the context of preferential trade agreements, the danger of net welfare losses from net trade diversion arises only if the relevant barriers are rent-creating. If the barriers are cost-escalating, then preferential liberalisation will always increase welfare, even if the preferential partner does not have the world's lowest costs. This second argument is elaborated in Adams *et al.* (2003).

To date, most modellers have made an *a priori* judgement about which treatment is appropriate (*e.g.*, Hertel 2000, Brown, Deardorff and Stern 2000, Dee and Hanslow 2001), but the truth is likely to lie in between, and to differ from sector to sector. Pure rents are relatively rare in practice, but it is easy to imagine them being a component of the returns to international finance and telecommunications companies, for example, given the artificial barriers to new entry in those sectors in many economies. On the other hand, it is easy to imagine how the trade restrictions built into the international system of bilateral air service agreements frustrate the ability of airlines to reap network economies, and thus increase their real costs of doing business.

Ideally, the empirical work involved in estimating the economic effects of the barriers should give insights as to whether they are rent-creating or cost-escalating. For example, if the restrictions are believed to create rents, then the relevant measure of performance to use in the econometric analysis would be price/cost margins. If the restrictions were believed to raise costs, then the relevant performance measure would be a measure of costs or productivity. Even more ideally, each study should use a range of performance measures to identify what types of effects are being created. In practice, only one or two measures of performance are used, and not always the most appropriate ones in hindsight.

Where restrictions are believed or shown to raise real resource costs, there is a subsidiary set of questions to answer. Do the restrictions raise fixed costs, sunk costs, or ongoing operating costs? And what is the commodity or primary factor composition of the real resource costs so created? In practice, little information is likely to be provided on these subsidiary questions in the process of estimating the barriers. But this will be a fruitful area for different modellers to take different theoretical approaches in their applications, and to test the implications accordingly.

Thus additional work on estimating barriers to services trade is warranted, not only to increase the sectoral and economy coverage of the estimates, but also to give additional insights into the types of economic effects that are being created.

6. Trade Restrictiveness Indexes – Some Results

In its initial phase, the Australian research focused on barriers to market access and derogations from national treatment, and quantified restrictions affecting trade in the following services sectors:

- banking services in 38 economies (McGuire 1998, McGuire and Schuele 2000, Kalirajan *et al.* 2000);
- telecommunications services in 136 economies (Warren 2000a, 2000b);
- maritime services in 35 economies (Kang 2000, McGuire, Schuele and Smith 2000);
- wholesale and retail distribution in 38 economies (Kalirajan 2000);
- education services in 29 economies (Kemp 2000);
- professional services (accounting, architecture, engineering, legal) for up to 34 economies (Nguyen-Hong 2000); and

- foreign direct investment in a variety of services sectors in 15 APEC member economies (Hardin and Holmes 1997).

More recently, the work has extended 'beyond the border' into the effects of regulatory regimes in three important service industries – air passenger transport, telecommunications and electricity supply. Doove *et al.* (2001) drew on the OECD's rigorous assessment of regulatory regimes in these three sectors (Gonenc and Nicoletti 2000, Boylaud and Nicoletti 2000, Steiner 2000) and extended it to range of non-OECD economies.

Index scores were calculated separately for domestic and foreign service suppliers. A foreign index measures all the restrictions that hinder foreign firms from entering and operating in an economy. It covers both discriminatory and non-discriminatory restrictions. A domestic index represents restrictions that are applied to domestic firms and it generally only covers non-discriminatory restrictions (for most services, restrictions do not discriminate against domestic firms). The difference between the foreign and domestic index scores is a measure of discrimination against foreigners. Figure 1 provides a stylised illustration of a typical trade restrictiveness index.

The index methodology also distinguished whether a restriction applied to:

- establishment – the ability of service suppliers to establish a physical outlet in a territory and supply services through those outlets; or
- ongoing operations – the operations of a service supplier after it has entered the market.

Restrictions on establishment often included licensing requirements for new firms, restrictions on direct investment in existing firms and restrictions on the permanent movement of people. Restrictions on ongoing operations often included restrictions on firms conducting their core business, the pricing of services and the temporary movement of people.

Generally, the results from the restrictiveness indexes showed that Asian and South American economies had medium to high index scores. These economies were also found to be the most discriminatory against foreign service suppliers. European and North American economies tended to have low to medium index scores. Nevertheless, there were some important exceptions to these general trends, as some of the following examples illustrate.

Figure 1. A typical trade restrictiveness index

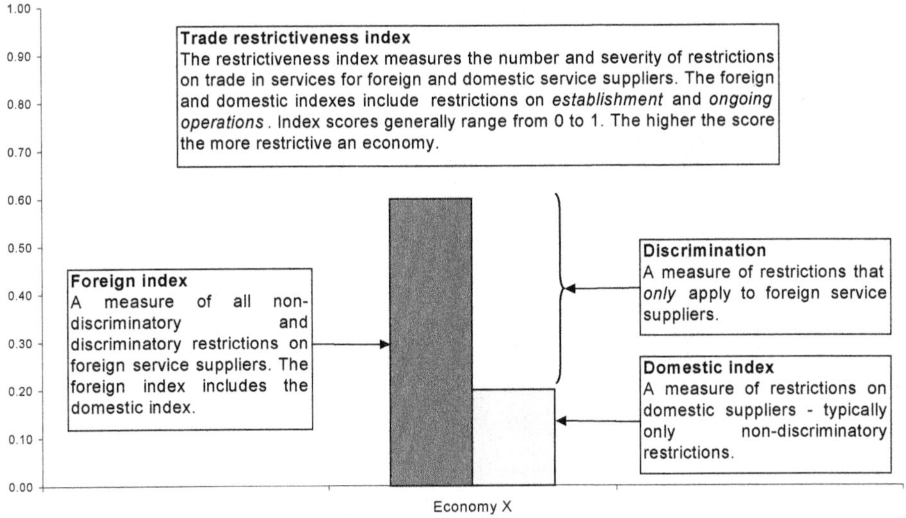

6.1. *Banking*

Figure 2 gives a summary of the index scores for banking services in selected economies. In computing the banking index, it was recognised that prudential regulation plays a vital role in ensuring the systemic stability of a banking system. Even though it may raise the operating costs of banks, it is not designed to restrict trade. The index was therefore compiled over non-prudential regulation (as listed in table 3), consistent with the 'prudential carve-out' of the GATS.

One important qualification is that the information on non-prudential restrictions covering trade in banking services was as at 31 December 1997, prior to significant banking reforms in many economies (including in Australia).

Figure 2 shows that at the time the information was collected, the Asian economies with the most restricted trade in banking services – India, Indonesia, Malaysia and the Philippines – also tended to be those that discriminated most against foreign entrants. Australia's index incorporates its restrictions on foreign equity participation in Australian banks. Australia's foreign banking index score, although relatively low, exceeds that for the United States, Canada and members of the European Union (not shown), primarily for this reason.

Figure 2. Banking restrictiveness indexes for selected Asia Pacific economies, South Africa and Turkey[1]

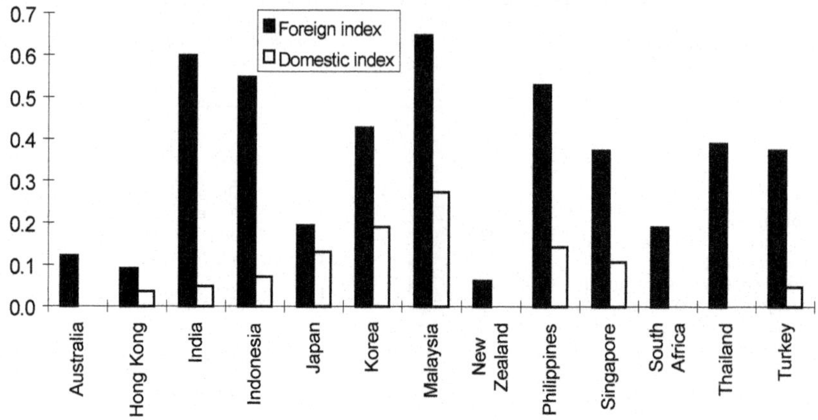

[1] The higher the score the more restrictive an economy. Scores range from 0 to 1.

Source: McGuire and Schuele (2000).

The potential significance of discrimination against foreign entrants in banking is illustrated in figure 3. This shows that economies with fewer restrictions against foreign entrants tend to have higher GNP *per capita.*

Figure 3. Banking foreign restrictiveness indexes and GNP per capita at PPP prices (1996)[1]

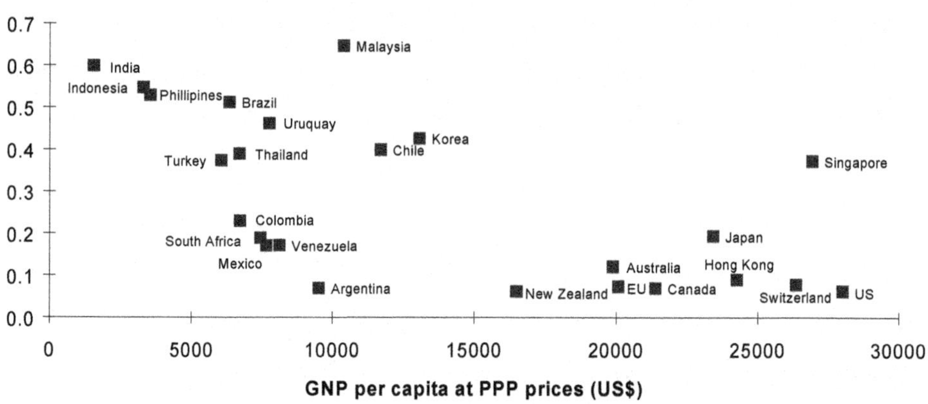

[1] Purchasing power parity (PPP) prices based on World Bank surveys undertaken since 1993. GNP *per capita* at PPP prices is used. GNP *per capita* using official exchange rates tends to undervalue low and middle income economies with relatively low prices (World Bank 1998).

Source: McGuire and Schuele (2000).

Other studies find a similar relationship between the openness of trade and income. Levine (1996) found that economies with financial systems that are better at performing key financial services functions tend to be economically developed, have higher income *per capita* and grow at a faster pace than those with less developed financial systems. PECC (1995) found a positive relationship between wealth and openness, in that APEC economies with a higher number of GATS commitments also tend to have higher GDP *per capita*.

6.2. *Telecommunications*

Figure 4 gives a measure of the total trade restrictiveness index scores for telecommunications in the top twenty services trading nations in 1997. The figure shows a high degree of variation, 'reflecting the continuing resistance among many economies to the liberalisation of their telecommunications markets' (Warren 2000a, p. 79).

Figure 4. Telecommunications trade restrictiveness index for the top-20 services trading nations, 1997[1]

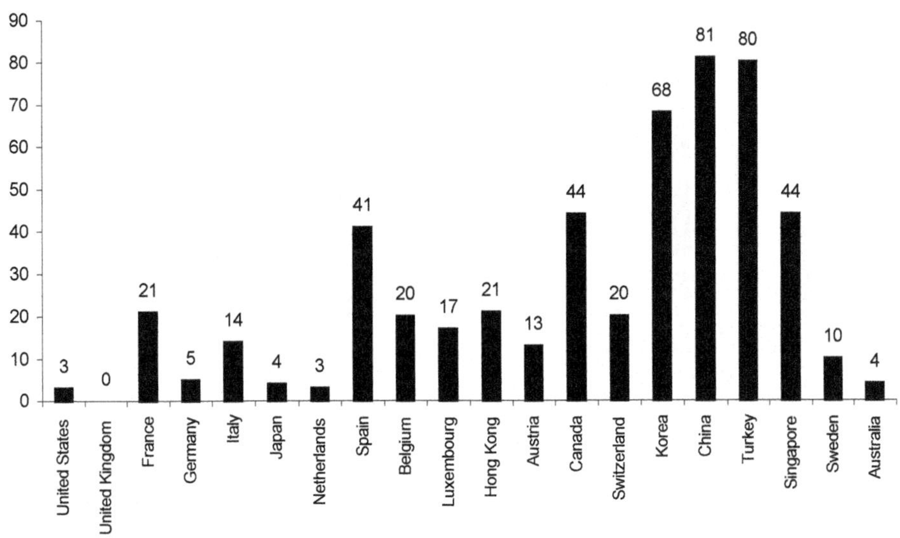

[1] The higher the score, the greater the degree to which an industry is restricted. The maximum score is 100 percent. The index is a simple unweighted average of scores for five components measuring restrictions on market access and national treatment in commercial presence and cross-border trade in fixed line and mobile telephony markets.

Source: Warren (2000a).

As with banking, there is a relatively strong correlation between the extent of trade restrictiveness and the level of *per capita* income. The high restrictiveness score for China, for example, is typical of that for a number of low and medium income economies. It also contributes to some of the modelling results highlighted later in the paper.

6.3. *Maritime*

In maritime, there tends to be less difference than in banking or telecommunications in the extent of trade restrictiveness between developed and developing economies. All of the 35 economies studied were found to maintain significant restrictions on new entrants, particularly foreign ones, in their maritime services markets (figures 5, 6 and 7). This was based on information on restrictions ranging from 1994 to the end of 1998, in areas such as cabotage, cargo sharing, government treatment of liner shipping conferences, and port services.

Figure 5. Maritime restrictiveness indexes for selected Asia Pacific economies and Turkey[1]

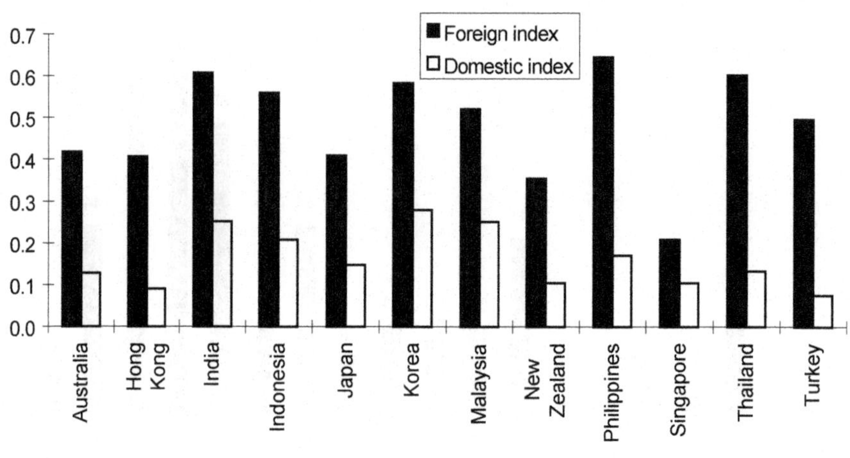

[1] The higher the score the more restrictive an economy. Scores range from 0 to 1.

Source: McGuire, Schuele and Smith (2000).

Figure 6. Maritime restrictiveness indexes for selected American economies[1]

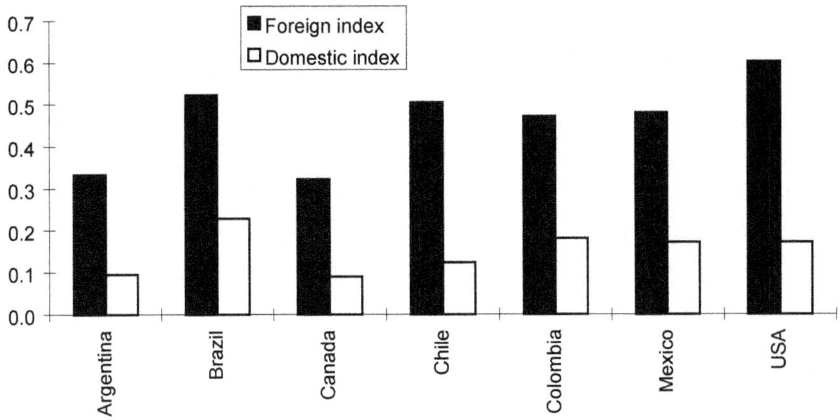

[1] The higher the score the more restrictive an economy. Scores range from 0 to 1.

Source: McGuire, Schuele and Smith (2000).

Figure 7. Maritime restrictiveness indexes for European economies[12]

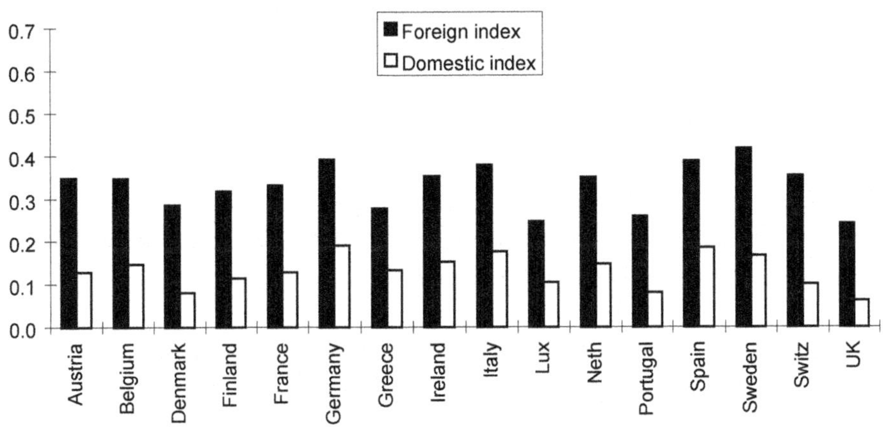

[1] The higher the score the more restrictive an economy. Scores range from 0 to 1.
[2] Inland waterways are covered by this study.

Source: McGuire, Schuele and Smith (2000).

Among the developed economies, the United States stood out as having a particularly restrictive trade regime. The Merchant Marine Act 1920 (the Jones Act) requires that all goods transported by water between U.S. ports be carried in U.S. owned, operated, built and crewed ships. The United States reserves the right to impose retaliatory measures on routes served by U.S. ships as well as routes served by foreign ships but carrying U.S. cargo.

The European economies tended to have lower restrictions on maritime services than the United States, although some of them, such as Luxembourg, are land-locked so the only meaningful restrictions were those applying to inland waterways.

7. Price and Quantity Impacts – Some Results

Australian research has estimated the effects of market access and national treatment restrictions on:

- the price-cost margins of banking services for 27 economies (Kalirajan *et al.* 2000);
- the price-cost margins for distribution services for 18 economies (Kalirajan 2000);
- the price-cost margins for engineering services for 20 economies (Nguyen-Hong 2000);
- the cost and price-cost margins for international air services (Johnson *et al.* 2000);
- the trade margins for maritime services (Kang 2000); and
- the cost and quantity for telecommunications services for up to 136 economies (Trewin 2000 and Warren 2000b).

The following examples show the limited extent to which the weights attributed to the components of the trade restrictiveness index have been able to be reestimated during the econometric stage.

It has typically not been possible to estimate the effects of trade restrictions on the performance of domestically owned and foreign owned firms separately. Since it has been argued that these firms are producing differentiated products, there should be no presumption that the prices of their services are equal in a given economy. Unfortunately, the information on ownership in the datasets used is either non-existent, or patchy at best. Thus the exercises have typically only identified impacts on a sample average of domestic and foreign firms. This constitutes an unfortunate theoretical inconsistency in the empirical work to date.

7.1. *Banking*

In Kalirajan *et al.* (2000), the effects of trade barriers on banking performance were examined in a two-stage process:

- first, the price performance of banks was 'corrected' for the influence of two key elements of prudential supervision – capital and liquidity requirements;
- then the influence of trade restrictions and other factors was examined on this 'corrected' price measure.

While the activities of banks have diversified enormously over recent years, a key banking function is still financial intermediation between depositors and borrowers. The raw price measure chosen was the net interest margin on this intermediation activity. The model, based on Saunders and Schumacher (1997a, 1997b), examined the main influences on financial intermediation activity.

The first stage was a firm-level estimation across a range of economies:

> Net interest margin = f [capital, liquidity, non-interest operating expenses (net of other operating income), economy dummy variables]

where all variables were measured as ratios and in natural log form. The net interest margin (including account service fees) was expressed as a ratio of interest earning assets. Capital (common stock, preferred stock and retained earnings), liquidity (cash and due from banks) and net non-interest operating expenses were expressed as ratios to total assets.

The capital and liquidity measures were the actual holdings of individual banks, on the assumption that these largely reflect prudential requirements. It was felt that using actual capital and liquidity ratios was the best that could be done, in the absence of data to compute each bank's actual reserve and liquidity requirements based on risk-weighted (rather than simple total) assets.

The inclusion of net non-interest expenses corrected for differences in the cost structures of different banks.

The second stage was a pure cross-country estimation:

> 'Corrected' interest margin = f [interest rate volatility, market structure, measures of trade policy]

where the 'corrected' interest margin was an average measure across all the banks in that economy. It was calculated from the results of the first stage estimation as the sum of the constant term and the coefficient on the relevant economy dummy in that equation.

Interest rate volatility was included because it increases interest rate risk for banks and reduces bank profit. It was measured as the variance of annualised quarterly deposit interest rates over the last 3 years. Market structure was included because greater bank concentration was expected to increase bank profits. It was measured as a four firm concentration ratio in lending assets.

The results in Kalirajan *et al.* (2000) suggested that higher capital or liquidity requirements would both raise the 'price' of intermediation services – the net interest margins of banks – although the result for liquidity requirements is highly insignificant. However, these estimates were only a partial measure of the effects of prudential regulations, which are not aimed at reducing the price of banking services, but at ensuring systemic stability. The results in Kalirajan *et al.* (2000) showed the incidental cost of such regulations, in terms of reducing bank profits, but they did not show the corresponding benefits.

Some insight into the benefits of prudential regulation is provided by Barth, Caprio and Levine (2002). They examined the effects of their regulatory variables on several measures of bank performance, including bank development (bank credit to the private sector as a share of GDP) and the probability of experiencing a banking crisis. They concluded that the stringency of capital regulations was not very closely linked with bank performance or stability, neither generally nor in particular institutional or regulatory environments. Instead, they found that regulations that encourage and facilitate private monitoring of banks tended to boost bank performance, while those that encourage diversification reduced the probability of suffering a systemic crisis. Their measure of capital stringency included such things as whether risks were properly accounted for, and whether capital requirements were officially verified, rather than the size of the capital requirements *per se* (as used in Kalirajan *et al.* 2000). Their finding on capital stringency raises questions about the conventional wisdom that such measures are beneficial.

Dee (2003b) extended the framework of Kalirajan *et al.* (2000) to also include the index measures of prudential supervision compiled by Barth, Caprio and Levine (2002) in the second stage of the estimation. Of the potential trade barrier and prudential variables, two were estimated to be significant – the policy variable measuring the extent of trade barriers to foreign entrants, and the measure of the extent to which foreign operators have actually entered the market. Trade barriers were estimated to increase prices, and actual foreign entry to reduce them. The results differed somewhat from those of Barth, Caprio and

Levine (2002), who found that only contestability, and not actual foreign entry, affected banking performance.

None of the bank supervisory variables were significant. As noted, these policies are designed to ensure system stability and integrity, not to reduce prices. The results were reassuring in that these supervisory practices did not appear to raise costs significantly as a secondary consequence. As in Barth, Caprio and Levine (2002), measures that encouraged private monitoring (7b and 7d) were instead estimated to reduce net interest margins, although the effect in Dee (2003b) was not significant. Barth, Caprio and Levine (2002) provide further evidence of how these policies contribute to banking system development and stability.

The econometric results from Dee (2003b) can be used to calculate the 'tax equivalents' of restrictions on banking activities. This is done by comparing the predicted values for net interest margins under current policy settings with the predicted values were policies to be set at their most (or more) liberal. The results give the percentage by which net interest margins are inflated as a result of the restrictions, and are shown in table for selected other economies (based on their 1997 policy settings).

Table 4. Tax equivalents of market access and national treatment restrictions on banking

	Trade barriers – market access	Trade barriers – national treatment	Low foreign ownership	Total
		Percent		
Chile	15.45	3.16		18.61
Indonesia	3.66	24.30		27.96
Korea	10.05	11.67		21.72
Philippines	7.45	19.93	3.59	30.97
Singapore	5.53	13.28		18.81
Thailand	0.00	17.85		17.85
Australia	0.00	3.53		3.53
France	0.00	0.50		0.50
Japan	6.81	0.12		6.93
Sweden	0.00	0.50		0.50
United States	0.00	0.12		0.12

Source: Dee (2003b).

The first two columns of table 4 show the tax equivalents of services trade restrictions. As noted, the tax equivalents of the non-discriminatory market access restrictions show the tax penalty imposed on domestic entrants. The tax equivalents of the national treatment restrictions show the additional penalty imposed on foreign entrants by discriminatory trade measures. Thus the total tax equivalent faced by foreign entrants is given by the sum of the first two columns in table 4. Note that the breakdown of the tax equivalents into their discriminatory and non-discriminatory components is based on the *a priori* assignment of weights in the restrictiveness index, rather than on econometric estimation. This is because there was insufficient in-sample variation in the non-discriminatory index to identify its effects econometrically.

Also potentially affecting the prices of banking services are factors that fall outside the narrow definition of services trade barriers. The econometric results in Dee (2003b) suggested that it was not just the contestability of the market for banking services that mattered, but also the actual extent of foreign ownership. The third column of table 4 captures the potential effects on banking prices if the actual extent of foreign ownership of banking assets were raised to the sample average of 18 percent. The currently low foreign ownership in the Philippines is estimated to add about 4 percent to the prices of banking services. Low foreign ownership was found to be more significant for the South East European economies.

Overall, the restrictions on banking services are estimated to have raised the prices of banking services in some developing economies by up to 30 percent. Clearly, there are significant potential gains from further reform in this area.

7.2. *Professions*

Nguyen-Hong (2000) estimated a model of the performance of engineering firms, in order to estimate the effects of trade restrictions on firm profitability, correcting for all the other factors that are likely to affect profitability in the sector. Extending models of profitability by Mueller (1986), the potentially relevant control variables were:

- market share of the particular firm;
- extent of overall market concentration;
- R&D spending, as an indicator of product differentiation;
- recent sales growth;
- diversification;
- absolute size;
- cost of capital.

Nguyen-Hong (2000) found that, correcting for other influences, non-discriminatory domestic barriers to establishment had a significant and negative effect on the price-cost margins of engineering firms. Discriminatory barriers to foreign establishment and ongoing operation had a significant and positive effect on price-cost margins.

The negative coefficients were taken as tentative evidence that the nature of the associated trade restrictions was primarily to raise the real costs of doing business. Thus the non-discriminatory restrictions, such as local licensing and accreditation requirements, were likely to raise costs, but the discriminatory nationality, residency and other restrictions placed on foreign professionals were likely to protect incumbent engineering professionals from competition and to create rents. In practice, both sorts of restrictions are likely to have independent effects on both prices and costs. The net impacts found by Nguyen-Hong would therefore understate the total impacts of the restrictions on competitiveness and efficiency.

Nguyen-Hong (2000) showed how the econometric results could be used to estimate the direct 'cost impact' of non-discriminatory restrictions and the 'price impact' of discriminatory restrictions for each economy in the sample.

The relative effects of the discriminatory and non-discriminatory restrictions were able to be identified by entering the foreign and domestic index measures together into the same regression. Therefore, multicollinearity was controlled for and the resulting coefficient estimates are not overstated.

The resulting price and cost impacts of restrictions on engineering services are shown in table 5, for selected economies. The results suggest that non-discriminatory barriers to establishment could raise the costs of engineering services by up to 5 percent. Discriminatory barriers to foreign entry could create rents for local companies, raising the prices of engineering services relative to costs by up to 10 percent. While the separate effects on the profits of engineering firms may be offsetting, both effects are likely to have adverse consequences for the economy as a whole.

While the results suggest that liberalising restrictions on engineering services may not be a high priority in many economies, they also hint at the potential gains from loosening regulatory restrictions on the more heavily regulated legal and accounting professions. For these sectors, Nguyen-Hong (2000) showed that the trade restrictiveness indexes tended to be significantly higher than for engineering.

7.3. *Other Sectors*

As with the restrictiveness index results, Asian and South American economies were generally found to have medium to high price and cost effect measures.

Table 5. Price- and cost-raising effects of barriers to trade in engineering services

	Price impact			Cost impact
	Foreign barriers to establishment	Foreign barriers to ongoing operation	All foreign barriers	Domestic barriers to establishment
		Percent		
Malaysia	11.3	0.7	12.0	5.3
Indonesia	9.9	0.3	10.2	3.2
Singapore	4.9	0.2	5.0	0.8
Australia	2.1	0.7	2.8	2.1
France	0.3	0.6	0.9	0.7
Japan	3.1	3.4	6.6	2.2
Sweden	5.9	0.9	6.8	0.7
United States	5.1	2.2	7.4	3.8

Source: Nguyen-Hong (2000).

European and North American economies tended to have low to medium price and cost effect measures.

A summary of the results from the trade restrictiveness index and econometric work has been included in the Productivity Commission's annual Trade and Assistance Review publications. These publications, along with detailed data on the trade restrictiveness indexes and results from the econometric studies, are available without charge on the Productivity Commission's website at *www.pc.gov.au/research/memoranda/servicesrestriction/index.html*.

8. Modelling Services Trade Liberalisation

8.1 *Studies to Date*

Few of the early multi-country studies recognised FDI as a mode of services delivery (table 6). Petri (1997) was a pioneering exception. Of those multi-country studies that did include FDI, few contained more than a single aggregate services sector. This reflects the constraints on model size associated with modelling FDI in a multi-sector, multi-country context. These constraints are still relevant.

In addition, many of the earlier multi-country studies took their estimates of barriers to services trade from the very early pioneering work of Hoekman (1995). His study combined an index measure of barriers to services trade, derived from GATS schedules, with 'guestimates' of the tax equivalents of those barriers. It therefore suffered from the incomplete coverage of GATS schedules, and lacked an econometric basis for the tax equivalents. More recent work by

Table 6. Selected CGE studies of services trade liberalisation

Study	No. of services sectors	Modes of services delivery		Barriers to modes of delivery		Source of estimates of services trade barriers
		FDI	Other	FDI	Other	
Multicountry studies						
Brown *et al.* (1996)	5	X	√	X	√	Hoekman (1995)
McKibbin and Wilcoxen (1996)	1	X	√	√ (in-direct)	√	Assumed
Petri (1997)	1	√	√	√	X	Hoekman (1995)
Hertel *et al.* (1999)	5	X	√	X	√	Hoekman (1995) and Francois and Hoekman (1999)
Robinson *et al.* (1999)	6	X	√	X	√	Hoekman (1995)
Hertel (2000)	8	X	√	X	√	Francois and Hoekman (1999)
Brown and Stern (2001)	1	√	√	√	√	Francois and Hoekman (1999)
Benjamin and Diao (2000)	1	X	√	X	√	Assumed
Chadha (2001)	8	X	√	X	√	Hoekman (1995)
Dee and Hanslow (2001)	1	√	√	√	√	Kalirajan *et al.* (2000) and Warren (2000b)
Verikios and Zhang (2001)	6	√	√	√	√	Kalirajan *et al.* (2000) and Warren (2000b)
Single country studies						
Konan and Maskus (2002)	14	X	√	X	√	Zarrouk (2000), Balhous and Nabli (2000), World Bank (2000), *etc.*
Jensen, Rutherford and Tarr (2003)	20	√	√	√	√	Zemnitsky (2001) and assumed

Source: See table for references.

Brown and Stern (1999), Dee and Hanslow (2001) and Verikios and Zhang (2001) has begun, in a limited way, to make use of the more comprehensive estimates available.

Two recent, single-country studies by Konan and Maskus (2002) and Jensen Rutherford and Tarr (2003) have been able to combine a much more disaggregated treatment of the services sector with much more detailed and country-specific measures of barriers to services trade. In Jensen, Rutherford and Tarr (2003), the estimates of barriers to services trade were based on the methodology of Findlay and Warren (2000). Konan and Maskus (2002) did not include a treatment of FDI, because in Tunisia's highly regulated economy, FDI was prohibited in many key services sectors, and they judged there was no way to predict how responsive sectors that were inactive in the benchmark would be to FDI in the liberalised environment. Jensen, Rutherford and Tarr (2003) judged FDI from new multinational service providers to be possible in 11 of their sectors (all in services), and modelled it accordingly.

8.2. *Australian Research*

The FTAP model has been used to examine the impact of multilateral liberalisation of services trade. It was developed by the Productivity Commission and is a 19 region (covering economies in Asia, North and South America and the European Union) by 3 sector (agriculture and food, manufacturing and services) computable general equilibrium model of the world economy. The FTAP model was developed from the Global Trade Analysis Project (GTAP) model (Hertel 1997), with the addition of some structure necessary to support the analysis of services liberalisation. A fuller discussion of the theoretical considerations in modelling services policy issues is contained in Dee (2003a).

The theoretical structure of the model covers both FDI and portfolio investment. The model's database contains estimates of FDI stocks and activities of FDI firms on a bilateral basis. The treatment of FDI allows for the examination of the comprehensive removal of restrictions on all modes of service supply, including restrictions on services delivered via commercial presence. Hanslow, Phamduc and Verikios (1999) fully document the structure of the FTAP model.

The first version of the FTAP model was indicative only in its treatment of barriers to services trade. An average of the estimates of barriers to trade in telecommunications and banking services, taken from Kalirajan *et al.* (2000) and Warren (2000b), was taken to be typical of barriers for the model's services sector as a whole. An area for further research will be to disaggregate FTAP's single services sector into its separate service industries and to model trade barriers for these industries separately.

Because of evidence that barriers to trade in banking and telecommunications services raised prices above costs in those sectors, services trade barriers were incorporated into FTAP as tax equivalents. Restrictions on establishment were incorporated as taxes on capital. Restrictions on ongoing operations were incorporated as taxes on the output of FDI firms and the exports of firms supplying via the other modes of delivery. Different 'tax' rates applied to domestic and foreign-owned firms, reflecting discriminatory treatment of foreign-owned entities. The model structure ensured that the revenues (or rents) from these 'taxes' were divided appropriately between the government and private agents.

In future, cost-raising restrictions will also be incorporated. But one implication of the current treatment is that the gains from services trade liberalisation are probably understated. As noted, if services trade barriers raise prices above costs and create rents for incumbent firms, liberalisation will yield 'triangle gains' associated with improvements in allocative efficiency, along with redistributive effects associated with the elimination of rents to incumbents. But if trade barriers raise the real resource cost of doing business, liberalisation could lead to 'rectangle gains' associated with a saving of real resources. And rectangle gains are likely to exceed triangle gains by a significant margin.

Dee and Hanslow (2001) used the FTAP model to find that the world as a whole would be projected to be better off by more than US$260 billion annually (in current dollar terms) as a result of eliminating all post-Uruguay Round trade restrictions. About US$130 billion would come from liberalizing services trade, of which US$100 billion would accrue in China. US$50 billion would come from agricultural liberalization, and US$80 billion from liberalization of manufactures. These were the projected gains in real income about 10 years after the liberalization had occurred and the associated resource adjustments had taken place.

Dee and Hanslow also projected the benefits of partially liberalizing services trade. The results showed that the greatest global benefits would come from liberalizing market access restrictions rather than national treatment restrictions (refer to table 7).

This is in contrast with the presumption widely found in the goods trade literature that the greatest gains would come from removing discrimination. In services, if restrictions on national treatment are removed while significant barriers to market access remain, the danger is that an economy will simply hand monopoly rents to foreign operators without gaining offsetting benefits in the

Table 7. Effects of partial services liberalisation on world real income[1]

	Remove restrictions on market access	Remove restrictions on national treatment	Both[2]
		US$ billions	
Remove restrictions to establishment	56.8	3.7	64.2
Remove restrictions on ongoing operations	25.6	12.9	39.3
Both[2]	98.8	19.3	133.4

[1] Projected gains in real income about 10 years after the liberalization had occurred and the associated resource adjustments had taken place.

[2] Because of interaction effects between types of partial liberalization, the figures for 'Both' are not additive.

Source: Dee and Hanslow (2001).

form of lower prices to domestic users. This is similar to the danger pointed out by Francois and Wooton (2001), and is part of what lies behind the FTAP results shown in table 7.

The results also showed that it would be difficult to find an outcome where at least some economies gained and none lost from partial liberalization, when it involved only removing one class of restriction (market access, national treatment, establishment or ongoing operations). This suggested that the best strategy for liberalization may be to negotiate gradual reductions in all types of restrictions simultaneously.

Dee, Hanslow and Phamduc (2003) looked at the question of which sectors would gain from multilateral services trade liberalization. An economy's services sector itself may not lose from liberalization because there are competing forces at work.

- Not all services trade barriers discriminate against foreign services suppliers, so the service sector could expand because of new domestic entry.
- Some services trade barriers restrict inward FDI, so the service sector could expand because of new foreign entry.
- Some services barriers discriminate against foreign services delivered cross-border, so the services sector could contract in the face of additional import competition.
- Services trade liberalisation could benefit downstream using industries, and the service sector may lose out in the competition for domestic resources (*e.g.*, labour).

The net effect was likely to be an expansion in the services sectors in economies where domestic services restrictions were high initially. Again, this is in contrast to liberalization of goods trade, and makes the political economy of services trade reform somewhat different.

The benefits to services sectors in economies such as China were projected to be particularly large, because of the focus of the initial work on barriers to banking and telecommunications, and the particularly high barriers to telecommunications trade in China. When trade restrictions in sectors such as maritime are also taken into account, the sectoral and economy breakdown of gains are likely to be more even.

Verikios and Zhang (2001) also used the FTAP model to analyze the sectoral impacts of removing restrictions on trade in financial and communication services separately. They found that the total gain in world income from liberalizing both sectors would be US$47 billion (in current dollars), with about US$24 billion of this coming from liberalizing communications services and US$23 billion from financial services.

9. Agenda for Further Research

The modelling of services trade in FTAP will be expanded to include the price and cost estimates for sectors beyond banking and telecommunications. More sectoral detail will also be incorporated in FTAP, so as to be able to model the benefits of liberalising each service sector separately and analyse the benefits of cross-sectoral trade offs.

More work is also required to model the movement of people. Dee and Hanslow (2001) lumped barriers to the permanent movement of people together with other barriers to FDI, and barriers to the temporary movement of people together with barriers to the other three modes of service delivery, but did not model either the temporary or permanent movement of people directly. This approach was adequate when the focus of attention was on barriers to FDI. But barriers to the movement of people *per se* is an issue of intense interest, especially to developing economies. If it is to be modelled directly, then the underlying flows of people will also need to be modelled. Winters (2002) summarises an important first step in this direction.

Finally, more work is needed to characterise domestic regulatory regimes across economies for selected industries, and to examine the interactions between services trade barriers and domestic regulatory regimes.

References

1. Adams, R., Dee, P., Gali, J. and McGuire, G. 2003, *The Trade and Investment Effects of Preferential Trading Arrangements – Old and New Evidence*, Productivity Commission Staff Working Paper, Canberra, May.
2. Bahlous, M. and Mustapha, K.N. 2000, 'Financial Liberalisation and Financing Constraints on the Corporate Sector in Tunisia', Working Paper No. 2005, Economic Research Forum for the Arab Countries.
3. Barth, J., Caprio, G. and Levine, R. 2002, 'Bank Regulation and Rupervision: What Works Best?', mimeo, World Bank, January.
4. Benjamin, N. and Diao 1998, 'Liberalising services trade in APEC: A general equilibrium analysis with imperfect competition', *Pacific Economic Review*, 5(1), pp. 49–75.
5. Boylaud, O. and Nicoletti, G. 2000, *Regulation, Market Structure and Performance in Telecommunications*, Working Paper No. 237, ECO/WKP(2000)10, Economics Department, OECD, Paris, 12 April.
6. Brown, D., Deardorff, A. and Stern, R. 1996, 'Modelling multilateral trade liberalisation in services', *Asia Pacific Economic Review*, 2(1), pp. 21–34.
7. Brown, D., Deardorff, A. and Stern, R. 2000, 'CGE modelling and analysis of multilateral and regional negotiating options', paper presented at conference on Issues and Options for the Multilateral, Regional and Bilateral Trade Policies of the United States and Japan, 5–6 October, University of Michigan, Ann Arbor.
8. Brown, D. and Stern, R. 2001, 'Measurement and modelling of the economic effects of trade and investment barriers in services', *Review of International Economics*, 9(2), pp. 262–86.
9. Chadha, R. 2001, 'GATS and developing countries: A case study of India', in Stern, R. (ed.), *Services in the International Economy*, University of Michigan Press, Ann Arbor, pp. 245–66.
10. Claessens, S., Demirgüç-Kunt, A. and Huizinga, H. 2001, 'How does foreign entry affect domestic banking markets?', *Journal of Banking and Finance*, 25, pp. 891–911.
11. Clark, X., Dollar, D. and Micco, A. 2002, 'Maritime Transport Costs and Port Efficiency', Mimeo, World Bank.
12. Deardorff, A. and Stern, R. 1997, 'Measurement of Non-tariff barriers', OCDE/GD(97)129, OECD, Paris.
13. Dee, P. 2003a, 'Modelling the policy issues in services trade', *Economie Internationale*, 94-95, forthcoming.
14. Dee, P. 2003b, 'Services Trade Liberalisation in South East European Countries', mimeo prepared for OECD, June.
15. Dee, P., Hardin, A, and Holmes, L. 2000, 'Issues in the application of CGE models to services trade liberalisation', in C. Findlay and T. Warren (eds), *Impediments to Trade in Services: Measurement and Policy Implications*, Routledge, London, pp. 267–86.
16. Dee, P. and Hanslow, K. 2001, 'Multilateral liberalisation of services trade', in Stern, R. (ed.), Services in the International Economy, University of Michigan Press, Ann Arbor, pp. 117–39.
17. Dee, P., Hanslow, K. and Phamduc, T. (2003), 'Measuring the cost of barriers to trade in services', in Ito, T. and Krueger, A. (eds), *Services Trade in the Asia-Pacific Region*, NBER-East Asia Seminar on Economics, Volume 11, University of Chicago Press, Chicago, pp. 11–43.

18. Doove, S., Gabbitas, O., Nguyen-Hong, D. and Owen, J. 2001, *Price Effects of Regulation: International Air Passenger Transport, Telecommunications and Electricity Supply*, Productivity Commission Staff Research Paper, Ausinfo, Canberra.
19. Eschenbach, F. and Francois, J. 2002, 'Financial Sector Competition, Services Trade and Growth', CEPR Discussion Paper No. 3573.
20. Ethier, W, and Horn, H. 1991, 'Services in international trade', in E. Helpman and A. Razin (eds), *International Trade and Trade Policy*, MIT Press, Cambridge Massachusetts, pp. 223–44.
21. Findlay, C. and Warren, T. (eds) 2000, *Impediments to Trade in Services: Measurement and Policy Implications*, Routledge, London and New York.
22. Fink, C., Mattoo, A. and Neagu, C. 2001, *Trade in International Maritime Services: How Much Does Policy Matter?*, Working Paper No. 2522, World Bank, Washington DC.
23. Fink, C., Mattoo, A. and Rathindran, R. 2002, 'Liberalizing Basic Telecommunications: Evidence from Developing Countries', paper presented at OECD-World Bank Services Experts Meeting, OECD, Paris, 4-5 March.
24. Francois, J. and Hoekman, B. 1999, 'Market access in the service sectors', Tinbergen Institute, manuscript, cited in B. Hoekman 2000, 'The next round of services negotiations: identifying priorities and options', *Federal Reserve Bank of St Louis Review*, 82(4), pp. 31–47.
25. Francois, J. and Schuknecht, l. 2000, 'International Trade in Financial Services, Competition and Growth Performance', Centre for International Economic Studies Paper No. 6.
26. Francois, J.F. and Wooten, I. 2001, 'Imperfect competition and trade liberalisation under the GATS', in R. Stern (ed.), *Services in the International Economy*, University of Michigan Press, Ann Arbor, pp. 141–56.
27. Gonenc, R. and Nicoletti, G. 2000, *Regulation, Market Structure and Performance in Air Passenger Transport*, Working Paper No. 254, ECO/WKP(2000)27, Economics Department, OECD, Paris, 3 August.
28. Hanslow, K., Phamduc, T. and Verikios, G. 1999, 'The structure of the FTAP model', Research Memorandum, Productivity Commission, Canberra, December.
29. Hardin, A. and Holmes, L. 2000, 'Assessing barriers to services sector investment', in Findlay, C. and Warren, T. (eds) 2000, *Impediments to Trade in Services: Measurement and Policy Implications*, Routledge, London and New York, pp. 52–70.
30. Hertel, T. 1997, Global Trade Analysis: *Modelling and Applications*, Cambridge University Press, Cambridge.
31. Hertel, T. 2000, 'Potential gains from reducing trade barriers in manufacturing, services and agriculture', *Federal Reserve Bank of St Louis Review*, 82(4), pp. 77–99.
32. Hertel, T., Anderson, K., Francois, J. and Martin, W. 1999, 'Agriculture and Non-Agricultural Liberalisation in the Millenium Round', paper presented at the Global Conference on Agriculture and the New Trade Agenda from a Development Perspective: Interests and Options in the WTO 2000 Negotiations, World Bank and WTO, Geneva, 1-2 October.
33. Hoekman, B. 1995, 'Assessing the General Agreement on Trade in Services', World Bank Discussion Paper No, 307, World Bank, Washington DC.
34. Jensen, J., Rutherford, T. and Tarr. D. 2003, 'Economy-wide and Sector Effects of Russia's Accession to the WTO', paper prepared for the Allied Social Science Meetings, Washington DC, 3-5 January.

35. Johnson, M., Gregan, T., Gentle, G. and Belin, P. 2000, 'Modelling the benefits of increasing competition in international air services', in Findlay, C. and Warren, T. (eds) 2000, *Impediments to Trade in Services: Measurement and Policy Implications*, Routledge, London and New York, pp. 119–51.
36. Kalirajan, K. 2000, *Restrictions on Trade in Distribution Services*, Productivity Commission Staff Research Paper, Ausinfo, Canberra.
37. ———, McGuire, G., Nguyen-Hong, D. and Schuele, M. 2000, 'The price impact of restrictions on banking services', in Findlay, C. and Warren, T. (eds) 2000, *Impediments to Trade in Services: Measurement and Policy Implications*, Routledge, London and New York, pp. 215–30.
38. Kang, J. 2000, 'Price impact of restrictions on maritime transport services', in Findlay, C. and Warren, T. (eds) 2000, *Impediments to Trade in Services: Measurement and Policy Implications*, Routledge, London and New York, pp. 189–200.
39. Karsenty, G. 2000, 'Assessing trade in services by mode of supply', in P. Sauvé and R. Stern (eds), *GATS 2000: New Directions in Services Trade Liberalisation*, Brookings Institution, Washington DC, pp. 33–56.
40. Kemp, S. 2000, 'Trade in education services and the impacts of barriers to trade', in Findlay, C. and Warren, T. (eds) 2000, *Impediments to Trade in Services: Measurement and Policy Implications*, Routledge, London and New York, pp. 231–44.
41. Konan, D. and Maskua, K. 2002, 'Quantifying the Impact of Services Liberalisation in a Developing Country', paper presented at the Economic Research Forum Ninth Annual Conference, October.
42. Levine, R. 1996, 'Foreign banks, financial development and economic growth', in Barfield, C.E. (ed.), *International Financial Markets: Harmonization versus Competition*, American Enterprise Institute Press, Washington DC.
43. Lucas, R.E. 1976, 'Econometric policy evaluation: A critique', in Brunner, K. and Meltzer, A. (eds), *The Phillips Curve and the Labour Market*, Vol. 1, Carnegie-Rochester Conferences in Public Policy, North-Holland, Amsterdam.
44. Markusen, J. 1995, 'The Boundaries of Multinational Enterprises and the Theory of International Trade', *Journal of Economic Perspectives*, 9(2), pp. 169–89.
45. Mattoo, A., Rathindran, R. and Subramanian, A. 2001, 'Measuring Services Trade Liberalisation and its Impact on Economic Growth: An Illustration', World Bank Working Paper No. 2655, World Bank.
46. McGuire, G. 1998, *Australia's Restrictions on Trade in Financial Services*, Productivity Commission Staff Research Paper, Ausinfo, Canberra.
47. McGuire, G. and Schuele, M. 2000, 'Restrictiveness of international trade in banking services', in C. Findlay and T. Warren (eds), Impediments to Trade in Services, Measurement and Policy Implications, Routledge, London and New York, pp. 201–214.
48. ———, Schuele, M., and Smith, T. 2000, 'Restrictiveness of international trade in maritime services', in Findlay, C. and Warren, T. (eds) 2000, *Impediments to Trade in Services: Measurement and Policy Implications*, Routledge, London and New York, pp. 172–88.
49. McKibbin, W. and Wilcoxen, P. 1996, 'The role of services in modelling the global economy', *Asia-Pacific Economic Review*, 2, pp. 2–13.
50. Mueller, D. 1986, *Profits in the Long Run*, Cambridge University Press, USA.

51. Nguyen-Hong, D. 2000, Restrictions on Trade in Professional Services, Productivity Commission Staff Research Paper, Ausinfo, Canberra.
52. PECC (Pacific Economic Cooperation Council) 1995, *Survey of Impediments to Trade and Investment in the APEC Region*, PECC, Singapore.
53. Petri, P.A. 1997, 'Foreign Direct Investment in a Computable General Equilibrium Framework', paper prepared for the conference, Making APEC work: Economic Challenges and Policy Alternatives, 13-14 March, Keio University, Tokyo.
54. Robinson, S., Wang, Z. and Martin, W. 1999, 'Capturing the Implications of Services Trade Liberalisation', invited paper at Second Annual Conference on Global Economic Analysis, Ebberuk, Denmark, 20-22 June.
55. Saunders, A. and Schumacher, L. 1997a, 'The Determinants of Bank Interest Rate Margins: An International Study', George Washington University, Washington DC.
56. Saunders, A. and Schumacher, L. 1997a, 'The Determinants of Bank Interest Margins in Mexico's Post-Privatisation Period', George Washington University, Washington DC.
57. Steiner, F. 2000, *Regulation, Industry Structure and Performance in the Electricity Supply Industry*, Working Paper No. 238, ECO/WKP(2000)11, Economics Department, OECD, Paris, 12 April.
58. Trewin, R. 2000, 'A price-impact measure of impediments to trade in telecommunications services', in Findlay, C. and Warren, T. (eds) 2000, *Impediments to Trade in Services: Measurement and Policy Implications*, Routledge, London and New York, pp. 101–18.
59. Verikios, G. and Zhang, X-G. 2001, *Global Gains from Liberalising Trade in Telecommunications and Financial Services*, Productivity Commission Staff Research Paper, Ausinfo, Canberra.
60. Warren, T. 2000a, 'The identification of impediments to trade and investment in telecommunication services', in C. Findlay and T. Warren (eds) 2000, *Impediments to Trade in Services: Measurement and Policy Implications*, Routledge, London and New York, pp. 71–84.
61. Warren, T. 2000b, 'The impact on output of impediments to trade and investment in telecommunications services', in C. Findlay and T. Warren (eds) 2000, *Impediments to Trade in Services: Measurement and Policy Implications*, Routledge, London and New York, pp. 85–100.
62. Winters, L.A. 2002, 'The Economic Implications of Liberalising Mode 4 Trade', paper prepared for Joint WTO-World Bank Symposium on The Movement of Natural Persons (Mode 4) Under the GATS, WTO, Geneva, 11-12 April.
63. World Bank 1998, *World Bank Atlas*, World Bank, Washington DC.
64. World Bank 2000, *Tunisia: Social and Structural Review 2000: Integrating into the World Economic and Sustaining Economic and Social Progress*, World Bank, Washington DC.
65. World Bank 2001, *World Development Report 2000/2001: Attacking Poverty*, Oxford University Press, New York.
66. Zarrouk, J. 2000, 'Regulatory Regimes and Trade Costs', in Hoekman. B. and Zarrouk, J. (eds), *Catching Up with the Competition: Trade Opportunities and Challenges for Arab Countries*, University of Michigan Press: Ann Arbor.
67. Zemnitsky, A. 2001, 'Non-tariff Barriers in Russian Services Sectors', mimeo.

NON-TARIFF MEASURES IN SERVICES MEASURING GAINS FROM MOVEMENT OF SKILLED PERSONNEL

Soumodip Sarkar[1]
Universidade de Évora

1. Introduction

Rapidly integrating goods and capital markets, along with technological advances and diminishing transportation costs, have connected international economies as never before. The continuous decline in barriers to trade have led tradable good prices across nations with price differentials of traded goods rarely exceeding a ratio of 2.

Yet the paradox remains that one of the greatest and most direct boosts to welfare arises from the liberalization of cross border labor services an issue which remains mostly hidden in the agenda of most trade liberalization talks. This despite economic logic that point to gains from cross border labor services to all agents involved. There is no trickle down welfare effects for the development economist to worry about. The gains go directly to the cross-border migrant worker. Through increased remittances and financial investments, the labor exporting country gains. Besides other dynamic effects on the return of the workers[2], there is an increase in the stock of human capital, often entrepreneurial. Likewise the host countries gain from lower factor costs that reduce production costs helping maintain the competitiveness of the economy.

Thus the irony remains that while barriers to trade in goods and many services have come down over the last decades, the temporary movement of natural persons (TMNP) or mode 4 trade in services gets very little attention. Indeed today the movement of people (excluding tourism) is well below levels experienced in the late nineteenth century, and migration rates are well below cross border flow of goods and investment. About 3 percent of the world's population is living outside their country of birth whereas global exports of goods are almost a fifth of GDP[3] and financial flows well above 10 percent. For

---

[1] The author is Associate Professor, Department of Business, Universidade de Évora, Portugal. The author may be contacted *via* email at *ssarkar@uevora.pt.*

[2] Edward Turner of the University of California, Davis, has quantified the multiplier effect: for every dollar sent home from the United States by a Mexican immigrant, \$3 more is generated in the form of construction material, food or contract work.

[3] Calculated from the Appendix to World Bank's: Global Economic Prospects 2004.

instance in the United States the number of permanent legal immigrants in 2002 at around 1 million is less than it was in 1914 when it stood at 1.2 million.[4] Trade in goods has seen the gradual convergence of prices of the tradable goods,[5] but the labor factor embodied in them continues to have a divergence of as much as 25 to 1[6] between the developed and developing nations.

Data from the worker remittances to developing countries is persuasive. In 2002, worker's remittances to developing countries stood at $80 billion, accounting for 1.3 percent of their GDP. For countries of southern Asia, the remittance inflow for 2002 stood at $16 billion, accounting for 2.5 percent of GDP.[7] This capital flow is considerably higher than official development assistance, and second only to FDI inflows as a source of external funding, as can be seen from the figures in Table 1.

Table 1. Remittances received by developing countries in 2001

	All Developing	Low Income	Low Middle Income	Upper Middle Income
as percent of GDP	1.3	1.9	1.4	0.8
as percent of IDE received	42.4	213.5	43.7	21.7
as percent of Official Aid	260.1	120.6	361.7	867.9

Source: Global Development Finance, 2003

In this paper we use back of the envelope calculations to estimate welfare gains of the reduction of quotas on the temporary immigration in the information and communications technology (ICT) sector where developed countries shortages of highly skilled workers have been often highlighted.

We find that if an experimental visa scheme is launched in the United States of issuing 140,000 visas for ICT workers (equal to the number of approved H1 B petitions in the computer systems design and related service' category in 2001), then net welfare increases substantially. Assuming that the rest of the developed world combined issues a similar number of visas, then for the 12-year period of this simulation, the average annual net gains would be around $38 billion. Further assuming that around 40 percent of the wage earnings are remitted, then the additional average annual remittance would be about $15 billion almost

[4] From Immigration and Naturalization Services (USA): "2002 Yearbook of Immigration Statistics" Table 1.

[5] Although wedges still remain the price ratio between countries has been reported to be no higher than 2. For a discussion on this, see Dani Rodrick (2002) "Feasible Globalizations", NBER Working Paper, No. W9129, August 2002.

[6] Even higher if one compares the average hourly wage rate of $30 in Germany to the 30 cent hourly wage rate in India or China.

[7] World Bank: Global Economic Prospects 2004, pages 148-149.

doubling the current remittance inflows to Asia. Furthermore the mode 4 workers under this scheme would at its maximum represent about 0.4 percent of current US labour force.

This paper is organized as follows. Section 2 puts the growth of trade, especially in services in perspective. In section 3, after a review of relevant literature, we calculate the gains from our visa scheme in the ICT sector. Section 4 carries our conclusions.

2. Growth of International Trade

For many countries trade has been the engine of growth. The share of world exports to GDP in 2002 was almost 20 percent, while in some countries this ratio is much higher. In East Asia for instance, the trade-GDP ratio is approximately 62 percent.

The growth rate of world trade has been more that twice the growth rate of world GDP. Thus in the decade of 1991-2000 while world GDP growth rate was 2.6 percent, the growth rate of world exports was more than double at 6.3 percent. For certain countries the growth rate of exports is even more impressive. As a block, East Asian exports for instance grew at an annual average of 12.0 percent during the period 1993-2002 (World Bank data).

2.1 *And the Increasing Importance of Trade in Services*

Services are the fastest growing sector of the global economy, accounting for more than 50 percent of the GDP of developing countries and significantly more for the developed economies. As table 1 illustrates world service trade grew at a faster rate (7 percent) in the period 1990-2000 that the growth rate of merchandise trade. The value of merchandise trade however remains almost 4 times of service trade. It is interesting to note as well that in the global downturn of 2001, service trade[8] shrunk by much less than goods trade, as shown in table 2.

Table 2. Exports of merchandise and commercial services: 1990-2002

	Value	**Growth Rate**	**Annual Percent Change**			
	2002	1990-2000	1999	2000	2001	2002
Merchandise Exports	6240	6	4	13	-4	4
Commercial Services	1540	7	3	6	-1	5

Source: World Bank

[8] All data in this section is derived from the World Bank

While world trade in services has grown at an annual average rate of 7 percent over the decade of 1990, the share of developing countries in trade in commercial services and their growth rate has been even faster. This share rose from 18.2 percent in 1990 to 22.5 percent in 2002. The growth rate of service trade of developing countries was an annual average of 9 percent in the decade of 1990 compared with an average of 7 percent for developed countries. The story is even more impressive for certain countries like China which more than tripled its share of global trade in services in a bit over a decade. In 1990 its share stood at 0.7 percent while in 2002 it rose to an impressive 2.4 percent. The corresponding figures for India were 0.6 percent and 1.3 percent, driven to a great extent by a boom in the exports of IT related services. The annual average growth rate of service exports of these two countries in the decade of 1990s were 18 percent and 14 percent more, than thrice and more than twice the world growth rate for these two countries respectively. Figure 1 gives a perspective on the relative size of major trading nations and groups in commercial service trade as well as the latest available data on growth rate.

Figure 1. Selected Regional and Country Share and Growth Rates of Commercial Service Exports

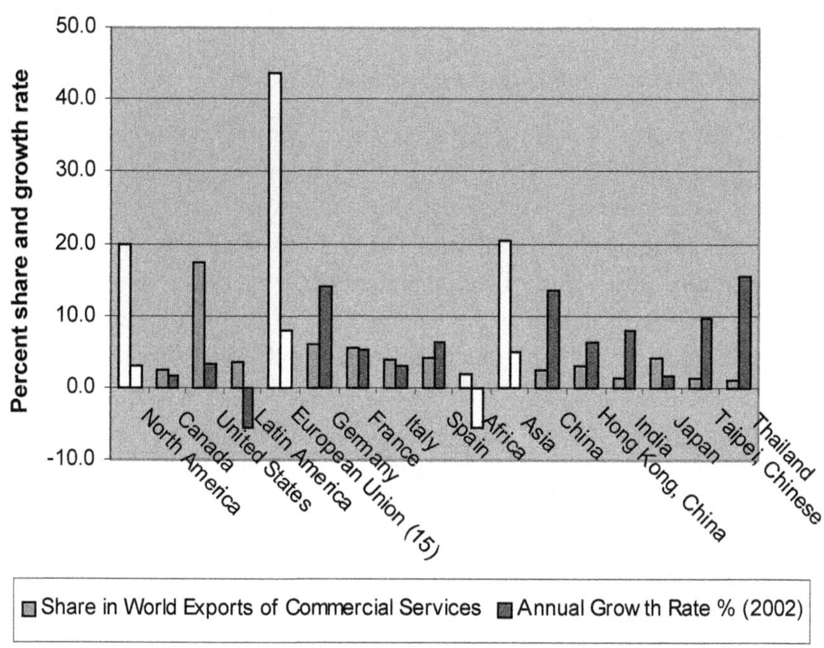

While trade in merchandise has been considered an engine of growth for many countries[9], the service sector exports of commercial services is no less important for development. Among the fastest growing sectors of many economies are services such as telecommunications, software and finance. Efficiency in financial services implies better allocation of resources, while efficiency in telecommunications generates economy wide benefits because is a vital intermediate input. Software development is the foundation of modern knowledge based economy.[10]

2.2. *Coverage and "Modes Of Supply"*

The General Agreement on Trade and Services (GATS) of the WTO that covers all internationally traded services[11] has defined four ways in which a service can be traded. These are known as "modes of supply"[12]. Mode 1 covers services supplied from one country to another officially known as "cross-border supply." Consumers remain in home country while the supplier is located in a different country. The delivery of the service can be effected by telephone, fax, internet, courier, *etc.* International telephone calls, freight transport services are examples of Mode 1 trade. It is in many ways similar to the traditional notion of trade where both the consumer and producer remain in their countries while the service is exchanged.

Mode 2 trade in services takes the form of consumer moves from one country, making use of a service in another country and is officially known as "consumption abroad." Some illustrations of Mode 2 trade in services are tourism, medical treatment of non-residents, ship-repair abroad *etc.* Mode 3 trade, officially known as "commercial presence," includes for instance a company from one country setting up subsidiaries or branches to provide services in another country. Banking, Insurance (and in general trade in diverse financial services), commercial presence abroad *etc.* are all part of Mode 3 trade.

Finally, mode 4 trade covers individuals traveling from their own country to supply services in another, officially known as "temporary movement of natural

[9] See for instance the World Bank's "The East Asian Miracle: Economic Growth and Public Policy" Oxford University Press , World Bank 1993.

[10] For more, see Chapter 3 of the World Bank's Global Economic Prospects, 2002.

[11] The only two exceptions are services provided to the public in the exercise of governmental authority, and, in the air transport sector, traffic rights and all services directly related to the exercise of traffic rights.

[12] For a full definition and statistical treatment of the modes of supply, see the UN's Manual of Statistics of International Trade in Services, 2003.

persons" (TMNP). Thus migrant construction workers in the Middle East, short term employment of foreign doctors, nurses software professionals etc are all part of Mode 4 trade. Intra-corporate staff (in general short term employment of foreign staff in overseas operations) is particularly relevant in the GATS context since many countries refer to this sub category in their schedules of commitments.

Table 3 below gives a break down of world exports (in percentage terms) of commercial services in 1990, 1995 and 2001, according to the three major categories of trade in services: transportation, travel and 'other commercial services'.

Table 3. World exports of commercial services by category, 1990, 1995 and 2001

	1990 (%)	1995 (%)	2001 (%)
Transportation	28.5	25.2	23.4
Travel	33.8	33.6	31.8
Other commercial services	37.6	41.1	44.8

Source: WTO

As seen from the data, the 'other' category is predominant in commercial service trade. This category includes items like communication and insurance (approximately 5 percent each), financial trade (10 percent), construction (7 percent), royalties and license fees (12 percent).

3. Barriers to TMNP: An Analysis of the Economic Impact of Mode 4

3.1. *Trade and Factor Price Equalization*

Ohlin (1933) argued that with trade would factor prices of the trading nations tend to converge. Samuelson (1948, 1949) showed the circumstances under which factor prices would actually become equal.[13] A classic result by Mundell (1957) demonstrates that international factor mobility can actually act as a substitute for international trade in goods and services. That is to say the presentation of this paper by the researcher is in an analytical sense similar to the paper being sent as hard-copy or by e-mail or even a video presentation.

However, a standard trade model for goods is different from trade in services through capital or labor movements. For one thing trade in services through factor movements change given factor endowments (a standard assumption in the classical trade literature is that the gains are based on given factor endowments). Also, trade is not a substitute for factor mobility but is rather represented by the

[13] One of the major theoretical results of the Heckscher-Ohlin model is the Factor Price Equalization theorem. This theorem states that under certain conditions free trade leads to complete equalization of production factor rewards independently of factor mobility.

movement of factors.[14] As further noted by Chanda, when speaking of labor movements, it is important to disaggregate labor into skill levels. Thus a labor abundant country such as India is both an exporter of unskilled labor (to many parts of the Middle East) as well as skilled labor in the ICT services.

The differences aside, the same motivation that drives trade in goods is also behind trade in services, *i.e.*, comparative advantage. Thus a relative abundance of skilled or highly skilled labor would give rise to a comparative advantage in the production (and consequent export of) goods intensive in such factors, as well as trade, *i.e.*, temporary movement of natural persons in this labor category.

3.2. *Size and the Barriers to Mode 4 Trade*

Being the interface between migration and international trade, the study of Mode 4 in its various aspects has been a rather neglected field of research. As one recent OECD study complains (OECD 2003), there has been no intellectual or statistical approach developed that accurately gauges the impact of workers under Mode 4. The problem is compounded by the difficult in even estimating the extent of mode 4 trade. Trade in services is normally measured from data from the balance of payment statistics. For Mode 4, BOP statistics break labor flows into three categories: labor income (foreign workers), worker remittances and finally migrant transfers (flow of goods and changes in financial assets associated with international migration). None of these categories correspond well with Mode 4 definition. One estimate (Kartsenty, 2000) has put Mode 4 trade in 1997 at $30 billion, or approximately 1.4 percent of service trade that year. Recent estimates by the WTO[15] figures Mode 4 trade to be a little over 1 percent of world services trade.

While we can argue with the statistical methodology employed for the veracity of these figures, Mode 4 trade still remains one of the smallest component of service trade, and arguably one of the most difficult to study. These small figures hide the dynamic impact to both the host and the exporting country through various externalities such as labor market prices, corporate incomes, skill and knowledge transfers *etc.*

The major barriers to market access conditions and constraints on the MNP can be briefly summarized under the following categories:

---

[14] See Chanda (1999) page 11.

[15] WTO (2002): "GATS, Mode 4 and the Pattern of Commitments: Background Information – WTO Secretariat," April 2002.

> Economic Needs Test (ENTs) and labor certification tests. This implies that potential host country nations can deny market access to foreign nationals at their discretion. The most common justification for denial is that similarly qualified nationals are available. The onus lies on the prospective employer to demonstrate that no equally qualified nation is available. The administration of such tests cause significant delays and add to the costs of the prospective employer.

The second barrier arises from issues relating to granting of visas and work permits. The administrative processes are cumbersome, expensive, stringent and generally lack transparency. A third barrier arises from recognition of qualifications. This especially hurts developing countries since professional standards are considered low by developed country standards. The last category of barriers arises from a differential treatment of domestic and foreign natural persons. This most typically arises from temporary foreign nationals having to contribute to social security systems of the host country and yet not having the payments refundable on their departure.

While barriers to trade in goods continue to decline barriers to service trade and especially Mode 4 trade remain high. A look at the member countries GATS schedule shows that the levels of commitments vary strongly across the modes of supply. Almost 43 percent of the entries of Mode 4 commitments have been for intracorporate transfers followed by executives (28 percent) and business visitors (23 percent). Only 4 percent of all horizontal entries cover low skilled persons. It is further interesting to note that the commitments scheduled by developing and developed countries are similar. Both groups seem reluctant to undertaking liberal commitments for Mode 4.

3.3. *Gains from Liberalization of Restrictions on Mode 4 Trade*

While progress is being made in the statistical information gathering of Mode 4 trade, measuring the economic impact of a liberalization of mode 4 trade remains a relatively unexplored field of research. This is unlike quantification of gains from liberalization of service trade overall where there is a considerable body of research, especially in telecommunications and finance service sectors.[16]

One estimate of gains from liberalization of Mode 4 trade was made by Winters, 2001, which showed that an increased international labor mobility could generate gains of over $300 billion per year. Among others, the estimate was based on an assumption that 50 million developing country workers worked

[16] For one literature survey see OECD (2002).

abroad in any given year. A later Winters study in 2002 and companion pieces, concluded that an increase in developed country quotas on inward movement of both unskilled and skilled temporary workers equivalent to 3 percent of the host country workforce would generate an aggregate annual gain of $156 billion.

Another study on welfare gains from Mode 4 liberalization was undertaken by Rodrick, which rests on a temporary work visa scheme with a quota set at 3 percent of developed countries work force. Under the scheme, both skilled and unskilled workers from developing countries would be allowed employment in the developed countries for 3-5 years to be replaced by a new group upon their return. Rodrick estimates a gain of $200 billion annually under this scheme, much more than the expected gain from the Doha agenda.

3.4. *Gains From Increase in Mode 4 Trade: A Preliminary Case Study for the ICT Sector*

In this presentation, I eschew general equilibrium analyses, preferring back of the envelope calculations to estimate gains from an increase in the visa cap for highly skilled information and communication technology (ICT) workers. In what follows I first simulate the net gains from an the issuance of an additional 140,000 visas for ICT workers in the United States, not taking into account all the dynamic (namely the positive economies to the exporting nation) gains. The rest of the developed economies, most notably the European Union and Japan are then assumed to take a further 140,000 skilled workers in the ICT sector, not a wholly unrealistic assumption given the published shortages of workers in this sector. The simulation results that I arrive are merely indicative of welfare gains from mode 4 trade in a highly critical sector of the global economy.

The ICT sector has been highlighted by various studies as suffering from domestic workforce shortages. I choose this sector for my initial analyses for three simple reasons.[17] First, the data I use in terms of the temporary migration numbers is fairly realistic. Second, there is an elastic supply of labor (in the stock of ICT workers in countries such as India and China). This further implies that the temporary withdrawal of these skilled people from the developing country economy would have arguably less negative impact to the domestic economy than say the departure of other highly skilled personnel that is in shortage.[18] Finally, at a policy level, if liberalization of movements of natural persons in

---

[17] Indeed most initial offers of market access of mode 4 has been for ICT sector workers.

[18] The departure of a few doctors from a developing country hospital is likely to have a very negative impact on its functioning, perhaps even leading to the temporary closure of some departments.

such a critical sector to the economy is difficult, then it is doubtful that within the short term at least we shall see any Mode 4 liberalizations, especially of non-skilled labor of which developing countries have a very large pool.

The information technology sector[19] has been widely reported to be suffering from a shortage of skilled workers both in the United States and in Europe. In fact one study by IDC predicted a shortfall of over 1.7 million jobs in Europe alone for the year 2003. In the United States, it was largely to this skills shortage that H1 B visas (workers with "speciality occupations") had been increased from 65,000 in October 2000 to 195,000. This cap is now expected to be reduced to 65,000 from the 1st of November of 2003.

The actual or expected shortage of ICT workers in the United States is however still a matter of debate. For instance IEEE-USA, a professional society representing more than 235,000 electrical, electronics, computer and software engineers, deny any shortage claims. A recent estimate shows that currently in the United States, there are about 10.3 million IT workers.[20] It is illustrative of the need for IT specialists, that according to the INS, for the year October 1999-September 2000, the top ten H1-B petitions were all filed by technology companies.[21] Cyclical downturns notwithstanding, there seem little doubt that the rapid expansion of IT, both as an intermediate as well as a final product to the US economy, that the shortage for ICT workers would be increasingly felt. The trend towards outsourcing, is a search for lower labor cost, especially in the highly labor intensive side of the ICT industry. While this trend cannot be controlled, liberalizing labor movement in this sector could indeed help to reduce chances of relocation of US firms.

Let us assume that we implement an ICT Mode 4 trade scheme where short-term visa allocations are made for ICT jobs for a further 140,000 annually. This number corresponds to the number of approved H1 B petitions in the 'computer systems design and related service' category in 2001. These additional 140,000 visas would be valid for a short term, say 3-5 years, after which the temporary worker returns to his country of origin, to be replaced by another 140,000 workers. Let us put this system in place for a total of 12 years, which would enable a cycle of nine generations of workers to stay on an average of 4 years

---

[19] Note that besides there being no one single 'IT job' there is also a varying degree of labor intensity associated with different tasks. This implies that within this ICT sector, developing countries could have a comparative advantage in data processing or even computer programming, but at a comparative disadvantage in systems analysis.

[20] ITAA: 2003 Workforce Survey, May 2003

[21] Reported in OECD Study: "Current Regimes for Temporary Movement of Service Providers Case Study: The United States of America", February 2003. TD/TC/WP(2002)23/FINAL

each. Thus the number of the temporary foreign ICT workers under this scheme would go to 0 at the end of the 12th year (beginning of the 13th).

Figure 2 below illustrates the simulation of the visa scheme. The number (stock) of skilled foreign workers under the ICT visa scheme (without renewal) who would be working in the United States at any given year describes a concave function. For 6 years under this scheme, the number of workers would be the maximum at 58,000. For a total labor force population of around 140 million and a population of 280 million, at a maximum this scheme would have around 0.4 percent of the labor force consisting of temporary Mode 4 ICT workers.

Figure 2. Stock of TMNP in ICT Sector, USA

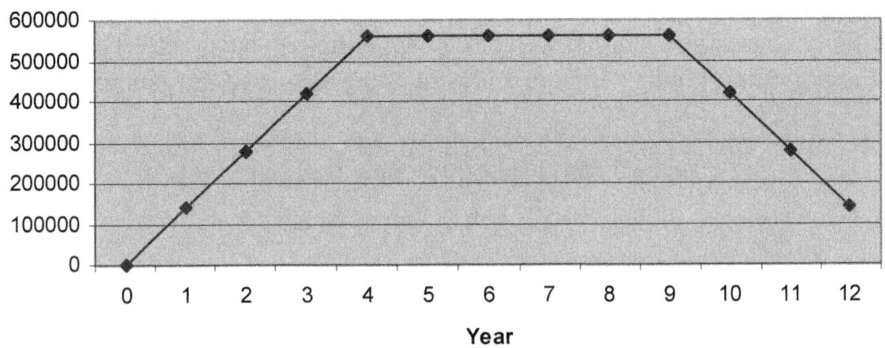

We begin with an assumed income differential of $50,000 in the ICT sector.[22] Let us further assume that the wage rate for ICT workers in the labor exporting nation increases at an annual rate of 15 percent compared to an annual increase for ICT workers in the United States of 5 percent (thus the annual differential decreases due to the increased demand as well as the tightening of labour markets of the exporting country). The income differential between workers in the two nations, at the end of this period of 12 years at these rates would be is significantly reduced at around $27,000. If we were to persist further with the simulation, then with the assumed rates of wage rise, there would no cost advantage after 15 years.[23] Thus the competitiveness of high skilled labour from

---

[22] From author's own research. Based on an average figure across various ICT jobs which are competitive given current market and technology conditions.

[23] These differentials are roughly consistent with industry analysts. The Economist (July 19, 2003), quoted an Indian industry figure predicting an erosion of the wage differential between IT workers in India and the United States in 15 years.

developing countries would be greatly diminished over the period of this experimental visa scheme.

The net static gain to the trading countries in any given year would be the increase in productivity associated with the movement of labor from the low wage to the high wage country. I assume that there are no productivity losses as workers move from the developing country to the developed.[24] In which case, the gain would be given by the stock of workers times the income differential. The cumulative net gains from such a visa experiment would result in gains of around $227 billion in the 12 years of the scheme. If one was to include the European Union (some of whose individual countries have implemented special visas schemes for skilled IT workers) and some other developed nations, then the gains to the world economy could well be over $450 billion over the twelve year period. In annual terms, this translates into net gains of $38 billion. These gains are fairly conservative in that we ignore the multiple dynamic effects principally to the exporting country.[25] Figure 3 illustrates the simulated net gain function.

Figure 3. Net Mode 4 (ICT) Gains Trade with USA

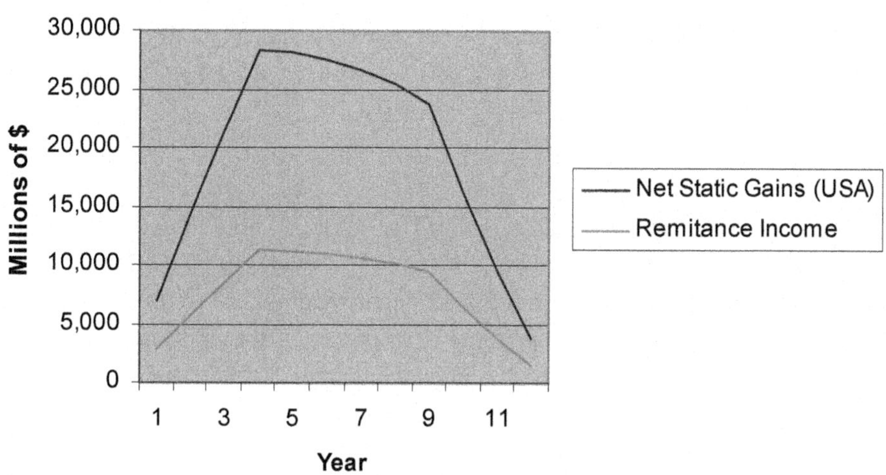

---

[24] Indeed under the present US immigration scheme whereby foreign workers have to be similar existing wages, it would be economically nonsense for a firm to pay a temporary immigrant worker the same pay of the productivity was less. Winters (2001), in his simulation assumed that for various reasons, three quarters of the wage gap persisted even after the cross border migration.

[25] Many of the Indian IT software companies with an international presence were started by Indians who had earlier worked in the United States. The same is true for many internet startups in China.

The benefits of this Mode 4 trade are obvious for the labor exporting country. The average annual exports of $38 billion represents about 1.5 percent of Asian GDP from whose economies most of the ICT workers would be expected to come, or about 5.7 percent of its exports. To take one specific country example, if even 50 percent of the IT workers were to come from India then this would imply gains representing approximately 3.6 percent of her GDP or about 41 percent of her current exports.

Further assuming that around 40 percent of the wage earnings are remitted, then the average additional annual remittance income would be about $15 billion, more than the remittance received in 2002 by East Asia ($11 billion) and almost equal that of South Asia ($16 billion).

4. Conclusions

The core 'tenet' of gains from trade lies in exploiting, for mutual benefits, the differences between nations. These differences could be in terms of factor abundance (relative), consumer preferences *etc.* and giving rise to comparative advantage. With high wage differentials one would expect these wages to converge given that trade in labor is embodied in the trade of goods. However this hasn't happened, and particularly in view of the shortage of skilled labor in certain sectors economic logic dictates that trade (Mode 4) would be beneficial for the trading partners.

This paper simulates the advantages of such a trade in one specific area, ICT. We simulate the advantages of issuing a limited number of visas (which at the most wouldn't account for more that 0.4 percent of the labor force say in the United States (and a similar figure for the European Union). Yet the gains are enormous as shown in our simulations. While the exact are merely indicative of the potential net gains, it is suggestive of enormous welfare gains from Mode 4 trade in this sector at least. Since our figures exclude the dynamic potential effects of cross border trade in services, we are possibly underestimating the true long run benefits.

Research in the area of mode 4 remains in its infancy for various reasons. Poor availability of valid data, being the interface of two areas of research: international trade and immigration being two important ones. Yet this is one area where potential gains are enormous, but yet have not made its way in any serious manner in the agenda of trade meetings. It is time perhaps to do so.

Bibliography

1. Chanda, Rupa (1999), "Movement of Natural Persons and Trade in Services: Liberalizing Temporary Movement of Labor under the GATS", Indian Council for Research on International Economic Relations, India (*www.icrier.res.in*)
2. IDC "Europe's Growing IT skills Crisis", IDC Executive Summary, 2000.
3. Karsenty, Guy (2000), Assessing Trade in Services by Mode of Supply", in Sauvé, Pierre, and Stern, Robert (Edits) GATS 2000: New Directions in Services Trade Liberalization, the Brookings Institution, Washington DC.
4. Mundell, R.A. (1960) "The Pure Theory of International Trade" American Economic Review, Vol. 40, pp. 301-322
5. OECD (2000), Quantification of Costs to national Welfare from Barriers to Service Trade: A Literature Review. TD/TC/WP(2000) 24/FINAL
6. OECD (2003), "Service Providers On The Move: The Economic Impact Of Mode 4," March 2003
7. Ohlin B. (1933). Interregional and International Trade. Harvard University Press, Cambridge. Mass.
8. Samuelson, Paul A., "International Trade and the Equalization of Factor Prices," *Economic Journal*, June 1948.
9. Samuelson, Paul A., "International Factor Price Equalization Once Again," *Economic Journal*, June 1949.
10. Winters, L. Alan, (2001), "Assessing the Efficiency Gain from Further Liberalization: A Comment", in Sauvé, P., Subramaniam, A., (Editors), *Efficiency, Equity and Legitimacy: The Multilateral Trading System and the Millenium*, Chicago University Press, Chicago, 2001.
11. Winters, L. Alan, (2002), *The Economic Implications of Liberalising Mode 4 Trade*, Joint WTO-World Bank Symposium on 'The Movement of Natural Persons (Mode 4) under the GATS', WTO, Geneva, 11-12 April, 2002.
12. Winters, L. Alan, Walmsley, Terrie L., Wang, Zhen Kun, Grynberg, Roman, (2002), *Negotiating the Liberalisation of the Temporary Movement of Natural Persons*, 2002.
13. Winters, L. Alan, Walmsley, Terrie L., (2002), *Relaxing the Restrictions on the Temporary Movement of Natural Persons: A Simulation Analysis*, 2002.

   UNCTAD: "Increasing the participation of Developing Countries through the Liberalization of Market Access in GATS Mode 4 for Movement of Natural Persons Supplying Service. Note by the UNCTAD secretariat", June 2003. TD/B/COM.1/EM.22.

ASSESSING THE POTENTIAL BENEFIT OF TRADE FACILITATION: A GLOBAL PERSPECTIVE

John S. Wilson

World Bank [1]

Catherine L. Mann

Institute for International Economics [2]

Tsunehiro Otsuki

World Bank [3]

1. Introduction

The relationships between trade facilitation, trade flows, and capacity building are complex and challenging, to assess empirically and in implementation. Even the first step—relating trade facilitation and trade flows—encounters the problem of definition and measurement of trade facilitation. However, as tariffs come down, assessing how other factors affect trade has increasing policy relevance. Once trade facilitation is defined and measured, the challenge is to estimate its effects on trade flows. An economy's trade will change not only through its own trade facilitation reforms, but also the reforms of its trading partners. Differences in the relative magnitude of trade facilitation efforts on trade, as calculated by category of trade facilitation effort or group of trading partners, could point to negotiating and capacity building focus. This paper measures and estimates the relationship between trade facilitation and trade flows, considering the relationships from a variety of perspectives. The hope is that the outcome will help inform policy decisions and capacity building choices.

Empirical research on the issue of trade facilitation faces three challenges: defining and measuring trade facilitation; choosing a modeling methodology to

---

[1] Transport Unit and Urban Development Department (TUDTR), the World Bank, 1818 H Street, NW, Washington, DC.

[2] Institute for International Economics, 1750 Massachusetts Ave NW, Washington, DC.

[3] Development Research Group (DECRG), the World Bank, 1818 H Street, NW, Washington, DC. The author may be contracted *via* email at *totsuki@worldbank.org*. The views expressed here are those of the authors and should not be attributed to the World Bank or the Institute for International Economics.

estimate the importance of trade facilitation for trade flows; and designing a scenario to estimate the effect of improved trade facilitation on trade flows.

- It is important to *define and measure trade facilitation* with the objectives in mind of informing policy and aiding capacity building. Accordingly, we consider four aspects of trade facilitation effort: ports, customs, regulations, and e-business (which is a proxy for the service sectors of telecommunications and financial intermediation, which are key for all types of trade). Simply benchmarking a country's condition in these four areas with respect to the global average and best practice yields insights for capacity building and policy attention.

- The *modeling methodology* is particularly important because it has to account for the fact that both export and import trade flows will be affected by trade facilitation efforts, and that the effect of trade facilitation will differ depending on the trading patterns of the economies being examined. Accordingly, we include trade facilitation measures for economies as importers and as exporters. Investigating the stability of the estimated relationship across directions of trade (north-south, south-south) adds insight on which measures may be most important for addressing capacity building.

- The *scenario design* needs to account for differences among economies relative to best practice. Accordingly, we consider scenarios where each economy improves toward best practice by an economy-specific amount.

So as to assist in policy design and capacity building, the presentation of results allows an economy to judge the potential outcome of trade facilitation efforts unilaterally, by region, and multilaterally. Since each economy is characterized by four unique trade facilitation measures, each of these measures bears a unique relationship to global best, and each economy has a unique trading pattern, the determination of which trade facilitation effort might yield the greatest increase in trade is unique to each economy.

Finally, the juxtaposition in multilateral forums of trade facilitation discussions and tariff negotiations points to the need to assess the relationship between these two approaches as they affect trade flows. In this paper we offer some insights on these issues using a sample of 75 economies.

2. Overview of Previous Work

2.1. *Definition of Trade Facilitation*

There is no standard definition of trade facilitation in public policy discourse. In a narrow sense, trade facilitation efforts simply address the logistics of moving goods through ports or more efficiently moving documentation associated with cross-border trade. In recent years, the definition has been broadened to include the environment in which trade transactions take place, transparency and professionalism of customs and regulatory environments, as well as harmonization of standards and conformance to international or regional regulations. These move the focus of trade facilitation efforts "inside the border" to domestic policies and institutional structures where capacity building can play an important role. In addition, the rapid integration of networked information technology into trade means that modern definitions of trade facilitation need to encompass a technological concept as well.

In light of this broadening definition of trade facilitation, our definition of trade facilitation incorporates relatively concrete "border" elements, such as port efficiency and customs administration, and "inside the border" elements, such as domestic regulatory environment and the infrastructure to enable e-business usage.

2.2. *Measuring the Impact of Trade Facilitation*

The empirical literature on trade facilitation is limited; it is outlined in more detail in Wilson, Mann, and Otsuki (2003) (henceforth WMO). Briefly, however, the tendency in work previous to WMO is first, to discuss what researchers would like to measure, but not to find measures or estimate their impact on trade (Maskus, Wilson, and Otsuki (2001), Asia Pacific Foundation of Canada (1999)). Second, some use a single measure of trade facilitation to estimate effects of trade facilitation on trade.

These latter estimates suggest large gains from trade facilitation efforts. A 3 percent reduction in landed costs applied to intra-APEC merchandise trade, as might be obtained by electronic documentation, reduces trade costs by US$60 billion.[4] A 1 percent reduction in import prices for the industrial economies and the newly industrializing economies of Korea, Chinese Taipei and Singapore, and a 2 percent reduction for the other developing economies, yield an increase in APEC merchandise trade of 3.3 percent—meaning the elasticity of trade

[4] See Paperless Trading: Benefits to APEC (2001), page 18.

facilitation efforts to trade flows is greater than 1.[5] Considering global estimates, a 1 percent reduction in the cost of maritime and air transport services in the developing economies could increase global GDP some US$7 billion (1997 dollars). If trade facilitation is considered in a broader sense to include an improvement in wholesale and retail trade services, an additional US$7 billion could be gained by a 1 percent improvement in the productivity of that sector.[6]

Other authors consider more specific categories of trade facilitation effort or a more limited economy set. Hertel, Walmsley and Itakura (2001) find that greater standards harmonization for e-business and automating customs procedures between Japan and Singapore increase trade flows in overall between these economies as well as their trade flows with the rest of the world. Hummels (2001) finds that each day saved in shipping time in part due to a faster customs clearance is worth 0.5 percentage point reduction of *ad valorem* tariff. Fink, Mattoo, and Neagu (2002a) examine the effect of anticompetitive practices in port services and other transport services on unit shipping cost. Freund and Weinhold (2000) find that a 10 percent increase in the relative number of web hosts in an economy would have increased trade flows by one percent in 1998 and 1999. Fink, Mattoo, and Neagu (2002b) find that a 10 percent decrease in the bilateral price of phone calls is associated with an 8 percent increase in bilateral trade. Moenius (2000) finds that bilaterally-shared and country-specific standards on goods trade promote trade. Otsuki, Wilson, and Sewadeh (2001a, 2001b) find that 10 percent tighter food standards in the European Union would reduce African exports of certain cereals, nuts, and dried foods by a range of 5 to 11 percent, depending on the category.

WMO change these approaches to estimating the effect of trade facilitation on trade flows by constructing four measures of trade facilitation and estimating the independent effects of these four on the trade flows among a broad group of economies in the Asia Pacific region. WMO use cross-country survey data on the business and policy climate in each APEC member to construct numerical measures of trade facilitation for each APEC member for port efficiency, customs environment, regulatory environment and , e-business usage (a proxy for service sector infrastructure important for trade). They find that the elasticity of increased port efficiency of importing economies is larger than the elasticity of improved customs environment or superior service sector infrastructure. A unilaterally applied more stringent regulatory environment will reduce an

[5] Assessing APEC Trade Liberalization and Facilitation: 1999 Update, Economic Committee, September 1999, page 11.

[6] See UNCTAD, E-Commerce and Development Report 2001, tables 8-11, page 33-36.

economy's imports. In simulations, they find that for the APEC economies as a group, improving port efficiency, customs environment and service sector infrastructure measures of the below-APEC-average economies half-way up to the APEC average for each trade facilitation measure yields an increase in trade of some 20 percent. Although on average the port efficiency indicator is the most important for trade facilitation, since each economy has a unique set of indicators and pattern of trade, more detailed analysis of the simulation results shows that for some members of APEC, a trade facilitation measure other than ports may be the best to target for capacity building to improve that economy's trade.

3. Data in This Study

3.1. *Rationale for These Indicators of Trade Facilitation*

The first essential task in the quantitative analysis of trade facilitation is to develop measures of trade facilitation. WMO present four distinct areas of focus that meet policymakers' needs for specificity on how to approach trade facilitation efforts. They are: (1) port efficiency, (2) customs environment, (3) own regulatory environment, and (4) service sector infrastructure.

Port efficiency is designed to measure the quality of infrastructure of maritime and air ports. Customs environment is designed to measure direct customs costs as well as administrative transparency of customs and border crossings. Regulatory environment is designed to measure the economy's approach to regulations. Service sector infrastructure[7] is designed to measure the extent to which an economy has the necessary domestic infrastructure (such as telecommunications, financial intermediaries, and logistics firms) and is using networked information to improve efficiency and to transform activities to enhance economic activity.[8]

Besides the observation that these categories match areas for policy-maker attention, these trade facilitation measures also match several GATT articles and appear in the list of Singapore issues in the Doha Development Agenda, and therefore have salience for WTO negotiations. The *port efficiency* measure has been constructed in accordance to GATT article V (freedom of transit). This article says that freedom of movement is to be assured for goods, which should be allowed to move *via* the most convenient route, should be exempt from customs or transit duties, and should be free from unnecessary delays or

[7] WMO used a different terminology- e-business usage- for this category.

[8] For further discussion of the relationship between domestic infrastructure and e-commerce, see Mann, Eckert, and Knight (2000).

restrictions. *Customs environment* here consists of components that have their basis in the GATT article VIII. GATT article VIII states that in order to minimize impediments to trade due to customs procedures, fees charged by customs officials must be limited to the approximate cost of customs services. Also, there should not be substantial penalties for minor breaches of customs regulations such as clerical errors. *Regulatory environment* issues are contained in GATT article X which discusses Publication and Administration of Trade Regulations. This article comes from the basic transparency obligation that requires prompt publication of laws and regulations affecting imports and exports so that foreign governments and traders may clearly understand them.

3.2. *Constructing the Measures Used in This Study*

This paper builds on the WMO methodology and categories of trade facilitation. However, because this paper broadens the set of economies for analysis to 75, the cross-country survey data on business and policy climate that are used to construct the four indicators for each economy are somewhat different from the data used to construct the indicators in WMO. Specifically, we drop data sources that have limited country coverage (Clark, Dollar and Micco (2001) and Transparency International), but include Kaufmann, Kraay and Zoido-Lobaton (2002) (henceforth KKZ) which has a wider country coverage. Therefore, we rely on three sources – World Economic Forum, Global Competitiveness Report 2001-2002 (henceforth GCR); IMD Lausanne, World Competitiveness Yearbook 2002 (henceforth WCY); and KKZ. See the Appendix for a more complete description of the sources and each of their methodologies for collecting and preparing data about an economy.

Because the survey scales of the sources differ, we must put all survey data from the three sources on comparable basis. In contrast to WMO, we index each observation of a raw series (which is an observation representing an economy) to the maximum of all the economies' value for the raw series (*e.g.*, global best practice). WMO used the mean of all economies as a benchmark for each of the indexes. We use the maximum as a benchmark since this easily indicates how far a country's performance is from the best practice country whose indexed value is 1.0.

Two survey data inputs are used to form each of the trade facilitation measures. We use multiple survey inputs into each trade facilitation indicator to avoid depending too heavily on any one survey question or source.

The next step in creating the trade facilitation indictors involves collecting these indexed inputs into the four specific trade facilitation indicators. A simple average of the two indexed inputs is used for transparency of method, and also because there is no specific argument (theoretical or statistical) to choose a different aggregation method. Therefore:

- Port efficiency for each economy *J* is the average of two indexed inputs from GCR:
  - Port facilities and inland waterways
  - Air transport
- Customs environment for each economy *J* is the average of two indexed inputs from GCR:
  - Hidden import barriers
  - Irregular extra payments and bribes
- Regulatory environment for each economy *J* is constructed as the average of indexed inputs from WCY and KKZ:
  - Transparency of government policy is satisfactory (WCY)
  - Control of Corruption (KKZ)
- Service sector infrastructure for each economy *J* is from GCR:
  - Speed and cost of internet access
  - Effect of internet on business

Within each of the trade facilitation categories, the correlation of the inputs that go into the final index are high, but less than one suggesting robustness of the methodology of using more than one survey indicator to construct the indicator. As well, this raises confidence that the indicator is correctly assessing each economy on that particular indicator of trade facilitation. Correlation coefficients of the inputs to the indicators are 0.802, 0.820, 0.696, and 0.658 for categories of port efficiency, customs environment, regulatory environment and service sector infrastructure, respectively.

Table 1 and Figures 1 to 4 (one for each trade facilitation indicator) report information about these indicators. Table 1 shows, for each input as well as for the trade facilitation indicator, the mean, standard deviation, and minimum value along with economies of best and worst practice. For best practice Singapore and Finland stand out. Worst practice is well distributed among many economies and regions of the world. The figures show the indexed inputs for regional groups of economies for each specific trade facilitation indicator.[9] Each indexed input is

[9] These regional indicators use a simple average of the region. An average weighted by trade or GDP would no doubt yield somewhat different results. There is no clear interpretation of alternative weighted aver ages. Moreover, these regional indexes are not used in estimation.

Table 1. Summary statistics for values of trade facilitation indicators

Category	Indexed inputs	Source	Mean	Std. Dev.	Min	Min. Importer	Max	Max. Importer
Port Efficiency	Ports Facilities	GCR	.636	.189	.261	Bolivia	1.000	Singapore
	Air Transport	GCR	.710	.166	.229	Slovak Republic	1.000	Singapore
Aggregate Index			.673	.169	.345	Bolivia	1.000	Singapore
Customs Environment	Hidden Import Barriers	GCR	.702	.167	.368	Paraguay	1.000	Finland
	Bribery	GCR	.689	.175	.343	Bangladesh	1.000	Iceland
Aggregate Index			.695	.163	.384	Paraguay	0.979	Finland
Regulatory Environment	Transparency of Government Policies	WCY	.619	.205	.089	Argentina	1.000	Finland
	Control of Corruption	KKZ	.746	.140	.530	South Africa	1.000	Finland
Aggregate Index			.689	.139	.353	Venezuela	1.000	Finland
Service sector infrastructure	Speed and Costs of Internet Access	GCR	.629	.162	.348	Vietnam	1.000	Finland
	Effect on Internet on Business	GCR	.719	.102	.481	Greece	1.000	Finland
Aggregate Index			.674	.121	.482	Mauritius	1.000	Finland

Source: Authors' calculation based on Global Competitiveness Report 2001-2002, Kaufmann, Kraay and Zoido-Lobaton (2002) and World Competitiveness Yearbook 2002.

Figure 1. Two indexed inputs to port efficiency

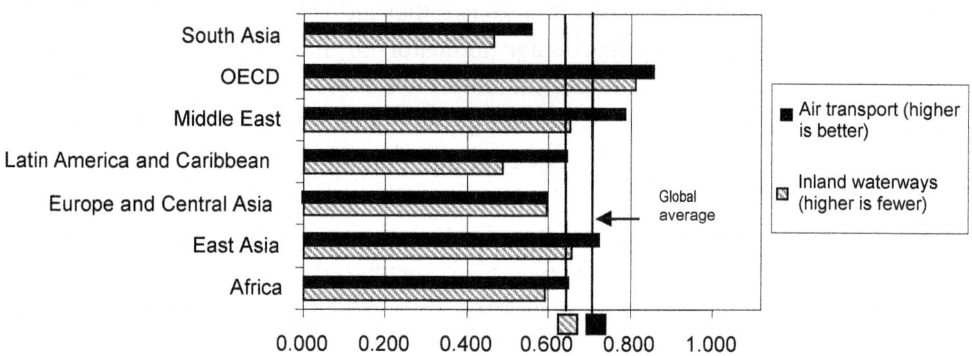

Source: Authors' calculation based on Global Competitiveness Report 2001-2001.

Figure 2. Two indexed inputs to customs environment

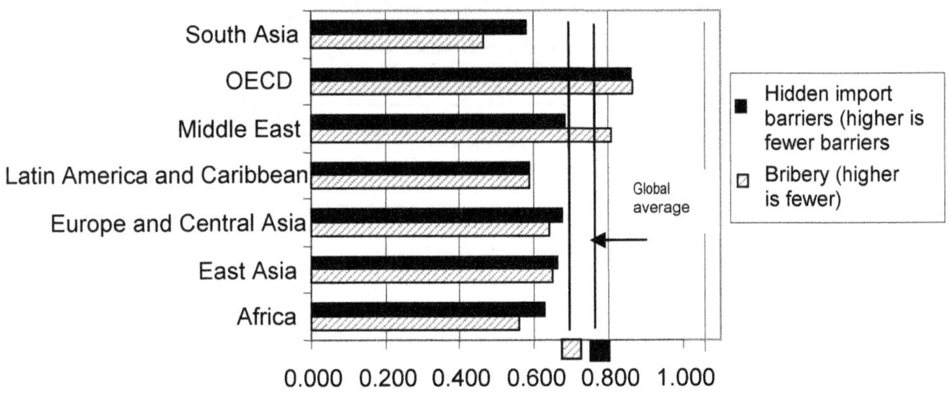

Source: Authors' calculation based on Global Competitiveness Report 2001-2001.

Figure 3. Two indexed inputs to regulatory environment

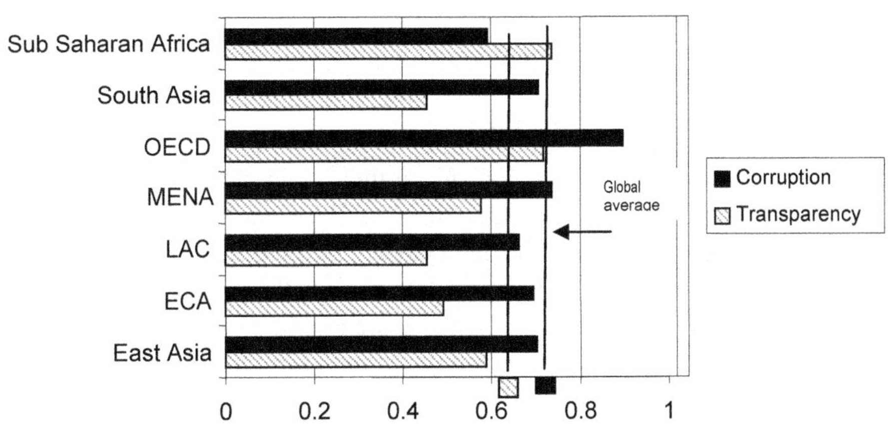

Source: Authors' calculation based on Kaufmann, Kraay and Zoido-Lobaton (2002) and World Competitiveness Yearbook 2002.

Figure 4. Two indexed inputs to service-sector infrastructure

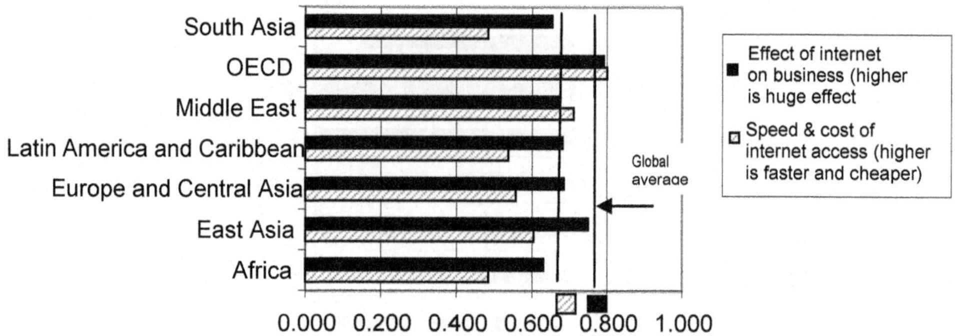

Source: Authors' calculation based on Global Competitiveness Report 2001-2001.

represented by a horizontal bar. The longer the bar extends to the right toward the maximum of 1.0, the higher ranked the region is in the category of trade facilitation. A vertical line is drawn at the average value. If a bar extends beyond the average for the particular trade facilitation measure, that indexed input for that region represents a condition superior to the average for all economies. For example, Figure 1 shows that OECD, Middle East and North Africa (MENA)[10] and East Asia regions are above the global average in terms of the two indexed inputs for port efficiency.

3.3. *Trade Flows and Other Variables*

We use bilateral trade flow data available at the Commodity and Trade Database (COMTRADE) of the United Nations Statistics Division, for 2000 and 2001. We focus our attention on trade in manufactured goods, defined as commodities in categories 5 to 8 in SITC 1 digit industry except those in category 68 (non-ferrous metals). Our trade flow data aggregate the trade flows over the manufactured goods for a given importer-exporter pair.[11]

Tariff data were derived from the Trade Analysis and Information System (TRAINS) of the United Nations Conference on Trade and Development (UNCTAD). We use the weighted average of applied tariff rates for the manufactured goods in 2000 and 2001 under the above definition where bilateral trade values corresponding to each tariff line are used as the weight. The data on

[10] Data are available only for Egypt, Jordan, and Israel.

[11] Standard International Trade Classification. Revision 1 is used for our definition.

gross national product (GNP) and *per capita* GNP were derived for years 2000 and 2001 from the World Development Indicators published by the World Bank.

4. The Econometric Model and Results

4.1. *An Aside on the Gravity Model*

The gravity model of international trade flows, which we use, is a common approach to modeling bilateral trade flows. It is enjoying a resurgence of interest given its natural kinship with current interests in the relationship between geography and trade. The standard gravity formulation includes various measures of market size (GDP, population, GDP *per capita* to account for intra-industry trade effects that may be associated with economies of similar incomes but varied tastes), measures of remoteness (distance and adjacency), and measures of kinship (regional trade arrangements, and language/ethnic similarities). To this basic formulation, we will add tariffs as well as the trade facilitation indicators and some additional factors, as described further below.

Despite the empirical success of gravity models to mimic trade patterns, there are serious questions as to the theoretical validity of the gravity model formulation. Some studies attempt to add additional structural elements to the gravity model to better reflect real world observations. These mainly concern the heterogeneity of traded goods in quality and price by origin, and price differentials associated with border and transportation costs. Anderson (1979) develops a gravity model in line with a general equilibrium framework. He incorporates into a gravity model consumers' preferences over goods that are differentiated by region of origin, assuming the constant elasticity of substitution (CES) structure on consumers' preferences. Anderson and von Wincoop (2003) additionally introduce the border costs as premiums on the export prices. Balistreri and Hillberry (2001) extend the results of the Anderson and von Wincoop's gravity model to estimate the transport and border costs separately by distinguishing consumers' and producers' price indices.

4.2. *Our Gravity Model Specification*

Using a standard gravity model as reviewed above, the basic structure of our specific gravity equation is the following:

$ln(V_{JI}^{t}) = b_1 ln(100+TARIFF_{JI}^{t}) + b_2\ lnPE_J + b_3 lnRE_J + b_4 lnSI_J + b_5 lnPE_I + b_6 lnCE_I + b_7 lnREI_I + b_8 lnSI_I + b_9 ln(GNP_I^t) + b_{10} ln(GNP_J^t) + b_{11} ln(GNPPC_I^t) + b_{12} ln(GNPPC_J^t) + b_{13} ln(DIST_{IJ}) + b_{14} D_{ADJ} + b_{15}\ D_{ASEAN} + b_{16} D_{NAFTA} + b_{17}\ D_{LAIA} +$

$b_{18}\, D_{AUNZ} + b_{19}\, D_{MERCOSUR} + b_{20} D_{EU} + b_{21} D_{ENG} + b_{22} D_{FRC} + b_{23} D_{SPN} + b_{24}\, D_{ARB} +$
$b_{25}\, D_{CHN} + b_{26}\, D_{GMN} + b_{27}\, D_{POR} + b_{28}\, D_{RUS} + b_{29}\, D_{2000} + \varepsilon_{JI}{}^{t}$ (1)

where I and J stand for the importer and exporter respectively, and t denotes trading years (t=2000, 2001). Parameter b's are coefficients. The term $\varepsilon_{JI}{}^{t}$ is the error term, assumed to be normally distributed with mean zero. The value of manufactures exports from economy J to I is denoted as V_{JI} (so exporter to importer). The term $TARIFF_{JI}$ denotes applied tariff rate in the percent *ad valorem* term that is specific to the trading partners I and J and year t. The inclusion of the tariff variable is useful for reducing omitted variable biases. It is particularly important for some nations since unlike the EU whose tariff policies are harmonized, applied tariff rates generally vary across most other economies and possibly across their exporting partners.

The terms PE_J, RE_J and SI_J denote exporting_economy J's indicators of port efficiency, regulatory environment, and service sector infrastructure. Similarly, PE_I, RE_I and SI_I stand for the same trade facilitation measures in the importing economy. For the importing economy we include one additional measure *i.e.*, "customs environment" or CE_I. We use "customs environment" only for the importers since in bilateral trade customs is more relevant as a factor affecting imports than exports.

This set of trade facilitation variables is different than in WMO. There, we included only PE_I, RE_I, SI_I , and CE_I. That is, for economy I we considered only the effect on imports of unilateral trade facilitation. Economy I's exports improved indirectly when its trading partners improved their trade facilitation efforts. In this formulation, we take explicit account of the fact that economy J' s exports (as well as its imports) will improve through its own trade facilitation efforts.

The term GNP denotes gross national product and *GNPPC* denotes *per capita* GNP, where both are expressed in 1995 US dollar terms. Geographical distance between capital cities I and J is denoted as $DIST_{IJ}$. Dummy variables are included to capture the effect of preferential trade arrangements, language similarity and adjacency. The trade arrangements dummies include NAFTA (D_{NAFTA}), ASEAN (D_{ASEAN}), LAIA (D_{LAIA}), AUNZ (D_{AUNZ}), *MERCOSUR*($D_{MERCOSUR}$) and EU (D_{EU}). The language dummies include English (D_{ENG}), French(D_{FRC}), Spanish(D_{SPN}), Arabic(D_{ARB}), Chinese (D_{CHN}), German(D_{GMN}), Portuguese (D_{POR}) and Russian (D_{RUS}). The adjacency dummy D_{ADJ} takes the value of one if economy I is adjacent to economy J and zero otherwise. Additionally a dummy for year 2000 is included in the model to control for time-specific shocks.

Table 2 shows the simple correlations among the included variables. All four trade facilitation variables are rather highly correlated with each other and rather highly correlated with *per capita* income of the importer. This is to be expected, first because the trade facilitation indicators are different facets of overall trade facilitation, and second because some of the elements of trade facilitation (administrative transparency, available resources to build quality ports, and so on) are more prevalent in higher income economies.

These relatively high correlations between trade facilitation and income and the use of a single-year observation for the construction of the trade-facilitation indicators in cross-section regression analysis points to the potentially ambiguous causal relationship between trade facilitation and trade. We cannot exclude the possibility that greater bilateral trade will lead to higher values of trade facilitation measures rather than the postulated reverse relationship as estimated. Port efficiency, customs environment and service sector infrastructure may induce reforms that improve with an economy's import and export flows and the estimated coefficients for these variables would be biased upwards if this endogeneity is present.

A logical approach to the endogeneity problem is (1) to employ instrumental variables for the trade facilitation variables so the error term does not correlate with trade facilitation measures, and/or (2) to extend the trade facilitation data to a multiple year series and to use time-lagged measures of trade facilitation as explanatory variables. Good instruments should be sufficiently exogenous to decision makers or pre-determined, and should uniquely capture the characteristics of each trade facilitation indicator. Given the very large number of economies, finding good instruments is difficult, and data are lacking. We have already used such data exhaustively as inputs to form our trade facilitation indicators. The implication of the use of time-lagged measures was investigated in more depth in WMO using the smaller and more data rich APEC sample, yielding weak evidence that endogeneity was not too large an issue.

Further methodological issue arise from not having time-varying trade facilitation indicators. We cannot use a fixed effects model to isolate country specific effects that are correlated but not specific to trade facilitation. Whereas WMO used a fixed-effects model to account for the variation across exporting economies, here the use of country's trade facilitation measures as an exporter will make it impossible to use fixed-effects for exporting economies. The time-varying gravity variables and the dummy variables will absorb variation other than that caused by differences in trade facilitation such that the trade facilitation variables appropriately capture the country specific effect associated only with trade facilitation. Although, we re-open the endogeneity box with this rationale.

Table 2. Correlation matrix of key variables for gravity model

	Trade	Tariff	Port Efficiency	Customs Environ-ment	Regulatory Environ-ment	Service sector infrastructure	GNP of Importer	GNP of Exporter	Per capita GNP of Importer	Per capita GNP of Exporter	Distance
Trade	1										
Tariff	-0.154	1									
Port Efficiency	0.239	-0.311	1								
Customs Environment	0.221	-0.335	0.767	1							
Regulatory Environment	0.078	-0.295	0.600	0.709	1						
Service sector infrastructure	0.255	-0.362	0.784	0.762	0.608	1					
GNP of Importer	0.444	-0.171	0.444	0.398	0.064	0.490	1				
GNP of Exporter	0.614	-0.024	-0.040	-0.051	-0.015	-0.051	-0.064	1			
Per capita GNP of Importer	0.255	-0.399	0.795	0.858	0.570	0.787	0.491	-0.055	1		
Per capita GNP of Exporter	0.399	-0.099	-0.026	-0.031	-0.009	-0.032	-0.036	0.504	-0.035	1	
Distance	-0.364	0.063	-0.091	-0.128	-0.081	-0.074	-0.019	0.013	-0.129	-0.115	1

Source: Authors' calculation.

In the end, our estimation can only be improved when panel data with a sufficiently long time series in trade facilitation variables become available, which would allow direct attention to endogeneity and application of fixed-effect modeling.

4.3. *Regression Results*

The approach used here, which constructs a set of distinct trade facilitation indicators and deploys them in a gravity model of trade, is generally successful. Table 3 displays regression results. The first column includes the estimated coefficients and standard errors for the model under the specification in Equation (1). The second column includes those for the specification with aggregate FTA and language dummies (*i.e.*, membership of any FTA, or any common language). The model was run using an ordinary least squares (OLS). The coefficients for the four trade facilitation measures are statistically significant and the estimated coefficients differ for the different trade facilitation indicators. From a policy perspective, these differences in estimated elasticity's of trade flows with respect to trade facilitation indicator implies that different approaches to trade facilitation will differentially affect trade of individual economies and of all economies in the sample as a whole. The estimates are robust to the choice of dummy for language and regional arrangement.

Before considering the trade facilitation indicators, it is worthwhile to consider tariffs. Higher tariffs have a significant and the expected negative effect (with −1.2 coefficient) on trade. The coefficient on tariffs is similar to that of distance. In *ad valorem* terms, the elasticity of tariff is −1.1 at the global average level of tariff rates – *i.e.*, 1 percent reduction in *ad valorem* tariff from the global average (from 8.5 percent to 7.5 percent) will increase the trade flow by 1.1 percent and a 1 percent reduction in distance (80 kilometers from the global average) would yield a 1.3 percent increase in trade flow. These figures are useful benchmarks against which to compare the coefficients on the trade facilitation indicators.

Port efficiency of both the importer and the exporter is positively associated with trade; that is, an improvement in the indicator toward best practice is associated with an increase in trade flows. Comparing the effect of port efficiency on imports *vs*. exports, we note that the coefficient is higher for exporters than importer, which implies that global trade flows get a bigger boost when the exporters' port efficiency improves. So for economies and regions that are well below the global best practice, such as Bolivia and Slovak Republic (from Table 1) there is great potential for improvement in terms of port

Table 3. Regression results

	Model 1		Model 2	
	Coef.	**Std. Err.**	**Coef.**	**Std. Err.**
Constant	-10.641***	1.558	-10.771***	1.549
Tariff Rates	-1.155***	0.318	-1.163***	0.318
Port Efficiency of Importer	0.307*	0.163	0.338*	0.160
Port Efficiency of Exporter	0.924***	0.148	0.938***	0.146
Customs Environment of Importer	0.472**	0.199	0.486*	0.199
Regulatory Environment of Importer	0.281*	0.144	0.264	0.144
Regulatory Environment of Exporter	0.620***	0.132	0.580***	0.131
Service sector infrastructure of Importer	0.729***	0.224	0.657**	0.224
Service sector infrastructure of Exporter	1.943***	0.216	1.943***	0.217
GNP of Importer	0.915***	0.014	0.915***	0.014
Per capita GNP of Importer	-0.182***	0.037	-0.210***	0.037
GNP of Exporter	1.246***	0.014	1.241***	0.014
Per capita GNP of Exporter	-0.226***	0.029	-0.251***	0.029
Geographical Distance	-1.258***	0.025	-1.225***	0.025
Adjacency dummy	0.336***	0.114	0.426***	0.108
Membership Dummy for any FTA			-0.021	0.078
ASEAN Membership Dummy	0.509***	0.190		
NAFTA Membership Dummy	-0.645	0.501		
LAIA Membership Dummy	0.593***	0.154		
AUNZ Membership Dummy	1.118	0.858		
MERCOSUR Membership Dummy	0.229	0.302		
EU Membership Dummy	-0.515***	0.106		
Dummy for any Common Language			0.823***	0.061
English Language Dummy	0.808***	0.089		
French Language Dummy	-1.413***	0.500		
Spanish Language Dummy	0.598***	0.098		
Arabic Language Dummy	-1.223	0.992		
Chinese Language Dummy	1.747***	0.406		
German Language Dummy	-0.826	0.505		
Portuguese Language Dummy	0.569	0.986		
Russian Language Dummy	2.026***	0.362		
Year 2000 dummy	-0.031	0.039	-0.038	0.039
Adjusted R-squared	0.758		0.755	
Number of the observations	7,904		7,904	

Note: The significance levels at 10%, 5% and 1% are denoted by "*", "**", and "***", respectively.

Source: Authors' calculation.

efficiency. Moreover, the range of performance on this measure of trade facilitation is the largest among the trade facilitation indicators (again see

Table 1). So, the opportunities for increased trade from improvements in this measure of trade facilitation could be quite large.

Customs environment also has a significantly positive effect on trade of the importing economy with an elasticity of 0.47, which is smaller than that for tariffs. Although the two metrics are different (*ad valorem* for tariffs and survey indicator for customs), the sign and size of elasticity present support for the attention to this as a Singapore issue. Trade facilitation is a possible avenue for reducing the cost of imports through customs improvements even as tariffs remain where they are.

Improving the regulatory environment of the importer and exporter has a positive and significant association with trade with coefficients of 0.28 and 0.62, respectively. As with ports, the magnitude of the coefficient is larger for the exporter than for the importer. The sign of the coefficient for regulatory environment of importer is reversed from that in WMO. In contrast that paper, the survey inputs used to construct regulatory environment indicator in this analysis are more unambiguously trade-promoting. Regulatory transparency and control of corruption (the two inputs) reduce unnecessary information costs of trading and reduce barriers to private business.

Improving indicators of service sector infrastructure are positive and significantly associated with trade among the studied economies. Similar to port efficiency and regulatory environment, service sector infrastructure have a more significant positive effect on the exporters than for importers. The elasticity of the exporters' service sector infrastructure is the highest among all trade facilitation measures (1.94). This high elasticity should come as no surprise since the role of the services-sectors in trade facilitation is important.[12]

It is notable that for all the trade facilitation indicators that are paired (that is, are estimated for both exporters and importers), the coefficient for exporters exceeds that for importers. There are several reasons why this might be the case. First, in the sample of economies, there are 30 developed economies (North) and 45 developing economies (South). Thus, the sample is weighted toward developing economies where the elasticity of improvement in trade facilitation indicators is likely to be higher than for the developed economies whose trade facilitation indicators are already high. Second, the pattern of trade in general is

---

[12] Other research investigates the relative magnitude of service sector liberalization compared to manufactures and agricultural liberalization in the context of the Uruguay Round and the Doha Development Agenda. Several researchers conclude that liberalization of services trade would yield at least as large an increase in GDP than does liberalization of manufactures trade, and much larger than liberalization of agriculture trade. See the discussion and sources in Mann, Rosen and APEC (2001, 2002), pages 33-35.

South-North (even if the value of trade North-North is larger). So, the estimated coefficients would tend to pick up the higher elasticity of trade from the South to the North.

To further investigate this issue, as well as to shed light on the potential for capacity building in the area of trade facilitation in the south, we examined the gravity model using several sub-sets of the 75 economies bilateral trade. Specifically, we re-estimated the gravity model on south-to-north trade and on south-to-south trade. Table 4 presents the results for the trade facilitation indicators for two sub-panels. Also repeated in the table for convenience are the values of the coefficients from the full panel.

Comparing across the three panels, several points emerge. In the South-to-North panel, many of the variables added to the gravity model for the North (as importer) are not significant – tariffs, port efficiency, the customs environment, and (nearly) the regulatory environment. The lack of significance on tariffs

Table 4. Regression results (south to south and south to north trade)

	Full sample	South to north trade	South to south trade
Tariff rates	-1.555***	-1.512	-1.5***
Port Efficiency of Importing Economy	0.307*	0.344	-0.283
Port Efficiency of Exporting Economy	0.924***	0.845***	0.949***
Customs Environment of Importing Economy	0.472**	1.041	0.202
Regulatory Environment of Importing Economy	0.281*	-1.120*	0.816***
Regulatory Environment of Exporting Economy	0.620***	2.437***	0.827***
Service sector infrastructure of Importing Economy	0.729***	2.134***	0.866
Service sector infrastructure of Exporting Economy	1.943***	2.124***	3.133***
Adjusted R-squared	0.758	0.702	0.649
Number of the observations	7,904	2,188	3,094

Note: The significance levels at 10%, 5% and 1% are denoted by "*", "**", and "***", respectively.

Source: Authors' calculation.

suggests that tariffs are not a major impediment to South-to-North trade. The fact that the trade facilitation indicators are nearer to global best in the North means that the other variables in the gravity model (such as GDP) dominate in estimation. On the other hand, the service sector infrastructure indicator has a higher coefficient than in the full sample for both importer and exporter, corroborating work cited earlier on the benefits of more Webhosts and lower telecommunications costs for trade. The high coefficient on regulatory environment in the exporting economy (South) would support a focus on capacity building in this area in the South.

Second, compare the South-to-South panel with the other two samples. Tariffs are once again significant, suggesting that south-to-south trade is more affected by tariffs than is south-to-north trade. Regulatory environment appears to be very important for both directions of trade. Looking at all the indicators, the coefficient estimated on the exporter is larger than the full sample and larger than for the importer in the restricted sample, suggesting that trade facilitation efforts and capacity building could play a complementary role in export promotion in the south.

Finally, given the juxtaposition in the Doha Agenda of tariff negotiations and Singapore trade facilitation issues, it is interesting to apply the regression results to the question of tariffs *vs.* trade facilitation. The data used in the estimation indicates an average 8.5 percent tariff rate. Figure 5 suggests that a complete tariff elimination would be associated with an increase in trade flow equivalent to a 15.6 percent (or 5.2 percent) improvement in port efficiency by importer (or exporter) or a 10.2 percent improvement in customs environment by the importer or an increase in indicator of service sector infrastructure by 6.6 percent (importer) or 2.5 percent (exporter). In terms of regulatory environment the same trade gains from a complete tariff cut is equivalent to 17.0 percent (7.8 percent) improvement of regulatory environment by importer (exporter).

4.4. *Implications of Geographical Characteristics*

Geographical characteristics such as being landlocked or an island can affect trade. Frankel and Rose (2000) included dummy variables for those geographical characteristics to allow for the intercept term to vary accordingly. We additionally allow for the coefficient for trade facilitation indicators to vary according to those characteristics. Our particular interest is whether ports play more important role in the import and export of landlocked economies, or whether ports play a less important role for island economies. Ports may play a less important role in trade between economies that share land borders. We perform this analysis by additionally introducing cross-product terms between the port efficiency indicators and these geographical characteristics based on the main regression model.

Figure 5. Changes in trade facilitation measures to have an equivalent increase in trade flow to a total elimination of tariffs in manufacture

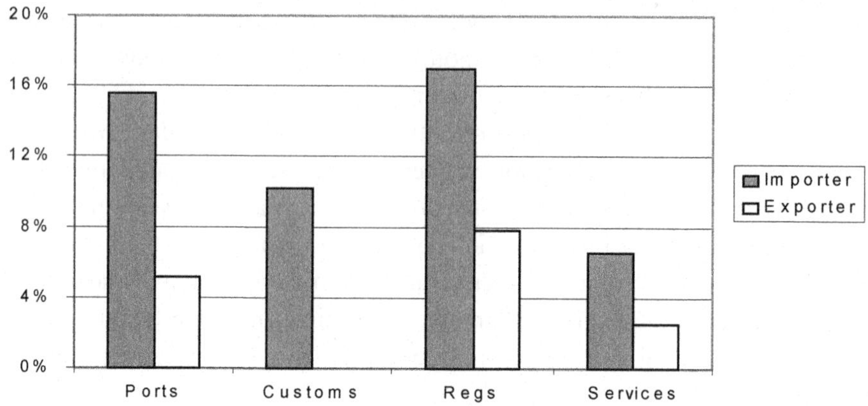

Source: Authors' calculation.

Landlocked, island, and adjacency variables are used here to differentiate the effect of port efficiency. Table 5 indicates the results for varied specifications. In the first three columns one characteristic is considered at a time. In the fourth column landlockedness and island are jointly considered as these characteristics are mutually exclusive. The last column allow for the coefficients for port efficiency to vary with respect to all the three characteristics. Consider first geographical adjacency. As expected, for economies that share land borders, ports are less important than for economies that do not. Interpreting the estimates for landlocked and island is more difficult. For landlocked economies, the importance of ports is as important for both import and export as in non-landlocked economies since the product terms are insignificant. Landlocked economies are disadvantaged in maritime transport but may have developed ground and air transport infrastructure and our port efficiency indicator is a combination of both types of ports. For island economies, it appears that ports are more important for their import and less important for their export compared to non-island economies. This result is difficult to interpret, but is consistent with some research that finds that small island economies are disadvantaged in export trade because they cannot offer a scale of production sufficiently large to compete in international markets or be part of an international value chain in production (Winters, 2004).

Table 5. The effect of port efficiency by geographical characteristics

Port Efficiency of Importer	0.333** (0.165)	0.311* (0.163)	0.368** (0.164)	0.303* (0.165)	0.357** (0.166)
Landlockedness* Port Efficiency of Importer	-0.157 (0.783)			-0.128 (0.783)	-0.126 (0.781)
Island* Port Efficiency of Importer		1.198** (0.604)		1.223** (0.606)	1.307** (0.605)
Adjacency* Port Efficiency of Importer			-1.360*** (0.409)		-1.333*** (0.410)
Port Efficiency of Exporter	0.940*** (0.149)	0.866*** (0.149)	1.007*** (0.149)	0.982*** (0.150)	1.057*** (0.150)
Landlockedness* Port Efficiency of Exporter	0.268 (0.836)			0.229 (0.835)	0.424 (0.835)
Island* Port Efficiency of Exporter		-2.000*** (0.612)		-2.107*** (0.614)	-2.038*** (0.612)
Adjacency* Port Efficiency of Exporter			-1.582*** (0.388)		-1.592*** (0.389)
Customs Environment of Importer	0.461** (0.200)	0.461** (0.199)	0.431** (0.199)	0.444** (0.200)	0.402** (0.199)
Regulatory Environment of Importer	0.283** (0.144)	0.294** (0.143)	0.279* (0.143)	0.288** (0.144)	0.287** (0.143)
Regulatory Environment of Exporter	0.619*** (0.132)	0.608*** (0.132)	0.607*** (0.132)	0.624*** (0.132)	0.610*** (0.132)
Service sector infrastructure of Importer	0.713*** (0.225)	0.745*** (0.224)	0.753*** (0.224)	0.764*** (0.225)	0.791*** (0.225)
Service sector infrastructure of Exporter	1.936*** (0.217)	2.002*** (0.218)	1.944*** (0.216)	1.867*** (0.218)	1.874*** (0.217)
Tariff Rates	-1.161*** (0.319)	-1.239*** (0.318)	-1.127*** (0.318)	-1.205*** (0.318)	-1.177*** (0.318)
Landlockedness Dummy	0.328 (0.794)			0.324 (0.793	0.386 (0.791)
Island Dummy		-0.260 (0.483)		-0.263 (0.370)	-0.222 (0.370)
Adjacency Dummy	0.329*** (0.114)	0.331*** (0.113)	-0.955*** (0.235)	0.329*** (0.114)	-0.953*** (0.235)
Adjusted R-squared	0.759	0.761	0.760	0.760	0.761

Note: The significance levels at 10%, 5% and 1% are denoted by "*", "**", and "***", respectively.

Source: Authors' calculation.

4.5. *Robustness of the OLS Estimators*

OLS estimation imposes the assumption that the error term is identically distributed. This assumption often is inappropriate for grouped data where the error term is heterosckedastic. Robustness of the OLS estimated standard error of the coefficients is examined by using heterosckedasticity-robust variance. The second column of Table 6 reports the Huber/White sandwich estimator of variance which is used without specifying a cluster (group) of the sample (see White (1980) for the procedure). In the third and fourth column a cluster is formed with respect to importer and exporter, respectively. As an alternative approach, we performed weighted least squares (WLS) by correcting the error term for heterosckedasticity by using the estimated variance for importer (the fifth column) or exporter (the sixth column). These results are compared with the main result displayed in the first column. Standard error is acceptably robust across those specifications. The significance of the key variables generally remains. The WLS coefficients are also similar to the OLS ones while a few coefficients turn insignificant.

5. Potential Benefits from Trade Facilitation: Simulation Results

5.1. *Simulation Design and Aggregate Results*

The gravity model approach allows us to consider how much trade among the 75 economies might be increased under various scenarios of improved trade facilitation and/or tariff reduction. We will examine scenarios that focus on improved port efficiency, improved customs environment, improved service sector infrastructure, and regulatory environment. Our objective in the simulations is to help inform policymakers on which specific trade facilitation initiatives might have the greatest potential to increase trade and economic well-being.

We follow the simulation strategy presented in WMO, which uses a formula to design a unique program of reform for each economy in the sample. The formula brings the *below-average* economies in the group *half-way* to the average for the entire set of economies. We focus on the *below-average* economy on the grounds that donor attention and capacity building efforts should be extended to this group. It is not that the economy with the best practice should not try to do better; it is just that limited multilateral resources are not best utilized that way.

We choose an improvement of *half-way* to the average because there are limited development resources and improvements take time. Dramatic improvements are possible, but it is not realistic to presume a scenario whereby all economies in the sample are assumed to achieve best practice as measured by

Table 6. Robustness check for the OLS estimator

Variable	OLS	Huber/ White	Huber/ White	Huber/ White	WLS	WLS
Tariff Rates	-1.155*** (0.318)	-1.155*** (0.399)	-1.155 (0.868)	-1.155** (0.561)	-1.467*** (0.343)	-0.483** (0.246)
Port Efficiency of Importer	0.307* (0.163)	0.307* (0.161)	0.307 (0.414)	0.307 (0.204)	0.246 (0.157)	0.473*** (0.119)
Port Efficiency of Exporter	0.924*** (0.148)	0.924*** (0.166)	0.924*** (0.179)	0.924 (0.978)	0.913*** (0.142)	0.537*** (0.137)
Customs Environment of Importer	0.472** (0.199)	0.472** (0.198)	0.472 (0.480)	0.472* (0.259)	0.472** (0.193)	1.112*** (0.147)
Regulatory Environment of Importer	0.281* (0.144)	0.281** (0.141)	0.281 (0.304)	0.281* (0.145)	0.288** (0.138)	-0.069 (0.107)
Regulatory Environment of Exporter	0.620*** (0.132)	0.620*** (0.144)	0.620*** (0.163)	0.620 (0.867)	0.594*** (0.127)	0.180 (0.118)
Service sector infrastructure of Importer	0.729*** (0.224)	0.729*** (0.241)	0.729 (0.771)	0.729*** (0.262)	0.647*** (0.227)	0.494*** (0.166)
Service sector infrastructure of Exporter	1.943*** (0.216)	1.943*** (0.234)	1.943*** (0.242)	1.943 (1.270)	1.831*** (0.208)	2.336*** (0.189)
GNP of Importer	0.915*** (0.014)	0.915*** (0.015)	0.915*** (0.044)	0.915*** (0.018)	0.931*** (0.014)	0.892*** (0.010)
Per capita GNP of Importer	-0.182*** (0.037)	-0.182*** (0.038)	-0.182* (0.099)	-0.182*** (0.056)	-0.183*** (0.037)	-0.227*** (0.028)
GNP of Exporter	1.246*** (0.014)	1.246*** (0.015)	1.246*** (0.020)	1.246*** (0.082)	1.239*** (0.014)	1.169*** (0.012)
Per capita GNP of Exporter	-0.226*** (0.029)	-0.226*** (0.030)	-0.226*** (0.032)	-0.226 (0.197)	-0.231*** (0.028)	-0.153*** (0.022)
Geographical Distance	-1.258*** (0.025)	-1.258*** (0.022)	-1.258*** (0.048)	-1.258*** (0.092)	-1.238*** (0.025)	-1.143*** (0.018)
Robust Standard Error Cluster	No	Yes No	Yes Importer	Yes Exporter		
Weighted Least Square Cluster					Yes Importer	Yes Exporter
Adjusted R-squared	0.759	0.759	0.759	0.759		
Chi-squared against all b being zero					26,755	38,700

Note: The significance levels at 10%, 5% and 1% are denoted by "*", "**", and "***", respectively.

Source: Authors' calculation.

the nation with the highest score on a particular measure of trade facilitation.[13] Since each economy has a specific value for each trade facilitation indicator, each economy that is below-average on that indicator will improve by a different amount so as to get half-way to average. Our simulation approach acknowledges the differential potential for improvement revealed by Table 1. This approach contrasts with the here-to-fore standard approach to simulation design where all economies improve trade facilitation measures by a given percentage, such as when trade costs are 'shocked' by, say, 1 percent in a CGE model.

Therefore, the economies for which we will simulate an improvement in trade facilitation will differ by the trade facilitation indicator. However, because trade facilitation links exporters and importers, all economies enjoy an increase in trade among each other even when only some have an improvement in their trade facilitation indicator. Having the coefficients for both importer's and exporter's trade facilitation measures enables us to simulate the change in trade flow from different perspectives: the country itself and the group as a whole. Figure 6 shows the various pieces of the simulation.

From the standpoint of a specific economy, improvement, say, in port efficiency should increase both its own imports and exports. The same can be expected for regulatory environment, and service sector infrastructure, as well as customs on the import side. But, an economy will export more not only from its own-reforms, but also because of reforms undertaken by its trading partners as importers. Thus export gains are the sum of the simulated effect on exports of unilateral reform and of import reforms undertaken by the country's trading partners. On the import side, an economy's imports increase first on account of its unilateral import reforms, and secondarily on account of the reforms undertaken by its trading partners as exporters. Examining the relative gains to trade from unilateral reforms as compared to partner's reforms, and on exports *vs.* imports, and across trade facilitation indicators offers three dimensions of potential insight to policymakers, donors, and the private sector.

Table 7 summarizes the results for the simulations and presents the results for the 75 economies as a whole. In total, the collection of simulations on the four trade facilitation indicators yields an increase in trade among the 75 economies worth about $377 billion, representing an increase of about 9.7 percent in total

[13] Moreover, it is the case that in the course of the simulation, the 'average' target will rise, and we do not take account of this endogeneity. By restricting the improvement to half-way to average, we limit to some degree these second round effects.

Figure 6: Simulation Analysis: Improvements in Trade Facilitation and Change in Trade Flows

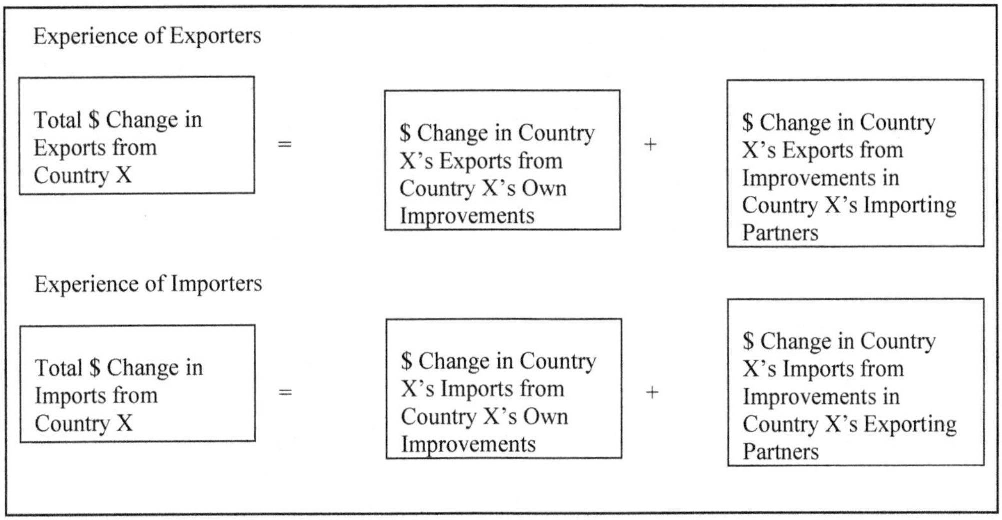

Table 7. Overview of simulation: bring below-average members half-way up to the global average (Change in trade flow in $ billion)

	Importer's change in trade facilitation	Exporter's change in trade facilitation	Total
'Border' Measures			
Port Efficiency	23.40 (0.6%)	84.53 (2.2%)	106.93 (2.8%)
Customs Environment	32.87 (0.8%)		32.87 (0.8%)
'Inside-the Border' Measures			
Service sector infrastructure	36.64 (0.9%)	117.38 (3.0%)	154.02 (4.0%)
Regulatory Environment	24.39 (0.6%)	58.86 (1.5%)	83.25 (2.1%)
Grand Total	117.30 (3.0%)	259.77 (6.7%)	377.06 (9.7%)

Source: Authors' calculation.

trade among these economies. About $107 billion of the total gain comes from the improvement in port efficiency and about $33 billion emanates from the improvement in customs environment. The gain from the improvement in regulatory environment is $83 billion. The largest gain comes from the improvement in service sector infrastructure ($154 billion), which is consistent with the broad concept of services infrastructure that this variable is designed to capture.

Table 8 summarizes the change in trade flow by region, by trade facilitation indicators, and by own *vs.* trading partners' reforms. All this detail can be combined in several ways to give different perspectives on which regions gain the most and why. One cut, exports and imports by region and by trade facilitation indicator, is shown in Figures 7 and 8. Figure 9 show increases in exports from domestic and partner reforms by region and by trade facilitation indicator.

5.2. *Exports and Imports by Region*

The first perspective on the detail is which region gains the most from what kinds of trade facilitation improvement and as an exporter or importer, and whether through own or trading partner reforms (as defined in Figure 6). To summarize: In all of these scenarios, the gains from own-reforms are much larger, whether as importer or exporter, and the gains as an exporter from own-reforms are dramatic. With respect to regions, the largest gainers (in percentage terms) are generally South Asia and Eastern Europe and Central Asia, with Latin American and Caribbean not far behind in terms of potential increases. In contrast, and on account of their relatively lower integration in global trade, Middle East and North Africa and Sub-Saharan Africa do not see much of improvement in their trade experience, either as exporters or importers. The results for Middle East and North Africa and for Sub-Saharan Africa must be viewed with caution as the number of economies with data from these two regions is quite limited.[14]

Considering *port efficiency,* South Asia gains the most as an exporter (12.1 percent increase in trade) followed by East Europe and Central Asia (ECA) (9.5 percent). The bulk of South Asia gains come from increased exports due to its own improvements (11.5 percent) as opposed to only 0.4 percent export gain due to its importing partners' improvement in port efficiency. South Asia's percentage gain is the highest because the region's average port efficiency is the lowest of all the regions. The "half-way to the average" scenario will consequently lead to a significant improvement in port efficiency in South Asia, which will have a large export promotion effect in the region. An examination of the detail from the simulation finds that in the South Asia region, Bangladesh accrues the highest percentage gain (32.5 percent) whereas India has the maximum gain in dollar amount ($2.3 billion). A similar pattern occurs in ECA

---

[14] The economies from MENA are Egypt, Jordan, and Israel. For SSA, data are available only for Mauritius, Nigeria, and South Africa.

Table 8. Detail of simulation results

Region	Initial Trade	Port efficiency: Importer Change, percent	Port efficiency: Exporter Change, percent	Port efficiency: Total Change, percent	Customs environment: Total Change, percent	Regulatory environment: Importer Change, percent	Regulatory environment: Exporter Change, percent	Regulatory environment: Total Change, percent	Service sector infrastructure: Importer Change, percent	Service sector infrastructure: Exporter Change, percent	Service sector infrastructure: Total Change, percent	Combined Effect: Total Change, percent
–Experience of Exporters												
East Asia	753	0.5	7.0	7.6	0.8	0.6	3.3	3.9	0.9	10.8	11.7	24.0
East Europe and Central Asia	139	0.8	8.7	9.5	0.9	0.7	5.5	6.1	1.4	12.1	13.5	30.0
Latin America and Caribbean	179	0.6	7.3	7.9	0.9	0.8	3.6	4.4	0.8	6.0	6.8	20.0
Middle East and North Africa	26	0.4	0.2	0.6	0.7	0.5	0.1	0.6	0.7	0.7	1.4	3.3
OECD	2735	0.6	0.0	0.7	0.8	0.6	0.6	1.3	1.0	0.0	1.0	3.8
South Asia	36	0.4	11.7	12.1	0.8	0.5	6.9	7.4	0.7	19.2	20.0	40.3
Sub-Saharan Africa	12	0.4	1.1	1.4	0.6	0.5	2.8	3.3	0.8	4.8	5.6	10.9
Total	3879	0.6	2.2	2.8	0.8	0.6	1.5	2.1	0.9	3.0	4.0	9.7
–Experience of Importers												
East Asia	620	1.5	2.7	4.2	2.2	1.1	2.1	3.3	2.7	4.4	7.0	16.7
East Europe and Central Asia	165	3.1	1.8	4.9	3.2	2.7	1.3	4	5.3	2.4	7.7	19.8
Latin America and Caribbean	260	2.9	1.3	4.2	3.4	2.4	1.4	3.8	2.9	1.8	4.7	16.1
Middle East and North Africa	32	0.2	1.0	1.3	1.3	0.1	1.1	1.2	0.7	2.1	2.8	6.6
OECD	2761	0.0	2.2	2.2	0.1	0.2	1.4	1.6	0.1	2.9	3.0	6.9
South Asia	21	3.1	1.4	4.5	5.8	3.3	1.5	4.8	6.8	2.5	9.3	24.4
Sub-saharan Africa	20	1.5	1.5	3.0	3.0	1.8	1.3	3.1	3.5	2.6	6.1	15.2
Total	3879	0.6	2.2	2.8	0.8	0.6	1.5	2.1	0.9	3.0	4.0	9.7

Source: Authors' calculation.

Figure 7. Change in exports by region

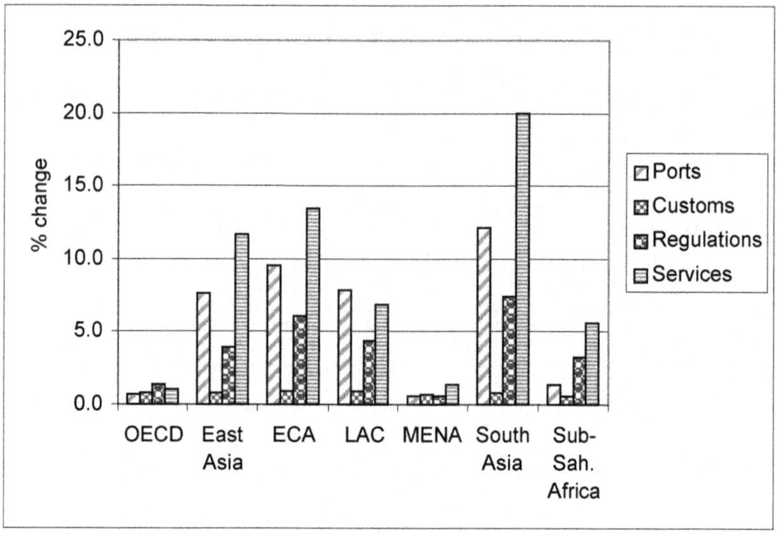

Source: Authors' calculation.

Figure 8. Change in imports by region

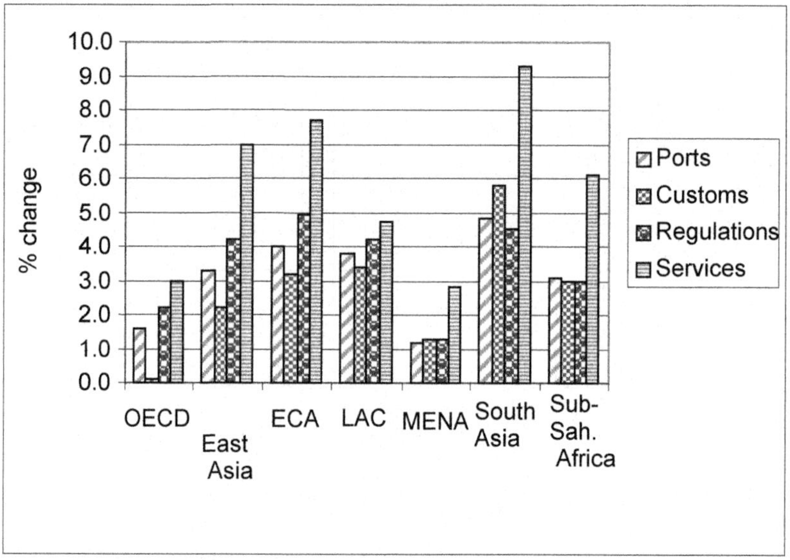

Source: Authors' calculation.

Figure 9. Change in manufacturing exports 'half-way to the global average' scenario: gains from domestic and partners' reform

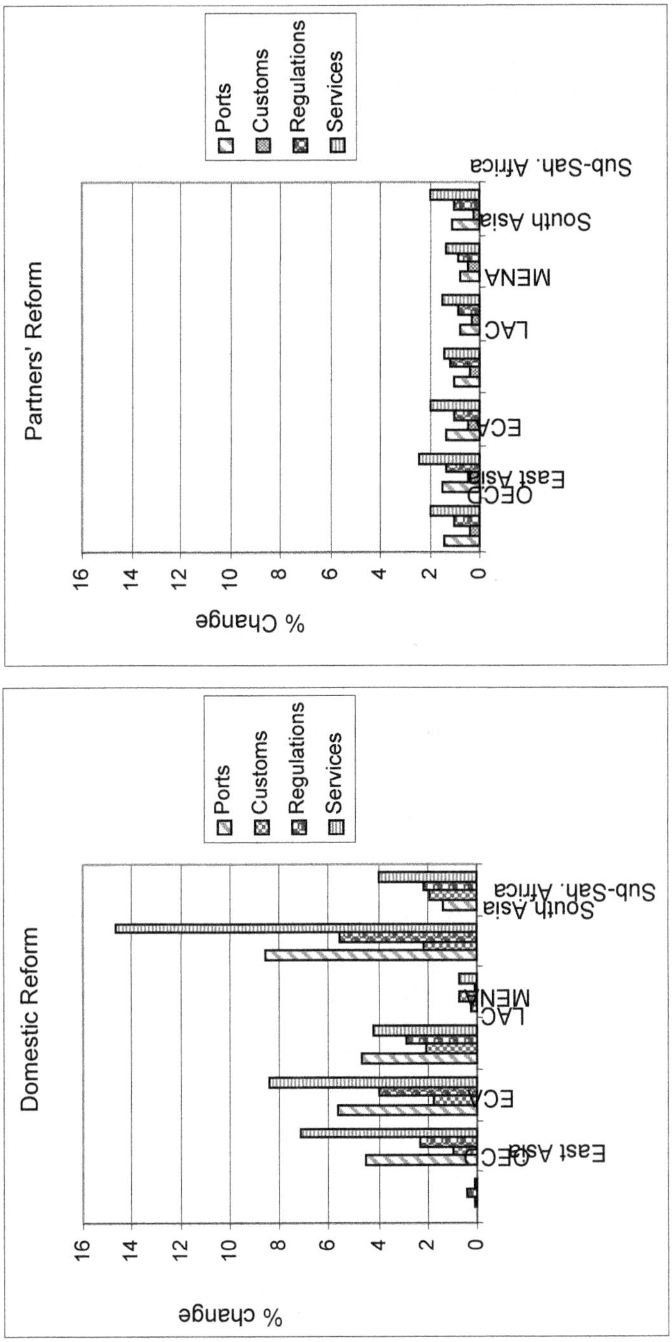

Source: Authors' calculation.

Source: Authors' calculation.

region, with the export gains from its own improvements at 8.7 percent *versus* only 0.8 percent increase in exports due to improvement in ports by its importing partners. In the ECA region the highest export gain is attained by Hungary in the amount of $3.0 billion (13.4 percent change) and Slovak Republic gains the most in terms of percentage (28.8 percent or $2.4 billion gain).

Examining the importer's side (as defined in Figure 6), regional variation in trade gains in percentage is much smaller for imports than exports. Four out of the seven regions will have an increase of more than 4 percent. The ECA obtains the highest import gain (4.9 percent) followed by South Asia (4.5 percent). ECA has an increase in imports of 3.1 percent from improving its own ports, and an additional 1.8 percent increase in imports from its exporting partners' improvement in their port efficiency. For South Asia these percentages are slightly lower: the gains from the partners improvement (1.4 percent) is less than from own improvement (3.1 percent). As an example of the country detail from these simulations, in ECA the largest increase in imports from own and partners' reforms turns out to be Hungary and Slovak Republic. Hungary in terms of dollar amount ($1.5 billion) and Slovak Republic in terms of percentage (12.3 percent). In South Asia, India obtains the largest import gain in dollar amount ($0.79 billion) and Sri Lanka attains the maximum percentage gain (5.7 percent). Thus, improvement in port efficiency is found to provide an economy a dual benefit by promoting both imports and exports.

Considering the *customs environment*, all the regions increase exports from the improvements in customs of the trading partners. This indicator is a good place to show the value of examining the simulation results from the standpoint of exporters or importers and at both regional and country detail. In principle, as exporters, economies gain when their partner's engage in reforms. But, the simulations suggest that the increase in trade coming from the improvement in the country's own customs environment exceeds the increase in trade when the improvement in customs is by the exporters. At least this is true when looking at the regions. Careful analysis of the country detail (where the individual nature of an economy's trading pattern is crucial for the simulations) could find a more nuanced result.

For example, as exporters, somewhat larger gains are enjoyed by Latin America and the Caribbean (LAC) and Eastern Europe and Central Asia (ECA), where both regions increase exports by 0.9 percent. In terms of country detail, in the ECA region Russia gains the most with an amount of $0.37 billion (2.2 percent) whereas Ukraine would have the highest percentage gain (4.5 percent). In the LAC region Brazil has the highest amount of export gain with $0.53

billion export gain whereas Panama would enjoy the highest export gain in term of percentage increase (5.1 percent).

As importers, the increase in trade from own-reforms as importers is more than double that for partner's reforms. South Asia accrues the highest percentage gain (5.8 percent). India gains in the amount of $0.98 billion (5.4 percent) and Sri Lanka gains by 16.9 percent with the amount of $0.25 billion. In South Asia only India and Sri Lanka turn out to be gainers while no data are available for Bangladesh.

Considering service sector infrastructure, the regional pattern is similar to that of ports, as is the source of the distribution of the gains. From the standpoint as exporter, South Asia gains the most (20.0 percent), with the largest export gain by percentage accrued by Bangladesh (30.6 percent) and India gets the maximum gain in dollar amount ($5.4 billion of exports. East Europe and Central Asia obtains 13.5 percent export gain from improvement in service sector infrastructure half-way up to the average. In the ECA region the largest export gain goes to Russia ($6.3 billion or 37 percent) from the improvement of service sector infrastructure. As in the case of ports, the lion's share of the gain comes from a country's own improvements, rather than improvements by their trading partners. South Asia gains 0.7 percent from the improvement of service sector infrastructure by its trading partners whereas from its own improvement of service sector infrastructure the export gain for South Asia is 19.2 percent.

If we look at the importers' experience, we find the same picture. South Asia gaining the most as importers (9.3 percent) followed by East Europe and Central Asia (ECA) (7.7 percent). Again in both regions gains are realized from improvement in service sector infrastructure in trading partners but relatively more imports arrive as a consequence of own improvements. In South Asia, India gains the most as importer ($1.7 billion or 9.6 percent). In the ECA region, Russia has the highest import gain ($3.2 billion or 16.9 percent).

Finally, considering the *regulatory environment* there is some change in the regional pattern, but not in the source of the gains. Examining first the perspective as exporters, an improved regulatory environment leads to a 7.4 percent and 6.1 percent export gains for South Asia and LAC, respectively, India contributes the most to the South Asia's gains ($2.4 billion) and Mexico contributes most to LAC's gains ($2.9 billion). Just as for the other trade facilitation measures, however, the source of the exports gain is predominantly on account of improvements in the exporter's own regulatory environment, rather than a change in the environment of its trading partners.

In the experience of importers, South Asia is the largest gainer in percentage (4.8 percent), followed by the ECA region (4.0 percent). In South Asia, India is the largest gainer in the amount and percentage ($0.93 billion (5.2 percent)). In the ECA region, Turkey is the largest gainer in the amount–$1.7 billion (6 percent), while Russia gains the largest in the percentage (6.5 percent). As before, the source of the gains comes from own-reforms, although the differences are less dramatic. For example, in the case of South Asia, 3.3 percent of the gain comes from own-reforms and 1.5 percent from reforms by trading partners.

The simulation result of the regulatory environment scenario is particularly sensitive due to the large positive coefficient of trade flow with respect to exporter's regulatory environment. The simulation result therefore should be viewed with care.

In overall, from improvement in all trade facilitation measures the highest export gain is attained by South Asia (40.3 percent) followed by the ECA region (30.0 percent). High gains for South Asia emanates from high export gains due to improvement in port efficiency, and service sector infrastructure. Likewise, the ECA region gains in its exports mainly from reforms in port efficiency and service sector infrastructure. In both cases, the gains come principally on account of their own improvements, rather than the improvements by trading partners. In the South Asia region, India has the highest dollar amount gain ($10.4 billion) and Bangladesh obtains the maximum percentage gain (68.3 percent). In the LAC region, Mexico accrues an export gain in the amount of $17.3 billion, *i.e.*, the highest in the region and Paraguay realizes a gain of 74.8 percent. Mexico and Paraguay's high gains again come from the improvement in ports and service sector infrastructure.

Looking globally, the highest export gain among all the economies due to the combined improvement of all trade facilitation measures is attained by China and it is in the amount of $120.7 billion. However, the East Asia region (which includes China) does not stand out in terms of export gains since the other economies in that region do not enjoy large export gains because many of the East Asian economies rank rather highly in terms of the trade facilitation indicators already and therefore are not "reforming" very much in these simulations.

In the global picture as importers, South Asia is the biggest gainer (24.4 percent) followed by the ECA region (19.8 percent). In South Asia region, India gains the most, accruing $4.4 billion or 24.5 percent. India gains in large amount as importer due the improvement in all the trade facilitation measures. In the ECA region, the big winner is Russia gaining a high amount from improvement in service sector infrastructure.

Finally, it is worthwhile to mention the results for the OECD economies, since they further emphasize the importance of the reforms by the developing economies. The simulations show that the OECD economies increase their imports when the developing economies improve their trade facilitation measures. Whereas the percentage increase in OECD trade as an importer (at 6.9 percent) is not particularly dramatic among regional groups, because the level of OECD trade is much larger than any other regional group's trade (at $2,761 billion it represents about three-quarter of the trade in the sample) the dollar value of gains is huge. It is worthwhile for developing economies to invest in their own trade facilitation because the increase in developing country exports will occur through the increased *ability to export* to the OECD market. The export gains will particularly accrue to the economies which have a drastic reform and those which are net exporters of manufacturing goods.

Does this observation regarding the magnitude of the OECD market mean that South-to-South trade facilitation efforts or regional integration efforts should be abandoned? No. The South-to-South sample discussed earlier shows the importance of improvements in trade facilitation efforts in the south, and suggests that the elasticity of trade facilitation efforts South-to-South could be quite large.

5.3. *Domestic and Partner Improvements*

The relative importance of own-reforms is further confirmed by Figure 9. The figure illustrates the simulated change in the sum of imports and exports by region from domestic reforms (left panel) and partners' reform (right panel) in trade facilitation. Comparing across trade facilitation areas, the relative importance of domestic trade facilitation measures differs significantly. The largest increase in trade comes from service sector infrastructure and port efficiency. However, these domestic reforms are consistent with the benefits to come from partner's reforms. So, the priority areas for domestic reform within an individual region are the same as those in the scenario of global or collective movement to raise capacity. This has relevance from the standpoint of consistency between objectives of the Doha Agenda and other regional or bilateral negotiations. Finally, this figure also indicates that the gains to developing economies will be much greater than those to the (high-income) OECD economies, because the developed economies in the OECD region are collectively much closer to best practice across all the indicators examined.

Importantly from the standpoint of balance of payments concerns, for most developing economies domestic reforms will yield more exports than imports – with a significant part of the gains resulting from the increased access to OECD markets. This focus on domestic reforms is somewhat different from the 'request-offer' procedure common in trade negotiations. As the exceptions, Africa and Middle East regions will have relatively small export gains compared to import gains - implying that they do not benefit from the increased access to OECD markets as much. The results suggest that trade facilitation reform should be implemented with particular care in these regions when the economies' major objective of the reform is export promotion and there are balance-of-payments concerns.

Finally, in considering the specific nature of capacity building, it is critical go to the country detail. The panels of Figure 10 show, for example, that Guatemala has a great potential for trade gains from its domestic reform in service sector infrastructure. In contrast, for Indonesia, the gains from regulatory reform dominate those associated with the enhancement of service sector infrastructure. Finally, in Nigeria, the reform in its customs system could have the most valuable outcome. Across all the economies considered, domestic reform will have much larger impact on total trade (imports plus exports).

6. Conclusions and Approach to Capacity Building Design

The analysis in this paper builds on the method developed in Wilson, Mann and Otsuki (2003). Four indicators of trade facilitation are developed: port efficiency, customs environment, regulatory environment, and e-commerce use by business (as a proxy for service sector infrastructure). These indicators are implemented in a gravity model of trade. Simulations are designed that take account of the differential character of trade facilitation in each economy as measured by each of the four categories. Using this set of indicators, modeling approach, and simulation design offers policymakers more information about what type of trade facilitation efforts might provide the largest gains in terms of increasing trade flow.

The improvements to this paper include broadening the economy set to 75 economies. In addition, a better measure of regulatory environment was constructed that is less ambiguous in interpretation of its impact on trade.

A particularly crucial improvement in this paper is to consider the effect on bilateral trade flow of trade facilitation reform both from the standpoint of the reforming economy's exports and its imports. In the earlier paper, an economy gained in exports on account of the improvements to its trading partner's trade facilitation efforts. In this new specification, an economy can increase its exports unilaterally through trade facilitation efforts. This will provide information that is useful if an economy looks to trade facilitation reforms as a strategy of export promotion.

Figure 10: Trade gains from domestic and partners' reform: economy examples

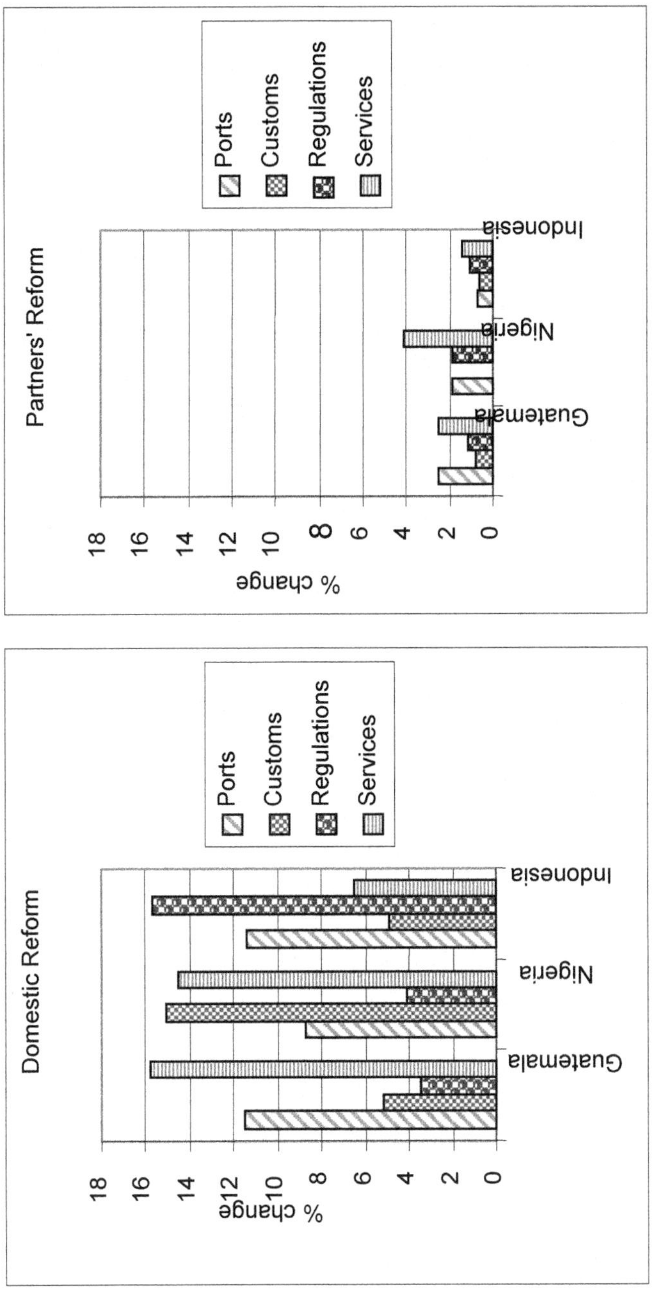

Source: Authors' calculation.

Source: Authors' calculation.

The total gain in trade flow in manufacturing goods from trade facilitation improvements in all four areas is estimated to be $377 billion; all regions gain in imports and exports. Most regions gain more in terms of exports than imports in large part through increasing exports to the OECD market. The most important ingredient in getting these gains, particularly to the OECD market, is the country's own trade facilitation efforts. In terms of regional analysis, South Asia has the greatest potential for both export and import growth, with export gains greater than import gains. In contrast economies in Africa and the Middle East have relatively small export gains compared to import gains because they are less integrated into the global trade in manufactures, and have less overall access to the OECD market. (The number of economies from these regions in the sample is small, so the results for these regions must be viewed with caution.)

The results also shed light on the GATT articles, Doha Development Agenda, and on the Singapore issues. Compliance with GATT Article V (freedom of transit) as proxied by the port efficiency indicator, and with Article VIII (fees and formalities connected with importation and exportation), as proxied by the customs environment indicator, would yield a $107 billion and $33 billion increase in manufacturing trade, respectively. Compliance with GATT Article X (publication and administration of trade regulations), as proxied by the regulatory environment indicator would yield an $83 billion increase in trade flow. Finally, with respect to services negotiations, improvements in service sector infrastructure could yield $154 billion increase in trade. These results should shed light on discussions at the WTO.

Finally, country-specific detail from these simulations, in conjunction with case studies and country-specific knowledge, could help inform and design capacity building to support trade. For example, Lane (2001) suggests that the Latin America region has been lagging behind in terms of customs environment. Our results confirm that LAC could gain from attention to customs. A case study from Peru showed that manual and paperwork-intensive systems resulted in a long clearance time for customs and limited transparency. But Peruvian customs reforms achieved remarkable gains in compliance, cost, and trade facilitation. So case study plus simulation detail, plus country-specific analysis could help other economies follow Peru's lead in reforms. Similarly, the analysis in this paper indicates that South Asia has a large scope for trade promotion from trade facilitation reform. In Bangladesh, a customs modernization program is helping to eradicate the corruption and inefficiency in fee collection. Rapid clearance for exports and their imported inputs, increased automation, efficient risk management systems and staff training are working to achieve this goal (World Bank 1999). Our results point not just to a need to focus on customs, but more broadly to address ports, regulatory environment, and particularly the domestic services infrastructure that support economic activity and trade. Further compilation of case studies in these areas would assist in capacity building efforts.

In conclusion, the results from this paper suggest that the scope and benefit of unilateral trade facilitation reforms are very large and that the gains fall disproportionately on exports. Combining the country detail from these simulations with case study analysis of specific reform efforts and the specifics of an economy's trade facilitation challenges can triangulate on a design strategy for capacity building to increase trade and economic well-being.

Data Appendix

Data come from the World Economic Forum, Global Competitiveness Report, 2001-02 (GCR); IMD Lausanne, World Competitiveness Yearbook 2002 (WCY); and Kaufmann, Kraay and Zoido-Lobaton (2002) (KKZ). All survey data in GCR comes from the World Economic Forum's Executive Opinion Survey. A total of 4,022 firms were surveyed. "In order to provide the basis for a comparative assessment on a global basis, it is essential that we interview a sufficient number of senior business leaders in individual economies and that the sample in each economy is not biased in favor of any particular business group. We have taken a number of steps to ensure this. First, we have asked each of our partner institutes, the organizations that administer the surveys in each economy, to start with a comprehensive register of firms. From this, they were asked to choose a sample whose distribution across economic sectors was proportional to the distribution of the country's labor force across sectors, excluding agriculture. They were then asked to choose firms randomly within these broad sectors (for example, by choosing firms at regular intervals from an alphabetic list), and to pursue face-to-face interviews, following up for clarifications where necessary. The employment distribution was taken from data in the 1998 *Yearbook of Labour Statistics* of the International Labour Office. The respondents to the survey are typically a company's CEO or a member of its senior management."

The WCY uses a 115 question survey sent to executives in top and middle management of firms in all 49 economies of the WCY. The sample size of each economy is proportional to GDP, and firms "normally have an international dimension." The firms are selected to be a cross section of manufacturing, service, and primary industries. There were 3532 responses to the Survey.

KKZ (2002) updates the data on governance that were developed in Kaufmann, Kraay and Zoido-Lobaton (1999) "Governance Matters." The database contains more than 300 governance indicators for 175 economies compiled from a variety of sources in 2000/2001. Six aggregate indicators are constructed corresponding to six basic governance concepts:

> Voice and Accountability, Political Stability, Government Effectiveness, Regulatory Quality, Rule of Law and Control of Corruption.

The various raw data series were chosen because of their relevance to the four concepts of trade facilitation.

- Port efficiency for each economy *J* is the average of two indexed inputs (all GCR):
  - Port facilities and inland waterways are :(1=underdeveloped, 7=as developed as the world's best, GCR)
  - Air transport is :(1=infrequent and inefficient, 7=as extensive and efficient as the world's best, GCR)
- Customs environment for each economy *J* is the average of two indexed inputs (all GCR):
  - Hidden import barriers other than published tariffs and quotas
  - Irregular extra payments or bribes connected with import and export permits
- Regulatory environment for each economy *J* is constructed as the average of four indexed inputs:
  - Transparency of government policy is satisfactory (WCY)
  - Control of Corruption (KKZ)
- Service sector infrastructure for each economy *J* is as the average of three indexed inputs (all GCR):
  - Speed and cost of internet access are: (1=slow and expensive, 7=fast and cheap)
  - Internet contribution to reduce inventory costs is: (1=no improvement, 7=huge improvement)

References

1. Anderson, James E. (1979). "A Theoretical Foundation for the Gravity Equation." *American Economic Review* 69: p.106-116.
2. Anderson, James E. and Eric van Wincoop (2003). "Gravity with Gravitas: A Solution to the Border Puzzle." American Economic Review v93, n1: 170-92.
3. Asia Pacific Economic Co-operation (APEC) (1999). *Assessing APEC Trade Liberalization and Facilitation: 1999 Update, Economic Committee*, September 1999. APEC: Singapore.

4. Asia Pacific Foundation of Canada (1999). *Survey on Customs, Standards and Business Mobility in the APEC Region.* APF Canada: Vancouver.
5. Balistreri, Edward J. and Russell H. Hillberry (mimeo). "Trade Friction and Welfare in the Gravity Model: How Much of the Iceberg Melts?" U.S. International Trade Commission, Washington, DC
6. Clark, Ximena, David Dollar and Alejandro Micco. (2002). "Maritime Transport Costs and Port Efficiency." World Bank Working Paper Series # 2781. The World Bank: Washington, DC
7. Dollar, David and Aart Kraay (2001). "Trade, Growth, and Poverty" World Bank Working Paper Series #2615. The World Bank: Washington, DC
8. Fink, Carsten, Aaditya Mattoo and Cristina Ileana Neagu (2002a). "Trade in International Maritime Services: How Much Does Policy Matter?" World Bank Economic Review v16, n1 (2002): 81-108.
9. Fink, Carsten, Aaditya Mattoo and Cristina Ileana Neagu (2002b). "Assessing the Role of Communication Costs in International Trade." World Bank Working Paper #2929. The World Bank: Washington, DC
10. Frankel, Jeffrey A and Rose, Andrew K. (2000). "Estimating the Effect of Currency Unions on Trade and Output." *National Bureau of Economic Research Working Paper* #7857.
11. Freund, Caroline and Diana Weinhold (2000). "On the Effect of the Internet on International Trade." International Finance Discussion Papers #693, Board of Governors of the Federal Reserve System.
12. Hertel, Thomas W., Terrie Walmsley; and Ken Itakura (2001). "Dynamic Effect of the "New Age" Free Trade Agreement between Japan and Singapore." *Journal of Economic Integration* v16, n4: p. 446-84.
13. Hummels, D. (2001). "Time as a Trade Barrier." Department of Economics, Indiana: Purdue University, Mimeo.
14. IMD (2000). *World Competitiveness Yearbook.* IMD: Lausanne.
15. Kaufmann, Daniel, Aart Kraay, and Pablo Zoido-Lobaton (2002). "Governance Matters II: Updated Indicators for 2000–01" World Bank Working Paper #2772, The World Bank: Washington, DC
16. Lane, Micahel (2001). *International Supply Chain Management and Customs. Peru Case*
17. *Study*, Washington, DC: The World Bank.
18. Mann, Catherine L., Sue E. Eckert, and Sarah Cleeland Knight (2000). *Global Electronic Commerce: A Policy Primer*, Washington: Institute for International Economics
19. Mann, Catherine L., Daniel H. Rosen, and APEC (2001, 2002). *The New Economy and APEC*,_Singapore: APEC Secretariat; reprinted (2002) Washington: Institute for International Economics.
20. Maskus, Keith E., John S. Wilson and Tsunehiro Otsuki (2001). "An Empirical Framework for Analyzing Technical Regulations and Trade" in *Quantifying the impact of technical barriers to trade: Can it be done?* Keith Maskus and John S. Wilson eds.
21. Messerlin, Patrick A and J. Zarrouk (1999). "Trade Facilitation: Technical Regulation and Customs Procedures." September 1999 for the WTO/World Bank Conference on Developing Countries in a Millennium Round.
22. Moenius, Johannes (2000). *Three Essays on Trade Barriers and Trade Volumes.* Ph.D. dissertation, University of California, San Diego.

23. Otsuki, Tsunehiro, John S. Wilson, and Mirvat Sewadeh (2001a) "What Price Precaution? European Harmonisation of Aflatoxin regulations and African groundnut exports."
24. *European Review of Agricultural Economics*, vol. 28, no. 3: 263-284.
25. Otsuki, Tsunehiro, John S. Wilson, and Mirvat Sewadeh (2001b). "Saving Two in a Billion: Quantifying the Trade Effect of European Food Safety Standards on African Exports." *Food Policy 26.*
26. United Nations Conference on Trade and Development (2001). *E-Commerce and Development Report.* UNCTAD: Geneva.
27. White, H. (1980). "A Heterosckedasticity-consistent Covariance Matrix Estimator and a Direct Test for Heteroscedasticity." Econometrica 48: 817-838.
28. Wilson, John S., Catherine L. Mann, and Tsunehiro Otsuki (2003). "Trade Facilitation and Economic Development: Measuring the Impact." World Bank Working Paper #2988. World Bank: Washington, DC
29. Winters, L. Alan (2004) "Globalization and Small Countries", presented at ASSA meetings, San Diego (January).
30. World Bank (1999). Project Appraisal Document on a Proposed Credit in the Amount of US$32 Million Equivalent to Bangladesh for an Export Diversification Project. The World Bank: Washington, DC.
31. World Economic Forum (2001). *Global Competitiveness Report.* World Economic Forum: Geneva.

BENEFITS OF TRADE FACILITATION: A QUANTITATIVE ASSESSMENT

Peter Walkenhorst and Tadashi Yasui

Organisation for Economic Co-operation and Development[1]

Executive Summary

Trade transaction costs (TTCs) related to border procedures vary depending on the efficiency and integrity of interacting businesses and administrations, the characteristics or kind of goods, and the size and type of businesses. Total costs may be seen as being composed of directly incurred costs, such as expenses relating to supplying information and documents to the related authority, and indirectly incurred costs, such as those arising from procedural delays. Empirical studies suggest that directly and indirectly incurred TTCs each amount to 1-15 percent of traded goods' value.

Moreover, empirical evidence suggests that TTCs for agro-food products are higher than those for manufactured goods, as agro-food shipments are subject to special border procedures, such as sanitary and phytosanitary controls. Also, small and medium-sized enterprises face cost-disadvantages. In light of this diversity in TTCs, the potential for the realisation of benefits from trade facilitation varies across economies, sectors, and types of traders. In cases where best practices are already applied, further efficiency gains will be difficult to achieve. But if border clearance costs are substantially above those encountered under best practices, room for improvement through suitable measures of trade facilitation will tend to exist.

The model-based analysis of the economic impacts of trade facilitation carried out in this study differs from earlier research by taking several salient features of import and export procedures into account. In particular, the differing characteristics of direct and indirect TTCs are represented, and economy-specific differences in trade facilitation potential are reflected according to empirical information on border waiting times and survey-based evidence on the quality of border processes. In addition, the higher TTCs for agro-food products and small and medium-sized enterprises are incorporated into the analysis.

The analysis does not evaluate the economic and trade impact of specific trade facilitation measures or instruments, such as those that might result from a

[1] The authors are analysts, respectively, in the Economics Department and the Trade Directorate, Organisation for Economic Co-operation and Development, 2 rue André-Pascal, F-75775 Paris Cedex 16, France. The views expressed in the paper are those of the authors' and do not necessarily represent those of the OECD or its Members. A related OECD study, entitled "Quantitative Assessment of the Benefits of Trade Facilitation" [TD/TC/WP(2003)31/FINAL], can be found on the following website: *http://www.oecd.org/trade*.

possible future WTO agreement on trade facilitation. Instead, the aim of the assessment is to better represent empirical characteristics of the border process in model-based analysis and to identify those features that crucially affect the results and that, therefore, deserve to be further explored in future analysis. Several scenarios of hypothetical, multilateral trade facilitation efforts are evaluated, focusing on the comparison of scenarios rather than the overall welfare gains that might result from trade facilitation.

For the purposes of this study, trade facilitation was assumed to lead to a reduction in TTCs by 1 percent of the value of world trade. This assumption is maintained across scenarios, in order to make it possible to meaningfully compare results. On this basis, aggregate welfare gains are estimated to amount to about US$40 billion worldwide, with all economies benefiting and non-OECD economies experiencing the biggest gains in relative terms. If the impact of trade facilitation on TTCs is taken to be more pronounced, then the welfare benefits will also be higher.

Earlier analysis often focused on the cost savings to traders and did not reflect the conceptual differences between direct and indirect TTCs, thereby ignoring macro-economic adjustment needs, such as re-deployment of redundant employees in the logistics sector, associated with direct TTCs. Incorporating these adjustment needs into the analysis provides a more nuanced assessment of the broader impact of trade facilitation and avoids creating inflated expectations concerning the potential benefits from reductions in TTCs. Moreover, the presence of these adjustment costs suggests that trade facilitation measures that focus on reducing indirect TTCs, notably border waiting times, might have a more marked impact on economic welfare than measures that aim at reducing documentation requirements and related direct TTCs. Furthermore, if the existing diversity of TTCs across economies, sectors and traders is represented, a larger share of the global benefits of trade facilitation of up to two-thirds of the total gains is obtained by developing economies than under an assumption of flat reductions in TTCs. Developing economies are also the prime beneficiaries from trade facilitation if the facilitation-generated welfare gains are related to GDP, as they tend to have considerable potential for reductions in TTCs and a relatively high trade to GDP ratio, so that reductions in the costs of importing and exporting affect them to a larger extent than many OECD members. However, the magnitude of the reported welfare gains has to be seen as an upper boundary of the actual gains that might be achievable, as investment needs to realise the assumed reductions in TTCs have not been incorporated into the quantitative analysis, due to lack of consistent, cross-economy information on the full range of costs associated with the implementation of trade facilitation measures.

1. Introduction

Reductions of tariff barriers in subsequent Rounds of international trade negotiations and changes in supply chain management practices, such as greater reliance on just-in-time deliveries, have resulted in a relative increase in the importance of border procedure-related trade transaction costs (TTCs) for international commerce and triggered keen public interest in trade facilitation efforts. The WTO Doha Development Agenda envisaged trade facilitation as a subject for possible multilateral negotiations, even though at the WTO Ministerial Meeting in Cancún no agreement on concrete negotiation steps was reached.

While quantification of the economic impacts of trade facilitation represents a major analytical challenge due to the complexity of the underlying issues, a limited number of studies have tried to assess the implications of efforts to reduce TTCs. This literature on TTCs and trade facilitation benefits has been reviewed in OECD (2002). The first objective of the present paper is to update and extend the earlier literature survey by synthesizing relevant recent studies that report estimates of TTCs and the effects of trade facilitation measures. Particular attention is thereby devoted to differences across economies, sectors, and types of traders. Secondly, reflecting the numerical estimates of the costs of specific border procedures and measures and the impact of facilitation efforts on these found in the literature, model-based analysis on the world-wide economic effects of trade facilitation is undertaken.

The modelling analysis differs from earlier research by taking several salient features of import and export procedures into account. In particular, the differing characteristics of direct and indirect TTCs are represented, and economy-specific differences in trade facilitation potential are reflected according to empirical information on border waiting times and survey-based evidence on the quality of border processes. In addition, the higher TTCs for agro-food products and small and medium-sized enterprises are incorporated into the analysis. Several scenarios of hypothetical, multilateral trade facilitation efforts are evaluated, focusing on the comparison of scenarios rather than the overall welfare gains that might result from trade facilitation.

The remainder of the paper is organised in four sections. Section 2 reviews available information on direct and indirect TTCs, with particular emphasis on differences among economies, traded products and types of traders. Section 3 then reports findings on the impact of trade facilitation efforts on TTCs, while section 4 describes different approaches that have been used to quantify the benefits of trade facilitation. Finally, section 5 discusses new estimates from model-based analysis that reflect the existing diversity among economies, sectors, and traders.

2. Estimates of Trade Transaction Costs

Trade transaction costs vary substantially. The OECD literature survey (OECD, 2002) found that such costs to businesses differ depending on the efficiency and integrity of interacting businesses and administrations, the characteristics or kind of goods, and the size and type of business. Total costs may be seen as being composed of directly incurred costs, such as expenses relating to supplying information and documents to the related authority, and indirectly incurred costs, such as those arising from procedural delays. The studies surveyed in OECD (2002) suggest that directly incurred TTCs involved in export and import procedures amount to 2-15 percent of traded goods' value,[2] and this range also emerged from a subsequent literature survey carried out by the Swedish Trade Procedures Council (SWEPRO, 2002). Some recent studies (METI, 1998; Haralambides and Londoño-Kent, 2002; and JETRO, 2002), however, suggest that directly incurred TTCs could in some cases be lower (Table 1) and amount to merely about one percent of the traded goods' value, so that the full range of direct cost estimates stretches from one to fifteen percent. All these estimates combine costs incurred on the import and the export side (Box 1).

Box 1: Trade Transaction Costs at the Export *Versus* the Import Side

Are the costs to businesses for clearing export procedures of a similar magnitude as those for complying with import procedures? Except for special cases, such as exports of dual-use goods, export procedures might be expected to be less costly and less time consuming than import procedures. Export procedures are often relatively simple, since customs inspections are rarely being undertaken and no special documents, such as rules of origin or health and safety certificates, need to be submitted. However, in a number of cases, pre-shipment inspection (PSI) leads to a shift of procedures from the importing to the exporting side. Indeed, more than a quarter of all WTO members — mainly developing economies in Asia, Africa, and Latin America — regularly use designated PSI-companies to inspect shipments at exporting locations for imports to PSI-using economies (WTO, 1999).

The available empirical studies suggest that TTCs are roughly the same on the import and the export side. According to a report by US-NCIT (1971), the absolute magnitude of documentation costs for exports is very similar to that for imports. A more recent World Bank survey of import and export procedures in CIS economies found for some economies that costs and delays on the import side exceeded those on the export side, while for other economies the inverse relationship prevailed (World Bank, 2002). Moreover, another survey found almost equal waiting times at borders of 3.5 days for imports to and 3 days for exports from Japan (MRI, 2001).

[2] Some of the reviewed studies did not explicitly distinguish between direct and indirect trade transaction costs or cover some indirect cost elements along with directly incurred costs.

Table 1. Selected studies reporting estimates of trade transaction costs

Study	Economy/ Region	Import/ Export	Direct costs		Indirect costs		Note
			Scope	Costs (%)*	Scope	Costs (%)**	
US-NCITD (1971)	USA	Average of imp. & exp. costs	Documentation; finance & insurance; carrier; and forward/broker	7.5%			Based on business survey.
SWEPRO (1985)	Sweden	Average of imp. & exp. costs	Documentation costs	4%			Estimated figures based on information from customs and business.
Ernst & Whinney (1987a,b)	Intra-EC	Imp. & exp. costs combined	Customs compliance costs	1.5%	Delays for road haulers & lost business	1-3%	Reservations have been expressed on the survey on lost business & road haulers. Indirect costs calculated by Secretariat.
EC (1989)	Intra-EC	Imp. & exp. costs combined	Documentation costs	3.5-15%			Methodology unclear.
UNCTAD (1994)	World		Costs for finance, customs; business information; transport & telecom	7-10%			Uses US-NCITD (1971), EC (1998) and other information sources. Coverage of direct and indirect costs.

Table 1. Selected studies reporting estimates of trade transaction costs–Continued

Study	Economy/ Region	Import/ Export	Direct costs Scope	Direct costs Costs (%)*	Indirect costs Scope	Indirect costs Costs (%)**	Note
METI (1998)	Japan	Imp. costs only	Costs for border procedures	0.5-2.4%			Based on a survey of Japanese manufacturing and trade companies.
Haralambides & Londoño-Kent (2002)	Between USA & Mexico	Imp. & exp. costs combined	Costs for handling, inspection, *etc.* for a) southbound, b) northbound	a) 0.8-2.1% b) 0.6-1.1%	Time delay	a) 1.6-4.0% b) 0.1-0.5%	Costs of time delay calculated based on Hummels (2001).
JETRO (2002)	Japan	Imp. costs only	Costs for import and port-related procedures a) EDI-use; b) non-ED-use	a) 0.5-0.8% b) 1.2%			Figures calculated by Secretariat.

[1] Due to differences in methodology as well as differing time periods during which particular studies were carried out, the estimates are not directly comparable. In particular, TTCs have been reduced over time in many economies as a result of trade facilitation efforts and technological progress, so that comparisons of TTC across time will tend to be misleading. Hence the purpose of the table is to report on different approaches that have been pursued and not to evaluate particular studies and their findings against each other.

[2] Percentage in terms of traded goods' value.

Source: Authors.

In addition, there are indirect TTCs, even though these are rarely expressed in monetary terms. As mentioned in OECD (2002), lengthy waiting times can result in loss of business opportunities and impose inventory-holding and depreciation costs on traders. Costs for inventory-holding include both the lost interest on capital tied up in goods at borders, as well as the need to keep larger buffer-stock inventories at the final destinations in order to accommodate possible variations in border clearance times. Depreciation captures costs related to spoilage of fresh produce, items with immediate information content, such as newspapers, and goods for which demand cannot be forecast well in advance, such as holiday toys or high-fashion apparel.

A recent World Bank publication reported evidence from the World Business Environment Survey on typical border waiting times for 80 economies (Batra, Kaufmann and Stone, 2003). The averages of typical time needed for release of imported cargo stretch from 1 to 24 days.[3] Assuming similar waiting times at the export side (Box 1), the range doubles to 2-48 days. These waiting times impose substantial costs on traders. Hummels (2001) investigated the willingness-to-pay of exporters for switching from slower ocean to faster air shipment and found that each day saved would be worth about 0.5 percent of the value of the traded goods. The largest share of these costs is due to depreciation and lost business opportunities. Combining Hummels' cost estimate with the border waiting times from the World Bank survey gives a range for the indirect TTCs of about 1-24 percent of traded goods' value. However, since only six of the 80 economies in the World Bank survey showed average import waiting times of 16 or more days, the "tail" in the sample's distribution is thin, and the range of the indirect TTCs might be thought of as being similar to the 1-15 percent for directly incurred costs.

2.1. *Economy-Specific Diversity*

A large part of the variation in TTCs is due to economy-specific differences. The cost differences seem closely related to the quality of border procedures, which in turn are heavily influenced by the trade facilitation efforts that governments have been pursuing. For example, among the 60 measures concerning "movement of goods" that have been proposed in the Menu of the APEC Trade Facilitation Action Plan, the implementation by economies ranges from zero to 50 measures (APEC, 2003a). It seems reasonable to expect that larger efforts at

[3] The average border waiting times were obtained by excluding survey responses that reported waiting times of more than 90 days.

trade facilitation are associated with lower TTCs, while less attention to improving the quality of border services will tend to result in higher costs of importing and exporting operations.

Unfortunately, truly comparable information on directly incurred TTCs is not available for a broad range of economies. In order nevertheless to try to estimate the economic and trade impacts of TTCs and trade facilitation across economies, analysts have recently used questionnaire-derived indicators of different aspects of border process quality as proxies for actual cost figures. For example, Wilson, Mann and Otsuki (2003) describe the extent and quality of trade facilitation efforts of economies in the APEC region by using survey information on port efficiency, customs environment, regulatory environment, and e-business practices. Each of these aspects is characterised through several indicators. For example, the quality of the customs environment is captured through indicators for the magnitude of import fees, transparency of import barriers, and perception of corruption. These indicators are normalised and then averaged to yield a proxy value for the quality of the customs environment across APEC economies.

This indicator-based methodology of deriving estimates for the quality of the customs environment can easily be generalised beyond APEC economies and applied to economies world-wide. Such a generalisation is pursued and used in this study for a broad set of border procedures (see the Annex for details on the construction of the "border process quality indicator"). The resulting estimates of border-process quality are to some extent subjective, reflecting the nature of the underlying information sources, and can only be indicative of the direct TTCs actually incurred by importing and exporting firms. But as will be discussed in section 3, the potential to improve border procedures through trade facilitation measures depends largely on the existing quality of border services, so that an estimate of the qualitative diversity of border procedures is necessary to appropriately assess the benefits from trade facilitation.

Differences in border process quality across the 102 economies for which indicator data are derived tend to be related to income levels (Figure 1). Economies with a higher *per capita* income generally score better with respect to border process quality than economies whose inhabitants are less well off. However, there are a number of examples of relatively poor economies scoring rather well, while several relatively rich economies show only mediocre performance with respect to the aggregate indicator of border process quality. In other words, a higher *per capita* income and the related availability of public financial resources explain differences in border process quality across economies to some extent, but the data suggest that low-income economies do

Figure 1. Economy-value of the border process quality-indicator in relation to *per capita* GDP (U.S. dollars, purchasing power parity)

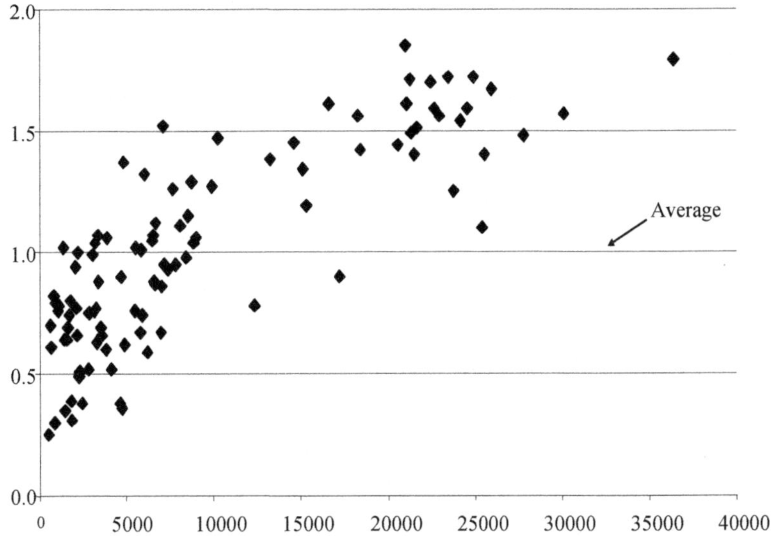

Note: A higher indicator value suggests a better border process quality. See the Annex for details.

Source: Authors.

not necessarily have to wait until they become rich before being able to adopt good border practices.

While the border process quality-indicator might be seen as being inversely related to directly incurred TTCs, border clearance times might serve as a proxy for indirect transactions costs. Figure 2 shows the relationship between waiting times, as reported in Batra *et al.* (2003), and *per capita* incomes. Higher *per capita* incomes are generally associated with shorter border waiting times, but considerable variation in waiting times, and by implication indirect TTCs, exists particularly for economies with a *per capita* income of less than US$9,000.

2.2. *Sector-Specific Diversity*

In addition to divergent integrity, transparency and efficiency of border procedures across economies, TTCs also depend on the type of goods that are imported and exported. In particular, for goods that are perishable by nature, such as agro-food products, delays and incongruities at the border can prove very costly. Moreover, agriculture and food products, fish, and forest and wood

Figure 2. Economy-average of number of days of import clearance time in relation to *per capita* GDP (U.S. dollars, purchasing power parity)

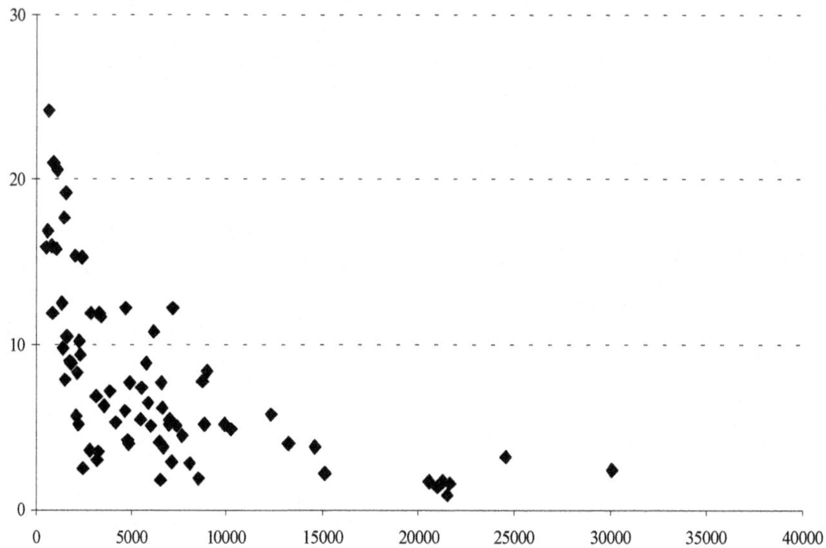

Source: Authors.

products are generally subject to additional border procedures and have to undergo documentary and physical inspection to ensure compliance with sanitary and phytosanitary requirements. This need for physical inspections, in particular, can lead to a considerable increase in border process fees and clearance times *per* consignment. Other goods undergo physical examination only according to prevailing risk management practices, which could mean that only a small fraction of containers is checked. Hence, the border clearance costs of these other goods tend on average to be significantly lower than those of agro-food and like products.

A recent study by the Japan External Trade Organization (JETRO) measured directly incurred costs and time for a "typical" container ship entering Japan (Table 2). The directly incurred costs and waiting time vary depending on whether the border procedures are paper-based or handled via electronic data interchange. But even though only about 20 percent of the containers on a "typical" ship are subject to mandatory sanitary and phytosanitary controls, 37-44 percent of the directly incurred costs and 18-22 percent of the time from entry to release of an "average" container are due to "special" procedures applicable to agriculture and food products.[4] And if, hence, the direct costs and waiting time for agro-food products are taken to account on average for roughly a third of the total costs of a shipment, TTCs for agro-food products turn out to be 50 percent higher than those for manufactured products.[5]

Table 2. Directly incurred costs and time required from port entry to release in Japan

	Costs (*JPY and percentage*)		Time (*hours and percentage*)	
	Paper-based	**EDI-based**	**Paper-based**	**EDI-based**
Common procedures for all goods	16,706 (63%)	10,197 (56%)	19.1 (82%)	12.8 (78%)
Special procedures for agro-food products[1]	9,864 (37%)	7,884 (44%)	4.2 (18%)	3.7 (22%)
Total	26,570 (100%)	18,081 (100%)	23.2 (100%)	16.5 (100%)

[1] Including animal/plant quarantine and food sanitary procedures.

Source: Authors based on JETRO (2002).

2.3. *Trader-Specific Diversity*

Trade transaction costs can vary also according to characteristics of the trader, such as the size of the trading firms. Smaller firms which engage less frequently than bigger competitors in cross-border transactions have several disadvantages: (i) they will tend to have fewer specialised personnel, so that they might have to devote relatively more resources towards acquiring knowledge on trade formalities and administering cross-border procedures; (ii) they might have weaker capital reserves, so that unforeseen delays at the border, tying-up a part of their working capital, can affect their liquidity and force them to seek expensive interim financing; and (iii) small firms might not have a sufficiently rich track record with customs authorities, so that they might be classified in a higher risk category and, hence, more frequently subjected to costly documentary and physical cargo checks (OECD, 2002; SWEPRO, 2003).

Yet, based on analysis of about 650 survey responses from Dutch firms, Verwaal and Donkers (2001) concluded that it is not firm size *per se*, but the size of international trade activities of firms that determines the level of TTCs. Hence, small firms with a focus on international markets are often able to reap the available benefits from economies of scale in border procedures. Moreover, small

[4] Similarly, according to a survey by Japan's Customs Tariff Bureau on the time required for release of imports (CTB, 2001), imported sea cargo subject to controlling agencies other than customs stays at borders for about 38 percent longer than other goods (about 94 hours *versus* about 68 hours).

[5] The extra cost ratio for agro-food products equals the total costs over the TTCs for manufactured products, *i.e.*, 100%/(100%-33.3%) = 1.5.

firms have often the opportunity to outsource customs-related activities to trading partners, logistical service providers or specialised international trade intermediaries in order to avoid size-related disadvantages they might otherwise face.

Nevertheless, in a study of customs procedures in the EU, Ernst & Whinney (1987a) found that firms with fewer than 250 employees incur TTCs that are 30-45 percent higher *per* consignment than those falling on bigger firms. One of the main reasons for the higher costs is that due to too infrequent transactions, small and medium sized enterprises (SMEs) are generally not able to participate in "simplified procedures", which according to Ernst & Whinney reduce TTCs by 50 percent. Similarly, the ability to participate in the Swedish "Stairways®" system is reported to have reduced TTCs of large-scale traders by up to 55 percent (SWEPRO, 2002).

3. Anecdotal Evidence on Benefits of Trade Facilitation

Trade transaction costs can not be entirely eliminated. Checks by customs and other controlling agencies are necessary to ensure that domestic regulations are implemented. But increasing the efficiency of border procedures can help to lower TTCs and, hence, shrink the wedge between domestic and international prices to the benefit of consumers and producers. Estimates of the potential medium-term income gains from trade facilitation have centred around 2-3 percent of the total value of traded goods (UNCTAD, 1994; APEC, 1999), even though much larger benefits might be reap in particular economies or regions (APEC, 2002). In some cases, a simple re-organisation of tasks and procedures might already make it possible to reap substantial benefits, while in others successful trade facilitation might require investments in physical infrastructure and human resources (Box 2).

Obviously, the potential for the realisation of benefits from trade facilitation varies across economies, sectors, and characteristics of traders. In cases where best practices are already applied, further efficiency gains will be difficult to achieve. But if TTCs are substantially above those encountered under best practices, room for improvement through suitable measures of trade facilitation will tend to exist.

Even though it is difficult to generalise from available information, the largest potential for improvements from trade facilitation seems to exist in developing economies. For example, a business survey conducted in the APEC region found that traders expected the largest benefits from hypothetical trade facilitation measures that would reduce transaction costs by 50 percent to materialise in the lower-income economies within the region (Table 3). The median responses to the questionnaire suggest that the trade facilitation efforts would yield reductions in total TTCs of 10.7 percent in industrialising APEC economies, compared with 7.8 percent in newly industrialised economies and 5.2 percent in industrialised economies. These results reflect to some extent the findings from section 2, namely that less developed economies tend to have less efficient customs services and, hence, more room for improvement.

Box 2: Costs to Implement Trade Facilitation Measures

Reducing TTCs through trade facilitation will in many cases involve upfront investments and higher operational expenses for governments and businesses. As customs services play a vital role for the functioning of border procedures, their modernisation and reform often constitutes an important element in promoting trade facilitation. The magnitude of the implementation costs varies according to the size of the customs service, existing customs infrastructure and available human resources. Moreover the general economic environment plays an important role. One frequent element of trade facilitation in developing economies is, for example, the introduction of automated customs systems, which crucially depends on the availability of functioning basic infrastructure, such as communication facilities and stable electricity supply.

Given the substantial costs involved, many developing economies appreciate assistance from bilateral and multilateral agencies to help them improve their customs services. In 1999, the World Bank extended 15 adjustment loans with components addressing customs reform (Wilson, 2001). For example, US$78 million was devoted to customs improvements in six south-eastern European economies and US$35 million towards export development in Tunisia. Moreover, a five year project for customs modernisation in Bolivia has been financed from several sources with about US$38 million since 1999, of which about US$25 million is being spend for institutional improvements and US$9 million for computerised systems (Gutierrez, 2001).

One major type of investment concerns customs automation systems. According to UNCTAD (2002), the costs of introducing automated customs system could sometimes be as high as US$20 million provided that economies develop their own system, and less than US$2 million for the widely-used Automatic System for Customs Data (ASYCUDA) system. In Chile, the total investment cost of implementing an automated customs system amounted to US$5 million in the early 1990s (WTO, 2000), while in Jamaica, the introduction of the ASYCUDA system in connection with overall requirements analysis, the development of software suites, data communication equipment and computers cost about US$5.5 million (Grant, 2001).

Once an improved customs system is running, there are operating expenses that in some economies are passed on to traders in the form of higher user fees, while in other economies these higher costs are financed from government budgets. Moreover, systems have to be updated from time to time in order to reflect the latest technological developments. The costs for such updates can be of a similar magnitude as the initial investments to introduce a new system. For example, Chinese Taipei updated its air cargo clearance system in 2000 at a cost of US$5 million, and is scheduled to improve its existing ocean-going cargo system in 2004 for about US$6.5 million (WTO, 2002). In the Philippines, updating the existing automated system from a DOS to a Windows-based platform cost about 40 percent of the original system installation (Bhatnagar, 2001).

Table 3. Estimates of reduction in trade transaction costs through customs-related trade facilitation

(weighted average of responses, in percent)

APEC economy group	Minimum estimate	Maximum estimate	Median estimate
Industrialised APEC economies	2.9	7.4	5.2
Newly industrialised APEC economies	5.3	10.7	7.8
Industrialising APEC economies	6.6	14.8	10.7

Source: APEC (2002).

The impact of trade facilitation measures on TTCs is likely to differ across products and transaction size. These differential effects were highlighted in a recent study by the Australian Department of Foreign Affairs and Trade (DFAT, 2001). The study investigated the potential for cost savings for businesses of changing from a paper-based to a paperless customs administration system. The savings estimates of the interviewed traders ranged from 1.5 percent for bulk sea shipments of coal to 15 percent for air shipments of fresh asparagus (Table 4). The differences seem partly due to the fixed costs of completing paperwork requirements manually, which are estimated to amount to US$75-125 *per* transaction irrespective of transaction-size.

Table 4. Estimate of savings from switch to paperless customs system

Product and transport mode	Typical volume	Cif-value of cargo (USD)	Estimate of savings (USD)	(percent)
Coal – bulk by sea	10 000 tons	520 000	7 800	1.5
Rice – bulk by sea	1 500 tons	810 000	17 820	2.2
Machine parts – by sea	20 foot container	175 000	5 425	3.1
Sugar – bagged by sea	1 500 tons	273 000	12 012	4.4
Fresh asparagus – by air	45 kg	1 370	206	15.0

Source: DFAT (2001).

Another means of trade facilitation is the establishment of a single window border automation system. Such a system makes it possible to minimise documentation cost by streamlining paperless processing needs of various regulatory agencies. In Singapore, the so-called TradeNet system was first conceived in the mid-1980s and is reported to have helped reduce the documentation cost borne by government and businesses by more than half (APEC, 2003b).

Several economies have experienced significant reductions in import clearance times following the implementation of trade facilitation measures. For example, in Japan significant reductions in the lead time from entry to release have been realised over the past decade. For air-cargo, the average processing time fell from 53 hours in 1991 to 26 hours in 2001, while for sea cargo the lead time was over the same period reduced from 168 hours to 74 hours (CTB, 2001). Similar progress has been reported for customs clearance time, which constitutes an important element in overall border procedures. In New Zealand, the institution of a multimedia electronic paperless clearance system has, over a four-year period, reduced customs processing times from ten days to an average of 12 minutes (WTO, 2003). Similarly, in Costa Rica, the switch towards single window warehouse clearing, electronic customs declaration, and risk management with automated method of selection made it possible to reduce customs clearance times from an average of six days in 1994 to 12 minutes (115 minutes in case of physical inspection) in 2000 (WTO, 2001). In Peru, different types of trade facilitation measures were pursued, with emphasis on staff training, the introduction of a code of conduct, and penalties for lack of integrity of customs officers. Through these initiatives, customs release times were shortened from 15-30 days to 2-48 hours (Lane, 2001).

4. Overview of Available Quantitative Studies on the Benefits of Trade Facilitation

There have been several studies that have tried to quantify the potential impact of trade facilitation on trade flows and income levels. Some researchers have based their analysis on the UNCTAD estimate that trade facilitation could result in savings equivalent to 2-3 percent of the value of traded goods (UNCTAD, 1994). Relating these savings to the value of international trade, the reduction in TTCs are estimated to amount to about US$1 billion *per* year for the former Soviet Union (Molnar and Ojala, 2003) and about US$60 billion annually for the APEC region (DFAT, 2001). As the savings are seen as reductions in previously existing inefficiencies that did not benefit the public or private sector, they are taken to represent income gains for traders and consumers. Furthermore, it might be expected that the reduced wedge between domestic and international prices will stimulate additional trade, further specialisation according to comparative advantage, and dynamic adjustments, so that the economic welfare gains will tend to be higher than those derived using existing trade flows as the basis for the calculations (SWEPRO, 2002).

Model-based analysis makes it possible to investigate the impacts of trade facilitation in more detail. Gravity model analysis, for example, has related trade flows among APEC economies to indicators of port efficiency, customs environment, regulatory environment, and e-business (Wilson, Mann and Otsuki, 2003). Assuming that trade facilitation would lead economies with below average indicator values to improve their performance half-way to the average of all APEC economies, intra-APEC trade would increase by US$254 billion, *i.e.*, 21 percent, *per* year. Using estimates of the effect of trade on *per capita* GDP (Dollar and Kraay, 2001), the facilitation-related expansion of trade suggests an increase in APEC average *per capita* GDP of 4.3 percent. This scenario analysis of improvements in trade-facilitation capacity that result in increases of performance halfway to the average has recently been extended beyond the APEC region. A study published in the World Bank's Global Economic Prospects Report suggests that such improvement in port efficiency, customs environment, regulatory environment, and service-sector infrastructure would increase trade among the 75 economies covered in the analysis by US$377 billion, *i.e.*, an increase of 9.7 percent of trade (Wilson, Bagai and Fink, 2003).

Another line of analysis has used computable general equilibrium (CGE) models to quantify the benefits from trade facilitation on a regional or world-wide basis. In these models, trade facilitation is generally represented as technical progress in trading activities, following the approach pursued by Hertel, Walmsley, and Itakura (2001). For example, when using a dynamic version of the GTAP model, APEC (1999) found that a reduction in TTCs of 1 percent in industrialised economies and 2 percent in developing economies would result in welfare gains of US$46 billion for the APEC region. On a world-wide basis, Francois, van Meil and van Tongeren (2003), using a modified version of the GTAP model that allows for imperfect competition in the manufacturing sector and assuming a uniform 1.5 percent reduction in TTCs, estimate the benefits of trade facilitation to amount to US$72 billion. A roughly comparable figure was obtained in OECD (2003), when evaluating a uniform 1 percent reduction in TTCs with the standard GTAP model under the assumption of perfect competition. Table 5 provides an overview of relevant CGE studies. Most of these investigations use flat reductions in TTCs across economies (or large groups of economies) and do not differentiate the trade facilitation effects by sector or type of trader. Moreover, the assumption of trade facilitation as being technical progress ignores any adjustment costs relating to employees that are no longer needed to process border documentation and, hence, tends to overestimate the benefits of trade facilitation. The following analysis uses a different set of assumptions concerning the potential for trade facilitation across economies, sectors, and traders, and the adjustment costs involved, and thereby aims to contribute to the refinement of quantitative assessments of trade facilitation.

Table 5. CGE-based studies of the benefits of trade facilitation

	Model characteristics			Scenario specification			Annual income gains[1]	
Study	**Base year**	**Competition**	**Dynamics**	**Regional coverage**	**Sector coverage**	**Reduction in trade value**	**(in USD billion)**	**(% of GDP)[2]**
Dee (1998)	1992	Imperfect	Dynamic	APEC	All goods and transport services	Uniform a) 5% b) 10%	a) 216 b) 442	a) 1.1 b) 2.3
APEC (1999)	1996	Perfect	Dynamic	APEC	All goods	By economy group a) 1% & 2% b) 2% & 3%	a) 45.8 b) 64	a) 0.25 b) 0.4
Hertel, Walmsley & Itakura (2001)	1995-2020	Perfect	Dynamic	Japan & Singapore	All goods	By goods sector 0.21-3.5%	6.6 (Japan) & 0.17 (Singapore)	0.16 (Japan) & 0.29 (Singapore)
UNCTAD (2001)	1997	Perfect	Static	Developed economies	a) Trade services b) Air & sea transport c) All services	Uniform 1%	a) 47.9 b) 6.1 c) 117.9	a) 0.22 b) 0.04 c) 0.54
APEC (2002)	1997	Perfect	Static	Intra-APEC trade	All goods	a) 5%[3] (uniform) b) 2.9-7.7%[3] (by economy group)	a) 154.0, b) 100.9-203.5	a) 0.98 b) 0.64-1.30

Table 5. CGE-based studies of the benefits of trade facilitation–Continued

Study	Base year	Model characteristics: Competition	Model characteristics: Dynamics	Scenario specification: Regional coverage	Scenario specification: Sector coverage	Scenario specification: Reduction in trade value	Annual income gains[1] (in USD billion)	Annual income gains[1] (% of GDP)[2]
Fox, Francois & Londoño-Kent (2003)	1997	Perfect	Static	Bilateral USA & Mexico trade	Goods shipped by truck	1% (northbound) & 5% (southbound)	1.4 (US) & 1.8 (Mex)	0.02 (US) & 0.47 (Mex)
Francois, van Meijl & van Tongeren (2003)	1997	Imperfect	Dynamic	World	All goods	Uniform a) 1.5% b) 3%	a) 72.3 b) 150.9	a) 0.25 b) 0.52
OECD (2003)	1997	Perfect	Static	World	All goods and services	Uniform 1%	76.4	0.26

[1] Due to methodological differences, the estimates are not directly comparable. See the individual studies for details.
[2] Calculated from GDP data if not available in the particular study.
[3] Reduction in trade transaction costs.

Source: Authors.

5. Model-Based Assessment of the Benefits of Trade Facilitation

As discussed in section 3, trade facilitation can reduce TTCs considerably, but the extent of the improvements depends, of course, on the measures and instruments that are put into place. Negotiations on trade facilitation in the WTO-context have been envisaged, but it seems virtually impossible to predict the outcome of such negotiations. In turn, it is not possible to forecast the impacts that a trade facilitation agreement might have on world trade and income. Instead, the aim of the following assessment will be to better represent empirical characteristics of the border process in model-based analysis and to identify those features that crucially affect the results and that, therefore, deserve to be further explored in future research. In other words, the focus will be more on the distribution of gains among groups of economies and on the comparison of results with those of existing studies than on the determination of the possible income gains from trade facilitation in absolute U.S. dollar terms.

5.1. *The Modelling Approach*

The analysis is carried out by using the well-established GTAP database and model. The latter is a static, multi-region, computable general equilibrium model that operates under assumptions of perfect competition and constant returns to scale. The model reflects bilateral trade flows, international transport margins, and economy and sector-specific rates of import protection. GTAP thereby makes it possible to determine changes in production, consumption, trade, and economic welfare from particular trade-related external shocks, such as changes in TTCs. A full description of the model can be found in Hertel (1997).

There is no representation of customs-activities or costs of border procedures in the model. Earlier GTAP-research on the impact of changes in border procedures has mostly assumed that trade facilitation takes the form of technical progress in trading activities, which can be incorporated in the model. According to this approach, trade facilitation makes it possible for traders to lose less of the value of the traded goods in transit, so that goods can be sold to consumers at the location of destination at lower prices (and/or generate higher returns for producers). This "iceberg-type" representation of TTCs seems very appropriate for indirect cost components, *i.e.*, border clearance times. If goods are in transit for a long time, a large part of their value "melts" away. Shortening the border clearance time through trade facilitation efforts would result in more of the product reaching its final destination.

However, the iceberg analogy appears to be less accurate for directly incurred TTCs, like the wage costs for providing necessary documentation. Trading firms have to buy the "form-filling" services from company-internal or external service providers. If trade facilitation leads to reduced form-filling needs, trading firms will encounter lower TTCs. But at the same time, the form-filling sector will experience a decline in the demand for its services and corresponding adjustment costs. The latter are not appropriately captured through an iceberg-type representation of TTCs.

These shortcomings have been realised, and Fox, Francois and Londoño-Kent (2003), for example, split the effects of TTCs into an iceberg and a tax component, when investigating the impact of trade facilitation at the US-Mexican border. The tax component is thought to represent the direct costs that firms incur due to border procedures. Traders are assumed to buy "logistics services" from public sector providers corresponding to an amount equal to the directly incurred TTCs.[6]

The analysis in this study follows the approach of Fox *et al.* by representing direct and indirect TTCs differently in the model. The indirect costs are modelled according to the iceberg-approach, while the direct costs are reflected in "logistics duties". The latter are split into charges applying at the export side and representing the direct TTCs in the exporting economy and levies that correspond to the direct TTCs in the importing economy. These additional duties are incorporated into the analysis by using the "Altertax" option, which makes it possible to change parameters in the model database. The procedure is designed to integrate additional information on policy variables into existing GTAP data aggregations (Malcolm, 1998).[7] Trade facilitation in the form of reduced direct TTCs is then modelled as a cut in export and import charges, which reduces TTCs, but also triggers adjustments in the government sector, due to the loss of revenues from logistics duties. These adjustments are associated with economic costs. For example, employees that used to work in documentation-processing but are no longer needed in this function might need to be retrained and moved to other jobs.

For presentational and computational purposes, a data aggregation with nine regions and three sectors is used. The regions are OECD Asia-Pacific, OECD Europe, OECD North America, Former Soviet Union, Latin America and Caribbean, Middle East and North Africa, Non-OECD Asia-Pacific, Sub-Saharan

[6] In practice, border procedures do in general not generate revenues for the government budget and logistics services are provided by private sector firms.

[7] Technically, the additional duties are incorporated in the database by applying appropriately sized "shocks" to tax variables at the export (parameter "txs") and the import (parameter "tms") side.

Africa, and a Rest of the World aggregate.[8] The sectors are agro-food, manufacturing, and services. In this study, trade facilitation is investigated in the context of agro-food and manufacturing trade, reflecting the focus of current WTO work.

5.2 *Scenario Analysis*

A number of salient observations in the earlier sections of this study are reflected in the modelling analysis:

- There are indirect and direct TTCs that show a similar range of magnitude (1-15 percent of the value of traded goods).
- Indirect transactions costs have an "iceberg"-character, while direct transactions costs can be seen as traders' expenditure on logistics services.
- Trade transactions costs vary considerably across economies, as suggested by empirical information on border waiting times and indicators of border process quality.
- Trade facilitation measures will tend to result in larger reductions of TTCs in economies where the latter are currently higher than in those that are closer to best practices already.
- Trade transactions costs are higher for agro-food products than for manufactured products.
- Small and medium-sized companies are confronted with higher TTCs than large companies.

Several scenarios are evaluated. In all cases, a re-calibrated version of the GTAP database that reflects direct TTCs in the form of additional logistics duties is used. As no consistent empirical information on these costs is available across economies, direct TTCs are taken to be inversely proportional to the value of the border process quality indicator, discussed above. In particular, the economy with the highest border process quality is associated with the low end of the range of direct TTCs, *i.e.*, 1 percent of traded goods' value. Conversely, the economy that showed the poorest performance with respect to the indicator of border process quality is assigned the highest observed TTCs, *i.e.*, 15 percent of the value of traded goods. Economies with intermediary performance are

[8] The latter is composed of economies, such as Cambodia, Malta and Papua New Guinea, that are not represented through economy-specific social accounting matrices in the GTAP database.

proportionally associated with intermediary cost estimates. Trade facilitation concerning direct TTCs is then represented as a reduction in logistics duties.

Trade facilitation with respect to indirect TTCs is modelled according to the iceberg approach. Indirect TTCs across economies are thereby assumed to be proportional to the border waiting times recently established in the World Bank survey discussed above.[9] Trade facilitation is assumed to lead to a shortening of these waiting times and, hence, a reduction in the associated costs.

Several assessments of hypothetical, multilateral trade facilitation efforts are undertaken, focusing on the comparison of scenarios rather than the overall welfare gains that might result from trade facilitation. A first set of experiments with the model addresses the question to what extent the empirical features listed above influence the modelling results. For this purpose, it is assumed that trade facilitation leads to a reduction in TTCs of 1 percent of the value of world-wide trade, of which half is taken to occur through savings in directly incurred TTCs and half through reductions in indirect TTCs. This assumption of a 1 percent reduction in global trade value is similar to those made in earlier quantitative research on the impact of trade facilitation.

In a baseline scenario (the "uniformity scenario"), TTCs for all economies, sectors and types of traders are assumed to fall by 1 percentage point of the value of traded goods. In other words, for an economy with rather efficient procedures and total TTCs (before the implementation of the assumed trade facilitation measures) of, for example, 3 percent, the post-facilitation TTCs would amount to 2 percent. For an economy with less efficient border services and, for example, pre-facilitation TTCs of 13 percent, the assumed trade facilitation efforts would bring border costs down to 12 percent of the traded goods' value.

In the scenarios that reflect economy and/or sector and trader diversity, the implementation of the hypothetical trade facilitation measures is assumed as resulting in a "closing of the gap" to best practices by a percentage common to all economies, sectors and types of traders. In cases where good practices are already applied, the assumed trade facilitation would result in reductions of TTCs by less than 1 percent, while the cuts in border costs would exceed 1 percent in cases where the currently existing TTCs are above average. For example, with a best practice of costs of 1 percent of the value of traded goods and a "convergence" factor of 20 percent, an economy with pre-facilitation TTCs of 3 percent would see a reduction in border costs by 0.4 percentage points to

[9] The World Bank survey did not report border waiting times for any of the OECD members in the Asia-Pacific region. To nevertheless cover these economies in the analysis, it was assumed that the border waiting times for Australia, Japan, Korea and New Zealand equal the average of the border waiting times in the OECD Europe and the OECD North America regions.

2.6 percent (20 percent of the gap between 1 percent and 3 percent of the value of traded goods). An economy with pre-facilitation costs of 13 percent would experience a drop in TTCs by 2.4 percentage points to 10.6 percent (20 percent of the gap between 1 percent and 13 percent of the value of traded goods). In other words, the implementation of the hypothetical trade facilitation measures would in this example result in reductions of TTCs that are six times higher in the low-efficiency than in the high-efficiency economy.

The diversity in TTCs across sectors is reflected through the assumption that border costs for agro-food products are 50 percent higher than those for manufacturing products. Similarly, it is assumed that SMEs face 50 percent higher TTCs than big enterprises. As the GTAP model does not distinguish between enterprises according to their size, the higher costs of SMEs are integrated into the economy-averages of TTCs, implying that economies with a higher share of SMEs in international trade face correspondingly higher TTCs. Information from APEC suggests that the share of SMEs in trading operations of non-OECD economies, such as China and Chinese Taipei, is 50-56 percent, while the corresponding share in OECD members, such as Australia, Japan, and the United States, is 10-29 percent (APEC, 1994). Based on this information, a differential of 25 percentage points in the share of SMEs is assumed to prevail between all OECD and non-OECD economies. In combination with the finding that SMEs face 50 percent higher TTCs, non-OECD economies are, *ceteris paribus*, assumed to have TTCs that are 12.5 percent higher than those in OECD members.

In addition to the "uniformity" scenario, three diversity scenarios are considered. A first model set-up reflects economy diversity but no sector or trader diversity ("economy diversity scenario"), a second scenario incorporates also sector diversity ("economy & sector diversity scenario"), and a third one deals with the full diversity across economies, sectors and traders ("economy, sector & trader diversity scenario"). In all three diversity scenarios, the convergence in TTCs following trade facilitation, *i.e.*, the degree to which a "closing of the gap" to best practice is achieved, is adjusted such that the global reduction in trade transactions costs amounts to 1 percent of the value of traded goods. This makes it possible to directly compare the uniformity and the three diversity scenarios.

A further scenario ("OECD only scenario") is closely related to the full diversity setting, but assumes that trade facilitation efforts are only undertaken in OECD members. For OECD members, the modelled reductions in TTCs are identical to those in the "economy, sector & trader diversity scenario", while no reduction is assumed to occur in non-OECD economies. The total reduction is, hence, less than 1 percentage point of world trade value. Table 6 summarises the assumptions of the modelling scenarios.

Table 6. Main scenario assumptions

	Uniformity scenario	Economy diversity scenario	Economy & sector diversity scenario	Economy, sector & trader diversity scenario	OECD-only scenario
Overall reduction of TTCs by 1% of the value of world trade	Yes	Yes	Yes	Yes	No
Reduction in TTCs differs across economies	No	Yes	Yes	Yes	Yes
Higher TTCs for agriculture and food products	No	No	Yes	Yes	Yes
Higher TTCs for small and medium-sized enterprises	No	No	No	Yes	Yes

Source: Authors.

Finally, a set of experiments with the full diversity setting is pursued that relax the assumption that trade facilitation leads to reductions in TTCs that correspond to 1 percentage point of the value of traded goods. A range of reductions amounting to 0.5-3 percent of traded goods' value is explored in order to evaluate the linkage between the assumed change in TTCs and overall welfare gains.

5.3. *Scenario Results*

The results from the modelling analysis indicate that the world income gains from a 1 percent reduction in TTCs would be considerable and amount to about US$40 billion with no losers (Table 7). However, this estimate is substantially below those from earlier studies. The result is partly due to the narrower focus of this study than, for example, OECD (2003), which also considered reductions in TTCs for services. But a second important factor that leads to the lower benefit estimate are adjustment costs in the logistics sector that are represented in the analysis through governmental revenue losses for the provision of logistics services. Indeed, less than 20 percent of the overall gains are due to trade facilitation-related reductions in direct TTCs, which are modelled as cuts in logistics duties, while more than 80 percent of the benefits derive from reductions in indirect TTCs, for which trade facilitation is represented as a pure efficiency gain in trading activities. If the characterisation of directly and indirectly incurred TTCs is appropriate, this finding suggests that trade facilitation measures that focus on reducing border waiting times might have a more marked impact on economic welfare than measures that aim at reducing documentation requirements and related direct TTCs.

Table 7. Scenario results on income effects of trade facilitation (million USD and percent of total)

	Uniformity	Economy diversity	Economy & sector diversity	Economy, sector & trader diversity	OECD-only
World-wide income gains	**38454**	**41844**	**42247**	**43259**	**14053**
- due to direct cost reduction	6041	7689	8119	8250	2650
- due to indirect cost reduction	32413	34155	34128	35009	11402
OECD	**69%**	**37%**	**37%**	**35%**	**103%**
OECD Asia-Pacific	8%	7%	7%	7%	22%
OECD Europe	43%	17%	17%	17%	45%
OECD North America	18%	13%	12%	11%	36%
Non-OECD	**31%**	**63%**	**63%**	**65%**	**-3%**
Former Soviet Union	2%	7%	7%	7%	-1%
Middle East & North Africa	5%	11%	11%	11%	0%
Latin America & Caribbean	5%	13%	13%	13%	-1%
Non-OECD Asia-Pacific	16%	24%	24%	24%	-1%
Sub-Saharan Africa	2%	7%	7%	7%	0%
Rest of World	1%	1%	1%	1%	0%

Source: Authors.

Another result concerns the distribution of income gains among regions that differs fundamentally between the uniformity and the three diversity scenarios. While under the assumption that trade facilitation leads to a uniform reduction of TTCs by 1 percentage point of the value of traded goods about 69 percent of the total gains accrue to OECD members, the incorporation of economy, sector and trader diversity leads to a marked shift of the benefits from trade facilitation towards non-OECD economies. This is because developing economies have, in general, less efficient border procedures and, hence, a bigger potential for improvements through trade facilitation, a larger part of their trade is in agro-food products, and a larger share of their traders are small and medium-sized enterprises. If the full diversity is considered, non-OECD economies obtain almost two-thirds of the global benefits from trade facilitation. This finding highlights the importance of incorporating the empirically observed diversity, and in particular diversity in the potential for improvements in border procedures across economies, into quantitative assessments of trade facilitation.

The large gains that developing economies could obtain from trade facilitation are further illustrated by linking the welfare gains in U.S. dollars to regional GDP (Table 8). In the "uniformity scenario", the gains from trade facilitation in developing economies already exceed those in OECD members in relative terms, as imports and exports account for a relatively large share of the economy in many developing economies, so that reductions in TTCs have a strong impact. If in addition the large potential for improvements through trade facilitation in non-OECD economies is considered, as in the diversity scenarios, the relatively larger impact on these economies becomes even more pronounced. Sub-Saharan Africa is the most striking example, with welfare gains in the full diversity scenario of more than 0.9 percent of GDP, *i.e.*, more than twelve times the OECD average in relative terms.

Table 8. Scenario results on income effects of a one percent reduction in trade transactions costs

(Percent of gross domestic product)

	Uniformity	Economy diversity	Economy & sector diversity	Economy, sector & trader diversity	OECD-only
World-wide income gains	**0.13%**	**0.14%**	**0.15%**	**0.15%**	**0.05%**
- due to direct cost reduction	0.02%	0.03%	0.03%	0.03%	0.01%
- due to indirect cost reduction	0.11%	0.12%	0.12%	0.12%	0.04%
OECD	**0.12%**	**0.07%**	**0.07%**	**0.07%**	**0.06%**
OECD Asia-Pacific	0.06%	0.06%	0.06%	0.06%	0.06%
OECD Europe	0.19%	0.08%	0.08%	0.08%	0.07%
OECD North America	0.08%	0.06%	0.06%	0.06%	0.06%
Non-OECD	**0.20%**	**0.44%**	**0.44%**	**0.47%**	**-0.01%**
Former Soviet Union	0.14%	0.48%	0.49%	0.51%	-0.02%
Middle East & North Africa	0.27%	0.64%	0.64%	0.67%	0.00%
Latin America & Caribbean	0.12%	0.33%	0.34%	0.36%	-0.01%
Non-OECD Asia-Pacific	0.25%	0.40%	0.40%	0.42%	0.00%
Sub-Saharan Africa	0.18%	0.85%	0.88%	0.92%	-0.02%
Rest of World	0.13%	0.21%	0.21%	0.22%	0.00%

Source: Authors.

Tables 7 and 8 also report results from the "OECD-only" scenario that assumes full diversity in TTCs, but limits trade facilitation efforts to OECD members. It turns out that non-OECD economies actually lose under these circumstances, as TTCs in the OECD area fall in absolute and relative terms and divert trade away from non-OECD economies. This effect outweighs any better market access that lower TTCs in OECD markets might offer to non-OECD economies. Hence, the benefits of trade facilitation accrue primarily to those economies that actively engage in it.

Concerning the size of the global benefits from trade facilitation in relation to the assumed reduction in TTCs, experiments with the full diversity setting suggest that the welfare gains are roughly proportional to the size of the assumed cut in TTCs (Figure 3). Trade facilitation efforts that lead to a reduction in TTCs that is twice as large as assumed in the above scenario analysis, for example, will result in welfare gains that are of about twice the size. However, the magnitude of these benefits has to be seen as an upper boundary of the actual gains that might be achievable, as investment needs to realise the assumed reduction in TTCs have not been incorporated into the quantitative analysis, due to lack of consistent cross-economy information.

Figure 3. Welfare gains under alternative assumptions on the extent of trade facilitation

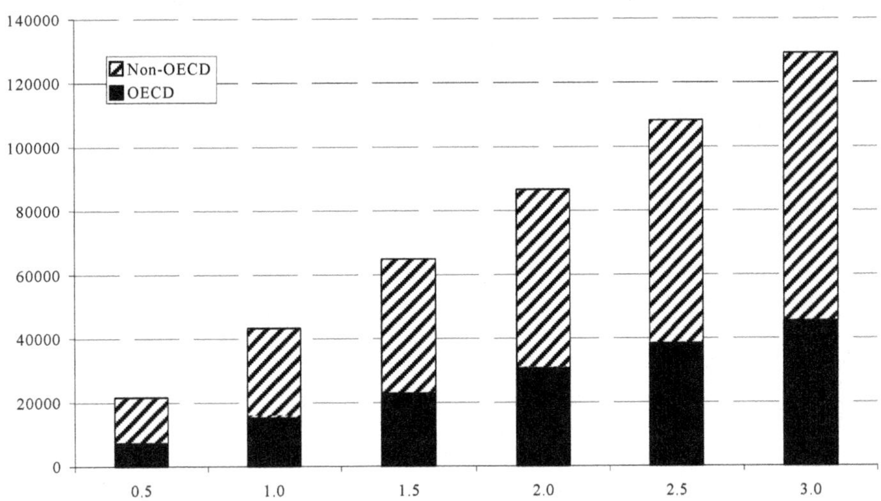

Assumed reduction in TTCs in terms of percentage points of traded goods value

Source: Authors.

References

1. APEC (Asia-Pacific Economic Co-operation), 1994. "The Highlights of the APEC Survey on Small and Medium Enterprises." Committee on Trade and Investment, Singapore.
2. APEC (Asia-Pacific Economic Co-operation), 1999. "Assessing APEC Trade Liberalization and Facilitation - 1999 Update." APEC Economic Committee. Bangkok.
3. APEC (Asia-Pacific Economic Co-operation), 2002. *Measuring the Impact of APEC Trade Facilitation on APEC Economies: A CGE Analysis.* APEC Economic Committee, Bangkok.

4. APEC (Asia-Pacific Economic Co-operation), 2003a. "Selection of Trade Facilitation Actions and Measures by Member Economies." Document 2003/SOM II/CTI/016, Committee on Trade and Investment, Khon Kaen/Thailand.
5. APEC (Asia-Pacific Economic Co-operation), 2003b. "Pioneering e-Trade: Singapore's Experience." Document 2003/SOM-II/CTI/064, Committee on Trade and Investment. Khon Kaen/Thailand.
6. Batra, G., D. Kaufmann, and A.H.W. Stone, 2003. *Investment Climate Around the World: Voices of the Firms from the World Business Environment Survey*. Washington, D.C.: The World Bank.
7. Bhatnagar, S., 2001. "Philippine Customs Reform." World Bank project report, Washington, D.C.
8. CTB (Japan's Customs and Tariff Bureau), 2001. "The 6th study on time required for release of imports (in Japanese)." Press Release. Tokyo.
9. Dee, P., 1998. "The Comprehensiveness of APEC's Free Trade Commitment", Session VIII in *The Economic Implications of Liberalizing*, Publication 3101, US International Trade Commission, Washington, D.C.
10. DFAT (Australia's Department of Foreign Affairs and Trade), 2001. "Paperless Trading Benefit to APEC, the Potential of the APEC Paperless Trading Initiative." Working Paper, Australian Department of Foreign Affairs and Trade, Canberra.
11. Dollar, D. and A. Kraay, 2001. *Trade, Growth and Poverty*. World Bank Working Paper Series No. 2615, World Bank, Washington, D.C.
12. Ernst & Whinney, 1987a. "The Costs of 'Non-Europe: Border Related Controls and Administrative Formalities", in European Commission: *Research on the Costs of 'Non-Europe' – Basic Findings*. Brussels, pp. 7-40.
13. Ernst & Whinney, 1987b. "The Cost of "Non-Europe: An illustration in the Road Haulage sector", in: European Commission: *Research on the Costs of 'Non-Europe' – Basic Findings*. Brussels, pp. 41-64.
14. European Commission, 1989. "COST 306 Final Report." Brussels.
15. Fox, A.K., J. Francois, and P. Londoño-Kent, 2003. "Measuring Border Crossing Costs and their Impact on Trade Flows: The United States-Mexican Trucking Case." Paper presented at the 6th conference on global economic analysis, Den Haag, Netherlands.
16. Francois, J., H. van Meil, and F. van Tongeren, 2003. "Economic Benefits of the Doha Round for the Netherlands." Project Report, Agricultural Economics Research Institute, The Hague.
17. Grant, L., 2001. "*Jamaica Customs Automated Services Online*." World Bank project report, Washington, D.C.
18. Gutierrez, J.E.O., 2001. "Customs Reform and Modernisation Program." Statement contributed to the WTO Workshop on Technical Assistance and Capacity Building in Trade Facilitation (10-11 May), Geneva.
19. Haralambides, H. and P. Londoño-Kent, 2002. "Impediments to Free Trade: The Case of Trucking and NAFTA in the U.S.-Mexican Border." Mimeo, Erasmus University, Rotterdam.
20. Hertel, T. (editor), 1997. *Global Trade Analysis: Modelling and Applications*. New York and Melbourne: Cambridge University Press.
21. Hertel, T., T. Walmsley, and K. Ikatura, 2001. "Dynamic Effects of the 'New Age' Free Trade Agreement between Japan and Singapore." *Journal of Economic Integration* 24: 1019-1049.

22. Hummels, D., 2001. "Time as a trade barrier." Working Paper, Purdue University, West Lafayette/Indiana.
23. IMD (Institute for Management Development), 2002. *World Competitiveness Yearbook.* Lausanne.
24. JETRO (Japan External Trade Organization), 2002. "Report on Market Access to Japan: Single Windows for Trade and Port-related Procedures (in Japanese)." Tokyo.
25. Lane, M., 2001. "International Supply Chain Management and Customs – Peru: a Case Study." World Bank report, Washington, D.C.
26. Malcolm, G., 1998. "Adjusting Tax Rates in the GTAP Database." GTAP technical paper No. 12, Center for Global Trade Analysis, Purdue University, West Lafayette.
27. Molnar, E. and L. Ojala, 2003. "Transport and Trade Facilitation Issues in the CIS-7, Kazakhstan and Turkmenistan. " Paper prepared for the Lucerne Conference of the CIS-7 Initiative (20-22 January), World Bank, Washington, D.C.
28. METI (Japan's Ministry of Economics, Trade and Industry), 1998. "Report on Asia-scale Industrial Structure Policies" (in Japanese). Tokyo.
29. MRI (Mitsubishi Research Institute), 2001. "Study on New Issues Concerning Economic Effects of Regional Integration" (in Japanese). Tokyo.
30. OECD (Organisation for Economic Co-operation and Development), 2002. *Business Benefits of Trade Facilitation.* Document TD/TC/WP(2001)21/FINAL, Paris.
31. OECD (Organisation for Economic Co-operation and Development), 2003. *Doha Development Agenda: Welfare Gains from Further Multilateral Trade Liberalisation with Respect to Tariffs.* Document TD/TC/WP(2003)10/FINAL, Paris.
32. SWEPRO (Swedish Trade Procedures Council), 1985. *Data Interchange in International Trade.* Stockholm.
33. SWEPRO (Swedish Trade Procedures Council), 2002. *Trade Facilitation: Impact and Potential Gains.* Stockholm.
34. SWEPRO (Swedish Trade Procedures Council), 2003. *Trade Facilitation from a Developing Country Perspective.* Stockholm.
35. Transparency International, 2002. *Global Corruption Report.* Berlin.
36. UN/CEFACT (United Nations Centre for Trade Facilitation and Electronic Business), 2001. "Compendium of Trade Facilitation Recommendations." Geneva.
37. UNCTAD (United Nations Conference on Trade and Development), 1994. "Fact Sheet 5." United Nations International Symposium on Trade Efficiency (17-21 October). Geneva.
38. UNCTAD (United Nations Conference on Trade and Development), 2001. "E-Commerce and Development Report." Geneva.
39. UNCTAD (United Nations Conference on Trade and Development), 2002. "UNCTAD Launches New E-Customs System." Press Release No. 40 (TAD/INF/PR40), Geneva.
40. US-NCITD (United States National Committee on International Trade Documentation), 1971. "Paperwork or Profits$? in International Trade." Washington, D.C.
41. Verwaal, E., and B. Donkers, 2001. "Customs Related Transactions Costs, Firm Size and International Trade Intensity." Erasmus Research Institute of Management Report No. 2001-13. Rotterdam School of Management, Rotterdam.
42. WEF (World Economic Forum), 2002. *Global Competitiveness Report.* Geneva.

43. Wilson, J.S., 2001. "Trade Facilitation Lending by the World Bank – Recent Experience, Research, and Capacity Building Initiatives." Paper Prepared for the Workshop on Technical Assistance and Capacity Building in Trade Facilitation (10-11 May), Geneva.
44. Wilson, J.S, S. Bagai, and C. Fink, 2003. "Reducing Trading Costs in a New Era of Security." Chapter 5 in Global Economic Prospects 2004 - *Realizing the Development Promise of the Doha Agenda.* Washington, D.C.: The World Bank.
45. Wilson, J.S., C.L. Mann, and T. Otsuki, 2003. *Trade Facilitation and Economic Development: Measuring the Impact.* World Bank Policy Research Working Paper No. 2988, Washington, D.C.
46. World Bank, 2002. "Costs of Doing Business Survey." World Bank Country Study, Washington, D.C.
47. WTO (World Trade Organization), 1999. "Report of the Working Party on Preshipment Inspection." Document G/L/300, Geneva
48. WTO (World Trade Organization), 2000. "Chile's Experience with the Modernization of Customs Administrations Based on the Use of Information Technology." Council of Trade in Goods Document G/C/W/239, Geneva.
49. WTO (World Trade Organization), 2001. "Trade Facilitation Experience Paper by Costa Rica." Council of Trade in Goods Document G/C/W/265, Geneva.
50. WTO (World Trade Organization), 2002. "The e-Customs Experience of the Separate Customs Territory of Taiwan, Penghu, Kinmen and Matsu." Council of Trade in Goods Document G/C/W/440, Geneva.
51. WTO (World Trade Organization), 2003. "Trade Facilitation: National Experience Paper from New Zealand." Council of Trade in Goods Document G/C/W/449, Geneva.

Annex: Deriving an indicator of border process quality

The approach for designing an indicator of border process quality is related to the method used by Wilson, Mann and Otsuki (2003). As no consistent data on direct TTCs is available across economies, Wilson *et al.* use survey-based information to derive indicators of TTCs. In constructing these indicators, different sources of survey information are used in order to reduce dependence on any one business survey. Yet unlike Wilson *et al.*, the border process quality indicator derived in this study does not exclusively rely on business perceptions of border transactions, but also incorporates information on government commitments towards trade facilitation.

There are four components of the indicator of border process quality. Three of these are constructed from survey information on different aspects of the border process environment, namely customs efficiency, hidden import barriers, and administrative integrity, obtained from three different information sources. The fourth component is based on the implementation of the nine trade facilitation instruments listed in the 2001-edition of the UN/CEFACT compendium of trade facilitation recommendations:

- *Customs efficiency*: Survey information on "Customs authorities do [do not] facilitate the efficient transit of goods?" Published in IMD, 2002. *World Competitiveness Yearbook*. Lausanne.
- *Hidden import barriers*: Survey information on "In your country, hidden import barriers, *i.e.*, barriers other than published tariffs and quotas, are an important problem [not an important problem]?" Published in WEF, 2002. *Global Competitiveness Report*. Geneva.
- *Administrative integrity*: Corruption perceptions index. Published in Transparency International, 2002. *Global Corruption Report*. Berlin.
- *Trade facilitation commitments*: Count of participation in or implementation of "trade facilitation instruments". Listing taken from UN/CEFACT, 2001. *Compendium of Trade Facilitation Recommendations*. Geneva.

In the surveys, business representatives were asked to rate the quality of the particular aspect of the border process environment, with a higher rating indicating greater satisfaction. As the scaling of the survey responses differs, such that survey responses on customs efficiency, for example, range from 1 to 10, while those on hidden import barriers range from 1 to 7, the raw data is normalised by dividing the data value for each individual economy by the average of the respective data series. A similar normalisation procedure is used for the indicator component representing trade facilitation commitments. Afterwards, the economy-related information in the four components is averaged to yield the indicator for border process quality.

Due to the different comprehensiveness of the information sources, sometimes economy-specific data are not available for all indicator-components. To avoid undue influence of any particular indicator-component, only those economies for which at least two indicator components are available were considered in the analysis. For the resulting sample of 102 economies, the economy-specific indicator of border process quality is derived as the simple average of the available components-data. Annex table 1 shows the correlation between the different indicator-components.

Annex table 1. Correlation between indicator-components[1] on border process quality

	Customs efficiency	Hidden import barriers	Admin-istrative integrity	Trade facilitation commitment
Customs efficiency	1.00	0.84	0.86	0.38
Hidden import barriers		1.00	0.86	0.55
Administrative integrity			1.00	0.54
Trade facilitation commitments				1.00

[1] normalised values at individual economy level.

Source: Authors.

The GTAP model that is used to undertake the quantitative analysis of the impact of trade facilitation distinguishes between 66 economies/regions (for details on the regional aggregation see *www.gtap.agecon.purdue.edu*). For the economies that are covered as part of wider regions rather than individual entities, the regional values of the components of the customs quality indicator are obtained as the simple averages of the component values for the economies within that GTAP-region. For example, the component values of Algeria, Egypt, Libya, and Tunisia are averaged to yield the component values for the GTAP-region "Rest of North Africa".

The value of the border process quality indicator for the 66 GTAP economies/regions ranges from 0.25 to 1.85, implying that the economy with the worst indicator value received a score in the rankings that was 75 percent below average, while the economy with the highest value scored 85 percent higher than the mean. These indicators form the basis for the derivation of world-wide estimates of direct TTCs in the quantitative trade facilitation analysis (see the corresponding section in the main body of the text).

USING DIRECTED ACYCLIC GRAPHS AND VAR ECONOMETRICS TO SIMULATE THE UPSTREAM AND DOWNSTREAM EFFECTS OF IMPOSITION OF AN IMPORT QUOTA: AN APPLICATION TO U.S. WHEAT-RELATED MARKETS

Ronald A. Babula, *U.S. International Trade Commission*[1]
Suchada V. Langley, *U.S. Department of Agriculture, Economic Research Service*
Agapi Somwaru, *U.S. Department of Agriculture, Economic Research Service*
Shiva S. Makki, *Ohio State University*

This paper applies a new econometric method to a reduced form time series model of wheat market and estimates market effects of imposing wheat quota on U.S. wheat and wheat products. The model is designed to reflect the dynamic quarterly effects on the U.S. wheat market and on U.S. wheat-related markets downstream of imposing a U.S. import quota on imports of (primarily Canadian) wheat.

Economic theory suggests that the U.S. wheat and its downstream markets interact and influence each other (Rich, Babula, and Romain 2002; Babula and Rich 2001). What is not theoretically evident, however, is just how, with what dynamic quarterly patterns, and to what ultimate degrees, that such interrelationships take place. While conventional theoretically-based or "structural" econometric models are equipped to address questions at static equilibria before and after an imposed shock, they often have little to say about what happens dynamically between pre- and post-shock equilibria (Sims 1980; Bessler 1980, pp. 110-111). Vector Autoregression (VAR) methods are well-equipped to address policy-relevant dynamic issues of what unfolds between pre- and post-shock equilibria. In addition, VAR econometric methods impose as few a priori theoretical restrictions as possible so as to permit the regularities in the data to reveal themselves (Bessler 1984).

Recent developments in VAR methodology were developed recently and first applied to agricultural economic issues by Bessler and Akleman (1998) and Haigh and Bessler (2003). These developments comprise a methodology that combines establishing lines of contemporaneous causality among economic variables using directed acyclic graphs or DAGs with Bernanke's (1986) well-

[1] The views expressed in this article are those of the authors. They are not the views of the U.S. International Trade Commission (USITC) as a whole nor any of its individual Commissioners, nor of the U.S. Department of Agriculture. The corresponding author, Ron Babula may be contacted *via* email at *ronald.babula@usitc.gov*.

known structural methods of vector autoregression or VAR modeling, and is hereafter denoted as the DAG/Bernanke VAR methodology. We present the methodology and its advantages over more traditional VAR modeling procedures below (for detailed derivations and summaries of VAR econometric methods see Sims (1980), Bessler (1984), Hamilton (1994, ch. 11) and Patterson (2000, ch. 14)).

Recently, Babula, Bessler, and Payne (2003, 2004) applied the reduced form DAG/Bernanke VAR methodology to a quarterly system of wheat-related markets. We adapt this model and use its results from simulation of the impulse response function and from analysis of forecast error variance or FEV decompositions to discern the dynamic effects of imposing a U.S. wheat import quota similar to that imposed on certain imports of Canadian wheat during the year ending September 11, 1995 (see Glickman and Kantor 1995; Canada-U.S. Joint Commission on Grains, 1995). The quarterly system of the seven wheat-related variables (hereafter denoted interchangeably by the parenthetical labels) is as follows:

1. Wheat price (PWHEAT)
2. Quantity of wheat demanded/supplied in the U.S. market (QWHEAT)
3. Wholesale price of wheat flour (PFLOUR)
4. Wholesale price for mixes and doughs (PMIXES)
5. Wholesale price of bread in first differences[2] (DIFPBREAD)
6. Wholesale price of wheat-based breakfast cereals (PCEREAL)
7. Wholesale price of cookies and crackers (PCOOKIES).

The model will provide information on the four "dynamic aspects" of how a shock in wheat market-clearing quantity of wheat influences wheat and its downstream markets: (1) direction of the responses, (2) magnitude of the responses, (3) patterns of responses, and (4) the strength of relationships among wheat-related variables. This is accomplished by first specifying a traditional VAR model of the seven quarterly wheat and wheat-related variables (hereafter, the "first-stage" VAR), and then applied the procedures of Bessler and Akleman (1998) and Haigh and Bessler (2003) to the first-stage VAR to render the DAG/Bernanke VAR model of the seven wheat-related variables and their causal ordering in contemporaneous time.

---

[2] For reasons presented below, evidence suggests that bread price is nonstationary and is modeled in first differences.

We examine the results from simulating this model's impulse response function in a way that mimics imposition of an import quota on U.S. wheat. The remainder of this paper is comprised of several sections. First, we summarize Babula, Bessler, and Payne's (2004) quarterly VAR model of the U.S. wheat and wheat product markets. We discuss an array of specification issues, including a rationale to use a VAR model and summarize a diagnostic evidence of its estimation. Second, we discuss the DAG/Bernanke VAR methodology (Bessler and Akleman (1998) and Haigh and Bessler (2003)), as applied the quarterly system of U.S. wheat and wheat product markets. We show the advantages of DAG methods in choosing an ordering of variables in contemporaneous time when confronted with several competing orderings. In the following two sections, we apply two well-known VAR econometric tools, analysis of selected impulse response simulations and forecast error variance (FEV) decompositions, to empirically estimate market price response multipliers and to illuminate the dynamic quarterly effects on the U.S. markets for wheat and wheat products from imposing a presumably quota-induced decrease in wheat on the model's impulse response function. A summary and conclusions follow.

1. The VAR Model: Specification, Data, Estimation, and Model Adequacy

The seven-equation system was estimated as a VAR model in logged levels (except for first difference in wholesale price of wheat (DIFPBREAD) because cointegration was not an issue as unit root test results suggest that six of the seven variables are likely stationary (in logged levels).

We applied Tiao and Box's lag selection methods to the above vector of endogenous variables, and evidence suggested a one-order lag structure. In other words, first-stage VAR model is as follows:

$$X(t) = a_0 + a_{x1}*PWHEAT(t\text{-}1) + a_{x,2}*QWHEAT(t\text{-}1) + {}_{x,3}*PFLOUR(t\text{-}1) + a_{x,4}*PMIXES(t\text{-}1) + a_{x,5}*DIFPBREAD(t\text{-}1) + a_{x,6}*PCEREAL(t\text{-}1) + a_{x,7}*PCOOKIES(t\text{-}1) + R_x(t) \quad (1)$$

Above, the parenthetical terms denote a value's time period: t for the current period and t-1 for the one-order quarterly lagged value. The a-terms are regression coefficient estimates. Of the two subscripts, x refers to the x-th equation, while the numeric subscript refers to a variable as assigned in equation (1). The nought-subscripted a-term refers to the intercept. X(t) = PWHEAT(t), QWHEAT(t), PFLOUR(t), PMIXES(t), DIFPBREAD(t), PCEREAL(t), and PCOOKIES(t). $R_x(t)$ are the x-th equation's estimated white noise residuals.

Each of the seven equations included a time trend and three seasonal binary ("dummy") variables (Babula, Bessler, and Payne 2004). Three event-specific binary variables were included in each VAR equation: the 1989 implementation of the Canada/U.S. Free Trade Agreement, the 1994 implementation of the North American Free Trade Agreement or NAFTA, and the U.S. tariff rate quotas imposed on U.S. imports of certain Canadian durum and non-durum wheat for the year ending September 11, 1995 (Babula, Bessler, and Payne 2004).

All data were defined for the June 1 - May 31 U.S. wheat "market year." Hence, a "split" year, say 2000/2001, refers to the U.S. market year beginning June 1, 2000 and ending May 31, 2001.[3] Babula, Bessler, and Payne (2004) collected quarterly market year data for the seven endogenous variables and estimated the VAR model over the 1986/87:1 through 2002/2003:2 period with ordinary least squares, which Sims (1980) and Bessler (1984) established as the appropriate estimator for VAR models. The VAR model was estimated in natural logarithms so that shocks to and impulse responses in the logged variables reflect approximate proportional changes in nonlogged variables.

Hamilton (p. 324-327) summarizes how a VAR model may be considered a reduced form of a structural econometric system. Hence, QWHEAT and the modeled wheat-related prices are not the quantities and prices specifically demanded or specifically supplied, but rather are prices and quantities that clear the market (Hamilton, pp. 324-327; Babula, Bessler, and Payne 2004). So a simulation's responses from a presumably quota-induced decline in QWHEAT are actually net changes after all, and sometimes countervailing, effects of supply and demand have played out (Babula, Bessler, and Payne 2004; Babula and Rich, p. 5, 2001).

Since detailed quarterly data on U.S. supply, consumption, or stocks were not available for wheat flour,[4] mixes and doughs, bread, wheat-based breakfast

---

[3] Throughout, the marketing year quarters are denoted by numerals to the right of the split year and colon. Considering 1998/99 as an example: 1998/99:1 refers to the quarter spanning June, July, and August of 1998; 1998/99:2 refers to the quarter spanning September, October, and November, 1998; 1998/99:3 refers to the quarter spanning December 1998, and January and February of 1999; and 1998/99:4 is the quarter spanning March, April, and May, 1999.

[4] The U.S. Department of Labor's Bureau of the Census (Labor, Census 1985-2002) publishes U.S. stocks and production of wheat flour in its quarterly and annual summary issues of *Current Industrial Reports, Flour Milling Products*. We followed Babula and Rich (2001) and Babula, Bessler, and Payne (2004) and did not use this data as the quality and accuracy of the data are in serious question. First, a major U.S. miller stated that the data on wheat flour stocks and production were unreliable in a telephone conversation. And second, these contentions were confirmed by the staff of the *Milling and Baking News* (pp. 1 and 19) in a front-page article concerning inaccuracies of these data.

cereals, and cookies/crackers, we followed Babula, Bessler and Payne (2004) and modeled wheat and downstream wheat product markets as reduced form price relationships (see also Babula and Rich 2001; Rich, Babula, and Romain 2002). The model was estimated as a VAR model where all seven endogenous variables except bread price were estimated in natural logarithms, and where bread price, because of evidence that logged levels were nonstationary, was incorporated in first differences of logged levels. This VAR framework was chosen over a vector error correction (VEC) model suggested by Johansen and Juselius (1990, 1992). This is because evidence emerged from the logged levels data to suggest that cointegration was likely not an issue, since all but one of the seven endogenous (in logged levels) were stationary (see Babula, Bessler, and Payne's (2004) for testing results and evidence which supported the choice of a VAR model (specified in equation 1) over a Johansen and Juselius (1990, 1992) VEC of the system).

1.1. *Sources of Quarterly Data and Data Issues*

QWHEAT, the U.S. market-clearing quantity of wheat, is the sum of beginning stocks, production, and imports, which are published by the USDA (2002, 2003).[5] Each equation's quarterly seasonal binary variables play an important role for two reasons. First, previous VAR econometric analyses on U.S. wheat-related markets have placed seasonal binaries in such equations to capture seasonal effects (USITC 1994, ch. II; Rich, Babula and Romain 2002, p. 103; and Babula and Rich 2001). And second, the seasonal binary variables capture the effects of an annually-recurring, production-induced QWHEAT spike in each market year's initiating quarter (Babula and Rich 2001).

All six prices were converted into market year quarterly data from monthly data and then placed into natural logarithms. A number of quarterly U.S. wheat-

---

[5] QWHEAT was defined to include (primarily Canadian) imports as well as U.S. supplies because of strong evidence that emerged from previous research that U.S. millers and merchants consider similarly classed consignments of Canadian and U.S. wheat as highly, if not perfectly, substitutable (U.S. International Trade Commission or USITC 1994, p. II.83 and appendix M; Babula and Jabara 1999 , pp. 90-91). This valuable evidence was based on highly reliable USITC questionnaire work, the reliability of which was enhanced by the USITC's option to subpoena non-respondents of the questionnaires (Babula and Jabara 1999, pp. 90-91). Previous research concluded that an increase in highly/perfectly substitutable imports of Canadian wheat had the same basic effects on U.S. price as increases in U.S.-produced supplies of wheat (USITC 1994, ch. II and appendix N; Babula and Jabara 1999, pp. 90-91). Consequently, we placed imports in with U.S. wheat supply to form QWHEAT, just as the researchers of quarterly U.S. wheat-related markets recently did (Rich, Babula, and Romain 2002; Babula and Rich 2001).

based product prices were calculated from the following monthly producer price indices (PPI) published by the U.S. Department of Labor, Bureau of Labor Statistics (Labor, BLS 2002): PFLOUR from the PPI for wheat flour (series no. PCU2041#1); PMIXES from the PPI for flour mixes and refrigerated and frozen doughs and batters (series no. PCU2045#6); PCEREAL from the PPI for wheat flakes and other wheat breakfast foods (series no. PCU2043#112); and PCOOKIES from the PPI for cookies and crackers (series no. PCU2052#). Quarterly DIFPBREAD data were obtained by taking monthly PPI data for bread (series no. PCU2051#1) from Labor, BLS (2002); converting data levels into market year quarterly values; logging these values; and then first-differencing the logged levels. Evidence provided by Babula, Bessler, and Payne (2004) from Ljung-Box portmanteau and Dickey-Fuller tests conducted on the VAR model's estimated residuals or innovations suggests that the VAR model is adequately specified by literature-established standards (2004).

1.2. *Directed Acyclic Graphs*

The above VAR modeling methods incorporates a lag structure which captures lagged causal relationships among PWHEAT, QWHEAT, PFLOUR, PMIXES, DIFPBREAD, PCEREAL, and PCOOKIES. The seven VAR variables are clearly correlated in contemporaneous time as well, although the VAR methods above do not address such contemporaneous correlation (Bessler 1984, p. 114). It is well known that ignoring causal orderings among a VAR's endogenous variables in contemporaneous time may produce impulse response simulations and FEV decompositions that may not represent observed market relationships (Sims; Bessler, p. 114; Saghaian, Hassan, and Reed, p. 104). DAG methods are an evidentially-based way of ordering variables in contemporaneous time.

Babula, Bessler, and Payne (2004) outlined the three principal ways which VAR econometric work has accounted for contemporaneous correlation. First is the Choleski factorization, the most traditionally applied method, where contemporaneous orderings are through imposition of a theoretically-based and recursive Wold causal ordering imposed on the VAR's variance/covariance matrix (Bessler 1984, p. 114; Bessler and Akleman 1998, p. 1144). Babula, Bessler, and Payne (2004) provided Choleski-based orderings of the same set of seven endogenous variables. The second approach is the application of Bernanke's structural VAR methods where prior notions of evidentially-based and/or theoretically-based causal orderings in contemporaneous time may be imposed on a VAR's endogenous variables (Bessler and Akleman , p. 1144). To compound the challenge of establishing a contemporaneous ordering with these two traditional VAR approaches is a factor of arbitrariness. There are several alternative and competing orderings to choose. Having noted that Choleski-ordered VAR models generate impulse response and FEV decomposition results that may vary with the Wold causal ordering chosen for the decomposition, Pesaran and Shin developed a third approach, a generalized impulse response analysis for VAR models (and for cointegrated models as well), that avoids orthogonalization of shocks and that generates order-invariant results. Bessler and Akleman (1998, p. 1144) noted that a potential problem with a Choleski-based approach is that the world may not be recursive, while a potential problem with Bernanke's approach is that the true contemporaneous ordering may in fact not be the optimal or most realistic choice. Doan (2002, p. 4) recommends caution when using Pesaran and Shin's generalized impulse response analysis because of difficulty in interpreting impulses from highly correlated shocks within a non-orthogonalized setting. Doan (2002, p. 4) adds that Pesaran and Shin's methods are equivalent to computing shocks with each variable in turn being set atop a Choleski ordering.

The DAG/Bernanke VAR approach offers a fourth approach that "nails-down" an evidentially supported optimal ordering from a set of competing alternatives. The DAG analysis of Scheines et. al. (1994) and Spirtes, Glymour, and Scheines (2000) is used to help in choosing a set of contemporaneous causal relations from a set of theoretically consistent alternatives, and then impose the evidentially-supported causal relations on a Bernanke-type structural VAR (see Babula, Bessler, and Payne (2004), Bessler and Akleman (1998) and Haigh, and Bessler (2003)). By engaging statistical evidence, this approach may avoid excessive reliance on recursive restrictions, expert opinions, and/or arbitrariness of choice in selecting among competing, yet theoretically consistent, contemporaneous orderings when using more traditional VAR modeling procedures (Babula, Bessler, and Payne 2004).

We applied the TETRADII PC algorithm to construct a DAG on innovations from their first-stage VAR model (DAG applications follow the theoretical work of Pearl (1995) and the TETRAD algorithms described in Spirtes, Glymour, and Scheines (2000). The PC algorithm begins with a general unrestricted set of relationships among the variables (errors from each VAR equation) and proceeds stepwise to remove edges between variables and to direct causal flow. Edges between variables are removed sequentially based on zero correlations or partial (conditional) correlations.

2. DAG Applications to Wheat and Wheat Products Markets

In sorting out how the seven wheat endogenous variables are ordered in contemporaneous time we follow Babula, Bessler, and Payne's (2004), Bessler and Akleman (1998), and Haigh and Bessler (2003). Hereafter, the seven variables are denoted interchangeably by the parenthetical Y-terms: PWHEAT (Y1), QWHEAT (Y2), PFLOUR (Y3), PMIXES (Y4), DIFPBREAD (Y5), PCEREAL (Y6), and PCOOKIES (Y7). The starting point is panel A of figure 1, the completely undirected graph of all possible edges among the seven variables. Panel B provides the edges that our analysis suggests as statistically nonzero at the chosen level (here 10%) of significance. There is a two-stage or possibly three-stage process for gleaning data-based evidence to establish contemporaneous causal orderings among the seven endogenous variables in contemporaneous time. First, we analyze unconditional correlations and eliminate all statistically zero edges, and retain all statistically nonzero correlations (see Scheines et. al. 1994; Spirtes, Glymour, and Scheines 2000). Second, we further analyze all remaining conditional correlations, eliminate the statistically zero ones and retain those which are statistically nonzero. Panel B in figure 1 provides the edges retained in these two stages. This figure indicates that some edges are directed, and some are undirected, giving rise to several competing systems of observationally equivalent contemporaneous causality relationships. Haigh and Bessler (2003) developed a method to optimally choose among such competing systems of ordered relations: they modified and applied Schwarz's (1978) loss metric, applied it to the alternative systems of causality, and then chose the system of causality which minimizes the Schwartz metric (panel C of figure 1 as detailed below). The metric-minimizing system of relationships (panel C, figure 1 as stated below) was imposed on the DAG/Bernanke model.

The quarterly, market year sample ranges from 1986/87:1 through 2002/2003:2, the estimation period for the VAR model. Innovations (ε_{it}) from our VAR outlined above provided the contemporaneous innovation matrix, Σ. Directed graph theory explicitly points out that the off-diagonal elements of the scaled inverse of this matrix (Σ or any correlation matrix) are the negatives of the partial correlation coefficients between the corresponding pair of variables, given the remaining variables in the matrix (Whittaker; Bessler and Akleman, p. 1146).

Table 1 provides the essentials for stages 1 and 2 (see also Babula, Bessler, and Payne's application of the analysis for more details). The correlation matrix (lower triangular innovation correlation matrix) was generated by the OLS-estimated VAR model. Each of the elements is a correlation coefficient denoted

Figure 1
Complete undirected graph (Panel A), TETRAD generated graph (Panel B), and final DAG (Panel C) on innovations from the VAR model of 7 wheat-related variables

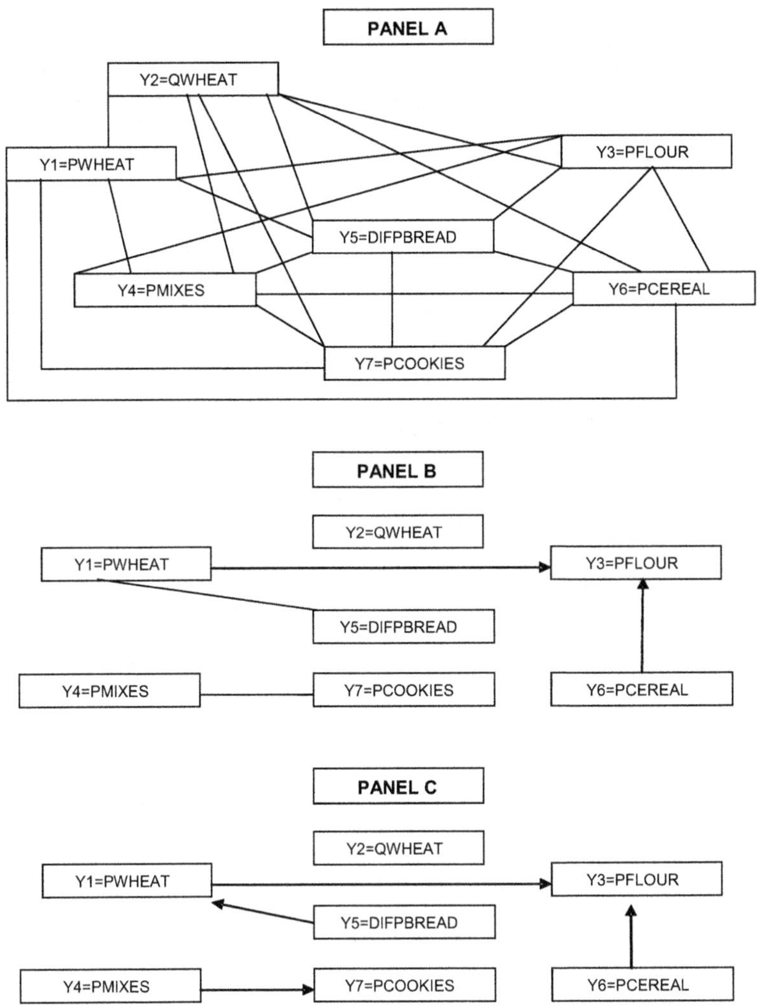

as "rho" with rho(1,3) [or rho(3,1) as they are symmetric and equal] denoting the correlation between Y1 and Y3. The p-values for these correlation coefficients are provided in the second lower triangular matrix. Basically, all edges with a p-value above 0.10 for the chosen 10% significance level are removed. This leaves the following five edges [bottom of table 1 and graphed in panel B of figure 1]:

Table 1. VAR model's correlation and covariance matrices and correlation P-values in lower-triangular form correlation and covariance matrix

Product Combinations	Correlation Coefficient	P-Values	Retained Edges* (10% significance level)
Y1*Y2	-0.44	0.0002	
Y1*Y3	0.92	0.0000	PRICE OF WHEAT → PRICE OF FLOUR
Y1*Y4	-0.05	0.7100	
Y1*Y5	0.23	0.0610	PRICE OF WHEAT – DIFPBREAD
Y1*Y6	0.10	0.4210	
Y1*Y7	-0.08	0.5120	
Y2*Y3	-0.42	0.0003	
Y2*Y4	0.09	0.4760	
Y2*Y5	0.02	0.8600	
Y2*Y6	-0.08	0.5200	
Y2*Y7	-0.06	0.6340	
Y3*Y4	-0.10	0.4130	
Y3*Y5	0.16	0.2130	
Y3*Y6	0.21	0.0580	PRICE OF CEREAL → PRICE OF FLOUR
Y3*Y7	-0.13	0.2990	
Y4*Y5	-0.05	0.6680	
Y4*Y6	-0.03	0.8290	
Y4*Y7	0.22	0.0800	PRICE OF MIXES – PRICE OF COOKIES
Y5*Y6	-0.15	0.2280	
Y5*Y7	-0.03	0.7840	
Y6*Y7	-0.14	0.2710	
			QWHEAT or Y2 = exogenous

Source: Authors' analyses of TETRAD II and regression results.

- PWHEAT(Y1)→ PFLOUR(Y3): A directed relationship where wheat price influences or causes flour price. Recall that rho(1,3) = +0.92 with a p-value of about zero.
- PCEREAL(Y6) → PFLOUR(Y3): A directed edge where the price of wheat-based breakfast cereals influences or causes wheat flour price. The rho(6,3) = 0.21 has a p-value of 0.085.
- PWHEAT(Y1) – DIFPBREAD(Y5): An undirected edge where wheat price and movements in bread prices are interrelated. The rho(5,1) of +0.23 has a

0.061 p-value. This edge has two observationally equivalent possibilities: Y5→ Y1 or Y1→ Y5.

- PMIXES(Y4) – PCOOKIES(Y7): An undirected edge where prices of mixes/doughs and of cookies/crackers are interrelated. The rho(7,4) of +0.22 has a 0.08 p-value. This edge also has two observationally equivalent possibilities: Y7→ Y4 or Y4→ Y7.
- QWHEAT (Y2) is exogenous.

These results generate the four plausible systems of causality as the unambiguous edges (first, third, and fifth) are combined with the ambiguous third and fourth edges with more than a single observational equivalent. One must choose among these four possible and competing systems of causal relations detailed in table 2. Table 2's non-intercept regressors and dependent variables are the respective variable's VAR-generated residual estimates. Hence, "Y1 = const, Y5" implies that Y5→ Y1 in contemporaneous time. An exogenous variable would have the intercept, const., as the only right-side regressor.

Table 2. Four alternative (Observationally Equivalent) systems of contemporaneous causal relations that emerge from TETRADII-suggested edges

System 1	**System 2**	**System 3**	**System 4**
Y1 = const.	Y1 = const.	Y1 = const., Y5	Y1 = const., Y5
Y2 = const.	Y2 = const.	Y2 = const.	Y2 = const.
Y3 = const., Y6, Y1	Y3 = const., Y6, Y1	Y3 = const., Y6, Y1	Y3 = const., Y6, Y1
Y4 = const.	Y4 = const., Y7	Y4 = const.	Y4 = const., Y7
Y5= const., Y1	Y5 = const., Y1	Y5 = const.	Y5 = const.
Y6 = const.	Y6 = const.	Y6 = const.	Y6 = const.
Y7 = const., Y4	Y7 = const.	Y7 = const., Y4	Y7 = const.
Schwarz value = -63.9	Schwarz value = -61.9	Schwarz value = -64.9	Schwarz value = -62.9

Notes.—Note that all equalities refer to regressions of the VAR model residuals of the endogenous variable against a constant or intercept, "const.", and the VAR model residuals of the other relevant variables. For example: the third equation in each system regresses the residuals of Y3 or PFLOUR against an intercept, the residuals of Y6 or PCEREAL, and the residuals of Y1 or PWHEAT. Note that Y1 through Y7 refer to the VAR model residuals of, respectively, PWHEAT, QWHEAT, PFLOUR, PMIXES, DIFPBREAD, PCEREAL, and PCOOKIES. See Schwarz (1978) and Haigh and Bessler (2002) for a details of how Schwarz's loss metric was applied to the above four competing systems of contemporaneous causal relations to score and then choose among them.

Source: Authors' application of Haigh and Bessler's (2003) regression methodology.

Schwarz's loss metric modified and adapted by Haigh and Bessler (2003) was used to score the four alternative, competing systems of causal relationships in table 2. The score for each model is provided in table 2, and is summarized in Haigh and Bessler (2003):

$$L^* = \log(|\Sigma^*|) + k\log(T)/T, \text{ where} \quad (2)$$

Σ^* is a diagonal matrix with diagonal elements of the variance/covariance

matrix associated with a linear representation of the disturbance terms from an acyclic graph fit to innovations from the VAR model. We chose the third system as it minimized the Schwarz loss metric (with the algebraically minimal value of -64.9). The following are the third system's relationships that were imposed onto the Bernanke structural VAR to form the DAG/Bernanke VAR model:

- DIFBPREAD or Y5→ PWHEAT or Y1.
- QWHEAT or Y2 is exogenous, as are the following that do not "receive" an arrow (← or →): PMIXES or Y4, DIFPBREAD or Y5, and PCEREAL or Y6.
- PCEREAL or Y6 →PFLOUR or Y3 ← PWHEAT or Y1.
- PMIXES or Y4 → PCOOKIES or Y7.

Imposing these relationships resolves the problem of contemporaneous correlation.

3. Analysis of Impulse Responses and FEV Decompositions to Discern Effects of a U.S. Wheat Import Quota

The impulse response function is well-known for its usefulness in simulating, over time, the effect of a shock in one of the system's series on itself and on other series in the system (Bessler 1984; Hamilton 1994, ch. 11). Such is accomplished by converting the VAR model into its moving average (MA) representation, the parameters of which are complex combinations of the VAR regression coefficients (Bessler 1984; Hamilton 1994, ch. 11). By imposing a one-time exogenous shock on one of the VAR variables, one may obtain a sort of dynamic map of how the modeled endogenous variables respond to the shock (Goodwin, McKenzie, and Djunaidi). More specifically, examination of the impulse response patterns simulated under a decline in QWHEAT, as explained below, can illuminate the dynamic nature and patterns of quarterly responses of the VAR model's endogenous variables when a U.S. import quota on wheat is imposed.

Using literature-established methods, multipliers are calculated from each simulation's statistically nonzero responses that emerge from the two simulations (a PWHEAT increase and a QWHEAT decrease and described below). The multipliers are similar to elasticities and indicate history's long run average percentage change in a responding variable per percentage change in a shock variable. Sign is important: a positive multiplier suggests that each percentage change in the shock variable directionally coincided with the shock variable changes, while a negative multiplier suggests that a variable response was in the opposite direction of the shock (readers interested in multiplier calculation methods are refereed to Babula, Bessler, and Payne (2004)).

Following Bessler, Yang, and Wongcharupan (2002, p. 819), Babula, Bessler, and Payne (2004) did not calculate confidence intervals on the impulse response functions. Although not a difficult task for a VAR ordered with a Choleski decomposition, calculating standard errors of impulse response functions for a Bernanke structural VAR was beyond the scope of this paper, and is left for future research. Yet clearly, one needs some sort of an indicator of impulse significance, such as provided by the routines of Kloek and VanDijk, which have been built into Doan's (1996) package for Choleski-ordered VAR impulse simulations. This is because often only a very small subset of all (here 12) calculated impulses typically achieves significance and these sets of statistically significant impulses comprise what are known as the duration times for the quarterly response patterns (see Babula and Bessler 1987 as an example). Previous research has used only impulses which were statistically nonzero when calculating the multipliers of response (Rich, Babula, and Romain 2002; Babula and Rich 2001). Fortunately, Rich, Babula, and Romain (2002) modeled the same endogenous wheat-based system as a Choleski-ordered VAR model, applied the Monte Carlo methods of Kloek and VanDijk to impulse response simulations of the a presumably quota-induced QWHEAT decline, and determined the sets (duration times) of statistically nonzero impulses. And further, impulse response patterns of Rich, Babula, and Romain (2002) were very similar to those generated by our DAG/Bernanke VAR. To calculate multipliers of response for our DAG/Bernanke VAR model's impulse response simulations, we applied the duration times (4-5 quarters) of statistically nonzero impulses (see Babula, Bessler, and Payne (2004)'s updated work of the Rich, Babula, and Romain (2002)) to the impulse responses which emerged from simulating our DAG/Bernanke VAR model under a similar QWHEAT-shock experiment.

We imposed a presumably quota-induced QWHEAT decline on the reduced form DAG/Bernanke VAR model and examined the dynamic aspects of quarterly response patterns in PWHEAT, PFLOUR, PMIXES, PCEREAL, and PCOOKIES.[6] Given the reduced form nature of the DAG/Bernanke VAR model, there is some subjective leeway in identifying the source of QWHEAT decrease imposed as the model's shock (Babula, Bessler, and Payne 2004; Babula and Rich, 2001, p. 10). While the quota-induced nature of the QWHEAT shock is valid and accepted in recent literature, the shock could have arisen from other sources – perhaps a decline in yield on the supply side or a decline in demand – since the DAG/Bernanke VAR model's estimated reduced-form relations quantity (QWHEAT) is neither quantity specifically supplied or demanded, but rather the quantity that clears the market after a full interplay of all, and often counterbalancing, demand and supply adjustments (Hamilton 1994, ch. 11; Babula, Bessler, and Payne 2004; and Babula and Rich 2001, pp. 10-11). So other sources could have generated the same shock.

As expected, the decline in QWHEAT elicited about a year's worth of wheat price increases, with the quarterly price increases taking a bell-shaped pattern. On average historically, each percentage drop in QWHEAT elicited a 0.7 percent rise in wheat price. Flour price increased for about a year with the drop in QWHEAT: increases took on a pattern of rising quarterly magnitudes and registered increases of 0.3 percent for each percentage drop in QWHEAT. The impulse response results suggest that the fall in QWHEAT would have little effect further downstream beyond the flour market, and effects would be confined to a the approximate time frame of a single crop cycle or market year. Yet Doan (1996, p. 8.13) strongly cautions against use of impulse response analysis alone, and suggests an accompanying analysis of FEV decompositions provided below.

---

[6] The size of the decline imposed and simulated was an orthogonalized standard error decrease of 9.7 percent. Yet it is well known from previous research that such VAR models as ours is linear, and given this linearity, the size of the shock is irrelevant. For example, by the model's linearity, once can characterize the effects of a 20 percent QWHEAT shock by simply multiplying the impulse response results from a 10 percent shock by the scaler 2.0. Likewise, one can characterize the effects of a 10 percent increase by simply taking the impulse response results from a 10 percent QWHEAT decline and multiplying the results by -1.0. The linear model provides the same multiplier regardless of shock size and shock sign. See Babula, Colling, and Gajewski (1994, p. 377). As well, we followed Babula, Bessler, and Payne (2004) and Rich, Babula, and Romain (2002) and do not analyze the dynamic attributes of DIFPBREAD response. This variable was included for purposes of adequacy of specification, and since it was necessary to so-include it in first differences, interpretation of this variable's impulses is not straightforward.

3.1. *Analysis of Forecast Error Variance Decompositions*

Analysis of decompositions of forecast error variance or FEV is a well-known VAR innovation accounting method for discerning relationships among the modeled system's time series (Sims; Bessler). Bessler (p. 111) noted that analysis of FEV decompositions is closely related to Granger causality analysis: not only do FEV decompositions suggest the simple existence of a causal relationship among two variables as does Granger causality analysis, but FEV decompositions go further and provide insight on the dynamic timing of such a relationship (Babula, Bessler, and Payne 2004; Babula and Rich 2001). Since a modeled endogenous variable's FEV is attributed at alternative horizons to shocks in each modeled variable (including itself), analysis of FEV decompositions not only provides evidence of the simple existence of a relationship among two variables, but it also illuminates the strength and dynamic timing of such a relationship (Bessler 1984, p. 111; Babula, Bessler, and Payne 2004; Babula and Rich, 2001, pp. 14-15; Saghaian, Hassan, and Reed, p. 107). Table 3 provides the FEV decompositions generated model for the seven wheat-related variables (see also Babula, Bessler, and Payne's (2004)). These FEV decompositions reflect the causal relationships embedded in both the lagged VAR model and the chosen causal ordering among the seven variables in contemporaneous time using Bessler and Akleman's (1998) DAG/Bernanke VAR modeling methods. A variable is endogenous (exogenous) when large (small) proportions of its FEV are attributed to variation of other modeled variables (itself) (Bessler 1984).

Babula, Bessler, and Payne (2004) provide an exhaustive analysis of these FEV decomposition results, which we do not replicate here: we refer interested readers to their article. We limit focus here on the FEV decomposition patterns relevant to the imposition of an import quota on U.S wheat. More specifically, we focus on how QWHEAT changes reflective of a wheat import quota's imposition, and subsequent PWHEAT movements, influence each other as well as the downstream wheat-related value added prices. Other results are mentioned when of interest.

Given that wheat production is climatically driven, and that part of QWHEAT is produced in the Canadian market, it is no surprise that wheat quantity is highly exogenous, here at the shorter run horizon. At horizons of four quarters or less, from 61 percent to 84 percent of QWHEAT behavior is explained by own-variation. As the time horizon lengthens, QWHEAT becomes more endogenous where own-variation explains only about half of its variation. The second most

Table 3. Decompositions of forecast error variance generated by the DAG/Bernanke VAR model

Variable explained	Horizon	PWHEAT	QWHEAT	PFLOUR	PMIXES	DIFPBREAD	PCEREAL	PCOOKIES
		Percent of forecast error variance explained by						
PWHEAT	1	79.92	5.22	3.32	0.47	10.35	0.31	0.41
	2	66.08	8.74	8.12	0.84	14.28	0.92	1.03
	4	47.85	12.45	15.59	1.11	18.14	2.63	2.25
	6	38.86	13.77	20.50	1.19	19.08	4.47	3.12
	8	34.46	14.11	21.34	1.24	19.10	6.10	3.65
	9	33.21	14.13	21.82	1.25	10.01	6.78	3.80
QWHEAT	1	12.40	84.38	1.54	0.18	1.46	0.00	0.03
	2	17.34	73.56	4.34	0.21	4.38	0.08	0.06
	4	19.03	60.80	9.56	0.25	9.15	0.79	0.42
	6	18.04	54.40	12.94	0.32	11.52	1.91	0.88
	8	16.94	51.00	14.84	0.38	12.55	3.06	1.23
	9	16.52	49.94	15.41	0.40	12.81	3.57	1.34
PFLOUR	1	75.36	2.28	8.70	2.21	9.30	2.09	0.16
	2	64.71	5.24	8.82	3.19	14.70	2.78	0.54
	4	46.34	9.53	14.31	3.27	20.64	4.47	1.44
	6	37.25	11.24	18.05	2.98	22.16	6.26	2.06
	8	33.11	11.74	19.80	2.82	22.32	7.84	2.38
	9	31.99	11.80	20.64	2.72	22.15	9.47	2.45
PMIXES	1	2.23	0.30	3.89	86.94	6.17	0.1	0.36
	2	6.06	0.87	5.87	70.20	9.03	0.29	0.67
	4	12.10	0.94	6.05	70.45	9.17	0.50	0.80
	6	14.95	1.31	6.,14	67.23	9.10	0.49	0.79
	8	15.74	2.05	6.96	64.24	9.56	0.55	0.89
	9	15.78	2.40	7.43	62.98	9.78	0.64	0.99

Table 3. Decompositions of forecast error variance generated by the DAG/Bernanke VAR model–Continued

Variable explained	Horizon	PWHEAT	QWHEAT	PFLOUR	PMIXES	DIFPBREAD	PCEREAL	PCOOKIES
DIFPBREAD	1	0.89	2.48	0.00	1.43	95.98	0.05	0.02
	2	1.42	2.87	0.04	2.51	91.74	0.10	0.09
	4	2.49	2.91	0.13	3.03	90.94	0.20	0.30
	6	3.25	2.85	0.14	3.01	89.87	0.24	0.64
	8	3.6	2.90	0.25	2.98	88.85	0.24	1.08
	9	3.67	2.95	0.35	2.97	88.51	0.25	1.31
PCEREAL	1	0.00	0.14	0.25	0.46	0.76	97.89	0.50
	2	0.07	0.12	0.68	0.64	2.53	94.58	1.38
	4	0.43	0.10	1.16	0.58	6.51	87.25	3.97
	6	0.68	0.11	1.13	0.51	9.38	80.94	7.25
	8	0.72	0.16	1.04	0.55	11.22	75.68	10.63
	9	0.70	0.19	1.01	0.59	11.90	73.41	12.20
PCOOKIES	1	1.46	1.76	0.17	8.48	2.95	0.04	85.15
	2	2.70	1.72	0.52	9.63	5.69	0.07	79.68
	4	5.42	1.28	0.79	9.06	10.58	0.10	72.76
	6	7.68	1.04	0.64	7.95	15.36	0.08	67.24
	8	9.14	1.13	0.70	7.06	19.54	0.10	62.34
	9	9.61	1.26	0.84	6.71	21.27	0.13	60.19

important factor of QWHEAT variation is PWHEAT, which explains up to 19 percent of QWHEAT behavior. Wheat and flour prices collectively explain from 30 to 32 percent of QWHEAT variations at the longer run horizons. As well, bread price variation accounts for up to 13 percent of QWHEAT behavior.

Wheat price has exogeneity patterns similar to those of QWHEAT: the price is highly exogenous at shorter run horizons, where own-variation explains up to 80 percent of its behavior. This exogeneity declines at longer run horizons, with own-variation accounting for about a third of its behavior.

QWHEAT and PWHEAT movements collectively explain the preponderance of the variation in both variables: up to 97 percent of QWHEAT and up to 87 percent of PWHEAT. Such clearly suggests that QWHEAT and PWHEAT are heavily dependent on each other, and that a QWHEAT decline from a quota would elicit a response in wheat price as well.

FEV decompositions in table 3 coincide with impulse response results, and suggest that flour price is heavily influenced by QWHEAT changes (perhaps from a quota) and from any subsequent movements in wheat price elicited by the QWHEAT changes. PFLOUR is highly endogenous, with no more than about 21 percent of its behavior explained by own-variation. A quota-induced fall in QWHEAT and any ensuing changes in PWHEAT would collectively explain up to nearly 80 percent of flour price behavior at horizons of 1-2 quarters, and from 44 to 56 percent of flour price behavior at horizons beyond two quarters. Movements of bread price explain a noticeable 21-22 percent of flour price variation at horizons beyond two quarters. Generally speaking, FEV decompositions and impulse response results suggest that shocks in QWHEAT, perhaps quota-induced, and subsequent changes in wheat price heavily impact the wheat flour market downstream.

Recent VAR econometric research on U.S. wheat-related markets conclude that the importance of wheat market shocks (changes in QWHEAT and PWHEAT) lessens as the level of downstream processing for a wheat-related, value-added market rises (Babula, Bessler, and Payne 1994; Babula and Rich 1981). Wheat-related costs take on decreasing shares of production costs as the level of processing rises: for example, FEV decompositions suggest that QWHEAT and PWHEAT movements collectively explain from 43 percent to 80 percent of PFLOUR variation, and for no more than about 11 percent of PCOOKIES variation. So a quota-induced fall in QWHEAT and subsequent changes in wheat price are expected to have generally lessened market effects the further one proceeds downstream from the wheat farm gate.

Beyond the flour market, FEV decompositions in table 3 support impulse response results and suggest that a quota-induced change in QWHEAT, and any elicited PWHEAT changes, are likely to have, at most, moderate influences on wheat-related prices. Presumably quota-induced changes in both wheat market variables account for no more than about 18 percent of PMIXES behavior; no more than about 11 percent of PCOOKIES behavior; and negligible proportions of the variation in DIFPBREAD. And what influence that the presumably quota-induced wheat market changes do have on the downstream mixes/doughs and cookies/crackers markets occur at the longer run horizons beyond a single market year or crop cycle (4-5 quarters). Perhaps such longer horizons are required for downstream market agents to alter long term contracts (purchases/sales) and to adjust fixed capital investment levels (Babula, Bessler, and Payne 2004). Note that these longer run downstream effects on these two markets did not emerge from the impulse response results.

Also of note is that beyond the flour market, variation in bread price does noticeably influence prices of wheat-related and value-added products. Bread price movements account for up to more than 10 percent of the variation in the prices of mixes/doughs, wheat-based breakfast cereals, and cookies/crackers. In fact, table 3 suggests that bread price variation contributes noticeably to the explanation of the behavior of all seven VAR variables, with little feedback from the other six variables to the explanation of bread price variation (for more details, see Babula, Bessler, and Payne (2004)). Bread price was the only variable that generated clear evidence of a unit root. This may imply that bread price is an efficient price where there is no appreciable predictability of its behavior from its past, as with any random walk, and where the best prediction is its current value. The bread market, compared with the other represented markets, appeared very competitive with its homogenous product (represented by the chosen PPI), the large number of U.S. bread producers, and with its near-universal product consumption by more than 90 percent of American households (Babula, Bessler, and Payne 1994). This may fulfill Samuelson's (1965) arguments that the bread market may be relatively more efficient than the wheat-based markets represented in the DAG/Bernanke VAR model; that as an efficient price, bread prices do not return to a constant historical mean, while other wheat-related prices do; and that bread price may constitute a widely-watched "informational" variable upon which the grain-based foods industry base decisions (Babula, Bessler, and Payne 2004). That is, Babula, Bessler, and Payne (2004) argued that producers of the less competitively structured markets for other wheat-based, value-added markets may look to bread price behavior for guidance in administering their other wheat-based value-added product prices – an argument which they admit is conjectural and would constitute a productive area of future research.

4. Summary and Conclusions

We analyzed DAG/Bernanke VAR model's impulse response function and forecast error variance (FEV) decompositions in order to discern the market impacts of imposing a U.S. import quota on wheat and wheat products, resembling that imposed on certain U.S. imports of Canadian wheat during the year ending September 11, 1995.

The impulse response function of the reduced-form DAG/Bernanke VAR model was simulated for a presumably quota-induced decline in the available quantity of wheat. Results suggest that on average historically, each percent decline in wheat quantity would elicit a 0.7 percent rise in wheat price and a 0.3 percent rise in flour price over the period of about a single market year, without having much of an effect on the markets further downstream.

Analysis of FEV decompositions, combined with the impulse response results, suggested that a presumably quota-induced fall in wheat demand and supplies would elicit an ensuing change in wheat price, and movements in both of these wheat market variables would in turn have certain effects on downstream markets. As with the impulse response results, the FEV decompositions suggest that a quota-induced wheat market shocks will appreciably affect flour price, although these FEV results suggest that such price of flour (PFLOUR) influence would extend beyond the time frame of a single market year suggested by the impulse results. And while impulse response results suggested that a quota -induced decline in QWHEAT would have little or no downstream effects beyond the wheat flour market, FEV decompositions suggested that there would be some effects on the mixes/doughs and cookies/crackers markets, and generally at longer term horizons beyond a single market year.

As with Babula, Bessler, and Payne, we also encountered evidence that suggested a one-way causal relationship from bread price movements to all six other endogenous variables with little or no causal feedback from these six variables to bread price behavior. Combined with other econometric evidence cited above, these results suggest that the bread market may be more competitive and perhaps more efficient than the other markets in the VAR model, and that bread price may serve as a "flagship" or "informational" variable upon which the agents from other less efficient and less competitive wheat-related markets may base business decisions.

References

1. Babula, R. and D. Bessler. "Farmgate, Processor, and Consumer Price Transmissions in the Wheat Sector." *Journal of Agricultural Economics Research* 41,3(1987):23-29.
2. Babula, R., P. Colling, and G. Gajewski. "Dynamic Impacts of Rising Lumber Prices on Housing-Related Prices." *Agribusiness: An International Journal* 10(1994):373-388.
3. Babula, R., D. Bessler, and W. Payne. "Dynamic Relationships Among U.S. Wheat-Related Markets: Applying Acyclic Graphs to a Time Series Model." *Journal of Agricultural and Applied Economics* 36,1(April, 2004): 1-22.
4. Babula, R. and C. Jabara. "The Wheat War of 1994: Comment." *Canadian Journal of Agricultural Economics* 47(1999):89-98.
5. Babula, R., and K. Rich. "Time Series Analysis of the U.S. Durum Wheat and Pasta Markets." *Journal of Food Distribution Research* 32,2(2001):1-19.
6. Bernanke, B. "Alternative Explanations of the Money-Income Correlation." *Carnegie-Rochester Conference Series on Public Policy* 25(1986):45-100.
7. Bessler, D. "An Analysis of Dynamic Economic Relationships: An Application to the U.S. Hog Market." *Canadian Journal of Agricultural Economics* 32(1984):109-124.
8. Bessler, D. and D. Akleman. "Farm Prices, Retail Prices, and Directed Graphs: Results for Pork and Beef." *American Journal of Agricultural Economics* 80,5(1998):1144-1149.
9. Bessler, D., J. Yang, and M. Wongcharupan. "Price Dynamics in the International Wheat Market: Modeling with Error Correction and Directed Acyclic Graphs." *Journal of Regional Science* 42,2(2002):793-825.
10. Canada-U.S. Joint Commission on Grains. *Preliminary Report*. Ottawa, Canada and Washington DC: Canada-U.S. Commission on Grains, June, 1995.
11. Doan, T. "Generalized Impulse Responses." *The RATSletter* 15(July, 2002):4.
12. Doan, T. *RATS Users' Manual, Version 4*. Evanston, IL: Estima, 1996.
13. Glickman, D., and M. Kantor. "Joint Statement from Agriculture Secretary Dan Glickman and Ambassador Michael Kantor Regarding U.S.-Canadian Grain Issues." U.S. Department of Agriculture, Office of Communications, Release no. 0658.95, Washington DC, September 12, 1995.
14. Goodwin, H.L., A. McKenzie, and H. Djunaidi. "Which Broiler Part is the Best Part:" *Journal of Agricultural and Applied Economics* 35,1(December, 2003):forthcoming.
15. Haigh, M., and B. Bessler. "Causality and Price Discovery: An Application of Directed Acyclic Graphs." *Journal of Business* (2003): forthcoming.
16. Hamilton, J. *Time Series Analysis*. Princeton, NJ: Princeton University Press, 1994.
17. Johansen, S. and K. Juselius. "Maximum Likelihood and Inference on Cointegration: With Applications to the Demand for Money." *Oxford Bulletin of Economics and Statistics* 52(1990):169-210.
18. Johansen, S. and K. Juselius. "Testing Structural Hypotheses in Multivariate Cointegration Analysis of the PPP and UIP for UK." *Journal of Econometrics* 53(1992):211-244.

19. Jonnala, S., S. Fuller, and D. Bessler. "A GARCH Approach to Modeling Ocean Grain Freight Rates." *International Journal of Maritime Economics* 4(2002): 103-125.
20. Kloek, T. and H. VanDijk. "Bayesian Estimates of Equation System Parameters: An Application of Monte Carlo." *Econometrica* 46(1978):1-20.
21. Milling and Baking News Staff. "Census Revisions Alter Semolina, Wheat Flour Production." *Milling and Baking News*, May 16, 2000, pp. 1 & 19.
22. Patterson, K. *An Introduction to Applied Econometrics: A Time Series Approach*. New York: Palgrave (St. Martin's Press), 2000.
23. Pearl, J. "Causal Diagrams for Empirical Research." *Biometrica* 82 (December 1995): 669-710.
24. Rich, K., R. Babula, and R. Romain. "Chapter 5: The Dynamics in the Wheat and Wheat Products Sector: U.S.-Canada Comparisons." In W. Koo and W. Wilson, Eds., *Agricultural Trade Under CUSTA*. Hauppauge, NY: Nova Science Publishers, Inc., 2002, pp. 93-118.
25. Sagharian, S., M. Hassan, and M. Reed. "Overshooting of Agricultural Prices in Four Asian Economies." *Journal of Agricultural and Applied Economics* 34,1(2002):95-109.
26. Samuelson, P. "Proof that Properly Anticipated Prices Fluctuate Randomly," *Industrial Management Review* 6(1965):41-49.
27. Scheines, R., P. Spirtes, C. Glymour, and C. Mee: TETRADII: *Tools for Causal Modeling*. Pittsburgh, PA: Carnegie Mellon University, 1994.
28. Schwarz, G. "Estimating the Dimension of a Model." *Annals of Statistics* 6(1978):461-464.
29. Sims, C. "Macroeconomics and Reality." *Econometrica* 48(1980):1-48.
30. Spirtes, P., C. Glymour, and R. Scheines. *Causation, Prediction, and Search*. New York: Springer-Verlag, 2000.
31. Tiao, G. And G. Box. "Modeling Multiple Time Series: With Applications." *Journal of the American Statistical Society* 76(1978):802-816.
32. U.S. Department of Agriculture, Economic Research Service (USDA, ERS). "Wheat Outlook," WHS-0103, January 14, 2003, p. 12. Source of QWHEAT data from 2001/2002:3 through 2002/2003:2.
33. U.S. Department of Agriculture, Economic Research Service (USDA, ERS). *Wheat Situation and Outlook Yearbook*, 2002. WHS-2002. Source of QWHEAT data from 1985/86:1 through 2001/2001:2.
34. U.S. Department of Labor, Bureau of Labor Statistics (Labor, BLS). Producer price index data based. Retrieved from www.bls.gov, on January 31, 2002.
35. U.S. International Trade Commission (USITC). *Wheat, Wheat Flour, and Semolina, Investigation No. 22-54*. USITC Publication no. 2794. Washington, DC: USITC, July 1994.
36. U.S. Department of Labor, Bureau of the Census (Labor, Census). *Current Industrial Reports, Flour Milling Products* (various quarterly and yearly issues). Quarterly 1997-2002 data from various quarterly issues; quarterly 1985-1996 data calculated from monthly data from annual summaries. Washington, DC: 1985-2001.
37. Whittaker, J. *Graphical Models in Applied Multivariate Statistics*. Chichester, UK: Wiley, 1990.

LIBERALIZING QUOTAS ON TEXTILES AND CLOTHING: HAS THE ATC ACTUALLY WORKED?

Joseph F. Francois

Tinbergen Institute[1]

Dean Spinanger

Institute for World Economics[2]

1. Introduction

The Ministerial Declaration at Punta Del Este that launched the Uruguay Round stated in pure, sugar-coated diplomatic understatements that the "Negotiations in the area of textiles and clothing shall aim to formulate modalities that would permit the eventual integration of this sector into GATT on the basis of strengthened GATT rules and disciplines."[3] What was probably interpreted by some to be a direct thrust at the jugular of quotas on imports of textiles and clothing products from developing countries, was no doubt interpreted by others to be a brief to finagle and to finesse an elimination that was not meant to be one. But it really cannot be denied that the bottom line of GATT-speak was nothing else than the launching of negotiations to achieve an Agreement on Textiles and Clothing (ATC) to lead to the elimination of almost 40 years of discriminatory protection in violation of the basic precepts of the GATT system.

The textile and clothing (T&C) sectors had long been treated as a very special case within the world trading system, with their own regulatory framework. This was first institutionalized in the beginning of the 1960s with the Short Term Arrangements (STA) regarding international trade in cotton textiles. The STA aimed at an "orderly" (GATT-speak for keeping markets closed for as long as possible) opening of restricted markets to avoid (for the importing industrialized countries) detrimental market disruptions (GATT-speak for trade-induced structural adjustment). The definition of "market disruption" adopted by the Contracting Parties in 1960 entailed the possibility of singling out imports of

[1] The author may be contacted through the Tinbergen Institute, Rotterdam, the Netherlands via email at *francois@few.eur.nl*.

[2] The author may be contacted through the Institute for World Economics, Kiel, Germany via email at *dspinanger@ifw.uni-kiel.de*.

[3] In biblical terms this is in essence saying that "the world was not created in a day." And how long did it take to create the world?

particular products from particular countries as the disrupting source. This opened the door for the series of bilaterally negotiated quota restrictions that became the rule in the following the Long Term Arrangement (LTA) in 1962. Details on the subsequent evolution of the system are provided in Table 1.

Table 1. A progression of acronyms from STA to ATC

Date	Action taken
1955: December	Japan (MITI) unilaterally restrains exports of cotton fabrics and clothing to the United States "to promote mutually beneficial relations".
1957: January	Five year agreement reached with Japan on limiting overall textile exports to the United States.
1958: November	United Kingdom signs "voluntary" limitation on cotton T&C products with Hong Kong, by threatening otherwise imposition at lower than prevailing volume levels.
1959: September	United Kingdom signs similar restraint agreements with India and Pakistan.
1960: November	GATT Contracting Parties recognize the problem of "market disruption", even if it is just threatened; serves as "excuse" for establishing future NTBs.
1961: July	The Short Term Arrangement (STA) is agreed.
1962: February	The Long Term Arrangement (LTA) is agreed, to commence October 1, 1962, and last for five years.
1963–64	The United States tries and fails to secure an international agreement on wool products.
1965: June	The United States tries and fails to negotiate restraints on Japanese wool products.
1966: June	The United Kingdom implements a global quota scheme in violation of the LTA – the LTA providing only for product-specific restraints.
1967: April	Agreement is reached to extend the LTA for three years.
1969–71	United States negotiates VERs with Asian suppliers on wool and man-made fibers.
1970: October	Agreement is reached to extend the LTA for three years. It was later extended three months more, to fill the gap until the MFA came into effect.
1973: December	The MFA is agreed, to commence January 1, 1974, and to last for four years.
1977: July–December	The European Economic Community and the United States negotiate bilateral agreements with developing countries prior to agreeing to extension of the MFA.
1977: December	The MFA is extended for four years.
1981: December	The MFA is renewed for five years. The United States, under pressure from increased imports resulting from dollar appreciation, negotiates tough quotas.
1986: July	The MFA is extended for 5 years, to conclude with Uruguay Round.
1991: July	The MFA is extended pending outcome of the Uruguay Round negotiations.

1993: December	The Uruguay Round (UR) draft final act provides for a 10-year phase-out of all MFA and other quotas on textiles in ATC. MFA extend until UR comes into force.
1995: January 1	1st ATC tranche liberalized by importing countries – 16% of 1990 import volume.
1998: January 1	2nd ATC tranche liberalized by importing countries – 17% of 1990 import volume.
2002: January 1	3rd ATC tranche liberalized by importing countries – 18% of 1990 import volume.
2005: January 1	4th ATC tranche liberalized by importing countries – 49% of 1990 import volume.

Source: Based on Francois, Glismann, and Spinanger (2000).

By the start of the 1970s, it had become apparent that the multiplicity of makeshift arrangements protecting the T&C industries in industrialized countries, but inhibiting these industries in developing countries, would have to be replaced. Ultimately the Multifibre Arrangement (MFA) was agreed upon and put into effect as of January 1, 1974. Its product coverage was extended to non-cotton textiles and clothing. The final MFA (*i.e.*, # IV) was extended several times until the Agreement on Textiles and Clothing as an integral part of the Uruguay Round agreement came into force.

Like the preceding arrangements, the MFA provided rules for the imposition of quotas, either through bilateral agreements or unilateral actions, when surges of imports caused market disruption, or the threat thereof, in importing countries. In the years leading up to the Uruguay Round Agreements, six developed participants actively applied quotas under the MFA – the EU, the U.S., Canada, Norway, Finland and Austria. These were aimed almost exclusively at imports from developing countries. Sweden liberalized its textile and clothing regime in 1991 and withdrew from the MFA agreement.[4] However, it had to effectively rejoin this regime when it joined the European Union. Two other developed country participants, Japan and Switzerland, did not impose MFA quotas, but instead restricted themselves to "signaling" a readiness to apply quotas by the act of being signatories to the MFA agreement, combined with (active) import surveillance.

[4] In the years following Sweden's EU accession in 1995, when it had to reintroduce quotas on T&C imports from developing counties, it continued to follow a course of trying to open up niches in this wall of protection. Not even when Sweden – with other Nordic members - tried to loosen the restrictiveness of the quotas on baby clothes within the EU was a consensus to be found in the Community. And it was particularly in this area that families were being burdened with the high costs of quota rents.

As shown by Winters (1994), import surveillance can, at least in concentrated industries, induce a fall in import levels as producers in the affected exporting countries try to forestall the imposition of explicit quotas. The restrictiveness of the applied quotas, whether under the defunct MFA or the still-prevailing ATC regime, varies from product to product, and from supplier to supplier, and aggregate measures are highly uncertain.

The Uruguay Round Agreement on Textiles and Clothing (ATC) has required a gradual phase out of the quota restrictions carried over from the MFA regime, as detailed in Table 2. The integration of the products covered by the agreement was to be achieved in three stages under a ten-year transition period. The first stage called for the integration of products comprising not less than 16 percent of the total volume of each member's 1990 imports of the products listed in the annex to the Agreement. The second stage, beginning in year 4, required the integration of a further 17 percent. The third stage, beginning in year 8, required that another 18 percent of imports be brought under normal GATT rules.

Table 2. Integration scheme for textiles and clothing

	Integration (Base: 1990 import volume of the products listed in annex)	**Growth rate of residual quotas** (Base: Previously agreed MFA growth rates of quotas)
Stage I. (January 1, 1995)	16%	16% higher growth rate than initially (Ex: 3% to 3.48%)
Stage II. (January 1, 1998)	Further 17% (total 33%)	Increase by 25% (Ex: 3.48% to 4.35%)
Stage III. (January 1, 2002)	Further 18% (total 51%)	Increase by 27% (Ex: 4.35% to 5.52%)
End of the 10 year transition period (January 1, 2005)	Remaining 49% (total 100%)	

Unfortunately, each importing country was free to choose the products it would integrate at each stage, the only constraint being that they had to encompass products from each of the four groupings: tops and yarn, fabrics, made-up textile products, and clothing. Products that remained restricted during the transition period were to benefit from a progressively increasing quota. The previously applied MFA quota annual growth rates were to be scaled up by a factor of 16 percent in the first stage – for instance, from 3 percent to ($3\times1.16 =$) 3.48% – an additional 25 percent in the second stage, and yet another 27 percent in the third stage. This turned a 3 percent initial annual growth rate to 5.52 percent in the third stage.

In theory, at the end of the ten-year transition period, all remaining quantitative restrictions on textiles and clothing (carried over from the MFA regime) are to be terminated. The process was meant to be smooth, with a gradual phase-out of restrictions. In reality, there has been worry in policy communities that much of the quota liberalization has been backloaded until the very end of the 10-year phase-in period. This is due partly to disingenuous graduation (*i.e.*, the graduation of products not actually restricted) in the first phases of the ATC.

2. Quota Rents and Effective Preference Erosion

In addition to backloading, an additional area of concern related to the implementation of the ATC and associated Uruguay Round MFN-tariff reductions has been the scope for preference erosion, especially for the least developed African countries. Virtually all African countries have entered into contractual preference arrangements with the European Union, and obtain preferential treatment for certain exports in the United States and Japan, as well as in other developed country markets under GSP schemes.[5] There has consequently been a concern that implementation of the market access results of the Uruguay Round would diminish rather than augment their trade and economic prospects (Blackhurst *et al.* 1996).

The actual scope for general preference erosion for African Lomé (now Cotonou) countries is very limited. Over half of the EU's imports from African countries are petroleum and other fuels, already bound duty-free, and agricultural and industrial products divide the rest. Access for industrial products is the main area where the EU's MFN-tariff reductions will have any impact. Even here, almost three-quarters of African exports to the European Union already enter at rates of less than 3 percent, and this percentage could rise to 80 percent. For these products, the margin of preference afforded under Lomé is likely to be consumed in large part by associated administrative costs.[6]

---

[5] The ACP-EC Fourth Lomé Convention covers Sub-Saharan African countries with the exception of South Africa and "free trade" agreements covering North African countries. These arrangements are detailed in GATT (1993a, pp. 44-46). In 1993, about two-thirds of Africa's exports were shipped to the European Union. The Lomé Convention has since been renegotiated/replaced by the Cotonou Agreement.

[6] The Uruguay Round negotiating group on market access considered that tariffs at or below 3 percent were "nuisance" tariffs. Herin (1986) found that the costs associated with meeting the origin requirements for EFTA exporters to the European Union led to payment of MFN duties on one-quarter of EFTA's exports to the EU. Manchin (2004) reports similar results, at a 4 percent threshold, for EU trade preferences under Cotonou.

Though not through tariffs, there is scope for relative preference erosion of another sort under the ATC. This is because at the start of the ATC phase-out, some countries and regions faced much greater restrictions than others. The lower-income suppliers in India and elsewhere in South Asia, in particular, faced negative preferences, in the sense that they faced greater effective restrictions than suppliers from East Asia and elsewhere. The distributional effect of the MFA restrictions was thus to discriminate between those developing countries covered by "Lomé" (or rather its successor), and against suppliers like India and Pakistan. Even where some least developed countries were favoured by preferential access, this was been largely at the expense of other least developed countries.

The European Union has addressed the problem of relative preference erosion following ATC quota elimination, to some extent, with the "Everything But Arms" initiative.[7] With the exclusion of agricultural trade, the poorest developing countries now receive duty-free access to the European market, although the value of these preferences is questionable (see Manchin 2004). Most other developing countries also receive some preferences, with the result that several Latin American countries (Mexico, Caribbean producers) also receive or are soon to receive steep preferences. This pattern is illustrated in Tables 3 and 4. These tables offer a "best guess", based on data derived from WTO MFN schedules, European Union data, and U.S. tariff data, of the pattern of tariffs on textiles and clothing trade that will prevail in the brave new world of post-ATC T&C trade. We have also assumed in the Table that the Free Trade Area of the Americas (FTAA) is implemented.

The pattern that emerges is as follows. The elimination of ATC quotas, and the accession of China to the WTO, means that textile and clothing trade is likely to shift dramatically toward both China, and also the Indian sub-continent. The MFA and ATC have, in effect, been serving as a negative preference system, helping other developing country suppliers at the expense of these two potentially dominant suppliers. The system of preferences in place on tariffs will, to some extent, compensate for the loss of implicit margins provided by the ATC quotas. However, we can also expect that, with further reductions in T&C tariffs under Doha negotiations, the shift of T&C trade to the more competitive

[7] Because of agricultural product exclusions, the joke has been that this is better called Everything but Farms.

Table 3. Bi-lateral Tariffs for Textiles Trade: MFN Basis and Including Major Regional Agreements and Preference Schemes as of 2001

	Importing Region →																								
Exporters	Aus	NZ	Chn	HKG	Jap	Kor	Tai	ASEAN5	Vnm	Bgl	Ind	SA	Can	Mex	USA	CBI	ATP	Braz	MERC	Chl	OLA	EU	Tur	AMEt	RfW	Sav
Australia (Aus)		0.0	15.6	0.0	0.4	2.6	1.7	5.1	33.3	18.1	23.0	50.0	10.7	4.3	9.5	0.0	10.8	17.0	18.7	11.0	18.9	2.2	1.2	7.2	16.5	11.1
New Zealand (NZ)	0.0		15.6	0.0	0.8	2.9	0.7	4.6	7.6	15.6	20.1	3.2	2.4	1.6	4.1	11.7	10.0	10.9	9.3	11.0	18.5	0.2	0.1	1.2	26.1	7.1
China (Chn)	24.6	16.6		0.0	10.0	9.5	7.8	13.9	36.4	36.1	33.8	26.7	18.3	18.8	8.7	12.3	17.7	17.9	18.9	11.0	14.7	9.5	9.7	18.2	15.6	16.3
Hong Kong (HKG)	13.0	5.1	25.6		12.3	8.3	12.6	19.3	35.1	35.7	36.8	28.9	21.4	26.1	12.3	18.5	18.0	18.0	19.4	11.0	16.4	12.5	9.3	17.0	9.2	17.7
Japan (Jap)	14.5	2.6	27.7	0.0		8.0	5.9	11.9	36.6	30.6	32.3	37.4	13.9	14.8	10.8	8.7	14.8	15.9	16.3	11.0	12.4	7.9	8.7	10.6	8.9	14.5
Korea (Kor)	17.7	4.3	26.6	0.0	9.1		6.0	15.4	33.8	33.7	37.2	32.3	14.8	14.9	13.2	13.2	16.4	16.1	17.1	11.0	16.2	10.2	9.2	14.8	11.3	15.8
Chinese Taipei (Tai)	12.9	5.5	26.6	0.0	6.1	7.4		15.6	31.2	34.4	37.5	44.9	17.0	15.5	12.4	12.6	15.3	17.0	17.8	11.0	17.3	10.3	9.3	18.3	11.6	16.3
ASEAN5	10.6	5.3	22.3	0.0	6.4	7.5	4.2	9.7	22.2	27.6	34.5	32.3	16.6	14.3	12.6	9.4	16.4	16.5	16.8	11.0	17.4	10.0	9.0	14.1	10.6	14.3
Vietnam (Vnm)	23.2	19.4	21.9	0.0	9.5	8.0	7.7	8.5		10.4	31.0	28.2	19.6	26.9	8.1	0.0	6.3	19.1	18.2	11.0	18.3	8.8	9.4	10.2	10.9	13.4
Bangladesh (Bgl)	0.9	8.1	8.8	0.0	5.8	7.8	5.0	8.0	13.6		40.0	48.5	21.3	21.6	12.1	19.9	11.9	14.3	8.5	11.0	17.4	0.0	0.5	10.6	9.3	12.2
India (Ind)	12.4	7.5	11.6	0.0	6.4	8.0	4.2	8.7	13.6	10.4		23.5	15.0	16.4	7.7	9.1	16.5	16.4	16.5	11.0	17.8	7.0	5.5	16.7	9.6	10.9
South Asia (SA)	21.4	6.0	13.3	0.0	4.4	8.0	3.5	8.0	13.6	10.6	37.4	19.9	15.2	17.4	10.5	20.0	19.8	17.5	18.3	11.0	17.4	7.7	7.5	17.4	11.3	13.5
Canada (Can)	7.5	6.6	15.5	0.0	10.9	8.0	6.8	12.2	0.4	37.5	36.8	49.2		0.0	0.0	0.0	0.0	0.0	0.0	0.0	0.0	7.4	8.3	10.2	8.2	12.4
Mexico (Mex)	13.5	14.1	15.2	0.0	10.0	7.9	2.6	11.4	40.0	10.4	30.5	62.3	0.0		0.0	0.0	0.0	0.0	0.0	0.0	0.0	2.0	6.6	7.4	8.4	13.0
USA	12.6	5.4	17.8	0.0	9.1	7.7	5.1	10.6	26.8	31.6	36.6	40.3	0.0	0.0		0.0	0.0	0.0	0.0	0.0	0.0	8.0	8.2	16.4	9.9	13.6
CBI	27.3	23.5	33.3	0.0	12.8	8.0	12.6	14.3	13.6	10.4	40.0	1.4	21.1	0.0	0.0		0.0	0.0	0.0	0.0	0.0	0.0	10.1	8.0	9.5	14.6
Andean Trd.Pact (ADP)	23.2	10.2	18.7	0.0	5.6	5.5	6.2	17.2	12.6	6.6	26.7	5.7	15.1	0.0	0.0	0.0		0.0	0.0	0.0	0.0	0.0	7.1	14.8	7.1	12.3
Brazil (Bra)	18.3	0.3	19.4	0.0	0.8	23.3	7.7	5.8	0.0	0.0	30.2	34.5	14.2	0.0	0.0	0.0	0.0		0.0	0.0	0.0	7.7	5.8	20.3	8.7	10.7
MERCOSUR (MERC)	13.4	5.2	15.1	0.0	0.4	5.1	1.5	2.7	13.4	10.4	23.3	4.9	10.4	0.0	0.0	0.0	0.0	0.0		0.0	0.0	1.7	3.4	9.4	8.4	8.9
Chile (Chl)	20.0	12.1	16.9	0.0	0.6	4.6	10.3	11.7	15.0	10.4	31.0	7.6	13.3	0.0	0.0	0.0	0.0	0.0	0.0	0	0.0	3.0	7.8	24.3	0.7	12.3
Other Latin A. (OLA)	8.8	0.4	15.8	0.0	4.4	7.4	3.3	2.2	13.6	10.4	28.4	1.5	16.6	0.0	0.0	0.0	0.0	0.0	0.0	0.0		6.9	7.8	6.7	0.5	9.9
European Union (EU)	12.2	5.8	21.6	0.0	7.9	7.7	8.0	9.8	31.4	31.6	32.9	37.6	12.7	15.8	9.5	13.8	15.5	14.6	15.4	11.7	16.0		8.5	25.2	9.4	15.0
Turkey (Tur)	13.9	11.1	16.2	0.0	8.9	8.0	4.2	5.7	40.0	32.5	22.6	31.8	15.5	14.5	12.2	10.7	14.8	16.4	18.6	11.0	15.1	0.0		15.8	12.5	14.1
Africa /Mideastt (AME)	12.6	9.8	12.4	0.0	6.3	5.6	5.5	6.2	26.1	7.5	33.2	51.9	13.5	15.2	11.8	7.6	14.4	15.5	14.6	11.0	13.4	0.0	0.0	18.2	7.8	13.3
Rest of World (RoW)	25.0	14.0	21.8	0.0	8.6	7.9	8.9	9.0	28.8	37.4	32.4	37.5	16.1	16.0	11.8	16.1	15.2	15.8	17.0	11.0	14.6	7.3	7.1	13.2	11.1	16.1
Simple average (Sav)	14.4	8.0	18.2	0.0	6.3	7.4	5.7	9.9	21.5	20.0	30.7	29.7	13.4	13.8	8.7	12.9	14.6	14.8	16.0	10.6	16.6	5.4	6.7	13.8	10.1	13.2

Table 4: Bi-lateral Tariffs for Clothing Trade: MFN basis and including major regional agreements and preference schemes as of 2001

	Importing Region →																								
Exporters	Aus	NZ	Chn	HKG	Jap	Kor	Tai	ASEAN5	Vnm	Bgl	Ind	SA	Can	Mex	USA	CBI	ATP	Bra	MERC	Chl	OLA	EU	Tur	AMEt	ROW	Sav
Australia (Aus)		0.0	28.5	0.0	13.2	6.0	12.3	8.1	45.5	10.2	9.4	34.8	14.1	33.6	9.7	0.0	6.5	15.7	23.3	11.0	19.3	8.1	3.1	17.4	30.1	14.4
New Zealand (NZ)	0.0		23.3	0.0	14.4	5.6	11.0	4.1	2.9	10.2	4.6	17.7	8.7	10.1	5.6	0.0	6.1	20.0	22.7	11.0	9.0	6.2	3.9	11.7	25.1	9.4
China (Chn)	29.8	25.2		0.0	12.5	8.0	11.2	8.9	49.9	37.4	34.4	44.3	20.5	29.1	11.3	14.2	19.4	20.2	20.9	11.0	20.3	11.1	7.4	22.1	19.1	19.5
Hong Kong (HKG)	27.1	24.1	32.2		13.2	8.0	13.1	14.8	49.3	36.5	38.4	20.5	21.8	34.8	12.7	11.4	20.0	20.1	20.7	11.0	20.0	12.5	7.0	28.0	14.5	20.5
Japan (Jap)	25.5	23.4	33.0	0.0		8.0	13.7	18.6	49.9	10.2	40.0	47.4	19.6	34.8	11.5	10.7	19.9	19.9	20.0	11.0	19.4	11.7	9.7	20.6	15.2	19.7
Korea (Kor)	25.1	24.1	31.2	0.0	12.3		13.0	17.5	49.5	37.4	40.0	34.5	21.7	33.9	14.9	22.4	19.9	20.0	20.9	11.0	20.5	10.6	6.8	20.7	20.7	21.1
Chinese Taipei (Tai)	15.6	21.6	32.3	0.0	10.7	8.0		14.7	46.7	37.3	39.8	61.4	21.8	32.6	15.3	24.6	18.7	20.0	20.7	11.0	21.2	11.4	7.5	27.6	12.3	21.3
ASEAN5	30.4	25.1	32.6	0.0	11.5	8.0	13.0	4.6	46.8	34.5	35.7	31.9	22.0	34.1	14.5	12.5	18.9	20.1	21.0	11.0	19.7	12.2	9.7	19.2	17.0	20.2
Vietnam (Vnm)	32.1	25.6	30.9	0.0	12.4	8.0	13.4	2.3		10.2	40.0	2.2	21.2	34.0	15.3	25.0	20.0	20.1	20.2	11.0	8.0	10.1	13.4	13.7	12.7	16.1
Bangladesh (Bgl)	29.8	22.4	31.4	0.0	13.2	8.0	13.5	0.4	29.4		40.0	49.6	21.9	30.7	12.5	25.0	19.8	23.8	20.2	11.0	8.9	0.0	12.5	15.7	16.7	18.3
India (Ind)	31.0	25.9	32.2	0.0	12.0	7.8	12.4	8.1	29.4	10.2		34.6	21.5	34.9	12.8	16.8	20.0	20.0	20.5	11.0	20.4	8.6	11.0	17.7	16.3	17.4
South Asia (SA)	26.8	23.4	29.4	0.0	11.8	7.9	6.0	5.7	29.4	10.2	22.3	32.5	21.5	34.4	13.9	24.5	17.3	20.0	22.0	11.0	19.8	8.9	8.7	15.8	18.6	17.7
Canada (Can)	26.5	24.8	28.4	0.0	14.3	6.2	13.8	16.2	50.0	10.2	40.0	17.1		0.0	0.0	0.0	0.0	0.0	0.0	0.0	0.0	9.4	9.5	19.5	21.0	16.8
Mexico (Mex)	25.7	25.5	0.0	0.0	12.7	8.0	14.6	9.0	29.4	0.0	0.0	19.2	0.0		0.0	0.0	0.0	0.0	0.0	0.0	0.0	2.5	13.2	13.5	16.7	12.2
USA	23.8	23.0	28.8	0.0	12.5	7.2	13.0	14.1	49.8	37.3	40.0	40.1	0.0	0.0		0.0	0.0	0.0	0.0	0.0	0.0	11.4	12.2	22.0	12.9	18.6
CBI	31.8	26.3	31.0	0.0	12.1	8.0	12.5	1.8	29.4	10.2	0.0	18.0	22.0	0.0	0.0		0.0	0.0	0.0	0.0	0.0	0.0	13.4	4.3	12.3	15.3
Andean Trd Pact (ATP)	27.8	22.0	0.0	0.0	12.0	8.0	11.0	2.3	29.4	10.2	0.0	14.3	22.0	0.0	0.0	0.0		0.0	0.0	0.0	0.0	0.0	0.6	11.7	12.1	13.7
Brazil (Bra)	24.6	26.5	30.5	0.0	13.1	5.3	13.1	10.4	29.4	10.2	0.0	18.0	19.1	0.0	0.0	0.0	0.0		0.0	0.0	0.0	7.4	2.3	20.2	4.8	13.3
MERCOSUR (MERC)	6.5	2.3	22.2	0.0	15.9	5.4	9.6	5.6	29.4	7.7	1.6	38.1	11.9	0.0	0.0	0.0	0.0	0.0		0.0	0.0	3.0	2.3	2.6	8.5	11.7
Chile (Chl)	13.1	0.0	0.0	0.0	12.3	5.0	0.0	0.5	29.4	10.2	0.0	19.4	16.4	0.0	0.0	0.0	0.0	0.0	0.0		0.0	7.8	2.1	10.7	4.7	10.8
Other Latin .A. (OLA)	2.1	0.0	0.0	0.0	-2.4	7.4	11.3	4.5	29.4	10.2	0.0	18.0	21.8	0.0	0.0	0.0	0.0	0.0	0.0	0.0		8.1	9.9	8.0	3.4	11.7
European Union (EU)	25.2	24.2	28.7	0.0	12.6	6.8	13.4	12.5	46.3	35.2	26.8	39.7	20.7	34.6	12.4	17.4	19.2	19.9	21.0	11.1	20.2		8.4	28.2	11.1	19.8

Table 4: Bi-lateral Tariffs for Clothing Trade: MFN basis and including major regional agreements and preference schemes as of 2001–Continued

	Importing Region →																									
Exporters	Aus	NZ	Chn	HKG	Jap	Kor	Tai	ASEAN5	Vnm	Bgl	Ind	SA	Can	Mex	USA	CBI	ATP	Bra	MERC	Chl	OLA	EU	Tur	AMEt	ROW	Sav
Rest of World (Rest of world)	32.3	25.8	29.6	0.0	13.2	6.9	13.3	2.9	35.4	9.0	17.3	35.0	21.8	34.0	14.9	23.5	11.2	19.2	20.0	9.6	12.4	12.2	8.3	18.2	17.9	17.8
Simple average (Sav)	23.0	19.7	22.7	0.0	11.6	6.8	11.2	8.1	35.4	16.9	20.4	31.0	17.4	28.5	10.5	17.3	17.1	18.3	20.0	10.5	17.4	7.2	7.8	17.3	15.2	16.5
Turkey (Tur)	31.6	26.0	22.0	0.0	13.0	5.7	12.6	11.8	29.4	10.2	31.6	50.2	21.7	33.6	12.8	20.9	18.2	20.0	16.4	11.0	0.2	0.0		24.2	22.3	17.8
Africa /Mideast (AME)	30.2	25.9	9.7	0.0	12.4	7.6	9.0	4.0	39.9	17.0	9.1	36.1	21.3	33.2	12.9	9.5	17.3	19.2	19.6	11.1	6.8	0.0	0.0	19.0	14.7	16.1

exporters will be accelerated. The next section examines the magnitude of T&C quota wedges, and their evolution since the end of the Uruguay Round.

3. A Quantitative Assessment of ATC Quota Margins

We next turn to an estimation of the price effects of the ATC quotas. Our data are for the value of bilateral trade in textiles and in clothing between the high-income OECD countries as importers and 86 countries and regions as exporters.[8] We also have data on trade-weighted tariffs (adjusted for trade preferences as well as we can) for this set of importer-exporter pairings. Trade data are drawn from GTAP6, while protection data come from a mix of WTO, UNCTAD, and CEPII data on tariffs, augmented to reflect U.S. preference schemes in the Western hemisphere.

Our approach is to first assume CES import demand. From the first order conditions, this implies the following as a functional determinant of imports of good x from country i and into country j.

$$x_{ij} = \left[\frac{\alpha_{ij}}{P_{ij}}\right]^{\sigma} P_j^{\sigma-1} E_j \qquad (1)$$

In equation (1), P_{ij} is the price of x_{ij} while P_j is the CES price index, E_j is country j expenditure on all imports of x and σ is the elasticity of substitution. From equation (1), relative import demands can then be written as a function of relative prices and CES expenditure weights α. This is shown in equation (2).

[8] The regions are: Australia; New Zealand; Rest of Oceania; China; Hong Kong; Japan; Korea; Chinese Taipei; Rest of East Asia; Indonesia; Malaysia; Philippines; Singapore; Thailand; Vietnam; Rest of Southeast Asia; Bangladesh; India; Sri Lanka; Rest of South Asia; Canada; United States; Mexico; Rest of North America; Colombia; Peru; Venezuela; Rest of Andean Pact; Argentina; Brazil; Chile; Uruguay; Rest of South America; Central America; Rest of Latin America; Rest of the Caribbean; Austria; Belgium; Denmark; Finland; France; Germany; United Kingdom; Greece; Ireland; Italy; Luxembourg; Netherlands; Portugal; Spain; Sweden; Switzerland; Rest of EFTA (basically Norway); Rest of Europe; Albania; Bulgaria; Croatia; Cyprus; Czech Republic; Hungary; Malta; Poland; Romania; Slovakia; Slovenia; Estonia; Latvia; Lithuania; Russian Federation; Rest of Former Soviet Union; Turkey; Rest of Middle East; Morocco; Rest of North Africa; Botswana; South Africa; Rest of South African Customs Union; Malawi; Mozambique; Tanzania; Zambia; Zimbabwe; Rest of SADC; Madagascar; Uganda; Rest of Sub Saharan Africa.

$$
\begin{aligned}
\frac{x_{ij}}{x_{kj}} &= \left[\frac{\alpha_{ij}}{\alpha_{kj}}\right]^{\sigma}\left[\frac{P_{kj}}{P_{ij}}\right]^{\sigma} \\
&= \left[\frac{\alpha_{ij}}{\alpha_{kj}}\right]^{\sigma}\left[\frac{\tau_{kj}P^{*}_{kj}}{\tau_{ij}P_{ij}}\right]^{\sigma}
\end{aligned} \tag{2}
$$

In equation (2), the τ term is a composite of any factors driving a wedge between world prices P^* and internal prices P.

To arrive at our estimating equation, we take logs of equation (2), and add terms for tariffs $(1+t)$ and ATC quota price margins Ω in place of the generic trading cost term τ. This yields equation (3).

$$
\begin{aligned}
&\ln(x_{ij}) - (\ln x_{kj}) = \sigma[\ln(\alpha_{ij}) - \ln(\alpha_{kj})] + \sigma[\ln(1+t_{kj}) - \ln(1+t_{ij})] + \sigma[\ln(\Omega_{kj}) - \ln(\Omega_{ij})] + \varepsilon_{ik,j} \\
&\textit{where} \quad \Omega \geq 1
\end{aligned} \tag{3}
$$

We estimate equation (3) using non-linear least squares, on the assumption that relative expenditure weights are comparable across OECD countries, once we control for trading costs. This involves minimizing equation (3), including the imposition of our lower bounds on the Ω terms and our assumption about the α terms, as shown in equation (4).

$$
\begin{aligned}
&\min \sum_{j,j\neq i,k} \sum_{h} (\varepsilon_{h,j})^2 \\
&s.t. \quad \{\ln(x_{ij}) - (\ln x_{kj})\} - \{\sigma[\ln(\alpha_i) - \ln(\alpha_k)] + \sigma[\ln(1+t_{kj}) - \ln(1+t_{ij})] + \sigma[\ln(\Omega_{kj}) - \ln(\Omega_{ij})]\} = \varepsilon_{ik,j} \\
&\qquad \ln(\Omega_{ij}) \geq 0
\end{aligned} \tag{4}
$$

In equation (4), the error terms are indexed over the set of possible exporter pairings *ik*. We have implemented the estimation problem in GAMS.

The regression results and the estimated values of the Ω coefficients are reported in Tables 5 and 6. ATC coefficients are only reported for countries where quotas are actually in place, and where such quotas are at least 50 percent filled across some product categories. Hence we do not measure the impact of monitoring or similar regimes. We have estimated these values both with an unrestricted substation elasticity (*i.e.*, where we estimate the substitution elasticity σ in addition to the ATC coefficients and expenditure weights) and also with the additional restriction that the substitution elasticities equal the new set

Table 5. NLS estimates of ATC price wedges for textiles

	Preferred – unrestricted model, estimated sigma=4.3			**Restricted model, imposed sigma=7.5**		
	Canada	**USA**	**EU15**	**Canada**	**USA**	**EU15**
China	1.332	1.508	1.883	1.166	1.262	1.402
Hong Kong	1.000	1.000	1.423	1.000	1.000	1.204
South Korea	1.000	1.049	1.407	1.000	1.019	1.184
Chinese Taipei	1.000	1.000	1.000	1.000	1.000	1.000
Rest of South East Asia	1.000	1.000	1.211	1.000	1.000	1.103
Indonesia	1.224	1.290	1.437	1.130	1.150	1.216
Malaysia	1.199	1.231	1.483	1.110	1.115	1.229
Philippines	1.018	1.000	1.454	1.026	1.000	1.231
Singapore	1.000	1.000	1.000	1.000	1.000	1.000
Thailand	1.133	1.080	1.400	1.071	1.042	1.187
Vietnam †	1.000	1.485	0.000	1.000	1.260	1.000
Bangladesh	1.000	1.000		1.000	1.000	
India	1.000	1.148	1.190	1.006	1.096	1.082
Sri Lanka	1.000	1.000		1.000	1.000	
Rest of South Asia	1.028	1.070	1.382	1.014	1.037	1.211
Columbia		1.000			1.000	
Peru			1.000			1.000
Argentina			1.000			1.000
Brazil	1.000	1.000	1.000	1.000	1.000	1.000
Uruguay	1.000	1.000		1.000	1.000	
Rest of Central America	1.000	1.000		1.000	1.000	
Rest of Caribbean	1.000	1.000		1.000	1.000	
Rest of FTAA	1.000	1.000		1.000	1.000	
Bulgaria		1.033			1.002	
Czech Republic	1.115	1.419		1.052	1.212	
Hungary	1.511	1.538		1.251	1.257	
Poland		1.471		1.000	1.234	
Romania	1.137	1.179		1.064	1.079	
Slovakia	1.595	1.809		1.301	1.387	
Turkey	1.135	1.065		1.057	1.019	
Rest of Middle East		1.000			1.000	
South Africa	1.000			1.000		

Rest of SACU	1.000			1.000		
Rest of SADC	1.123	1.000		1.066	1.000	
Rest of Sub-Saharan Africa		1.151			1.070	
	R-squared .781, Obs 66516, F 1466.178 (Pr>F, 0.000)			R-squared .780, Obs 66516, F 1467.766		

Note: F statistic for restriction on sigma is 267.973, (Pr>F, 0.00).

All estimates involve NLS estimates, based on pair-wise regressions of textile imports for 2001 into high income OECD countries. The set of ATC coefficients, in both regressions, is significant at the .001 level. The unrestricted model fits the data better, also at the .001 level. Restricted values are from Hertel, Hummels, Ivanic, and Keeney (2003). Quotas are treated with a price effect only if some categories have at least 50% quota fill rates. Blank values indicate no regime, or monitoring only. A value of 1 indicates non-binding regime.

†Vietnam in 2000 had negotiated a trade treaty with the U.S. However, this was not approved until later 2001, and implemented in 2002. Hence, Vietnam is subject here to column 2 (non-MFN) tariffs, combined with other monitoring requirements and restrictions on investment and trade. The Vietnam estimates represent the impact of this treatment, *vis-à-vis* MFN tariffs.

Table 6: NLS estimates of ATC price wedges for clothing

	Preferred – unrestricted model, estimated sigma=5.1			**Restricted model, imposed sigma=7.4**		
	Canada	**USA**	**EU15**	**Canada**	**USA**	**EU15**
China	1.309	1.590	1.573	1.204	1.376	1.339
Hong Kong	1.000	1.000	1.130	1.000	1.000	1.078
South Korea	1.000	1.000	1.363	1.000	1.000	1.214
Chinese Taipei	1.000	1.000	1.000	1.000	1.000	1.000
Rest of South East Asia	1.000	1.000	1.093	1.000	1.000	1.056
Indonesia	1.000	1.000	1.176	1.000	1.000	1.108
Malaysia	1.000	1.000	1.192	1.000	1.000	1.116
Philippines	1.000	1.000	1.403	1.000	1.000	1.248
Singapore	1.000	1.000	1.000	1.000	1.000	1.000
Thailand	1.006	1.022	1.265	1.010	1.019	1.162
Vietnam †	1.000	1.563	1.000	1.000	1.368	1.000
Bangladesh	1.000	1.000		1.000	1.000	
India	1.000	1.096	1.117	1.000	1.072	1.072
Sri Lanka	1.000	1.000		1.000	1.000	
Rest of South Asia	1.000	1.000	1.174	1.000	1.000	1.148
Columbia		1.000			1.000	
Peru			1.000			1.000
Argentina			1.000			1.000
Brazil	1.184	1.080	1.000	1.119	1.050	1.000
Uruguay	1.000	1.009		1.000	1.007	
Rest of Central America	1.000	1.000		1.000	1.000	
Rest of Caribbean	1.000			1.000	1.000	

Rest of FTAA	1.000	1.000	1.000	1.000
Bulgaria		1.043		1.018
Czech Republic	1.046	1.378	1.019	1.234
Hungary	1.000	1.149	1.000	1.090
Poland		1.487		1.302
Romania	1.266	1.322	1.164	1.200
Slovakia	1.257	1.353	1.148	1.211
Turkey	1.000	1.024		1.011
Rest of Middle East		1.000		1.000
South Africa	1.000			
Rest of SACU	1.000		1.000	
Rest of SADC	1.000	1.000	1.000	1.000
Rest of Sub-Saharan Africa		1.000		1.000
	R-squared .738, Obs 66204, F 1170.288 (Pr>F, 0.000)		R-squared .737, Obs 66204, F 1171.196	

Note: F statistic for restriction on sigma is 270.794, (Pr>F, 0.00)

All estimates involve NLS estimates, based on pair-wise regressions of clothing imports for 2001 into high income OECD countries. The set of ATC coefficients, in both regressions, is significant at the .001 level. The unrestricted model fits the data better, also at the .001 level. Restricted values are from Hertel, Hummels, Ivanic, and Keeney (2003). Quotas are treated with a price effect only if some categories have at least 50% quota fill rates. Blank values indicate no regime, or monitoring only. A value of 1 indicates non-binding regime.

†Vietnam in 2000 had negotiated a trade treaty with the U.S. However, this was not approved until later 2001, and implemented in 2002. Hence, Vietnam is subject here to column 2 (non-MFN) tariffs, combined with other monitoring requirements and restrictions on investment and trade. The Vietnam estimates represent the impact of this treatment, *vis-à-vis* MFN tariffs.

of GTAP elasticities (Hertel, Hummels, Ivanic and Keeney 2003). While we reject this restriction based on an F-test, these values are relevant for those working with the standard GTAP model and parameter set.

The ATC coefficients are converted to ad valorem equivalents in Table 7 and compared to country values for 1997 from Dimaranan and McDougal (2002). A further comparison is made to 1992 estimates on a regional basis, again using the Dimaranan and McDougal value, and also Francois, McDonald, and Nordstrom (1995) in Table 8. The clear pattern is one of general liberalization since the beginning of the ATC process, with a few notable exceptions.

Most notable is China. Both the EU and the United States have estimated tax equivalent rates that are the same for clothing as at the start of the 1990s. In addition, the regime for textiles is even more restrictive than it was in the early 1990s. This can be interpreted as implying that quota growth rates under the ATC have simply failed to keep up with the mix of supply and demand side growth since the liberalization process started. In addition, Vietnam, which was not a major player in world markets over the decade of the 1990s, now faces far greater restrictions from the United States. In part, this reflects changes in the U.S.-Vietnam relationship. In 1992, Vietnam was still subject to Smoot-Hawley (column 2) tariff rates. With the implementation of the U.S.-Vietnam agreement in 2001-2002, and subsequent action by the U.S. to limit textile and clothing trade, new quotas, have essentially replaced the old tariffs.

Another notable increase is North American protection against textiles and clothing from Central Europe. Again, in the course of the early 1990s these countries were emerging from the fog of communism, and were not major players on world markets. While individual countries from this group behind the "iron curtain" were able to improve their shares in U.S. imports up through 2002, on average these countries could only maintain their total share of U.S. T&C imports. A more detailed examination of the quota and trade categories involved shows that the North American regimes are protecting domestic producers of wool fabrics, suits, and related items. This protection is quite high. Finally, several countries have been largely graduated toward a liberal trade regime. This includes many of the lower income Asian and African suppliers.

Table 7. Comparison of country estimates: 1997 and 2001

	ATC Export Tax Equivalent Rate, fraction of f.o.b. value (world prices)			
	United States			
	Textiles		Clothing	
	1997	2001	1997	2001
China	20.0	20.8	33.0	27.3
Hong Kong	1.0	0.0	10.0	0.0
South Korea	2.4	1.9	1.9	0.0
Chinese Taipei	2.2	0.0	7.5	0.0
Indonesia	8.1	13.0	7.8	0.0
Malaysia	8.1	10.3	7.8	0.0
Philippines	6.5	0.0	7.8	0.0
Singapore	0.0	0.0	0.6	0.0
Thailand	8.3	4.0	13.2	1.9
Vietnam †	6.9	20.6	7.1	26.9
India	9.8	8.8	34.2	6.7
Sri Lanka	15.3	0.0	8.1	0.0
Latin America	7.2	0.0	5.3	0.7
Central European Associates	6.9	16.3	5.0	15.0
Turkey	7.0	1.9	4.9	1.1

Table 7. Comparison of country estimates: 1997 and 2001–Continued

	ATC Export Tax Equivalent Rate, fraction of f.o.b. value (world prices) **European Union**			
	Textiles		Clothing	
	1997	2001	1997	2001
China	12.0	28.7	15.0	25.3
Hong Kong	1.0	16.9	10.0	7.2
South Korea	1.6	15.5	0.6	17.6
Chinese Taipei	6.9	0.0	5.9	0.0
Indonesia	6.3	17.7	6.0	9.7
Malaysia	6.3	18.7	6.0	10.4
Philippines	5.7	18.7	6.0	19.9
Singapore	0.6	0.0	0.2	0.0
Thailand	6.4	15.8	7.8	14.0
Vietnam	7.5	0.0	7.2	0.0
India	12.0	7.6	15.2	6.7
Sri Lanka	5.5	0.0	6.4	0.0
Latin America	3.1	0.0	5.2	0.0
Central European Associates	0.0	0.0	0.0	0.0
Turkey	1.5	0.0	0.0	0.0

†Vietnam in 2000 had negotiated a trade treaty with the U.S. However, this was not approved until later 2001, and implemented in 2002. Hence, Vietnam is subject here to column 2 (non-MFN) tariffs, combined with other monitoring requirements and restrictions on investment and trade. The Vietnam estimates represent the impact of this treatment, *vis-à-vis* MFN tariffs. Since the U.S. imposed quotas immediately after implementing the trade agreement, these also provide a rough approximation of current import quota price effects.

Source: 2001 estimates are from author's calculations, 1997 estimates are Francois and Spinanger (2002) as summarized in Dimaranan *et al.* (2002). 2001 estimates are based on the restricted elasticity columns in Tables 3 and 4.

Table 8. Comparison of regional estimates: 1992, 1997 and 2001

	ATC Export Tax Equivalent Rate, fraction of f.o.b. value (world prices)					
	United States					
	Textiles			Clothing		
	1992	1997	2001	1992	1997	2001
China	15.5	20.0	20.8	28.7	33.0	27.3
East Asia	8.5	4.8	5.5	19.8	7.1	3.2
South Asia	15.5	12.6	4.4	28.7	21.2	3.4
Latin America	8.6	7.2	0.0	16.8	5.3	0.7
Middle East/Africa	4.4	0.5	0.2	7.7	0.6	0
Eastern Europe	6	6.9	16.3	11.9	5.0	15.0
Rest of world	3.6	7.0	1.9	6.7	4.9	1.1

Table 8. Comparison of regional estimates: 1992, 1997 and 2001–Continued

	ATC Export Tax Equivalent Rate, fraction of f.o.b. value (world prices) **European Union**					
	Textiles			Clothing		
	1992	1997	2001	1992	1997	2001
China	21.5	12.0	28.7	26.5	15.0	25.3
East Asia	11.5	4.7	11.5	19.9	5.5	8.8
South Asia	21.5	8.8	3.8	26.5	10.8	3.4
Latin America	12.4	3.1	0.0	15	5.2	0.0
Middle East/Africa	6.0	0.3	0.0	7.2	0.0	0.0
Eastern Europe	8.6	0.0	0.0	10.8	0.0	0.0
Rest of world	5.2	1.5	0.0	6.7	0.0	0.0

Source: 2001 estimates are from author's calculations, 1997 estimates are Francois and Spinanger (2002) as summarized in Dimaranan *et al.* (2002), and 1992 estimates are from Chyc *et al.* (1994) and USITC (1993) as summarized in Francois, McDonald and Nordstrom (1995). 2001 estimates are based on the restricted elasticity columns in Tables 3 and 4.

Was the lifting of the fog of communism also instrumental in increasing EU T&C imports from Eastern European countries? Here the overall picture definitely shows that the share of T&C imports coming from Eastern Europe increased during this period (by roughly 3 percentage points). Of course, it must be realized that numerous European countries had already been tapping this natural – that is being right next door (as in the case of Mexico for the United States) – offshore production base for years. Particularly in the case of Germany and Sweden had the Eastern European countries been serving as an important offshore sourcing base for clothing products since the late 1970s - all this being driven by liberal offshore production legislation. For instance, in the case of Sweden, Eastern European countries accounted for roughly 10 percent of its clothing imports in 1980, only to see this slowly reduced to 5 percent by 1990. However, this downward trend was then reversed and by the time the third ATC liberalization tranche was effected as of January 1, 2002 (see Table 1) almost 17 percent of Sweden's clothing imports were sourced in Eastern Europe.

Despite these trends it must not be neglected that both in the case of the United States and the EU the underlying trends revealed that those countries in Eastern Europe lying farther to the east (*e.g.* Bulgaria, Rumania, Ukraine) profited the most in recent years. This implies that locations were being sought which offered the cheapest labor costs. If this production demand component remains dominant, then it could imply that countries like China will (as has been shown in numerous studies) profit the most. However, if time becomes an ever more important factor in determining sourcing decisions then nearness could develop into the key factor determining where T&C products are produced. (See Andriamananjara *et al.*, 2004).

4. Summary and Conclusions

The paper has examined the evolution of the ATC through 2001. The ATC quotas have been in phase-out mode since 1995. A key message from these calculations is that the problem of China's (PRC) T&C sector integration has been deferred. This means that the potential still exists for a substantial surge in China's exports after 2005. Such a surge in Chinese exports would of course mean lost market share for most other developing countries. Of course, this will only happen if other economies do not attempt to take advantage of specific contingent protection rules included in China's protocol of accession. These permit other WTO members to keep protectionist pressure up against China (PRC) for 15 years. They cover special anti-surge clauses for T&C products (4 years), general anti-surge clauses (12 years) and treatment of China as "a non-market economy" in antidumping cases (15 years). Icing the cake is the fear that anti-dumping measures against China (PRC) will also be on the increase. The pattern of ATC quotas across regions suggests that the next few years will be very interesting indeed.

References[9]

1. Baughman, L. R. Mirus, M. Morkre, and D. Spinanger (1997). Of Tyre Cords, Ties, and Tents. *World Economy* 4: 407–434.
2. Chyc, K., M. Gelhar, D. Gray, T. Hertel, E. Ianchivichina, B. McDonald, and M. Tsigas (1996). The GTAP Database. In T. Hertel (ed.), *Global Trade Analysis*, Cambridge: Cambridge University Press.
3. De Melo, J., and A.L. Winters (1993). Price and Quality Effects of VERs Revisited: A Case Study of Korean Footwear Exports. *Journal of Economic Integration* 8: 33–57.
4. Andriamananjara, S, J. Dean, D. Spinanger (2004) Trading Textiles and Apparel: Developing Countiries in 2005. GTAP Conference, World Bank, Washington D.C., mimeo.
5. Dimaranan, Betina V., and Robert A. McDougall (2002). Global Trade, Assistance, and Production: The GTAP 5 Data Base. Center for *Global Trade Analysis*, Purdue University.
6. Francois, J.F., H.H. Glismann, and D. Spinanger (2000). The Cost of EU Trade Protection in Textiles and Clothing. Kiel Working Papers 997, August.
7. Francois, J.F., and A. Strutt (1999). Post Uruguay Round Tariff Vectors For GTAP Version 4. Erasmus University manuscript.

---

[9] Contains some relevant sources not explicitly noted in text.

8. Francois, J.F. (2000). Assessing the Results of General Equilibrium Studies of Multilateral Trade Negotiations. UNCTAD/ITCD/TAB/4, UNCTAD Policy Issues in International Trade and Commodities Study Series, UNCTAD:Geneva, October.
9. Francois, J. B. McDonald, and H. Nordstrom (1995). Assessing the Uruguay Round. In W. Martin and L. Alan Winters (eds.), *The Uruguay Round and the Developing Economies*, World Bank Discussion Paper 307. Washington, D.C.
10. Harrison, G.W., T.F. Rutherford, and D.G. Tarr (1995). Quantifiying the Uruguay Round. In W. Martin and L.A. Winters (eds.), *The Uruguay Round and the Developing Economies*, World Bank Discussion Paper 307. Washington, D.C.
11. Hertel, T.W., W. Martin, K. Yanagishima, and B. Dimaranan (1995).,Liberalizing Manufactures in a Changing World Economy. In W. Martin and L.A. Winters (eds.), *The Uruguay Round and the Developing Economies*, World Bank Discussion Paper 307. Washington, D.C.
12. Hertel, T., D. Hummels, M. Ivanic, and R. Keeney (2003). How Confident Can We Be in CGE-Based Assessments of Free Trade Agreements? GTAP Working Paper 26.
13. Krishna, K., and L.H. Tan (1997). The Multifibre Arrangement in Practice: Challenging the Competitive Framework.'In D. Robertson (ed.), *East Asian Trade After the Uruguay Round*, Cambridge.
14. McDougall, R. (ed.) (2001). *The GTAP Database – Version 5*. Global Trade Analysis Center: Purdue University.
15. Reinert, K.A., and D.W. Roland-Holst (1997). Social Accounting Matrices. In J.F. Francois and K.A. Reinert (eds.), *Applied Methods for Trade Policy Analysis: a Handbook*, Cambridge University Press: New York.
16. Smith, M.A.M (1977). Capital Accumulation in the Open Two-Sector Economy. *The Economic Journal* 87 (June): 273–282.
17. Smith, M.A.M. (1976). Trade, Growth, and Consumption in Alternative Models of Capital Accumulation. *Journal of International Economics* 6 (November): 385–388.
18. Spinanger, D. (2002). RTAs and Contingent Protection: Are Anti-Dumping Measures (ADMs) Really an Issue? Paper presented at WTO Regional Seminar on *Regionalism and the Multilateral Trading System*, Geneva, 26 April.
19. Srinivasan, T.N., and J.N. Bhagwait (1980). Trade and Welfare in a Steady-State. Chapter 12 in J.S. Chipman and C.P Kindelberger (eds.), *Flexible Exchange Rates and the Balance of Payments*, North-Holland Publishing.
20. U.S. International Trade Commission (1993). *The Economic Effect of Significant U.S. Import Restraints*. USITC: Washington.
21. World Trade Organization – WTO (2000). *Annual Report 2000*. Geneva.
22. Yang, Y., (1994), *Trade Liberalization and Externaltities: A General Equilibrium Assessment of the Uruguay Round*. Mimeo, Australian National University.

ESTIMATING TARIFF EQUIVALENTS OF CORE AND NON-CORE NON-TARIFF MEASURES IN THE APEC MEMBER ECONOMIES

Mitsuyo Ando

Keio University[1]

1. Introduction

In contrast with successful tariff reduction as a result of periodic rounds of multilateral trade negotiations, non-tariff measures (NTMs) have been a growing problem for international trade. Tariffs, which are recognized to be economically preferred form of protection, are visible and relatively easy to negotiate over. In contrast, NTMs are in general not tractable in terms of their price and other protective effects while they highly distort the behavior of producers and consumers, and consequently trade patterns.

As Deardorff and Stern (1998) point out, NTMs have various characteristics: first, they reduce the quantity of imports and increase the price of imports. Second, they could change the elasticity of demand for imports. Third, the effectiveness of NTMs could vary over time according to the change in market conditions. Fourth, the uncertainty in implementation of NTMs, especially such as antidumping (AD) and countervailing (CV) measures, could restrict potential trade. Fifth, they bring about welfare costs as well as resource costs such as administrative costs or rent seeking related costs. These non-transparent and obscure features of NTMs make them difficult to control and monitor. At the same time, such uncertain characteristics of NTMs have attracted governments and domestic industries lobbying for protection.

Regardless of the serious concern on NTM issues, not so many studies have empirically measured the economic impact of NTMs, partly because of several fundamental problems. First, a basic difficulty is how to define their range. A number of scholars have claimed that NTMs should include various measures other than tariffs that distort international trade or raise the welfare cost,

[1] The author may be contacted through Keio University, Faculty of Economics, 2-15-45 Mita, Minato-ku, Tokyo 152-0004, Japan, via email at *andomitsuyo@hotmail.com* The author would like to thank the participants of the 8th convention of the East Asian Economic Association as well as the participants of the APEC capacity-building workshop on quantitative methods for assessing NTMs and trade facilitation for helpful comments and suggestion. I also would like to thank Takamune Fujii for initial consultation and research assistance.

regardless of whether border type or internal type.[2] There, however, is a large degree of difference in interpretation over what constitutes NTMs and what can be treated as legitimate measures of government policies. For instance, AD/CV measures or technical measures such as technical regulations and sanitary and phytosanitary (SPS) regulations have been controversial issues.[3] Since NTMs are not necessarily barriers to trade, *i.e.*, non-tariff barriers (NTBs), and include trade-distorting measures such as subsidies as well, a certain part of distortion on prices or price differentials due to the use of some measures could be justified as far as at the reasonable levels. Second, as discussed above, it is hard to identify their economic impact explicitly, due to their non-transparent and open-ended effects on prices, trade patterns, and welfare. Third, the most critical problem is a lack of statistical information on NTMs. The currently available database with fairly comprehensive data of NTMs is solely the United Nations Conference on Trade and Development (UNCTAD) database, Trade Analysis and Information System (TRAINS). Although this database has some drawbacks, it provides the information on Harmonized System (HS) product categories (tariff lines) subject to NTMs for a number of economies.[4]

Most of the previous empirical studies on NTMs for trade in goods have employed an inventory approach based on indices such as frequency ratios and import coverage ratios.[5] Frequency ratios indicate the portion of HS tariff lines subject to NTM(s), irrespective of whether and how much the products are actually imported while import coverage ratios imply the share of imports subject to NTM(s), *i.e.*, import-weighted frequency ratios.[6] Although these indices serve to observe the pervasiveness of NTMs and to identify those sectors on which NTMs concentrate, they could provide no information on either the degree of protection or the economic impact of NTMs on prices, trade, and welfare.

In addition, few empirical studies have taken into account the use of non-core NTMs[7] such as technical measures despite the fact that they are likely to cause

---

[2] For example, Baldwin (1970, p5) addresses that a nontariff-distorting policy is any measure (public or private) that causes internationally traded goods and services, or resources devoted to the production of these goods and services, to be allocated in such a way as to reduce potential real world income.

[3] Some economies argue that these measures represent policies with legitimacy under multilateral agreement, and should not be treated as NTMs.

[4] See footnote 16 for discussion over the deficiency of this database.

[5] See, for instance, Laird and Yeats (1990a), OECD (1997), PECC (2000), and Ando (2002) for empirical studies based on inventory approach.

[6] See Laird (1997) and OECD (1997) for other possible weights as well as the discussion on various weights.

[7] The next section explains what non-core NTMs include more precisely.

more serious problems than before.[8] As will be discussed in the following sections, the way of applying various core and non-core NTMs differs from economy to economy, and such a diversity suggests that NTMs, including non-core NTMs, be measured by type.

Considering all the facts discussed above, the study attempts to present the methodology to empirically measure the economic impact of core NTMs as well as non-core NTMs in terms of tariff equivalents by the type of measures. To estimate tariff equivalents of by-type NTMs, the paper focuses on the price differentials between the c.i.f. price of imports and the domestic producer price of the domestic substitutes, and uses by- type frequency ratios of NTMs to decompose tariff equivalent of overall NTMs. The types of NTMs examined in the study are price control measures, auto-licensing measures, quantity control measures, monopolistic measures, and technical measures, based on the UNCTAD classification.[9] The estimates of tariff equivalents of by-type NTMs reveal that, though they may still be tentative in terms of their accuracy because of problems in quality of price differential data, all types of measures, *i.e.*, both core NTMs and non-core NTMs, could provide a certain degree of protection for domestic producers.

The remaining sections are organized as follows: section 2 provides literature survey on the measurement of NTMs, including the discussion on the range of NTMs, to explain the framework of measuring tariff equivalents of NTMs. Section 3 investigates to what extent and what types of NTMs are implemented in the 13 APEC economies after explaining how to construct by-type frequency ratios of core and non-core NTMs. Section 4 presents the methodology to estimate tariff equivalents by each type of NTMs, using price differentials and frequency ratios. Section 4 also discusses data construction and data sources used in our study. Then, the empirical results and implications are presented in section 5, and the conclusion is in section 6.

2. Literature Survey on the Measurement of NTMs

This section first discusses the range of NTMs. As already mentioned, there is no consensus on the range of NTMs, and thus we compare what types of measures are included among major classifications of NTMs and some major trade

---

[8] See Maskus and Wilson (2001) for theoretical papers on technical measures.

[9] Financial control measures are not included as no economy in the analysis reports the use of these measures.

agreements. The latter part of this section provides empirical methodology of measuring NTMs, focusing on the tariff equivalent approach.

2.1. *The Range of NTMs*

Table 1 presents a list of NTMs included in the classifications proposed by UNCTAD, Deardorff and Stern (1998), and Baldwin (1970) as well as in the GATT/WTO agreement and major bilateral/regional agreements.[10] The table classifies measures into seven large categories and their sub-categories: large categories are 1. price control measures, 2. financial control measures, 3. automatic licensing measures, 4. quantity control measures, 5. monopolistic measures, 6. technical measures, and 7. other government policies. Multilateral and bilateral/regional agreements shown in Table 1 are of the GATT/WTO, APEC's Osaka Action Agenda, New Zealand-Singapore Closer Economic Partnership, US-Jordan FTA (US-Jordan Free Trade Agreement), EU-Mexico FTA (EU-Mexico Free Trade Agreement), AFTA (ASEAN Free Trade Area), NAFTA (North American Free Trade Agreement), MERCOSUR (El Mercado Comun del Sur), US-Israel FTA (US-Israel Free Trade Area Agreement), and CER (Australia-New Zealand Closer Economic Relations Agreement).

Any measure in the list could distort international trade in goods directly or indirectly. The UNCTAD classification categorizes NTMs into three types of measures defined as core NTMs, which are price control measures, financial control measures, and quantity control measures, and three types of other measures, which include auto-licensing measures, monopolistic measures, and technical measures.[11] We call the latter types of measures non-core NTMs. There is a notable difference in the UNCTAD classification from the Deardorff-Stern classification and the Baldwin classification. The UNCTAD classification focuses on only import distorting measures such as import quantity control measures and price control measures. On the other hand, the Deardorff-Stern classification and the Baldwin classification cover not only import related measures but also export related measures as well as domestic institutions and policies that may result in distorting international trade. Therefore, the range of NTMs included in these classifications is wider than in the UNCTAD classification.

---

[10] The table basically targets NTMs for trade in goods and does not cover NTMs for trade in services.

[11] The definition of core NTMs by OECD is different from the one by UNCTAD; OECD (1997) defines only both price control measures and quantitative restrictions as core NTMs.

Table 1. The list of NTMs identified in the NTM classifications and major multilateral and bilateral/regional trade agreements

	NTMs' classifications			Multi-lateral	Bilateral/regional								
	UNC-TAD	Deardorff & Stern	Baldwin	GATT/WTO	Osaka Action Agenda	NZ-Singapore	US-Jordan	EU-Mexico	AFTA	NAFTA	MERCOSUR	US-Israel	CER
1. Price control measures													
(1) Administrative pricing	◎			◎	◎					◎			
minimum import prices	○			○	○					○			
(2) Voluntary export price restraint	◎									◎			
(3) Variable charges	◎	◎			◎	◎			◎				◎
variable levies on imports	○	○			○								○
variable levies on exports					○								
variable components	○												
compensatory elements	○												
flexible import fees	○												
(4) Anti-dumping measures	◎	◎	◎	◎		◎		◎		◎		◎	◎
anti-dumping investigations	○	○		○		○							
anti-dumping duties	○	○	○	○		○							
price undertakings	○												
(5) Countervailing measures	◎	◎		◎				◎		◎			◎
countervailing investigations	○	○		○									
countervailing duties	○	○		○									
price undertakings	○												
(6) Selective indirect taxes		◎	◎										

Table 1. The list of NTMs identified in the NTM classifications and major multilateral and bilateral/regional trade agreements–Continued

	NTMs' classifications			Multi-lateral	Bilateral/regional								
	UNC-TAD	Deardorff & Stern	Baldwin	GATT/WTO	Osaka Action Agenda	NZ-Singapore	US-Jordan	EU-Mexico	AFTA	NAFTA	MERCOSUR	US-Israel	CER
2. Finance control measures													
(1) Advance payments requirements	◎	◎	◎										
advance import deposit	○	○											
cash margin requirement	○												
advance payment of customs duties	○												
refundable deposits for sensitive product categories	○												
(2) Multiple exchange rates	◎	◎	◎										
(3) Restrictive official foreign exchange allocation	◎	◎	◎										
prohibition of foreign exchange allocation	○												
bank authorization	○												
(4) Regulations concerning terms of payment for imports	◎	◎							◎				
(5) Transfer delays, queuing	◎												
3. Automatic licensing measures													
(1) Automatic license	◎			◎									
(2) Import monitoring	◎												
retrospective surveillance	○												

Table 1. The list of NTMs identified in the NTM classifications and major multilateral and bilateral/regional trade agreements–Continued

	NTMs' classifications			Multi-lateral	Bilateral/regional								
	UNC-TAD	Deardorff & Stern	Baldwin	GATT/WTO	Osaka Action Agenda	NZ-Singapore	US-Jordan	EU-Mexico	AFTA	NAFTA	MERCOSUR	US-Israel	CER
prior surveillance	○												
prior surveillance product categories	○												
(3) Surrender requirement	○												
4. Quantity control measures													
(1) Non-automatic licensing	◎	◎		◎	◎			◎				◎	◎
license with no specific ex-ante criteria	○												
license for selected purchasers	○												
license for specified use	○												
- linked with export trade	○												
- for purpose other than exports	○												
license linked with local production	○	○		○					○				
- purchase of local goods	○	○		○									
- local content requirement	○	○		○									
- barter or counter trade	○	○		○									
license linked with non-official foreign exchange	○			○									
- external foreign exchange	○			○									
- importers own foreign exchange	○			○									

Table 1. The list of NTMs identified in the NTM classifications and major multilateral and bilateral/regional trade agreements–Continued

	NTMs' classifications			Multi-lateral	Bilateral/regional								
	UNC-TAD	Deardorff & Stern	Baldwin	GATT/WTO	Osaka Action Agenda	NZ-Singapore	US-Jordan	EU-Mexico	AFTA	NAFTA	MERCOSUR	US-Israel	CER
license combined with or replaced by special authorization	○												
prior authorization for sensitive product categories	○												
(2) Import quotas (import restrictions)	◎	◎	◎	◎	◎	◎		◎	◎	◎	◎	◎	◎
global quotas	○	○		○									
- unallocated	○												
- allocated to exporting economies	○			○									
bilateral quotas	○	○		○									
seasonal quotas	○			○									
quotas linked wit export performance	○			○									
quotas linked with purchase of local goods	○			○									
quotas for sensitive product categories	○	○		○									
quotas for political reasons (embargo)	○												
(3) Prohibition	◎	◎		◎	◎	◎			◎	◎			
suspension of issuance licenses	○												
seasonal prohibition	○												

Table 1. The list of NTMs identified in the NTM classifications and major multilateral and bilateral/regional trade agreements–Continued

	NTMs' classifications			Multi-lateral	Bilateral/regional								
	UNC-TAD	Deardorff & Stern	Baldwin	GATT/WTO	Osaka Action Agenda	NZ-Singapore	US-Jordan	EU-Mexico	AFTA	NAFTA	MERCOSUR	US-Israel	CER
temporary prohibition	○												
import diversification	○												
prohibition on the basis of origin	○												
prohibition for sensitive product categories	○												
prohibition for political reasons (embargo)	○												
(4) Export restraint arrangements	◎	◎		◎	◎	◎							
voluntary export restraint arrangements	○	○		○	○	○							
orderly marketing arrangements	○	○											
multi-fiber arrangement (MFA)	○			○						○			
- quota agreement	○												
- consultation agreement	○												
- administrative cooperation agreement	○												
export restraint arrangements on textiles outside MFA	○												
(5) Enterprise-specific restrictions	◎												
selective approval of importers	○												
enterprise-specific quota	○												

Table 1. The list of NTMs identified in the NTM classifications and major multilateral and bilateral/regional trade agreements–Continued

	NTMs' classifications			Multi-lateral	Bilateral/regional								
	UNC-TAD	Deardorff & Stern	Baldwin	GATT/WTO	Osaka Action Agenda	NZ-Singapore	US-Jordan	EU-Mexico	AFTA	NAFTA	MERCOSUR	US-Israel	CER
(6) Export restrictions (*e.g.*, export quotas, export taxes, prohibition)													
5. Monopolistic measures													
(1) Single channel for imports	◎	◎	◎	◎						◎			
state trading administration	○	○	○	○									
sole importing agency	○	○											
single channel for imports for sensitive product categories	○												
exclusive franchises		○											
(2) Compulsory national services	◎	◎											
compulsory national insurance	○	○											
compulsory national transport	○	○											
6. Technical measures													
(1) Technical regulations	◎	◎	◎	◎	◎	◎	◎	◎	◎	◎	◎		◎
product characteristics requirements	○												
marking (trademarks) requirements	○	○		○						○			
labeling requirements	○	○		○									○

Table 1. The list of NTMs identified in the NTM classifications and major multilateral and bilateral/regional trade agreements–Continued

	NTMs' classifications			Multi-lateral	Bilateral/regional								
	UNC-TAD	Deardorff & Stern	Baldwin	GATT/WTO	Osaka Action Agenda	NZ-Singapore	US-Jordan	EU-Mexico	AFTA	NAFTA	MERCOSUR	US-Israel	CER
packaging requirements	○	○		○									
testing, inspection and quarantine requirements	○			○		○	○						○
information requirements	○			○		○		○		○			
safety and industrial standards and regulations		○		○			○	○					○
health and sanitary regulations and quality standards		○		○		○		○		○	○	○	○
advertising and media regulations		○								○			
(2) Pre-shipment inspection	◎			◎									
(3) Special customs formalities	◎	◎	◎	◎	◎	◎	◎	◎	◎	◎			◎
custom valuation procedures		○		○		○		○	○				○
customs classification procedure		○		○		○		○	○				○
customs clearance procedures		○		○		○		○					○
(4) Obligation to return used product	◎									◎			
7. Other government policies													
(1) Subsidies to export and import competing industries		◎	◎	◎	◎	◎		◎				◎	◎

Table 1. The list of NTMs identified in the NTM classifications and major multilateral and bilateral/regional trade agreements–Continued

	NTMs' classifications			Multi-lateral	Bilateral/regional								
	UNC-TAD	Deardorff & Stern	Baldwin	GATT/ WTO	Osaka Action Agenda	NZ-Singapore	US-Jordan	EU-Mexico	AFTA	NAFTA	MERCOSUR	US-Israel	CER
(2) Government procurement policies		◎	◎	◎	◎	◎	◎	◎		◎	◎	◎	◎
(3) Government industrial policy and regional development measures		◎											
(4) Government financed research and development and other technology policies		◎											
(5) National systems of taxation and social insurance		◎											
(6) Macroeconomic policies		◎							◎	◎			
(7) Competition policies		◎			◎	◎		◎	◎	◎			◎
(8) Foreign investment policies		◎	◎	◎	◎			◎	◎	◎	◎		◎
(9) Foreign corruption policies		◎	◎	◎	◎								
(10) Immigration policies		◎	◎										

Data source UNCTAD (2001), Deardorff and Stern (1998), and Baldwin (1970) for the NTM classifications, and original agreements for multilaratel and bilateral/regional agreements, which are available from Australian Department of Foreign Affairs and Trade (1983), Israel Ministry of Foreign Affairs (1985), NAFTA Secretariat (1994), WTO (1994), APEC Secretariat (1995), ASEAN Secretariat (1998), EU (2000), Jordan-U.S. Free Trade Agreement Website (2000), Ministry of Industry and Trade (2000), and Secretaria del MERCOSUR (2002).

Note: ◎ stands for NTMs identified in large categories and ○ in the sub-categories.

The table also clearly presents what types of measures are identified in multilateral and bilateral/regional agreements. Some include a specialized section for NTMs and explicitly define their range while others do not. Many of the agreements in the table cover policy measures categorized into price control measures, quantity control measures, technical measures, and other government policies. The measures identified in more than six out of nine agreements are anti-dumping measures, import quotas (import restrictions), export restrictions, technical regulations, special customs formalities, subsidies, government procurement policies, competition policies, and foreign investment policies that could distort trade patterns. In contrast, few agreements cover financial control measures, automatic licensing measures, and monopolistic measures. What the agreements include may reflect the main purpose of individual agreement. For example, US-Jordan FTA and US-Israel FTA do not cover a wide range of trade policies probably since they are principally motivated by the political issues to maintain and promote the peace and security in the Middle East. On the other hand, NZ-Singapore Closer Economic Partnership and CER, for instance, cover many trade-distorting measures because their principal purpose is to deepen the economic integration through more free environments for trade and so on.

The range of NTMs would continue to expand furthermore, as PECC (2000) and Bosworth (1999) discuss, if governments implement new policies or measures to protect domestic industries from foreign competition.

2.2. *The Empirical Methodology of Measuring NTMs*

Deardorff and Stern (1998) classify various methods of measuring NTMs as follows: frequency-type measures based on inventory listings of observed NTMs; price-comparison measures, focusing on differentials between domestic price and the reference price of compared good, in terms of the price relatives or tariff equivalents expressed as a percentage difference; quantity-impact measures based on econometric estimates of the models of trade flows; and measures of equivalent nominal rates of assistance.[12] As discussed in the previous section, the methods most often applied in empirical studies are frequency-type measures. They are useful in investigating the pervasiveness of NTMs, but they cannot provide information on either the economic impact of NTMs or the degree of protection that NTMs provide for domestic producers. As the paper applies price comparison measures in terms of tariff equivalents, this sub-section focuses on

[12] See also Laird and Yeats (1990b) and Laird (1997) for methods of measuring NTMs for trade in goods.

the discussion over the empirical approach to estimate tariff equivalents of NTMs.

There are two approaches usually employed to empirically measure NTMs in terms of tariff equivalents, assuming that compared goods are homogeneous. The first approach is based on the price differentials between the c.i.f price of imported goods and the domestic price or between the c.i.f price of imported goods and the domestic price of the domestic substitutes. This approach assumes that all the price differentials are attributed to trade protection, namely, tariffs and NTMs. Sazanami, Urata, and Kawai (1995), for example, estimated the degree of trade protection in Japan by comparing the c.i.f import unit values with domestic producers' unit values of the domestic substitutes, and obtained tariff equivalents of NTMs by subtracting tariffs from tariff equivalents of overall trade protection.

The second approach is based on price differentials between the domestic (retail) price and the overseas reference price of the same goods. The price used as overseas reference price is usually either the domestic (retail) price of the same goods in foreign exporting economy or the lowest domestic price among all foreign exporters. This approach attributes price differentials to various barriers, including inefficient distribution systems within an economy. Campbell and Cossette (1994), for instance, compare Canadian domestic prices of such supply-managed products as diary products, chicken and turkey with constructed measures of reference prices charged by low-cost foreign suppliers. A basic difference between the two approaches is that the latter includes transport costs while the former does not.[13]

Both of the approaches introduced above are to estimate tariff equivalents of NTMs for trade in goods. There are several studies that have attempted to estimate "tariff equivalents" of the relative degree of restriction to trade in services as well. For example, Hoekman (1995) estimated "tariff equivalents" of barriers to trade in services, using a set of benchmark, 'guess-estimates' of "tariff equivalents", and frequency ratios of impediments to trade in services.[14] He first arbitrarily defined a set of benchmark 'guess-estimates' of "tariff equivalents" for each sector to express an economy that is highly restricted with respect to market access.[15] Then, he estimated "tariff equivalents" for each sector by multiplying benchmark values by frequency ratios. Although the estimated values of "tariff equivalents" calculated by this procedure do not indicate that the prices are

[13] See Deardorff and Stern (1998) for more detailed explanation of these approaches.

[14] See also Holmes and Hardin (2000) for indices of restriction to foreign direct investment for APEC economies estimated by similar approach to Hoekman's.

[15] A value of 200% was arbitrarily chosen for the most restricted sectors while values between 20% and 50% were assigned to more open sectors.

higher by the rates than the prices in the absence of restriction, they are useful to obtain the indication of the relative degree of restriction in service trade across economies and sectors.

This paper basically follows the same framework as Sazanami, Urata, and Kawai (1995) to estimate tariff equivalents of NTMs by type, focusing on the price differentials between the price of imports and the domestic producer price of the substitutes. To obtain the magnitude of price differentials due to both tariffs and NTMs, *i.e.*, tariff equivalents of total trade protection, we first calculate price differentials by comparing the c.i.f. unit value of imports with domestic producer's unit value of the domestic substitute, and divide them by the c.i.f. price of imports. Then, tariff equivalents of overall NTMs can be obtained by subtracting tariffs from them. Finally, this paper also incorporates Hoekman's approach in the sense that frequency ratios are used into our estimation to obtain tariff equivalents by each type of measures, unlike prior works. We decompose tariff equivalents of overall NTMs by the five types of NTMs, using frequency ratios of NTMs. This procedure allows us to have the estimated degree of protection provided by each type of NTMs including non-core NTMs. The following sections present our procedure to obtain by-type frequency ratios as well as to estimate tariff equivalents of by-type NTMs.

3. The Pervasiveness of NTMs in the APEC Member Economies

To identify incidences of both core and non-core NTMs by type needs to use the information on NTMs at the most disaggregated levels[16] available from the UNCTAD database (TRAINS).[17] After describing how to construct by-type frequency ratios with such information, this section briefly discusses the features of the pervasiveness of core and non-core NTMs in the 13 APEC member

---

[16] The most disaggregated levels are HS eight-digit for Australia, Canada, Chile, China, Mexico, New Zealand, Singapore, and the United States, HS nine-digit for Indonesia, Japan, and Malaysia, and HS 10-digit for Korea and Thailand.

[17] The deficiency of this database is known as follows: first, the reliance on data may be doubtful since the underlying information is reported by a government of each economy and is not sent back to confirm its accuracy. PECC (2000) points out that the information on NTMs that have already removed is still included in some cases. Second, because of the lack of strong commitment on reporting NTMs, the types of measures reported are inconsistent among economies. While some economies provide detailed information on NTMs, others do not cooperate or do not properly report existing NTMs. In the case of economies with only a few types of NTMs reported, the small number of incidences does not necessarily mean low protection provided by NTMs. Third, the database does not have enough information on the types of technical measures (except technical regulations).

economies, based on the detailed frequency ratios. Economies included in the study are China, Indonesia, Thailand, Malaysia, Korea, Singapore, Japan, Australia, New Zealand, Chile, Mexico, Canada, and the United States. Notice that the latest years of NTM data available from UNCTAD (2001) are different across economies: the years are 2000 for Canada, 1994 for Singapore and Thailand and 1996-1999 for other APEC economies.

3.1. *Constructing Method of By-Type Frequency Ratios of NTMs*

To construct by-type frequency ratios, first of all, variable measures reported by each economy are categorized into the following types as they are inconsistent across economies: 1. Price control measures, 1-(1) Administrative pricing, 1-(3) Variable charges, 1-(4) Anti-dumping (AD) measures, 1-(5) Countervailing (CV) measures, 3. Automatic licensing measures, 4. Quantity control measures, 4-(1) Non-automatic licensing measures, 4-(2) Import quota, 4-(3) Import prohibition, 4-(4) Export restraint agreements, 5. Monopolistic measures, 5-(1) Single channel for imports, 6. Technical measures, 6-(1) Technical regulations, and 6-(3) Special customs formalities.[18] Table A1 in the Appendix shows measures reported by Japan, where figures in the first column indicate the classified types of measures.[19] Second, according to the categorization, we count the number of HS tariff lines subject to each type of NTMs at the most disaggregated level for each economy. Finally, a frequency ratio (F_{ji}) of j type of measures for sector/commodity i is obtained as follows:

$$F_{ji} = T_{ji} / T_i \cdot 100 \tag{3-1}$$

where T_i is the total number of tariff lines belonging to sector/commodity i and T_{ji} is the number of tariff lines subject to j type of NTMs among tariff lines belonging to sector/commodity i.

HS tariff lines of each economy are categorized into 21 sectors as the example of Japan shows (Table A2).[20] Table A2 presents, in addition to frequency ratios

---

[18] Financial measures are not included because no economy in the analysis reports their use.

[19] See Ando (2002, Table A-2) for tables with reported measures and the categorization conducted as the first procedure for each of other economies in the analysis. They are all available upon request.

[20] 21 sectors at the HS two-digit level are as follows: 1. HS Chapter 01-05, 2. HS Chapter 06-14, 3. HS Chapter 15, 4. HS Chapter 16-24, 5. HS Chapter 25-27, 6. HS Chapter 28-38, 7. HS Chapter 39-40, 8. HS Chapter 41-43, 9. HS Chapter 44-46, 10. HS Chapter 47-49, 11. HS Chapter 50-63, 12. HS Chapter 64-67, 13. HS Chapter 68-70, 14. HS Chapter 71, 15. HS Chapter 72-83, 16. HS Chapter 84-85, 17. HS Chapter 86-89, 18. HS Chapter 90-92, 19. HS Chapter 93, 20. HS Chapter 94-96, and 21. HS Chapter 97.

expressed as a percentage level, the total number of tariff lines in each of 21 sectors as well as the number of tariff lines subject to each type of measures in each sector in the case of Japan.[21] To easily make a comparison across economies, Table 2 provides summarized table with frequency ratios by type and by six industries: agriculture and food industry, chemicals, metals, light industry, machinery and transport equipment, and others.

3.2. *Features of the Use of NTMs*

Frequency ratios in terms of 21 sectors as well as of 6 sectors reveal that there are substantial differences across economies in the way of applying NTMs. The features observed for the 13 APEC member economies can be summarized as follows[22]: first, compared to developing economies, developed economies with lower tariff protection implement NTMs more pervasively instead of tariffs possibly to protect domestic producers.[23] In particular, they implement much less transparent types, *i.e.*, non-core NTMs such as technical measures, more pervasively. In the case of developing economies, they do not frequently use NTMs except China; China uses as many types of measures as administrative pricing, non-automatic licensing, import quotas, import prohibition, single channel for imports, and technical regulations, applying direct trade-distorting measures more frequently.

Second, some economies implement various types of NTMs together with relatively low coverage while others use a smaller number of types with high coverage. For instance, Japan implements many types of NTMs together for its protecting sectors particularly in agriculture and food industry though each of by-type frequency ratios is not extremely high. In contrast, Australia uses only a few types of NTMs but applies them to almost all products in its protecting sectors. In the case of agriculture and food sectors, the frequency ratio of technical regulations is as high as 100 percent. That is, any of the products included in these sectors should pass technical regulations in addition to other NTMs.

---

[21] See Ando (2002, Table A-1) for tables with frequency ratios for 21 sectors in other economies in the analysis. They are all available upon request.

[22] See Ando (2002) for much more detailed description on the use of NTMs in each of the 13 APEC member economies.

[23] See Table A3 in the Appendix for bounded tariffs, applied tariffs and so on in 1996, 2000/2001, 2003.

Table 2. Frequency ratios by the type of NTMs for the 13 APEC economies: Summary table for six sectors

Sector	Number of tariff lines	1	1-(1)	1-(3)	1-(4)	1-(5)	3	3-(1)	3-(2)	4	4-(1)	4-(2)	4-(3)	4-($)	5	5-(1)	6	6-(1)	6-(3)
China (1997)																			
Total	6911	**0.41**	0.41							**9.75**	2.82	5.06	2.66		**0.23**	0.23	**11.36**	11.36	
Agriculture and food processing	980	**1.02**	1.02							**9.29**	3.37	1.12	5.20		**1.43**	1.43	**4.90**	4.90	
Chemicals	1341	**0.30**	0.30							**8.13**	0.30	0.97	7.16				**1.79**	1.79	
Iron and steel	655									**15.27**	15.27						**30.08**	30.08	
Light industry	1713	**0.23**	0.23							**4.50**	2.92	2.86	0.58		**0.12**	0.12	**9.17**	9.17	
Machinery and transport equipment	1849	**0.11**	0.11							**14.71**		14.66	0.54				**17.41**	17.41	
Others	373									**6.70**			4.56				**9.92**	9.92	
Indonesia (1999)																			
Total	7252	**0.18**			0.18		**0.58**	0.58		**1.75**	**1.54**		0.21		**0.10**	0.10	**10.81**	10.81	
Agriculture and food processing	1046						**2.29**	2.29		**2.49**	2.49						**67.21**	67.21	
Chemicals	1378	**0.15**			0.15					**2.32**	1.23		1.09		**0.29**	0.29	**5.44**	5.44	
Iron and steel	826	**1.33**			1.33					**4.24**	4.24								
Light industry	2074						**0.87**	0.87		**0.43**	0.43								
Machinery and transport equipment	1517									**1.32**	1.32								
Others	411									**1.22**	1.22				**0.73**	0.73	**1.46**	1.46	

Table 2. Frequency ratios by the type of NTMs for the 13 APEC economies: Summary table for six sectors–Continued

Sector	Number of tariff lines	The type of NTMs 1	1-(1)	1-(3)	1-(4)	1-(5)	3	3-(1)	3-(2)	4	4-(1)	4-(2)	4-(3)	4-($)	5	5-(1)	6	6-(1)	6-(3)
Thailand (1994)																			
Total	6837						**1.67**		1.67	**9.65**	8.61		1.45		**0.09**	0.09	**20.14**	20.14	
Agriculture and food processing	1044						**10.92**		10.92	**8.72**	8.62		0.86		**0.57**	0.57	**78.45**	78.45	
Chemicals	1219									**0.66**	0.08		0.57				**38.23**	38.23	
Iron and steel	646									**1.39**	1.39						**0.93**	0.93	
Light industry	1700									**24.82**	24.12		0.71				**0.35**	0.35	
Machinery and transport equipment	1821									**5.82**	3.02		3.90				**4.39**	4.39	
Others	407									**5.90**	5.90								
Malaysia (1996)																			
Total	8596	**0.02**			0.02					**8.82**	8.34	0.02	0.52		**0.14**	0.14	**3.51**	3.51	
Agriculture and food processing	1252									**14.22**	12.70	0.16	1.44		**0.96**	0.96	**19.73**	19.73	
Chemicals	1824	**0.11**			0.11					**5.26**	5.21		0.05				**0.11**	0.01	
Iron and steel	1052									**4.56**	4.56								
Light industry	2116									**7.04**	7.04								
Machinery and transport equipment	1887									**11.98**	11.61		0.64				**2.76**	2.76	
Others	465									**13.12**	10.11		3.01				**0.22**	0.22	

Table 2. Frequency ratios by the type of NTMs for the 13 APEC economies: Summary table for six sectors–Continued

Sector	Number of tariff lines	The type of NTMs 1	1-(1)	1-(3)	1-(4)	1-(5)	3	3-(1)	3-(2)	4	4-(1)	4-(2)	4-(3)	4-($)	5	5-(1)	6	6-(1)	6-(3)
Korea (1996)																			
Total	6374	**0.27**			0.27					**0.02**	0.02								
Agriculture and food processing	1036																		
Chemicals	1273	**0.08**			0.08					**0.08**	0.08								
Iron and steel	652																		
Light industry	1488	**0.60**			0.60														
Machinery and transport equipment	1534																		
Others	391	**1.79**			1.79														
Singapore (1994)																			
Total	5829						**3.31**	3.31		**15.78**	14.98		1.10				**2.40**	2.40	
Agriculture and food processing	891						**21.66**	21.66		**48.93**	48.15		1.46				**2.36**	2.36	
Chemicals	1067									**29.43**	29.43		0.09				**0.19**	0.09	
Iron and steel	627																		
Light industry	1562									**2.82**	2.82		0.06						
Machinery and transport equipment	1312									**6.63**	4.42		2.21				**8.99**	8.99	
Others	370									**10.54**	7.57		5.14						

Table 2. Frequency ratios by the type of NTMs for the 13 APEC economies: Summary table for six sectors–Continued

Sector	Number of tariff lines	1	1-(1)	1-(3)	1-(4)	1-(5)	3	3-(1)	3-(2)	4	4-(1)	4-(2)	4-(3)	4-($)	5	5-(1)	6	6-(1)	6-(3)
Japan (1996)																			
Total	9032	**0.73**		0.72	0.01		**0.55**	0.55		**19.19**	17.34	2.35			**1.76**	1.76	**26.58**	26.58	
Agriculture and food processing	1954	**1.54**		1.54			**2.10**	2.10		**15.66**	14.69	3.28			**6.40**	6.40	**56.91**	56.91	
Chemicals	1308	**0.08**		0.08						**7.42**	0.23	7.19			**1.68**	1.68	**65.83**	65.83	
Iron and steel	835	**4.19**		4.07	0.12					**36.17**	36.05	0.12					**4.67**	4.67	
Light industry	3043									**32.04**	32.04				**0.33**	0.33	**5.78**	5.78	
Machinery and transport equipment	1451									**1.93**		1.93			**0.07**	0.07	**6.89**	6.89	
Others	441						**2.04**	2.04		**5.67**		5.67			**0.23**	0.23	**25.62**	25.62	
Australia (1999)																			
Total	5818	**0.33**			0.28	0.07				**3.44**	2.29		1.17				**19.97**	19.97	
Agriculture and food processing	733	**0.55**			0.14	0.55				**8.19**	2.18		6.14				**100.00**	100.00	
Chemicals	1044	**0.48**			0.48					**6.42**	5.56		0.86				**8.05**	8.05	
Iron and steel	588	**0.34**			0.34					**0.34**			0.34						
Light industry	1641	**0.36**			0.36					**1.20**	1.20						**0.54**	0.54	
Machinery and transport equipment	1457	**0.14**			0.14					**2.54**	2.54						**22.31**	22.31	
Others	325									**4.31**	0.62		3.69				**3.38**	3.38	

Table 2. Frequency ratios by the type of NTMs for the 13 APEC economies: Summary table for six sectors–Continued

	Number	The type of NTMs																	
	of tariff	1					3			4					5		6		
Sector	lines		1-(1)	1-(3)	1-(4)	1-(5)		3-(1)	3-(2)		4-(1)	4-(2)	4-(3)	4-($)		5-(1)		6-(1)	6-(3)
New Zealand (1999)																			
Total	7246	**1.09**			1.01	0.11				**19.35**	19.28		0.07				**23.46**	23.46	
Agriculture and food processing	1037	**0.96**			0.87	0.29				**65.67**	65.67						**44.55**	44.55	
Chemicals	1275									**31.14**	21.14						**9.96**	9.96	
Iron and steel	788	**0.13**			0.13					**2.28**	2.28								
Light industry	2093	**2.77**			2.77					**8.03**	7.79		0.24				**8.41**	8.41	
Machinery and transport equipment	1639	**0.55**			0.24	0.31				**5.06**	5.06						**56.07**	56.07	
Others	414	**0.24**			0.24					**13.29**	13.29						**3.86**	3.86	
Chile (1999)																			
Total	5854	**0.51**		0.51						**8.78**	6.51		2.99				**32.71**	32.58	28.25
Agriculture and food processing	853	**3.52**		3.52						**25.56**	20.05		8.21				**97.66**	97.66	96.48
Chemicals	1171									**14.43**	12.89		3.07				**63.79**	63.11	60.46
Iron and steel	593									**0.84**	0.84						**0.51**	0.51	
Light industry	1556									**1.41**	0.84		0.58				**8.61**	8.61	7.20
Machinery and transport equipment	1349									**5.93**	1.63		4.37				**13.64**	13.64	
Others	332									**6.02**	5.72		0.30				**4.22**	4.22	3.31

Table 2. Frequency ratios by the type of NTMs for the 13 APEC economies: Summary table for six sectors–Continued

Sector	Number of tariff lines	The type of NTMs 1	1-(1)	1-(3)	1-(4)	1-(5)	3	3-(1)	3-(2)	4	4-(1)	4-(2)	4-(3)	4-($)	5	5-(1)	6	6-(1)	6-(3)
Mexico (1999)																			
Total	11319						**0.71**	0.71		**10.55**	10.46	0.09					**48.05**	48.05	
Agriculture and food processing	1068									**24.53**	24.53						**78.18**	78.18	
Chemicals	3208						**0.34**	0.34		**22.44**	22.13	0.31					**62.47**	62.47	
Iron and steel	1153						**1.56**	1.56		**0.87**	0.87						**18.21**	18.21	
Light industry	2164						**2.22**	2.22		**0.09**	0.09						**69.55**	69.55	
Machinery and transport equipment	3264						**0.06**	0.06		**4.47**	4.47						**21.75**	21.75	
Others	462						**0.22**	0.22		**11.69**	11.69						**37.88**	37.88	
Canada (2000)																			
Total	8175									**21.83**	15.23	0.24		6.41			**1.38**	1.38	
Agriculture and food processing	1397									**56.19**	56.19	0.29					**0.29**	0.29	
Chemicals	1390									**2.73**	1.58	1.15					**3.24**	3.24	
Iron and steel	883									**34.31**	34.31						**0.57**	0.57	
Light industry	2103									**30.05**	5.23			24.82					
Machinery and transport equipment	2009									**0.05**	0.05						**2.94**	2.94	
Others	393									**6.62**	6.11			0.51					

Table 2. Frequency ratios by the type of NTMs for the 13 APEC economies: Summary table for six sectors–Continued

Sector	Number of tariff lines	The type of NTMs 1	1-(1)	1-(3)	1-(4)	1-(5)	3	3-(1)	3-(2)	4	4-(1)	4-(2)	4-(3)	4-($)	5	5-(1)	6	6-(1)	6-(3)
USA (1999)																			
Total	10176	**6.75**			6.48	1.58				**9.65**	8.89	0.68	0.08				**25.29**	25.29	
Agriculture and food processing	1785	**2.52**			2.02	0.78				**26.39**	26.16	0.22					**61.85**	61.85	
Chemicals	2018	**4.86**			4.86	0.10				**4.76**	1.19	3.22	0.35				**10.41**	10.41	
Iron and steel	982	**23.73**			23.73	12.63				**0.10**			0.10				**0.51**	0.51	
Light industry	2681	**1.08**			0.52	0.63				**13.17**	13.17						**30.70**	30.70	
Machinery and transport equipment	2205	**12.34**			12.15	0.18				**0.45**	0.45						**18.00**	18.00	
Others	505	**1.98**			1.98					**10.10**	10.10						**6.93**	6.93	

Data source: Author's calculation, based on the information available from UNCTAD (2001).

Note: The types of NTMs are as follows:

Large category	Sub-category			
1: Price control measures	1-(1): Administrative pricing	1-(3): Variable charges	1-(4): AD measures	1-(5): CV measures
3: Automatic licensing measures	3-(1): Automatic license	3-(2): Import monitoring		
4: Quantity control measures	4-(1): Non-automatic licensing	4-(2): Import quotas	4-(3): Import prohibition	4-(4): Export restraint arrangements
5: Monopolistic measures	5-(1): Single channel for imports			
6: Technical measures	6-(1): Technical regulations	6-(3): Special custom formalities		

Third, both developing and developed economies commonly protect agriculture and food sectors by explicit and implicit trade distorting NTMs though protecting sectors vary across economies, reflecting each economy's policy.

4. Estimation of Tariff Equivalents of By- Type NTMs

This section explains how to estimate tariff equivalents of by-type NTMs, using by-type frequency ratios, and also describes data sources used in the estimation.

4.1. *Estimation Procedures*

Estimating tariff equivalents of NTMs by type and commodity requires three steps. The first step is to calculate the magnitude of price differential due to NTMs. Let p_i^M and p_i^D be the c.i.f. price of imports and the domestic producer price of the domestic substitutes of commodity i ($i = 1, \cdots, 21$), respectively. PD_i^T stands for the magnitude of price differential induced by both tariffs and NTMs for commodity i. Then, PD_i^T can be calculated as follows:

$$PD_i^T = 100 \times (p_i^D - p_i^M) / p_i^M . \tag{4-1}$$

Notice that a critical assumption for this procedure is the homogeneity of imported goods and the domestic substitutes. As Deardorff and Stern (1998) discuss, this method is valid to the extent that the domestic and imported goods are perfect substitutes so that they both sell the same price in the domestic market. If imported goods are of higher quality than domestic goods in the same industry, for example, this measure would find negative protection.

Let t_i be the import tariff rate for commodity i. Denote by PD_i^N the magnitude of price differential due to NTMs for commodity i. Then, PD_i^N can be obtained by subtracting t_i from PD_i^T calculated in equation (4-1).

$$PD_i^N = PD_i^T - t_i \tag{4-2}$$

The second step is to estimate the price distorting effect of each type of NTMs, using PD_i^N obtained in the first step and frequency ratios of NTMs. The types of NTMs examined in the study are 1:price control measures, 3: auto-licensing measures, 4:quantity control measures, 5:monopolistic measures and 6:technical measures.[24] Denote by F_{ji} the frequency ratio of j type of

[24] The number of types follows the typology in Table 1. Type 2 could be financial measures but is omitted since no economy in the analysis reports them.

NTMs for commodity i ($j = 1,3,4,5,6$). The base-case regression equation is as follows:

$$PD_i^N = \alpha + \sum_j \hat{\beta}_j F_{ji}. \qquad (4\text{-}3)$$

where α stands for the intercept and $\hat{\beta}_j$'s are the estimated coefficients of price distorting effect of each type of NTMs. Notice that the price distorting effect of j-type NTMs, β_j, is assumed to be common across sectors. In addition to the base-case regression, we also control income levels by adding variables such as GDP *per capita* (the ratio to GDP *per capita* in the United States) or a developing economy dummy to take into account the fact that there seems to be more cases with negative price differentials due to the quality difference between imported goods and domestic goods treated as comparable goods in developing economies. Considering possible heteroskedasticity problem due to analysis of cross-section data, the White estimator of variance is used for these regressions.

The final step is to calculate by-type tariff equivalents for 21 commodities. Denote by TE_{ji} tariff equivalent of j-type NTMs for commodity i. By multiplying $\hat{\beta}_j$ by F_{ji}, TE_{ji} is finally estimated.

$$TE_{ji} = \hat{\beta}_j F_{ji}. \qquad (4\text{-}4)$$

Although $\hat{\beta}_j$ are assumed to be common across sectors, F_{ji} reflect sector specific effects to some extent. Therefore, TE_{ji} estimated by multiplying $\hat{\beta}_j$ by F_{ji} could be interpreted as tariff equivalents of a certain type of measures for a certain commodity.

4.2. *Data Description*

Domestic producer unit prices in local currency are calculated by dividing values by quantities. Values of domestic production are available from United Nations (various years) at the ISIC four-digit level (rev.2 and rev.3),[25] and quantities of domestic production are from United Nations (1998a) at the ISIC six-digit level (rev.2).[26] The years of domestic production data

[25] Values of domestic production are in ISIC rev. 3 for Australia, Canada, Indonesia, Japan, Korea, and Singapore while in ISIC rev. 2 for others. As for economies with value data at the ISIC rev. 3 code, value data are first converted to ISIC rev. 2 and then matched with quantity data at the ISIC rev. 2 code.

[26] As quantity data are based on more disaggregated classification, they are aggregated to be matched with production value data. Some quantity data are unable to be aggregated because their measuring units are different across commodities.

are the same or available years that are the closest to those of NTM data.[27]

Similarly, c.i.f. import unit prices are calculated by dividing values by quantities. Values and quantities of imports are from United Nations (1998b) at the SITC four-digit level for New Zealand, Malaysia, Thailand, and Singapore and from GTI (various years) at the HS four-digit level for all other economies. The years of import data are the same as those of domestic production data.

Import tariff rates at the HS two-digit level are obtained by first aggregating the data at the most disaggregated levels, which are available from UNCTAD (1999), to the HS six-digit level, and then re-aggregating them up to the HS two-digit level by taking simple average.[28] The years of tariff data are the same or available years that are the closest to those of NTM data.

Frequency ratios by type and by 21 commodities are constructed as the previous section explains, based on the information on NTMs at the most disaggregated levels available from UNCTAD (2001). As already mentioned, the latest years of NTM data available from UNCTAD (2001) vary from economy to economy: the years are 2000 for Canada, 1994 for Singapore and Thailand, and 1996-1999 for others.

To calculate the price differentials between c.i.f. import prices and domestic producer prices, sectors at the ISIC four-digit code are matched with those at the HS (SITC) four-digit code. Exchange rates (period average), which are from the World Bank (2001), are used for economies where currencies for import data and domestic production data are different. Then, the magnitude of price differentials due to NTMs is obtained by subtracting tariff rates from that of price differentials due to both tariffs and NTMs at the HS four-digit level. In obtaining the magnitude of price differentials for 21 commodities, we take the simple average of those at the HS four-digit level according to the commodity classification of NTM data.[29]

---

[27] The years of domestic production data are as follows: 1998 for Indonesia, 1997 for Australia, Chile, and China, 1996 for Japan, Korea, and Malaysia, 1995 for Canada, Mexico, and United States, 1994 for Thailand and Singapore, and 1993 for New Zealand.

[28] Tariffs are basically MFN tariffs. Information on preferential tariffs under bilateral/regional agreements is not incorporated in calculating import tariff rates at HS two-digit level.

[29] Extremely large values of the magnitude of price differentials at the HS four-digit level are omitted when the simple average of price differentials is calculated by commodity. Such data would be attributed to large differences in quality between import goods and the domestic substitutes that are matched as same goods to obtain price differentials.

5. Empirical Results and the Implication

This section presents preliminary empirical results of estimating tariff equivalents of NTMs by type, and discusses the implication. In order to calculate tariff equivalents, price distorting effects of five types of NTMs (β_j) were first estimated by regressing the magnitude of price differentials attributed to NTMs (PD_i^N) by frequency ratios of NTMs (F_{ji}). Table 3 shows the estimated coefficients for price distorting effect ($\hat{\beta}_j$), based on the regression equation (4-3) with and without control variable, GDP *per capita* (the ratio to GDP *per capita* in the United States), which provide several findings.[30] First, the estimated coefficients for all types of measures are positive. They imply that core NTMs as well as non-core NTMs have positive price distorting effects, do raise the prices of imports, and provide a certain degree of protection for domestic producers. Although non-core NTMs, *i.e.*, automatic licensing measures, monopolistic measures, and technical measures, have not been empirically measured in many previous studies, these results suggest that they significantly affect international trade, and their protective effects should not be neglected at all.

Second, price control measures have the largest estimated coefficient of price distorting effect among all types of measures. This implies that price control measures increase directly and indirectly the price of imports most if the frequency ratios are the same. For example, AD/CV measures directly raise the domestic price of imports by the rate of AD/CV duty. They may also indirectly increase the price through a reduction of potential trade volume from export economy even if they are not actually imposed, due to uncertainty of their implementation. Although price control measures are not as pervasive as quantity control measures are, the increase in the use of AD/CV measures would be definitely harmful to international trade.

Third, quantity control measures, which are another core NTMs, show much smaller price distorting effect. This would be because they include not only direct trade restrictive measures such as quota and prohibition but also very indirect ones like non-automatic licensing measures, which are the most frequently used ones among quantity control measures.

Let us move to the results of estimated tariff equivalents. Table 4 displays the estimated tariff equivalents by five types of measures for 21 sectors, which are based on $\hat{\beta}_j$ estimated with the control variable. Half of the economies in the analysis have nine or more sectors with tariff equivalents of overall NTMs by

---

[30] Although developing economy dummy is also used to control income levels instead of GDP *per capita*, the results are not shown because they are similar to the ones shown in Table 3.

Table 3. Price distorting effects of five types of NTMs (Dependent variable: tariff equivalents of overall NTMs)

Variable	Equation (1)	Equation (2)
C	155.95[1] (4.61)	99.61 (1.51)
Price control measures	13.08[2] (2.44)	11.95[3] (1.91)
Auto-licensing measures	4.12 (1.08)	5.81[3] (1.96)
Quantity control measures	0.20 (0.15)	0.12 (0.09)
Monopolistic measures	11.87 (0.87)	6.55 (0.39)
Technical measures	0.91 (0.54)	0.91 (0.55)
GDP *per capita*		129.71 (0.95)
R-squared	0.033	0.0445
Number of observations	123	123

[1] Statistically significant at the 0.01 level.
[2] Statistically significant at the 0.5 level.
[3] Statistically significant at the 0.1 level.

t-values are in parentheses.

more than 10 percent: Australia, Chile, China, Japan, Mexico, New Zealand, and the United States. This leads to several interesting insights since all of them, except China, are either developed economies or economies with a number of free trade agreements (FTAs) or bilateral/regional agreements. First of all, developed economies do effectively implement NTMs to protect domestic industries. In particular, they significantly use non-core NTMs such as technical measures in addition to core NTMs. Non-core NTMs, especially technical measures, are of much less transparent type and are government policies with legitimacy under multilateral trading rules. However, the positive and high equivalent rates indicate that they could do provide a certain degree of protection for domestic producers as disguised trade restriction. Even if tariffs have been successfully reduced, the reduced protection would be easily offset by these high equivalent rates of NTMs, including non-core NTMs.

Table 4. Tariff equivalents of NTMs by type for 21 commodities

Commodities	1 Price control measures	3 Automatic licensing	4 Quantity control measures	5 Monopolistic measures	6 Technical measures	1+4 Core NTMs	3+5+6 Non-Core NTMs	1+3+4+5+6 Overall NTMs
	China							
Live animals & products	0.0	0.0	1.4	0.0	0.7	1.4	0.7	2.1
Vegetable products	23.0	0.0	0.8	11.1	3.3	23.8	14.4	38.2
Animal & vegetable oils	0.0	0.0	3.4	0.0	36.9	3.4	36.9	40.3
Products of food industry	9.9	0.0	1.0	19.0	4.5	10.9	23.6	34.5
Mineral products	51.4	0.0	0.5	0.0	12.8	51.9	12.8	64.7
Chemicals	0.0	0.0	1.1	0.0	0.2	1.1	0.2	1.2
Plastic & plastic materials	20.5	0.0	0.6	0.0	8.6	21.2	8.6	29.8
Skin, raw material	0.0	0.0	0.0	0.0	17.8	0.0	17.8	17.8
Wood & wood products	10.6	0.0	2.0	0.0	3.2	12.5	3.2	15.8
Pulp & paper	0.0	0.0	0.7	0.0	28.9	0.7	28.9	29.6
Textiles	3.4	0.0	0.6	1.2	7.4	4.0	8.6	12.6
Footwear, umbrellas	0.0	0.0	0.0	0.0	0.0	0.0	0.0	0.0
Cement, ceramic, *et al.*	0.0	0.0	0.0	0.0	0.0	0.0	0.0	0.0
Precious stones	0.2	0.0	0.0	0.0	0.0	0.0	0.0	0.0
Base metals & products	0.0	0.0	1.9	0.0	27.5	1.9	27.5	29.3
Ordinary machinery	1.9	0.0	1.5	0.0	16.3	3.4	16.3	19.7
Transport equipment	0.0	0.0	3.7	0.0	19.8	3.7	19.8	23.5
Precision machinery	0.0	0.0	1.2	0.0	10.9	1.2	10.9	12.1
Firearms	0.0	0.0	12.3	0.0	0.0	12.3	0.0	12.3
Various manufactured goods	0.0	0.0	0.0	0.0	6.2	0.0	6.2	6.2
Art, antiques, *et al.*	0.0	0.0	0.0	0.0	0.0	0.0	0.0	0.0

Table 4. Tariff equivalents of NTMs by type for 21 commodities–Continued

Commodities	1 Price control measures	3 Automatic licensing	4 Quantity control measures	5 Monopolistic measures	6 Technical measures	1+4 Core NTMs	3+5+6 Non-Core NTMs	1+3+4+5+6 Overall NTMs
				Indonesia				
Live animals & products	0.0	14.9	0.0	0.0	87.3	0.0	102.2	102.2
Vegetable products	0.0	15.0	0.0	0.0	77.7	0.0	92.6	92.6
Animal & vegetable oils	0.0	0.0	0.0	0.0	84.8	0.0	84.8	84.8
Products of food industry	0.0	12.9	1.0	0.0	13.6	1.0	26.5	27.5
Mineral products	0.0	0.0	0.3	10.9	3.0	0.3	14.0	14.3
Chemicals	2.3	0.0	0.3	2.6	6.2	2.6	8.8	11.4
Plastic & plastic materials	0.0	0.0	0.2	0.0	1.3	0.2	1.3	1.5
Skin, raw material	0.0	0.0	0.0	0.0	0.0	0.0	0.0	0.0
Wood & wood products	0.0	0.0	0.0	0.0	0.0	0.0	0.0	0.0
Pulp & paper	0.0	0.0	0.5	0.0	0.0	0.5	0.0	0.5
Textiles	0.0	7.8	0.0	0.0	0.0	0.0	7.8	7.8
Footwear, umbrellas	0.0	0.0	0.0	0.0	0.0	0.0	0.0	0.0
Cement, ceramic, *et al.*	0.0	0.0	0.1	0.0	0.0	0.1	0.0	0.1
Precious stones	0.0	17.6	0.0	0.0	0.0	0.0	17.6	17.6
Base metals & products	15.9	0.0	0.5	0.0	0.0	16.4	0.0	16.4
Ordinary machinery	0.0	0.0	0.2	0.0	0.0	0.2	0.0	0.2
Transport equipment	0.0	0.0	0.3	0.0	0.0	0.3	0.0	0.3
Precision machinery	0.0	0.0	0.0	0.0	0.0	0.0	0.0	0.0
Firearms	0.0	0.0	0.0	0.0	0.0	0.0	0.0	0.0
Various manufactured goods	0.0	0.0	0.0	0.0	0.0	0.0	0.0	0.0
Art, antiques, *et al.*	0.0	0.0	0.0	0.0	0.0	0.0	0.0	0.0

Table 4. Tariff equivalents of NTMs by type for 21 commodities–Continued

Commodities	1 Price control measures	3 Automatic licensing	4 Quantity control measures	5 Monopolistic measures	6 Technical measures	1+4 Core NTMs	3+5+6 Non-Core NTMs	1+3+4+5+6 Overall NTMs
				Thailand				
Live animals & products	0.0	0.0	1.5	0.0	78.1	1.5	78.1	79.6
Vegetable products	0.0	0.0	0.6	1.6	82.4	0.6	84.0	84.6
Animal & vegetable oils	0.0	503.5	1.8	0.0	91.3	1.8	594.8	596.6
Products of food industry	0.0	76.9	1.2	12.0	42.3	1.2	131.2	132.4
Mineral products	0.0	0.0	0.9	0.0	11.3	0.9	11.3	12.2
Chemicals	0.0	0.0	0.1	0.0	44.2	0.1	44.2	44.3
Plastic & plastic materials	0.0	0.0	0.0	0.0	2.7	0.0	2.7	2.7
Skin, raw material	0.0	0.0	0.0	0.0	0.0	0.0	0.0	0.0
Wood & wood products	0.0	0.0	6.7	0.0	0.0	6.7	0.0	6.7
Pulp & paper	0.0	0.0	0.0	0.0	0.0	0.0	0.0	0.0
Textiles	0.0	0.0	4.0	0.0	0.0	4.0	0.0	4.0
Footwear, umbrellas	0.0	0.0	0.0	0.0	2.6	0.0	2.6	2.6
Cement, ceramic, *et al.*	0.0	0.0	1.6	0.0	2.2	1.6	2.2	3.8
Precious stones	0.0	0.0	0.9	0.0	0.0	0.9	0.0	0.9
Base metals & products	0.0	0.0	0.2	0.0	0.8	0.2	0.8	1.0
Ordinary machinery	0.0	0.0	0.4	0.0	4.7	0.4	4.7	5.1
Transport equipment	0.0	0.0	3.3	0.0	4.8	3.3	4.8	8.1
Precision machinery	0.0	0.0	0.1	0.0	0.0	0.1	0.0	0.1
Firearms	0.0	0.0	0.0	0.0	0.0	0.0	0.0	0.0
Various manufactured goods	0.0	0.0	0.5	0.0	0.0	0.5	0.0	0.5
Art, antiques, *et al.*	0.0	0.0	3.1	0.0	0.0	3.1	0.0	3.1

Table 4. Tariff equivalents of NTMs by type for 21 commodities–Continued

Commodities	1 Price control measures	3 Automatic licensing	4 Quantity control measures	5 Monopolistic measures	6 Technical measures	1+4 Core NTMs	3+5+6 Non-Core NTMs	1+3+4+5+6 Overall NTMs
	Malaysia							
Live animals & products	0.0	0.0	3.9	0.0	17.1	3.9	17.1	21.0
Vegetable products	0.0	0.0	1.2	16.3	48.4	1.2	64.7	65.9
Animal & vegetable oils	0.0	0.0	0.5	0.0	0.0	0.5	0.0	0.5
Products of food industry	0.0	0.0	1.2	4.5	0.2	1.2	4.7	6.0
Mineral products	0.0	0.0	1.1	0.0	0.0	1.1	0.0	1.1
Chemicals	0.0	0.0	0.8	0.0	0.2	0.8	0.2	1.0
Plastic & plastic materials	3.8	0.0	0.4	0.0	0.0	4.2	0.0	4.2
Skin, raw material	0.0	0.0	0.0	0.0	0.0	0.0	0.0	0.0
Wood & wood products	0.0	0.0	3.5	0.0	0.0	3.5	0.0	3.5
Pulp & paper	0.0	0.0	0.4	0.0	0.0	0.4	0.0	0.4
Textiles	0.0	0.0	0.5	0.0	0.0	0.5	0.0	0.5
Footwear, umbrellas	0.0	0.0	0.3	0.0	0.0	0.3	0.0	0.3
Cement, ceramic, *et al.*	0.0	0.0	0.0	0.0	0.0	0.0	0.0	0.0
Precious stones	0.0	0.0	1.2	0.0	0.0	1.2	0.0	1.2
Base metals & products	0.0	0.0	0.6	0.0	0.0	0.6	0.0	0.6
Ordinary machinery	0.0	0.0	0.7	0.0	3.8	0.7	3.8	4.5
Transport equipment	0.0	0.0	4.9	0.0	0.2	4.9	0.2	5.1
Precision machinery	0.0	0.0	0.2	0.0	0.0	0.2	0.0	0.2
Firearms	0.0	0.0	12.3	0.0	0.0	12.3	0.0	12.3
Various manufactured goods	0.0	0.0	1.2	0.0	0.4	1.2	0.4	1.5
Art, antiques, *et al.*	0.0	0.0	0.0	0.0	0.0	0.0	0.0	0.0

Table 4. Tariff equivalents of NTMs by type for 21 commodities–Continued

Commodities	1 Price control measures	3 Automatic licensing	4 Quantity control measures	5 Monopolistic measures	6 Technical measures	1+4 Core NTMs	3+5+6 Non-Core NTMs	1+3+4+5+6 Overall NTMs
				Korea				
Live animals & products	0.0	0.0	0.0	0.0	0.0	0.0	0.0	0.0
Vegetable products	0.0	0.0	0.0	0.0	0.0	0.0	0.0	0.0
Animal & vegetable oils	0.0	0.0	0.0	0.0	0.0	0.0	0.0	0.0
Products of food industry	0.0	0.0	0.0	0.0	0.0	0.0	0.0	0.0
Mineral products	41.0	0.0	0.0	0.0	0.0	41.0	0.0	41.0
Chemicals	0.0	0.0	0.0	0.0	0.0	0.0	0.0	0.0
Plastic & plastic materials	5.7	0.0	0.0	0.0	0.0	5.7	0.0	5.7
Skin, raw material	0.0	0.0	0.0	0.0	0.0	0.0	0.0	0.0
Wood & wood products	0.0	0.0	0.0	0.0	0.0	0.0	0.0	0.0
Pulp & paper	0.0	0.0	0.0	0.0	0.0	0.0	0.0	0.0
Textiles	12.4	0.0	0.0	0.0	0.0	12.4	0.0	12.4
Footwear, umbrellas	0.0	0.0	0.0	0.0	0.0	0.0	0.0	0.0
Cement, ceramic, *et al.*	0.0	0.0	0.0	0.0	0.0	0.0	0.0	0.0
Precious stones	0.0	0.0	0.0	0.0	0.0	0.0	0.0	0.0
Base metals & products	0.0	0.0	0.0	0.0	0.0	0.0	0.0	0.0
Ordinary machinery	0.0	0.0	0.0	0.0	0.0	0.0	0.0	0.0
Transport equipment	0.0	0.0	0.0	0.0	0.0	0.0	0.0	0.0
Precision machinery	0.0	0.0	0.0	0.0	0.0	0.0	0.0	0.0
Firearms	0.0	0.0	0.0	0.0	0.0	0.0	0.0	0.0
Various manufactured goods	0.0	0.0	0.0	0.0	0.0	0.0	0.0	0.0
Art, antiques, *et al.*	0.0	0.0	0.0	0.0	0.0	0.0	0.0	0.0

Table 4. Tariff equivalents of NTMs by type for 21 commodities–Continued

Commodities	1 Price control measures	3 Automatic licensing	4 Quantity control measures	5 Monopolistic measures	6 Technical measures	1+4 Core NTMs	3+5+6 Non-Core NTMs	1+3+4+5+6 Overall NTMs
				Singapore				
Live animals & products	0.0	135.6	9.4	0.0	5.3	9.4	140.9	150.3
Vegetable products	0.0	250.3	6.8	0.0	0.0	6.8	250.3	257.2
Animal & vegetable oils	0.0	0.0	12.3	0.0	0.0	12.3	0.0	12.3
Products of food industry	0.0	0.0	0.9	0.0	2.3	0.9	2.3	3.2
Mineral products	0.0	0.0	0.0	0.0	0.0	0.0	0.0	0.0
Chemicals	0.0	0.0	4.6	0.0	0.1	4.6	0.1	4.8
Plastic & plastic materials	0.0	0.0	0.0	0.0	0.0	0.1	0.0	0.1
Skin, raw material	0.0	0.0	2.3	0.0	0.0	2.3	0.0	2.3
Wood & wood products	0.0	0.0	0.0	0.0	0.0	0.0	0.0	0.0
Pulp & paper	0.0	0.0	1.0	0.0	0.0	1.0	0.0	1.0
Textiles	0.0	0.0	0.2	0.0	0.0	0.2	0.0	0.2
Footwear, umbrellas	0.0	0.0	0.8	0.0	0.0	0.8	0.0	0.8
Cement, ceramic, *et al.*	0.0	0.0	0.0	0.0	0.0	0.0	0.0	0.0
Precious stones	0.0	0.0	0.0	0.0	0.0	0.0	0.0	0.0
Base metals & products	0.0	0.0	0.0	0.0	0.0	0.0	0.0	0.0
Ordinary machinery	0.0	0.0	0.6	0.0	8.1	0.6	8.1	8.6
Transport equipment	0.0	0.0	2.4	0.0	22.2	2.4	22.2	24.6
Precision machinery	0.0	0.0	0.8	0.0	0.0	0.8	0.0	0.8
Firearms	0.0	0.0	12.3	0.0	0.0	12.3	0.0	12.3
Various manufactured goods	0.0	0.0	1.5	0.0	0.0	1.5	0.0	1.5
Art, antiques, *et al.*	0.0	0.0	3.1	0.0	0.0	3.1	0.0	3.1

Table 4. Tariff equivalents of NTMs by type for 21 commodities–Continued

Commodities	1 Price control measures	3 Automatic licensing	4 Quantity control measures	5 Monopolistic measures	6 Technical measures	1+4 Core NTMs	3+5+6 Non-Core NTMs	1+3+4+5+6 Overall NTMs
				Japan				
Live animals & products	61.0	19.0	6.1	118.2	88.5	67.1	225.7	292.8
Vegetable products	4.3	23.8	0.6	30.4	82.3	4.9	136.5	141.4
Animal & vegetable oils	0.0	0.0	0.9	0.0	82.4	0.9	82.4	83.3
Products of food industry	0.0	0.0	0.0	0.0	0.0	0.0	0.0	0.0
Mineral products	0.0	25.3	0.2	3.2	29.1	0.2	57.5	57.7
Chemicals	1.2	0.0	1.1	14.1	73.7	2.3	87.7	90.0
Plastic & plastic materials	0.0	0.0	0.2	0.0	11.0	0.2	11.0	11.1
Skin, raw material	0.0	0.0	2.7	0.0	33.8	2.7	33.8	36.5
Wood & wood products	0.0	0.0	2.0	0.0	28.7	2.0	28.7	30.7
Pulp & paper	0.0	0.0	0.0	0.0	14.2	0.0	14.2	14.2
Textiles	0.0	0.0	5.3	3.1	0.0	5.3	3.1	8.5
Footwear, umbrellas	0.0	0.0	0.1	0.0	0.0	0.1	0.0	0.1
Cement, ceramic, *et al.*	0.0	0.0	0.0	0.0	7.9	0.0	7.9	7.9
Precious stones	0.0	0.0	0.0	0.0	3.5	0.0	3.5	3.5
Base metals & products	50.1	0.0	4.4	0.0	4.3	54.5	4.3	58.8
Ordinary machinery	0.0	0.0	0.2	0.7	2.8	0.2	3.4	3.6
Transport equipment	0.0	0.0	0.6	0.0	5.4	0.6	5.4	6.1
Precision machinery	0.0	0.0	0.1	0.0	18.1	0.1	18.1	18.2
Firearms	0.0	0.0	12.3	0.0	39.1	12.3	39.1	51.4
Various manufactured goods	0.0	0.0	0.0	0.0	16.8	0.0	16.8	16.8
Art, antiques, *et al.*	0.0	0.0	1.8	0.0	0.0	1.8	0.0	1.8

Table 4. Tariff equivalents of NTMs by type for 21 commodities–Continued

	1	3	4	5	6	1+4	3+5+6	1+3+4+5+6
Commodities	**Price control measures**	**Automatic licensing**	**Quantity control measures**	**Monopolistic measures**	**Technical measures**	**Core NTMs**	**Non-Core NTMs**	**Overall NTMs**
				Australia				
Live animals & products	0.0	0.0	3.0	0.0	91.3	3.0	91.3	94.3
Vegetable products	0.0	0.0	0.5	0.0	91.3	0.5	91.3	91.8
Animal & vegetable oils	0.0	0.0	0.0	0.0	91.3	0.0	91.3	91.3
Products of food industry	23.2	0.0	0.0	0.0	91.3	23.2	91.3	114.5
Mineral products	0.0	0.0	0.0	0.0	4.6	0.0	4.6	4.6
Chemicals	0.0	0.0	1.0	0.0	9.3	1.0	9.3	10.3
Plastic & plastic materials	27.0	0.0	0.0	0.0	0.0	27.0	0.0	27.0
Skin, raw material	0.0	0.0	2.9	0.0	0.0	2.9	0.0	2.9
Wood & wood products	0.0	0.0	0.0	0.0	0.0	0.0	0.0	0.0
Pulp & paper	19.3	0.0	0.0	0.0	0.0	19.3	0.0	19.3
Textiles	2.4	0.0	0.0	0.0	0.8	2.4	0.8	3.2
Footwear, umbrellas	0.0	0.0	0.0	0.0	0.0	0.0	0.0	0.0
Cement, ceramic, *et al.*	7.3	0.0	0.0	0.0	0.0	7.3	0.0	7.3
Precious stones	0.0	0.0	0.0	0.0	0.0	0.0	0.0	0.0
Base metals & products	4.1	0.0	4.2	0.0	0.0	8.2	0.0	8.2
Ordinary machinery	1.3	0.0	0.0	0.0	27.4	1.3	27.4	28.7
Transport equipment	5.2	0.0	2.0	0.0	0.0	7.2	0.0	7.2
Precision machinery	0.0	0.0	0.0	0.0	14.0	0.0	14.0	14.0
Firearms	0.0	0.0	8.7	0.0	0.0	8.7	0.0	8.7
Various manufactured goods	0.0	0.0	0.2	0.0	1.9	0.2	1.9	2.1
Art, antiques, *et al.*	0.0	0.0	0.0	0.0	0.0	0.0	0.0	0.0

Table 4. Tariff equivalents of NTMs by type for 21 commodities–Continued

Commodities	1 Price control measures	3 Automatic licensing	4 Quantity control measures	5 Monopolistic measures	6 Technical measures	1+4 Core NTMs	3+5+6 Non-Core NTMs	1+3+4+5+6 Overall NTMs
				New Zealand				
Live animals & products	5.3	0.0	12.3	0.0	0.0	17.6	0.0	17.6
Vegetable products	0.0	0.0	12.3	0.0	49.5	12.3	49.5	61.8
Animal & vegetable oils	0.0	0.0	6.2	0.0	0.0	6.2	0.0	6.2
Products of food industry	24.3	0.0	3.2	0.0	60.5	27.5	60.5	88.1
Mineral products	0.0	0.0	0.8	0.0	0.0	0.8	0.0	0.8
Chemicals	0.0	0.0	5.4	0.0	10.3	5.4	10.3	15.7
Plastic & plastic materials	0.0	0.0	0.2	0.0	6.2	0.2	6.2	6.4
Skin, raw material	0.0	0.0	4.7	0.0	0.0	4.7	0.0	4.7
Wood & wood products	0.0	0.0	6.6	0.0	2.4	6.6	2.4	9.0
Pulp & paper	0.0	0.0	0.0	0.0	0.0	0.0	0.0	0.0
Textiles	0.0	0.0	0.4	0.0	6.3	0.4	6.3	6.6
Footwear, umbrellas	541.4	0.0	0.1	0.0	68.7	541.5	68.7	610.2
Cement, ceramic, *et al.*	27.7	0.0	0.3	0.0	0.0	28.0	0.0	28.0
Precious stones	0.0	0.0	0.9	0.0	0.0	0.9	0.0	0.9
Base metals & products	1.5	0.0	0.3	0.0	0.0	1.8	0.0	1.8
Ordinary machinery	4.2	0.0	0.2	0.0	74.3	4.4	74.3	78.7
Transport equipment	24.1	0.0	3.2	0.0	0.0	27.3	0.0	27.3
Precision machinery	0.0	0.0	0.0	0.0	0.0	0.0	0.0	0.0
Firearms	0.0	0.0	4.4	0.0	0.0	4.4	0.0	4.4
Various manufactured goods	6.3	0.0	1.9	0.0	7.6	8.2	7.6	15.8
Art, antiques, *et al.*	0.0	0.0	0.0	0.0	0.0	0.0	0.0	0.0

Table 4. Tariff equivalents of NTMs by type for 21 commodities–Continued

	1	3	4	5	6	1+4	3+5+6	1+3+4+5+6
Commodities	Price control measures	Automatic licensing	Quantity control measures	Monopolistic measures	Technical measures	Core NTMs	Non-Core NTMs	Overall NTMs
				Chile				
Live animals & products	0.0	0.0	3.5	0.0	90.3	3.5	90.3	93.8
Vegetable products	4.1	0.0	5.2	0.0	91.0	9.3	91.0	100.3
Animal & vegetable oils	585.9	0.0	0.2	0.0	84.1	586.1	84.1	670.3
Products of food industry	20.7	0.0	0.7	0.0	86.6	21.4	86.6	108.0
Mineral products	0.0	0.0	0.1	0.0	5.3	0.1	5.3	5.4
Chemicals	0.0	0.0	2.2	0.0	71.6	2.2	71.6	73.8
Plastic & plastic materials	0.0	0.0	0.1	0.0	3.2	0.1	3.2	3.2
Skin, raw material	0.0	0.0	0.0	0.0	0.0	0.0	0.0	0.0
Wood & wood products	0.0	0.0	0.2	0.0	73.0	0.2	73.0	73.3
Pulp & paper	0.0	0.0	0.9	0.0	0.0	0.9	0.0	0.9
Textiles	0.0	0.0	0.1	0.0	5.3	0.1	5.3	5.4
Footwear, umbrellas	0.0	0.0	0.0	0.0	0.0	0.0	0.0	0.0
Cement, ceramic, *et al.*	0.0	0.0	0.0	0.0	0.0	0.0	0.0	0.0
Precious stones	0.0	0.0	0.0	0.0	0.0	0.0	0.0	0.0
Base metals & products	0.0	0.0	0.1	0.0	0.5	0.1	0.5	0.6
Ordinary machinery	0.0	0.0	0.1	0.0	8.9	0.1	8.9	9.1
Transport equipment	0.0	0.0	3.3	0.0	0.0	3.3	0.0	3.3
Precision machinery	0.0	0.0	0.5	0.0	37.0	0.5	37.0	37.5
Firearms	0.0	0.0	10.4	0.0	0.0	10.4	0.0	10.4
Various manufactured goods	0.0	0.0	0.1	0.0	2.0	0.1	2.0	2.1
Art, antiques, *et al.*	0.0	0.0	3.5	0.0	13.0	3.5	13.0	16.6

Table 4. Tariff equivalents of NTMs by type for 21 commodities–Continued

Commodities	1 Price control measures	3 Automatic licensing	4 Quantity control measures	5 Monopolistic measures	6 Technical measures	1+4 Core NTMs	3+5+6 Non-Core NTMs	1+3+4+5+6 Overall NTMs
				Mexico				
Live animals & products	0.0	0.0	6.6	0.0	63.0	6.6	63.0	69.6
Vegetable products	0.0	0.0	0.9	0.0	77.5	0.9	77.5	78.5
Animal & vegetable oils	0.0	0.0	3.0	0.0	27.7	3.0	27.7	30.6
Products of food industry	0.0	0.0	2.6	0.0	80.1	2.6	80.1	82.7
Mineral products	0.0	0.0	1.7	0.0	3.8	1.7	3.8	5.5
Chemicals	0.0	0.9	3.3	0.0	65.5	3.3	66.3	69.6
Plastic & plastic materials	0.0	7.9	0.2	0.0	12.8	0.2	20.7	20.9
Skin, raw material	0.0	0.0	0.0	0.0	74.9	0.0	74.9	74.9
Wood & wood products	0.0	14.2	0.0	0.0	51.2	0.0	65.4	65.4
Pulp & paper	0.0	0.0	0.0	0.0	13.4	0.0	13.4	13.4
Textiles	0.0	12.5	0.0	0.0	89.1	0.0	101.6	101.7
Footwear, umbrellas	0.0	28.8	0.0	0.0	72.3	0.0	101.1	101.1
Cement, ceramic, *et al.*	0.0	28.0	0.0	0.0	18.5	0.0	46.5	46.5
Precious stones	0.0	0.0	0.0	0.0	8.8	0.0	8.8	8.8
Base metals & products	0.0	9.1	0.1	0.0	16.6	0.1	25.7	25.8
Ordinary machinery	0.0	0.0	0.2	0.0	15.8	0.2	15.8	16.0
Transport equipment	0.0	3.3	2.8	0.0	12.2	2.8	15.4	18.3
Precision machinery	0.0	0.0	0.8	0.0	47.4	0.8	47.4	48.2
Firearms	0.0	0.0	11.5	0.0	31.5	11.5	31.5	42.9
Various manufactured goods	0.0	2.5	0.1	0.0	60.3	0.1	62.9	62.9
Art, antiques, *et al.*	0.0	0.0	0.0	0.0	38.0	0.0	38.0	38.0

Table 4. Tariff equivalents of NTMs by type for 21 commodities–Continued

Commodities	1 Price control measures	3 Automatic licensing	4 Quantity control measures	5 Monopolistic measures	6 Technical measures	1+4 Core NTMs	3+5+6 Non-Core NTMs	1+3+4+5+6 Overall NTMs
				Canada				
Live animals & products	0.0	0.0	12.3	0.0	0.0	12.3	0.0	12.3
Vegetable products	0.0	0.0	12.0	0.0	0.8	12.0	0.8	12.8
Animal & vegetable oils	0.0	0.0	0.0	0.0	0.0	0.0	0.0	0.0
Products of food industry	0.0	0.0	0.0	0.0	0.0	0.0	0.0	0.0
Mineral products	0.0	0.0	0.2	0.0	0.0	0.2	0.0	0.2
Chemicals	0.0	0.0	0.4	0.0	2.6	0.4	2.6	3.1
Plastic & plastic materials	0.0	0.0	0.0	0.0	4.0	0.0	4.0	4.0
Skin, raw material	0.0	0.0	8.7	0.0	0.0	8.7	0.0	8.7
Wood & wood products	0.0	0.0	0.0	0.0	0.0	0.0	0.0	0.0
Pulp & paper	0.0	0.0	0.0	0.0	0.0	0.0	0.0	0.0
Textiles	0.0	0.0	4.8	0.0	0.0	4.8	0.0	4.8
Footwear, umbrellas	0.0	0.0	2.2	0.0	0.0	2.2	0.0	2.2
Cement, ceramic, *et al.*	0.0	0.0	0.0	0.0	0.0	0.0	0.0	0.0
Precious stones	0.0	0.0	0.2	0.0	0.0	0.2	0.0	0.2
Base metals & products	0.0	0.0	4.2	0.0	0.5	4.2	0.5	4.7
Ordinary machinery	0.0	0.0	0.0	0.0	1.9	0.0	1.9	1.9
Transport equipment	0.0	0.0	0.1	0.0	11.6	0.1	11.6	11.7
Precision machinery	0.0	0.0	0.0	0.0	0.0	0.0	0.0	0.0
Firearms	0.0	0.0	4.3	0.0	0.0	4.3	0.0	4.3
Various manufactured goods	0.0	0.0	0.9	0.0	0.0	0.9	0.0	0.9
Art, antiques, *et al.*	0.0	0.0	0.0	0.0	0.0	0.0	0.0	0.0

Table 4. Tariff equivalents of NTMs by type for 21 commodities–Continued

Commodities	1 Price control measures	3 Automatic licensing	4 Quantity control measures	5 Monopolistic measures	6 Technical measures	1+4 Core NTMs	3+5+6 Non-Core NTMs	1+3+4+5+6 Overall NTMs
	U.S.A.							
Live animals & products	14.3	0.0	1.9	0.0	90.4	16.2	90.4	106.6
Vegetable products	26.7	0.0	8.2	0.0	20.2	34.9	20.2	55.1
Animal & vegetable oils	0.0	0.0	1.7	0.0	0.0	1.7	0.0	1.7
Products of food industry	46.2	0.0	1.0	0.0	62.7	47.1	62.7	109.8
Mineral products	52.0	0.0	0.1	0.0	0.0	52.1	0.0	52.1
Chemicals	30.1	0.0	0.7	0.0	11.5	30.9	11.5	42.4
Plastic & plastic materials	189.6	0.0	0.0	0.0	0.0	189.6	0.0	189.6
Skin, raw material	0.0	0.0	2.7	0.0	21.1	2.7	21.1	23.8
Wood & wood products	0.0	0.0	7.6	0.0	0.0	7.6	0.0	7.6
Pulp & paper	0.0	0.0	0.0	0.0	0.0	0.0	0.0	0.0
Textiles	21.7	0.0	1.5	0.0	46.1	23.2	46.1	69.3
Footwear, umbrellas	0.0	0.0	0.8	0.0	2.7	0.8	2.7	3.5
Cement, ceramic, *et al.*	4.0	0.0	0.0	0.0	0.6	4.0	0.6	4.6
Precious stones	0.0	0.0	0.0	0.0	0.0	0.0	0.0	0.0
Base metals & products	283.6	0.0	0.0	0.0	0.5	283.6	0.5	284.1
Ordinary machinery	195.5	0.0	0.0	0.0	15.0	195.5	15.0	210.5
Transport equipment	120.5	0.0	0.1	0.0	56.0	120.6	56.0	176.6
Precision machinery	29.3	0.0	0.1	0.0	2.6	29.4	2.6	32.0
Firearms	0.0	0.0	12.3	0.0	0.0	12.3	0.0	12.3
Various manufactured goods	8.6	0.0	0.5	0.0	11.5	9.1	11.5	20.7
Art, antiques, *et al.*	0.0	0.0	1.8	0.0	0.0	1.8	0.0	1.8

Data source: Author's calculations.

How effectively the listed developed economies provide protection for domestic producers by implementing core and non-core NTMs is, however, somewhat different between Japan and Australia, New Zealand, and the United States. Japan implements various types of both core and non-core NTMs together. Particularly for such commodities as agricultural products, mineral products, and chemicals, as many as four or more types of measures are applied together, which results in high equivalent rates of overall NTMs. On the other hand, Australia, New Zealand, and the United States do not implement so many types of measures as Japan does. Instead, these economies apply AD/CV measures to their protective sectors in addition to technical measure and quantity measures with their high coverage, ending up with high equivalents of overall NTMs. For instance, tariff equivalents of AD/CD measures are quite high for footwear sector in New Zealand and for base metal sector in the United States. As already discussed, AD/CV measures directly raise the domestic price of imports by the rate of AD/CV duty and may also indirectly increase the price through a reduction of potential trade volume due to the uncertainty of their implementation, irrespective of whether they are actually imposed.

Second, economies participating in a number of FTAs or bilateral/regional agreements, such as Chile, Mexico, and the United States, have high tariff equivalents of overall NTMs. Chile and Mexico, in particular, show very high equivalent rates of technical measures. The shares of tariff equivalents of non-core NTMs exceed 70 percent of those of overall NTMs for 13 out of 17 sectors subject to NTMs in Chile and for all sectors in Mexico. Because they have already had multiple FTAs and have applied lower preferential tariff rates than MFN tariff rates to the member economies, they would heavily implement NTMs, especially technical measures, as a means of protecting domestic industries.

Third, developing economies in the analysis do not heavily use NTMs for most of the commodities except agriculture and food products. Malaysia does not show high equivalents of NTMs even in agriculture and food industry aside from vegetable products. With regards to other industries, there are only a few cases with tariff equivalents of overall NTMs of more than 10 percent, such as mineral products and chemicals in Indonesia and Thailand. China is an exception among developing economies in the sense that it applies various types of NTMs to many sectors; frequently used measures are price control measures (administrative pricing), quantity control measures, and technical measures. China still tends to significantly implement more directly affective measures. Unlike developed economies, however, the equivalent rates of overall NTMs for all sectors in China are less than 40 percent except for mineral products.

Fourth, agriculture and food processing is heavily protected by NTMs, particularly by technical measures in most of the APEC member economies in the study. There is a difference, however, between developed economies and developing economies in what types of products are protected by NTMs. Developed economies are more likely to apply NTMs to agricultural products, partly reflecting a policy to protect domestic producers from cheaper imports. On the other hand, developing economies are more likely to protect food processing, partly reflecting infant industry protection policy.

There are a few economies we have not discussed above: Canada, Korea, and Singapore. These economies have only a few measures reported as NTMs and also show relatively low tariff equivalents. While Singapore could be called as rather liberalized economy in terms of trade in goods, the results for Canada and Korea have to be cautiously interpreted. Moreover, the years in this analysis are older for some economies due to the availability of NTM data as explained in section 3. Considering the growing interests in technical measures such as technical regulations and SPS regulations since the Uruguay Round, tariff equivalents of these measures in some economies might be higher and more serious issues at present.

6. Conclusion

This paper has attempted to demonstrate how to measure the economic impact of both core and non-core NTMs in terms of tariff equivalents by the type of measures, focusing on the price differentials between the prices of imports and the domestic producer prices of the domestic substitutes and on by-type frequency ratios. The types of NTMs examined in the paper are core NTMs, that is, price control measures and quantity control measures, and non-core NTMs, *i.e.*, auto-licensing measures, monopolistic measures, and technical measures.

We found that both core and non-core NTMs do provide a certain degree of protection for domestic producers in the APEC economies. We also obtained several other findings. First, developed economies with lower tariff protection do significantly protect domestic industries by implementing NTMs, in particular non-core NTMs such as technical regulations or SPS regulations. Japan implements various types of NTMs, in particular several types of non-core NTMs. On the other hand, Australia, New Zealand, and the United States effectively protect domestic industries by applying technical measures as well as AD/CV measures with their high coverage though they do not implement so many types of measures as Japan does. Such high tariff equivalents of NTMs could easily offset the benefits of tariff reduction.

Second, economies with a number of FTAs such as Chile and Mexico also significantly protect domestic industries by implementing NTMs, especially technical measures. They would implement various technical measures to protect domestic industries, possibly compensating for lower protection in terms of preferential tariffs.

Third, developing economies except China do not heavily depend on NTMs in most sectors except for agriculture and food processing. China applies various types of NTMs to many sectors.

Fourth, agriculture and food processing are heavily protected by NTMs, particularly technical measures in most of the APEC economies in the analysis though there is a difference between developed economies and developing economies in what types of products are protected in agriculture and food processing. Developed economies are more likely to apply NTMs to agricultural products while developing economies to protect food processing.

Our empirical results could be improved by conducting better matching between value data and quantity data to calculate unit values of domestic production if more disaggregated data of domestic production were available. Moreover, because of the differences in statistical codes among ISIC rev.2, ISIC rev.3, and HS (SITC), the quality of some price differentials would be doubtful. With more disaggregated data and more qualified data, the quality of unit values as well as the price differentials would be improved, and as a result estimates of tariff equivalents of NTMs would be improved.

The results could be improved by using more recent data as well. Due to the availability of NTM data, the years in the analysis are inconsistent among the 13 APEC economies, and are pretty old for a few economies. Moreover, the years of price differential data are inconsistent with (older than) those of NTM data due to the deficiency of domestic production data for some economies. If more recent data were available, these problems would be solved.

Another possibility to apply this methodology is first to calculate the price distorting effect of each type of NTMs by focusing on a specific economy with more finely disaggregated data, for instance, Japan, and then to estimate tariff equivalents of NTMs in other APEC economies by using the estimated coefficients in that economy.

An extension to this study would be to measure the economic impact of removing NTMs within the framework of CGE model.

References

1. Ando, M., 2002, The pervasiveness of non tariff measures in APEC countries. *COE Discussion Paper*, No.0201, Keio University, Tokyo.
2. APEC Secretariat, 1995, *The Osaka Action Agenda Implementation of the Bogor Declaration*. APEC Secretariat, Singapore.
3. ASEAN Secretariat, 1998, *AFTA Reader Vol.5: The Sixth ASEAN Summit and the Acceleration of AFTA*. ASEAN Secretariat, Jakarta.
4. Australian Department of Foreign Affairs and Trade, 1983, *Australia New Zealand Closer Economic Relations Trade Agreement*. Australian Department of Foreign Affairs and Trade, Commonwealth of Australia, Canberra.
5. Baldwin, R. E., 1970, *Nontariff Distortions of International Trade*. Brookings Institution, Washington D.C.
6. Bosworth, M., 1999, Non-tariff measures as trade barriers: yesterday's problem or what?. paper presented at *The OECD Workshop with Non-Member Economies on Barriers to Trade in Goods and Services in the Post-Uruguay Round Context*.
7. Campbell, K. and R. Cossette, 1994, *A Study of Canada's Non-Tariff Trade Barriers: The Tariff Equivalents of Quantitative Import Restrictions*. Research Branch, Canadian International Trade Tribunal, Ottawa.
8. Deardorff, A. V., 1987, Why do governments prefer nontariff barriers?. *Carnegie-Rochester Conference Series on Public Policy*, 26.
9. Deardorff, A. V. and R. M. Stern, 1998, Measurement of Nontariff Barriers. University of Michigan Press, Ann Arbor, MI.
10. European Union, 2000, *Decision No.2/2000 of the EC/Mexico Joint Council of 23 March 2000*. European Union, Brussels.
11. Global Trade Information Services, 2002, *World Trade Atlas*. GTI, Columbia, SC.
12. Hoekman, B., 1995, Assessing the general agreement on trade in services. In Martin, W. and L. A. Winters eds. The Uruguay round and the developing economies. *World Bank Discussion Paper*, 307, World Bank, Washington D.C.
13. Holmes, L. and A. Hardin, 2000, Assessing barriers to services sector investment, In Findlay, C. and T. Warren eds. *Impediments to Trade in Services: Measurement and policy implications*. Routledge, London.
14. Hufbauer, G. C. and K. A. Elliott, 1994, *Measuring the Costs of Protection in the United States*. Institute for International Economics, Washington D.C.
15. Israel Ministry of Foreign Affairs, 1985, *Agreement on the Establishment of a Free Trade Area between the Government of Israel and the Government of the United States of America*. Israel Ministry of Foreign Affairs, Government of Israel, Jerusalem.
16. Jordan-U.S. Free Trade Agreement Website, The, 2000, *Agreement between the United States of America and the Hashemite Kingdom of Jordan on the Establishment of a Free Trade Area*. Jordan-U.S. Free Trade Agreement Website, http://www.jordanusfta.com.
17. Laird, S. and A. J. Yeats, 1990a, Trends in nontariff barriers of developed countries, 1966-1986. *Weltwirtschaftliches Archiv*, 126.
18. Laird, S. and A. J. Yeats, 1990b, *Quantitative Methods for Trade Barriers Analysis*. Macmillan Press, London.
19. Laird, S., 1997, Quantifying commercial policies. In Francois, J.F. and K. A. Reinert eds. *Applied Methods for Trade Policy Analysis*. Cambridge University Press, Cambridge.

20. Maskus, K. M. and J. S. Wilson eds., 2001, *Quantifying the Impact of Technical Barriers to Trade: Can It Be Done?* University of Michigan Press, Ann Arbor, MI.
21. Ministry of Trade and Industry, 2000, *Agreement between New Zealand and Singapore on a Closer Economic Partnership*. Ministry of Trade and Industry, Government of Singapore, Singapore.
22. NAFTA Secretariat, 1994, *North American Free Trade Agreement*. NAFTA Secretariat, Washington D.C.
23. Organization for Economic Cooperation and Development, 1997, *Indicators of Tariff and Non-tariff Trade Barriers*. OECD, Paris.
24. Pacific Economic Cooperation Council, 2000, *Non-tariff measures in goods and services trade*. PECC, Singapore.
25. Sazanami, Y., S. Urata and H. Kawai, 1995, *Measuring the Costs of Protection in Japan*. Institute for International Economics, Washington D.C.
26. Secretaria del MERCOSUR, 2002, *Listado de Instrumentos Juridicos del MERCOSUR*. Secretaria del MERCOSUR, Ulguay.
27. United Nations, 1998a, *Industrial Commodity Statistical Yearbook*. UN, New York.
28. United Nations, 1998b, *International Trade Statistics Yearbook*. UN, New York.
29. United Nations, 2002, *International Yearbook of Industrial Statistics*. UN, New York.
30. United Nations Conference on Trade and Development, 1996, *A Users' Manual for TRAINS (Trade Analysis and Information System)*. UNCTAD, Geneva.
31. United Nations Conference on Trade and Development, 1999, *TRAINS (CD-ROM) 1999 winter version*. UNCTAD, Geneva.
32. United Nations Conference on Trade and Development, 2001, *TRAINS (CD-ROM) 2001 spring version*. UNCTAD, Geneva.
33. World Bank, 2001, *World Development Indicators (CD-ROM)*. World Bank, Washington D.C.
34. World Trade Organization, 1994, *General Agreement on Tariffs and Trade 1994*. World Trade Organization, Geneva.

Table A1. Reported NTMs: The case of Japan

Categorized type	Description	Categorized type	Description
0	Tariff quota	5-(1)	State monopoly of imports
0	Seasonal tariff rates	5-(1)	Sole importing agency
1-(3)	Variable charges	6-(1)	Technical requirements
1-(4)	Antidumping duties	6-(1)	Product characteristics requirements to protect human health
3-(1)	Automatic license	6-(1)	Product characteristics requirements to protect environment
4-(1)	Non-Automatic license	6-(1)	Product characteristics requirements to protect wildlife
4- (1)	Authorization	6-(1)	Marking requirements to protect environment
4- (1)	Authorization for wildlife protection	6-(1)	Labeling requirement for human health protection
4- (1)	Authorization to ensure national security	6-(1)	Testing, inspection and quarantine requirements
4- (1)	Authorization for political reasons	6-(1)	Technical measures, n.e.s.
4- (2)	Global quota		
4- (2)	Quota for sensitive products		

Note: The categorization of measures above is conducted by author.

Table A2. Frequency ratios by type and sector: The case of Japan

Sector	Number of total tariff lines in sectors	1 Price control measures			3 Automatic licensing measures		4 Quantity control measures			5 Monopolistic measures		6 Technical measures	
			1-(3) Variable changes	1-(4) AD measure		3-(1) Auto licensing		4-(1) Non-auto licensing	4-(2) Import quota		5-(1) Single channel imports		6-(1) Technical regulation
1 Live animals	549	**28**	28		**18**	18	**273**	271	47	**99**	99	**532**	532
		5.1%	5.1%		**3.3%**	3.3%	**49.7%**	49.4%	8.6%	**18.0%**	18.0%	**96.9%**	96.9%
2 Vegetable products	561	**2**	2		**23**	23	**27**	10	17	**26**	26	**506**	506
		0.4%	0.4%		**4.1%**	4.1%	**4.8%**	1.8%	3.0%	**4.6%**	4.6%	**90.2%**	90.2%
3 Animal & vegetable oils & fats	82						**6**	6				**74**	74
							7.3%	7.3%				**90.2%**	90.2%
4 Products of food industry	762												
5 Mineral products	207				**9**	9	**3**		3	**1**	1	**66**	66
					4.3%	4.3%	**1.4%**		1.4%	**0.5%**	0.5%	**31.9%**	31.9%
6 Chemicals	1025	**1**	1				**93**	3	90	**22**	22	**827**	827
		0.1%	0.1%				**9.1%**	0.3%	8.8%	**2.1%**	2.1%	**80.7%**	80.7%
7 Plastic & plastic materials	283						**4**		4			**34**	34
							1.4%		1.4%			**12.0%**	12.0%
8 Skin, raw material	173						**38**	38				**64**	64
							22.0%	22.0%				**37.0%**	37.0%
9 Wood & wood products	213						**34**	34				**67**	67
							16.0%	16.0%				**31.5%**	31.5%
10 Pulp & paper	174											**27**	27
												15.5%	15.5%
11 Textiles	2087						**902**	902		**10**	10		
							43.2%	43.2%		**0.5%**	0.5%		
12 Footwear, umbrellas	145						**1**	1					
							0.7%	0.7%					
13 Cement, ceramic, *et al.*	173											**15**	15
												8.7%	8.7%
14 Precious stones	78											**3**	3
												3.8%	3.8%

Table A2. Frequency ratios by type and sector: The case of Japan–Continued

Sector	Number of total tariff lines in sectors	**1 Price control measures**			**3 Automatic licensing measures**	**4 Quantity control measures**			**5 Monopolistic measures**			
			1-(3) Variable changes	**1-(4) AD measure**	**3-(1) Auto licensing**		**4-(1) Non-auto licensing**	**4-(2) Import quota**		**5-(1) Single channel imports**		**6-(1) Technical regulation**
15 Base metals & base metal products	835	**35** **4.2%**	34 4.2%	1 0.1%		**302** **36.2%**	301 36.0%	1 0.1%			**39** **4.7%**	39 4.7%
16 Ordinary machinery	991					**18** **1.8%**		18 1.8%	**1** **0.1%**	1 0.1%	**30** **3.0%**	30 3.0%
17 Transport equipment	152					**8** **5.3%**		8 5.3%			**9** **5.9%**	9 5.9%
18 Precision machinery	308					**2** **0.6%**		2 0.6%			**61** **19.8%**	61 19.8%
19 Firearms	21					**21** **100.0%**		21 100.0%			**9** **42.9%**	9 42.9%
20 Various manufactured goods	206										**38** **18.4%**	38 18.4%
21 Art, antiques, *et al.*	7					**1** **4.3%**		1 4.3%				

Data source: Author's calculation, based on the information available from UNCTAD (2001). Note: The figures expressed as a percentage level indicate frequency ratios by type and sector, and the figure above them show the number of tariff lines subject to NTM in each sector.

Table A3. Bound tariffs and applied tariffs in the 13 APEC member economies

	1996	2000/2001	2003	1996	2000/2001	2003
		China			Indonesia	
WTO bound rate (%): simple average	n.a.	n.a.	11.0		37.2	37.2
WTO bound rate (%): import-weighted	n.a.	n.a.				
Applied rate (%): simple average	23.0	15.3	11.0	13.9	7.3	7.2
Applied rate (%): import-weighted						
Bound tariff lines (%)	n.a.	n.a.		93.9	93.9	93.9
Specific tariff lines		52 (7111)	52 (7445)		5 (7290)	12 (7542)
		Thailand			Malaysia	
WTO bound rate (%): simple average		39.7	28.2		17.2	17.2
WTO bound rate (%): import-weighted						
Applied rate (%): simple average	17.0	15.4	13.8	9.0	9.2	9.3
Applied rate (%): import-weighted				7.0	3.0	2.9
Bound tariff lines (%)		73.1	68.4		61.8	61.8
Specific tariff lines		90 (5903)	93(6204)			83 (10458)
		Korea			Singapore	
WTO bound rate (%): simple average	27.6	19.5	17.7	10.0	6.5	5.3
WTO bound rate (%): import-weighted	15.4	9.6	10.2		3.0	3.1
Applied rate (%): simple average	14.4	13.7	13.3	0.0	0.0	0.0
Applied rate (%): import-weighted	10.9	8.3	9.0		0.0	0.0
Bound tariff lines (%)	90.4	91.8	91.4	70.0	85.0	94.3
Specific tariff lines		21 (11176)	31 (11261)		4 (5859)	4 (6036)

Table A3. Bound tariffs and applied tariffs in the 13 APEC member economies–Continued

	1996	2000/2001	2003	1996	2000/2001	2003
		Japan				
WTO bound rate (%): simple average	8.8	8.0				
WTO bound rate (%): import-weighted	7.4	3.6	3.5			
Applied rate (%): simple average		8.2	7.5			
Applied rate (%): import-weighted	5.0	2.5	2.5			
Bound tariff lines (%)		98.9	98.9			
Specific tariff lines		656 (9036)	661 (9303)			
		Australia			New Zealand	
WTO bound rate (%): simple average	15.9	11.0	10.3		12.0	12.0
WTO bound rate (%): import-weighted		11.8	9.3			
Applied rate (%): simple average	6.1	4.4	4.3	5.7	3.7	3.6
Applied rate (%): import-weighted		4.4	4.1			
Bound tariff lines (%)	96.1	95.4	96.5		99.9	99.9
Specific tariff lines			0.3		198 (7108)	58 (7078)
		Chile			Mexico	
WTO bound rate (%): simple average	25.0	25.1	25.1		36.2	36.2
WTO bound rate (%): import-weighted						
Applied rate (%): simple average	11.0	9.2	5.9		16.2	16.4
Applied rate (%): import-weighted					3.1	2.8
Bound tariff lines (%)		100.0	100.0		100.0	100.0
Specific tariff lines		0 (5867)	0 (7901)		55 (11396)	58 (11809)

Table A3. Bound tariffs and applied tariffs in the 13 APEC member economies–Continued

	1996	2000/2001	2003	1996	2000/2001	2003
		Canada			U.S.A.	
WTO bound rate (%): simple average		5.6	5.1	6.4		5.2
WTO bound rate (%): import-weighted			5.0	3.4		1.7
Applied rate (%): simple average		4.4	4.0	6.4	5.5	5.2
Applied rate (%): import-weighted	1.3	0.9	1.0	3.4	2.8	1.7
Bound tariff lines (%)		99.7	99.7		99.9	99.9
Specific tariff lines			396			
		386 (8182)	(8515)			

Data sources: APEC Individual Action Plan (2000, 2001, and 2003) for each country (available at http://www.apec-iap.org).

Notes: Data for 2000 are of 2000 or 2001.

Bound tariff lines (%) present the shares in total tariff lines in corresponding sectors.

Figures in parenthesis for specific tariff lines are the total number of tariff lines in corresponding sectors.

WTO bound rates for Indonesia in 2003 are of 2001.

WTO bound rates for Malaysia are the simple average of tariffs on industrial products.

In calcurating applied tariffs in Thailand, the ad valorem equivalents of specific tariffs are assumed to be 30 percent for rice and 20% and 25% for sugar.

ESTIMATING THE TARIFF-EQUIVALENT OF NTMS

Judith M. Dean
U.S. International Trade Commission[1]

Robert Feinberg
American University

Michael Ferrantino
U.S. International Trade Commission

1. Introduction

With the steady decrease in world-wide tariffs accomplished in the various rounds of multilateral trade negotiations over the past several decades, the attention of both policy-makers and economists has turned to the role played by non-tariff methods of protection. Especially for the purpose of negotiations, it is important that the impacts of these NTMs be quantified. Yet this has proven difficult. Variation across economies in product prices is due to many factors of which NTMS are just one. In addition, the many types of NTMs–quotas, non-automatic licensing, bans, prior authorization for protection of human health, local content requirements, among others–defy the development of a simple uniform method to convert the effect of these quantity controls into tariff-equivalents.

Deardorff and Stern (1997) present both a survey of past work in this area and a clear guide to methodological approaches to the problem. They also give a detailed exposition of the calculation of the tariff-equivalent of NTMs using data on individual products, and allowing for different types of NTMs, market competition, and product substitutability. More recently, Bradford (2001) uses OECD data on specific product prices across economies to elicit percentage

[1] Judith Dean and Michael Ferrantino are associated with the Office of Economics, U.S. International Trade Commission. Robert Feinberg is (currently visiting Scholar at the USITC) affiliated with the American University in Washington, DC. The views expressed in this article are those of the authors. They are not the views of the U.S. International Trade Commission (USITC) as a whole nor any of its individual Commissioners. The authors may be contacted *via* email at *judith.dean@usitc.gov*, *robert.feinberg@usitc.gov*, and *michael.ferrantino@usitc.gov*, respectively. We would like to gratefully acknowledge the help of Larry Chomsisengphet, Shakira van Savage, and Saba Zeleke for their excellent work compiling data for this project. We have also benefited from several discussions with other members of the USITC NTM project. Finally, we thank Rod Ludema for his contribution to this project as Visiting Scholar at the USITC, 2001-2002.

markups due to protection. Using retail margins and export margins from IO tables to represent distribution and transport costs, Bradford calculates producer prices for products in a number of OECD economies, and compares them to the calculated minimum producer price (plus transport costs). If this ratio is larger than the margin due to an economy's tariff on the product, then the larger ratio is taken to represent the aggregate price effect of both tariffs and NTMs.

In the same spirit as Bradford, this paper attempts to estimate the percentage increase in specific product prices across economies due to NTMs. It differs in three key respects. First, price data is drawn from the EIU CityData. This allows estimation over a very large group of products, covering a wide range of industrial and developing economies. Second, explicit data on the incidence of NTMs by economy and by product are used. We draw on two databases for data on NTM incidence–UNCTAD TRAINS data, and the compilation of measures described in Manifold and Donnelly (2004). Third, we develop a differentiated products model which yields an estimating equation. This equation allows us to estimate directly the effect of NTMs on retail prices, while controlling for tariffs, distribution costs, and transport costs. This preliminary draft presents estimates for three GTAP sectors (apparel, shoes, and processed foods), for 18 economies/regional groups. We illustrate the econometric methodology which we plan to extend to a more complete range of sectors, and which we expect to be of use to others studying this issue.

2. Modeling NTMs

The EIU CityData contains prices on more than 160 products and services in 123 cities in 79 economies, since 1990. This offers a unique opportunity to discern the effects of NTMs by comparing goods prices on specific products globally at a point in time. Consider the domestic economies with a tariff and an import quota on a good x. Assume good x is produced perfectly competitively in all economies, good x from all sources are considered perfect substitutes for each other, and foreign economies have no trade barriers on these products. Following Deardorff and Stern (1997), we could calculate the gap between the domestic "inside the border" price of imported x, P_d^m, and the c.i.f. price of imported x, P_c^m, as a percentage of the latter. Netting out the *ad valorem tariff*, τ, yields

$$TE = [(P_d^m - P_c^m)/P_c^m] - \tau = \rho \qquad (1)$$

where ρ is the tariff-equivalent (TE) of the rent premium attributable to the domestic economies import quota.

There are several features of the EIU data which make it difficult to calculate TEs using (1). EIU CityData prices are retail prices, *e.g.*, the retail prices of good x in Atlanta and in Berlin. Thus, these prices include distribution costs, C, and transport costs, C_T. They also do not reflect the price of the imported good only, but are composites of both domestically-produced goods and imported goods. Thus, the retail price of good x in Atlanta (Berlin) will be a composite of the retail prices of American-made (German-made) x and imported x, and will reflect the tariffs and import quotas maintained by the United States (EU) on good x. One could adapt (1) to account for these features. If we maintain the assumption that domestic and imported x are perfect substitutes, and we assume that distribution costs are identical for the domestic and imported good within the same economy, then we can express the TE of the domestic economy's import quota now as:

$$TE = [((P_R - P_R^*) - (C - C^*) - C_T) / P_D^*] - (\tau - \tau^*) + \rho^* = \rho \qquad (1)'$$

where R = retail price and * indicates foreign economy variables. However, (1)′ shows that an estimate of the TE of the domestic economy's import quota, ρ, now requires a knowledge of the TE of the foreign economy's import quota, ρ^*. This is clearly unavailable. In addition, (1)′ requires accurate data on domestic and foreign distribution costs.

Another difficult problem arises because use of (1) or (1)′ assumes that domestic and foreign retail prices refer to the same product, or composite of products. Suppose good x was a business shirt. The EIU data gives "brand store" and "chain store" prices for men's business shirts. However, within each of these categories, shirts may be further differentiated by quality, by source economy (Italian shirts *vs.* Chinese shirts), or by features (button-down collars, top-stitching detail, *etc.*). If shirts are really a differentiated product, then the composite price in Berlin could differ from that in Atlanta simply because the sources of imported shirts (or shares from those sources, or varieties bought from those sources) differ between the two cities. These differences could lead to a positive quota premium, even if there were no quota on imported shirts. One could adjust (1)′ for less than perfect substitutes. However, to make a comparison between retail price in Atlanta and Berlin, one would have to know the bilateral trade patterns of the US and Germany, to be sure that the German price composite accurately reflected the same mixture of imported shirts as that of the United States.

To address these issues, we develop a differentiated products model of retail prices in a city.[2] Suppose that the EIU price of a good x in city i is the simple average of all of the varieties of good x found in retail stores in city i. Let the number of varieties consumed in city i and produced in city j be n_{ij}. Then the average price of the varieties from city j (consumed in city i) will be

$$P_{ij} = \left[\sum_{k=1}^{n_{ij}} (P_{j(k)} + \mu_{ij} + t_{ij} + r_{ij}) \right] \Big/ n_{ij} \tag{2}$$

where $P_{j(k)}$ denotes the "ex factory" price of variety k produced in city j, μ_{ij} denotes the retail markup in city i on variety k produced in city j, and C_{ij}, t_{ij}, and r_{ij}, are the transport cost, specific tariff and NTM rent, respectively, on imports from j. (These are assumed to be the same across varieties from the same source city, hence no k subscript).

Let N_i be the total number of varieties consumed in city i, and let M be the total number of cities. Then the EIU price of good x in city i can be written as a weighted average of the average prices from each source city j:

$$P_i^R = \sum_{j=1}^{M} \theta_{ij} P_{ij} \tag{3}$$

where the weights $\theta_{ij} = (n_{ij} / N_i)$ are the share of total varieties consumed in city i from each source j. Substituting (2) into (3) yields:

$$P_i^R = \frac{1}{N_i} \sum_{j=1}^{M} \sum_{k=1}^{n_{ij}} (P_{j(k)} + \mu_{ij} + C_{ij} + t_{ij} + r_{ij}) \tag{4}$$

If all cities consume the same varieties, then $n_{ij} = n_j, N_i = N$. Given this assumption equation (4) can be written as:

$$P_i^R = \overline{P} + \overline{\mu} + \sum_{j=1}^{M} \theta_j (C_{Tij} + t_{ij} + r_{ij}) \tag{5}$$

where $\overline{P} = \frac{1}{N_i} \sum_{j=1}^{M} \sum_{k=1}^{n_{ij}} P_{j(k)}$, $\overline{\mu} = \frac{1}{N_i} \sum_{j=1}^{M} \sum_{k=1}^{n_{ij}} \mu_{ijk}$, and $\theta_j = n_j / N$. Equation (5) gives a relationship between the EIU price in city i and the NTM rent on trade between city i and every other city. Tariffs and NTMs are imposed at the economy level. Thus, for any pair of cities i and j located in the same economy, for any good k, we have $t_{ik} = t_{jk}$, and similarly $r_{ik} = r_{jk}$. Equation (5), along with this set of restrictions, forms the basis of our empirical estimation.

[2] We are indebted to Rod Ludema for this formulation.

3. Estimation

Equation (5) could be estimated for each product separately, using a cross-section of cities, in a given year. The term $\overline{P}$ would become the constant in the regression, representing the average "ex factory" price of the product, and would be the same across all cities (given the assumptions above). The mark-up due to distribution costs, $\overline{\mu}$, could be proxied by a vector of city-specific characteristics that we expect to influence retail mark-ups, $Z_{i.}$. Transport costs (C_T) would be proxied by a measure of distance (d). Since it is unlikely that data on the domestic economy's NTMs on good x *with each partner economy* are available, we could instead estimate the aggregate rent premium. One way to do this is to create a dummy variable, NTM_K ,which equals one if a city is located in an economy with an NTM on good x, and zero otherwise. This yields the following estimating equation:

$$P_i^R = \alpha_0 + \alpha_1 Z_i + \alpha_2 \left(\sum_{j=1}^{M} \theta_j d_{ij} \right) + \alpha_3 \left(\sum_{j=1}^{M} \theta_j t_{ij} \right) + \alpha_4 \left(\sum_{K=1}^{\overline{K}} \eta_K DUM_K \cdot NTM_K \right) \tag{6}$$

where DUM_K are economy dummy variables, which are equal to one if city i is in economy K and zero otherwise.

There are systemic problems with estimation of (6) for a single good across all cities in the sample. It is clear that the prices in each city are not independent of each other. These equations represent a sort of reduced form model from a system describing demand and supply for product k in a given city. But the market for good k is a global market, so prices in all cities reflect the determinants of the global market price in a given time t. For example, an increase in the cost of cotton fabric globally, would impact the price of men's business shirts in all cities in a given year. In effect, (6) is really a system of equations, where the implicit final equation shows the global market clearing at the prevailing retail prices in all cities. Thus, the estimation of (6) must include a correct ion for contemporaneous correlation. In addition, large economies' trade barriers will likely impact prices in smaller economies. Though the specification in (6) assume that only the domestic economy's own trade barriers affect its prices, large exporting or importing economies move global prices, thereby affecting prices in all other smaller economies. This implies another implicit link between prices across cities.

To address these systemic issues, we estimate (6) using pooled cross-city, cross product data. Since the objective is to determine an NTM estimate for each GTAP sector, we pool data across all products in a given sector contained in the

EIU CityData.[3] Cities are grouped into regions, where regions represent either one economy (*e.g.*, China), or a group of related economies (*e.g.*, the EU 15).[4] The pooled specification is given in (6)′:

$$\mathbf{P}_r^s = \boldsymbol{\alpha}_0'\mathbf{D}_r + \alpha_{1r}\mathbf{Z}_r + \alpha_{2r}\boldsymbol{\theta}_r'\mathbf{d}_r + \alpha_{3r}\boldsymbol{\theta}_r'\mathbf{t}_r + \alpha_{5r}\mathbf{DUM}_r \cdot \mathbf{NTM}_r \qquad (6)'$$

where bold type indicates a $((ixk)x1)$ vector, s and r indicate sector and region, respectively. $\mathbf{D}_r$ is a vector of product-specific dummy variables, thus $\boldsymbol{\alpha}_0$ will contain estimates of the "average ex-factory prices of the products within the sector." Equation (6)′ is estimated for each sector using SUR, with a correction for region-specific heteroskedasticity.

There are several advantages of using this pooled SUR approach. First, it corrects for contemporaneous correlation between prices in each city for product k (*e.g.*, shirts), in a given year, and between prices for products in the same sector (*e.g.*, shirts, trousers, dresses, *etc.*). It may also, in part, capture the inter-relationship between large economy trade barriers and small economy prices. Second, it is flexible enough to yield region-specific parameters (indicated by subscript r on parameters in equation (6)′). In particular, a direct output of the estimation is an economy-specific estimate of the average percentage increase in price due to economy j's NTMs on products in a given sector.[5] Third, it allows us to use dummy variables to capture the impact of NTMs, despite the limitations of the data on other explanatory variables. Since some explanatory variables vary only across economies rather than cities, a regression on a single product causes collinearity between the NTM dummy and these explanatory variables for regions containing a single economy. If there is variation in an economy's NTMs across products within a sector, pooling across these products avoids this collinearity problem.

4. Data

All data were obtained for the year 2001. Prices of all products are taken from the EIU CityData. Prices designated as "supermarket" or "chain store" were used rather than "mid-priced" or "branded store." Three variables were chosen to proxy the local markup on a product in a given city: GDP *per capita*, wages in a

---

[3] Sectors are defined in appendix 1.

[4] Regions are defined as a single economy whenever there are a sufficient number of city observations available. If only one city was available for an economy, that economy was grouped with other economies based on (a) a common trade policy, or (b) regional proximity and a similar level of development. Regions are defined in appendix 2. The number of cities available for each economy is also reported in appendix 2.

[5] These parameters must be corrected for bias. See discussion below.

non-traded service, and housing rental costs. Wages on a non-traded service and the price of a non-traded good such as housing may give some indication of local distribution costs. GDP *per capita* may give an indication of the size of the retail margin that a market can bear. Based on availability across cities, we use the hourly wage for maid service and rental on a one-bedroom furnished apartment to represent service wages and housing rental.[6] Both of these variables are from the EIU CityData, while GDP *per capita* is calculated from the World Bank WDI Database.[7] Sensitivity tests were run for alternate proxies, such as rental on furnished 3 bedroom apartments, and monthly wages for maid service. GNI *per capita* was also used as an alternate measure of purchasing power. The results appear insensitive to the choice of proxies for retail markup.

Transport costs are proxied by GDP-weighted great-circle distance, now commonly used in the gravity model literature to reflect remoteness. The specification in (6)′ calls for a weighted distance measure, with weights representing the share of varieties produced in city j, θ_{ij}, in economy K. Finding a proxy for θ_{ij} is difficult. One could assume that θ_{ij} is proportional to partner economy K's share of global output of the good, or partner economy K's share of global exports of the good. Alternatively one might assume that θ_{ij} is proportional to the domestic economy's share of imports from partner economy K. Data for most of these proxies is not readily available across a large number of products and economies. In estimating (6)′, we do not include any proxy for θ_{ij}. If the share of varieties from any economy K is positively correlated with GDP of economy K, then GDP-weighted distance may adequately represent the specification in (6)′.

Products in the EIU CityData were matched with products at the HS 4-digit (or HS 6-digit level where possible), in order to obtain tariff and NTM data.[8] Tariff data were obtained from the UNCTAD TRAINS database using WITS. In most cases these data are for 2001, though for some economies the latest available information was from 1997-1999. The specification in (6)′ calls for data on specific tariffs levied on good k imported from city j (in economy K), weighted by θ_{ij}. For simplicity, we chose to use unweighted MFN *(ad valorem)* tariffs in our estimation. Where economies are members of a customs union (*e.g.*, Mercosur) or economic union (*e.g.*, the EU), the CET was used. Note that

[6] Rental on commercial property is available widely for industrial economies only. In some developing economies these rentals may not be representative of the costs of doing business locally.

[7] Unfortunately city income *per capita* is only readily available for the United States. Hence the estimation uses economy level data.

[8] The corresponding products and HS codes are shown in the appendix.

most economies impose tariffs on a particular good globally, making distinctions with respect to MFN partner economies, and with respect to partners in preferential trade agreements. If the domestic economy imposes the same tariff on good k on all partner economies, and these partners produced all varieties of good k, then the specification in (6)′ would reduce to simply $\alpha_3 t$. Thus, the more an economy trades with its MFN partners, and the larger share of global varieties produced by these partners, the better approximation the MFN tariff will be to the specification in (6)′. The use of *ad valorem* instead of specific tariff is simply due to data availability.

Data on NTMs were obtained from two sources. A dummy variable was created using the TRAINS database, which takes a value of 1 if an economy has any type of "Quantity Control Measure" recorded for a product, and zero, otherwise. This includes import quotas, prohibitions, non-automatic licensing, VERs, prior authorizations for human or animal health, environment, *etc.* [9] Another dummy variable (MD) was created based on the entries in the compilation described in Manifold-Donnelly (2004). This dummy variable took a value of 1 if the MD showed the presence of an import restriction, import quota or prohibition, import license, import surcharges or customs measures considered to be impediments to trade.

While the TRAINS measure and the Manifold-Donnelly measure were chosen to reflect similar types of NTMs, the databases are likely to reflect different–perhaps complementary–information. TRAINS records the presence of NTMs as reported by official governments. The entries in Manifold-Donnelly are constructed largely from complaints from the private sector about impediments to trade in a particular economy. Thus, we introduce these two measures using four different specifications. In the first and second specification, we introduce, respectively, the TRAINS and MD dummy variables alone. The third specification includes both dummy variables, and assesses their net impact on a region's prices.[10] Finally, the fourth specification introduces a composite dummy which takes a value of 1 if either the TRAINS or MD dummy variable records the presence of a reported NTM.

---

[9] This designation refers to Control Measures designated as 6100-6900 in the TRAINS database.

[10] In two cases, only one dummy will enter the regression: if either dummy variable shows no NTMs in the sector; if both NTM dummies are identical.

5. Results

In this paper, we investigate the impact of NTMs on three GTAP sectors: apparel (28), shoes (29), and processed food (25). Estimates of the tariff equivalents of the NTMs in each of these sectors are reported in tables 1-3, respectively. Testing revealed that estimation of (6)′ with continuous variables in logs rather than levels fit the data best. Thus, these estimates are obtained from log-linear regressions.[11] (Full regression results are not reported, but may be obtained from the authors upon request.) Ideally, we would like to allow the coefficients on distance, tariff, and the retail margin proxy variables to vary across regions. However, the lack of sufficient variation in these variables across some regions prevented estimation of region-specific parameters. We were able to allow the regional retail margin variables to have product-specific parameters. For example, we were able to allow children's, men's, and women's shoes to respond differently to the retail margin proxy variables.

As shown by Halvorson and Palmquist (1980), the coefficients on the NTM dummy variables in (6)′ may be transformed into the percentage markup in price (tariff-equivalent) by taking the anti-log of the coefficient and subtracting 1. Kennedy (1981) notes that the Halvorson/Palmquist transformation is biased upward, and develops a correction.[12] More recently van Garderen and Shah (2002) argue that the Kennedy correction should be used with an approximate unbiased variance estimator to construct t-statistics.[13] Thus, the TE estimates in tables 1-3 are constructed using the Kennedy transformation. Statistical significance is determined using standard errors calculated from the van Garderen and Shah approximate unbiased variance estimator. The first two columns of each table report the regions for which the TRAINS Database or the MD compilation record NTMs on at least one product in at least one economy

---

[11] It is important to note that a log-linear version of (6)′ looks very similar to the specification which would emerge from a homogeneous products-perfect competition model. In that case, retail prices would simply be

$P_r = P_w(1+\mu)(1+\tau)(1+\delta)(1+\rho)$, where μ, τ, δ, and ρ are the percentage markups due to distribution costs, tariffs, transport costs and the NTM, respectively. Taking logs of both sides yields: $\ln P_r = \ln P_w + \ln\tilde{\mu} + \ln\tilde{\tau} + \ln\tilde{\delta} + \ln\tilde{\rho}$, where ~ indicates one plus the variable.

[12] Using this transformation the tariff-equivalent (in percent) is $TE = 100 * [\exp(\hat{c} - 0.5 * \hat{V}(\hat{c})) - 1]$, where c, V are coefficient, and variance, respectively, and ^ indicates estimated value.

[13] Van Garderen and Shah argue that the Kennedy transformed estimator is itself biased, but that this bias goes to zero asymptotically as the sample size grows. They also suggest this is true for their own approximate unbiased variance estimator is:

$\tilde{V}(TE) = 100^2 * [\exp(2\hat{c})][\exp(-\hat{V}(\hat{c})) - \exp(-2\hat{V}(\hat{c}))]$ They demonstrate that the difference between this estimator and the exact unbiased variance estimator approaches zero as the sample grows larger.

within a region. Note that even if both databases record NTMs for a region, they may refer to different products and or economies within that region. The next four columns give the TEs under each of the four alternate NTM specifications. Only TEs which are positive and significant at the 10 percent level or above are reported in the tables.

5.1. *Apparel*

Both TRAINS and MD report a number of regions with NTMs on apparel. Notably, both databases record NTMs for the United States, the EU, and Canada–the three industrial economies (regions) with well-known VER agreements restricting many apparel products under the ATC. However, other regions also appear to have some quantitative restrictions. Both databases record NTMs for MERCOSUR and for Turkey and the Middle East,[14] and both record no NTMs for China. For the other regions, the databases give diverging conclusions. This suggests that the two databases may be providing different information–official, tariff-line records *vs.* broad product level complaints from exporting economies.

For the Canada, the EU and the United States, the TE estimates are plausible, when compared to the estimates in previous literature.[15] Canadian retail prices on apparel with NTMs are 20 to 35 percent higher (on average) than apparel products with no NTMs. For the EU, apparel retail prices are 19 to 34 percent higher due to the EU's NTMs. Estimates for the US show slightly smaller values than Canada and the EU. US NTMs on apparel raise US apparel retail prices between 17 and 24 percent, relative to apparel products with no NTMs.

Latin America and the Former Soviet Union and Eastern Europe also register rather large TEs due to NTMs. Estimates for MERCOSUR suggest that when an economy in this region has an NTM on apparel, its prices are between 31 and 39 percent higher than economies without NTMs on apparel. Economies in Mexico/Central America with NTMs have 137-152 percent higher prices on apparel than those without, while Other Latin American economies experience 56-66 percent higher prices due to their NTMs. Estimates for economies with NTMs in the FSU and Eastern Europe show much smaller TEs of 25-32 percent.

---

[14] MD have very little data for this region, while the TRAINS database has data on all but one (see appendix 2.) Thus, TE estimates may differ widely between specifications (1) and (2), and may not be feasibly estimated in specifications (3) and (4). This problem occurs in all three sectors discussed in the paper.

[15] See, for example, Khaturia, et al. (2001), USITC (2002), Francois and Spinanger (2000).

Table 1. Apparel

		Policy data		Increase in price due to own NTM[1] (%)			
		TRAINS	MD	TRAINS	MD	TRAINS & MD	COMPOSITE
				(1)	(2)	(3)	(4)
REGION	**Economy**						
1a	Southern Africa	x					
1b	Other Sub-Saharan Africa						
2	Australia/New Zealand						
3	EU	x	x	19	31	31	34
4	FSU and E. Europe		x		32	28	25
5	Other Latin America		x		63	57	66
6	MERCOSUR	x	x	36		39	31
7	Mexico/ Central America		x		152	137	146
8	Southeast Asia		x				
9	South Asia	x					
10	East Asia	x		31		37	43
11	China						
12	Canada	x	x	20	28	32	35
13	Japan		x		68	79	71
14a	Turkey and Middle East[3]	x	x	88	18	([2])	38
14b	North Africa						
15	EFTA						
16	US	x	x		17	22	24
Obs.				1164	1114	1164	1174

[1] Estimates corrected using Kennedy (1981) correction. Standard errors corrected using Van Garderen-Shah (2002) approximate unbiased variance estimator. Only estimates which are positive and significant at the 10 percent level or above are shown. Estimates rounded to the nearest integer.
[2] The ITC database has no information on a number of economies in this region. Thus, inclusion of this NTM dummy was not possible.
[3] The range of estimates is wide because the two databases have data on different economies within this region.

Oddly, Japan is estimated to have 68-79 percent markups on apparel products with NTMs. Yet, in other literature (and in the TRAINS database) Japan is said to have no NTMs on apparel imports (Yang, 1994). Another anomaly appears is East Asia, which shows TE estimates ranging from 31-43 percent. These results suggests that perhaps the NTM variable is picking up some economy-fixed effects, such as variation in cost-of-living, which have not been adequately controlled for by the retail margin variables. In that case, these estimates are likely to be overstated. This reinforces the importance of modifying the estimation to allow for region-specific responses to all variables.

5.2. *Shoes*

In table 2, both databases show the FSU and Eastern Europe, MERCOSUR, Turkey and the Middle East, and the United States as having NTMs on shoes. They also both agree that the two African regions, Other Latin American economies, Southeast Asia, China and Canada have no NTMs (as defined above) on shoes. Only the NTMs of MERCOSUR and Mexico/Central America show consistently positive and statistically significant effects on retail prices. If an economy in MERCOSUR has NTMs on shoes, prices are 93-99 percent higher than economies without NTMs on shoes. The price premium for an economy with NTMs on shoes in the Mexico/Central America region is 38-48 percent.

5.3. *Processed Food*

Many economies are reported to have NTMs on processed food according to both databases (table 3). According to the TRAINS database, these NTMs are more often than not non-automatic licenses or prior authorizations for the protection of human or plant health. The databases agree that Southern Africa, the EU, Other Latin America, MERCOSUR, and Southeast Asia all have NTMs on some processed food products in some economies within each region, while China has none.

Only the NTMs of Southern Africa and Other Latin America have positive, statistically significant effects on processed food prices. In Southern Africa, an NTM on a processed food product raises the price by 53-54 percent above those processed food products with no NTMs. In Other Latin America, three out of four specifications indicated positive TEs on processed food, but only the composite specification yielded a positive and significant estimate. If an economy in this region has an NTM on processed food products this specification indicates a 13 percent price increase over those economies without NTMs on

Table 2. Shoes

		Policy data		Increase in price due to own NTM[1] (%)			
		TRAINS	MD	TRAINS	MD	TRAINS & MD	COMPOSITE
				(1)	(2)	(3)	(4)
REGION	**Economy**						
1a	Southern Africa						
1b	Other Sub-Saharan Africa						
2	Australia/New Zealand	x					
3	EU	x					
4	FSU and E. Europe	x	x				
5	Other Latin America						
6	MERCOSUR	x	x	97	99	93	95
7	Mexico/ Central America		x		48	40	38
8	Southeast Asia						
9	South Asia	x					
10	East Asia	x					
11	China						
12	Canada						
13	Japan		x				
14a	Turkey and Middle East	x	x	82		([2])	
14b	North Africa	x					
15	EFTA	x					
16	US	x	x				
Obs.				415	402	419	422

[1] Estimates corrected using Kennedy (1981) correction. Standard errors corrected using Van Garderen-Shah (2002) approximate unbiased variance estimator. Only estimates which are positive and significant at the 10 percent level or above are shown. Estimates rounded to the nearest integer.

[2] The ITC database has no information on a number of economies in this region. Thus, inclusion of this NTM dummy was not possible.

Table 3. Processed foods

		Policy data		Increase in price due to own NTM[1] (%)			
		TRAINS	MD	TRAINS	MD	TRAINS & MD	COMPOSITE
				(1)	(2)	(3)	(4)
REGION	**Economy**						
1a	Southern Africa	x	x	54		54	53
1b	Other Sub-Saharan Africa	x					
2	Australia/New Zealand	x					
3	EU	x	x				
4	FSU and E. Europe	x					
5	Other Latin America	x	x				13
6	MERCOSUR	x	x				
7	Mexico/ Central America	x					
8	Southeast Asia	x	x				
9	South Asia	x					
10	East Asia	x					
11	China						
12	Canada	x					
13	Japan	x		([3])		([3])	([3])
14a	Turkey and Middle East		x				([2])
14b	North Africa	x					
15	EFTA	x					
16	US	x					
Obs.				1418	1178	1328	1433

[1] Estimates corrected using Kennedy (1981) correction. Standard errors corrected using Van Garderen-Shah (2002) approximate unbiased variance estimator. Only estimates which are positive and significant at the 10 percent level or above are shown. Estimates rounded to the nearest integer.
[2] The ITC database has no information on a number of economies in this region. Thus, inclusion of this NTM dummy was not possible.
[3] Missing data on other explanatory variables rendered estimation of the TE of this NTM impossible.

these products. Since product standards on food for the protection of human health are common across many economies, these estimates may help delineate cases where either the standards or the implementation of those standards acts as a trade barrier.

6. Conclusions, Caveats and Extensions

The preliminary results shown for the apparel, shoes and processed foods sectors, suggests that this econometric approach may yield useful estimates of the tariff-equivalents of NTMS. Regressions for all three sectors fit the data fairly well, explaining between 80 and 95 percent of the variation in the data. Interestingly, the method of introducing the NTM variables into the regression did not seem to be critical to the estimation of the tariff-equivalent of these barriers. While the four different specifications did yield a range of estimates for the tariff-equivalent of the NTMs, the range was not usually very wide–roughly 5 to 10 percentage points for a given region and product. In addition, the four specifications nearly always yielded similar conclusions as to which regions' NTMs have significant effects on prices and which do not.

While these results are encouraging, there are a number of caveats that suggest further work needs to be done. Given the imperfect nature of the proxies used to capture retail margins and transport costs, it would make sense to allow region-specific responses to these variables. At present, limitations in the data prevent this. As a result, the TE estimates may actually pick up economy-specific cost-of-living effects which have not been adequately represented by the other variables. In addition, estimation of the coefficients on a number of the other variables–such as the tariff and GDP *per capita*–are consistently not significant or wrong-signed. Where the data does allow region-specific parameters, this problem often disappears. However, instead the TE estimates for some economies become absurdly inflated. In future work, we will attempt to iron out these problems, and to extend our estimates to a large number of other sectors.

References

1. Bradford, S. (2001). "Paying the Price: the Welfare and Employment Effects of Protection in OECD Countries," Working Paper, Brigham Young University.
2. Deardorff, A. and R. Stern (1997). "Measurement of Non-Tariff Barriers," Economics Dept. Working Paper No. 179, OECD.
3. Economics Intelligence Unit (2002). EIU CityData., *www.eiu.com*.
4. Francois, J. and D. Spinanger (2000). "The Cost of EU Trade Protection in Textiles and Clothing," manuscript.

5. Halvorsen, R. and R. Palmquist (1980). "The Interpretation of Dummy Variables in Semi logarithmic Equations," *American Economic Review* 70, 474-5.
6. Kennedy, P. (1981). "Estimation with Correctly Interpreted Dummy Variables in Semi logarithmic Equations," *American Economic Review* 71, 801.
7. Kathuria, S., and A. Bhardwaj (2001), "The Export Tax Equivalents of Quota Restrictions in the Indian Textile and Garment Industries," World Bank Working Paper.
8. Manifold, D., and W. Donnelly (2004), "A Compilation from Multiple Sources of Measures which May Affect Trade," this volume, Chapter 2.1.
9. van Garderen, K.J. and C. Shah (2002). "Exact Interpretation of Dummy Variables in Semilogarithmic Equations," *Econometrics Journal* 5, 149-159.
10. USITC (2002). *The Economic Effects of Significant Import Restraint, Third Update, 2002.* USITC, Publication No. 3519.
11. Yang, Y. (1994). "The Impact of MFA Phasing Out on World Clothing and Textile Markets," *The Journal of Development Studies*, 20 (4) 1994, 892-915.

APPENDIX 1. EIU Citydata product/GTAP/HTS concordances

GTAP Sector	EIU CityData Product	HTS	GTAP Sector	EIU CityData Product	HTS
4	Apples (1 kg)	080810	21	Margarine, 500g	151710
4	Bananas (1 kg)	080300	21	Olive oil (1 l)	1509
4	Carrots (1 kg)	070610	21	Peanut or corn oil (1 l)	150890, 151529
4	Lemons (1 kg)	080530			
4	Lettuce (one)	070511	22	Butter, 500 g	040510
4	Mushrooms (1 kg)	070951	22	Cheese, imported (500 g)	0406
4	Onions (1 kg)	070310	22	Milk, pasteurized (1 l)	040120
4	Oranges (1 kg)	080510	22	Yoghurt, natural (150 g)	040310
4	Potatoes (2 kg)	070190			
4	Tomatoes (1 kg)	070200	23	White rice, 1 kg	100630
10	Eggs (12)	040700	24	Sugar, white (1 kg)	1701
14	Fresh fish (1 kg)	0302	25	Cocoa (250 g)	180500
			25	Cornflakes (375 g)	190410
19	Beef: ground or minced (1 kg)	0201, 0202	25	Drinking chocolate (500 g)	180610
19	Beef: roast (1 kg)	0201, 0202	25	Frozen fish fingers (1 kg)	160420
19	Beef: stewing, shoulder (1 kg)	0201, 0202	25	Flour, white (1 kg)	110100
19	Beef: filet mignon (1 kg)	0201, 0202	25	Ground coffee (500 g)	0901
19	Lamb: chops (1 kg)	0204	25	Instant coffee (125 g)	0901

APPENDIX 1. EIU citydata product/GTAP/HTS concordances–Continued

GTAP Sector	EIU CityData Product	HTS	GTAP Sector	EIU CityData Product	HTS
19	Lamb: leg (1 kg)	0204	25	Orange juice (1 l)	2009
19	Lamb: Stewing (1 kg)	0204	25	Peaches, canned (500 g)	200870
19	Beef: steak, entrecote (1 kg)	0201, 0202	25	Peas, canned (250 g)	200540
19	Veal: chops (1 kg)	0201, 0202	25	Sliced pineapples, canned (500 g)	200820
19	Veal: fillet (1 kg)	0201, 0202	25	Spaghetti (1 kg)	190219
19	Veal: roast (1 kg)	0201, 0202	25	Tea bags (25 bags)	090230
			25	Tomatoes, canned (250 g)	200210
20	Bacon (1 kg)	021012	25	White bread, 1 kg (mid-priced	190590
20	Chicken: fresh (1 kg)	0207			
20	Chicken: frozen (1 kg)	0207	26	Beer, local brand (1 l)	220300
20	Ham: whole (1 kg)	021011	26	Beer, top quality (330 ml)	220300
20	Pork: loin (1 kg)	0203	26	Cognac, French VSOP (700 ml)	220820
20	Pork: chops (1 kg)	0203	26	Gin, Gilbey's or equivalent (700 ml)	220850
26	Liqueur, Cointreau (700 ml)	220870	31	Daily local newspaper	490210
26	Vermouth, Martini & Rossi (1 l) 1	220510	31	Paperback novel (at bookstore)	4901
26	Wine, common table (1 l)	220421	31	International weekly news magazine	490290
26	Wine, fine quality (700 ml)	220421			
26	Wine, superior quality (700 ml)	220421	32	Regular unleaded petrol (1 l)	2710
26	Mineral water (1 l)	220110			
26	Tonic water (200 ml)	220210	33	Dishwashing liquid (750 ml)	340220
26	Cigarettes, local brand (pack of 20)	240220	33	Insect-killer spray (330 g)	380810
26	Cigarettes, Marlboro (pack of 20)	240220	33	Laundry detergent (3 l)	340220

APPENDIX 1. EIU citydata product/GTAP/HTS concordances–Continued

GTAP Sector	EIU CityData Product	HTS	GTAP Sector	EIU CityData Product	HTS
26	Pipe tobacco (50 g)	240310	33	Soap (100 g)	340111
			33	Aspirins (100 tablets)	291822
28	Socks, wool mixture	6115	33	Hand lotion (125 ml)	330430
28	Tights, panty hose	6115	33	Lipstick (deluxe type)	330410
28	Women's cardigan sweater	6110	33	Shampoo & conditioner in one (400 ml)	330510
28	Boy's jacket, smart	620331-620333	33	Toothpaste with fluoride (120 g)	330610
28	Business suit, two piece, med. weight	620311, 620312	33	Kodak colour film (36 exposures)	370231
28	Boy's dress trousers	620341, 620343			
28	Child's jeans	620342	37	Frying pan (Teflon or equivalent)	732393
28	Dress, ready to wear, daytime	6204	37	Razor blades (five pieces)	821220
28	Girl's dress	6204			
28	Business shirt, white	620520. 620530	38	Compact car (1300-1799 cc)	8703
28	Mens raincoat, Burberry type	620112, 620113	38	Deluxe car (2500 cc upwards)	8703
28	Women's raincoat, Burberry type	620212, 620213	38	Family car (1800-2499 cc)	8703
			38	Low priced car (900-1299 cc) 2	8703
29	Child's shoes, dresswear	640420			
29	Men's shoes, business wear	640420	40	Television, colour (66 cm)	852812
29	Child's shoes, sportswear	640411	40	Personal computer (64 MB)	847141
29	Women's shoes, town	640420			
			41	Batteries (two, size D/LR20)	8506
31	Toilet tissue (two rolls)	481810	41	Electric toaster (for two slices)	851672
31	Facial tissues (box of 100)	481820	41	Light bulbs (two, 60 watts)	853922
			41	Compact disc album	852432

APPENDIX 2. Regional groups used in estimation (number of cities in parentheses)

Region #	Region Name	Region #	Region Name	Region #	Region Name
1.1	**Southern Africa**	**4**	Hungary (1)	**7**	Guatemala (1)
	Zimbabwe (1)		Poland (1)		Panama (1)
	South Africa (1)		Romania (1)		
			Russia (2)	**8**	**SE Asia**
1.2	**Rest of SSA**				Indonesia (1)
	Cameroon (1)	**5**	**Rest of South America**		Malaysia (1)
	Cote D'Ivoire[1] (1)		Chile (1)		Philippines (1)
	Gabon (1)		Colombia (1)		Thailand (1)
	Kenya (1)		Venezuela (1)		Vietnam (2)
	Nigeria (1)		Peru[1] (1)		
	Senegal[1] (1)		Ecuador (1)	**9**	**South Asia**
					Bangladesh (1)
2	**AUS/NZ**	**6**	**MERCOSUR**		India (2)
	Australia (5)		Argentina (1)		Sri Lanka[1] (1)
	New Zealand (2)		Brazil (2)		Pakistan (1)
			Paraguay (1)		
3	**EU-15 (23)**		Uruguay (1)	**10**	**East Asia**
					Hong Kong (1)
4	**Russia/EE**	**7**	**Mexico and CA**		South Korea (1)
	Azerbaijan[2] (1)		Mexico (1)		Singapore (1)
	Czech Republic (1)		Costa Rica (1)		Chinese Taipei (1)

APPENDIX 2. Regional groups used in estimation (number of cities in parentheses)–Continued

Region #	Region Name	Region #	Region Name	Region #	Region Name
11	**China (5)**	**14.2**	**North Africa**		
			Morocco (1)		
12	**Canada (4)**		Egypt (1)		
			Tunisia (1)		
13	**Japan (2)**				
		15	**EFTA**		
14.1	**Turkey & Middle East**		Iceland (1)		
	Turkey (1)		Norway (1)		
			Switzerland (2)		
	Israel[2] (1)				
	Bahrain[1] (1)	**16**	**USA (16)**		
	Jordan[1] (1)				
	Saudi Arabia[1] (3)				

[1] No data available for this economy in the ITC NTM Database.
[2] No recent data available for this economy in the TRAINS Database.

ESTIMATION OF NOMINAL AND EFFECTIVE RATES OF PROTECTION

Jungho Yoo

Korea Development Institute

1. Background: Concepts of Nominal and Effective Rates Of Protection

When imports of a good are restricted by tariff or non-tariff barriers, the domestic price of the good tends to rise above the border price, the price that the good commands when it arrives at the border. Nominal rate of protection (NRP) is the rate by which the domestic price of the good exceeds the border price. Let t stand for nominal rate of protection. It may then be expressed as:

$$t_j = \frac{P_j}{P_j*} - 1, \text{j} = 1, 2, \ldots, \text{K}, \tag{1}$$

where subscript *j* refers to the j-th good, *K* is the number of tradable goods, P stands for the price of a given good, and * indicates the variables "before" imposition of tariffs or non-tariff measures.

NRP is not a good indicator of how much the domestic producers are protected by the tariff or non-tariff measure that gave rise to the NRP. For domestic producers, of greater interest than the price rise is the rise in value added, that remains of a unit value of output after the cost of intermediate inputs is deducted. A better indicator of the protection accorded to the domestic producers is the effective rate of protection (ERP), which is the rate by which the value added increases after the imposition of protective measures. Let *z* stand for ERP. It may then be expressed as:

$$z_j = \frac{VA_j}{VA_j*} - 1, \text{j} = 1, 2, \ldots, \text{K}, \tag{2}$$

where VA stands for value added and other symbols have the same meaning as before. A word of caution is in order here. The statement that "the value added increases" does not mean that protection can somehow create more value added out of the same quantities of inputs as does a rise in productivity. In fact the physical input-output relation will be assumed to remain the same in this paper before and after the imposition of tariffs or non-tariff measures. What is meant is that the "price" of value added rises as a result of protection not the "quantity" of value added.

How a set of NRPs changes the ERP of a given good is shown in the following equation. For the moment it will be assumed that intermediate inputs are all tradable goods and that tariff is the only protective measure employed. Shortly, these assumptions will be done away with.

$$z_j = \frac{(1+t_j) - \sum_i a_{ij} * (1+t_i)}{1 - \sum_i a_{ij} *} - 1 = \frac{t_j - \sum_i a_{ij} * t_i}{1 - \sum_i a_{ij} *} \quad (3)$$

where a_{ij} stands for the amount of input of Good i required to produce a unit value, say, a dollar's worth, of Good j. In the first expression on the right hand side the denominator represents the value added before imposition of tariffs for a unit value of output j, and the numerator the value added after the imposition. The first term in the numerator shows that the price of the output increases by t_j times 100 percent, and the second term shows how much the costs of intermediate inputs increase, each increasing by t_i times 100 percent. Hence, not just the tariff on Good j but the tariffs on other goods of intermediate inputs have to be taken into account in order to see how a given set of tariffs changes the value added for the producers of Good j. It should be noted that the small country assumption was made here and will be maintained throughout the paper.

Effective rate of protection can be less than zero, a case of negative z_j. This would arise, if a given set of tariffs raises the cost of the intermediate inputs, the second term, more than the price of output, the first term in the numerator of equation (3). A negative z_j means that the net effect of the protection is to reduce the value added of good j, hurting the domestic producers, although the t_j, the nominal rate of protection, may be positive.

As a practical matter of estimation, however, a negative effective rate of protection may be estimated for certain goods, even when protection increases the valued added. It will happen, if the denominator of equation (3) is negative in value, while the numerator is positive. A positive numerator means that the price of the good is greater than the cost of production after imposition of tariffs, and a negative denominator means that the cost of production is greater than the price before the imposition. This would be the case, if production of the good in question is not commercially viable without protection but only survives thanks to protection. Though rare, this possibility should not be ignored in estimating the effective rates of protection.

2. Estimation of Nominal Rates of Protection

It would be simple to estimate the NRP, if tariffs were the only protective barrier that restricts imports and applied to all imports without exception. In reality there are other barriers restricting imports such as quantitative restrictions, import approval or recommendation system, safety standards, hygienic standards, other special laws and so on. Also, the government may exempt or rebate tariffs when imports are used for some specified purposes such as production of exports, research and development, or other purposes that are deemed desirable in the economy. Hence, the rates in the tariff schedule are more often than not a poor indicator of the nominal rate of protection. It would be ideal if domestic prices and border prices were known, as the domestic prices would bear all of the effects of tariff and non-tariff measures of protection. Of course, the information is not readily available but has to be collected through a survey, and the survey is not always accurate.

This consideration suggests three possible candidates from which to choose one as the estimate of NRP for an industry. One candidate is "legal tariff," *i.e.*, the tariff rate on the tariff schedule, and the other is "actual tariff" which may be obtained by dividing the tariff revenue on an import good by the value of imports. The third one is "tariff equivalent", the ratio of domestic price to border price less one, both prices obtained through a survey.

2.1. *The Survey*

The survey was conducted in 1990 on 766 8-digit level KSIC (Korea Standard Industrial Classification) products in the mining and manufacturing sectors. They accounted for 85 percent of the outputs of the two sectors. Respondents were establishments with 10 or more employees. It was decided that these producers must know better than others the domestic and border prices of the goods that they produce, whether competing with imports or exporting. The survey covered all establishments with 100 or more employees. Others with fewer employees were ranked by amount of shipments, and those ranked high were included in the survey ahead of others until 70 percent of the total shipments of the product was reached. A total of 6,547 establishments were surveyed.

Each establishment was asked to pick three specifications of a product that they produced most and to supply for each specification both the domestic price before indirect taxes and the border price. A product even at 8-digit level industrial classification varies a great deal in price depending on specifications regarding the shape, size, structure, functions, and so on. The border price here refers to c.i.f. (cost, insurance, freight) price in the case of import-competing goods and f.o.b. (free on board) price for export goods.

Given the purpose of the survey, only those responses with both domestic and border prices could be used. The survey produced 11,203 such responses at the "specification" level on 757 8-digit KSIC products. The establishments that provided the useful responses accounted for 38 percent of the total shipments of those establishments with ten or more employees in the mining and manufacturing sectors.

For the ratio of domestic price over border price of agricultural commodities, Korean government's report on tariff equivalents in 1991 to Negotiating Group on Agriculture of the Uruguay Round was relied on. For fishery and forestry products, the comparison between domestic and border price could not be made, and only legal and actual tariffs were considered as the candidates for the nominal rate of protection.

2.2. *Concordance*

In estimating the effective rates of protection the nominal rates were going to be applied on the input-output (I-O) tables that were regularly estimated and published by Bank of Korea. This means that the legal tariff rate, actual tariff rate, and tariff equivalent have to be found for each of the goods-producing I-O industries so that one of the three candidates may be chosen to be the estimate of nominal rate of protection. Therefore, two concordances were necessary: one between I-O industries and SITC (Standard International Trade Classification) or HS (Harmonized System) by which the tariff rates were going to be collected; the other between I-O industries and 8-digit KSIC by which the tariff equivalent for a product would be found through a price survey.

The I-O table used in the estimating ERP had 161 industries in total with 122 of them producing goods. However, estimation of NRPs, explained in the following, was first conducted at a more finely defined level of 402 I-O industries with 316 of them producing goods. The estimates at this level are then aggregated to obtain NRPs for the 122 I-O industries.

2.3. *Selection of Nominal Rates of Protection*

At the level of 402 I-O industries the estimation of NRP was to select one as the estimate among three candidates, namely, legal tariff, actual tariff, and tariff equivalent. Legal tariff (LT) for an industry was obtained by taking a simple average of the tariffs on the goods belonging to the industry. Actual tariff (AT) was obtained by dividing the tariff revenue on imports of the goods belonging to the industry by the imports. Tariff equivalent (TE) was obtained through the survey as explained earlier. TE can be greater or smaller than either LT or AT. But LT is supposed to be greater than AT for a good, since only exemption can make the two differ from each other. When an average was taken of the tariffs on more than one goods belonging to the same industry, it may happen that LT is found to be less than AT in some exceptional cases. Care should be taken in such cases.

What had to be done was to select among the three candidates, without knowing, the one that best represents the "true" price gap between domestic and border prices of the goods belonging to an industry. The selection took into consideration the industry's trade-characteristics, that is, how actively traded were the goods and, if they were, whether they mostly competed with imports or were exported. An I-O industry was considered import-competing, if its import dependency is greater than 10 percent. Here, import dependency is the ratio of imports to domestic consumption, which is an industry's outputs plus imports minus the sum of exports and inventory increase. For such an import-competing industry the estimation procedure, to be described in the following, assumed that the determination of domestic prices of the goods belonging to the industry was influenced by import prices. Then, the problem of selecting the NRP among the three candidates boils down to making a judgment on whether it was the tariffs or non-tariff measures that gave rise to the price gap between domestic and border prices. An industry was called export-oriented, if the share of exports in the industry's output exceeds 10 percent. For export-oriented industries it was assumed that the domestic prices of their outputs were more likely to be influenced by the export prices than by legal and actual tariffs on imports. An industry could be both import-competing and export-oriented, with both of its export share and import dependency being greater than 10 percent. In such cases all three candidates should be considered equally likely to represent the price gap. An industry may be neither import-competing nor export-oriented. Then, import restrictive measures may have little influence on the price gap. In any case it should be noted that the small-country assumption was made regarding foreign demand and supply.

2.3.1. *Selection Rules for Import-Competing Industries*

a) TE > LT

This is a case of tariff equivalent (TE) found to be greater than legal tariff (LT), that is, the domestic price was found to exceed import price by more than what can be explained by tariffs. If there was one or more non-tariff measures (NTM) restricting imports, TE was chosen to be the NRP. If there was none, LT was chosen. In some instances, even though there was no NTM, when the survey results looked robust, for example, in view of the number of responses, then TE was chosen to be the NRP.

b) LT > TE > AT

The first inequality shows that, according to the price survey, the domestic price exceeded border price by less than the legal tariff. This was taken as an indication that legal tariff was ineffective in affecting the determination of the domestic price, perhaps, because of extensive exemptions. So it was decided that the choice to be made was between TE and AT. As in a), if there was some NTMs, TE was selected. If there was none, AT was selected.

c) AT > TE > 0

Since AT was the tariff rate that was actually applied, the domestic price was supposed to be higher than the border price by at least AT. This means that the first inequality cannot hold, if the goods belonging to the industry in question were homogeneous. For this reason, the inequality was taken as an indication that least two different kinds of goods, 1 and 2, belong to the industry. Let's suppose Good 1 was imported, but Good 2 was not, because TE was smaller than AT for Good 2. Then, it was possible to obtain the inequality, even if the actual tariff rates were the same for the two goods. For, then, the AT for the industry would reflect only the AT on imported Good 1, while the obtained TE for the industry was an average of the AT on Good 1 and TE on Good 2 that was not imported.

In this case the information available on sub-industries that constitute 402 I-O industries was taken into consideration. If a sub-industry were import-competing that had a big weight in output supply of the industry in question, AT was chosen as the NRP; if it were not import-competing, TE was chosen. Even though a NTM existed, it did not affect the selection, since an AT greater than TE implied that the NTM was less of a barrier than tariff. If there was a reason to question the validity of the price survey, the possibility was not ignored that TE may have been temporarily lower than AT at the time of the survey.

d) 0 > TE

The inequality implies that the domestic price is lower than the border price, a situation not likely to arise for import-competing goods. One possibility was that the import price was higher because the imported goods was of higher quality compared to domestic goods. In case import dependency was rather high for the industry in question this possibility was taken to be the reason, and AT (> 0) was chosen to be the NRP. If the industry was export-oriented as well as import-competing by the definitions adopted in the above and domestic goods appeared to be competitive, TE (< 0) was selected as the NRP.

2.3.2. *Selection Rules for Export-Oriented Industries*

For the goods belonging to export-oriented industries, TE was mostly chosen to be the NRP. This was not just because the domestic prices are supposed to be mostly influenced by export prices. Another important reason was that for most export-oriented industries the survey results looked robust because of many respondents. The number of respondents who supplied both domestic and border prices, who were mostly exporters, were usually many times greater than that for the import-competing industries.

In many instances TE was much greater than LT or AT, an implausible phenomenon at first look for export-oriented industries. However, for many of such industries there were NTMs, indicating that their domestic markets were protected, for example, automobile industry. Another reason why the domestic prices may exceed the export price very much would be the monopoly power in the market, for example, in TV industry. In such cases LT was chosen to be the NRP for the reason that it reflects the protective measures. In other cases such as clothing industries that were very much export-oriented, LT was chosen for the same reason, although high domestic prices compared to foreign price were plainly observed. In some export-oriented industries such as cotton fabrics and silk fabrics where TEs not only were smaller than LT or AT but were slightly less than zero, TEs were chosen as the NRPs.

In selecting an NRP among legal tariff, actual tariff, and tariff equivalent it is difficult to devise a rule that can be mechanically followed that anticipates all factors affecting the price gap between domestic and border prices. As apparent in this explanation, it is almost unavoidable to make some judgment, often without sufficient information.

3. Estimation of Effective Rates of Protection

3.1. *Cleaning the I-O tables of Indirect Taxes*

What is left to do in estimating ERPs is to apply the NRPs to the I-O tables. The tables, however, had to be revised and a new set of I-O coefficients estimated before the application. One reason was that the estimation of ERPs could be distorted because of the indirect taxes included in the I-O transactions. When an indirect tax is levied on a good, it makes the industry's output appear greater in value terms and, therefore, the value added. When a good on which an indirect tax is levied is used as an intermediate input into the production of other goods, the indirect tax inflates the cost of the intermediate input, making the value added of these other goods appear that much smaller.[1] Therefore, the I-O tables had to be cleaned of the indirect taxes so that ERP estimates may not be affected by them. For this purpose indirect taxes had to be subtracted from the two tables, the sum of which was the I-O Table: Transactions Table of Domestic Goods and Services and Transactions Table of Imported Goods and Services.

The Transactions Table of Domestic Goods and Services was cleaned as follows. From Bank of Korea the flows of Value-Added Taxes among the cells of the Table were obtained, and they could simply be subtracted from the table. Other indirect taxes were grouped into "proportional indirect tax," Special Consumption Tax and Alcohol Tax, and "Other Indirect Taxes." For each of these three groups the amount of tax revenue collected from each industry was available. The domestic Transactions table was cleaned of Proportional Indirect Tax and Other Indirect Tax, for each of these taxes, by deflating an industry's sales of inputs to other industries and to the final demand sector by the same implicit tax rate, which was calculated under the assumption that all the transactions were taxed by the same rate. In subtracting Special Consumption Tax and Alcohol Tax from the domestic Transactions table, it was taken into consideration that the inputs into the production of exports were exempted of the two taxes. (See the subsection 3.2 in the following.)

The Transactions Table of Imported Goods and Services had to be cleaned differently, because the indirect taxes were not separately available but only their sum was, which was called "import tax", while the sum was available for each industry. Also, a care was taken for the inter-industry transactions that did not include import tax, since rebates were allowed of the indirect taxes on imported inputs that went into the production of export goods. (See the subsection 3.2 in the following.)

3.2. *Domestic Price Based I-O Table*

The other reason why the I-O coefficients had to be revised to estimate ERPs was that the transactions reported in the I-O tables were a sum of two kinds of transactions that were valued differently. Because of the tariff rebate system,

[1] For more detailed discussion see Corden (1971), especially Section III, Ch.3.

exporters and producers of the inputs that went into the production of exports could draw back the tariffs they paid on imported goods. This means that the values of some intermediate inputs for which producers could claim tariff rebates were valued in the border prices and others were valued in domestic prices. Thus, the next thing to do after cleaning the I-O tables of indirect taxes was to have the different transactions be revalued on the same valuation base, that is, the base of domestic prices. Two explanations are in order. One is how this was done; the other is why the valuation base chosen was that of domestic prices. Domestic prices were chosen to be the valuation base of all transactions of the I-O table for the simple reason that the border prices were not available for services, the non-tradable, and, therefore, the service transactions could not be revalued in border prices. So it was decided that the traded goods transactions valued in border prices be revalued in domestic prices and summed together with the other transactions that were already expressed in domestic prices.

The transactions valued in border prices were the inputs of traded goods that went into the production of export goods and exports themselves. The amount of intermediate input i into export good j was estimated by multiplying the input coefficient a_{ij} of the industry j by its exports, E_j. The product a_{ij} x E_j was then inflated in value by the nominal rate of production for industry i, and this was summed with the other part of intermediate input i that was already valued in domestic price. This was done for both Transactions Table of Domestic Goods and Services and Transactions Table of Imported Goods and Services. For the domestic transactions table, E_j was also inflated by the nominal rate of protection for goods j. Then these two transactions tables were added together to obtain a new I-O table, all transactions of which were now valued in domestic prices. An industry's total output had to be newly estimated by summing across all industries the industry's supplies of inputs to them and its sales to the final demand sector. Lastly, a new set of I-O coefficients for each industry was obtained by dividing the inputs by the newly estimated total output for the industry.

The valuation base of this new set of I-O coefficients was domestic prices and they were free of indirect taxes. If we let a_{ij} stand for the new set of I-O coefficients, eq. (3) can be rewritten as follows.

$$z_j = \frac{VA_j}{VA_j*} - 1 = \frac{1 - \sum_i a_{ij}}{\frac{1}{1+t_j} - \sum_i \frac{a_{ij}}{1+t_i}} - 1 \qquad (4)$$

3.3. *Treatment of Non-Traded Goods*

So far it has been assumed for simplicity that no non-traded inputs are required in the production of traded goods. In an empirical study like this one they simply cannot be assumed away but somehow have to be dealt with. Two methods exist: Corden's and Balassa's. To describe these methods, it would be convenient to use some symbols. Let *i* and j indicate traded goods, of which there are K in number. Let *m* and *n* indicate non-traded goods, of which there are N in number. As before,

a_{ij} = required input of traded good *i* for the production of unit value of good *j*,

a_{mj} = required input of non-traded good *m* for the production of unit value of good *j*,

a_{in} = required input of traded good *i* for the production of unit value of non-trade good *n*,

a_{mn} = required input of non-traded good *m* for the production of unit value of non-traded good n.

3.3.1 *Corden's ERP*

Corden notes that "the prices of non-traded goods, just like the prices of the primary factors, are determined within the system while – given the small country assumption – the prices of traded goods are given as parameters"[2]. According to him, while the immediate effect of a protective measure on good *j* is to raise the price of good *j* and its domestic production, this in turn increases the demand for, therefore, the prices of the non-traded goods required in producing good *j*. The prices of traded goods required in producing good *j*, however, would not be affected under the small country assumption, as they depend only on the effect of protective measures on them and their border prices.

The effect of a protection does not end in the industry protected but extends to other industries producing non-traded goods that are required in the production of the protected industry. Thus, Corden suggests that effective protection should measure not only the effect on the value added of the protected industry but also the effects on the values added of those industries producing the non-traded goods that are required in the production of the protected industry.[3]

---

[2] Corden (1971), p.152

[3] In his words, "To obtain the value-added share for out formula all direct contributions by primary factors should in principle be summed with all indirect contributions by primary factors through non-traded inputs." *Ibid.*, p.159

How do we get at the values added of those industries producing the non-traded goods that are required in the production of the protected industry? The inputs into the production of a unit value of Good j may be expressed as follows:

$$a_{1j}\, a_{2j}\, \ldots\, a_{Kj}\, a_{K+1\,j}\, a_{K+2\,j}\, \ldots\, a_{K+N\,j}\, a_{vj}, \tag{5}$$

where the first K inputs are traded inputs and the next N inputs are non-traded inputs and a_{vj} stands for value added by industry j. What Corden suggests is that an ERP should measure not only a_{vj} but also the values added that are directly and indirectly incorporated in a_{mj} for m = K+1, K+2, … K+N. The values added directly and indirectly incorporated in a_{mj} can be found by endlessly decomposing the non-traded inputs as follows. In the first round, a_{mj} can be decomposed into three parts that are indirectly required in producing Good *j* through non-traded good *m*: traded inputs, non-traded inputs, and value added. This is done for all a_{mj} for m = K+1, K+2, … K+N. In the second round, each of these indirectly required non-traded inputs are again decomposed into three parts of inputs. In the next round, these indirectly required non-traded inputs in the second round can further be decomposed. As the non-traded inputs are decomposed in this fashion endlessly, the non-traded inputs a_{mj} vanish and are successfully decomposed into two parts: indirectly required inputs of traded goods and indirectly incorporated values added that are created in the industries producing non-traded goods.

We can imagine collecting the inputs of traded goods at every round of the decomposition. Let r_{im} stand for this collection of the inputs of Good *i* that are directly and indirectly required in producing of a unit value of *m*. Then, a unit value of non-traded good *m* can be decomposed as follows:

$$1 = \sum_i r_{im} + r_{vm}\,. \tag{6}$$

The first term on the right hand side is the sum of all directly and indirectly required traded inputs in the production of a unit value of *m*. The second term r_{vm} is the sum of the value added in industry *m* and all values added that are created in the industries that produce the indirectly required non-traded inputs into *m*.

Now a unit value of Good j can be expressed as follows:

$$1 = \sum_i a_{ij} + \sum_m a_{mj} + a_{vj} = \sum_i a_{ij} + \sum_m \sum_i r_{im}a_{mj} + \sum_m r_{vm}a_{mj} + a_{vj} \tag{7}$$

where $r_{im}a_{mj}$ represents inputs of traded goods *i* that go indirectly into the production of *j* through non-traded good *m*, and $\sum_i r_{im}a_{mj}$ the inputs of all traded goods that go indirectly into the production of *j* through one non-traded good, m. Then, the second term on the right hand side of the second equality, $\sum_m \sum_i r_{im}a_{mj}$ represents the inputs of all traded goods that go indirectly into production of j through all non-traded goods. The next term $\sum_m r_{vm}a_{mj}$ represents the values added incorporated in the non-traded inputs. The equation shows that the sum of non-traded inputs $\sum_m a_{mj}$ is decomposed into these two terms in the last expression.

Corden's ERP of an industry *j* measures not only the effect of protection on *j's* value added, a_{vj}, but also the effects on the values added incorporated in the non-traded inputs a_{mj}, $r_{vm}a_{mj}$, for every non-traded input *m*. Thus, Corden's VA*j* in (4), the value added on domestic valuation base after imposition of protective measures may be expressed as:

$$VA(C)_j = 1 - \sum_i a_{ij} - \sum_m \sum_i r_{im}a_{mj} \tag{8}$$

The border price counterpart, Corden's VAj* in (4), may be expressed as:

$$VA(C)_j{}^* = \frac{1}{1+t_j} - \sum_i \frac{a_{ij}}{1+t_i} - \sum_m \sum_i \frac{r_{im}a_{mj}}{1+t_i}. \tag{9}$$

In the first term on the right hand side, the unit value of *j's* output is deflated by the NRP to get the unit value before the imposition of protective measures. Similarly, the price rises of traded inputs caused by the protective measures are deflated in the second term, and the indirect inputs of traded goods through non-traded inputs are also deflated. Then, the Corden's ERPs were obtained by substituting (8) and (9) into (2).

3.3.2. *Balassa's ERP*

Imposition of tariffs or non-tariff measures on Good *j* tends to increase its production and its price, and this lead to an increased demand for intermediate inputs, as before. But, unlike Corden, Balassa assumes that the increased demand for the non-traded intermediate inputs does not result in increases in their prices. When a set of tariffs or non-tariff measures are imposed on all traded goods, the prices of non-traded goods will rise only to the extent that the prices of traded inputs go up because of the protective measures.[4] This means that the value added of the industries producing non-traded goods is not assumed to rise in price.

Hence, Balassa's ERP of a traded good *j* is concerned only with how much the value added of industry *j* is affected. Thus, Balassa's VA*j* in (4) may be written

$$VA(B)_j = 1 - \sum_i a_{ij} - \sum_m a_{mj} \tag{10}$$

---

[4] Balassa and Associates (1971), Appendix A.

The border price counterpart VAj* in (4) may be written

$$VA(B)_j^* = \frac{1}{1+t_j} - \sum_i \frac{a_{ij}}{1+t_i} - \sum_m \sum_i \frac{r_{im} a_{mj}}{1+t_i} - \sum_m r_{vm} a_{mj} \quad (11)$$

Comparing these two equations with equations (8) and (9), one can see that the values added incorporated in non-traded inputs are excluded in Balassa's ERP and included in Corden's ERP.

4. Estimation Results and Policy Implications

4.1. *NRPs*

Nominal rates of protection were found to be much greater than tariffs. For all traded goods the NRP in 1990 was 25.9 percent, whereas the legal and actual tariff rates were, respectively, 12.4 percent and 10 percent. It shows that the non-tariff measures were very important restraints on imports. This was especially the case with regard to agricultural goods, for which NRP was 101.3 percent while the actual tariff rate was only 11.6 percent. For the manufactures, the NRP and actual tariff were, respectively, 20.5 percent and 10 percent, while they become 13.6 percent and 9.7 percent, when food products were excluded.

4.2. ERPs

The average effective rate of protection of all industries for producing traded goods for domestic sales was estimated to be 34.5 percent by the Corden method and 47 percent by the Balassa method. The rates for the agricultural sector were 160 percent and 183 percent, respectively. For the manufacturing sector they were 15.9 percent and 22.7. The ERP for agricultural sector was nearly ten times as large as that for the manufacturing sector in 1990. (See tables 1 and 2).

As expected, the ERP estimates show much greater variation in its magnitude. The standard deviation of ERPs was more than three times as large as that for NRPs.

Some industries had negative ERPs, that is, their values added declined after the imposition of tariffs and non-tariff measures. An example was textile industry, for which NRPs on the intermediate inputs were relatively low but the NRP for its output was still lower. The low NRP on textile products may have been the result of the policy to promote clothing industry, an important export industry still in 1990, by keeping the input prices low. For footwear and electrical machinery including consumer electronics, which are also important export industries, ERPs were estimated to be much higher than the manufacturing average.

Table 1. ERP estimates by KSIC 3-digit industries – Corden Method

(unit: %)

KSIC 3-digit Industries	ERP	NRP	NRP, Average for Inputs	Inputs/ Output
All industries	34.5	28.3	24.3	60.3
Agriculture	159.7	101.9	24.1	42.6
Forestry	6.4	7.5	19.4	8.3
Fishing	15	13.9	10.5	24.2
Mining	-2.1	0.4	11.8	17.9
Manufacturing	15.9	21.4	24.5	64.2
Food	27.5	81.4	99.0	75.3
Beverage	10.6	24.2	38.1	49.3
Tobacco	99.9	40.0	11.1	67.4
Textiles	-12.3	3.8	12.9	64.0
Clothing	22.3	13.0	8.1	65.6
Leather	-11.8	4.6	10.0	75.1
Footwear	23.3	12.5	8.3	71.8
Wood	-1.1	3.5	5.8	66.9
Furniture	-2.3	4.2	8.6	59.3
Pulp, paper	7.7	7.8	7.9	64.4
Printing	-7.0	1.8	12.2	45.9
Industrial chemicals	13.7	11.3	9.9	62.9
Other chemicals	42.6	26.1	14.6	58.7
Oil refining	14.5	9.0	6.1	65.5
Petrol., coal products	4.0	2.2	1.7	76.7
Rubber products	6.0	8.6	10.7	56.0
Plastic products	1.3	12.4	18.6	64.0
Pottery, china	6.2	7.7	9.8	41.7
Glass	11.1	10.7	10.2	42.7
Other nonmetal min. prods.	3.4	4.9	6.4	50.8
Iron & steel	0.6	2.8	3.6	73.8
Nonferrous metal	6.3	5.0	4.4	68.4
Fabricated metal	6.7	6.9	7.1	57.8
Nonelectrical mach	24.9	17.9	12.3	55.9
Electrical mach.	47.3	25.3	14.2	66.4
Transport equip.	11.5	13.0	13.9	63.8
Prof., science. Equip.	26.0	20.9	17.0	57.1
Miscellaneous mfg.	10.8	11.3	11.6	56.6
All Industries ex. Ag.	14.9	20.7	24.3	62.1
Mfg. ex. Foods	14.7	11.9	10.2	62.4

Table 2. ERP estimates by KSIC 3-digit industries – Balassa Method

(unit: %)

KSIC 3-digit Industries	ERP	NRP	NRP, Average for Inputs	Inputs/ Output
All industries	47.0	28.3	20.7	71.0
Agriculture	183.2	101.9	20.5	49.9
Forestry	6.5	7.5	16.4	9.8
Fishing	17.1	13.9	7.5	33.6
Mining	-2.5	0.4	7.1	30.0
Manufacturing	22.7	21.4	21.0	75.4
Food	52.5	81.4	85.6	87.1
Beverage	15.1	24.2	29.3	64.2
Tobacco	123.9	40.0	10.1	73.7
Textiles	-15.9	3.8	11.5	72.2
Clothing	30.6	13.0	7.1	74.9
Leather	-67.7	4.6	63.7	55.0
Footwear	31.8	12.5	7.5	79.3
Wood	-1.7	3.5	5.0	77.9
Furniture	-3.5	4.2	6.9	73.9
Pulp, paper	11.4	7.8	6.7	76.0
Printing	-9.3	1.8	9.5	59.2
Industrial chemicals	21.1	11.3	8.2	75.9
Other chemicals	73.5	26.1	11.2	76.1
Oil refining	16.4	9.0	5.7	69.6
Petrol., coal products	7.1	2.2	1.5	86.8
Rubber products	7.6	8.6	9.2	65.3
Plastic products	1.8	12.4	16.1	74.1
Pottery, china	8.3	7.7	7.2	56.5
Glass	14.5	10.7	7.8	56.3
Other nonmetal min. prods.	4.8	4.9	5.0	65.0
Iron & steel	0.8	2.8	3.2	81.0
Nonferrous metal	9.3	5.0	3.8	78.7
Fabricated metal	9.5	6.9	5.9	70.0
Nonelectrical mach	35.7	17.9	9.9	69.3
Electrical mach.	73.0	25.3	12.0	78.2
Transport equip.	17.6	13.0	11.6	76.3
Prof., science. Equip.	37.7	20.9	13.8	70.4
Miscellaneous mfg.	14.4	11.3	9.7	67.6
All Industries ex. Ag.	20.7	20.7	20.8	73.2
Mfg. ex. Foods	20.3	11.9	8.8	73.5

Also, negative ERPs of different classes were estimated for some industries, which arise because value added at border prices was negative. In other words, the costs of intermediate inputs for the industries would have been greater than the output price, had there been no protection on the output, and they could not have survived. Examples were "meat and meat products" and "dairy products".

The heavy protection of these food-processing industries was inevitable, if the livestock industry were to be protected at all.

4.2.1. *ERP for Export Production*

It should be noted that the ERP is for the production for domestic market only. A typical industry produces its output for both domestic sales and exports, however. Hence, for many industries an ERP estimate is not a good measure of how much their value added rises in price. If this measure is desired for all sales, a weighted average of the ERP estimated and zero, the ERP for export sales, may be taken, with weights being the domestic sales for the former and export sales for the latter.

Since protective measures cannot raise the export price for an industry, the largest value the ERP for the industry's production for exports can attain is zero. And, this can be attained, only if the tariff rebate system succeeds in making all intermediate inputs available at the border prices for the industry. Otherwise, the ERP for export producing activities would be negative, implying that the value added would decline when protective measures are imposed on the system.

4.3. Implicit Income Transfer and Protection Tax

4.3.1. *Implicit Income Transfer*

The estimation procedure making use of an I-O table makes it possible to estimate implicit income transfers that protective measures give rise to. As mentioned earlier, the NRP is the rate by which domestic price of a good exceeds the border price. By applying the NRP to an industry's total supply to the domestic users, one can estimate what may be called "gross implicit income transfer", the amount of extra payments that the users make to the industry because of the protective measures.

The estimated gross implicit income transfer to all goods-producing industries was about 18 trillion won for 1990, (Table 3) which was slightly bigger than 10 percent of GDP for the year. (The average exchange rate was 707.97 won *per* U.S. dollar for the year.) Nearly 43 percent of the total accrued to the agriculture and 56 percent to manufacture.

"Net implicit income transfer", the difference in the values added before and after protective measures, which accrues to primary factors taking part in an industry's production, can also be estimated. The total to all goods-producing industries was estimated to be about 10.7 trillion won, of which nearly 65 percent accrued to the agriculture and 34 percent to the manufacture.

Table 3. Income Transfer Estimates

	Gross Income Transfer (bil. won)	Proportion in Output Value (%)	Distribution (%)	Net Income Transfer (bil. won)	Distribution (%)
All industries	18,053.0	10.2	100.0	10,755.8	100.0
Agriculture	7,720.5	49.2	42.8	6,944.7	64.6
Forestry	41.6	5.6	0.2	32.6	0.3
Fishing	181.3	7.8	1.0	148.3	1.4
Mining	5.5	0.3	0.0	-25.8	-0.2
Manufacturing	10,104.2	6.8	56.0	3,656.0	34.0
Food	2,929.2	22.8	16.2	316.7	2.9
Beverage	368.2	11.6	2.0	82.1	0.8
Tobacco	169.7	8.4	0.9	138.1	1.3
Textiles	87.8	0.8	0.5	-101.1	-0.9
Clothing	215.7	2.6	1.2	127.4	1.2
Leather	13.9	1.1	0.1	-8.9	-0.1
Footwear	19.1	2.4	0.1	10.0	0.1
Wood	35.9	2.6	0.2	-3.8	0.0
Furniture	31.4	3.3	0.2	-6.9	-0.1
Pulp, paper	211.7	5.4	1.2	74.0	0.7
Printing	31.7	1.6	0.2	-65.2	-0.6
Industrial chemicals	343.2	5.7	1.9	154.3	1.4
Other chemicals	1,084.7	14.0	6.0	730.1	6.8
Oil refining	364.2	6.0	2.0	202.6	1.9
Petrol., coal prod.	34.9	2.1	0.2	14.5	0.1
Rubber products	80.2	1.9	0.4	24.4	0.2
Plastic products	200.7	5.2	1.1	7.6	0.1
Pottery, china	7.4	3.0	0.0	3.5	0.0
Glass	51.3	6.0	0.3	30.4	0.3
Other nonmetal Mineral prods.	166.3	4.1	0.9	56.8	0.5
Iron & steel	192.2	1.5	1.1	10.3	0.1
Nonferrous metal	62.2	2.5	0.3	24.6	0.2
Fabricated metal	209.8	3.6	1.2	85.8	0.8
Nonelectric mach.	982.4	11.0	5.4	603.8	5.6
Electrical mach.	1,287.9	6.3	7.1	808.6	7.5
Transport equip.	673.2	6.2	3.7	215.6	2.0
Prof., science. Equip.	144.5	9.7	0.8	77.4	0.7
Miscellaneous mfg.	104.8	3.0	0.6	43.5	0.4
All Industries ex. Ag.	15,210.8	6.4	57.2	3,811.1	35.4
Mfg. ex. Foods	7,175.0	5.2	39.8	3,339.4	31.1

4.3.2. *Implicit Protection Tax*

Protective measures, of course, raise not just domestic prices but the import prices as well. The extra payments the domestic users make because of the rise in import prices were estimated to be 3.5 trillion won, about one half of which was tariff revenue. These income transfers do not accrue to domestic producers, whom the protective measures intended to help, but to the government and importers. But the payments are made out of the users' pockets, and in this sense the sum of extra payments through the price rises in both domestic and foreign goods may be called "implicit protection tax". The implicit protection tax was 21.6 trillion won, compared to 34 trillion won of the central government's total expenditure for the year.

4.4. *Policy Implications*

What the findings of an exercise like this imply for an economy's trade and other policies would differ from one country to another. In any case, the numbers estimated may facilitate the discussion and help focus on the desirable and undesirable impacts of protective measures. In general, given the estimates of NRPs, ERPs, income transfers, and protection taxes, and so on, policy makers and economists can ask if the estimates are more or less the intended results in terms of absolute magnitudes and relative magnitudes among the industries. If they are not what is intended, the next question would be, whether or not intended results can be achieved by utilizing the available policy tools.

The relatively high NRPs and ERPs, and the large sums of implicit income transfers and protection taxes were estimated, especially in the case of agricultural sector, for the Korean economy 1990. The estimates make one wonder if the policy makers would have had taken the same protective measures, had they known what the consequences would be.

The estimates raise questions about the protective measures as policy tools. The benefits accruing to domestic producers, which protection is intended to provide, may be represented by net implicit income transfers. It was found that the net transfer of about 10.7 trillion won was effected through levying an implicit protection tax of nearly twice its size, 21.6 trillion won. The effective rates of protection were found to differ widely across the industries, and for some they were negative. The question is if the large protection tax is worth the resulting incentive structure, which may be far from what is intended. Another question is if the structure of ERPs can at all be manipulated to policy makers' liking by selecting tariffs and non-tariff measures.

The findings also raise a serious question about the impact of the protective measures on the export incentives. It is well known that import duties have the same effects as export duties. In the context of this empirical study, it may be said that, the greater the ERPs, the greater is the bias against exports. A producer would be indifferent between domestic sales and export sales, if the ERP for export production can be raised to the same level as that for domestic production. The required amount of subsidies for this purpose can be estimated by multiplying an industry's exports by the ERP estimate for the industry. The amount for all manufacturing industries excluding food industry, not to speak of agricultural sector, would be 2.9 trillion won. Even if the outstanding loans at the end of the same year made by deposit money banks to exporters were all forgiven, it would not have been sufficient to make domestic producers indifferent between domestic sales and export sales, for the total loans were less than 2 trillion won.

References

1. Balassa and Associates (1971), *The Structure of Protection in Developing Countries*, Baltimore: The Johns Hopkins Press.
2. Corden, W. M. (1971), *The Theory of Protection*, London: Oxford University Press.
3. Yoo, J. (1993), "The Political Economy of Protection Structure in Korea" in Ito and Krueger (eds.) *Trade and Protectionism* (NBER-East Asia Seminar on Economics Vol. 2), Chicago: The University of Chicago Press.
4. Yoo, J., Hong, and Lee (1993), *Protection and Distortion of Incentive Structure: Estimation of Nominal and Effective Rates of Protection*, Korea Development Institute (in Korean).

Appendix Table 1. Estimation Results – Corden Method

I-O Industries	ERP	NRP, Output	NRP, Average for Inputs	Inputs/ Output
1. Unmilled rice	499.6	311.0	26.2	39.8
2. Barley, wheat and other cereals	916.2	275.3	15.6	71.2
3. Vegetables	13.4	15.4	25.2	16.7
4. Fruits	140.1	98.8	11.5	32.1
5. Other edible crops	867.8	390.0	48.1	58.3
6. Non-food crops	8.4	12.0	25.0	21.7
7. Livestock breeding	144.6	43.5	22.9	83.1
8. Sericulture	76.9	64.0	23.6	24.2
9. Agricultural services	-7.0	0.0	20.5	25.4
10. Forest planting and conservation	10.0	11.1	13.6	30.2
11. Forestry products	6.2	7.3	20.7	7.1
12. Fishing	13.0	12.4	10.6	25.8
13. Aquaculture	21.9	19.8	9.8	17.7
14. Coal mining	-1.0	1.0	10.5	17.2

Appendix Table 1. Estimation Results – Corden Method–Continued

I-O Industries	ERP	NRP, Output	NRP, Average for Inputs	Inputs/ Output
15. Iron ore	-1.6	1.0	13.9	16.8
16. Nonferrous metal ores mining	-2.5	1.0	13.7	22.1
17. Crude oil and natural gas				
18. Stone, sand and gravel	-4.7	-2.3	12.7	13.9
19. Limestone, ceramic and refractory minerals	-3.0	1.7	13.9	27.6
20. Other nonmetallic minerals	0.2	3.4	13.9	23.4
21. Meat and meat products	-346.6	121.6	45.4	119.4
22. Dairy products	-214.7	333.5	48.5	208.3
23. Conned or preserved fruits and vegetables	-29.0	4.7	31.0	56.2
24. Processed seafood products	-3.8	7.8	13.7	66.6
25. Polished rice		311.0	296.1	99.2
26. Polished barley		292.3	108.4	172.9
27. Flour and cereal preparations	-17.5	54.3	95.1	63.8
28. Sugar	58.2	27.4	16.6	74.2
29. Bread, confectionery product and noodles	-26.7	2.2	30.2	50.8
30. Seasonings	-19.3	6.7	22.5	62.2
31. Animal and vegetable oils and fats, and allied products	-73.3	15.0	164.0	37.2
32. Other food preparations	-73.6	5.7	69.5	55.4
33. Prepared livestock feeds	-43.5	10.5	51.1	57.1
34. Alcoholic beverages	4.8	23.0	43.3	47.2
35. Soft drinks	19.0	25.8	32.1	52.1
36. Tobacco products	99.9	40.0	11.1	67.4
37. Cotton yarn	-12.0	2.9	13.8	57.7
38. Silk yarn	-66.3	8.0	59.4	59.1
39. Woolen yarn	-33.3	3.3	26.9	60.8
40. Hempen Yarn	-5.9	11.0	20.2	64.7
41. Chemical fiber yarn	-23.0	10.6	22.9	73.2
42. Other fiber yarn and thread	-0.5	5.7	9.5	61.9
43. Cotton fabrics	-15.5	-1.7	5.1	66.9
44. Silk fabrics	-19.4	-0.3	7.9	69.8
45. Woolen fabrics	37.3	22.6	12.3	58.9
46. Hempen fabrics	-1.3	7.3	9.9	76.5
47. Chemical fiber fabrics	-15.9	1.1	10.5	64.4
48. Other fiber fabrics	-20.2	-1.3	9.7	63.1
49. Knitted fabrics	16.4	12.0	9.7	64.9
50. Fiber bleaching and dyeing	-9.2	0.0	12.5	42.4
51. Knitted products	20.1	12.7	8.3	63.2
52. Cordage, rope and fishing nets	-21.1	0.5	13.1	63.3
53. Miscellaneous fabricated textile products	8.2	7.0	6.4	66.3
54. Wearing apparels and dress accessories	26.6	13.5	7.8	69.4
55. Leather and fur products	-11.8	4.6	10.0	75.1
56. Leather products	23.3	12.5	8.3	71.8
57. Lumber	-6.1	1.6	4.8	70.6
58. Plywood	5.3	6.4	6.9	69.1

Appendix Table 1. Estimation Results – Corden Method–Continued

I-O Industries	ERP	NRP, Output	NRP, Average for Inputs	Inputs/ Output
59. Wooden furniture	-2.3	4.2	8.6	59.3
60. Other wood products	-3.0	1.4	5.7	51.4
61. Pulp	-2.2	2.0	6.0	51.2
62. Paper	21.1	10.5	5.6	68.5
63. Paper products	-2.0	5.8	10.7	61.8
64. Printing and publishing	-7.0	1.8	12.2	45.9
65. Basic chemicals	3.0	7.6	10.4	62.4
66. Other basic organic chemicals	15.2	11.2	9.4	69.5
67. Synthetic resins	48.7	22.8	10.9	68.5
68. Synthetic rubber	15.4	13.0	11.9	69.2
69. Basic inorganic chemicals	12.2	10.0	8.1	53.0
70. Chemical fibers	10.1	10.7	11.0	67.5
71. Chemical fertilizers	6.2	8.8	10.0	68.2
72. Agricultural chemicals	-12.0	0.7	7.9	63.8
73. Pharmaceuticals	27.6	23.2	17.9	45.3
74. Cosmetics and toothpaste	372.1	94.6	19.1	78.6
75. Dyestuffs, pigments and paints	8.7	10.7	12.0	61.0
76. Soap and synthetic detergents	162.6	45.0	13.8	79.0
77. Other chemical products	27.3	16.8	11.0	64.9
78. Synthetic resins products	1.3	12.4	18.6	64.0
79. Naphtha	22.7	11.1	5.3	66.7
80 .Fuel oils	14.3	8.5	5.3	64.2
81. Other petroleum products	11.2	11.2	11.2	74.2
82. Coal products	4.0	2.2	1.7	76.7
83. Rubber products	6.0	8.6	10.7	56.0
84. Pottery china and earthenware	6.2	7.7	9.8	41.7
85. Glass and glass products	11.1	10.7	10.2	42.7
86. Clay products for construction	16.5	13.0	8.8	45.7
87. Cement	10.2	8.0	5.6	47.7
88. Cement products	-7.5	0.0	6.4	54.0
89. Other ceramic and nonmetallic mineral products	11.3	8.4	5.6	51.2
90. Iron manufacturing	-3.8	1.5	3.9	69.2
91. Steel ingots and semi-finished products	0.0	2.3	2.9	78.7
92. Hot rolled steel products	0.9	2.5	3.1	74.2
93. Cold rolled steel products	1.0	3.9	4.8	75.5
94. Steel tubes and pipes	20.2	8.4	4.5	75.1
95. Iron and steel foundry products and forgings	-4.2	1.1	5.9	52.6
96. Nonferrous metal ingots	3.9	3.6	3.5	65.3
97. Primary nonferrous metal products	8.0	5.9	5.0	70.4
98. Metal furniture and household metal articles	18.7	12.9	8.9	59.4
99. Metal products for construction	-5.1	1.3	6.3	55.7

Appendix Table 1. Estimation Results – Corden Method–Continued

I-O Industries	ERP	NRP, Output	NRP, Average for Inputs	Inputs/ Output
100. Other metal products	23.5	13.8	7.5	60.7
101. Power generating machinery and boilers	36.8	25.1	15.0	53.5
102. Metal working and processing machinery	29.6	19.9	11.7	54.5
103. Industrial machinery	11.6	11.9	12.1	57.9
104. Office and service industry machinery	92.0	39.5	15.4	68.5
105. Other general industrial machinery and equipment	15.0	12.4	10.5	57.5
106. General machinery parts	12.2	10.8	8.9	42.5
107. Household electrical appliances	181.6	61.5	19.4	74.0
108. Electrical industrial apparatus	9.2	10.9	11.9	62.6
109. Other electrical equipment, and supplies	26.7	15.7	10.2	66.6
110. Household electrical appliances	93.7	35.6	14.5	73.4
111. Electronic appliances	-6.7	10.3	18.3	68.2
112. Electronic components	3.6	9.2	12.8	61.4
113. Communication equipment	67.0	35.3	15.3	61.3
114. Shipbuilding and repairing	-20.7	1.5	14.1	63.8
115. Railroad vehicles	-19.4	0.1	17.1	53.4
116. Motor vehicles	16.7	14.8	13.8	64.1
117. Aircraft	-0.3	3.3	5.4	63.4
118. Other transportation equipment	7.2	12.5	15.4	64.6
119. Measuring and medical instruments	15.6	14.3	13.1	54.1
120. Photographic and optical instruments	43.4	30.4	19.3	53.9
121. Watches and clocks	25.4	21.7	19.6	63.8
122. Miscellaneous manufactured products	10.8	11.3	11.6	56.6

Appendix Table 2. Estimation Results – Balassa's ERP

I-O Industries	ERP	NRP, Output	NRP, Average for Input	Inputs/ Output
1. Unmilled rice	564.2	311.0	22.4	46.7
2. Barley, wheat and other cereals	1193.4	275.3	14.2	77.9
3. Vegetables	13.9	15.4	21.8	19.3
4. Fruits	161.7	98.8	9.0	41.2
5. Other edible crops	1097.3	390.0	41.8	67.0
6. Non-food crops	8.9	12.0	21.3	25.4
7. Livestock breeding	671.3	43.5	19.8	96.4
8. Sericulture	79.7	64.0	21.3	26.9
9. Agricultural services	-8.0	0.0	15.1	34.5
10. Forest planting and conservation	11.3	11.1	10.8	38.1
11. Forestry products	6.3	7.3	17.8	8.3
12. Fishing	15.1	12.4	1.6	36.2
13. Aquaculture	23.6	19.8	7.4	23.6

Appendix Table 2. Estimation Results – Balassa's ERP–Continued

I-O Industries	ERP	NRP, Output	NRP, Average for Input	Inputs/ Output
14. Coal mining	-1.1	1.0	6.3	28.6
15. Iron ore	-2.1	1.0	6.9	34.7
16. Nonferrous metal ores mining	-3.4	1.0	7.3	41.3
17. Crude oil and natural gas				
18. Stone, sand and gravel	-5.2	-2.3	7.6	23.0
19. Limestone, ceramic and refractory minerals	-4.1	1.7	8.1	47.4
20. Other nonmetallic minerals	0.3	3.4	8.5	38.1
21. Meat and meat products	-172.5	121.6	39.0	139.0
22. Dairy products	-147.6	333.5	39.2	257.5
23. Conned or preserved fruits and vegetables	-40.5	4.7	25.4	68.6
24. Processed seafood products	-5.5	7.8	11.8	77.0
25. Polished rice		311.0	278.3	105.5
26. Polished barley		292.3	103.7	180.8
27. Flour and cereal preparations	-23.4	54.3	83.3	72.8
28. Sugar	82.6	27.4	15.1	81.8
29. Bread, confectionery product and noodles	-34.9	2.2	24.6	62.3
30. Seasonings	-29.7	6.7	18.5	75.4
31. Animal and vegetable oils and fats, and allied products	-86.2	15.0	130.9	46.6
32. Other food preparations	-94.2	5.7	59.1	65.1
33. Prepared livestock feeds	-54.0	10.5	44.5	65.5
34. Alcoholic beverages	6.8	23.0	32.6	62.6
35. Soft drinks	27.0	25.8	25.2	66.3
36. Tobacco products	123.9	40.0	10.1	73.7
37. Cotton yarn	-14.8	2.9	12.1	65.8
38. Silk yarn	-84.6	8.0	51.7	67.9
39. Woolen yarn	-40.7	3.3	24.1	67.9
40. Hempen Yarn	-7.3	11.0	18.2	71.9
41. Chemical fiber yarn	-33.8	10.6	20.5	81.8
42. Other fiber yarn and thread	-0.7	5.7	8.4	70.6
43. Cotton fabrics	-20.1	-1.7	4.6	74.4
44. Silk fabrics	-24.6	-0.3	7.3	76.2
45. Woolen fabrics	43.9	22.6	11.2	65.1
46. Hempen fabrics	-1.6	7.3	9.3	81.8
47. Chemical fiber fabrics	-20.7	1.1	9.3	72.6
48. Other fiber fabrics	-24.9	-1.3	8.8	70.1
49. Knitted fabrics	20.3	12.0	8.8	71.7
50. Fiber bleaching and dyeing	-12.0	0.0	9.5	55.9
51. Knitted products	26.7	12.7	7.3	72.3
52. Cordage, rope and fishing nets	-27.1	0.5	11.6	71.5
53. Miscellaneous fabricated textile products	10.4	7.0	5.7	73.6
54. Wearing apparels and dress accessories	38.5	13.5	6.9	78.9
55. Leather and fur products	-67.7	4.6	63.7	55.0
56. Leather products	31.8	12.5	7.5	79.3
57. Lumber	-8.9	1.6	4.3	79.6

Appendix Table 2. Estimation Results – Balassa's ERP–Continued

I-O Industries	ERP	NRP, Output	NRP, Average for Input	Inputs/ Output
58. Plywood	8.1	6.4	6.0	80.0
59. Wooden furniture	-3.5	4.2	6.9	73.9
60. Other wood products	-4.6	1.4	4.3	68.4
61. Pulp	-3.1	2.0	4.8	64.5
62. Paper	36.0	10.5	4.7	81.5
63. Paper products	-2.7	5.8	9.2	71.8
64. Printing and publishing	-9.3	1.8	9.5	59.2
65. Basic chemicals	4.6	7.6	8.6	75.2
66. Other basic organic chemicals	22.0	11.2	8.3	78.8
67. Synthetic resins	83.0	22.8	9.2	81.5
68. Synthetic rubber	26.4	13.0	10.1	82.0
69. Basic inorganic chemicals	17.9	10.0	6.3	67.9
70. Chemical fibers	17.4	10.7	9.2	81.1
71. Chemical fertilizers	9.4	8.8	8.6	78.9
72. Agricultural chemicals	-19.1	0.7	6.5	77.3
73. Pharmaceuticals	43.4	23.2	12.4	65.3
74. Cosmetics and toothpaste	-642.0	94.6	13.3	112.4
75. Dyestuffs, pigments and paints	11.8	10.7	10.3	71.2
76. Soap and synthetic detergents	956.6	45.0	11.3	96.4
77. Other chemical products	38.2	16.8	9.6	74.9
78. Synthetic resins products	1.8	12.4	16.1	74.1
79. Naphtha	25.0	11.1	5.1	69.8
80. Fuel oils	15.9	8.5	5.0	67.8
81. Other petroleum products	15.6	11.2	10.2	81.5
82. Coal products	7.1	2.2	1.5	86.8
83. Rubber products	7.6	8.6	9.2	65.3
84. Pottery china and earthenware	8.3	7.7	7.2	56.5
85. Glass and glass products	14.5	10.7	7.8	56.3
86. Clay products for construction	22.0	13.0	6.8	59.3
87. Cement	15.7	8.0	4.0	66.1
88. Cement products	-10.0	0.0	5.3	65.5
89. Other ceramic and nonmetallic mineral products	17.0	8.4	4.2	67.4
90. Iron manufacturing	-5.6	1.5	3.4	79.4
91. Steel ingots and semi-finished products	0.0	2.3	2.7	85.4
92. Hot rolled steel products	1.1	2.5	2.8	80.3
93. Cold rolled steel products	1.3	3.9	4.4	82.3
94. Steel tubes and pipes	29.1	8.4	4.1	82.8
95. Iron and steel foundry products and forgings	-5.3	1.1	4.9	63.2
96. Nonferrous metal ingots	5.9	3.6	2.9	77.3
97. Primary nonferrous metal products	11.7	5.9	4.4	79.6
98. Metal furniture and household metal articles	26.9	12.9	7.4	71.7
99. Metal products for construction	-7.0	1.3	5.2	67.8
100. Other metal products	34.0	13.8	6.3	72.9
101. Power generating machinery and boilers	54.5	25.1	11.7	68.5

Appendix Table 2. Estimation Results – Balassa's ERP–Continued

I-O Industries	ERP	NRP, Output	NRP, Average for Input	Inputs/ Output
102. Metal working and processing machinery	45.5	19.9	9.1	70.4
103. Industrial machinery	17.0	11.9	9.8	71.1
104. Office and service industry machinery	154.3	39.5	13.0	81.2
105. Other general industrial machinery and equipment	19.9	12.4	8.9	67.9
106. General machinery parts	16.8	10.8	6.5	58.2
107. Household electrical appliances	450.7	61.5	16.0	89.5
108. Electrical industrial apparatus	13.2	10.9	10.1	73.9
109. Other electrical equipment, and supplies	38.7	15.7	8.8	76.9
110. Household electrical appliances	163.8	35.6	12.6	84.8
111. Electronic appliances	-9.0	10.3	16.3	76.3
112. Electronic components	5.1	9.2	10.8	72.9
113. Communication equipment	100.6	35.3	12.6	74.2
114. Shipbuilding and repairing	-45.8	1.5	10.7	83.7
115. Railroad vehicles	-26.8	0.1	13.8	66.2
116. Motor vehicles	24.9	14.8	11.6	75.9
117. Aircraft	-0.3	3.3	5.1	67.1
118. Other transportation equipment	11.7	12.5	12.7	78.2
119. Measuring and medical instruments	22.3	14.3	10.5	67.9
120. Photographic and optical instruments	64.4	30.4	15.1	68.9
121. Watches and clocks	36.6	21.7	16.7	74.8
122. Miscellaneous manufactured products	14.4	11.3	9.7	67.6

RULES OF ORIGIN IN THE WORLD TRADING SYSTEM AND PROPOSALS FOR MULTILATERAL HARMONIZATION

Antoni Estevadeordal

Inter-American Development Bank [1]

Kati Suominen

Inter-American Development Bank [2]

1. Introduction

Rules of origin (RoO) are a powerful trade policy instrument arbitrating the market access of goods and guiding firms' outsourcing, export, and investment decisions around the world. Feared to risk important distortions in global trade and investment patterns, RoO are gaining growing policy attention at the multilateral level. In preparation for the Doha Trade Round, the Committee on Regional Trade Agreements of the World Trade Organization (WTO) is for the first time raising preferential RoO to a systemic issue in the negotiation agenda. Meanwhile, the WTO Committee on Rules of Origin is making strides towards finalizing the process of harmonizing non-preferential RoO at the global level.

The recently heightened attention to RoO begs a boost to the still incipient understanding of the types and implications of the colorful mosaic of RoO regimes governing global commerce. Also required are constructive policy prescriptions for tackling RoO's potentially distortionary effects on trade and investment flows. These are the tasks of this paper. We seek to accomplish six objectives, in particular: (1) to provide an overview of the objectives, types, and effects of rules of origin (RoO) used around the world; (2) to present a comparative analysis of the preferential RoO regimes in some of the main preferential trading arrangements (PTAs) in Europe, the Americas, Asia-Pacific, Africa, and the Middle East; (3) to measure the degree of restrictiveness and selectivity of product-specific RoO employed in the various RoO regimes; (4) to

---

[1] The author may be contacted through the Inter-American Development Bank; Intergration, Trade and Hemispheric Issues Division; Integration and Regional Programs Department, *via* email at *antonie@iadb.org* .

[2] The author may be contacted through the Inter-American Development Bank; Intergration, Trade and Hemispheric Issues Division; Integration and Regional Programs Department, *via* email at *ksuominen@consultant.iadb.org* . The opinions expressed herein are those of the authors and do not necessarily reflect the official position of the institution they represent.

capture the extent of flexibility instilled in RoO regimes by various regime-wide RoO and also by *ad hoc* measures that we term "RoO innovations"; (5) to explore the effects of RoO on aggregate trade and trade in intermediates; and (6) to put forth recommendations for minimizing the frictions created by RoO on global commerce. Our primary focus is on preferential RoO; however, we do include non-preferential RoO in the analysis.

This paper makes three main arguments. First, the design of rules of origin regimes has important implications to trade flows: the more restrictive the RoO, the larger the trade diversion and other negative economic effects they create. Second, despite an ostensive *de facto* global convergence toward a few ostensibly similar preferential RoO regime models, even slight existing inter-regime differences can have important implications to firms' outsourcing and investment decisions the world over, and potentially lead to the rise of exclusive trade- and investment-diverting hubs. Third, the Doha Trade Round presents a unique and most timely opportunity for attacking the distortions generated by restrictive and divergent RoO through multilateral means. The Doha negotiators should take decisive measures to address RoO as a major distortionary trade and investment policy instrument and do so in four concrete ways: (1) to give a forceful push for finalizing the harmonization of non-preferential RoO; (2) to commit themselves to harmonizing preferential RoO with the relatively unrestrictive non-preferential RoO as the blueprint; (3) to forge in a multilateral mechanism to monitor and enforce the transparent application of RoO; and (4) incorporate RoO in the negotiations over trade-related investment measures (TRIMs).

The first section of this paper discusses the purposes of RoO, lays out the different types of product-specific and regime-wide RoO, presents the latest empirical evidence on the economic effects of RoO, and explores the broader policy implications of these findings. The second section examines the prevalence of the different types of RoO in a hundred RoO regimes employed around the world. The third section draws analytical comparisons between the different RoO regimes by their level of restrictiveness. Section four presents some of the key results of Estevadeordal and Suominen (2004a) on the trade effects of RoO. The fifth section elaborates on RoO innovations particularly from PTAs forged in recently by the European Union and Singapore, respectively. Section six makes predictions of the evolution of the global preferential RoO panorama, and makes policy recommendations on multilateral measures to counter the distortionary effects of RoO. Section seven concludes.

2. Purposes and Effects of Rules of Origin

2.1. *Purposes of RoO*

There are two types of rules of origin, non-preferential and preferential RoO. Non-preferential RoO are used to distinguish foreign from domestic products for the purpose of applying several other trade policy instruments, such as anti-dumping and countervailing duties, safeguard measures, origin marking requirements, discriminatory quantitative restrictions or tariff quotas, and/or rules on government procurement.

Preferential RoO are employed in PTAs and in the context of generalized systems of preferences (GSP) to define the conditions under which the importing economy will regard a product as originating in an exporting economy that receives preferential treatment from the importing economy. The economic justification for preferential RoO is to curb trade deflection–to avoid products from non-preference receiving countrues from being transshipped through a low-tariff PTA or GSP partner to a high-tariff one. RoO are a feature of virtually all PTAs around the world, affecting the nearly 50 percent of world trade that is conducted on a preferential basis.[3]

However, since preferential RoO can serve as an effective means to deter transshipment, they can give rise to uses beyond the efforts to avert trade deflection. Indeed, RoO are emerging as a widespread trade policy instrument with the proliferation of PTAs around the world that can work to offset the benefits of the on-going multilateral lowering of tariff and non-tariff barriers.[4] Most prominently, RoO can be employed to favor intra-PTA industry linkages over those between the PTA and the rest of the world (ROW), and, as such, to

---

[3] RoO are an inherent feature of free trade agreements (FTAs) where the member states' external tariffs diverge and/or where the members wish to retain their individual tariff policies *vis-à-vis* the rest of the world (ROW). The Asia-Pacific Cooperation (APEC) forum is a prominent exception, with its members employing their respective domestic RoO (OECD 2002). APEC is based on a principle of open regionalism–extending tariff preferences on an MFN basis–which renders the need for preferential RoO obsolete. RoO would be unnecessary in a customs union (CU) with a common external tariff (CET) that covered the whole tariff universe. However, in practice, RoO are widely used in CUs, either as a transitory tool when moving toward the CET, or as a more permanent means of covering product categories where reaching agreement on a CET is difficult, for instance due to large tariff differentials between the member countries.

[4] Analysts engaged in the nascent yet rigorous debate on RoO are increasingly picking up on the political economy of RoO; see Krueger (1993); Krishna and Krueger (1995); Jensen-Moran (1996); Garay and Estevadeordal (1996); Stephenson (1996); Scollay (1996); Ju and Krishna (1998); Appiah (1999); Falvey and Reed (2000); Estevadeordal (2000); Duttagupta (2000); Duttagupta and Panagariya (2001); Lloyd (1996, 2001a, 2001b); Rodriguez (2001); Brenton and Manchin (2002); Flatters (2002); Garay and Cornejo (2002); Hirsch (2002); Krishna (2002); Estevadeordal and Suominen (2003, 2004ab); and contributions in Cadot *et al.* (2004).

indirectly protect PTA-based input producers *vis-à-vis* their extra-PTA rivals (Krueger, 1993; Krishna and Krueger, 1995). Stringent RoO can compel intra-PTA firms with low-cost extra-PTA supply sources to turn to higher-cost inputs produced within the PTA in order to obtain preferential treatment for their final products, particularly in sectors where preferential margins are wide. As such, RoO liken a tariff on the intermediate product levied by the importing economy (Falvey and Reed 2000; Lloyd 2001), and can even be used by one PTA member to secure its PTA partners' input markets for the exports of its own intermediate products (Krueger 1993; Krishna and Krueger 1995).

If RoO introduce a price wedge in the intermediate market, they could be expected to engender opposition by downstream producers intent on retaining their extra-PTA low-cost supply sources while still qualifying for the PTA-conferred preferential treatment. However, there are two reasons why downstream producers may accept or even favor stringent RoO. First, RoO may simply be the price that downstream producers have to pay for the PTA: despite risking costly trade diversion, restrictive RoO can help placate protectionist sectors so as to render PTA formation politically feasible (Duttagupta 2000). Second, downstream producers that are not globally the most competitive ones yet intent on exporting to the PTA partner's market can draw contingent benefits from stringent RoO, and, as such, be willing to shoulder the heightened production costs. For instance, should the linkages between different stages of production in the industry be tight, extra-PTA final goods producers would likely be hard-pressed to locate approriate components witin the PTA and remain competitive *vis-à-vis* the intra-PTA producers in the PTA market. Even if extra-PTA firms were to locate in the PTA market *via* tariff-jumping-like "RoO-jumping", discrimination would continue until the regional sourcing met the RoO (Graham and Wilkie 1998).

RoO can thus be used to meet the political economy goal of extending protection to both intra-PTA input and final goods producers. In an en econometric study of the determinants of the restrictiveness of the RoO in the North American Free Trade Agreement (NAFTA), Estevadeordal (2000) shows that the same political economy factors that drive tariff protection also drive RoO.[5] Furthermore, given that RoO hold the potential of increasing local

---

[5] Suominen (2004), arguing that restrictive RoO tend to be accompanied by long phase-outs in PTAs due to RoO's being an imperfect substitute to the MFN tariff, obtains similar results in a study of the EU-Mexico FTA. Flatters (2002) reaches similar conclusions in a non-econometric analysis of the Southern African Development Community RoO, as do Estevadeordal and Suominen (2003) in a study of European Union's extra-regional FTAs with South Africa, Mexico, and Chile.

sourcing and affecting the locational decisions of investors, governments can use RoO to encourage investment in certain strategic or high-value sectors–for instance in order to create lucrative jobs (Jensen-Moran 1996; Hirsch 2002).

2.2. *Types of RoO*

Besides the theoretical notions of how RoO can serve political economy ends, there are two immediate indications that RoO are a matter beyond resolving the trade deflection problem: (1) negotiations over preferential RoO in PTAs are generally prolonged and contentious; and (2) rather than employing simple, value added or change in tariff heading-RoO across the tariff universe, integrating governments are adopting highly complex RoO and often a combination of different RoO criteria to govern any given products. This part surveys the various existing types of product-specific and general, regime-wide RoO.

2.2.1. *Product-Specific RoO: Five Main Components*

The Kyoto Convention recognizes two basic criteria to determine origin: wholly obtained or produced, and substantial transformation.[6] The wholly obtained or produced-category applies only to one PTA member, and asks whether the commodities and related products have been entirely grown, harvested, or extracted from the soil in the territory of that member, or manufactured there from any of these products. The rule of origin is met through not using any second-economy components or materials. Most economies apply this strict and precise definition.

The substantial transformation-criterion is more complex, involving four main components that can be used as stand-alone or in combinations with each other. The precision with which these components define RoO in PTAs today contrasts sharply with the vagueness of the substantial transformation-criterion as used by the United States since 1908 through the inception of the Canada-US Free Trade Agreement (CUSFTA) and, subsequently, NAFTA (Reyna 1995: 7).[7]

[6] The Revised Kyoto Convention is an international instrument adopted by the World Customs Organization (WCO) to standardize and harmonize customs policies and procedures around the world. The WCO adopted the original Convention in 1974. The revised version was adopted in June 1999.

[7] The old criterion basically required the emergence of a "new and different article" from the manufacturing process applied to the original article. It was, however, much-criticized for allowing–and indeed requiring–subjective and case-by-case determinations of origin (Reyna 1995: 7).

The first component of the substantial transformation criterion is a change in tariff classification (CTC) between the manufactured good and the inputs from extra-PTA parties used in the productive process. The CTC may require the product to alter its chapter (2 digits under the Harmonized System), heading (4 digits), sub-heading (6 digits) or item (8-10 digits) in the exporting economy.

The second criterion is an exception attached to a particular CTC (ECTC). ECTC generally prohibits the use of non-originating materials from a certain sub-heading, heading, or chapter.

The third criterion is value content (VC), which requires the product to acquire a certain minimum local value in the exporting economy (or, alternatively, to remain below a certain ceiling percentage of value originating in the non-member economies). The value content can be expressed in three main ways: as the minimum percentage of value that must have been added in the exporting economy (domestic or regional value content, RVC); as the difference between the value of the final good and the costs of the imported inputs (import content, MC); or as the value of parts (VP), whereby originating status is granted for products meeting a minimum percentage of originating parts out of the total.

The fourth RoO component is technical requirement (TECH), which requires the product to undergo certain manufacturing operations in the originating economy. TECH requires or prohibits the use certain input(s) and/or the realization of certain process(es) in the production of the good.[8] It is a particularly prominent feature in RoO governing textile products.

Table 1 summarizes the frequency of the various product-specific criteria in 93 PTAs–6 customs unions and 87 FTAs–around the world. The change of heading-requirement is the staple of PTAs. It is used either as stand-alone or in tandem with other RoO criteria. Also frequently used are the import content (usually ranging from 30 to 60 percent), value of parts, and technical requirements. Adding analytical complexity albeit administrative flexibility is that many RoO regimes provide two alternative RoO for a given product, such as a change of chapter or, alternatively, a change of heading + RVC.

2.2.2. *Regime-Wide RoO*

Besides product-specific RoO, RoO regimes vary by the types of general RoO they employ–including in the degree of *de minimis*, the roll-up principle, and the type of cumulation.

---

[8] TECH can be highly discretional given that lack of classification tools to objectively guarantee sufficient transformation in the production of the good.

Table 1. Frequency of various product-specific criteria

PTAs	Criterion				
		VALUE CONTENT			
	CTH	MC	RVC	VP	TECH
Customs unions (6)	6	2 (60-40%)	2 (35-60%)	-	-
FTAs and Other PTAs (87)	83	68 (60-30%)	7 (25-65%)	67	74

Source: World Trade Organization (2002).

Note: MC criterion refers to the maximum percentage of non-originating inputs that can be incorporated in a product; the RVC criterion, which can be considered the inverse of MC, refers to the minimum percentage of regional inputs required for a product.

First, most PTAs contain a *de minimis* rule, which allows for a specified maximum percentage of non-originating materials to be used without affecting origin. The *de minimis* rule inserts leniency in the CTC or TECH criteria by making it easier for products with non-originating inputs to qualify.

Second, the roll-up or absorption principle allows materials that have acquired origin by meeting specific processing requirements to be considered originating when used as input in a subsequent transformation. That is, when roll-up is allowed, non-originating materials are not taken into account in the calculation of the value-added of the subsequent transformation.

Third, cumulation allows producers of one PTA member to use non-originating materials from another PTA member (or other members) without losing the preferential status of the final product. There are three types of cumulation. Bilateral cumulation operates between the two PTA partners and permits them to use products that originate in the other PTA partner as if they were their own when seeking to qualify for preferential treatment. Diagonal cumulation means that economies tied by the same set of preferential origin rules can use products that originate in any part of the area as if they originated in the exporting economy. Full cumulation extends diagonal cumulation. It provides that economies tied by the same set of preferential origin rules among each other can use goods produced in any part of the area, even if these were not originating products. All the processing done in the zone is then taken into account as if it had taken place in the final economy of manufacture.[9] As such, diagonal and full

[9] In bilateral cumulation, the use of the partner country components is favored; in diagonal cumulation, all the beneficiary trading partners of the cumulation area are favored. While diagonal cumulation and, even more so, bilateral cumulation, promote the use of materials originating within the FTA, full cumulation is more liberal than diagonal cumulation by allowing a greater use of third-country materials. It is, however, rarely used.

cumulation can notably expand the geographical and product coverage of a RoO regime. Table 2 illustrates the frequency of general RoO provisions around the world.

Table 2. Frequency of general RoO provisions

PTAs	DE MINIMIS	TYPE OF CUMULATION			ROLL-UP
		Bilateral	Diagonal	Full	
Customs unions (6)	3	6	0	0	2
FTAs and other PTAs (87)	85	87	58	8	81

Source: World Trade Organization (2002).

Whereas *de minimis*, roll-up, and cumulation allow for leniency in the application of RoO, there are three provisions that may have the opposite effect–increase the stringency of RoO.[10]

First, most PTAs contain a separate list indicating the operations that are in all circumstances considered insufficient to confer origin, such as preservation during transport and storage, as well as simple operations of cleaning, sorting, painting, packaging, assembling, and marking and labeling.

Second, many PTAs prohibit duty drawback–preclude the refunding of tariffs on non-originating inputs that are subsequently included in a final product exported to a PTA partner market. Many developing economies in particular employ drawback in order to attract investment and to encourage exports. However, drawback in the context of a PTA is viewed as providing a cost advantage to the PTA-based producers who gear their final goods to export over producers selling their final good in the domestic market.[11] The end of duty drawback entails an increase in the cost of non-originating components for PTA-based final goods producers. As such, the end of drawback in the presence of cumulation may encourage intra-PTA producers to shift to suppliers in the cumulation area (WTO 2002).

Third, PTAs may impose high administrative costs stemming from the method of certifying the origin of goods. The main models of certification employed in PTAs are self-certification by exporters, certification by an industry umbrella group, and certification by the exporting economy government–or various combinations of the three. The more numerous the bureaucratic hurdles

---

[10] To be sure, some economies argue that a system of cumulation merely introduces another layer of discrimination, since non-participating economies are not eligible for its benefits.

[11] Cadot, de Melo and Olarreaga (2001) show that duty drawback may have a protectionist bias for reducing the interest of producers to lobby against protection of intermediate products.

and the higher the costs for an exporter to obtain an origin certificate, the lower the incentives to seek PTA-conferred preferential treatment.

2.3. *Effects of RoO*

What, then, can the complex instrument of RoO do? That RoO can be employed for distributive, political economy purposes does not automatically mean they divert resources from the most efficient uses. However, analysts of the potential trade effects of RoO have produced resounding evidence that RoO impose important administrative costs and increase production costs to parties applying them. Both types of costs introduce protectionist biases that undercut the unfettered flow of commerce. We consider each in turn.

2.3.1. *Administrative Costs of RoO*

The administrative costs of RoO stem from the procedures required for ascertaining compliance with the requirements of the RoO regime. These are essentially book-keeping costs–first and foremost the costs for the exporter of certifying the origin of a good prior to its export to the territory of another PTA member–and the costs to the partner economy customs of verifying the origin of goods. The different certification mechanisms impose divergent costs on firms; moreover, while in some economies certification is free of charge, in many the costs are hardly trivial. In Brazil, for instance, the cost of obtaining certification for a single shipment from a certifying agency is estimated to range between US$6 and US$20; in Chile, the cost is US$7. Koskinen (1983) estimates the administrative costs for Finnish exporters under the European Community-European Free Trade Association (EFTA) FTA at 1.4 percent to 5.7 percent of the value of export transactions.[12] Holmes and Shephard (1983) find the average export transaction from EFTA to the EC to require 35 documents and 360 copies.[13] Administrative costs are important even in regimes operating on self-certification: in a recent study, Cadot *et al.* (2002) disentangle NAFTA's non-RoO and RoO-related administrative costs, finding the latter to approximate two percent of the value of Mexican exports to the US market. The verification costs of RoO to member governments have yet to receive empirical scrutiny; however,

---

[12] In another pioneering study, Herin (1986) puts the cost of obtaining the appropriate documentation to meet the RoO at three to five percent of the FOB value of the good in the context of EFTA.

[13] Quoted in Herin (1986).

such costs could be expected to rise particularly for economies party to several complex and divergent RoO regimes.

2.3.2. *Production Costs of RoO*

The production costs of RoO arise from the various technical criteria imposed by the RoO regime. They start playing a role in trade flows when they encourage the use of intra-PTA inputs at the expense of extra-PTA ones even if the latter were cheaper. Should this occur, RoO could be expected (1) to divert trade in intermediates to the PTA area; and (2) to moderate the potential for a PTA to boost aggregate trade between the members due to raising the costs for final goods producers. Pioneering empirical evidence supports these hypotheses. Estevadeordal and Suominen (2004a) carry out the most extensive effort as yet to capture the trade effects of RoO by employing a 155-economy gravity model. In a cross-section study for 2001, they find that regimes with restrictive RoO and with high degrees of sectoral selectivity discourage aggregate trade flows and encourage trade in intermediates, while regime-wide RoO that allow for flexibility in the application of the product-specific RoO, such as cumulation, drawback, and self-certification facilitate aggregate trade flows–and, as such, counteract restrictive RoO's negative effects on trade. The study also finds that exporters learn to apply RoO over time. The results will be discussed in greater detail in section V of this paper.

Other, single-regime studies have reached similar results. Appiah (1999), employing a three-country, multisector Computable General Equilibrium (CGE) model, argues that NAFTA RoO distort trade flows and undercut welfare. Cadot *et al.* (2002) and Cadot *et al.* (2004) find that Mexican exports to the United States have been undermined by restrictive NAFTA RoO. James (2004) posits that NAFTA preferences and restrictive RoO have undercut Asian textile and apparel exports to the United States. Flatters and Kirk (2004) note that restrictive SADC RoO work against efficiency gains that the members would reach through outsourcing outside the PTA area. Augier *et al.* (2004) examine cumulation, arguing that without cumulation, trade among PTA partners would be up to 52 percent lower than expected; the impact is particularly notable in intermediate goods.

2.4. *Policy Implications of RoO's Effects*

The findings on the effects of RoO have four immediate policy implications. First, RoO can reduce the utilization rates of the PTA- or GSP-provided preferences. Estevadeordal and Miller (2002) document "missed preferences"–*i.e.*, utilization rates below 100 percent–between the United States and Canada, which they attribute to the tightening of the pre-FTA RoO under NAFTA launched in 1994 (figure 1). Cadot *et al.* (2002) link the mere 64 percent utilization rate of NAFTA preferences to stringent RoO. Indeed, already in the context of the NAFTA predecessor, the US-Canada FTA, Canadian producers were reported to have opted to pay the tariff rather than going through the administrative hurdles to meet the RoO (Krueger 1995). In the EU context, Brenton and Manchin (2002), albeit not operationalizing RoO, attribute the low utilization rates of the EU's trading partners in the textile sector to excessive stringency of EU RoO.

Figure 1. From USA-Canada FTA to NAFTA: Rules of Origin and Utilization Rates

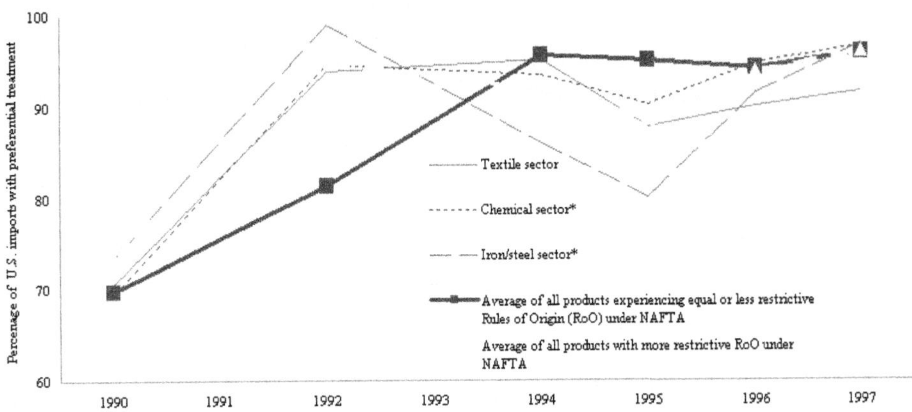

Note: 1991 and 1993 data points linearly interpolated.
Source: Estevadeordal and Miller (2002)

Second, from a legal standpoint, preferential RoO are feared to breach Article XXIV of the General Agreements on Tariffs and Trade (GATT), which in paragraph 8(b) defines a free trade area as "a group of two or more customs territories in which the duties and other restrictive regulations of commerce...are eliminated on substantially all the trade between the constituent territories in products originating in such territories."[14] Indeed, the WTO has recently recognized RoO to be part of "other regulations of commerce (ORCs); ambiguities remain as to the meaning of "substantially all the trade".[15] Since

[14] Italics added.

[15] See, for instance, WTO (2002b).

RoO have implications to extra-PTA parties' access to the PTA market, they also risk violating paragraph 5 of Article XXIV that prohibits PTAs that raise barriers toward the rest of the world from the pre-PTA levels. The WTO Negotiation Group on Rules is in effect advocating a case-by-case analysis of the potentially restrictive effects of preferential RoO on extra-PTA parties (WTO 2002b).

Third, besides the short-run trade effects, RoO may in the longer run cause investment diversion. This occurs when extra-PTA final goods producers "jump" the RoO by locating plants within a PTA region in order to satisfy the RoO even if the PTA region was not the most optimal location for investment. RoO can also produce investment diversion within the PTA area. For one, should final goods producers be hard-pressed to locate approriate components in the PTA area and remain competitive, they may simply choose to locate to the territory of the largest PTA market and the one with the lowest external tariffs–such as the United States in the context of NAFTA–and continue importing third-economy inputs required for the final product.[16] Two, producers located in the PTA member with the lowest production costs can be placed in a disadvantage when the RoO are based on RVC, which is easier to meet in PTA members with higher production costs. As such, RoO may encourage investment to a large hub economy that may well be an inefficient producer, and perpetuate the hub given the agglomeration effects of foreign direct investment. Rodriguez (2001) shows formally that RoO can lead to distortions in production structures within the PTA area. To be sure, RoO-induced investment can also help counteract RoO's effects: should extra-PTA input producers locate to the PTA area to take advantage of higher rents, they could crowd the market, augment supply, and thus drive the price of inputs down.

Fourth, the relevance of RoO *per se*–and their importance as a constraint on commerce and guide for investment thereby–decreases with the lowering of MFN tariff barriers by PTA members. With the production and administrative costs imposed by RoO rising to unsustainably high levels, final goods producers would rather import their inputs from the ROW and sell their output at their home market than produce to the PTA partner's market at high input costs. However, the higher a PTA member's MFN tariff, the greater the preferential margin offered to its PTA (or GSP) partners, and thus the greater the willingness of firms in the partner economies to comply with the RoO, including to shift to intra-PTA inputs and furnish the certifying documentation–and for firms in non-

[16] For example, a Mexican and a US firm selling at the US market and purchasing their inputs from outside the NAFTA region would be unequally treated under NAFTA, as the Mexican firm would be disadvantaged *vis-à-vis* the US firm by the former's failure to meet the RoO required to export to the US market (Graham and Wilkie 1998: 110).

PTA economies to engage in RoO-jumping foreign direct investment. This has rendered some analysts to suggest that the expanding spaghetti-bowl of overlapping PTAs and RoO regimes should be accompanied by the principle of open regionalism and/or replaced by customs unions or a hybrid arrangment between and CU and FTA altogether, lest the benefits of preferential trade liberalization be lost.[17]

3. Rules of Origin around the World

This section turns to examining the great variety of combinations of product-specific and regime-wide RoO used in selected PTAs in Europe, the Americas, Asia-Pacific, Africa, and the Middle East, as well as in PTAs between these regions. We subsequently discuss the structure of non-preferential RoO. The latter part of this section presents an analytical, comparative assessment of (1) the relative restrictiveness of the product-specific RoO governing different economic sectors in the different RoO regimes, and (2) the degree of flexibility instilled in the various RoO regimes by the regime-wide RoO.

3.1. *Comparing the Structure of RoO Regimes in Five Regions*

3.1.1. *Europe: Expansion of the PANEURO System*

The RoO regimes employed today across the EU's FTAs are highly uniform *vis-à-vis* each other. This owes largely to the European Commission's recent drive to harmonize the EU's existing and future preferential RoO regimes in order to facilitate the operations of EU exporters dealing on multiple trade fronts, and to pave the way for particularly the EU's East European FTA partners to draw greater benefits from EU-provided preferential treatment *via* diagonal cumulation–that was precluded by the lack of compatibility among the EU's RoO regimes. The harmonization efforts pertained to product-specific and regime-wide RoO alike. They extended to the RoO protocols with the EFTA members that dated from 1972 and 1973, as well as across the EU's FTAs forged in the early 1990s in the context of the Europe Agreements with Bulgaria, Czech Republic, Estonia, Hungary, Latvia, Lithuania, Poland, Slovakia, and Romania.[18] The work culminated in 1997 in the launch of the Pan-European (PANEURO) system, which established identical RoO protocols and product-specific RoO across the EU's existing FTAs, providing for diagonal cumulation among the

---

[17] See Bergsten (1997); Wonnacott (1996).

[18] See Driessen and Graafsma (1999) for review.

participating economies thereby. The Commission's regulation 46 of January 1999 reiterates the harmonized protocols, outlining the so-call single list RoO. Overall, the PANEURO RoO are highly complex, combining CTC mainly at the heading level with exceptions, VC, and TECH, and varying markedly across economic sectors.

Since 1997, the PANEURO model has become incorporated in the EU's newer FTAs, including the Euro-Mediterranean Association Agreements, the Stabilization and Association Agreements with Croatia and the Former Yugoslav Republic of Macedonia, the EU-Slovenia FTA, as well as the extra-regional FTAs with South Africa, Mexico, and Chile. Also the RoO of the EU's generalized system of preferences (GSP) and the 2000 Cotonou Agreement with the African Caribbean, and Pacific (ACP) developing economies approximate the single list, PANEURO model. EFTA's recently concluded FTAs with Mexico and Singapore also follow the PANEURO model; however, the EFTA-Singapore RoO provide in many sectors–such as plastics, rubber, textiles, iron and steel products, and some machinery products–an alternative, 50 percent import content RoO that either does not exist in the PANEURO model, or is in PANEURO set at lower and thus more demanding levels.

Overall, however, the harmonized RoO do not represent a dramatic break with those of the pre-1997 era. For example, the RoO in nearly three-quarters of the products (in terms of tariff sub-headings) in PANEURO and the original EU-Poland RoO protocol published in 1993 are identical. Both the new and the old versions combine CTC with VC and/or TECH. Indeed, the EU RoO feature remarkable continuity: the RoO of the European Community-Cyprus FTA formed in 1973 are strikingly similar to those used today. One notable difference between the older and the newer protocols is that the latter allow for an optional way of meeting the RoO for about 25 percent of the products, whereas the former specify mostly only one way of meeting the RoO (Estevadeordal and Suominen 2003a). The second option, alternative RoO, much like the first option RoO, combine different RoO criteria; however, the most frequently used alternative RoO is a stand-alone import content criterion.

3.1.2. *Americas: Four RoO Families*

There is much more variation across RoO regimes in the Americas. Nevertheless, distinct RoO families can be identified (Garay and Cornejo 2002). One extreme is populated by the traditional trade agreements such as the Latin American Integration Agreement (LAIA), which uses a general rule applicable across the board for all tariff items (a change in tariff classification at the heading level or, alternatively, a regional value added of at least 50 percent of the FOB export value). The LAIA model is the point of reference to RoO used in the Andean Community (CAN) and Caribbean Community (CARICOM). At the other extreme lie the so-called new generation PTAs such as NAFTA, which, in turn, is used as a reference point for the US-Chile, Mexico-Costa Rica, Mexico-Chile, Mexico-Bolivia, Mexico-Nicaragua, Mexico-Northern Triangle (El Salvador, Guatemala, and Honduras), Chile-Canada, and Mexico-Colombia-Venezuela (or G-3) FTAs; the NAFTA model is also widely viewed as the likeliest blueprint for the RoO of the Free Trade Area of the Americas (FTAA).[19] The RoO regimes in these agreements may require a change of chapter, heading, sub-heading or item, depending on the product in question. In addition, many products combine the change of tariff classification with an exception, regional value content, or technical requirement.

Mercosur RoO, as well as RoO in the Mercosur-Bolivia and Mercosur-Chile FTAs fall between the LAIA-NAFTA extremes. They are mainly based on change of heading and different combinations of regional value content and technical requirements. The Central American Common Market's (CACM) RoO regime can be seen as located between those of the Mercosur and NAFTA: it uses chiefly change in tariff classification only, but in a more precise and diverse ways than Mercosur due to requiring the change to take place at either the chapter, heading, or subheading level, depending on the product in question. In some products, CACM introduces exceptions; a handful of products are also governed by regional value content or technical requirements.

Notably, unlike the EU's extra-European FTAs that follow the PANEURO system, US bilateral FTAs with extra-Hemispheric partners–Jordan and Israel–diverge markedly from the NAFTA model, operating on VC alone. However, the RoO of the US-Singapore FTA are again more complex, likening the NAFTA RoO. Similarly, the RoO of the recently forged Chile-South Korea FTA also feature a high degree of sectoral selectivity *à la* NAFTA, and, indeed, the US-Chile FTA. Nonetheless, the RoO of the Chile-Korea regime are overall less complex than either NAFTA or US-Chile RoO, and also more reliant on the change in heading criterion than NAFTA that has a strong change in chapter-component and US-Chile FTA, which features an important change in subheading-component.

---

[19] NAFTA RoO enshrined in Chapter 4 constitute a maze of highly disaggregated trade regulations described in a 150-page long Annex.

3.1.3. *Africa, Asia, Middle East: Toward Selectivity From Across-The-Board RoO?*

The relative complexity of RoO in Europe and the Americas stands in contrast to the generality of RoO in many Asian, African, and Middle Eastern PTAs. Some of the main integration schemes in these regions–the ASEAN Free Trade Area (AFTA), Australia-New Zealand Closer Economic Relations Trade Agreement (ANZCERTA), Singapore-Australia Free Trade Agreement (SAFTA), and South Pacific Regional Trade and Economic Cooperation (SPARTECA) in Asia-Pacific; the Economic Community of West African States (ECOWAS), Common Market for Eastern and Southern Africa (COMESA), and Namibia-Zimbabwe FTA in Africa; and the Gulf Cooperation Council (GCC) in the Middle East–are based on an across-the-board VC rule that, when defined as RVC, ranges from 25 percent (in Namibia-Zimbabwe FTA) to 50 percent (ANZCERTA). Some of the agreements allow, or, indeed, require, the RoO to be based on import content. Most of these regimes also specify and alternative RoO based on the CTC criterion, most often change in heading or, in the case of ECOWAS that also has a relatively low RVC requirement at 30 percent, change in subheading.

However, the more recent RoO regimes in both Africa and Asia-Pacific carry RoO of high degrees of sectoral selectivity. The Southern African Development Community (SADC) RoO approximate the PANEURO model both in types of sectoral RoO and in sectoral selectivity. Moreover, there have been some initiatives to renegotiate COMESA RoO; such attempts may well eventually lead to greater selectivity. On the Asian front, the RoO of the Japan-Singapore Economic Partnership Agreement (JSEPA) are also complex, as evinced by the more than 200-page RoO protocol. However, much like in the Chile-Korea FTA, nearly half of JSEPA RoO are based on a simple change in heading-criterion, which makes the regime much less complex when contrasted with the PANEURO and NAFTA models. Furthermore, for many products JSEPA introduces an alternative, usually PANEURO-type, free-standing VC rule, which instills generality and flexibility to the agreement.

The inter-continental RoO regimes of the US-Singapore and Chile-Korea FTAs have delivered additional complexity to the Asia-Pacific RoO theater. RoO in these agreements tend to follow the NAFTA model yet be notably less complex overall, featuring a strong change of heading component. The future Mexico-Singapore, Canada-Singapore, Mexico-Korea, Mexico-Japan, and US-Australia FTAs, among others, will likely compound this trend. Meanwhile, further European overtures to the Asian front will likely bring the PANEURO model to accompany the NAFTA model in the region. The EFTA-Singapore

FTA attests to that; however, importantly and much like in JSEPA, the standard PANEURO package in the FTA is accompanied by the flexible, alternative import content RoO. Further intra-regional FTAs in Asia-Pacific, such as between Japan and Korea, between Korea and Singapore, and between ASEAN on the one hand, and China, Japan, and/or Korea, on the other, will allow to gauge whether a genuinely Asian RoO model *à la* JSEPA of greater generality than the EU or NAFTA models yet higher complexity than featured in the older, across-the-board RoO regimes might be emerging.[20] The future FTA between India and Singapore could bring further novel features to the Asian RoO panorama.

3.2. *Non-Preferential RoO*

Non-preferential RoO are used for purposes distinct from those of preferential rules. Even if an economy did not use preferential RoO, it would still apply some type of non-preferential RoO; these RoO apply to the roughly 55 percent of world trade that is conducted on a non-preferential basis (WTO 2003). Unlike preferential RoO that have thus far escaped multilateral regulation, non-preferential RoO have been under a process of harmonization since 1995 as mandated by the Uruguay Round's Agreement on Rules of Origin (ARO). The harmonization work, propelled precisely by growing concerns of the divergent national RoO's effects on unfettered trade flows, has been carried out under the auspices of the Committee on Rules of Origin (CRO) of the World Trade Organization (WTO) and the Technical Committee on Rules of Origin (TCRO) of the Brussels-based World Customs Cooperation Council, which has been responsible for the technical part of the work, including discussions on the RoO options for each product.

The harmonization drive was initially scheduled to be completed by July 1998. However, the deadline has been extended several times since then. The Technical Committee's work was concluded in 1999, with about 500 pending issues that could not be solved at the technical level being sent to the CRO in Geneva. As of June 2003, the process at the WTO had yet to reach a solution to some 93 issues; these affect an estimated fifth of the actual tariff subheadings of the entire tariff universe. In their current structure, the non-preferential RoO approximate the PANEURO and NAFTA models in sectoral specificity, yet are

---

[20] There have been impulses to establish separate, bilateral FTAs between ASEAN and Japan, China, and Korea rather than negotiating a single FTA encompassing all the players. Japan has reportedly also studied possible economic partnership agreements with Thailand and the Philippines, respectively.

less demanding than either of the two main RoO regimes. However, since several issues are still contested at the WTO, their final degree of complexity and restrictiveness remains to be gauged. What is clear is that the definition of the non-preferential RoO is driven by the same political economy considerations as the definition of preferential RoO; indeed, the harmonization work can be considered in part endogenous to the RoO regimes that already exist in the manifold PTAs around the world. We address the harmonization work in greater detail in section V.

3.3. *Depicting Product-Specific RoO Around the World*

Figure 2 centers on the first RoO component, the CTC criterion, in three of EU's RoO regimes (PANEURO–where the RoO are basically fully identical to those of the EU-South Africa FTA–and the RoO in the EU-Mexico and EU-Chile FTAs); the EFTA-Mexico RoO that approximate the EU-Mexico RoO; six RoO regimes based on the NAFTA model gaining prominence in the Western Hemisphere (NAFTA, US-Chile, Group of Three, and Mexico-Costa Rica, Mexico-Bolivia, and Canada-Chile FTAs); the RoO in the CACM-Chile FTA, the RoO regimes in the FTAs between Mercosur on the one hand, and Chile and Bolivia, on the other; the LAIA RoO; and the RoO in force in four PTAs in Africa (ECOWAS, COMESA, Namibia-Zimbabwe FTA, and SADC), five in Asia-Pacific (AFTA, Bangkok Agreement, ANZCERTA, JSEPA, and Chile-Korea FTA); the Gulf Cooperation Council in the Middle East; and US extra-hemispheric FTAs with Jordan and Israel. The two final sets of bars depict two potential outcomes of the harmonization process of the non-preferential RoO (as set to their "lowest" and "highest" levels of stringency, which will be discussed in the next section).[21]

The change of heading-criterion predominates EU RoO, whereas the RoO built upon the NAFTA RoO regime are based on change of heading and change of chapter-criteria at relatively even quantities. The US-Chile FTA stands somewhat apart for requiring only change in sub-heading for a substantial number of tariff lines. The Chile-CACM FTA diverges from the NAFTA model due to its marked change in heading-component, as do the Japan-Singapore and Chile-Korea FTAs. The other Asian PTAs considered here stand out for their generality–for using an across-the-board value content requirement exclusively.

---

[21] The figure is based on the first RoO only when two or more possible RoO are provided for a tariff heading or subheading. The recently published Chile-Korea and Japan-Singapore FTAs await future coding efforts.

Figure 2. Distribution of CTC criteria by agreement

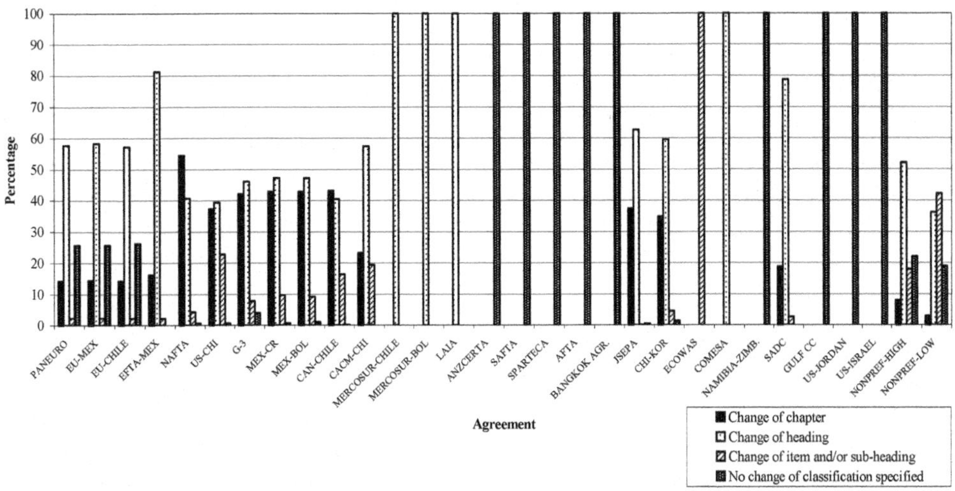

Source: Authors' calculations based on RoO protocols.

Except for the SADC, African RoO regimes are also marked by general, across-the-board CTC RoO, as are LAIA and Mercosur's FTAs with Chile and Bolivia that employ the change of heading-criteria across the RoO universe. In contrast to the PANEURO and NAFTA models, non-preferential RoO feature also a strong change of subheading-component. Another notable difference between the various FTAs is that some, such as ANZCERTA, employ the VC criterion across sectors, completely foregoing the use of the CTC-criterion. The EU does this in about a quarter of its RoO; the bulk (more than 80 percent) of these RoO are based on the wholly-obtained criterion used particularly in agricultural products, or on the import content-rule that imposes a ceiling of 40-50 percent to non-originating components of the ex-works price of the final product. The stand-alone import content RoO are used particularly frequently for optics, transportation equipment, and machinery and electrical equipment.

Table 3 centers on the tariff sub-headings governed by VC (including combinations of VC with CTC, and VC when employed as an alternative to a CTC criterion) in various RoO regimes, and, in particular, on the height of the VC criterion. The most usual level of VC is 40-50 percent, whether defined as MC or RVC; however, the permitted value of non-originating inputs of the price of the final product is as low as 15-30 percent in some products in the PANEURO and SADC regimes. The table also displays the various bases for calculation of the VC; differences in the method of calculation can have crucial

Table 3. VC criteria by agreement

PTA	Value Content Criterion (percent)		Basis for Calculation
	MC	RVC	
PANEURO (50)	50-30		Ex-works price[1]
PE (15)[2]	50-30		Ex-works price
EU-South Africa	50-30		Ex-works price
EU-Mexico	50-30		Ex-works price
EU-Chile	50-30		Ex-works price
EFTA-Mexico	50-30		Ex-works price
NAFTA		50-60	50 net cost; 60 transaction value[3]
US-Chile		35-45	35 build-up; 45 build-down[4]
Canada-Chile		50-60	50 net cost; 60 transaction value
G-3		50-55[5]	Transaction value
Mexico-Costa Rica		41.66-50	41.66 net cost; 50 transaction value
Mexico-Bolivia		41.66-50	41.66 net cost; 50 transaction value
Mexico-Chile		40-50	40 net cost; 50 transaction value
CACM		N/A	Transaction value
CACM-Chile		30	Transaction value
Mercosur	40	60	Fob export value[6]
Mercosur-Chile	40		Fob export value[7]
Mercosur-Bolivia	40		Fob export value
Andean Community	50[8]		Fob export value
Caricom-Dom. Rep.		N/A	Transaction value
LAIA	50		Fob export value
ANZCERTA		50	Factory cost[9]
SAFTA		30-50	Factory cost
SPARTECA		50	Factory cost
AFTA		40	Value of content
Bangkok Agreement		40	Ex-works[10]
Japan-Singapore	40	60	Export value[11]
US-Singapore		30-65	30-35 build-up; 45-65 build-down
Chile-Korea		30-45	30 build-up; 45 build-down
COMESA	60	35	60 value of materials; 35 ex-factory cost[12]
ECOWAS		30	Factory cost
Namibia-Zimbabwe		25	N/A
SADC	70-35		Ex-works price
Gulf Coop. Council		40[13]	Ex-works price
US-Jordan		35	Value of materials/processes[14]
US-Israel		35	Value of materials/processes

Table 3. VC criteria by agreement–Continued

PTA	Value Content Criterion (percent)		Basis for Calculation
	MC	RVC	
MEX-ISRAEL		35-45	35 net cost; 45 transaction value
NON-PREF.	60-40		Ex-works price

[1] Ex-works price means the price paid for the product ex works to the manufacturer in the Member States in whose undertaking the last working or processing is carried out, provided the price includes the value of all the materials (the customs value at the time of importation of the non-originating materials used, or the first ascertainable price paid for the materials in the Member State concerned) used, minus any internal taxes which are, or may be, repaid when the product obtained is exported.

[2] The PE model that is separated here for analytical purposes essentially involves the same product-specific RoO as PANEURO, while diverging somewhat from the PANEURO in the regime-wide RoO. It applies to some 15 FTAs, particularly to those forged by the EU and East European economies with Israel (WTO 2002).

[3] The transaction method is

RVC = (TV - VNM/TV) x 100

where

RVC is the regional value content, expressed as a percentage;

TV is the transaction value of the good adjusted to a F.O.B. basis; and

VNM is the value of non-originating materials used by the producer in the production of the good.

The net cost method is

RVC = [(NC – VNM)/NC] X 100

where

RVC is the regional value content, expressed as a percentage;

NC is the net cost of the good; and

VNM is the value of non-originating materials used by the producer in the production of the good.

[4] The build-down method is

RVC = [(AV B VNM)/AV] x 100;

the build-up method is:

RVC = (VOM/AV) x 100,

where RVC is the regional value content, expressed as a percentage;

AV is the adjusted value;

VNM is the value of non-originating materials used by the producer in the production of the good; and

VOM is the value of originating materials used by the producer in the production of the good.

[5] The initial VC for chs. 28-40 is 40 percent for the first three years, 45 percent during the fourth and fifth years, and 50 percent starting in year six. For chs. 72-85 and 90, VC is 50 percent for the first five years, and 55 percent starting year six.

[6] The MERCOSUR RoO is 60 percent RVC, and, additionally, change in tariff heading (Garay and Cornejo 2002). When it cannot be determined that a change in heading has taken place, the CIF value of the non-originating components cannot exceed 40 percent of the FOB value of the final good. Special RoO apply to selected sensitive sectors, including chemical, some information technology, and certain metal products.

[7] The requirement is that the CIF value of the non-originating materials does not exceed 40 percent of the of the FOB export value of the final good.

[8] A 50 percent MC rule applies to Colombia, Peru and Venezuela; products from Bolivia and Ecuador are governed by a 60 percent MC rule.

[9] The value added test and is based on the formula: Qualifying Expenditure (Q/E) / Factory Cost (F/C)
where
Q/E = Qualifying expenditure on materials + qualifying labor and overheads (includes inner containers); and
F/C = Total expenditure on materials + qualifying labor and overheads (includes inner containers).
The factory or works cost are essentially the sum of costs of materials (excluding customs, excise or other duties), labor, factory overheads, and inner containers.

[10] The agreement requires the value added ensuing from their production in Member States be not less than 40 percent of their final value "at the termination of the production phase". In addition, Member States citizens' share in the ownership of the producing plant is not to be less than 51 percent.

[11] The MC criterion is calculated from CIF and FOB as follows: NOM= MCIF/FOB *100, where NOM is the value content of non-originating materials, MCIF is the CIF value on non-originating materials, and FOB is the free on board value payable by the buyer to the seller.

[12] The origin protocol requires that either the cif value of non-originating materials does not exceed 60 percent of the total cost of the materials used in the production of the goods; or that the value added (the difference between the ex-factory cost of the finished product and the cif value of the materials imported from outside the Member States and used in the production) resulting from the process of production accounts for at least 35 percent of the ex-factory cost (the value of the total inputs required to produce a given product) of the goods.

[13] Besides the 40 percent RVC rule, member states' citizens' share of the plant that produced the product must be at least 51 percent.

[14] The RVC is calculated as the sum of (i) the cost or value of the materials produced in the exporting Party, plus (ii) the direct costs of processing operations performed in the exporting Party. It cannot be less than 35 percent of the appraised value of the article at the time it is entered into the other Party. The cost or value of materials produced in a Party includes: (i) the manufacturer's actual cost for the materials, (ii) when not included in the manufacturer's actual cost for the materials, the freight, insurance, packing, and all other costs incurred in transporting the materials to the manufacturer's plant, (iii) the actual cost of waste or spoilage (material list), less the value of recoverable scrap, and (iv) taxes and/or duties imposed on the materials by a Party, provided they are not remitted upon exportation. Where a material is provided to the manufacturer without charge, or at less than fair market value, its cost or value shall be determined by computing the sum of: (i) all expenses incurred in the growth, production, or manufacture of the material, including general expenses, (ii) an amount for profit, and (iii) freight, insurance, packing, and all other costs incurred in transporting the material to the manufacturer's plant. Direct costs of processing operations mean those costs either directly incurred in, or which can be reasonably allocated to, the growth, production, manufacture, or assembly, of the specific article under consideration. Such costs include, for example, (i) all actual labor costs involved in the growth, production, manufacture, or assembly, of the specific article, including fringe benefits, on-the-job training, and the cost of engineering, supervisory, quality control, and similar personnel, (ii) dies, molds, tooling and depreciation on machinery and equipment which are allocable to the specific article, (iii) research, development, design, engineering, and blueprint costs insofar as they are allocable to the specific article; and (iv) costs of inspecting and testing the specific article.

implications to the exporters' capacity to meet the RoO. The PE model that is separated here for analytical purposes essentially involves the same product-specific RoO as PANEURO, while diverging somewhat from the PANEURO in the regime-wide RoO. It applies to some 15 FTAs, particularly to those forged by the EU and East European economies with Israel (WTO 2002).

Capturing the full scale of variation in the RoO regimes requires a look at the various combinations of RoO components. Table 4 displays the RoO combinations in selected FTAs around the world. Particularly notable is the high degree of selectivity of PANEURO, NAFTA, and non-preferential RoO, as opposed to the Africa and Asian RoO that are set at the same values across sectors within a given agreement.

3.4. *Regime-Wide RoO*

Besides sectoral RoO, the different RoO regimes can be compared by their regime-wide RoO. Table 5 contrasts the various RoO regimes by their general, regime-wide RoO–*de minimis*, roll-up, cumulation, and drawback.

First, EU RoO regimes feature a higher *de minimis* than NAFTA and many other FTAs in the Americas, while there is no *de minimis* rule in Mercosur's FTAs and various FTAs in Asia and Africa. However, the principle does have exceptions in most regimes: for example, the EU's *de minimis* does not apply to textiles and apparel, except for allowing an 8 percent *de minimis* of the total weight of textile materials in mixed textiles products. In the EU-South Africa

FTA, *de minimis* is set at 15 percent but excludes fish and crustaceans, tobacco products, as well as certain meat products and alcoholic beverages. The NAFTA *de minimis* does not extend to the production of dairy produce; edible products of animal origin; citrus fruit and juice; instant coffee; cocoa products, and some machinery and mechanical appliances, such as air conditioners and refrigerators (Reyna 1995: 115-117). In textiles, the 7 percent *de minimis* refers to the total weight rather than cost of the input component. Chile-Korea FTA places *de minimis* at 8 percent, but requires the non-originating materials in chapters 1-24 of the Harmonized System to undergo a change in subheading prior to re-exportation.

Second, the roll-up principle is widely used around the world. For example, in NAFTA, a good may acquire originating status if it is produced in a NAFTA economy from materials considered as originating (whether such materials are wholly obtained or having satisfied a CTC or RVC criterion) even if no change in tariff classification takes place between the intermediate material and the final product. Similarly, the EU-Mexico FTA stipulates that "if a product which has

Table 4. Distribution of RoO combinations, selected PTAs (1st RoO only)

	EUROPE					AMERICAS									ASIA/PACIFIC							AFRICA				MIDDLE EAST			NON-PREF		
Requirement	PANEURO	EU-MEX	EU-CHI	EU PRE-97	EFTA-MEX	NAFTA	US-CHI	G3	MEX-CR	MEX-BOL	CAN-CHI	CACM-CHI	MERC-CHI	LAIA	ANZCERTA	SAFTA	SPARTECA	AFTA	BANGKOK	JSEPA	CHI-KOR	ECOWAS	COMESA	NAM-ZIMB.	SADC	GULF CC	US-JORDAN	US-ISRAEL	HIGHEST	LOWEST	**Requirement**
NC	0.39	0.39	0.39	0.20		0.54	0.51	4.05	0.55	0.95											0.51										NC
NC+BCTC	2.39	2.04	2.39	2.36																											NC+BCTC
NC+TECH	1.39	1.39	1.39	0.72			0.02																						0.72	9.62	NC+TECH
NC+BCTC+TECH	0.00	0.00	0.00	0.00																											NC+BCTC+TECH
NC+VC	11.46	10.91	11.90	11.08					0.02						100	100	100	100	100		0.78			100		100	83.94	100	11.48	0.06	NC+VC
NC+BCTC+VC	1.57	1.57	1.57	1.61																											NC+BCTC+VC
NC+VC+TECH	0.08	0.20	0.20	0.00																									0.34	0.5	NC+VC+TECH
NC+WHOLLY OBTAINED CHAPTER	7.62	7.62	7.62	3.24																							16.06		9.39	8.7	NC+WHOLLY OBTAINED CHAPTER
NC+WHOLLY OBTAINED HEADING	0.70	0.70	0.70	0.70																0.42											NC+WHOLLY OBTAINED HEADING
SUBTOTAL	*25.60*	*24.82*	*26.16*	*19.91*	*0.00*	*0.54*	*0.53*	*4.05*	*0.57*	*0.95*	*0.00*	*0.00*	*0.00*	*0.00*	*100.00*	*100.00*	*100.00*	*100.00*	*100.00*	*0.42*	*1.29*	*0.00*	*0.00*	*100.00*	*0.00*	*100.00*	*100.00*	*100.00*	*21.93*	*18.88*	**SUBTOTAL**
CI																													3.64	6.18	CI
CI+BCTC						0.02			0.04																				0.12	0.12	CI+BCTC
CI+TECH					2.17																				1.39				0.08	3.09	CI+TECH
CI+BCTC+TECH																															CI+BCTC+TECH
CI+VC																															CI+VC
CI+BCTC+VC						0.02																									CI+BCTC+VC
CI+VC+TECH																															CI+VC+TECH
SUBTOTAL	*0.00*	*0.00*	*0.00*	*0.00*	*2.17*	*0.04*	*0.00*	*0.00*	*0.04*	*0.00*	*0.00*	*0.00*	*0.00*	*0.00*	*0.00*	*0.00*	*0.00*	*0.00*	*0.00*	*0.00*	*0.00*	*0.00*	*0.00*	*0.00*	*1.39*	*0.00*	*0.00*	*0.00*	*3.84*	*9.39*	**SUBTOTAL**
CS	0.20	0.20	0.20	0.08		1.29	16.56	1.54	2.99	2.94	11.00	19.16									1.68	100			1.16				13.53	30.42	CS
CS+BCTC	0.00	0.00	0.00	0.00		2.52	5.57	0.73	2.14	1.32	1.60	0.20								0.05	0.47								0.64	0.92	CS+BCTC
CS+TECH	1.90	1.90	1.78	1.89		0.04	0.14	0.10		0.02																				1.41	CS+TECH
CS+BCTC+TECH	0.00	0.00	0.00	0.00		0.40	0.04	0.04	0.28	0.43																					CS+BCTC+TECH
CS+VC	0.27	0.27	0.27	0.37			0.42	4.60	4.25	4.24		0.03									2.11										CS+VC
CS+BCTC+VC	0.00	0.00	0.00	0.00		0.10	0.04														0.16										CS+BCTC+VC
CS+VC+TECH	0.00	0.00	0.00	0.00				0.04		0.26																					CS+VC+TECH
CS+BCTC+VC+TECH	0.00	0.00	0.00	0.00				0.83																							CS+BCTC+VC+TECH
SUBTOTAL	*2.37*	*2.37*	*2.25*	*2.34*	*0.00*	*4.35*	*22.77*	*7.88*	*9.66*	*9.21*	*12.60*	*19.39*	*0.00*	*0.00*	*0.00*	*0.00*	*0.00*	*0.00*	*0.00*	*0.05*	*4.42*	*100.00*	*0.00*	*0.00*	*1.16*	*0.00*	*0.00*	*0.00*	*14.17*	*32.75*	***SUBTOTAL***
CH	32.99	32.99	32.86	36.83	58.79	17.09	23.70	16.45	24.32	17.00	17.50	57.15	46.00	100.00						45.81	46.87		100		68.65				40.13	33.88	CH
CH+BCTC	4.60	5.13	4.56	4.57	7.22	19.18	11.19	13.45	19.66	14.27	17.10	0.26								14.46	9.12				3.35				11.64	2.22	CH+BCTC
CH+TECH	0.00	0.00	0.00	0.34		0.02	0.34	0.97		0.22			20.04							0.58	0.14								0.36		CH+TECH
CH+BCTC+TECH	6.66	6.66	6.66	6.68	9.04	0.14	0.44	0.26		1.74															6.52						CH+BCTC+TECH
CH+VC	13.01	12.68	12.78	13.58	6.1	3.54	3.25	2.01	2.67	2.17	3.40		9.99							1.66	2.95				0.13						CH+VC
CH+BCTC+VC	0.37	0.86	0.37	0.43	0.08	0.58	0.48		0.52	0.85										0.10	0.49										CH+BCTC+VC
CH+VC+TECH	0.00	0.00	0.00	0.00		0.10		8.06	0.02	10.01			23.97																		CH+VC+TECH
CH+BCTC+VC+TECH	0.02	0.02	0.02	0.02	0.03			4.82		0.89															0.03						CH+BCTC+VC+TECH
SUBTOTAL	*57.65*	*58.34*	*57.25*	*62.43*	*81.26*	*40.65*	*39.40*	*46.02*	*47.19*	*47.15*	*38.00*	*57.41*	*100.00*	*100.00*	*0.00*	*0.00*	*0.00*	*0.00*	*0.00*	*62.61*	*59.57*	*0.00*	*100.00*	*0.00*	*78.65*	*0.00*	*0.00*	*0.00*	*52.13*	*36.10*	***SUBTOTAL***
CC	2.16	2.16	2.16	2.28		30.95	23.18	21.09	31.05	21.80	29.50	22.94									22.49				0.68				7.86	2.78	CC
CC+BCTC	1.02	1.02	1.02	0.74	0.7	17.71	5.83	5.90	5.65	6.67	5.30	0.26								37.35	4.71								0.1	0.1	CC+BCTC
CC+TECH	0.04	0.04	0.04	0.04	0.05	0.02	0.06	5.43		6.30											0.08										CC+TECH
CC+BCTC+TECH	11.02	11.25	11.02	11.02	15.41	5.76	8.08	6.65	5.81	6.24	7.90										5.67				18.09						CC+BCTC+TECH
CC+VC	0.00	0.00	0.00	0.00			0.06	0.14	0.26	0.43											1.80										CC+VC
CC+BCTC+VC	0.00	0.00	0.00	0.00				0.00																							CC+BCTC+VC
CC+VC+TECH	0.00	0.00	0.00	0.00				2.67		1.24																					CC+VC+TECH
CC+BCTC+VC+TECH	0.00	0.00	0.00	0.00				0.20																							CC+BCTC+VC+TECH
SUBTOTAL	14.24	14.47	*14.24*	*14.08*	*16.16*	*54.44*	*37.21*	*42.08*	*42.77*	*42.68*	*42.70*	*23.20*	*0.00*	*0.00*	*0.00*	*0.00*	*0.00*	*0.00*	*0.00*	*37.35*	*34.75*	*0.00*	*0.00*	*0.00*	*18.77*	*0.00*	*0.00*	*0.00*	*7.96*	2.88	***SUBTOTAL***
TOTAL	100	100	100	99	100	100	100	100	100	100	93	100	100	100	100	100	100	100	100	100	100	100	100	100	100	100	100	100	100	100	**TOTAL**

CC = CHANGE IN CHAPTER

CH = CHANGE IN HEADING

CS = CHANGE IN SUBHEADING

ECTC = EXCEPTION TO CHANGE OF TARIFF CLASSIFICATION

VC = REGIONAL VALUE CONTENT

TECH = TECHNICAL REQUIREMENT

Calculations at 6-digit level of the Harmonized System.

Source: Authors' calculations and Devlin and Estevadeordal (2001).

Table 5. Regime-Wide RoO in selected PTAs

PTA	*De minimis (percentage)*	Roll-Up	Cumulation		Drawback Allowed?[vi]
			Bilateral	Diagonal	
PANEURO (50)	10	Yes	Yes	Yes (full in EEA)	No
PE (15)	10	Yes	Yes	Yes	No[1]
EU-South Africa	15	Yes	Yes	Yes with ACP (full with SACU)	Not mentioned
EU-Mexico	10	Yes	Yes	No	No after 2 years
EU-Chile	10	Yes	Yes	No	No after 4 years
EFTA-Mexico	10 (not chs. 50-63)	Yes	Yes	No	No after 3 years
NAFTA	7 (exceptions in agric. and ind. products; 7% of weight in chs. 50-63	Yes except automotive	Yes	No	No after 7 years
US-Chile	10 (except. in agric. and processed agr. products)	Yes	Yes	No	Not mentioned
G3	7 (7% of wt in chs. 50-63)	Yes	Yes	No	Not mentioned
Mexico-Costa Rica	7 (except. in chs. 4-15 and headings 0901, 1701, 2105, 2202)	Yes	Yes	No	No after 7 years
Mexico-Chile	8 (except. in agric. and ind. products; 9% of weight in chs. 50-63)	Yes	Yes	No	Not mentioned
Mexico-Bolivia	7 (not chs. 1-27 unless CS; not chs. 50-63)	Yes	Yes	No	No after 8 years
Canada-Chile	9 (except. in agric. and ind. products; 9% of weight in chs. 50-63)	Yes	Yes	No	Not mentioned
CACM-Chile	8 (not chs. 1-27 unless CS)	Yes	Yes	No	Not mentioned
CACM	10 until 2000; 7 from 2001 on (7% of weight in chs. 50-63)	N/A	Yes	No	Yes

Table 5. Regime-Wide RoO in selected PTAs–Continued

PTA	*De minimis (percentage)*	Roll-Up	Cumulation		Drawback Allowed?[vi]
			Bilateral	Diagonal	
Mercosur	Not mentioned	Yes except automotive	Yes	No	Yes (except automotive imports from Arg. and Braz.)
Mercosur-Chile	Not mentioned	Yes	Yes	No	Yes
Mercosur-Bolivia	Not mentioned	Yes	Yes	No	No after 5 years
Caricom	Not mentioned	Not mentioned	Yes	No	Possibly[2]
Caricom-DR	7	Not mentioned	Yes	No	Not mentioned
ANZCERTA	2	Yes	Yes	Yes (full)	Yes
SAFTA	2	Yes	Yes	No	Not mentioned
SPARTECA	2	Yes	Yes[3]	Yes (full)	Yes
AFTA	Not mentioned	Not mentioned	Yes	No	Yes
BANGKOK	Not mentioned	Yes	Yes[4]	No	Possibly[5]
Japan-Singapore	To be determined	Yes	Yes	No (Outward Processing allowed)[6]	Not mentioned
US-Singapore	10 (except. in various agric. products; 7% of weight in chs. 50-63)	Yes	Yes	No (OP and ISI allowed)[7]	Not mentioned
Chile-Korea	8 (not chs. 1-24 unless CS; 8% of weight in chs. 50-63	Yes	Yes	No	Not mentioned
COMESA	2[8]	Yes	Yes	No	Not after 10 years
ECOWAS	Not mentioned	Not mentioned	Yes	No	Not mentioned
SADC	10 (not chs. 50-63, 87, 98)	Yes	Yes	No	Not mentioned
Gulf CC	Not mentioned	Not mentioned	Yes	No	Not mentioned
US-Jordan	Not mentioned	Not mentioned	Yes	No	Not mentioned
US-Israel	Not mentioned	Yes	Yes	No	Yes

Table 5. Regime-Wide RoO in selected PTAs–Continued

PTA	*De minimis (percentage)*	Roll-Up	Cumulation		Drawback Allowed?[vi]
			Bilateral	Diagonal	
Canada-Israel	10 (except. in agric. and industrial products; 7% of weight in chs. 50-63)	Yes	Yes	Yes (with any third party with which both have an FTA, such as US)[9]	Not mentioned
Mexico-Israel	10 (except. in agric. and industrial products; 7% of weight in chs. 50-63)	Yes	Yes	No	Not mentioned

[1] Drawback not mentioned in Hungary-Israel, Poland-Israel, Slovenia-Croatia, Slovenia-FYROM. Drawback allowed for the first two years in EU-Palestinian Authority, two and one half years in EFTA- Palestinian Authority, three years in EFTA-FYROM, one year in Bulgaria-FYROM, 3 months in Turkey-FYROM, and two years in Israel-Slovenia.

[2] The Revised Treaty of Chaguaramas Establishing the Caribbean Community, including the CARCIOM Single Market and Economy stipulates that any member state needs to justify the need to apply an export drawback Council for Trade and Economic Development (COTED); COTED will review the use of drawback by members on an annual basis.

[3] When products from the South Pacific Islands that are exported to New Zealand are cumulated with Australian inputs, a minimum of 25 percent of "qualifying expenditure" from South Pacific Islands is required.

[4] Requires the expenditure on goods produced and labor performed *within the territory of the exporting* Member State in the manufacture of the goods to not less than fifty percent of the ex-factory or ex-works cost of the goods in their finished state (emphasis added).

[5] The agreement stipulates that "With respect to drawbacks within one year from the date of entry into force of this Agreement, the Standing Committee shall consider whether drawbacks on goods imported from third countries should be permitted in relation to products used in the manufacture of finished products for which concessions have been exchanged by the Participating States."

[6] Singapore's FTAs, including JSEPA, incorporate the outward processing (OP) principle tailored to accommodate Singapore's unique production pattern. The principle acknowledges that part of the manufacturing process (usually the lower value-added or labor intensive activities) may be outsourced to neighboring economies after the product has received initial processing in Singapore without the initial processing being discarded when calculating the final Singaporean content. That is, if in stage 1, production takes place in Singapore, in stage 2 in a foreign country, and in stage 3 again in Singapore; value of production acquired in both stages 1 and 3 will be counted as Singaporean content. Conventional RoO, in contrast, would not allow the activities in Singapore prior to outward processing to be counted towards the local content.

[7] Both OP and the integrated sourcing initiative (ISI) operate in the US-Singapore FTA. ISI applies to non-sensitive, globalized sectors, such as information technologies. Under the scheme, certain IT components and medical devices are not subject to RoO when shipped from either of the parties to the FTA. The scheme is designed to reflect the economic realities of globally distributed production linkages, and to further encourage US multinationals take advantage of ASEAN economies' respective comparative advantages.

[8] Mentioned in the section on trade remedies: one of the criteria for imposing a countervailing duty within the block is that the targeted subsidy is not less than the 2 percent de *minimis*.
[9] The FTA stipulates that "Where each Party has entered separately into a free trade agreement under Article XXIV of the GATT 1994 with the same non-Party before this Agreement enters into force, a good, which, if imported into the territory of one of the Parties under such free trade agreement with that non-Party, would qualify for tariff preferences under that agreement, shall be considered to be an originating good under this Chapter when imported into the territory of the other Party and used as a material in the production of another good in the territory of that other Party."

Sources: World Trade Organization (2002); ALADI (2002); FTA texts.

acquired originating status by fulfilling the conditions...is used in the manufacture of another product, the conditions applicable to the product in which it is incorporated do not apply to it, and no account shall be taken of the non-originating materials which may have been used in its manufacture."

Third, the EU's Pan-European system of cumulation applied since 1997 draws a clear distinction between the EU RoO regimes on the one hand, and most RoO regimes elsewhere in the world, on the other. The foremost diagonal cumulation regime in the world, the Pan-European system incorporates 16 partners and covers no fewer than 50 FTAs.[22] These include FTAs between EU and third parties, such as the members of the European Free Trade Agreement (EFTA), the central and eastern European economies, the Baltic economies, Slovenia, and Turkey, and also FTAs forged between the EU's partner economies–such as between Slovenia and Estonia. In concrete terms, the Pan-European system enables producers to use components originating in any of the participating economies without losing the preferential status of the final product. The EEA agreement between EU and EFTA permits full cumulation. The EU-South Africa FTA also provides for full cumulation. It incorporates the "single territory" concept, whereby goods originating from economies party with South Africa to the Southern Africa Customs Union (SACU) are considered as originating in the EU-South Africa FTA area. Notably, AFTA and ANZCERTA models provide for full cumulation, while the Canada-Israel FTA allows for cumulation with the two economies' common FTA partner, the United States. Singapore's FTAs incorporate the outward processing (OP) concept tailored to accommodate Singapore's unique economic features and its access to low-cost

[22] The participants in the PANEURO system of cumulation are the EU, Bulgaria, Czech Republic, Estonia, Hungary, Iceland, Lativia, Liechtenstein, Lithuania, Norway, Poland, Romania, Slovak Republic, Slovenia, Switzerland, and Turkey.

processing in neighboring economies; OP will be detailed in Section IV of this paper.

Fourth, EU's FTAs and FTAs in the Americas tend explicitly to preclude drawback. Nonetheless, both have allowed for a phase-out periods during which drawback is permitted. For instance, Mexico was allowed to employ drawback for the first two years under the EU-Mexico FTA, while Chile can do so through 2007, the fourth year of the FTA with the EU. NAFTA allowed Mexico to use drawback during the first seven years. NAFTA also provides for leniency in the application of the no-drawback rule by putting in place a refund system, whereby the producer will be refunded the lesser of the amount of duties paid on imported goods and the amount of duties paid on the exports of the good (or another product manufactured from that good) upon its introduction to another NAFTA member. AFTA, ANZCERTA, SPARTECA, the US-Israel FTA, CACM, and Mercosur's FTAs stand out for permitting drawback. However, in Mercosur *per se*, no-drawback rule does govern Argentine and Brazilian imports of intermediate automotive products when the final product is exported to a Mercosur partner.

3.5. *Administration of RoO*

The various RoO regimes diverge in their administrative requirements, particularly the method of certification (table 6).

The EU RoO regimes require the use of a movement certificate, EUR.1, that is to be issued in two steps–by the exporting economy government once application has been made by exporter or the exporter's competent agency, such as a sectoral umbrella organization. However, the EU regimes provide for an alternative certification method, the invoice declaration, for "approved exporters" who make frequent shipments and are authorized by the customs authorities of the exporting economy to make invoice declarations. NAFTA and a number of other FTAs in the Americas as well as the Chile-Korea FTA, meanwhile, rely on self-certification, which entails that the exporter's signing the certificate suffices as an affirmation that the items covered by it qualify as originating. The certification method in Mercosur, Andean Community, Caricom, AFTA, ANZCERTA, SAFTA, the Bangkok Agreement, JSEPA, and ECOWAS require certification by a public body or a private umbrella entity approved as a certifying agency by the government. However, unlike in the two-step model, the exporter is not required to take the first cut at filling out the movement

Table 6. Certification methods in selected PTAs

PTA	Certification method
PANEURO	Two-step private and public; limited self-certification
PE	Two-step private and public; limited self-certification
EU-South Africa	Two-step private and public; limited self-certification
EU-Mexico	Two-step private and public; limited self-certification
EU-Chile	Two-step private and public; limited self-certification
NAFTA	Self-certification
G3	Two-step private and public
US-Chile	Self-certification
Mexico-CR	Self-certification
Mexico-Bolivia	Self-certification (two-step private and public during first 4 years)
Canada-Chile	Self-certification
CACM-Chile	Self-certification
CACM	Self-certification
Mercosur	Public (or delegated to a private entity)
Mercosur-Chile	Public (or delegated to a private entity)
Mercosur-Bolivia	Public (or delegated to a private entity)
CAN	Public (or delegated to a private entity)
CARICOM	Public (or delegated to a private entity)
CARICOM-DR	Public (or delegated to a private entity)
LAIA	Two-step private and public
ANZCERTA	Public (or delegated to a private entity)
SAFTA	Public (or delegated to a private entity)
SPARTECA	Not mentioned
AFTA	Public (or delegated to a private entity)
BANGKOK	Public (or delegated to a private entity)
Japan-Singapore	Public (or delegated to a private entity)
US-Singapore	Self-certification
Chile-Korea	Self-certification
COMESA	Two-step private and public
ECOWAS	Public (or delegated to a private entity)
SADC	Two-step private and public
US-Jordan	Self-certification

Source: Authors' classification based on the texts of RoO protocols.

certificate, but, rather, to furnish the certifying agency with a legal declaration of the origin of the product.[23]

---

[23] The certificate in NAFTA and G3, CACM-Chile, will be valid for a single shipment or multiple shipments for a period of a year; in ANZCERTA and SAFTA, the certificate will be valid for multiple shipments for two years. In ECOWAS, certificate is not required for agricultural, livestock products and handmade articles produced without the use of tools directly operated by the manufacturer. In Mercosur-Chile, Mercosur-Bolivia, CARICOM-DR, ANZCERTA, and SAFTA, the certificate requires to be accompanied by a legal declaration by the final producer or exporter of compliance with the RoO. In CAN and CARICOM, declaration by the producer is required. In CARICOM, the declaration can be completed by the exporter if it is impossible for the producer to do so.

The self-certification model can be seen as placing to burden of proof essentially on the importing economy producers; as such, it arguably minimizes the role of the government in the certifying process, entailing rather low administrative costs to exporters and governments alike. In contrast, the two-step system requires heavier involvement by the exporting economy government and increases the steps that an exporter is to bear when seeking certification. To be sure, the invoice declaration system implemented by the EU facilitates exporting among frequent traders.

4. A Comparative Analysis of the Restrictiveness of RoO Regimes

4.1. *Restrictiveness of Product-Specific RoO*

The manifold RoO combinations within and across RoO regimes present a challenge for meaningful and rigorous cross-RoO comparisons. This paper seeks to draw such comparisons through a categorical index grounded on the plausible restrictiveness of a given type of RoO. First developed by Estevadeordal (2000) to examine NAFTA RoO, the index ranges from 1 (least restrictive) to 7 (most restrictive), and can be conceptualized as an indicator of how demanding a given RoO is for an exporter. The observation rule is based on two assumptions: (1) change at the level of chapter is more restrictive than change at the level of heading, and change at the level of heading more restrictive than change at the level of sub-heading, and so on; and (2) VC and TECH attached to a given CTC add to the RoO's restrictiveness.[24] While this paper builds on Estevadeordal's index to consider the restrictiveness of product-specific RoO, some modifications are made to the observation rule (specified in appendix I) to account for the structure of EU RoO–in particular the instances where the CTC criterion is not used.

Figure 3 reports the restrictiveness of RoO as calculated at the six-digit level of disaggregation in selected FTAs. The EU RoO regimes are again strikingly alike across agreements; indeed, the similarities are accentuated in comparison to the graphs above as the differences between the pre- and post-1997 RoO regimes in about a fifth of subheadings are too small to alter the restrictiveness code. For instance, in many products the only difference between the two sets of regimes is

[24] Given that the degree of restrictiveness is a function of *ex ante* restrictiveness rather than the effective restrictiveness following the implementation of the RoO, the methodology–much like that of Garay and Cornejo (2002)–is particularly useful for endogenizing and comparing RoO regimes. The methodology allows RoO to be analyzed in terms of their characteristics rather than their effects.

Figure 3. Restrictiveness of RoO in selected PTAs

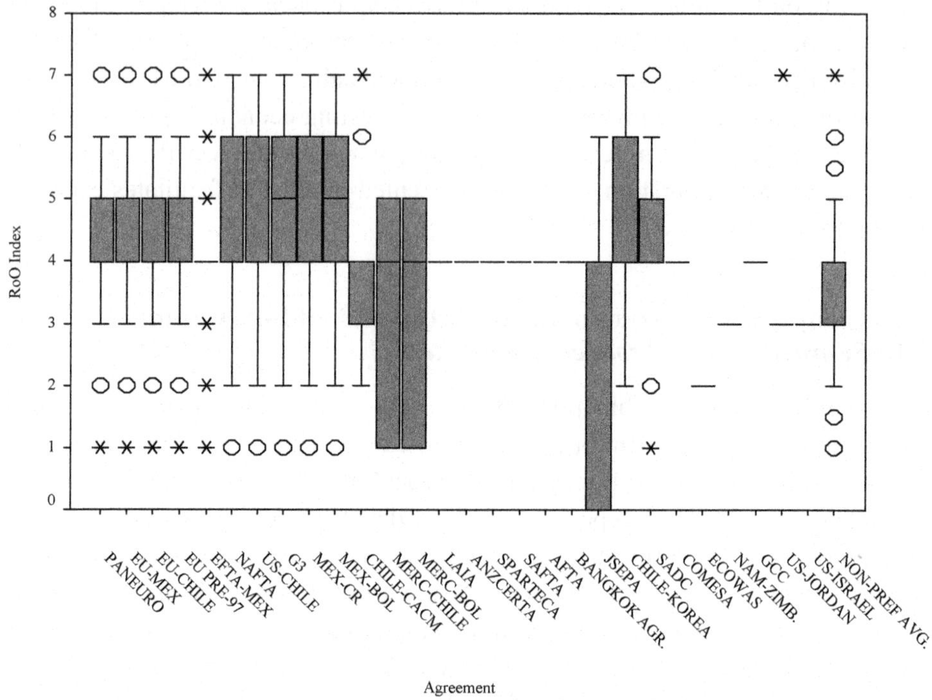

Note: Boxplots represent interquartile ranges. The line in the middle of the box represents the median 50th percentile of the data. The box extends from the 25th percentile to the 75th percentile, or through the so-called inter-quartile range (IQR). The whiskers emerging from the boxes extend to the lower and upper adjacent values. The upper adjacent value is defined as the largest data point less than or equal to x(75) + 1.5 IQR. The lower adjacent value is defined as the smallest data point greater than or equal to x(25) + 1.5 IQR. Observed points more extreme than the adjacent values are individually plotted (outliers and extreme values are marked using "x" and "o" symbols, respectively).

Source: Authors' calculations based on RoO protocols.

that a RoO requiring, say, a change of heading for a given product may also impose an ECTC under one regime while not doing so under another; such differences go uncaptured by the index employed here. The RoO regimes based on the NAFTA model, such as the G-3, are also highly alike. The Mercosur model pertinent to Mercosur-Chile and Mercosur-Bolivia FTAs is more general, yet still exhibiting more cross-sectoral variation in the restrictiveness of RoO than the LAIA model marked by the across-the-board change of heading RoO. However, diverging from each other, the NAFTA, Mercosur, and LAIA models evince the distinctive RoO families operated in the Americas.

The generality of the LAIA model is replicated by most Asian and African RoO regimes. However, some newer PTAs–Japan-Singapore, Chile-Korea, and SADC–feature high levels of cross-sectoral variation in RoO. Notably, the restrictiveness of Chile-Korea RoO resembles those of NAFTA and US-Chile RoO. The JSEPA model appears less restrictive than it is as about half of the tariff sub-headings in the agreement do not have RoO given that the parties have zero MFN tariffs in these sectors already; for these sub-headings, the graph simply assigns the value of zero. Non-preferential RoO similarly carry RoO of marked sectoral selectivity. However, the overall restrictiveness of the non-preferential model is lower than that of most preferential RoO regimes.

4.1.1. *Comparing the Restrictiveness of Sectoral RoO*

To what extent does the restrictiveness of RoO vary across economic sectors? Are some sectors more susceptible to the negative trade and investment effects of RoO than others?

We explore these questions by focusing on nine RoO regimes with inter-sectoral variation in RoO–the PANEURO, EFTA-Mexico, NAFTA, US-Chile, Chile-CACM, JSEPA, Chile-Korea, SADC, and non-preferential models. Table 7 reports the restrictiveness values aggregated by section of the Harmonized System that are established on the basis of these regimes.

Two issues stand out. First, the average restrictiveness value for the PANEURO RoO falls between 4 and 5, which correspond to the change of heading and change of heading plus regional value content criteria, respectively. As such, the index conveys the same message as the analysis above of the predominance of the change of heading rule in EU's RoO regimes. The average is somewhat higher for NAFTA, reflecting the use of the change in chapter criterion. EFTA-Mexico and Chile-CACM RoO are somewhat more lenient, while the restrictiveness of the SADC RoO is strikingly similar to the PANEURO model. Non-preferential RoO, here set at the average level of restrictiveness of RoO in sectors where agreement on one single RoO has yet to be identified, are less restrictive overall given the downward influence of the change of sub-heading and change of item criteria.

Second, the data reveal important variation in the degree of restrictiveness across economic sectors within the three regimes, as well as striking similarities in the variation of cross-sectoral restrictiveness within each agreement. Agricultural products and textiles and apparel are marked by a particularly high restrictiveness score in each regime, which provides precursory evidence that the restrictiveness of RoO may be driven by the same political economy variables

Table 7. Sectoral restrictiveness of sectoral RoO in selected PTAs

HS Section	PAN-EURO	EFTA-MEX	NAFTA	US-Chile	Chile-CACM	JSEPA	Chile-Korea	SADC	Non-Pref. Avg.
1. Live Animals	7.0	5.3	6.0	6.0	5.9	7.0	6.0	7.0	6.2
2. Vegetable Products	6.6	4.0	6.0	6.0	5.6	7.0	6.1	6.6	6.6
3. Fats and Oils	4.7	4.0	6.0	6.0	3.0	7.0	7.0	7.0	4.0
4. Food, Bev. and Tobacco	5.0	4.4	4.7	5.7	3.7	6.8	5.2	5.4	4.6
5. Mineral Products	3.5	3.5	6.0	3.9	5.3	6.6	5.4	4.0	4.8
6. Chemicals	3.9	3.8	5.3	2.6	2.6	3.7	4.0	4.0	2.5
7. Plastics	4.9	4.9	4.8	3.7	3.2	4.0	4.1	4.7	4.0
8. Leather Goods	3.3	3.5	5.6	5.0	3.7	4.0	4.9	3.8	3.4
9. Wood Products	2.9	2.9	4.0	4.1	3.2	4.0	4.1	4.8	3.3
10. Pulp and Paper	4.4	4.6	4.8	4.9	4.1	4.0	4.3	4.3	3.9
11. Textile and Apparel	6.1	6.1	6.9	5.9	4.5	6.0	5.5	6.1	3.4
12. Footwear	2.8	4.1	4.9	4.8	3.5	4.3	4.7	2.6	3.7
13. Stone and Glass	3.7	3.7	4.9	4.4	4.2	4.0	5.0	3.7	3.5
14. Jewelry	3.7	3.7	5.3	5.2	4.0	4.0	5.4	3.7	3.4
15. Base Metals	4.2	4.2	4.6	4.6	3.8	4.0	4.5	3.9	3.4
16. Machinery and Electrical Equipment	4.8	4.0	3.2	2.9	4.3	6.0	3.8	4.1	3.6
17. Transportation Equipment	4.7	4.2	4.8	4.2	3.4	4.0	4.3	3.8	3.8
18. Optics	5.0	4.4	4.0	4.5	4.0	4.0	4.3	3.9	3.5
19. Arms and Ammunition	4.0	4.0	4.7	5.5	4.0	4.0	4.8	3.1	4.0
20. Works of Art, Misc.	4.1	4.1	5.1	5.3	3.6	4.6	4.7	4.0	3.3
Average	4.5	4.2	5.1	4.8	4.0	4.9	4.9	4.5	3.9

Source: Authors' calculations based on the RoO protocols.

that arbitrate the level of tariffs particularly in the EU and United States. Non-preferential RoO exhibit similar patterns across sectors, communicating the operation of political economy dynamics also at the multilateral level. Yet, most sectors in the non-preferential RoO are less restrictive than their preferential counterparts.

The box-and-whisker plots in figure 4 provide a more nuanced look at the sectoral restrictiveness across four major recent RoO regimes–PANEURO, SADC, NAFTA, and Chile Korea FTA. The plots reveal some differences in the range of restrictiveness (or the lack of it) within sectors in each agreement. For instance, while PANEURO RoO and SADC RoO tailored to a good extent after the PANEURO model are nearly uniform with sections 13-21, NAFTA and

Figure 4. Profiles of Sectoral Restrictiveness of RoO in PANEURO, SADC, NAFTA, and Chile-Korea FTA

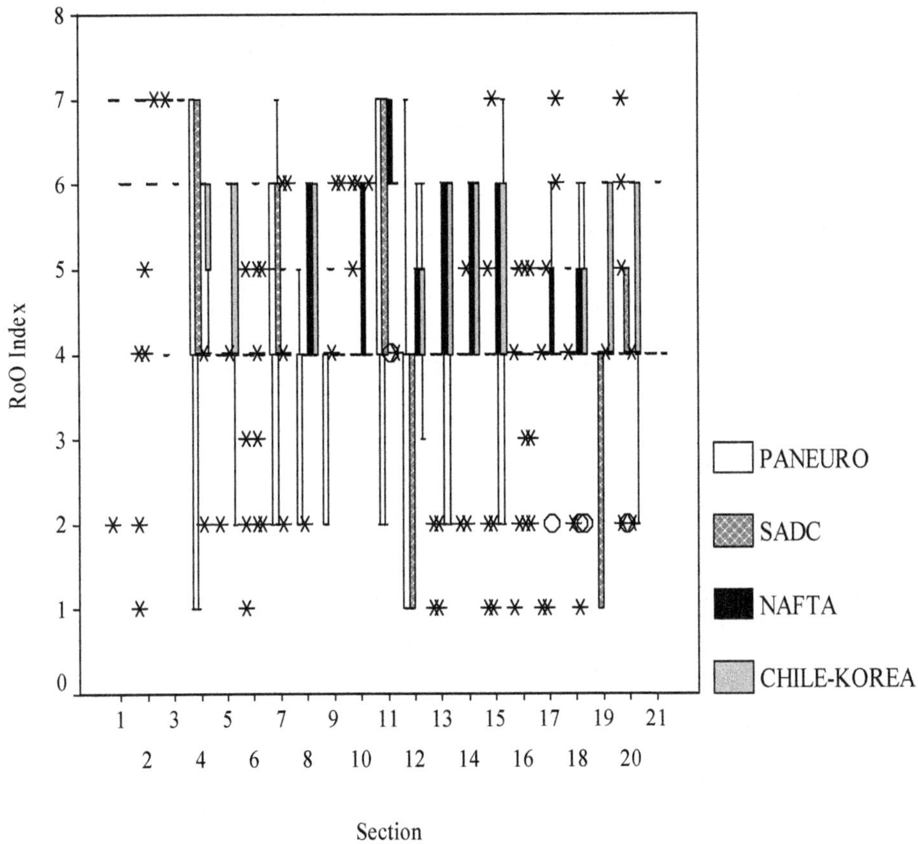

Note: Observed points more extreme than the adjacent values are individually plotted (outliers and extreme values are marked using "x" and "o" symbols, respectively).

Source: Authors' calculations based on the texts of EU, NAFTA, and SADC RoO protocols.

Chile-Korea RoO vary more within these sections–and tend to be more restrictive than the EU RoO. Meanwhile, EU and SADC RoO in foodstuffs (section 4) feature a wide range of restrictiveness values, while the NAFTA and Chile-Korea RoO are highly uniform in the sector. Also notable is the somewhat lower extent of intra-sectoral variation in the Chile-Korea FTA than NAFTA in some sectors, such as pulp and paper (section 10) and transportation equipment (section 17), which communicates the higher level of generality of the trans-Pacific regime.

The methodology is replicated in figure 5, which provides a look at the various potential outcomes of the harmonization process for non-preferential RoO–with the RoO set at the average, lowest, highest levels of restrictiveness.

The spread of restrictiveness values by sector is rather similar across the possible outcomes; neither are the overall restrictiveness values between the three possibilities are too divergent. Notably, however, unlike in many sectors in the PANEURO and NAFTA models, few sectors in non-preferential RoO feature a uniform RoO, but rather display great intra-sectoral selectivity.

Figure 5. Profiles of Sectoral restrictiveness of RoO in three potential non-preferential RoO regimes

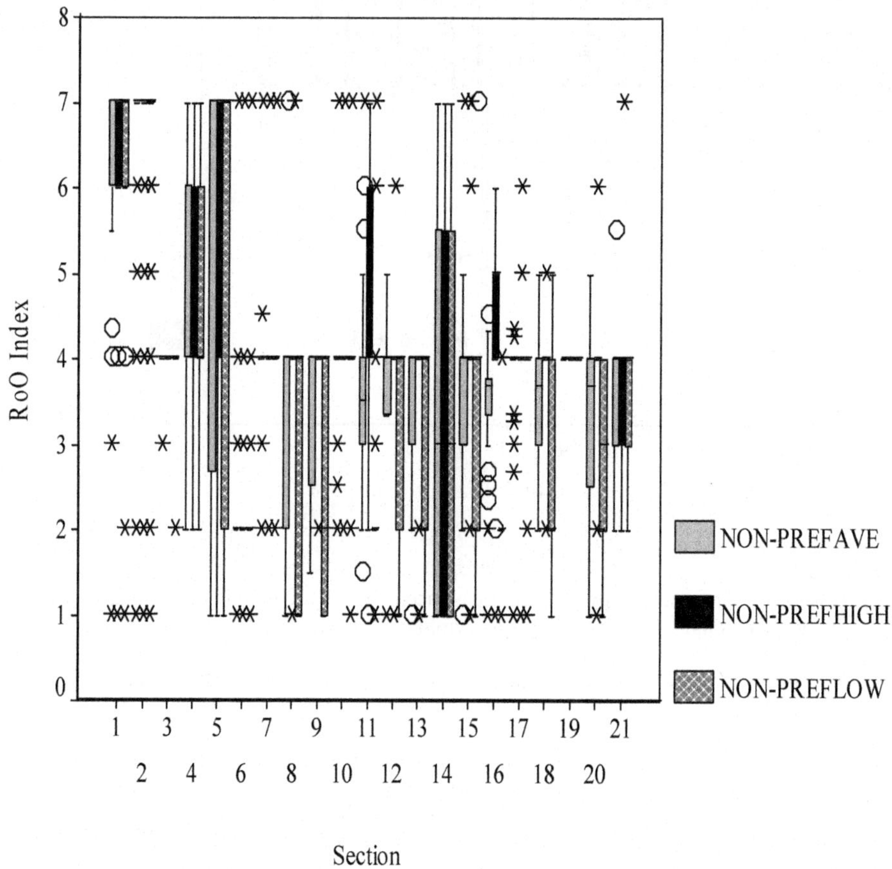

Note: Observed points more extreme than the adjacent values are individually plotted (outliers and extreme values are marked using "x" and "o" symbols, respectively).

Source: Authors' calculations based on the latest revisions to the non-preferential RoO.

4.1.2. *"Weighted" RoO: RoO's Coverage of Actual Trade Flows*

A look at RoO's coverage of tariff sub-headings provides an indication of the prevalence of various types of RoO and RoO of different degrees of stringency in and across RoO regimes. However, an analysis of the potential trade effects of RoO benefits from exploring the coverage of actual imports by different types of RoO. Table 8 presents such a "weighted" RoO measure of NAFTA, PANEURO, Chile-CACM, and SADC RoO based on weighting by US imports from NAFTA partners, EU's total imports, Chilean imports from CACM, and South African imports from SADC partners, respectively, in year 2000. The column next to each FTA specifies the deviation of the weighted RoO from the unweighted RoO, operationalized here as the share of the weighted RoO of the unweighted

Table 8. Weighted restrictiveness of PANEURO, NAFTA, Chile-CACM, and SADC RoO

HS Section	PAN-EURO	as share of unweighted	NAFTA	as share of unweighted	Chile-CACM	as share of unweighted	SADC	as share of unweighted
1. Live Animals	7.0	1.00	6.0	1.00	7.0	1.19	7.0	1.00
2. Vegetable Products	5.5	0.83	5.8	0.96	7.0	1.25	6.3	0.96
3. Fats and Oils	4.2	0.90	6.0	1.00	4.0	1.33	7.0	1.00
4. Food, Bev. and Tobacco	4.9	0.99	5.0	1.06	0.9	0.23	6.4	1.19
5. Mineral Products	2.4	0.68	5.3	0.88	0.0	0.00	4.0	1.00
6. Chemicals	4.1	1.04	4.9	0.93	4.1	1.56	4.0	1.00
7. Plastics	4.8	0.97	4.8	1.00	2.3	0.72	4.3	0.91
8. Leather Goods	3.5	1.06	5.5	0.98	2.0	0.54	4.0	1.05
9. Wood Products	2.5	0.85	4.0	1.00	0.0	0.00	5.0	1.04
10. Pulp and Paper	4.3	0.97	5.6	1.17	4.0	0.98	4.0	0.93
11. Textile and Apparel	6.6	1.09	6.8	0.98	6.9	1.54	4.5	0.74
12. Footwear	2.1	0.74	4.9	1.00	0.0	0.00	1.2	0.46
13. Stone and Glass	3.8	1.03	5.0	1.02	0.0	0.00	2.8	0.76
14. Jewelry	3.6	0.98	5.7	1.08	0.0	0.00	3.9	1.06
15. Base Metals	3.9	0.93	4.8	1.03	4.6	1.22	4.5	1.15
16. Machinery and Electrical Eq.	4.9	1.01	3.8	1.20	4.6	1.07	4.0	0.96
17. Transportation Equipment	4.6	0.98	4.8	0.99	0.0	0.00	3.7	0.97
18. Optics	5.2	1.04	4.1	1.02	5.0	1.25	3.8	0.98
19. Arms and Ammunition	4.0	1.00	4.8	1.02	0.0	0.00	0.0	0.00
20. Works of Art, Misc.	2.9	0.72	5.4	1.05	0.0	0.00	4.9	1.22
Average	*4.2*	*0.94*	*5.1*	*1.01*	*2.6*	*0.66*	*4.3*	*0.95*

Source: Authors' calculations based on the RoO protocols and UNCTAD TRAINS trade data for 2000.

one. When the share is 1, the RoO in the unweighted and weighted exercises are as restrictive; when the share rises above one, the weighted RoO is more restrictive. When the share is zero, the economy on whose imports the weights are generated has no incoming flows from the partners, as is the case in many sectors in the Chile-CACM FTA.

The table reveals striking similarity between the weighted and unweighted RoO. Indeed, the weighted RoO tend to be less restrictive than the unweighted RoO; this may in and of itself be an indication that stringent RoO stifle commerce.

The RoO index provides extremely useful means for capturing the restrictiveness of RoO. However, as a caveat, it should be kept in mind that restrictiveness of RoO is in practice highly specific to the product in question, with some of the nuances escaping the index. First, that RoO are formulated on the basis of the Harmonized System, which was not designed with a consideration for the determination of origin, can have important implications to some types of products. Even if a product undergoes a substantial transformation, it may still in practice fail to alter its tariff classification, and hence fail to meet the CTC test. The ostensibly simple change of heading criteria may thus be highly restrictive for some sectors where the intermediate and final goods are often classified under the same heading. This is the case particularly in the machinery sector. Second, the similarly seemingly simple stand-alone VC RoO can be problematic for producers to meet in the face of frequent fluctuations in exchange rates and changes in production costs; the VC rule is also particularly susceptible to subjectivity by the importing economy customs. The problems of calculating the production costs particularly of goods produced in multiple economies has led Lloyd (2001a) to recommend a value-added tariff in lieu of RoO–a tariff whose base is not the price of the imported article but rather the proportion of the value added outside the area.

4.2. *Comparing Regime-Wide RoO: A Facilitation Index*

Product-specific RoO in a given PTA absent of an across-the-board RoO can impose highly divergent requirements to the exporters of different goods. Furthermore, even an across-the-board rule applicable to all sectors will undoubtedly have more striking implications in some sectors than in others, depending on the product-specific features. However, as discussed above, RoO regimes employ several mechanisms to add flexibility to the application of the product-specific RoO. We strive to capture the combined effect of such mechanisms by developing a regime-wide "facilitation index". The index is based on five components: *de minimis*, diagonal cumulation, full cumulation, drawback, and self-certification. The maximum index value of 5 results when the permitted level of *de minimis* is 5 percent or higher and when the other four variables are permitted by the RoO regime in question. The minimum value of zero results when *de minimis* is below 5 percent and none of the other regime-wide RoO are included in the PTA. Each component provides one extra "point" to the index.

Figure 6 graphs the "facil index" values for PTAs. The PANEURO and NAFTA models are nearly at a par; the difference here is produced by coding NAFTA as allowing drawback, as it did for the first seven years for Mexico. The EU-South Africa and the Canada-Israel are the most "permissive" regimes, the former thanks to drawback and diagonal and full cumulation, and the latter because of self-certification, drawback and cumulation with the United States. Meanwhile, many regimes with an across-the-board RoO neither provide for *de minimis* nor feature many regime-wide provisions of flexibility; the most usually occurring regime-wide rule in these PTAs is drawback. Indeed, that regimes with most stringent RoO and highest degree of sectoral selectivity in RoO feature the highest facilitation values may evince counter-lobbying by producers jeopardized

Figure 6. Facilitation index for selected PTAs

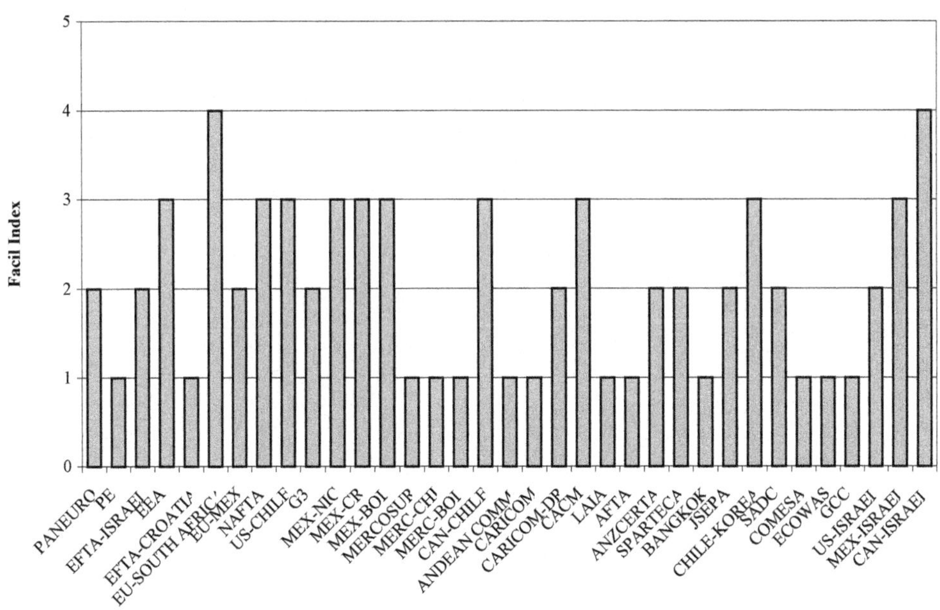

by stringent product-specific RoO. Given that the restrictiveness of product-specific RoO is likely a less salient issue in regimes employing an across-the-board RoO, political economy pressure for alleviating mechanisms could be hypothesized to be reduced at the time when RoO are negotiated.

Figure 7 summarizes the average restrictiveness of RoO (ROORI), the sectoral selectivity of RoO (ROOSD, operationalized as standard deviation in the product-specific RoO), and the facilitation index scores (Facil) for PTAs include included in the empirical specifications of this study. Correlation among the three variables evinces the use of restrictive and selective RoO and relatively flexible facilitation terms in the NAFTA- and PANEURO-type regimes.

Given that these regimes entered into force at different points in time (as specified in appendix IIa), the aggregate level of restrictiveness, selectivity, and facilitation around the world can be expected to alter over time. Indeed, (1) that a larger number of country pairs will be tied by a common RoO regime over time; and (2) that regimes with most restrictive and selective product-specific RoO and most lenient facilitation terms–such as NAFTA and the bulk of the EU's FTAs–emerged after the early 1990s mean that the "world average" restrictiveness and selectivity of RoO and level of facilitation should be increasing over time. Figures 8a-c confirm this, displaying the upward trend in the trade-weighted world averages of restrictiveness, selectivity, and facilitation for our sample of 1981-2001. Figures 9a-b reveal a similar patterns in the restrictiveness and selectivity in final goods in selected sectors.

Figure 7. Restrictiveness of RoO, standard deviation in RoO, and Facil Index Values in selected PTAs

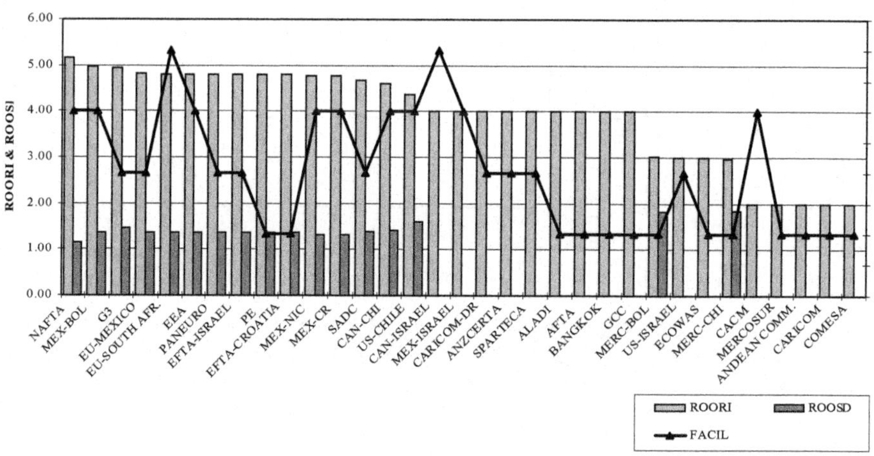

Source: Authors' calculations.

Figure 8a. Trade-weighted world average of restrictiveness of RoO, 1981-2001

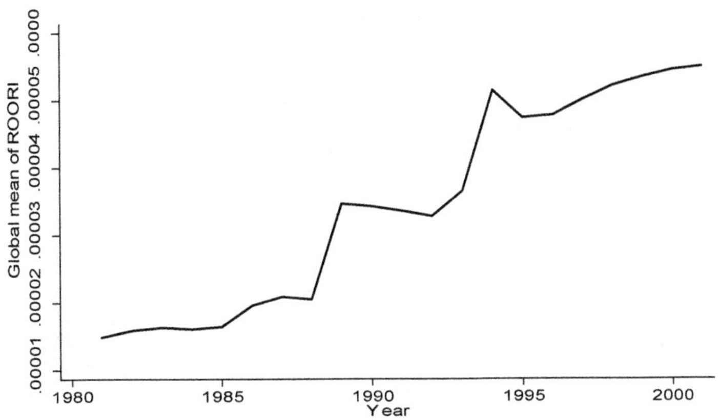

Figure 8b. Trade-weighted world average of sectoral selectivity of RoO, 1981-2001

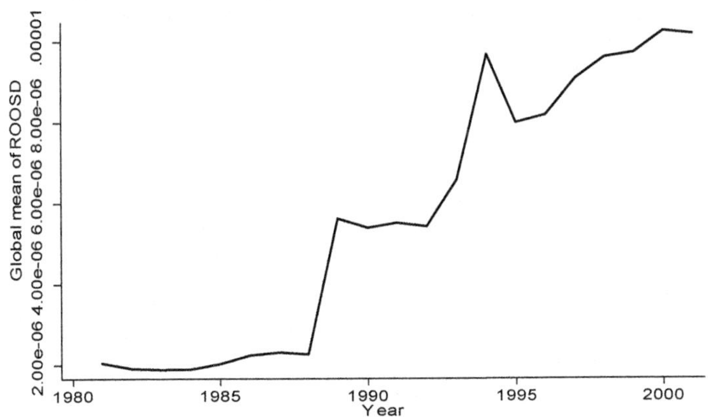

Figure 8c. Trade-weighted world average of facilitation in regime-wide RoO, 1981-2001

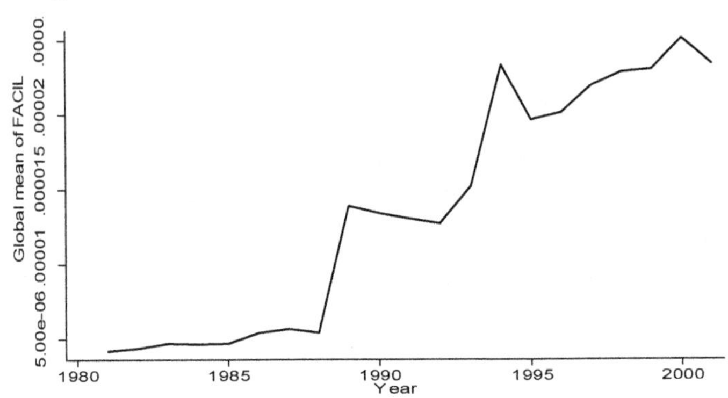

Source: Authors' calculations.

Figure 9a. Average Level of Restrictiveness of RoO by Sector, 1988-2001

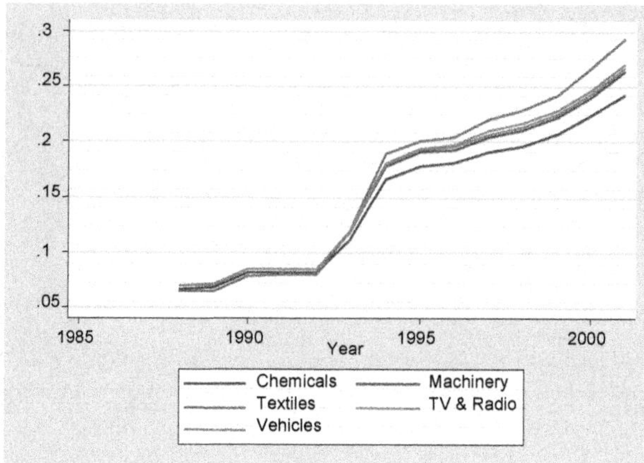

Figure 9b. Average level of standard deviation of RoO by sector, 1988-2001

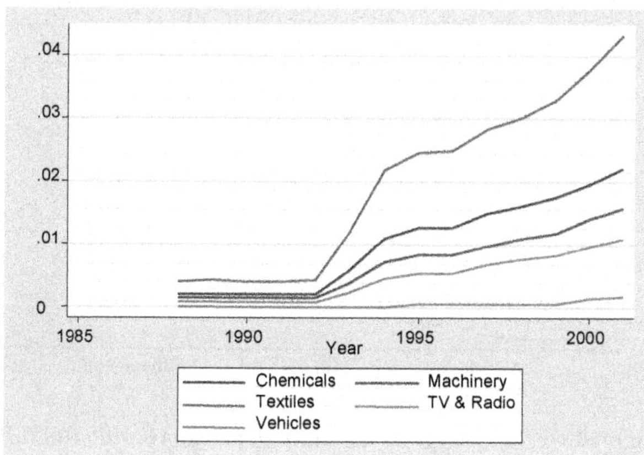

5. Trade Effects of RoO

A number of rigorous theoretical studies, such as Ju and Krishna (1998) and Duttagupta and Panagariya (2000), have explored the impact of different degrees of restrictiveness of RoO on aggregate trade flows as well as trade in inputs and final goods, respectively. The results have, however, remained rather inconclusive, relegating the impact of RoO on trade to an empirical matter.

The handful of existing empirical studies on RoO have given grounds to believe that stringent RoO undermine trade flows. Yet, the understanding of the effects of RoO on global commerce is still relatively incipient. However, in a recent study, Estevadeordal and Suominen (2004a) provide clarity to the trade effects of RoO. They employ a modified gravity model to assess the trade effects of (1) product-specific RoO of different degrees of restrictiveness and selectivity; and (2) the flexibility instilled in RoO regimes by different types of regime-wide RoO provisions. In other words, the study puts the RoO and Facil indices developed above to work. It examines two types of trade flows: aggregate imports, and as imports in intermediate goods in the chemical, machinery, textile, television and radio transmitter, and vehicle sectors. The data covers 155 countries and nearly a hundred PTAs (50 PTAs of the PANEURO system, 15 of the PE system, and 28 others specified in appendix IIa) for years 1981-2001 for aggregate trade, and 1988-2001 for trade in intermediates.

5.1. *Empirical Specification for Panel Regression*

Estevadeordal and Suominen (2004a) estimate the following basic gravity equation using OLS:

$$\ln(V_{ij}) = b_0 + b_1\ln(GDP_i) + b_2\ln(GDP_j) + b_3\ln(GDPPC_i) + b_4\ln(GDPPC_j) + b_5\ln(DIST_{ij}) + b_6(BORDER_{ij}) + b_7(COMLANG_{ij}) + b_8(COL_{ij}) + b_9(COMCOL_{ij}) + b_{10}(PTA_{ij}) + b_{11}\ln(ROORI_{ij}) + b_{12}(FACIL_{ij}) + \varepsilon \quad [1]$$

where

V_{ij} is the value of imports of economy i from economy j;

GDP_i is the exporter's GDP;

GDP_j is the importer's GDP;

$GDPPC_i$ is the exporter's GDP *per capita* ratio;

$GDPPC_j$ is the importer's GDP *per capita* ratio;

$DIST_{ij}$ is the distance between the capitals of the two countries and serves as a proxy for transportation costs;[25]

$BORDER_{ij}$ is a dummy that takes value 1 if economies i and j share a land border and 0 otherwise;

$COMLANG_{ij}$ is a dummy for cultural affinities, that takes value 1 when the two economies speak the same language;

COL_{ij} is a dummy that takes value 1 when one economy has been colonized by the other;

---

[25] Another useful control variable would be a "distance from major economic centers"-variable; according to Soloaga and Winters (2001), after controlling for distance between i and j, the further country i is from all its trading partners, the greater its imports will be from country j–*i.e.*, Australia and New Zealand will likely trade with each other more due to being far apart from any other trading partners than two other economies separated by the same distance (such as Poland and Spain) due to the latter having many trading partners nearby. We for now lack such distance data for all of the 155 economies in the sample.

$COMCOL_{ij}$ is a dummy that takes value 1 when the two economies have been colonized by the same colonial power;
PTA_{ij} is a dummy that takes value 1 when two economies belong to the same PTA;
$ROORI_{ij}$ is the average of the restrictiveness of RoO-values (as measured at the 6-digit level of disaggregation) of a PTA regulating trade between the two economies, and can take values anywhere between 1 and 7;
$FACIL_{ij}$ is the facilitation index of a PTA regulating trade between the two economies, and can take values anywhere between 1 and 5; and
ε is a normally-distributed error term.

A subsequent estimation replaces $ROORI_{ij}$ with $ROOSD_{ij}$, which is the standard deviation of ROORI values within a regime and geared to capturing the effects of "RoO peaks" in a regime.

Table 9 displays the results. The results on traditional gravity variables are largely as expected. The basic gravity model used in several studies to examine the effects of regional integration shows that PTAs have a positive effect on aggregate trade flows. However and as expected, rules of origin, a key market access provision in virtually all PTAs, has a negative sign and is significant at the 1 percent level. This is the first main finding of this paper: *restrictive product-specific RoO undermine aggregate trade*. Indeed, stringent RoO are key in countering the PTA-inspired boost to trade: the difference in the coefficient for the PTA variable in columns I and II (*i.e.*, 2.417-0.550 = 1.867) approximates the negative coefficient of the RoO variable (1.482).

Column III incorporates the FACIL variable. As expected, FACIL has a positive and significant effect on trade. This is the second main finding: *the combined effect of regime-wide variables that instill flexibility to the application of product-specific RoO boosts trade*. As such, facilitation terms foster the liberalizing logic of PTAs.[26]

Columns IV and V show that the results on RoO and FACIL hold also for the sub-sample of PTA pairs. Restrictive product-specific RoO undercut trade among PTA pairs.[27] The policy implication is clear: PTA members adopting stringent product-specific RoO are well-advised to adopt lenient regime-wide RoO.

---

[26] Note that ROORI and FACIL have an independent and additive rather than an interacting and synergistic effect on trade: in regressions not shown here, ROORI*FACIL interaction term was not significant even at the 5 percent level.

[27] To be sure, the facilation term may pick up and thus proxy for some other trade-enhancing variables of the PTAs, such as sturdy regulations on the use of emergency safeguards.

Table 9. Effects of Restrictive RoO and Sectoral Selectivity of RoO on Trade, 1981-2001

	Dependent Variable: Ln (Trade)					Dependent Variable: Ln(Trade)					
Independent Variables	All pairs 1981-2001			PTA Pairs 1981-2001		All Pairs 1981-2001		PTA Pairs 1981-2001		PTA Pairs 1991-2001	
	I	II	III	IV	V	VI	VII	VIII	XI	X	XI
ln(GDP_imp)	0.224	0.206	0.207	0.800	0.782	0.207	0.207	0.797	0.789	0.437	0.434
	(8.18)**	(7.55)**	(7.58)**	(9.86)**	(9.68)**	(7.58)**	(7.56)**	(9.80)**	(9.72)**	(4.86)**	(4.84)**
ln(GDP_exp)	0.464	0.403	0.406	0.530	0.480	0.405	0.403	0.532	0.512	-0.216	-0.197
	(10.58)**	(9.20)**	(9.27)**	(3.04)**	(2.76)**	(9.22)**	(9.17)**	(3.04)**	(2.93)**	(0.94)	(0.86)
ln(PerCap GDP_imp)	0.378	0.398	0.397	-0.533	-0.516	0.393	0.393	-0.532	-0.520	-0.568	-0.561
	(13.74)**	(14.51)**	(14.46)**	(8.82)**	(8.57)**	(14.31)**	(14.30)**	(8.79)**	(8.60)**	(9.00)**	(8.90)**
ln(PerCap GDP_exp)	0.601	0.659	0.657	-0.347	-0.304	0.649	0.650	-0.35	-0.327	0.106	0.102
	(14.40)**	(15.82)**	(15.76)**	(2.64)*	(2.32)**	(15.54)**	(15.56)**	(2.66)**	(2.49)*	(0.68)	(0.65)
ln(Distance)	-1.234	-1.222	-1.218	-1.158	-1.151	-1.231	-1.228	-1.183	-1.182	-1.253	-1.253
	(185.94)**	(183.73)**	(182.75)**	(47.45)**	(47.29)**	(185.22)**	(184.45)**	(49.01)**	(49.09)**	(45.61)**	(45.70)**
Common Border	0.27	0.238	0.244	0.504	0.481	0.241	0.245	0.507	0.489	0.539	0.519
	(10.32)**	(9.12)**	(9.37)**	(11.71)**	(11.19)**	(9.22)**	(9.37)**	(11.78)**	(11.34)**	(10.82)**	(10.40)**
Common Language	0.354	0.334	0.337	-0.031	-0.013	0.334	0.335	-0.013	-0.002	0.105	0.117
	(24.39)**	(23.07)**	(23.26)**	(0.54)	(0.23)	(22.99)**	(23.06)**	(0.23)	(0.04)	(1.68)	(1.87)
Colonial Rel.	1.287	1.295	1.294	0.802	0.765	1.285	1.282	0.846	0.819	1.055	1.014
	(41.74)**	(42.07)**	(42.04)**	(7.99)**	(7.63)**	(41.68)**	(41.60)**	(8.43)**	(8.17)**	(8.19)**	(7.87)**
Common Colonizer	0.643	0.618	0.627	0.715	0.720	0.625	0.632	0.685	0.676	0.621	0.613
	(39.11)**	(37.67)**	(38.11)**	(14.79)**	(14.93)**	(38.01)**	(38.38)**	(14.13)**	(13.97)**	(10.55)**	(10.44)**
PTA	0.550	2.417	2.341			0.879	0.643				
	(28.56)**	(38.53)**	(36.90)**			(36.51)**	(15.66)**				
ln(Restrictiveness Avg)		-1.482	-1.676	-0.637	-0.715						
		(31.26)**	(31.49)**	(6.91)**	(7.74)**						
ln(Restrictiveness Sd)						-0.942	-1.144	0.095	-0.048	-0.14	-0.252
						(22.71)**	(22.74)**	(1.13)	(0.55)	(1.49)	(2.63)**
Facil			0.189		0.474		0.181		0.376		0.319
			(8.02)**		(8.47)**		(7.10)**		(6.85)**		(5.53)**
Constant	2.597	-1.281	-1.363	-3.806	-3.336	-1.137	-1.067	-4.704	-4.779	19.176	18.351
	(2.59)**	(1.28)	(1.36)	(1.00)	(0.88)	(1.13)	(1.06)**	(1.23)	(1.25)	(3.83)*	(3.67)**
Observations	185497	185491	185491	11920	11920	185497	185497	11926	11926	8857	8857
Adjusted R-squared	0.73	0.73	0.73	0.88	0.88	0.73	0.73	0.88	0.88	0.88	0.88
Year FE	Yes	Yes	Yes	Yes	Yes	Yes	Yes	Yes	Yes	Yes	Yes
Importer and Exporter FE	Yes	Yes	Yes	Yes	Yes	Yes	Yes	Yes	Yes	Yes	Yes

Absolute value of t statistics in parentheses
* significant at 5%; ** significant at 1%

Columns VI-XI replace ROORI with ROOSD, providing the third major result: *high levels of sectoral selectivity in RoO undermine aggregate trade*. That FACIL has a positive and significant effect on trade provides further evidence that flexible regime-wide RoO can help boost aggregate trade flows.

The results are less resounding when ROOSD is examined in the sub-sample of PTA pairs. However, this is due to the construct of the data. Apart from the US-Canada FTA of 1989, all RoO regimes formed prior to 1991 in the sample feature an across-the-board RoO, which implies that the ROOSD values are basically zero until the 1990s. Indeed, column XI shows that ROOSD re-acquires its negative and significant sign when the sample is limited to the years of the rise of complex RoO regimes (1991-2001).

5.2. *RoO and Intermediate Imports: A Sectoral Approach*

The second key focus of Estevadeordal and Suominen is on intermediate trade in five sectors–chemicals, machinery, textiles, television and radio transmitters, and vehicles. They estimate the following equation using OLS:

$$\ln(INPUT_{ijs}) = = b_0 + b_1\ln(GDP_i) + b_2\ln(GDP_j) + b_3\ln(GDPPC_i) + b_4\ln(GDPPC_j) + b_5\ln(DIST_{ij}) + b_6(BORDER_{ij}) + b_7(COMLANG_{ij}) + b_8(COL_{ij}) + b_9(COMCOL_{ij})) + b_{10}\ln(ROORIFINAL_{ijs}) + b_{11}\ln(FACIL_{ij}) + \varepsilon \quad [2]$$

where

$INPUT_{ijs}$ is the value of intermediate imports of economy i from economy j in sector s; and $ROORIFINAL_{ijs}$ is the average of the restrictiveness of RoO-values (as measured at the 6-digit level of disaggregation) in final goods in sector s.

The other variables are defined as in [1].

The expectation is now that the key independent variable, $ROORIFINAL_{ijs}$, will be *positively* related to trade flows: stringent RoO in final goods should encourage trade in intermediates in the PTA area at the expense of outsourcing by the PTA partners from the ROW. FACIL should, as above, be positively related to trade flows between the partners.

Table 10 summarizes the regression results by the variables of interest. The key independent variables, ROORIFINAL and FACIL are, as expected, positively related to trade in intermediate goods. This is the fourth major result of Estevadeordal and Suominen (2004a): *the restrictiveness of RoO in final goods encourages trade in intermediate products*. This finding serves as evidence to the long-suspected impact of RoO on input trade–an impact that could divert trade in intermediates from ROW to the PTA area. Note that inclusion of the FACIL variable reduces the coefficient of the ROORIFINAL variable by precisely the amount of the coefficient of FACIL; as such, it appears to be the combined effect of ROORIFINAL and FACIL that serves to boost trade in intermediates.[28] This result stands in clear contrast to the regressions at the aggregate level, where ROORI and FACIL pulled in different directions.

Table 11 centers on the results of regressions where ROORIFINAL-variable is replaced by ROOSDFINAL, which measures the level of sectoral selectivity in the restrictiveness of RoO in final goods. The table shows that sectoral selectivity of RoO in final goods is positively and significantly related to trade in

[28] Thus, omitting either would lead to attributing too much weight to each individual variable.

intermediate goods. FACIL, meanwhile, continues to boost trade. This is the fifth key result of the study: RoO peaks in final goods encourage trade in intermediate products.

Table 10. Effects of RoO in final goods and facilitation terms on trade in intermediates, 1988-2001

Chemicals		
RoO Restrictiveness	0.984	0.339
	(64.96)**	(9.45)**
Facilitation Index		0.474
		(19.81)**
Observations	237708	237708
Adjusted R-squared	0.43	0.43
Machinery		
RoO Restrictiveness	0.928	0.496
	(67.56)**	(14.73)**
Facilitation Index		0.333
		(14.06)**
Observations	237715	237715
Adjusted R-squared	0.45	0.45
Television and Radio Transmitters		
RoO Restrictiveness	1.002	0.583
	(63.85)**	(15.25)**
Facilitation Index		0.326
		(12.01)**
Observations	237708	237708
Adjusted R-squared	0.47	0.47
Textiles		
RoO Restrictiveness	0.407	0.347
	(54.47)**	(18.31)**
Facilitation Index		0.050
		(3.42)**
Observations	237708	237708
Adjusted R-squared	0.30	0.30
Vehicles		
RoO Restrictiveness	1.000	0.603
	(59.63)**	(14.66)**
Facilitation Index		0.311
		(10.55)**
Observations	237708	237708
Adjusted R-squared	0.50	0.50

Absolute value of t-statistics in parentheses
* = significant at 5 percent level; ** = significant at 1 percent level
All regressions with year and exporter and importer fixed effects

Table 11. Effects of sectoral selectivity of RoO in final goods and facilitation terms on trade in intermediates, 1988-2001

Chemicals		
RoO Selectivity	4.321	3.695
	(81.61)**	(47.06)**
Facilitation Index		0.162
		(10.85)**
Observations	237721	237721
Adjusted R-squared	0.43	0.43
Machinery		
RoO Selectivity	5.519	4.605
	(82.05)**	(48.35)**
Facilitation Index		0.185
		(13.53)**
Observations	237721	237721
Adjusted R-squared	0.45	0.45
Television and Radio Transmitters		
RoO Selectivity	7.137	5.225
	(71.27)**	(40.05)**
Facilitation Index		0.330
		(22.82)**
Observations	237721	237721
Adjusted R-squared	0.47	0.47
Textiles		
RoO Selectivity	1.279	1.264
	(67.66)**	(43.90)**
Facilitation Index		0.006
		(0.66)
Observations	237721	237721
Adjusted R-squared	0.30	0.30
Vehicles		
RoO Selectivity	4.985	2.847
	(20.71)**	(11.76)**
Facilitation Index		0.682
		(56.12)**
Observations	237721	237721
Adjusted R-squared	0.50	0.50

Absolute value of t-statistics in parentheses
* = significant at 5 percent level; ** = significant at 1 percent level
All regressions with year and exporter and importer fixed effects

6. RoO "Innovations": *Ad Hoc* Mechanisms for Flexibility[29]

Empirical evidence shows that stringent and complex product-specific RoO can undercut the liberalizing potential of PTAs by reducing exporters' incentives to

---

[29] This section draws on Estevadeordal and Suominen (2004b).

seek to qualify for PTA-conferred preferential treatment. However, RoO regimes with the most restrictive and complex RoO tend also to contain regime-wide provisions that instill flexibility to the application of product-specific RoO, potentially counteracting the negative incentives of restrictive RoO.

This section focuses on further, innovative features in some recent RoO regimes that can alleviate the impact of stringent RoO, and which future RoO regime-builders in particularly North-South PTAs might be well-advised to consider: (1) a phase-in period for a stringent value content RoO; (2) permanent deviations for an economy or set of economies from the RoO regime that would otherwise apply; (3) flexibility in the ways of calculating value content; and (4) tariff preference levels (TPLs) employed when the partner lacks intermediate product industries. While most regimes employing these provisions make them applicable to all members, some regimes provide them asymmetrically, for instance to accommodate some economy-specific idiosyncrasies in production structures or to provide greater leniency to a developing member economy when the parties' development levels differ drastically. As noted above, drawback is one such provision. For example, intra-Mercosur automotive imports from Argentina and Brazil are not allowed to have used drawback; the provision should help put vehicle producers in Paraguay and Uruguay at a par with the larger Mercosur partners, and possibly encourage investment in the automotive sector in these smaller economies. The following reviews the uses of each of these innovative provisions.

6.1. *RoO Phase-Ins*

Some regimes have adopted what are in many cases highly detailed product-specific provisions that allow for phasing in of the RoO. Mercosur-Chile FTA provides a seven-year adjustment period for Paraguay to start applying the FTA's import content RoO of 40 percent in selected headings across a host of sectors such as food products, chemicals, plastics, textiles, apparel, footwear, base metals, and machinery. During the period, Paraguay applies a 60 percent import content rule. Mercosur-Bolivia FTA allows Bolivia to export to Mercosur some selected goods at 50 percent import content for the first five years, and others at 60 percent for three years as opposed to the 40 percent that will subsequently take effect. For its part, Paraguay can export to Bolivia at 60 percent import content for the first three years.

Also the EU's extra-European agreements with Mexico and Chile allow for some product-specific deviations from the PANEURO standard for a certain period of time.[30] In the case of the EU-Mexico FTA, these pertain to one whole chapter (knitted apparel) and to 25 headings (or subheadings) in chemicals, textiles, footwear, machinery, and vehicles, and endure from two to six years prior to converging to the benchmark RoO. Some are explicitly applicable to Mexico only; the most notable exceptions favoring Mexico involve three headings in vehicles (road tractors and semi-trailers; public transport vehicles; and motor vehicles for transport of goods), for which Mexico applies a 55 percent VC for an annual quota of 2,500 units through 2002, followed by a 50 percent VC on the quota through 2006. This contrasts with the 60 percent VC that will be applied otherwise and following year 2006.[31] In footwear, RoO is more restrictive for the EU than in its other FTAs: the same RoO applies as in the FTAs with Chile and South Africa up to a certain quota, while the rest of EU exports to the Mexican market are regulated by much more stringent RoO.

The RoO phase-ins are fewer in the case of the EU-Chile FTA, pertaining to textiles and bicycles for the first three years of the agreement. For two headings in man-made staple fibers (chapter 55), the rule of origin is more lenient prior to the phase-in. In special woven fabrics (chapter 58), the RoO is stricter prior to the phase-in, whereas in headgear (chapter 65), the initial RoO requires a VC instead of a change in heading. In bicycles (chapter 87), the initial RoO requires a VC rather than an ECTC, which sets in three years into the agreement.

6.2. *Permanent Reductions in the Level of RVC*

A second means to add leniency to the RoO protocol are permanent deviations for an economy or a set of economies from the RoO regime that would otherwise apply. The RoO of the Andean Community allows the less developed members, Bolivia and Ecuador, to use non-originating components up to 60 percent of the value of the final good, as opposed to the 40 percent applicable to the other members. LAIA allows the less developed partners to use non-originating components of up to 60 percent of the value of the final good, as opposed to 50 percent applying to the rest of the members. In COMESA, products of importance to economic development to the partner economies (selected headings in mineral products, chemicals, machinery, and optical instruments) enjoy a 25 percent RVC, as opposed to the across-the-board 35 percent RVC that otherwise applies.

---

[30] For detailed treatment of the EU's extra-regional FTAs, see Estevadeordal and Suominen (2003).

[31] A similar alleviating exception applies to three other headings in vehicles and two headings pertinent to piston engines in chapter 84, but only through the year 2004.

Also the EU-Mexico and EU-Chile FTAs allow for permanent deviations from the single list, PANEURO model. Although the deviations are rather minor, the fact that most of them feature a less stringent rule of origin than that on the PANEURO model suggests, much like the RoO phase-ins do, that both Mexico and Chile achieved some favorable sectoral outcomes in the RoO bargaining with the EU. Notably, in both cases, the divergences apply to selected industrial products only (*i.e.*, selected headings in chapters 25-97).[32]

6.3. *Options for Calculating Value Content*

Some regimes have created innovative optional means of calculating value content. In SADC, the more developed members may allow the less developed members to count as originating processes that are usually left outside the value content calculation. Regimes modeled after NAFTA provide a number of optional ways of calculating RVC in vehicles when the producer uses pre-defined intermediate goods from Chapters 40 and 84, as well as for calculating the RVC for these intermediate goods.[33]

However, it is Singapore's FTAs that incorporate perhaps the most innovative and comprehensive mechanisms to add flexibility to the calculation of the value content, and, in particular, to help the many Singaporean industries that have extensive outsourcing ties to qualify for the preferential treatment provided by its PTA partners: outward processing (OP) and integrated sourcing initiative (ISI). OP is recognized in all of Singapore's PTAs, while ISI is incorporated in the US-Singapore FTA. The concept of OP enables Singapore to outsource part of the manufacturing process, usually the lower value-added or labor-intensive activities, to the neighboring economies, yet to count the value of Singaporean

[32] For Chile, most deviations are in machinery and mechanical appliances, and electrical machinery and equipment. For Mexico, the bulk of the deviations are in apparel; footwear; machinery and mechanical appliances; electrical machinery and equipment; vehicle parts; and optical instruments. The RoO in these sectors were modified in order to accommodate the lack of raw materials, components, and local production in Mexico (Holbein *et al.* 2002).

[33] The producer of a vehicle can calculate the RVC by may average the calculation over the fiscal year by using any one of the following categories: (a) the same model line of vehicles in the same class of vehicles produced in the same plant in the territory of a party; (b) the same class of motor vehicles produced in the same plant in the territory of a party; and (c) the same model line of motor vehicles produced in the territory of a Party. Meanwhile, the producer can calculate the RVC intermediate goods for vehicles by (a) averaging the calculation over the fiscal year of the motor vehicle producer to whom the good is sold, over any quarter or month, or over its fiscal year, if the good is sold as an aftermarket part; (b) calculating the average separately for any or all goods sold to one or more motor vehicle producers; or (c) calculating separately those goods that are exported to the territory of the other party.

production done prior to the outsourcing activity toward local, Singaporean content when meeting the RoO required by the export market. Table 12 illustrates the process.

Table 12. Operation of Outward Processing in Singapore's FTAs

Stage 1	Stage 2	Stage 3	
Singapore →	Foreign Country →	Singapore →	Exported

Conventional RoO → Stage 3 = Local Content

Recognition of OP → Stage 1 + Stage 3 = Local Content

Although the OP concept applies only to products with a value added rule, it is credited to have encouraged higher value activities to be retained in Singapore, while outsourcing labor-intensive and low-value processes.

For its part, ISI operating in the US-Singapore FTA applies to non-sensitive, globalized sectors, such as information technologies. Under the scheme, certain IT components and medical devices are not subject to RoO when shipped from either of the parties to the FTA. The scheme is designed to reflect the economic realities of globally distributed production linkages, and to further encourage US multinationals take advantage of ASEAN countries' respective comparative advantages.

6.4. *Tariff Preference Levels*

The fourth *ad hoc* mechanism to add leniency to a RoO regime is Tariff Preference Levels (TPLs). TPLs allow goods that would not otherwise satisfy the RoO protocol to qualify for the preferential treatment up to some pre-specified annual quotas. Above these levels, non-originating goods become subject to the importer's MFN tariff. Most commonly applying to textiles and apparel, TPLs are employed particularly in the NAFTA-model RoO regimes. They are generally extended by all parties to all other parties, made available by any given party on a "first-come, first-served"-basis. Some other regimes employ what could be viewed as a modified form of TPLs, allocating the quotas not fully free of RoO, but against some more lenient product-specific RoO. For instance, SADC provides quotas at more lenient RoO for the textile and apparel exports of Malawi, Mozambique, Tanzania, and Zambia (MMTZ countries) to SACU for a period of five years.

In sum, particularly the more recent RoO regimes have incorporated various provisions to add flexibility to the application of RoO beyond that provided by the more widely used instruments of *de minimis*, roll-up, and cumulation, and drawback. These *ad hoc* provisions can be of great importance to countries with limited production base and in the absence of relatively cheap input providers in the PTA area–and should, as such, be taken into serious consideration by RoO regime-builders in particularly North-South PTAs.

7. The Future of the Global RoO Panorama: Toward a De Jure Harmonization of Preferential RoO?

The global RoO panorama is evolving rapidly with the proliferation and expansion of PTAs with divergent RoO regimes around the world, as well as with the on-going tailoring of the non-preferential RoO at the WTO. Against the backdrop of heightening global competition, even subtle the differences between RoO regimes can have important implications to firms' calculations of the most feasible export and outsourcing decisions. When RoO and the differences between RoO regimes discourage the pursuit of least costly strategies, RoO counteract the trade-creating potential of PTAs and ultimately undercut the provision of cheapest, most efficiently produced goods to consumers.

This section strives addresses these concerns in three parts: it (1) lays out a potential evolution of the global preferential RoO panorama; (2) discusses the prospects for harmonizing non-preferential RoO; and (3) proposes to counter the potentially distortionary effects of preferential RoO through harmonizing these RoO at the multilateral level.

7.1. *Future Global RoO Theater*

7.1.1. *Preferential RoO: Convergence toward a Bipolar RoO World?*

The mosaic of RoO regimes populating the globe will likely undergo three developments in the near future.

First, the PANEURO model will not only consolidate its hold in the European theater, but also expand to FTAs forged between the EU (and other PANEURO adherents) with extra-European partners, most immediately with MERCOSUR and the various Southern Mediterranean economies. The PANEURO model itself will likely continue unaltered: although the EU is launching a process to evaluating its RoO regime, as of May 2003, no major retailoring of the model was planned. Minor changes may take place to accommodate changing production patterns in Europe, but these may well be done for instance by adjusting the 10 percent standard *de minimis*, rather than altering the product-specific RoO.

To be sure, developments on the broader political landscape of Europe will have implications to the PANEURO system: the accession of ten new EU members means that the bulk of the FTAs carrying the PANEURO model will disappear, with the partner economies' bilateral trade ties becoming governed by the customs union. The EU plans to subsequently extend the PANEURO system to the Southern Mediterranean economies and Israel through a single convention signed simultaneously by all the participants. The adjustment by many new developing partner economies to the PANEURO system will be smoothened by the fact that the model already applies to them under EU's GSP scheme. Thus, the "formalization" of the PANEURO model in further, extra-regional and inter-continental PTAs will likely work to entrench the existing supply relations with the EU's partners. The attraction of the model to the EU's partner economies is the possibility for eventual accession to the PANEURO system of cumulation. Cumulation in EU's GSP, currently allowed for member economies within ASEAN, South Asian Association for Regional Cooperation (SAARC), Andean Community, and CACM, will be modified to permit cumulation also between Andean Community and CACM members.

Second, the Western Hemisphere will likely become covered by a NAFTA-type RoO regime as a result of the Free Trade Area of the Americas-process. Much like in the case of PANEURO, the NAFTA RoO model–which, after all, is not dramatically different from that of the PANEURO model–will undoubtedly affect the shape of RoO regimes in the Asia-Pacific region, given that it is the NAFTA-model adherents (Canada, Chile, Mexico, and the United States) that are the most enthusiastic Western Hemisphere nations to build cross-Pacific FTAs. The Chile-Korea FTA that incorporates NAFTA-type RoO yet is somewhat less complex and restrictive may well presage the type of RoO resulting from the melding of the NAFTA model with the interests of East Asia's thus far foremost engines of inter-continental integration–Japan, Korea, and Singapore.

Third, further integration and renegotiation of prior PTAs in Asia, Africa, and the Middle East can well spawn RoO of greater selectivity, as evinced by SADC and JSEPA. Although such selectivity would likely follow the types and levels of sectoral restrictiveness of RoO in place in Europe and the Americas, the final outcome will likely resemble JSEPA RoO or CACM's revised RoO, with the relatively general change of heading RoO (or VC) being interspersed by some exceptions, combinations with VC (or change of heading), and technical requirements, albeit to a more moderate extent than in the PANEURO or NAFTA models.

In sum, the expanding geographical reach of the PANEURO model; the convergence toward a single FTAA RoO regime in the Americas; the rise of the inter-continental FTAs between European and Western Hemisphere partners on the one hand, and partners in other regions, on the other; as well as third parties' entering in PTAs with one another can be expected to lead to the application of two to three relatively similar RoO regimes on the global level. Indeed, as seen above, the main poles of RoO regimes, NAFTA and PANEURO models, come out rather similar when abstracted to the level of sectoral restrictiveness and regime-wide facilitation index. This potential *de facto* harmonization dynamic, along with (1) the harmonization of the non-preferential RoO at the WTO, and (2) the fact that many RoO regimes particularly in the Asia-Pacific and African PTA theaters are thus far relatively simple, with the same RoO often applying across the board, could facilitate eventual convergence toward a single global preferential RoO regime. Such an outcome of global RoO convergence would be particularly beneficial to the "spoke" economies that implement divergent RoO regimes across their FTA partners, rather than applying a single, uniform RoO regime in operations across partners, as is done by the EU hub and, within the Americas, by the US and Mexico hubs.

7.1.2. *Non-Preferential RoO: Awaiting the Final Push for Harmonization*

The rapid evolution of the preferential RoO panorama stands in contrast to the glacial progress of the non-preferential RoO negotiations. Although the painstaking and laudable process of tackling the RoO of the about 5,000 products defined in the Harmonized System at the 6-digit level is today nearing in its final stages, the prospects for a rapid conclusion are dimmed by the fact that the remaining issues are also the politically most sensitive ones. The main sticking points as of June 2003 can be divided into three broad categories: (1) issues going to the very heart of the fundamental differences between the WTO members in the conceptualization of some product-specific RoO, as reflected by the differences between their preferential RoO regimes particularly in machinery; (2) broader differences in trade policy concepts between the members, such as issues pertaining to sanitary and phytosanitary standards, the exclusive economic zone, and trademarks; and (3) disagreements over the application of RoO in anti-dumping actions.[34]

First, the NAFTA and PANEURO models diverge on the RoO for assembled machinery, electrical equipment, vehicles, airplanes, and ships. The NAFTA

[34] The following draws on interviews with WTO and WCO officials and on Thorstensen (2002).

model assigns basically all RoO a CTC component, whereas the PANEURO model leaves a quarter of RoO without CTC and bases such RoO on a stand-alone VC (or TECH). This difference is particularly prominent in machinery. The United States favors CTC and/or TECH as the most appropriate types of RoO in machinery, while the EC supports a RoO based on value added. Neither type of RoO is without faults. The VC rule is difficult to implement particularly in complex products made of parts from several sources; it also provides for relatively high degrees of subjectivity by the importing economy customs when verifying origin. Meanwhile, the CTC rule is straight-forward to implement and thus reduces the margin for administrative error and the likelihood that the implementation of RoO becomes politicized. However and as noted above, CTC, if implemented at the level of tariff heading, is nearly impossible to meet in many machinery products given that the parts and the final good inherently originate from the same tariff heading. For its part, TECH is criticized for lacking clarity and transparency.

Besides assembled industrial products, there are several other contested sectoral RoO involving agricultural and industrial products alike, first and foremost pizzas, refined vegetable oils, fruit juices, wines, cement, pharmaceuticals, leather, and iron and steel. The main issues at stake on these front are two-fold: (1) the type of processing or manufacturing that suffices to confer origin; and (2) the extent to which a given economy's input share in a final product suffices to assign origin to that economy and not others whose materials are used in the product. The former is the most commonly disputed question; however, the debate on some products such as pharmaceuticals involve both issues.

The second challenge facing the non-preferential talks concerns the relationship of RoO to other international trade policy instruments such as sanitary standards and trademark often governed by their own WTO agreements. There are three main issues. One, the definition of RoO will have implications to the application of many other international trade policy instruments; thus the beneficiaries of the other agreements will have a stake in the harmonization process. Two, RoO negotiators are up against the major task of making RoO as closely compatible with the other WTO agreements as possible. Three, movement on the RoO front can be contingent on movement on issues larger than RoO. There are several such broader issues:

- Trademarks are protected as intellectual property by the Agreement on Trade-Related Aspects of Intellectual Property Rights (TRIPs). One of the key issues surrounding trademarks and RoO concerns coffee. Colombia is particularly insistent on its trademark "100% Colombian Coffee"; other coffee producers, such as Brazil, oppose the 100% rule on coffee due to producing blends. This poses a challenge for reconciling harmonization work with the TRIPs Agreement

- Geographic indications, also covered by TRIPs, affect RoO particularly in wines and liquors. As on trademarks, RoO would have to be made compatible with TRIPs.
- Origin marking requirements will be affected by the how origin is defined on the RoO front; yet, the marking requirements tend to be stricter than RoO. Although the purposes of origin markings are distinct from the purposes of RoO, the application of the two sets of rules becomes problematic if they conflict.
- Export subsidies that encourage eligible producers to import raw materials, process them, and subsequently re-export them, subsidized, to the raw material producer economies–a practice that undercuts domestic producers' market share in these economies. The issue is particularly pertinent to refined sugar.
- Sanitary and phytosanitary (SPS) standards. The SPS Agreement stipulates that the health standards for food products should be defined in ways that would not create new barriers to trade. The key question is how to comply with this provision in a world where a given food product may contain inputs from various different economies with differing health standards–and differences in the uses of chemicals, antibiotics, hormones, and genetically modified seeds. Although the objectives of the SPS Agreement and the ARO differ, their provisions should be compatible with each other.
- Codex Alimentarius defines the international norms for food products, informing consumers of the ingredients and processes involved in the production of the final product. It basically defines origin on the grounds of processing. However, the RoO negotiations will complicate the labeling requirements, as they have given rise to several proposals to define origin especially for meat products, such as on the basis of economy where the animal was born, raised, or slaughtered, or where the meat was processed.[35]
- Disagreement over the exclusive economic zone (EEZ) in the affects origin definition for fish products. While all WTO members agree that fish caught within 12 nautical miles from the shore of a member is accorded the origin of

[35] Moreover, that consumers have recently become more demanding of the information on the origin of meat and the type of processing that can be employed will likely have important implications to the Codex and the definition of RoO alike (Thorstensen 2002).

that economy, the origin of products obtained from the EEZ extending 200 nautical miles from a member's coast is disputed. Most developing economies favor RoO that confers origin to the economy in whose EEZ the fish was caught, while the EC supports a RoO that determines origin of fish caught in the EEZ by the origin of the vessel.

Another broad issue complicating RoO talks is economy-specific textile quotas, whereby proving and claiming origin is crucial for obtaining a share of the quota. However, the abolishing of textile quotes in 2005 under the Multifiber Agreement (MFA) will relegate non-preferential RoO in textiles to much reduced importance, as no longer will members require to prove origin with the purpose of accessing a quota.

The third and perhaps the most important question holding up the harmonization process revolves around application of RoO in anti-dumping investigations. ARO states that non-preferential rules are to be the basis for antidumping actions. However, some member economies, such as the United States, Korea, and Japan, argue that the calculation of the margin of dumping–the wedge between the price of the exported good and its value in the domestic market–as *per* the Agreement on Anti-Dumping is based on the concept of exporting economy and not on the economy of origin. Should this concept be employed, the determination of origin would be unnecessary: the final exporter of a good that has passed through production in various economies on its way to the importer's market would be the subject of antidumping investigations by the importer. However, since economies would under this notion be able to use their own concept of origin for antidumping investigations without considering the harmonized RoO, they would also be able to define "exporter" in broader terms than allowed by the multilateral non-preferential rules, and hence target every economy through which a good has passed with the same antidumping investigation–rather than targeting only the economy that RoO define as the economy origin. Applying harmonized RoO in anti-dumping actions is resisted also because of the changes that this would require the member to make in their respective domestic anti-dumping legislations.

A related problem is circumvention of anti-dumping actions. It takes place when an exporter, in an effort to circumvent an antidumping measure by an importer, exports dumped components to the importer's market and produces the final good within the borders of the importer. Alternatively, the exporter ships dumped goods to a third economy and proceeds to export from the third economy to the importer, thus subjecting the third economy to antidumping action by the importer, rather than being itself the subject. Harmonized RoO would allow for resolving numerous cases of circumvention, particularly of goods shipped from Asia to the US or EU markets, and help deter anticircumvention activities (Thorstensen 2002). However, that RoO would do so also gives rise to opposition to harmonizing them.

In sum, that the non-preferential RoO continue contested still today, eight years after the harmonization work was launched, attests to the complexity of interests seeking to affect the definition of origin around the world. Although the CRO has been able to define a RoO for most products, it has been compelled to send the most complex and politically sensitive pending issues–ones that cannot be resolved at the technical level–to the highest instance of the WTO negotiations, the General Council, in order for the member economy ambassadors to reach a political solution. Besides raising the profile of RoO talks, various ways are being envisioned at the WTO to facilitate the resolution of the pending issues. The first is to simply devise ambiguous language that leaves some room for subjective interpretations yet establishes an effective regulation. Two, the difference between the EC and the United States in RoO in machinery can be solved by adopting both types of rules as interchangeable alternatives to govern a given product. Third, the Doha Round could help engender solutions to the bigger issues hampering the finalization of the harmonization program, such as antidumping and the definition of trademarks. Fourth, RoO are a particularly prominent area for compromises and logrolling: negotiators can achieve gains in some sectors by yielding in others. A clear prioritization of issues by each member economy would help produce a productive give-and-take bargaining process.

7.2. *Harmonizing Preferential RoO: A Boost to Open Regionalism*

7.2.1. *Problems with the multi-regime RoO world*

Less well-known than the harmonization of non-preferential RoO are ARO's provisions on preferential RoO enshrined in the Common Declaration with Regard to Preferential Rules of Origin. The declaration spells out the intent by the ARO signatories to bring also preferential RoO under a harmonization program and use the harmonized non-preferential RoO as the blueprint in the process. Thus far, however, preferential PTA RoO have fallen under the responsibility of the WTO Committee on Regional Trade Agreements rather than being dealt with by the CRO. For their part, GSP RoO are the responsibility of the Committee on Trade and Development.

To be sure, some might argue that the entrenchment of the preferential RoO regimes since the mid-1990s, the ostensive *de facto* convergence in RoO regimes, and the overall lowering of tariffs around the world have made harmonization of non-preferential RoO increasingly irrelevant. However, we posit that there are two particularly compelling reasons for pursuing the harmonization of preferential RoO.

First, non-preferential RoO, if used as the benchmark for harmonizing preferential RoO, are, as seen above, less restrictive and complex than any of the main RoO regimes. As such, replacing the existing RoO in most preferential schemes would enhance the prospects for open regionalism around the world. In forthcoming work, we seek to estimate the impact of ROO in trade should all preferential RoO be set at the levels of non-preferential RoO.

Second, even subtle differences among RoO regimes can result in the formation of trade-and investment-diverting hubs. Even in a simple world with two main and rather similar RoO regimes, FTAA tailored after NAFTA and PANEURO models, three important differences would continue affecting producers and exporters in both hubs and in particularly in economies that are spokes of both of the hubs.

One, as noted above, a central difference between the PANEURO and NAFTA models is the type of RoO governing some manufacturing sectors, particularly machinery, where the PANEURO model employs a stand-alone VC rule, while NAFTA model relies on its staple RoO of CTC, often accompanied by VC. This difference can have important effects on economic decisions. For example, a small Chilean exporter seeking to access both FTAA and EU markets and who lacks, as is often the case for a small economy, intermediate products in Chile will likely have to choose between producing to either market rather than to both given the difference in RoO: switching production patterns and outsourcing relations according to the RoO regime may simply be too cumbersome and costly. A major European car company might present another example. Such a company would likely be deterred from the FTAA market should the restrictiveness of RoO rise to levels above 50 to 60 percent value content, as the remaining share of outsourcing is done in Europe. Thus, in order to qualify for FTAA-conferred preferential treatment, European car companies would have to create outsourcing linkages in the Americas and/or encourage their European suppliers to set up shop in the Western Hemisphere; however, both options feature a time lag which can give a crucial foothold to US car companies in the continent.

The second major difference between the two poles is the use of cumulation; the PANEURO model has gained prominence to a great extent thanks to the lure of cumulation, while the PTAs in the Americas–and PTAs based on the NAFTA model–remain disconnected. However, the FTAA will in practice result in one major cumulation zone in the Western Hemisphere. Indeed, this prospect could stir some concerns of bipolar trade diversion–growth in intra-bloc trade within the American and Europe at the expense of the rest of the world–which is a real possibility as long as the pole members have restrictive RoO, positive MFN tariffs *vis-à-vis* the ROW, and/or are reachable only by paying high transportation costs.

Third, the differences between the PANEURO's two-step certification method and NAFTA's self-certification will likely remain. The EU is planning to facilitate certification by moving to electronically-issued certificates; however, the extra step a potential exporter must take in certifying origin through a governmental entity, particularly in some of the EU's partner economies where the costs of obtaining a certificate are notably high, may not only undercut exporters' incentives to seek PTA-conferred preferential treatment *per se*, but tilt export decisions in favor of PTAs operating on the self-certificate.

7.2.2. *Counteracting the Splintering of the RoO Panorama: Possibilities and Prospects*

While RoO *per se* in any given RoO regime are not necessarily "bad" for sound economic decisions, restrictive RoO can be. Furthermore, the existing differences in the restrictiveness of product-specific RoO and the regime-wide facilitation mechanisms between RoO regimes can and do make a difference in the decisions of economic actors in favor of less efficient outsourcing and investment strategies even in a simplified bi- or tripolar RoO world. But how can the potential frictions created by stringent RoO and by the differences between RoO regimes be reduced? How can entrepreneurs continue importing inputs from the cheapest sources, firms exploit cross-border economies of scale at lowest costs, and multinational companies make sweeping investment decisions based on economic efficiency rather than distortionary policies? What are the best ways to counter the development of trade- and investment diverting hubs in favor of globally free flow of goods, services, and investment?

Abolishing RoO altogether would certainly be the best and simplest means to counteract the impact of RoO. Another way to relegate RoO to irrelevance is by bringing MFN tariffs to zero globally. However, since these options are hardly politically palatable in the near future, a third possibility would be to harmonize preferential RoO at the global level. This would ensure that at least the required production patterns in a given sector would remain similar across export markets.[36] A further measure to accompany the harmonization work is the establishment of a multilateral mechanism to monitor member economies' application of preferential and non-preferential RoO alike in order to guarantee to minimize the politicization of RoO and their uses for distributional purposes.

What are the prospects for harmonization of preferential RoO? To be sure, harmonization would be no simple endeavor given the differences in the types of RoO around the world: even slight differences can be difficult to overcome due to political resistance by sectors benefiting from status quo. Meanwhile, it is not clear that a similarly strong exporter lobby would materialize to voice demands for harmonization. Perhaps most importantly, both the EU and the United States would likely in principle be reluctant to adopt each other's RoO. Both would also hold the practical concerns of the counterpart's seeking RoO that would allow it to transship *via* the common PTA partners, such as Mexico, to the other party's market.

However, the adoption of a globally uniform preferential RoO regime might not be as daunting as it might initially seem. There are four sources of optimism. First, the WTO members have already been able to sit down and compromise on harmonized non-preferential RoO–which not only evinces the existence of at least some reservoir of political will to tackle RoO, but also provides an immediately available and globally agreed RoO blueprint for harmonizing preferential RoO. And not only are non-preferential RoO negotiated and readily available as a model, but they make a good model: overall, they are less restrictive of commerce and less complex to implement than either the NAFTA- or PANEURO-type RoO. Some non-preferential RoO might, to be sure, require tightening if translated into preferential RoO in order for products to remain sufficiently differentiated for keeping PTAs what they are constructed to be, geographical areas of selective liberalization where deeper trade preferences are conferred to the partner economies than to the rest of the world. Moreover,

[36] Of course, qualifying for preferential treatment would even in the presence of harmonized RoO require tailoring outsourcing relations and production to the demands of the RoO of the PTA conferring the preferences. For example, a Chilean firm faced with a CH requirement in both the EU and US market would have to verify that when exporting to the EU, the CH is met by production in Chile (or in the Chile-EU FTA area). Similarly, should the product be governed by a 60% RVC rule, Chilean firm would need to ensure that the 60 percent arises from the EU-Chile FTA area when exporting to the EU, and from the Chile-US FTA area when exporting to the United States. The requirements would nonetheless be identical; hence, should all inputs and processes originate in Chile to begin with, the exporter would not have to make any adjustments according to the export market–as he/she would in the face of different RoO in the two markets. Meanwhile, harmonization would also reduce the time and effort required to learn about the RoO specific to a given export market.

loosening RoO markedly in some sectors to the levels of non-preferential RoO could risk a political backlash against PTAs by sensitive sectors. The handful of such potentially necessary sectoral exceptions notwithstanding, the ready availability of globally harmonized and relatively loose RoO should be fully exploited for harmonization of preferential RoO.

The second reason why harmonization of preferential RoO might not be farfetched is that preferential RoO would likely prove simpler to agree on than non-preferential RoO. Non-preferential RoO involve tracking down the production process all the way to the party where the good originates (*i.e.*, it is not enough to establish whether the exporter economy is the economy of origin or not as on the preferential RoO front), and can thus involve a great number of interested parties for a given rule in the negotiation process. Preferential RoO, meanwhile, have implications only to the exporter and the PTA partner: the good either originates in the PTA partner or it does not, with the "true" and ultimate origin in the latter case being immaterial. Moreover, unlike non-preferential RoO that are employed for the application of numerous other trade policy instruments, preferential RoO have few purposes beyond arbitrating markets access of goods to the PTA space. As such, their negotiation would unlikely involve as much consideration of the other WTO agreements as the harmonization of non-preferential RoO does.

Third, the growing attention at the WTO on PTAs and preferential RoO should propel constructive proposals for RoO that are most conducive to the march toward globally unfettered flow of commerce. For the first time in its history, the WTO Committee on Regional Trade Agreements has decided to consider RoO a "systemic" issue, as opposed both to individual PTA-issues such as prior considerations of the PANEURO system, and to issues that–whether systemic or individual–are not being prioritized by the CRTA. The concomitant growing interest by policy analysts and academia in RoO will add to the understanding of the operation and effects of different types of RoO.

Fourth, advances in Trade-Related Investment Measures (TRIMS) can help advance the harmonization of RoO, should RoO be considered, as they rightfully can and should be, as policies affecting investment decisions (Thorstensen 2002). Like TRIMS, RoO can be employed strategically as an incentive to attract investment and encourage exports–and exports with high local value. A sturdier multilateral regulatory framework on investment policies could help curb the strategic, trade- and investment-distorting uses of RoO.

In sum, harmonization of preferential RoO would be the most attainable means at present to counteract RoO's distortionary impact on trade and investment flows. Political will to negotiate preferential RoO will not be easy to muster in light of the entrenchment of RoO regime models and the interests supporting them, and simply due to the very full agendas of the WTO members. Of course, less problematic would be a lack of political will stemming from major advances in the reduction of tariffs at the multilateral level that would render preferential RoO increasingly irrelevant as arbitrators of trade and investment flows.

8. Conclusion

This paper has sought to cast light on the economy and the future evolution of global RoO panorama, and to present ways to compare RoO regimes by their levels of restrictiveness. We have argued that multilateral approaches to harmonize preferential RoO are increasingly pressing in the face of (1) the proliferation of PTAs, each with somewhat distinct RoO; and (2) the recent empirical evidence suggest strongly that restrictive RoO can and do divert trade and undermine the trade-creating potential of PTAs; and (3) the potential breach by the various RoO regimes of the tacit prohibition of "other restrictive regulations of commerce" put forth by Article XXIV of the GATT.

The negotiators of the Doha Trade Round should decisively tackle RoO as a distortionary trade and investment policy instrument, and to do so in four concrete ways. First, they should provide a forceful push for completing the task of harmonizing non-preferential RoO. Completing the harmonization process is all the more compelling in the face of growth of global commerce and the increasing fragmentation of global production, both of which would thrive under clear and uniform set of rules. Second, the Doha negotiators should launch the process of *de jure* harmonization of preferential rules of origin. The relatively high levels of restrictiveness of the main existing RoO regimes and the differences between them pose unnecessary policy hurdles to rational economic decisions and limit the potential of exporters to benefit from operating on multiple trade front simultaneously. As such, RoO hamper consumers access to the best goods at the lowest prices. Third, the Round should forge in a multilateral mechanism to monitor and enforce the transparent application of preferential and non-preferential RoO alike. And fourth, RoO should be incorporated in the TRIMs negotiations.

Preferential RoO matter only as long as there are MFN tariffs. Thus, the key to undercutting preferential RoO's negative trade effects lies ultimately in the success of multilateral liberalization. Should the multilateral trade rounds result in deep MFN tariff lowering and the proliferation of PTAs engender a dynamic of competitive liberalization worldwide, the importance of preferential RoO as gatekeepers of commerce would automatically begin to fade.

References

1. Appiah, Alex Jameson. 1999. "Applied General Equilibrium Model of North American Integration with Rules of Origin." PhD Dissertation. Simon Fraser University (Canada).
2. Asociación Latinoamericana de Integración (ALADI). 2002. *Inventario sobre Regímenes de Origen.* Montevideo: Secretaría General (julio).
3. Augier, Patricia, Michael Gasiorek, and Charles Lai-Tong. 2004. "The Impact of Rules of Origin on Trade Flows." In Cadot, Olivier, Antoni Estevadeordal, Akiko Suwa-Eisenmann, and Thierry Verdier, eds. *The Origin of Goods: A Conceptual and Empirical Assessment of Rules of Origin in PTAs.* Washington: IADB and CEPR (forthcoming).
4. Bergsten, C. Fred. 1997. "Open Regionalism." In C. Fred Bergsten, ed. *Whither APEC: The Progress to Date and Agenda for the Future.* Washington: Institute of International Economics.
5. Brenton, Paul and Miriam Manchin. 2002. "Making EU Trade Agreements Work: The Role of Rules of Origin." CEPS Working Document No. 183. Brussels: Centre for European Policy Studies (March).
6. Cadot, Olivier, Antoni Estevadeordal, Akiko Suwa-Eisenmann, and Thierry Verdier, eds. *The Origin of Goods: A Conceptual and Empirical Assessment of Rules of Origin in PTAs.* Washington: IADB and CEPR (forthcoming).
7. Cadot, Olivier, Antoni Estevadeordal and Akiko Suwa-Eisenmann. 2004. "An Assessment of Rules of Origin: The Case of NAFTA." In Cadot, Olivier, Antoni Estevadeordal, Akiko Suwa-Eisenmann, and Thierry Verdier, eds. *The Origin of Goods: A Conceptual and Empirical Assessment of Rules of Origin in PTAs.* Washington: IADB and CEPR (forthcoming).
8. Cadot, Oliver, Jaime de Melo, Antoni Estevadeordal, Akiko Suwa-Eisenmann and Bolormaa Tumurchudur. 2002. "Assessing the Effect of NAFTA's Rules of Origin." Mimeo.
9. Devlin, Robert and Antoni Estevadeordal. 2001. "What's New in the New Regionalism in the Americas?" In Victor Bulmer-Thomas, ed. *Regional Integration in Latin America and the Caribbean: The Political Economy of Open Regionalism.* London: ILAS.
10. Driessen, Bart and Folkert Graafsma. 1999. "The EC's Wonderland: An Overview of the Pan-European Harmonised Origin Protocols." *Journal of World Trade* 33, 4.
11. Duttagupta, Rupa. 2000. "Intermediate Inputs and Rules of Origin: Implications for Welfare and Viability of Free Trade Agreements." PhD Dissertation, University of Maryland, College Park.
12. Duttagupta, Rupa and Arvind Panagariya. 2001. "Free Trade Areas and Rules of Origin: Economics and Politics." Seminar Paper.
13. Estevadeordal, Antoni. 2000. "Negotiating Preferential Market Access: The Case of the North American Free Trade Agreement." *Journal of World Trade* 34, 1 (February).
14. Estevadeordal, Antoni and Eric Miller. 2002. "Rules of Origin and the Pattern of Trade between U.S. and Canada." Washington, DC: Integration, Trade and Hemispheric Issues Division, Inter-American Development Bank.

15. Estevadeordal, Antoni and Kati Suominen. 2003. "Rules of Origin in FTAs in Europe and in the Americas: Issues and Implications for the EU-Mercosur Inter-Regional Association Agreement." In Valladão, Alfredo G.A. and Roberto Bouzas (eds.), *Market Access for Goods & Services in the EU-Mercosur Negotiations*, Paris: Chaire Mercosur de Sciences Po. Also published in 2004 as INTAL-ITD Working Paper 15, Washington, DC: Inter-American Development Bank.
16. ________. 2004a. "Rules of Origin: A World Map and Trade Effects." In Cadot, Olivier, Antoni Estevadeordal, Akiko Suwa-Eisenmann, and Thierry Verdier, eds. *The Origin of Goods: A Conceptual and Empirical Assessment of Rules of Origin in PTAs*. Washington: IADB and CEPR (forthcoming).
17. ________. 2004b. "Rules of Origin in the World Trading System and Proposals for Multilateral Harmonization." Article submitted to *World Trade Review*.
18. Falvey, Rod and Geoff Reed. 2000. "Rules of Origin as Commercial Policy Instruments." Research Paper No. 2000/18. Centre for Research on Globalization and Labor Markets, University of Nottingham.
19. Flatters, Frank. 2002. "SADC Rules of Origin: Undermining Regional Free Trade." Paper prepared for the TIPS Forum, Johannesburg, 9-11 September.
20. ________ and Robert Kirk. 2004. "Rules of Origin as Tools of Development? Some Lessons from SADC." In Cadot, Olivier, Antoni Estevadeordal, Akiko Suwa-Eisenmann, and Thierry Verdier, eds. *The Origin of Goods: A Conceptual and Empirical Assessment of Rules of Origin in PTAs*. Washington: IADB and CEPR (forthcoming).
21. Garay, Luis and Rafael Cornejo. 2002. "Metodología para el Análisis de Régimenes de Origen: Aplicación en el Caso de las Américas." INTAL-ITD-STA Documento de Trabajo 8. Washington, DC: Inter-American Development Bank.
22. Garay, Luis Jorge and Antoni Estevadeordal. 1996. "Protection, Preferential Tariff Elimination and Rules of Origin in the Americas." *Integration and Trade 1*.
23. Graham, Edward M. and Christopher Wilkie. 1998. "Regional Economic Agreements and Multinational Firms: The Investment Provisions of the NAFTA." In Hafiz Mirza, ed. *Global Competitive Strategies in the New World Economy*. Cheltenham, UK; Northampton, MA: Edward Elgar.
24. Herin, Jan. 1986. "Rules of Origin and Differences between Tariff Levels in EFTA and in the EC." EFTA Occasional Paper No. 13. Geneva (February).
25. Hirsch, Moshe. 2002. "International Trade Law, Political Economy and Rules of Origin: A Plea for a Reform of the WTO Regime on Rules of Origin." *Journal of World Trade* 36, 2 (April).
26. James, William (2004), 'Rules of Origin, Tariff Discrimination and Trade Diversion: A Case Study of Asian Textiles and Apparel Exports', in Cadot, Olivier, Antoni Estevadeordal, Akiko Suwa-Eisenmann, and Thierry Verdier (eds.), *The Origin of Goods: A Conceptual and Empirical Assessment of Rules of Origin in PTAs*, Washington: IADB and CEPR.
27. Jensen-Moran, Jeri. 1996. "Trade Battles as Investment Wars: The Coming Rules of Origin Debate." *The Washington Quarterly* 19, 1 (Winter).
28. Ju, Jiandong and Kala Krishna. 1998. "Firm Behavior and Market Access in a Free Trade Area With Rules of Origin." NBER Working Paper No. 6857. Cambridge, MA: NBER.

29. Koskinen, Matti. 1983. "Excess Documentation Costs as a Non-Tariff Measure: An Empirical Analysis of the Effects of Documentation Costs." Working Paper. Swedish School of Economics and Business Administration.
30. Krishna, Kala and Anne O. Kruger. 1995. "Implementing Free Trade Areas: Rules of Origin and Hidden Protection." In Alan Deardorff, James Levinsohn and Robert Stern, eds. *New Directions in Trade Theory*. Ann Arbor: University of Michigan Press.
31. Krishna, Kala. 2002. "Understanding Rule of Origin." Mimeo (15 December).
32. Krueger, Anne O. 1993. "Free Trade Agreements as Protectionist Devices: Rules of Origin." NBER Working Paper No. 4352. Cambridge, MA: NBER.
33. ________. 1995. "Free Trade Agreements versus Customs Unions." NBER Working Paper No. W5084. Cambridge, MA: NBER.
34. Lloyd, Peter J. 1997. "Towards a Framework of Trade and Competition Policy." *Asia-Pacific Economic Review* 3, 2 (August).
35. ________. 2001a. "Rules of Origin and Fragmentation of Trade." In Leonard K. Cheng and Henryk Kierzkowski, eds. *Global Production and Trade in East Asia*. Boston, MA: Kluwer Academic Publishers.
36. ________. 2001b. "Country of Origin in the Global Economy." Paper delivered at PECC XIV, Hong Kong, 28-30 November 2001.
37. Organization for Economic Cooperation and Development (OECD). 2002. "The Relationship between Regional Trade Agreements and Multilateral Trading System: The Role of Rules of Origin." Working Party of the Trade Committee (19 June).
38. Reyna, Jimmie V. 1995. *Passport to North American Trade: Rules of Origin and Customs Procedures under NAFTA*. Colorado Springs: Shepard's/ McGraw-Hill, Inc.
39. Rodriguez, Peter. 2001. "Rules of Origin with Multistage Production." *The World Economy* 24, 1.
40. Roos, Alfred. 1996. "Rules of Origin in the EC Context: The Origin(al) Approach of the EC Commission." In Kees Jan Kuilwijk and Robert Wright, eds. *European Trade and Industry in the 21st Century: Future Directions in EC Law and Policy*. Beuningen, the Netherlands: Nexed Editions.
41. Scollay, Robert. 1997. "Preferential Rules of Origin, Regional Trading Arrangements and APEC." *Asia-Pacific Economic Review* 3, 2 (August).
42. Soloaga, Isidro and Alan Winters. 2001. "Regionalism in the Nineties: What Effect on Trade?" *North American Journal of Economics and Finance* 12.
43. Stephenson, Sherry. 1997. "The Economic Impact of Rules of Origin in the Asia-Pacific Region." *Asia-Pacific Economic Review* 3, 2 (August).
44. Suominen, Kati. 2004. "Selective Liberalization in Response to Globalization:
45. Rules of Origin as Determinants of Market Access Provisions in PTAs." *Integration and Trade* (forthcoming issue).
46. Thorstensen, Vera. 2002. "Regras de origem: as negociações e implicações para a política de comércio exterior." *Revista Brasileira de Comércio Exterior* 15, 73 (outubro-dezembro).
47. Wonnacott, Paul. 1996. "Beyond NAFTA–The Design of a Free Trade Agreement of the Americas." In J. Bhagwati and A. Panagariya, eds., *The Economics of Preferential Trading Agreements*. Washington, D.C.: the AEI Press, pp. 79-107.
48. World Trade Organization (WTO). 2002a. "Rules of Origin Regimes in Regional Trade Agreements." Committee on Regional Trade Agreements (5 April).

49. ________. 2002b. "Compendium of Issues Related to Regional Trade Agreements." Negotiating Group on Rules (August).

50. ________.2003. "Rules of Origin." Various Documents. *http://www.wto.org/english/tratop_e/roi_e/roi_e.htm*

APPENDIX I

Estevadeordal's (2000) observation rule yields a RoO index as follows:

$y = 1$ if $y^* \leq CI$
$y = 2$ if $CI < y^* \leq CS$
$y = 3$ if $CS < y^* \leq CS$ and VC
$y = 4$ if CS and $VC < y^* \leq CH$
$y = 5$ if $CH < y^* \leq CH$ and VC
$y = 6$ if CH and $VC < y^* \leq CC$
$y = 7$ if $CC < y^* \leq CC$ and TECH

where y^* is the latent level of restrictiveness of RoO (rather than the observed level of restrictiveness); CI is change of tariff classification at he level of tariff item (8-10 digits), CS is change at the level of sub-heading (6-digit HS), CH is change at the level of heading (4 digits), and CC is change at the level of chapter (2 digits HS); VC is a value content criterion; and TECH is a technical requirement.

There are a number of modifications to the observation rule in the case of those EU RoO for which no CTC is specified. First, RoO based on the import content rule are equated to a change in heading (value 4) if the content requirement allows up to 50 percent of non-originating inputs of the ex-works price of the product. Value 5 is assigned when the share of non-originating inputs is below 50 percent, as well as when an import content criterion is combined with a technical requirement. Second, RoO featuring an exception alone is assigned value 1 if exception concerns a heading or a number of headings, and 2 if the exception concerns a chapter or a number of chapters. Third, RoO based on the wholly-obtained criterion are assigned value 7.

The observation rule is admittedly somewhat crude for accounting for the subtleties of the EU RoO as it does not account for the "soft" CTC criterion used by the EU. However, it does allow for comparing the EU and NAFTA RoO regimes.

In the case of the non-preferential RoO, a RoO that requires change in item or a change in item and an exception and/or TECH is coded as 1. When a change in item plus VC is required, a 2 would be assigned; however, empirically, there are no such cases.

In subheadings where an agreement on the RoO has yet to be reached, up to four RoO proposals are taken into account and the averages formed on the basis of these; in the handful of categories where there are more than four proposals, the four proposals included into the calculations are selected so as to capture the range of different proposals and restrictiveness values.

APPENDIX IIA. PTAs included in the study, by year of entry into force and full name

PTA	Entry year	Full name/type
CACM	1961	Central American Common Market
CARIOM	1973	Caribbean Community
EU-ICELAND	1973	
EU-NORWAY	1973	
EU-SWITZERLAND	1973	
BANGKOK AGREEMENT	1976	
LAIA	1981	Latin American Integration Association
SPARTECA	1981	South Pacific Regional Trade and Economic Cooperation Agreement
ANZCERTA	1983	Australia-New Zealand Closer Economic Relations Trade Agreement
GULF CC	1983	Gulf Cooperation Council
US-ISRAEL	1985	
ECOWAS Trade Liberalisaztion Scheme	1990	Economic Community of West African States
NAMIBIA-ZIMBABWE	1992	
EFTA-CZECH REPUBLIC	1992	PANEURO
EU-CZECH REPUBLIC	1992	PANEURO
EU-HUNGARY	1992	PANEURO
EU-SLOVAK REPUBLIC	1992	PANEURO
EFTA-SLOVAK REPUBLIC	1992	PANEURO
EFTA-TURKEY	1992	PANEURO
EU-POLAND	1992	PANEURO
EU-BULGARIA	1993	PANEURO
AFTA	1993	ASEAN Free Trade Area
CEFTA	1993	Central European Free Trade Area/PANEURO
EFTA-BULGARIA	1993	PANEURO
EFTA-ISRAEL	1993	PE
EFTA-HUNGARY	1993	PANEURO
EFTA-POLAND	1993	PANEURO
EFTA-ROMANIA	1993	PANEURO
EU-ROMANIA	1993	PANEURO
BAFTA	1994	Baltic Free Trade Agreement/ PANEURO

APPENDIX IIA. PTAs included in the study, by year of entry into force and full name–Continued

PTA	Entry year	Full name/type
COMESA	1994	Common Market for Eastern and Southern Africa
EEA	1994	European Economic Area/ PANEURO
NAFTA	1994	North American Free Trade Agreement
GEORGIA-RUSSIA	1994	
G3	1995	Group of Three
EFTA-SLOVENIA	1995	PANEURO
EU-LATVIA	1995	PANEURO
EU-LITHUANIA	1995	PANEURO
EU-ESTONIA	1995	PANEURO
MEXICO-BOLIVIA	1995	
MEXICO-COSTA RICA	1995	
ROMANIA-MOLDAVIA	1995	
KYRGYZ REPUBLIC-KAZAKHSTAN	1995	
EFTA-ESTONIA	1996	PANEURO
EFTA-LATVIA	1996	PANEURO
EFTA-LITHUANIA	1996	PANEURO
SLOVENIA-LATVIA	1996	PANEURO
MERCOSUR-CHILE	1996	
GEORGIA-UKRAINE	1996	
GEORGIA-AZERBAIJAN	1996	
CZECH REPUBLIC-LITHUANIA	1997	PANEURO
POLAND-LITHUANIA	1997	PANEURO
SLOVAK REPUBLIC-ISRAEL	1997	PANEURO
SLOVENIA-ESTONIA	1997	PANEURO
CZECH REPUBLIC-ISRAEL	1997	PE
CZECH REPUBLIC-LATVIA	1997	PANEURO
SLOVAK REPUBLIC-LATVIA	1997	PANEURO
SLOVAK REPUBLIC-LITHUANIA	1997	PANEURO
SLOVENIA-LITHUANIA	1997	PANEURO
TURKEY-ISRAEL	1997	PE
CANADA-CHILE	1997	
CANADA-ISRAEL	1997	
MERCOSUR-BOLIVIA	1997	
CZECH REPUBLIC-ESTONIA	1998	PANEURO
HUNGARY-TURKEY	1998	PANEURO
ROMANIA-TURKEY	1998	PANEURO
SLOVAK REPUBLIC-ESTONIA	1998	PANEURO
SLOVAK REPUBLIC-TURKEY	1998	PANEURO
TURKEY-LITHUANIA	1998	PANEURO
CZECH REPUBLIC-TURKEY	1998	PANEURO

APPENDIX IIA. PTAs included in the study, by year of entry into force and full name–Continued

PTA	Entry year	Full name/type
HUNGARY-ISRAEL	1998	PE
POLAND-ISRAEL	1998	PE
SLOVENIA-CROATIA	1998	PE
SLOVENIA-ISRAEL	1998	PE
MEXICO-NICARAGUA	1998	
EU-TUNISIA	1998	
GEORGIA-ARMENIA	1998	
EU-SLOVENIA	1999	PANEURO
POLAND-LATVIA	1999	PANEURO
CHILE-MEXICO	1999	
TURKEY-BULGARIA	1999	
EFTA-MOROCCO	1999	
GEORGIA-KAZAKHSTAN	1999	
HUNGARY-LITHUANIA	2000	PANEURO
POLAND-TURKEY	2000	PANEURO
TURKEY-LATVIA	2000	PANEURO
TURKEY-SLOVENIA	2000	PANEURO
HUNGARY-LATVIA	2000	PANEURO
TURKEY-SLOVENIA	2000	PANEURO
EU-ISRAEL	2000	PE
SADC	2000	Southern African Development Community
EU-MEXICO	2000	
EU-SOUTH AFRICA	2000	
MEXICO-ISRAEL	2000	
EU-MOROCCO	2000	
NEW ZEALAND-SINGAPORE	2001	
PTAs not included in the gravity model (due to entering into force later than 1 January 2000)		
US-JORDAN	2001	
EFTA-MEXICO	2001	
HUNGARY-ESTONIA	2001	PANEURO
EFTA-CROATIA	2002	PE
EU-CROATIA	2002	PE
CACM-CHILE	2002	
JSEPA	2002	Japan-Singapore Economic Partnership Agreement
CHILE-COSTA RICA	2002	
CANADA-COSTA RICA	2002	
SAFTA	2003	Singapore-Australia Free Trade Agreement

EU-CHILE	2003	
EFTA-SINGAPORE	2003	
CHILE-SOUTH KOREA	2003	
US-CHILE	2003	
PTAs treated as "Perfect" CUs		
EC/EU	1958	European Community-European Union
EFTA	1960	European Free Trade Area
EU-MALTA	1971	
EU-CYPRUS	1973	
EU-TURKEY	1996	
FSRs	1999	CU of four Former Soviet Republics

Notes: The PANEURO system was launched in 1997. RoO protocols of FTAs forged prior to that by the EU were revised to be compatible with the PANEURO model.

Note: PE indicates RoO protocols that are basically identical to the PANEURO model I product – specific RoO, but diverge from the PANEURO model in some regime-wide provisions, most notably by not being part of the PANEURO system of diagonal cumulation.

Entry dates obtained from the World Trade Organization of American States.

APPENDIX IIb. Selected PTAs by member economy

PTA	Members
AFTA	Brunei, Darussalam, Cambodia, Indonesia, Laos, Malaysia, Myanmar, Philippines, Singapore, Thailand, Vietnam
ANZCERTA	Australia, New Zealand
BAFTA	Estonia, Latvia, Lithuania
BANGKOK AGREEMENT	Bangladesh, China, India, Republic of Korea, Laos, Sri Lanka
CACM	Costa Rica, El Salvador, Guatemala, Honduras, Nicaragua
CARICOM	Antigua and Barbuda, the Bahamas, Barbados, Belize, Dominica, Grenada, Guyana, Haiti, Jamaica, Montserrat, St. Lucia, St. Kitts and Nevis, St. Vincent and the Grenadines, Suriname, Trinidad and Tobago
CEFTA	Bulgaria, Czech Republic, Hungary, Poland, Romania, Slovak Republic, Slovenia
COMESA	Angola, Burundi, Comoros, Democratic Republic of Congo, Djibouti, Egypt, Eritrea, Ethiopia, Kenya, Madagascar, Malawi, Mauritius, Namibia, Rwanda, Seychelles, Sudan, Swaziland, Uganda, Zambia, Zimbabwe
EEA	EU, Iceland, Liechtenstein, Norway
EFTA	Iceland, Liechtenstein, Norway, Switzerland
ECOWAS	Benin, Burkina Faso, Cabo Verde, Ivory Coast, Gambia, Ghana, Guinea, Guinea Bissau, Mali, Liberia, Niger, Nigeria, Senegal, Sierra Leone, Togo, Namibia, Zimbabwe
FSRs	Belarus, Kazakhstan, Kyrgyz Republic, Russia

APPENDIX IIb. Selected PTAs by member economy–Continued

PTA	**Members**
G3	Mexico, Colombia, Venezuela
GULF CC	Bahrain, Kuwait, Oman, Qatar, Saudi Arabia, United Arab Emirates
JSEPA	Japan, Singapore
LAIA	Argentina, Bolivia, Brazil, Chile, Colombia, Cuba, Ecuador, Mexico, Paraguay, Peru, Uruguay, Venezuela
MERCOSUR	Argentina, Brazil, Paraguay, Uruguay
NAFTA	US, Canada, Mexico
SADC	Angola, Botswana, Lesotho, Malawi, Mauritius, Mozambique, Namibia, South Africa, Swaziland, Tanzania, Zambia, Zimbabwe
SAFTA	Singapore, Australia
SPARTECA	Australia, New Zealand, Cook Islands, Fiji, Kiribati, Marshall Islands, Micronesia, Nauru, Niue, Papua New Guinea, Solomon Islands, Tonga, Tuvalu, Vanuatu, Western Samoa

THE REASONS FOR AND THE IMPACT OF ANTIDUMPING PROTECTION: THE CASE OF PEOPLE'S REPUBLIC OF CHINA

Tianshu Chu

East-West Center

Thomas J. Prusa

Rutgers University

1. Introduction

Over the past few decades, the liberalization in international trade has progressed at rapid speed. Many traditional forms of barriers to trade, most importantly tariffs and quotas, have been reduced worldwide. Accompanying this great reduction in trade barriers has also been a great expansion in trade. Trade to GDP ratio has increased 86.1 percent from 1950 to 1990, and a large proportion is likely to be accounted by the reduction in trade barriers. (Bergoeing and Kehoe 2003). While tariffs and quotas have been and continue to be reduced, another type of trade barrier, antidumping, is being used more and more frequently as a measure of protection. (Prusa and Skeath, 2002). Further complicating the role of antidumping is the fact that the economies who are being affected by antidumping protection has changed over time; traditionally antidumping was used by and against developed economies, but over the past decade developing economies have emerged as frequent targets (and users) of antidumping (Prusa, 2001; Fu, 1997).

In this paper, we focus on the case of China, to explore the characteristics, the reasons for and implications of antidumping. China initiated trade liberalization about 25 years ago, and since has observed an accelerated increase in exports. Coincidental with its increased exports, China has also become the largest targeting economy of antidumping (AD) trade disputes. There are many aspects of AD that explain why China is more susceptible to antidumping, including its non-market economy (NME) status. Yet, as suggested by Blonigen (2003), even after controlling for all these unfavorable factors, China is subject to an inexplicably large number of antidumping attacks.

The literature on antidumping against China includes several articles that review the use of AD by EU (Vermulst and Graafsma, 1992; Liu and Vandenbussche, 2002; Mai, 2002; Eeckhout, 1997; Wang, 1999), and two that examine the United States AD cases (McGee, 1999; Kao, 1990). A recent working paper by Messerlin (2002) also discusses the characteristics of AD activity against China.

Our paper builds on the previous studies, and make new contributions in analyzing the reasons for China being so broadly and intensively targeted. In particular, the domestic characteristics of exports structure and industrial structures are examined. Our analysis also reveals that foreign direct investment (FDI) may be a significant factor explaining AD cases against China. There is also evidence that low concentration ratios in Chinese industries have contributed to the competitive price and low profit margins.

The next section discusses the characteristics of AD cases targeting Chinese imports. We then analyze the reasons for AD activity against China and discuss some implications for the Chinese economy. We make a few concluding comments in the final section.

2. Characteristics of AD Cases against China

We would like to establish a set of stylized facts about AD targeting China, focusing on the size, trend, intensity, and broadness.

2.1. *The Size and the Trend*

As it is well known, China is the largest target economy for AD cases. The total number of AD cases targeting China reached 457 by the end of 2001, making China's total only slightly lower that all of the EU economies combined. If current trends continue, China will surpass the EU in the near future. China is easily the largest target when compared with any individual economy.

In Table 1, we present the time series since 1980 of the top six economies affected by AD investigations. The United States was the top target economy during the early 1980s; it was then replaced by Japan who remained the most targeted economy during the rest of the 1980s. Since 1992, China has been the top targeted economy every year. Not only is it the largest affected economy, but also the number of cases against China easily surpasses the level of the United States and Japan when they were the leading targets. Overall even though China only become a significant target in the past ten years, its total number of AD cases has surpassed the United States and Japan, and China has emerged as the largest targeted economy.

Not only is the number of AD cases targeting China high, but also the trend is positive and increasing at a rapid rate. The number of cases against China was relatively small in the early to mid 1980s; since 1988, however, there has been a

Table 1. Top six antidumping targets, 1980-2001

	CHINA (PRC)	USA	SOUTH KOREA	JAPAN	USSR (FORMER)	CHINESE TAIPEI	OTHER	TOTAL
1980	1	20	.	5	.	.	43	69
1981	1	11	5	9	1	4	62	93
1982	8	20	17	19	.	5	148	217
1983	8	16	12	21	.	10	106	173
1984	6	13	9	19	2	7	95	151
1985	8	14	12	20	1	12	135	202
1986	6	14	11	18	.	11	100	160
1987	1	18	8	19	1	6	66	119
1988	5	10	12	18	.	8	69	122
1989	4	8	6	10	1	6	61	96
1990	12	18	11	13	3	11	97	165
1991	16	16	12	18	16	10	140	228
1992	31	26	25	14	19	15	190	320
1993	45	31	17	11	21	11	161	297
1994	44	14	8	7	37	5	119	234
1995	20	12	14	5	9	4	92	156
1996	43	21	11	6	11	9	123	224
1997	33	15	15	12	17	16	135	243
1998	28	15	24	13	21	10	136	247
1999	41	14	34	22	29	22	187	349
2000	43	13	22	9	18	16	157	278
2001	53	13	19	12	13	19	211	340
TOTAL	457	352	304	300	220	217	2633	4483

marked increase in the number of cases against China by both the EU and the United States (Vermulst and Graafsma, 1992).

In order to quantify this trend in AD filings we have applied a simple fixed effect OLS model:

$$n_{it} = a_i + b \times t + b_i \times t$$

where

n_{it} = number of cases filed against economy i at time t (*e.g.*, each year)

a_i = economy fixed effect

b_i = economy-specific trend

t = time trend

In table 2 we report our estimates. Note that our regression includes an time dummy for each economy; however, for space reasons we only report the parameters for the nine economies with statistically significant estimates. As shown it turns out, the time trend for most economies is insignificant; in addition, most economies with significant estimates have negative trends. There are only

Table 2. Filing trends over time

Levels	
Baseline Time Trend	280 [0.143]
(Japan)*Time Trend	-0.498 [0.185]**
(Indonesia)*Time Trend	0.923 [0.294]**
(South Korea)*Time Trend	0.41 [0.190]*
(Thailand)*Time Trend	0.451 [0.217]*
(PRC)*Time Trend	2.091 [0.185]**
(Czechoslovakia)*Time Trend	-0.847 [0.324]**
(Poland)*Time Trend	-0.402 [0.190]*
(Romania)*Time Trend	-0.382 [0.190]*
(New Zealand)*Time Trend	-0.496 [0.206]*
Observations	806
R-squared	0.81

Standard errors in brackets
*significant at 5 percent
** significant at 1 percent

Note: Only economies with statistically significant time trends reported

four economies showing positive trends: China, Indonesia, Korea and Thailand. The time trend for China is the steepest of all target economies. As can be seen in Figure 1, the other three economies with a positive coefficient have much milder slope in comparison with China. Moreover, as we will discuss later (Table 6) it is developing economies such as India and Mexico that are main contributors to the steep upward trend. Therefore, in the foreseeable future, China is likely to stay as the most named economy in AD filings and is going to see continuing increase in the share of total AD filings.

2.2. *The Intensity*

Because of China's growing international trade and growing size of the economy, it is perhaps not surprising to see it being named frequently in AD filings. After all, more trade may simply lead to more filings against it. The next question to

Figure 1. Filing trend over time

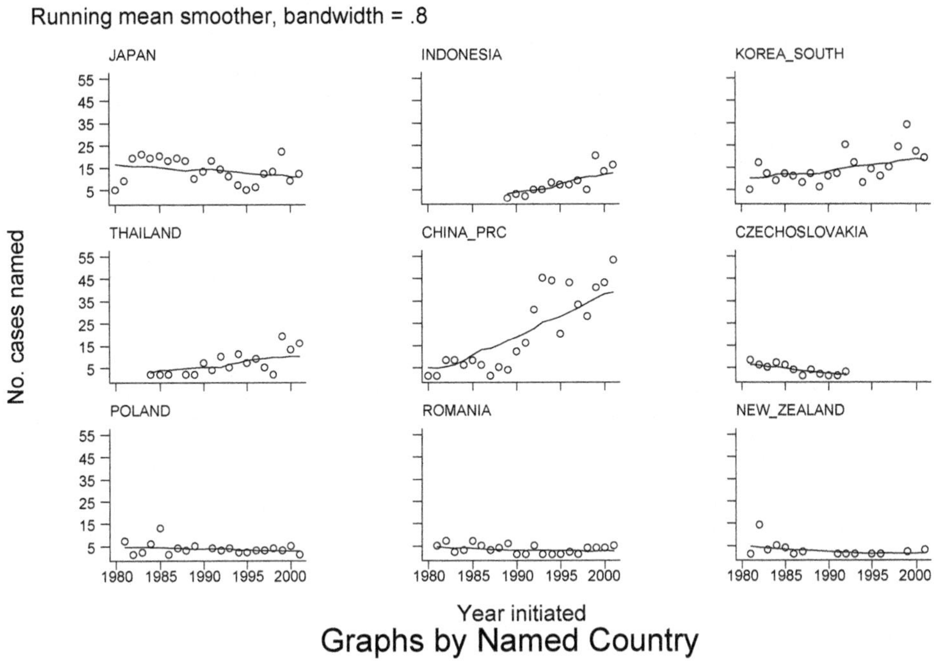

ask, then, is whether China is also being named more intensively than other economies given its trade value. The answer is positive.

The intensity of AD against China is high. As we have already shown China is the leading AD target. In terms of international trade, China ranks as the sixth largest in the world both in terms of exports and imports. This disparity suggests the intensity of AD use against China is high. To quantify this point we compute three indicators for intensity of being targeted for AD (Table 3). The first is the "AD-export" ratio, which is defined as an economy's share of AD cases in the world divided by its share in world exports. If an economy's AD-export ratio is above 1, it means that the economy is being targeted more than its share in exports.

Consider China's intensity number. China accounts for about 4.3 percent of total world exports in 2001, and an astounding 17 percent of all AD cases (1995-2002). Therefore, according to this measure China receives four times as much as AD investigations as one might predict given its share in world exports (AD-export ratio = 4). Korea, Indonesia, India and South Africa are also among the other high AD-export ratio economies.

Table 3. Top twenty antidumping targets and intensity measures, 1995-2002

Rank	Affected Economies	AD cases (95-02)	AD Share (%)	AD share/ Exports share	Affirmative Ratio (%)	Product of the two intensity measures
1	China, P.R.	308	14.3	4	69	2.76
2	South Korea	160	7.4	4.8	52	2.50
3	United States	115	5.3	0.4	58	0.23
4	China, Taipei	109	5	4	63	2.52
5	Indonesia	91	4.2	4.7	43	2.02
6	Japan	88	4.1	0.6	73	0.44
7	India	82	3.8	5.9	54	3.19
8	Thailand	81	3.8	3.4	59	2.01
9	Russia	77	3.6	2.1	71	1.49
10	Germany	70	3.2	0.3	46	0.14
11	Brazil	68	3.1	3.5	75	2.63
12	South Africa	46	2.1	4.3	52	2.24
13	Ukraine	46	2.1	7.1	83	5.89
14	Malaysia	40	1.9	1.3	59	0.77
15	United Kingdom	40	1.9	0.4	58	0.23
16	Italy	39	1.8	0.5	48	0.24
17	Spain	37	1.7	1	59	0.59
18	France	32	1.5	0.3	54	0.16
19	Singapore	32	1.5	1.3	72	0.94
20	Turkey	30	1.4	2.8	41	1.15

Note: Chinese and Indian exports share are 95-02 average, while others using 2002 share. The reason is that other economies do not exhibit significant changes in share of world trade.

A second indicator is an economy's affirmative ratio, which is defined as the number of measures (*i.e.*, duties levied) divided by the number of initiations targeting a particular economy. During the period of 1995-2002, 69 percent of all AD initiations against China received an affirmative final determination. While this number is high, there are several other economies that have even higher ratios, such as Japan, Russia, Brazil, Ukraine, and Singapore.

Our third intensity measure combines the first two in order to indicate the overall possibility of an economy's exports being subject to AD duties. This third measure is reported in the final column where we calculate the product of the first two measures. With this third measure, China ranks third, trailing Ukraine and India. However, one needs to remember that the total number of cases against India and Ukraine combined is only 40 percent of the total against China. In this sense, China exports bear the most significant brunt of AD protection.

One important caveat: one must recognize that all of the above three measures offer only crude estimates of AD intensity. There are a number of weaknesses in these measures, not the least is that none of them accurately measure the amount of trade being affected in any given case.

2.3. *The AD Measures*

The duties resulting from the final determination can be very high in AD cases against China. In many cases, the measures are prohibitive. For instance, Liu and Vandenbussche (2002) and Fu (1997) examine EU AD against China. The two studies look at different time periods but both find that the AD duties imposed by the EU are high. Liu and Vandenbussche (2002) report the average antidumping duty (ADD) is around 41 percent, ranging from 10 to 102 percent. Fu (1997) examines the trade impact of the duties and finds dramatic decreases in trade. For instance, after the EU imposed AD measures on Chinese exports of Tungstic Oxide and Tungstic Acid, and Barium Chloride in 1988, the exports of these products from China to the EU dropped by 96 percent in four years. Similarly, exports of small color televisions, polyester yarns and videotapes in cassettes dropped over 90 percent.

We have compiled antidumping duty (ADD) data for the United States against Chinese exports; our result indicates even higher ADD than observed by the EU against Chinese exports. Among the 60 AD cases for which we have information on ADD, 11 had ADD above 100 percent, and 6 of them the ADD was above 150 percent; 17 cases had ADD duties between 50 and 100 percent. Altogether, nearly half of US cases against China had ADD above 50 percent. The average ADD is 54 percent

The AD duties from the developing economies (what are often referred to as the new users) tend to be even higher than those applied by the EU and US. For example, Brazil currently has ADD imposed on 12 types of Chinese products, with margins ranging from 35.8 percent to 203.4 percent, with an average around 77 percent.

2.4. *The Sectors Being Named*

We also investigate the type of Chinese products that are targeted by AD investigations. Our results indicate that the range of industries that have been the targets for AD is amazingly wide. In terms of two-digit ISIC classification of industries, all 2-digit manufacturing industries have been targeted (Table 4). In terms of three-digit ISIC classification, 26 out of total 29 (3-digit) ISIC manufacturing industries. Such widespread coverage not only demonstrates China's diverse economy and widespread comparative advantage, but it also demonstrates how comprehensive and versatile tool antidumping can be, allowing an economy to protect virtually any filing industry, regardless whether the industry has comparative advantage.

Table 4. Chinese exports affected by AD by two-digit ISIC classification

Industries	Number of AD cases
35 – Manufacture of Chemicals and Chemical, Petroleum, Coal, Rubber and Plastic Products	158
38 – Manufacture of Fabricated Metal Products, Machinery and Equipment	105
32 – Textile, Wearing Apparel and Leather Industries	62
37 – Basic Metal Industries	55
36 – Manufacture of Non-Metallic Mineral Products, except Products of Petroleum and Coal	31
39 – Other Manufacturing Industries	21
31 – Manufacture of Food, Beverages and Tobacco	17
34 – Manufacture of Paper and Paper Products, Printing and Publishing	8
33 – Manufacture of Wood and Wood Products, Including Furniture	6
11 – Agriculture and Hunting	4
29 – Other Mining	4
23 – Metal Ore Mining	3

Despite the breadth of Chinese industries being targeted, the frequencies for some industries are particularly high. Four sectors account for 80 percent of all AD filings: "Manufacture of Chemicals and Chemical, Petroleum, Coal, Rubber and Plastic Products," "Manufacture of Fabricated Metal Products, Machinery and Equipment," "Textile, Wearing Apparel and Leather Industries," and "Basic Metal Industries." The first two sectors account for 55 percent of all AD filings. The filing trends suggest that the simple basic manufacturing industries which China has its greatest cost advantages are also the ones being hit the hardest by AD.

The most frequently targeted industries at the four-digit classification level are "Manufacture of basic industrial chemicals except fertilizers" and "Iron and steel basic industries," which together account for 25 percent of all filings. Activity against the other 4-digit sectors are fairly evenly spread out, with 19 sectors having been subject to 9 to 23 cases, and 37 sectors named from once to six times (Table 5).

Table 5. Chinese exports affected by AD by four-digit ISIC classification

Rank	Sector Description	ISIC4	No. AD cases
1	Manufacture of basic industrial chemicals except fertilizers	3511	80
2	Iron and steel basic industries	3710	46
3	Manufacture of other chemical products	3522	23
4	Manufacture of footwear, except vulcanized or molded rubber or plastic footwear	3240	19
5	Manufacturing industries not elsewhere classified	3909	19
6	Manufacture of fabricated metal products except machinery and equipment not elsewhere classified	3819	18
7	Manufacture of chemical products not elsewhere classified	3529	17
8	Manufacture of textiles not elsewhere classified	3219	15
9	Manufacture of cutlery, hand tools and general hardware	3811	15
10	Canning and preserving of fruits and vegetables	3113	14
11	Manufacture of glass and glass products	3620	14
12	Manufacture of motorcycles and bicycles	3844	14
13	Manufacture of wearing apparel, except footwear	3220	10
14	Manufacture of synthetic resins, plastic materials and man-made fibers except glass	3513	10
15	Manufacture of non-metallic mineral products not elsewhere classified	3699	9
16	Non-ferrous metal basic industries	3720	9
17	Manufacture of fertilizers and pesticides	3512	8
18	Manufacture of plastic products not elsewhere classified	3560	8
19	Manufacture of radio, television and communication equipment and apparatus	3832	8
20	Manufacture of electrical appliances and housewares	3833	7
21	Manufacture of electrical apparatus and supplies not elsewhere classified	3839	7
	All others		104

2.5. *The Filing Economies*

The next issue we examine is the question of who is targeting Chinese exports. We find that China has been targeted by a wide array of economies. Treating all EU members as one economy, there have been 25 economies that have launched AD investigation against Chinese exports.

Among the top initiators are: the United States, EU, India, Australia, Argentina, and Mexico; together they account for 72 percent of all AD cases filing against China. AD activity, therefore, is concentrated among a handful of major users. In order to examine whether there are significant differences in the filing intensity we computed each economy's filing intensity and relative filing intensity as:

$$Intensity_i = Number\ of\ filings\ against\ China_i \,/\, Imports\ from\ China_i$$
$$Relative\ Intensity_i = Intensity_i \,/\, Intensity_{US}$$

As shown in Table 6, South Korea, the United States and EU are among the least intensive economies using AD to target Chinese exports. Developed economies with high intensities are Australia and New Zealand, which are 8.4 and 11.5 times more likely to file an AD case relative to the United States. The truly large users are developing economies such as Argentina (relative intensity=46.8), Peru (42.4), India (18.1) and Mexico (15). Not surprisingly, these economies all compete in labor-intensive industries that are most likely losing (or have lost) comparative advantage in those industries to China.

Table 6. The initiating economies targeting Chinese exports

Initiator	Number of Filings	Exports from China (million US. dollars)	Intensity Relative to US
US	87	54359	1.0
EU	66	40953	1.0
India	55	1896	18.1
Australia	48	3570	8.4
Argentina	43	574	46.8
Mexico	43	1790	15.0
Canada	21	3346	3.9
Brazil	20	1351	9.2
South Africa	16	1049	9.5
Korea	14	12521	0.7
Peru	12	177	42.4
Turkey	12	674	11.1
Venezuela	10	443	14.1
New Zealand	8	435	11.5
All Others	19		

Source of exports data: Direction of Trade Statistics Yearbook 2002.

In summary, with respect to AD investigations targeting China we have shown that:

1. China constitutes the largest single economy being targeted by AD investigations;
2. The trend in using AD against China is positive and is growing faster than any other economy;
3. The intensity which Chinese exports are targeted is high; the likelihood that ADD are imposed is high;
4. When they are imposed, AD duties are very high, often prohibitive;

5. The sectors covered is broad, nearly comprehensive;
6. A large number of developing and developed economies target Chinese exports; filing intensities varies widely across filings economies.

While in some respects China is not unique as many developing economies have broadly similar stories of AD abuse, especially in terms of the high intensity and high likelihood of duties being levied. Taking all factors together, however, China clearly emerges as the economy most severely affected by AD.

3. The Reasons for High China's AD Intensity and High AD Duties

In this section, we investigate the reasons for the large number and high intensity of AD investigations targeting China, as well as the high AD duties in AD cases against China.

First we document the likely contributing factors that are shared with other economies, such as the strategic use of AD, NME status, the role of cumulation, and inexperienced and ineffective legal defenses. We then focus on a couple of factors that are very unique in China, the roles played foreign direct investment (FDI) through foreign invested enterprises (FEI) and the low concentration ratio in many Chinese industries.

3.1. *AD as A Learned Strategy for Domestic Firms Blocking Foreign Competition*

To what extent is AD a learned strategic behavior? How can we account the proliferation of AD across industries and across economies? Prusa and Skeath (2002) and Fu (1997) argue that it is likely that firms learn that AD can be used strategically to block foreign competition. In the case of China, because of its rapid increase in trade, the publicity about China is abundant. Publicity about China lowers the cost of acquiring information needed in the AD petition. We have examined the possibility of copying from the same industries across economies in launching AD investigations as an indication of an informational spillover. A simple measure is to check how many antidumping cases for the similar products occur within one year of one other in different economies (*e.g.*, similar case against Chinese exports by both EU and the United States within one year). If a case is launched shortly after a similar case by another economy, we will say the second "echoes" the initial filing.

We find that there have been 83 cases against China that could be said to echo. That is, these cases were initiated within one year of another economy initiating an AD case involving the same or very similar products. Cases involving textiles and footwear frequently echoed. For example, in the case of textiles, EU, Mexico, Turkey and Peru each launched AD investigations on a wide array of textile products within a short time frame.

We believe our measure is conservative in two senses. First, we restrict our measure to only one year, however, a span of 18 month or longer could be reasonably called an echoing period. Moreover, the learning could occur across wide array of products (echoing within an economy rather than between economies). For example, Mexico had AD investigations covering HS codes 52, 53, 54 and 55, and Peru had investigations covering "various fabrics." Simply put, it seems likely that the learning occur across industries, which is a type of learning that our measure does not capture.

Can AD initiation be a learned tactic for declining industries? This seems to be a very logical tactic for some industries. It is fairly commonly observed that AD investigations involved the same (or similar) line of products are filed repeatedly over time. Steel is perhaps the best example where both the United States and EU have filed AD investigations involving many types of Chinese steel over the past decade. Australia launched investigation on canned pear and peaches, and soon thereafter started investigation on canned tomatoes. In EU, the AD investigation against Chinese made cotton fabrics was initiated three times in 1994, 1996 and 1997.

Therefore, it seems that AD protection can be contagious across economies and becomes a learned behavior over time. If an AD action against foreign competitor can achieve an affirmative result with a high probability, or if it deters the imports through litigation costs, then AD is more likely to become a learned behavior. Unfortunately, this seems to be the case. According to various studies (Prusa and Skeath 2002, Fu 1997), AD investigations have successfully deterred imports and raised profitability of initiating firms, therefore, the economic rational for troubled firms to initiate AD is very strong.

3.2. *Non-Market Economy (NME) Status*

There are a few widely recognized reasons that Chinese exports receive disproportional amount of AD investigations. China's non-market economy status is arguably the most commonly cited explanation.

The GATT/WTO antidumping rules allow an investigating economy to not use the exporter's domestic prices when calculating the home market sales, input costs, *etc.* Being classified as a non-market makes it extremely difficult (virtually impossible) for exporting economy to defend itself. China has always been classified as a non-market economy. In the accession protocol to WTO, China agreed that this non-market treatment would not be phased out for another 15 years (will expire in 2016).

The argument is that China is not considered a market economy; thus Chinese domestic prices do not reflect the true cost of these inputs as determined in the markets. Therefore, during the investigation of antidumping case targeting China, the investigators do not have to use the Chinese domestic input prices in determining the cost of the production of the investigated product.

This practice renders greatly increases China's risk in dumping allegations because the low cost of labor services is its major comparative advantage for international trade. In practice, China's non-market economy status hands greater discretionary power to the investigators, who have the option to choose an economy with high prices when evaluating the cost of inputs in China. For example, in a recent investigation in brake rotors by the United States, the handling and freight cost was calculated using India cost. India is known for higher cost of transportation than most of its neighbors.[1] Therefore, using India price would increase the likelihood of affirmative result.

Even though non-market status contributed to unfavorable determination in AD investigations against China, it is probably not sufficient to explain the large number of cases targeting China (Blonigen, 2003). Even after controlling for China's non-market status, Blonigen still finds a significantly positive unexplained "China factor." Therefore, there are other factors that are not yet well captured or measured by economists that contribute significantly to China's being the largest targeted economy.

3.3. *Cumulation*

Cumulation is another factor that increases the number of cases against China. As is well known, China has experienced a rapid expansion of the international trade. Its share of world trade has increased seven-fold and China's volume of international trade increased 40-fold during 1977-2001.[2] With the rapid growth of international trade, it is inevitable that the China's import market share in a particular economy will rise rapidly from non-existent or very small to above the

---

[1] [Federal Register: January 8, 2003 (Volume 68, Number 5)][Page 1031-1038] [DOCID:fr08ja03-24] [A-570-846] Brake Rotors from the People's Republic of China: Preliminary, Results and Preliminary Partial Rescission of the Fifth Antidumping, Duty Administrative Review and Preliminary Results of the Seventh New Shipper Review.

[2] The data source is World Development Indicator 2003.

low threshold for cumulation. Therefore, even though Chinese imports in many products still capture only a small proportion of the market, with the cumulative assessment of the market share, China is included in the investigation even though China is not (at the time of the filing of the case) a significant exporter to foreign markets. Hansen and Prusa (1996) document that the mandatory cumulation in 1984 in the United States has led to significant increase in the possibility of finding injuries. Since most AD initiations against China have occurred since the late 1980s, therefore, cumulation has likely contributed to the large number of cases filed against China as well as the intensity against China.

3.4. *Weakness in Corporate Governance Prevents Effective Defense in AD Investigations*

It has been noted that, especially in the first decade of facing AD investigations, Chinese enterprises have not coordinated well or presented their case in an effective manner. This reflects the overall weakness of Chinese enterprises in terms of the backward corporate governance practice, and also the overall weakness of the nationwide legal infrastructure.

Chinese enterprises often do not respond in a timely manner, and cannot afford high cost for hiring lawyers of experiences, and in some cases just not responded at all. China has a tradition of having a weak legal system, and Chinese traditional values do not encourage litigation. The SOE status is much to account for this behavior, where the managers have little incentive to fight for the SOE's behalf where they personally have little stake. Moreover, even when some are willing to cooperate, they lack the authority as well as the necessary skill and information to respond effectively.

On top of this, the macro coordination effort still needs improvement. One piece of evidence is that among all 53 cases of the WTO dispute involving antidumping issues, none has been filed by China.[3] In fact, China is the only one economy among the top-ten target economies that has not filed a single WTO dispute on AD issues.

China was not eligible to file complaints to the WTO Dispute Settlement Body (DSB) before it became a member in 2002. Yet, of the approximately 200 AD cases targeting China annually, it is unlikely that all cases are handled in conformity with WTO laws. It is still unclear if China will begin to lodge some complains to DSB in the near future.

---

[3] See *http://www.wto.org/english/tratop_e/dispu_e/dispu_subjects_index_e.htm#bkmk4* for list of AD disputes.

It remains to see whether filing complaints has any impact on the cases initiated or not. If it does, as common sense would predict, then the fact that China does not use the DSB might lead the initiating economy over-reach in its efforts to levy ADD on cases against China. This issue is not a factor controlled in Blonigen's (2003) study that found a significant positive "China effect" in AD activity. Future research should examine whether WTO DSB has any deterrent effect on AD activity.

Table 7. Economies that initiated WTO disputes on antidumping measures

Initiating Economy	No. of disputes
European Community	9
Mexico	9
Brazil	7
India	5
Canada	5
United States	4
South Korea	4
Japan	3
All Others	14
of which China	0

Source: WTO official website,
http://www.wto.org/english/tratop_e/dispu_e/dispu_subjects_index_e.htm#bkmk4

3.5. *Foreign Direct Investment and the "Antidumping (AD) Triangle"*

Once China relaxed the regulations governing FDI in 1992 inward FDI has increased dramatically. Currently the foreign invested enterprises (FIE), the firms with FDI, account for roughly 50 percent of both Chinese imports and exports.

Blonigen (2000) documented that FDI is one means for a foreign firm to avoid a tariff or AD duty or what he refers to as tariff-jumping. We explore the related hypothesis that FDI might play an important role in explaining the large number of AD filings against Chinese exports. A significant amount of Chinese FDI has been from the four East-Asian Tigers and has resulted in Chinese-sourced exports have replaced exports from parent company home markets. It is natural to hypothesize that AD filings against China are also replacing AD filings against these economies. This is a particular type of tariff jumping by multinationals not previously discussed in the literature.

Due to data limitation, at this time we cannot fully explore the "AD triangle" hypothesis. What we can do, however, is document the correlation of FDI flow into China with the number AD filings against China. Our result shows that the number of AD filings against Chinese exports is increasing significantly in FDI. The estimating equation is:

$$n_t = a + b_1\, ln(FDI_t) + b_2\, ln(Exports_t) + b_3\, (Exchange\ rate_t) + e_t\,,$$

where

n_t = number of cases filed against China at time t (*e.g.*, each year)
FDI_t = inward flow FDI at time t
$Exports_t$ = Chinese exports at time t
$Exchange\ Rate_t$ = exchange rate (Yuan *per* dollar) at time t

Because the dependent variable is a count variable, we use Poisson regression model. As can be seen in Table 8, FDI is the only significant explanatory variable, and it is significant at the 99 percent level. Exports are statistically insignificant and the exchange rate has wrong sign.[4] As shown in Figure 3, the high correlation between FDI and AD filings is obvious. This simple regression lends strong support for the notion that Chinese FDI inflow plays an important role in the number of AD cases filed. This is also consistent with the proposed special type of tariff jumping, the "AD triangle."

Table 8. Poisson regression: Effects of FDI on AD filings

	Estimate	Std. Err.	t-stat	p-value	[99% Conf. Interval]	
FDI	0.7701904	.1495	5.15	0.000	.3848	1.155
Exports	0.1133838	.2241	0.51	0.613	-.4639	.6907
Ex. Rate	-.1553	.0863375	-1.80	0.072	-.3776	.0671
Constant	-1.050289	2.075	-0.51	0.613	-6.396	4.295

Number of obs = 17
LR chi2(3) = 175.27
Prob > chi2 = 0.0000
Pseudo R2 = 0.5758
Log likelihood = -64.568

3.6. *Low Concentration Ratio in Chinese Industries*

One particular feature of Chinese industries is their very low concentration ratios. Existing studies focus on the geographic concentration, which is high (Amiti and Wen 2002). However the market concentration is very low. Even though no much literature has been found on this, low concentration is a well-recognized fact, and in the *Tenth Five-year Plan on Industrial Structure Adjustment*, the fact that production concentration is low was recognized as one of the major

[4] When we test each explanatory variables individually, they are all-significant and have correct signs, but the FDI has the highest pseudo r-square value.

Figure 2. The antidumping duties imposed by the US on Chinese exports

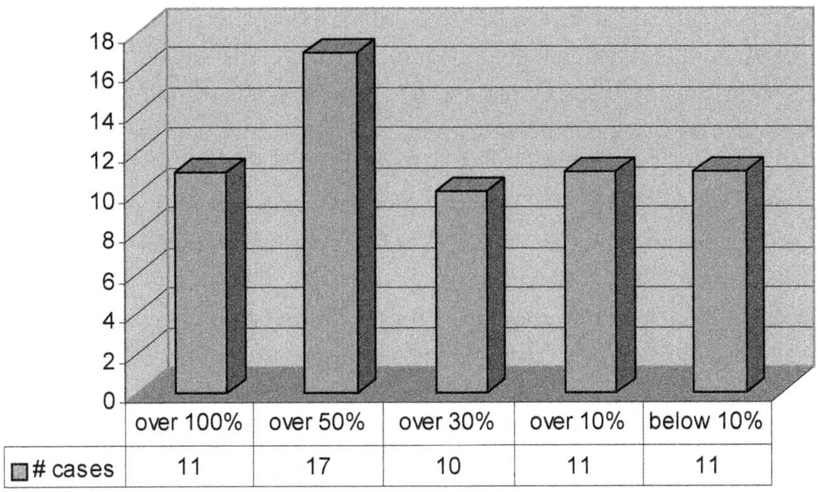

Figure 3. The AD filed against and the FDI in China

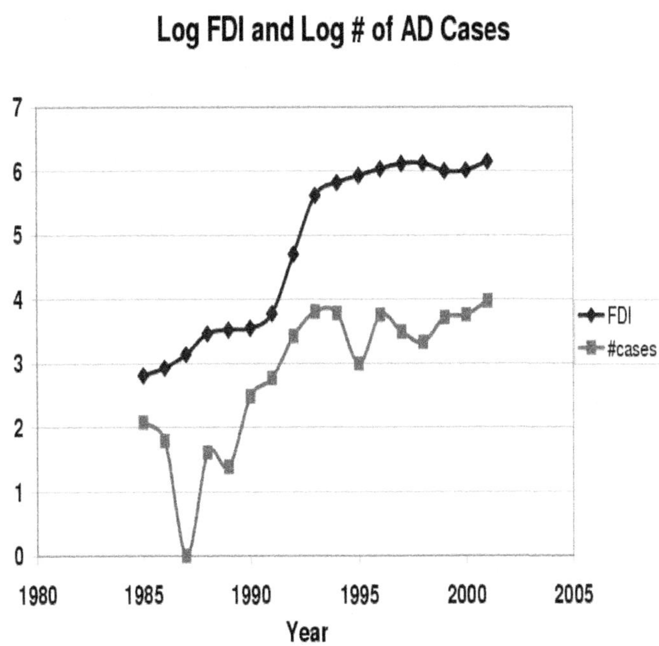

problems of current industrial structure in China. According to the analysis in the Third Industrial Census (National Statistic Bureau 2003), one of the major problem is "small and scattered scale of industrial organization."

A brief comparison can demonstrate the huge difference in concentration level in industries between China and the United States. In the United States, 50 largest industrial firms count for 23 percent of total production in manufacturing (in year 1997), and top 201 firms count for 60 percent of total.[5] Whereas in China, 375 largest firms produce 16 percent of total industrial output in 2001, and it takes an enormous number of 22,987 firms to produce 60 percent of total industrial output.[6] The difference is huge. Even though the U.S. data is for manufacturing only and China data is for all industries including manufacturing, utility and mining sectors, it does not affect the result much. In the United States, mining counts only 4 percent and utility counts for 9 percent of industrial output, thus it can only affect slightly the overall US concentration level presented above.[7] Therefore, the statistics strongly indicates that Chinese industries are far less concentrated than that of the United States.

Given very low production and market concentration, profitability of Chinese firms is reduced. The low profit margins, when facing AD investigation, which typically specify high profit margin when evaluating cost of production, can lead to higher imposed duties. This is still only a hypothesis and need further investigation whether its impact is significant enough leading to quantitative impacts on AD determinations. The low profit margin in Chinese firms can also lead to undercutting the exports prices, which will lead to more AD initiations.

The mirror problem of the low concentration and low profit margin in Chinese industries is the relatively high concentration ratio and higher profitability in many major AD initiating economies. In the highly concentrated industries, the firms exhibit more strategic behavior, and are more likely to utilize the tool of AD regulation to block the foreign competition. This has been confirmed by the study on EU AD (Liu and Vandenbussche, 2002) who document that the majority of AD files are filed by highly concentrated industries; in many cases monopolists and oligopolies in the EU market; a very small proportion (less than 15 percent) involve not so concentrated industries. This statistic also applies to the United States, another major user of AD, where the

[5] Data source: 1997 Economic Census, US Census Bureau.

[6] Data source: Table 13-1, China Statistical Yearbook, 2003.

[7] In fact, the utility sector in the United States is also very concentrated, with 4 largest firms counting 15 percent of total revenue of the sector. The mining sector is less concentrated, but with its 4 percent share of total output, it will produce only negligible impact on overall concentration level. Data source: 1997 Economic Census, US Census Bureau.

industrial concentration among industries using AD is high (Hansen and Prusa, 1996). In many respects, this finding illustrates one of the great ironies of AD regulation – instead of creating "fair" competition, it punishes the competitive international industries, and encourage uncompetitive domestic behavior.

4. Implications

It is a difficult task to evaluate the impacts of AD on China. One reason is the lack of data, but another is that the dynamic impacts are yet to be fully understood. For instance, the United States uses individual treatment, which often gives one (or a few Chinese exporters) smaller ADD and all other Chinese exporters, current or future, a very high ADD. In this case it not only alters the trade pattern, it also will affect the industrial structure in China. However, these effects are hard to use a formal treatment to estimate, therefore in this section we only discuss qualitatively some likely impacts of the large, growing, intensive, severe, and broad AD filings against Chinese exports.

The amount of Chinese exports affected by AD, among trade remedies, is the second largest, only trailing technical barriers. According to Yue (2003), the cumulated amount of exports that have been affected has reached 16 billion US dollars. Fu (1997) estimates that about 5 percent of Chinese exports to EU are affected by EU AD filings. This number is very large considering the strong deterring effect of AD investigation on imports. In comparison with tariffs, ADD are very high and target the particular products. As we have discussed in the intensity of AD from various economies, EU is modest in terms of intensity of filing, therefore, it is very likely in other economies, the trade affected will be much higher than 5 percent of total. Therefore, the amount of trade affected is very significant. The cost is also to employment, which will be adversely affected through the decrease in exports, which will further complicate China's continuing economic transition.

Moreover, learning from the lessons of antidumping, some Chinese manufactures have begun to form alliance, restricting the price of exports to the United States. For example, the apple cider producers in China now meet annually to determine the minimum price to the United States. It is natural to see more and more firms become aware and begin to charge higher export prices toward major users of AD. This might contribute toward increasing the concentration ratio in Chinese industries, or even create monopolies or oligopolies in exports markets.

Moreover, according to our finding on the role of FDI in explaining the AD filings, the multinationals or foreign investors are likely hurt by AD filings against Chinese exports.

Will China become a new important user of AD? We think yes. The number of cases filed by China is increasing rapidly. We have illustrated in Figure 4 the number of cases initiated by China, which has a clear positive trend. There is no evidence China has used AD as a retaliation toward economies filing AD against Chinese exports, however, it should be recognized that China has it own industries to protect, and it might find that AD can be a very convenient instrument for protection. The ongoing pressure of unemployment, and the fact that much needed expansion of Chinese export sector employment is constrained by the foreign AD filings, it is natural for China to use the same tool to retain employment. If this occurs, AD will lead to mutual welfare worsening effects.

Figure 4. Number of AD cases filed by China

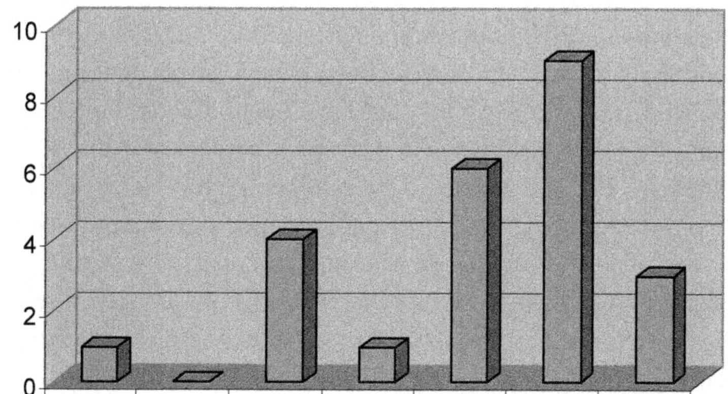

	1997	1998	1999	2000	2001	2002	2003
Number Filed	1	0	4	1	6	9	3

5. Conclusion

We have examined the case of AD filings for Chinese exports, the largest in the world, in this paper, and document the characteristics of these AD filings. We have shown that AD activity against China has involved and continues to involve a large number of filings; that AD use against China is increasing; that intensity of AD use against China is high; that Chinese cases often involve very high duty levels; that AD cases against China have broad industrial coverage, and have been initiated by many economies. We then analyze the possible causes and/or contributing factors for the use of AD against China. Besides common factors being recognized by other studies, such as non-market economy status and cumulation, we have found two important and unique contributing factors in China, the FDI inflow and the low concentration ratio in Chinese industries.

The FDI hypothesis is related with studies on tariff jumping, yet it is different that it involves not investing in the AD initiating economy, which might not have comparative advantage. Some of the FDI inflow to China might be from foreign firms that were subjected to anti-dumping, either in its home economy or a third economy that it had foreign investment, to relocate to China, which has not been subjected to AD filings yet and which has comparative advantages in these industries. We are not able to directly test this hypothesis; however, our result is consistent with it. It requires multi-economy study to further explore the validity of this hypothesis.

Our review of AD filings against China has confirmed that the AD practice can be very convenient and effective tool to deter trade and that it has a number of dynamic impacts that are hard to quantify. China is likely to follow other new users of AD if the filings against Chinese products continue to rise and obstruct the creation of employment in export sector to absorb unemployment from the dismantled industries as a result of WTO transition and other reforms. Should this happen, significant welfare costs will occur to both China and its trade partners.

References

1. Almstedt, Kermit W; Norton, Patrick M, 2000. "China's Antidumping Laws and the WTO Antidumping Agreement: (Including Comments on China's Early Enforcement of Its Antidumping Laws.)," Journal of World Trade, vol. 34, no. 6, December 2000, pp. 75-113.
2. Amiti, M. and M. Wen, 2002. "Spatial distribution of manufacturing in China," in Modeling the Chinese Economy, ed. By P. Lloyd and X. Zhang, London; Edward Elgar.
3. Bergoeing, R. and Kehoe, T. 2003. "Trade Theory and Trade Facts," Federal Reserve bank of Minneapolis, Research Department Staff Report 284, October 2003.
4. Blonigen , Bruce, 2003. "Evolving Discretionary Practices of U.S Antidumping Activity," NBER Working Paper No. w9625, April 2003
5. Blonigen , Bruce, 2000. "Tariff-Jumping Antidumping Duties," NBER Working Paper No. w7776, July 2000.
6. Blonigen, Bruce and Thomas J. Prusa, "Antidumping" in *Handbook of International Economics*, E. Kwan Choi and James Harrigan, eds. (Malden, MA, Blackwell Publishing), 2003.
7. China's Modernization and Open Economic Policy, edited by M. Dutta, Pei-Kang Chang, and Shao-Kung Lin. JAI Press, 1990, p. 333-36.

8. Chinese National Bureau of Statistics, 2003. "The current status, problems and solution of industrial structural adjustment," Analysis number 23 on Third Industrial Census. (Chinese).
9. Dong, Yi; Xu, Huijun; Liu, Fang, 1998. "Antidumping and the WTO: Implications for China," Journal of World Trade, vol. 32, no. 1, February 1998, pp. 19-27.
10. Eeckhout, Piet, 1997. "European Antidumping Law and China," European Integration online papers, vol.1, n° 7. *http://eiop.or.at/eiop/texte/1997-007.htm.*
11. Fu, Donghui, 1997. "EC Antidumping Law and Individual Treatment Policy in Cases Involving Imports from China," Journal of World Trade, vol. 31, no. 1, February 1997, pp. 73-105.
12. Gupta, P and A. Panagariya, 2003. Injury Investigations in Antidumping and the Super-Additivity Effect: A Theoretical Explanation, University of Maryland working paper.
13. Hansen, Wendy L. and Thomas J. Prusa, "Cumulation and ITC decision-making: The sum of the parts is greater than the whole," *Economic Inquiry*, 34, 1996, 746-769.
14. Huang, Thomas Weishing, 2002. "The Gathering Storm of Antidumping Enforcement in China," Journal of World Trade, vol. 36, no. 2, April 2002, pp. 255-83.
15. Kao, Hung-Yeh, 1990. "The Theory of Comparative Advantage: American Antidumping Procedure against Chinese Goods China's modernization and open economic policy. 1990, pp. 333-36,Research in Asian Economic Studies, vol. 2. (Greenwich, Conn. and London: JAI Press).
16. Liu, Xiang; Vandenbussche, Hylke 2002. "European Union Antidumping Cases against China: An Overview and Future Prospects with Respect to China's World Trade Organization Membership," Journal of World Trade, vol. 36, no. 6, December 2002, pp. 1125-44.
17. Mai, Y. H. 2002. "An Analysis of EU Antidumping Cases against China," Asia-Pacific Development Journal, vol. 9, no. 2, December 2002, pp. 131-50.
18. McGee, Robert W, 1999. "Antidumping Laws, the World Trade Organization and the People's Republic of China: The managerial process and impact of foreign investment in Greater China," Advances in Chinese Industrial Studies, vol. 6. pp. 141-55, (Stamford, Conn.: JAI Press).
19. Messerlin, Patrick A., China in the WTO: Antidumping and Safeguards, December, 2002, mimeo.
20. Prusa, Thomas J. and Susan Skeath, "The Economic and Strategic Motives for Antidumping Filings," *Weltwirtschaftliches Archiv*, 138(3), 2002, 389-413.
21. Prusa, Thomas J., "On the Spread and Impact of Antidumping," *Canadian Journal of Economics* 34(3), August 2001, 591-611.
22. Prusa, Thomas J., "The trade effects of U.S. antidumping actions," in *Effects of U.S. Trade Protection and Promotion Policies*, Robert C. Feenstra ed., (University of Chicago Press, Chicago, 1997).
23. Stahnke, Arthur A, 1981. "The West German System of Protection against Dumping by Centrally Planned Economies," ACES Bulletin, vol. 23, no. 1, Spr. 1981, pp. 1-24.
24. Tharakan, P.K.M., D. Greenaway and J. Tharakan, 1998, "Cumulation and Injury Determination of the European Community in Antidumping Cases," Weltwirtschaftliches Archiv, 134, 2, 320-339.
25. Vermulst, Edwin A; Graafsma, Folkert, 1992. "A Decade of European Community Antidumping Law and Practice Applicable to Imports from China," Journal of World Trade, vol. 26, no. 3, June 1992, pp. 5-60.

26. Wang, Jianyu, 1999. "A Critique of the Application to China of the Non-market Economy Rules of Antidumping Legislation and Practice of the European Union," Journal of World Trade, vol. 33, no. 3, June 1999, pp. 117-45.
27. Wang, Lei; Yu, Shengxing, 2002. "China's New Antidumping Regulations: Improvements to Comply with the World Trade Organization Rules," Journal of World Trade, vol. 36, no. 5, October 2002, pp. 903-20.
28. Yue, Hao, 2003. "A Study on the Unfairness of the International Antidumping," International Economic Cooperation, February, 2003. ISSN1002-1515 CN11-1583/F.

THE EXTENT AND IMPACT OF FINAL GOODS NON-TARIFF BARRIERS IN RICH COUNTRIES

Scott Bradford

Brigham Young University

1. Introduction

International trade negotiations have significantly reduced tariffs in rich economies, greatly increasing the relative importance of non-tariff barriers (NTBs). This has presented two challenges for trade analysts and negotiators alike. First, since NTBs are harder to measure than tariffs, we have become less sure about how much protection remains in rich economies. Second, since NTBs lack tariffs' transparency and are often embedded within complex domestic regulatory regimes, reducing NTBs generally requires more work than reducing tariffs does.

This extra work stems not just from more difficult and technical subject matter but also from more intense political opposition to deeper integration. The Uruguay Round took almost eight years, by far the longest round on record, because the agenda included trade in services, government procurement, customs procedures, standards, certification procedures, intellectual property, and binding dispute settlement. The Doha Round, which also includes a heavy dose of NTB discussions, was launched only after a failed attempt at Seattle two years earlier and has recently suffered a collapse in the talks.

Despite this opposition, the desire for more integration still drives policy. Nations continue to negotiate regional agreements, many covering behind-the-border measures. The European Union (EU) has moved furthest in eliminating national borders. Many in Europe, though, still believe that further deepening is required, and efforts to promote European integration continue.[1] The other major economies are also pursuing integration. The United States has moved beyond preferential trade agreements (PTAs) with Canada (CUSFTA) and Mexico (NAFTA) towards deeper ties with other nations in the Western Hemisphere and beyond. In late 2002, the United States concluded new PTAs with Chile and Singapore and announced its intention to negotiate several more. Japan, too,

[1] See for example "European single market has boosted wealth but more powers needed" *Financial Times* January 5th, 2003, page 4.

continues to implement measures to increase its international integration, through domestic deregulation and free trade agreements.

Given strong support for, and opposition to, reducing NTBs, we need to weigh the benefits of doing so. If they are small, then perhaps the time has come to place a lower priority on achieving deeper economic integration. On the other hand, if the barriers remain substantial, it could be worthwhile to invest considerable political capital in their elimination.

Assessing whether negotiating reducing NTBs is worthwhile involves two tasks: (1) Reliably measuring the height of NTBs, and (2) Using an economic model to infer the potential economic gains from their removal. Accordingly, we first present a new method for estimating tariff equivalents of NTBs for final goods in OECD economies. The analysis exploits detailed, comprehensive, and careful price comparisons. We also present some preliminary information on the policies behind the estimates. Then, we use an applied general equilibrium (AGE) model to provide a broad-brushed assessment of the impact of these NTBs.[2] The results imply that NTBs greatly restrict trade in OECD economies and that removing them would bring large gains to the world economy, for rich and poor economies alike. Thus, this research implies that continued efforts to negotiate the reduction of NTBs will indeed exceed the costs.

2. Measuring NTBs

The greatest obstacle to measuring the openness of markets accurately today is the fact that nations can protect their industries in many different ways that are difficult to measure. As trade agreements have caused reductions in tariffs, governments have relied on a variety of less visible but effective means for insulating domestic markets against foreign competition. These hidden barriers include subsidies, biased government procurement, lax antitrust enforcement, health and safety standards and other regulations, burdensome customs procedures, anti-dumping duties, and threats of protection. Even when not created with protectionist intent, these policies can inhibit international arbitrage, protect producers, and shrink the world economy.

---

[2] This analysis gives an overview of the size and shape of the protection forest, without describing individual trees. Assessing the effects of particular policies, however, is important future work since it would probably facilitate the negotiations that this paper implies are worthwhile.

2.1. *Other Approaches to Measuring NTBs*

In this section, we discuss three prominent approaches to measuring NTBs: (1) Counting NTBs and computing coverage ratios, (2) Inferring protection from trade flows, and (3) Inferring protection from price gaps. We then discuss our method.

2.1.1. *Compute NTB "Coverage Ratios"*

The United Nations has developed "NTB coverage ratios" by computing what percentage of products within a sector has an NTB. Unfortunately, this measure does not take account of how restrictive each barrier is. One sector may have many products that are subject to minor NTBs. Another sector may have just a few products with very restrictive NTBs. The first sector would have a much higher NTB coverage ratio, while we would expect the second sector to actually have more restrictive trade barriers. Also, the UN's accounting probably does not cover all NTBs. For instance, these coverage ratios do not include inefficient customs procedures, even though they probably significantly restrict a wide variety of imports.

2.1.2. *Infer protection from trade flows*

This approach seeks to measure the effects of NTBs by estimating their impact on the volume of trade in different industries. Researchers use models to predict trade patterns absent any barriers (on the basis of factors such as country size, distance from other economies, and factor endowments) and then use the gap between actual and predicted trade flows to infer protection. This method has the advantage of being able to capture the aggregate impact of all barriers combined, even ones not considered by NTB list-makers.[3] This approach, however, depends on having a trade model that can accurately account for all determinants of trade, besides barriers, which is an ambitious requirement. One wonders how much of the gap between predicted and actual flows results from barriers and how much results from model misspecification or data mismeasurement or both. The fact that one has to specify demand elasticities in order to convert the quantity shortfalls into tariff-equivalents introduces another source of uncertainty.

[3] One popular version of this approach is to use so-called gravity equations. For an excellent review of this methodology, see Frankel 1997.

2.1.3. *Price Gaps*

Like the second approach, this method has the virtue of capturing the full impact of all NTBs. It has the additional virtues of not relying on any single model and providing tariff-equivalent measures directly. Although it has pitfalls, we believe that the price gap approach has the most promise for measuring NTBs. With many possible barriers to trade, we believe that one can best account for all of them by using the information that prices concisely convey.

The basic philosophy behind this approach is that barriers to arbitrage across national borders should be considered barriers to trade.[4] If international markets are integrated, sellers cannot raise domestic prices above prices that would attract arbitrage from abroad. One needs to carefully account for unavoidable costs associated with shipping goods between economies. Once one has done this, however, if a price gap exists for equivalent goods in two different economies, then one can conclude that the higher-priced market is protected. Moreover, one can use the price gap as a measure of the extent of protection. Thus, a single number can give the total effect of all trade barriers. These gaps may be caused in part by policies that are not explicitly designed to impede trade, such as certification requirements that are more restrictive than is needed. No matter what the intent, however, which can be difficult to judge anyway, we presume that policies that segment national markets are trade barriers.[5]

The major problem applying this approach is obtaining appropriate price measures. Such efforts confront three major challenges. The first is comparing prices of equivalent goods. Even if they have the same name, goods may have very different levels of quality. Thus, surveyors need to work hard to ensure comparability. Many researchers have used unit values as price proxies because they are widely available. These can provide reasonable estimates of price gaps at very detailed classification levels (*e.g.*, Harmonized System 10-digit), but, at higher levels of aggregation, unit values are notoriously inexact measures of prices because of large quality differences in products.

A second challenge is using producer, rather than consumer, prices. Most price surveys are undertaken with a view to comparing costs to the consumer. In order to accurately gauge protection for producers, though, one should compare

---

[4] This does not depend on individual consumers engaging in arbitrage. Organized and well-informed trading companies and other international wholesalers can easily seize arbitrage opportunities.

[5] This notion corresponds to that of Knetter and Goldberg 1996, which argues that "A market is segmented if the location [sic] of the buyers and the sellers influences the terms of the transaction in a substantial way (*i.e.*, by more than the marginal cost of physically moving the good from one location to another)." (pp 3-4.)

producer prices. Data gathered at the retail level include non-traded value added, such as distribution margins and transportation costs. These prices may therefore provide an inaccurate picture of protection since they include elements that cannot be eliminated through arbitrage. The price of a pound of coffee purchased in a supermarket in Tokyo may be higher than a pound of the same brand of coffee purchased in New York, either because trade barriers raise the wholesale price of coffee or because the costs of distributing coffee in Tokyo are higher, or both. Since we seek to isolate the role of trade barriers, we need to compare producer, rather than consumer, prices.

A third challenge relates to the comprehensiveness of coverage. Samples of a few products gathered at selective retail outlets may not be representative of the full array of goods sold. In particular, many surveys focus heavily on consumer products sold at supermarkets and generally neglect to include capital and intermediate goods. Also, many international surveys were undertaken to establish differences in the cost of living experienced by business executives and their families. These naturally focus on a set of products that are not representative of all purchases.

2.2. Our Method[6]

Other studies have used price differentials as evidence of protection and to estimate the benefits of integration.[7] In this section, we discuss how we have tried to overcome the challenges mentioned above, in order to produce improved estimates of NTB protection and its effects. We use data in which every effort has been made to ensure comprehensive coverage and comparability. In addition, we have endeavored to compare producer prices by eliminating the effects of distribution margins. We also analyze the data at a fairly disaggregated level, to mitigate weighting problems.

We start with carefully matched retail prices that the OECD collects on a regular basis in order to calculate purchasing power parity (PPP) estimates. With the cooperation of member governments, OECD researchers regularly sample prices of over 3000 final goods. They make every effort to compare equivalent products across economies. For most manufactured goods, they compare the same make and model, or make comparisons from a list of two or more models when each item on that list is thought to be equivalent. For other manufactured

[6] See Bradford and Lawrence 2003 and Bradford 2003 for more discussion of the methodology and data presented in this paper and for welfare analyses of total protection.
[7] See in particular Hufbauer *et al.* 2002.

goods and food items, researchers rely on exact descriptions of the items to be priced. When they cannot find appropriate matches based on model or on descriptions, researchers from the economies involved travel abroad to determine which items would be most appropriate matches for the items in their country. This has occurred with grain, some vegetables, tobacco, textiles, footwear, stationary, and small housewares. The researchers also call upon the expertise of manufacturers, trade associations, and buyers for large stores in order to determine matches. On occasion, different goods that were "equivalent in use" have been compared. For instance, 220-volt bulbs in Europe have been matched with 120-volt bulbs in the United States.

Prices are collected from many markets and outlets at different times during the year in order to obtain a single annual, national average (World Bank 1993, p10). Also, prices of the average-sized purchase for that country were compared. After collecting the data, apparent mismatches in quality are dealt with either by refining the specifications or discarding the data (OECD 1995, p5). This method does not produce perfect data, but the scale of resources expended on accurate matching indicates that these are excellent measures of price differences for equivalent products.

The researchers aggregate the most detailed price data into categories called "basic headings." These are defined as "groups of similar well-defined commodities for which a sample of products can be selected that are both representative of their type and of the purchases made in participating countries" (OECD 1995, p5). Thus, a basic heading should not be too broad or too narrow. It should not be so broad that very different products are compared; it should not be so narrow that few economies in the sample sell it. For instance, seaweed is too narrow, and food is too broad.

In multilateral comparisons, one usually cannot find products that are representative of the category and typical of what is bought in every country, since consumers in different economies buy different mixes of products. Thus, while most items are priced in most or all of the economies, not every product in the sample is priced in each country. To be included in the sample, a product needs to be a "representative product" in at least one country and it must be sold in large enough quantities in at least one other country so as to be price-able. A "representative product" is one that accounts for a large share of that country's expenditure on that basic heading. For instance, cheddar is a representative product for the cheese basic heading in France but not for Italy. Cheddar cheese, however, is price-able in Italy. As long as economies price their own major products and a share of all other products, relative prices for each product and country can be calculated indirectly as well as directly. For details on how the prices are combined into one average price for each country see Eurostat-OECD PPP Programme 1996. There are about 200 basic headings. We obtained unpublished basic heading price data for 1999 and trimmed the sample to about 112 traded goods. We converted all prices to US dollars using the 1999 exchange rates. (See Table 1 for the list of categories).

We converted the consumer price measures to producer prices using data on margins–wholesale trade, retail trade, transportation, and taxes–which come from national input-output tables.[8] We did so for nine economies: Australia, Belgium, Canada, Germany, Italy, Japan, the Netherlands, the United Kingdom (UK), and the United States (US). Although we wanted to include more economies, such as France, the availability of detailed margins data determined which economies became part of the sample. We matched these margins with the OECD retail price data and derived estimates of producer prices by peeling off the relevant margins. Thus,

$$p_{ij}^{p} = \frac{p_{ij}^{c}}{1+m_{ij}}, \tag{1}$$

p_{ij}^{p}: the producer price of good *i* in country *j*,

p_{ij}^{c}: the consumer price of good *i* in country *j*, as taken from the OECD data,

m_{ij}: the margin for good *i* in country *j*, as taken from the national IO table.

Unfortunately, margins data only become available with a considerable time lag.[9] The producer price estimates were therefore obtained by assuming that distribution margins were the same percentage of overall value-added as they were in the most recent year for which data were available.

Producer prices allow us to get a sense of which industries in which economies have the lowest prices, but inferring the extent of insulation from foreign competition requires one more step: taking account of transport costs from one nation's market to another. A foreign good must travel from the foreign factory to the foreign border and then to the domestic border in order to compete with a domestic good.[10] Thus, one cannot infer protection simply by comparing

[8] Roningen and Yeats 1976 also use retail prices and adjust for taxes and transport costs, but they do not adjust for wholesale and retail trade margins, which significantly outweigh taxes and transportation.

[9] The margins data come from the following years: Australia, 95; Belgium, 90; Canada, 90; Germany, 93; Italy, 92; Japan, 95; Netherlands, 90; UK, 90; and US, 92.

[10] For a discussion of the importance of export margins, see Rousslang and To 1993.

Table 1. Products in the sample

Ingestible Products	Manufactured Household Goods	Capital Goods
Rice	Men's clothing	Structural metal products
Flour and other cereals	Ladies' clothing	Products of boilermaking
Bread	Children's clothing	Tools and finished metal goods
Other bakery products	Infant's clothing	Agricultural machinery and tractors
Pasta products	Materials, yarns, accessories, *etc.*	Machine tools for metal working
Other cereal products	Men's footwear	Equipment for mining, metallurgy
Fresh, frozen and chilled beef	Ladies' footwear	Textile machinery
Fresh, frozen and chilled veal	Children's and infant's footwear	Machinery for food, chemicals, rubber
Fresh, frozen and chilled pork	Furniture and fixtures	Machinery for working wood, paper
Fresh, *etc.* lamb, mutton and goat	Carpets and other floor coverings	Other machinery & mechanical equipment
Fresh, frozen and chilled poultry	Household textiles, other furnishings	Office and data processing machines
Delicatessen	Refrigerators and freezers	Precision instruments
Other meat preparations, extracts	Washing machines, driers, dishwashers	Optical instruments, photographic equip.
Other fresh, frozen, chilled meat	Cookers, hobs and ovens	Electrical equipment including lamps
Fresh, frozen or deep-frozen fish	Heaters and air-conditioners	Telecommunication & electrical equip. n.e.c.
Dried, smoked or salted fish	Vacuum cleaners, polishers, *etc.*	Electronic equipment, *etc.*
Fresh, frozen, deep-frozen seafood	Other major household appliances	Motor vehicles and engines
Preserved or processed fish & seafood	Glassware and tableware	Boats, steamers, tugs, platforms, rigs
Fresh, pasteurized, sterilized milk	Cutlery and silverware	Locomotives, vans, wagons
Condensed, powdered milk	Motorless kitchen & domestic utensils	Aircraft and other aeronautical equipment
Other milk products excluding cheese	Motorless garden appliances	Other transport equipment
Processed and unprocessed cheese	Electric bulbs, wires, plugs, *etc.*	
Eggs and egg products	Cleaning and maintenance products	
Butter	Other non-durable household goods	
Margarine	Drugs and medical preparations	
Edible oils	Other medical supplies	

Table 1. Products in the sample–Continued

Ingestible Products	Manufactured Household Goods	Capital Goods
Other animal and vegetable fats	Spectacle lenses and contact lenses	
Fresh fruit	Orthopedic and therapeutic appliances	
Dried fruit and nuts	Passenger vehicles	
Frozen and preserved fruit and juices	Motorcycles and bicycles	
Fresh vegetables	Tires, tubes, parts, accessories	
Dried vegetables	Motor fuels, oils and greases	
Frozen vegetables	Radio sets	
Preserved vegetables, juices, soups	Television sets, video recorders, *etc.*	
Potatoes and other tuber vegetables	Record-players, cassette recorders, *etc.*	
Potato products	Cameras and photographic equipment	
Raw and refined sugar	Other durable recreational goods	
Coffee and instant coffee	Records, tapes, cassettes, *etc.*	
Tea and other infusions	Sports goods and camping equipment	
Cocoa excluding cocoa preparations	Games, toys and hobbies	
Jams, jellies, honey and syrups	Films and photographic supplies	
Chocolate and cocoa preparations	Flowers, plants and shrubs	
Confectionery	Books	
Edible ice and ice-cream	Newspapers and other printed matter	
Salt, spices, sauces, condiments	Durable toilet articles and repairs	
Mineral water	Non-durable toilet articles	
Other soft drinks n.e.c.	Jewelry, watches and their repair	
Spirits and liqueurs	Travel goods and baggage items	
Wine (not fortified or sparkling)	Goods for babies, personal accessories	
Beer	Writing & drawing equipment & supplies	
Other wines and alcoholic beverages		
Cigarettes		

producer prices. The domestic producer price must be pcompared to the import price of the foreign good. We do not, however, have import price data that can be matched with the domestic price data. So, we infer the import price by combining data on export margins, also available from national input-output tables, with international transport costs.[11]

We could only get detailed data on international transport costs for Australia and the United States. Each of these economies reports import values for detailed commodities on both a basis that includes insurance and freight (c.i.f.) and one that does not–so-called free on board (f.o.b.). The c.i.f./f.o.b. ratio is a good measure of all the costs of shipping goods from abroad to these economies. For costs between other economies we simply average the costs of the United States with those of Australia. The ratios for both economies, however, are small, so that the gap between the two is also small. The average for all products for the United States is 1.05, while the overall average for Australia it is 1.09. Thus, for each detailed sector, we take the average of the two c.i.f./f.o.b. ratios and use this as an estimate for the international transport cost for that product for all the economies.

We use this data on export margins and international transport costs to compute import prices for each product and country, as follows. By adding the export margins to the producer prices, we calculated the export price for each product in each country. The lowest export price plus the common international transport cost is the import price. Thus, the export price is given by:

$$p_{ij}^{e} = p_{ij}^{p}(1 + em_{ij}), \tag{2}$$

p_{ij}^{e}: the export price of good *i* for country *j*,
em_{ij}: the export margin of good *i* for country *j*.

The import price is then given by:

$$p_{i}^{I} = p_{iM}(1 + tr_{i}), \tag{3}$$

p_{i}^{I} : the import price of good *i* (the same for each economy),
tr_{i}: the international transport margin for good *i*,

$p_{iM} = \min(p_{i1}^{e}, p_{i2}^{e}, \ldots, p_{i9}^{e})$, the minimum of the 9 export prices.

The ratio of each country's producer price to the import price gives us an initial measure of protection, pr_{ij}^{IN} :

[11] We have export margins for all countries except the UK, for which we used the Netherlands export margins. Export margins tend not to vary much by country, so we feel confident that using the Netherlands margins does not compromise our results.

$$pr_{ij}^{IN} = \frac{p_{ij}^{P}}{p_i^{I}}. \tag{4}$$

For a given good, these measures will differ from true protection if all of the economies in the sample have barriers to imports for that good. For such goods, the calculated import price will exceed the true import price to the extent that the low cost producer has barriers against imports. This will bias the protection estimates downward. By the same token, if just one of the nine has no barriers to imports in that good, then pr_{ij}^{IN} will approximate true protection, because, in this case, the price in the free trading country will approximate the import price. Since the sample includes Australia, Canada, and the United States, which are fairly free traders, the low price in the sample will approximate the import price the great majority of the time.

Nevertheless, we use data on trade taxes to correct, at least partially, for the possible downward bias. These tariff data come from the OECD tariff database. The final measure of total protection, pr_{ij}^{TOT}, is given by:

$$pr_{ij}^{TOT} = max(pr_{ij}^{IN}, 1 + tar_{ij}), \tag{5}$$

tar_{ij}: the tariff rate for good i in country j.

We simply use the fact that tariffs provide a lower bound on protection. If our initial measures do not exceed the overall tariff rate, then that tariff rate is used as the measure of protection. This happened about one-third of the time. After this correction, the only time that these protection measures will be biased downward is when all economies in the sample have NTBs against the rest of the world.

These measures provide estimates of the protective effect of all kinds of barriers–tariffs and NTBs alike. For our purposes, we want to focus on the impact of NTBs alone, so we perform one final, simple modification. We subtract out tariffs from these total protection numbers. Mathematically, NTB protection is given by

$$pr_{ij}^{NTB} = pr_{ij}^{TOT} - tar_{ij} = \max(pr_{ij}^{IN} - tar_{ij}, 1) \tag{6}$$

Note that, since we measure protection as a ratio of the world price, a value of 1 indicates no protection. Thus, we conclude that there is no NTB protection whenever $pr_{ij}^{IN} - tar_{ij} < 1 \Rightarrow pr_{ij}^{IN} < 1 + tar_{ij}$, that is, whenever the percentage by which the producer price exceeds the import price does not exceed the tariff rate.

Figure 1 shows a schematic example that illustrates this methodology. Suppose that there are three economies, with consumer prices as shown: Country A with the lowest and Country C with the highest. C's consumer price is nearly

Figure 1. NTB protection calculation: schematic example

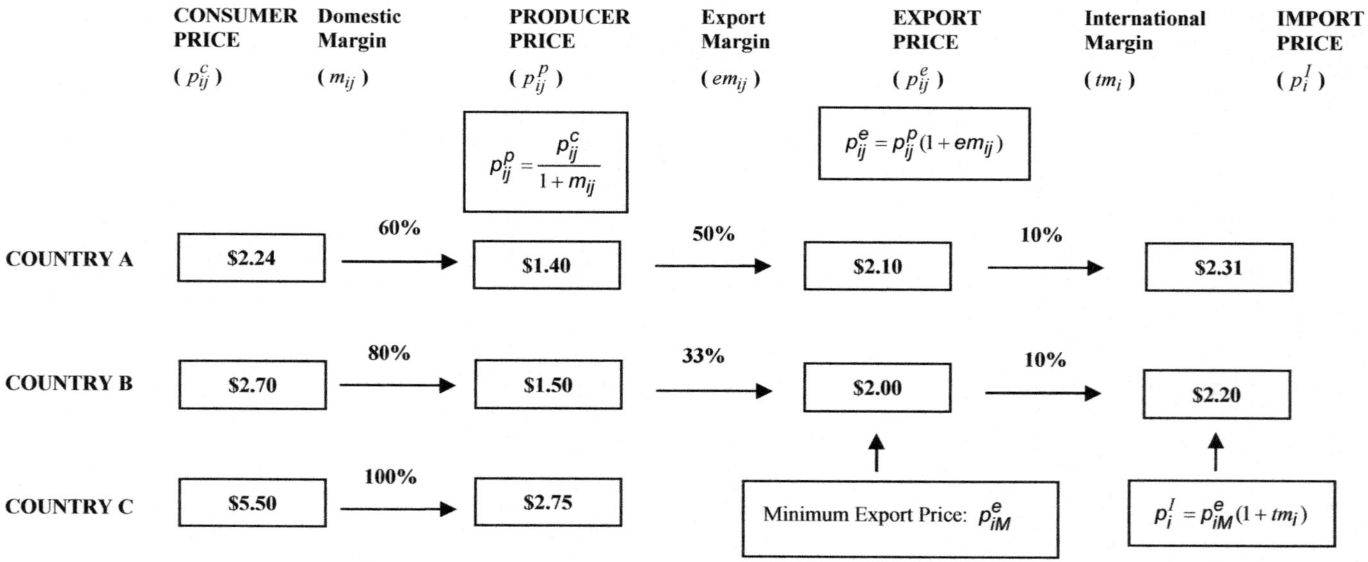

➔ NTB Protection in C = $\frac{p^p_{iC}}{p^I_i} - tar_{ij} = \frac{2.75}{2.20} - tar_{ij} = 1.25 - tar_{ij}$, *i.e.*, (25% - tariff rate), if the tariff rate is 25% or less. Otherwise, NTB protection is inferred to be zero.

Note: *i* indexes products, and *j* indexes countries.

2.5 times that of A, but such a facile comparison can mislead. After peeling off domestic distribution costs for this good, the ratio of C's producer price to A's is lower, though still large. As is often the case in reality, in this example, the country with the high consumer price also has the highest percentage domestic distribution margin. Converting to producer prices gets us closer to our goal, since these provide a clearer indication of how efficient producers in different economies are. Still, as discussed above, a straight comparison of producer prices would overstate protection, since doing so would not take account of the costs required to sell in foreign markets. So, to each of the producer prices, we add the unavoidable export margins and the international transport costs. Note that, because of its relatively small export margin, Country B ends up with the lower border price, even though its consumer and producer prices were higher than A's. In the end, the NTB protection level for C that we calculate is (25 percent - the tariff rate) (if the tariff rate is lower than that), a much smaller gap than that between the underlying consumer and producer prices.

3. Summary and Assessment

3.1. *Four Key Characteristics*

We believe that these measures, while not perfect, shed useful new light on NTB protection because they possess, to a large degree, four key characteristics: completeness, comprehensiveness, accuracy, and internationally comparability.

3.1.1. *Completeness*

Using price gaps enables one, in principle, to capture the combined effects of all NTBs, which can include any number of regulations and bureaucratic procedures. For example, a UN study analyzed how excess paperwork and cumbersome customs procedures impede the international flow of goods. The study points out that, in addition to direct costs, these regulations impose indirect costs, such as losses due to "deterioration or pilferage" while cargo is waiting to be cleared, or the "strong disincentive for potential exporters" imposed by complicated procedures. (See United Nations Conference on Trade and Development (1992).) The study estimated that these barriers imposed costs that averaged 10 percent to 15 percent, on top of any other trade barriers. Protection measures that rely on lists of individual barriers, such as the UN's own NTB measures, will tend to overlook subtle but real barriers such as these. Our method, however, will capture the protective impact of these barriers if one of the economies in our sample is free from them and, if this is not so, will partially capture such barriers (unless their price impact is exactly the same in each country).

3.1.2. *Comprehensiveness*

These measures cover all traded final goods, instead of a small subset thereof. Some other studies (such as Hufbauer and Elliott 1994) have limited their coverage to sectors in which protection had been previously thought to exist, without testing whether other sectors might enjoy well-disguised insulation from foreign competition. The approach in this paper allows us to construct a more comprehensive picture of final goods NTB protection in these economies. By the same token, this method does exclude non-final goods, which account for most output and trade. Nevertheless, final goods receive significantly more protection than do intermediate and primary products, so that this data probably covers most NTB protection.

3.1.3. *Accuracy*

Accuracy stems from comparing actual prices of identical or equivalent goods. Differences in quality have bedeviled attempts to use prices, except for certain homogeneous goods. The data here, on the other hand, have resulted from intensive multilateral efforts to correct for quality differences.

3.1.4. *International Comparability*

Many other estimates have only been derived for a single country at a time, making it difficult to rank economies in terms of openness. Our measures use the same data and apply the same method to each country in the sample, thus allowing us to make such rankings, for individual products, for aggregated categories, and for each country as a whole.

3.2. *Possible Concerns*

3.2.1. *Imperfect Competition*

Is it possible that market power could lead to estimates that do not really reflect NTBs? We argue that this is not so. If the domestic producer price exceeds the prevailing import price by more than the tariff rate, an NTB must support that gap, no matter how those prices came to be. Market power does not change this fact. With market power, a trade barrier may endogenously change prices, but the fact remains: an un-arbitraged gap between the domestic price and the tariff-inclusive import price cannot persist without NTBs that segment the domestic and world markets, and the gap measures the amount of NTB protection.

3.2.2. *Terms of Trade Effects*

A related concern is the impact of terms of trade effects, for which our method makes no adjustment. If an NTB drives down the import price, should we measure NTB protection with respect to the NTB-ridden import price or the free trade import price? For instance, suppose that the latter is 1.00 and that a country imposes an NTB of 0.2 that drives the domestic price to 1.10 and the import price to 0.90. Is the amount of NTB protection 22 percent ($\frac{1.1}{0.9}-1$) or 10 percent ($\frac{1.1}{1}-1$)? While the barrier only raises domestic prices by 10 percent, we believe that the amount of NTB protection is 22 percent. We hold to the view that the amount of the barrier is the gap (or ratio) between the domestic and import price. With the barrier in place, domestic consumers have to pay 22 percent more than people who can buy the good at world prices. Consider a more extreme case. Suppose in the above example that the domestic price remains at 1.00, while the import price gets driven to 0.80. One cannot reasonably conclude that NTB protection is zero simply because the domestic price did not move. In practice, the terms of trade rarely, if ever, move as much as in the above examples and will usually not matter. Even if one does want to correct for terms of trade effects, one does not observe the free trade import price, so speculation would drive the correction, and it would introduce a fair amount of uncertainty into the measures. Thus, for theoretical and practical reasons, we do not correct for terms of trade effects.

3.2.3. *Dumping*

Dumping can possibly bias our inferred import price downward, which would bias our protection measures upward. While protectionists make much of dumping, true cases of dumping in which firms sell goods overseas below cost are rare to non-existent. Most economists would agree that, the vast majority of the time, policymakers use anti-dumping duties as alternative ways to protect inefficient industries, not as justified defenses against a predatory threat. Even if such dumping occurs, and the resulting import price is lower than otherwise, that does not invalidate it as a proper benchmark. Again, barriers need to support gaps between domestic and import prices, even if the latter are artificially low.

3.2.4. *Demand Differences*

One may wonder whether these measures are valid if consumers in different economies have different demands. The question arises: If Country A's citizens have a higher demand for good *X* than do Country B's citizens, won't that drive up the price of good *X* in Country A in the absence of trade barriers? Answer: Only if there is a barrier in Country A that allows such a gap to emerge. If Country A and Country B are truly integrated, then good *X* will have one single demand curve, and the price will be the same everywhere. Demand differences without barriers cannot sustain price gaps.

3.2.5. *Price vs. Quantity Effects*

Finally, in deriving these estimates, we realize that there is no clear connection between tariff equivalents and the amount by which imports are reduced. Quantity changes depend on market structure and such key parameters as the elasticities of supply and of demand. Thus, a high NTB on a good with a low elasticity of demand may reduce imports by less than a small NTB on a good with a high elasticity of demand. We do not purport, however, to analyze prices and quantities at the same time. In order to assess the impact of the barriers on quantities, and thus on welfare, one would need a model of the particular sector in question. We claim that the cleanest, most effective way to measure NTB protection is to derive tariff equivalents and leave quantity and welfare analysis for the next step.

4. The Extent of NTB Protection

Table 2 presents the NTB data for the nine economies. Again, we report these as the ratio of the domestic producer price to the world price. Thus, a reading of 2.00 would be a protection rate of 100 percent. As mentioned above, the measures were constructed using 112 categories, but, to facilitate the presentation, we have aggregated up to 26 sectors, which correspond to the GTAP sectors that we will use in our AGE analysis below. We also report weighted geometric means for each country. We used the value of consumption as weights in constructing these means. Two factors motivated this choice: (1) Protection skews the value of consumption less than protection skews the value of production or of imports, and (2) The OECD reports the value of consumption along with its price data, so we had consumption data that exactly matches the protection aggregation.

Table 2. NTB estimates

	AUS	BEL	CAN	GER	ITA	JAP	NET	UK	US
Vegetables, fruit, nuts	1.055	1.031	1.046	1.257	1.036	2.048	1.000	1.317	1.203
Crops n.e.c.: Garden Products	1.000	2.231	3.227	1.956	1.326	2.478	1.197	2.529	1.524
Live Animals: Pets	1.000	1.081	1.000	1.321	1.113	2.305	1.000	1.473	1.000
Other Ag Products: Eggs	1.429	1.098	1.000	1.020	1.000	1.000	1.072	1.657	1.000
Fishing	1.137	1.181	1.114	1.206	1.000	1.398	1.000	1.056	1.301
Bovine cattle, sheep and goat, horse meat products	1.000	1.563	1.021	2.140	1.259	5.332	1.773	2.026	1.001
Meat products n.e.c.: Poultry, Pork	1.010	1.165	1.003	1.346	1.085	2.600	1.157	1.256	1.004
Vegetable oils and fats	1.313	1.472	1.204	1.249	1.087	2.348	1.000	1.000	1.447
Dairy products	1.274	1.164	1.237	1.022	1.065	1.759	1.056	1.081	1.145
Processed rice	1.000	1.067	1.000	1.028	1.023	2.773	1.000	1.000	1.119
Sugar	1.000	1.157	1.052	1.000	1.000	1.216	1.199	1.000	1.000
Food products n.e.c.	1.083	1.194	1.042	1.053	1.044	2.048	1.013	1.117	1.071
Beverages and tobacco products	1.488	1.012	1.166	1.004	1.009	1.519	1.047	1.234	1.063
Textiles	1.304	1.000	1.459	1.447	1.030	1.367	1.984	1.663	1.271
Wearing apparel	1.002	1.417	1.009	1.111	1.421	1.281	1.327	1.149	1.000
Leather products: Footwear	1.000	1.594	1.029	1.204	1.045	1.298	1.957	1.191	1.000
Wood products	1.000	1.096	1.000	1.000	1.000	2.103	1.119	1.396	1.000
Paper products, publishing	1.027	1.401	1.186	1.059	1.107	1.419	1.561	1.181	1.066
Petroleum, coal products	2.170	3.011	1.002	2.689	4.579	4.042	3.686	4.515	1.000
Chemical, rubber, plastic products	1.016	1.103	1.000	1.204	1.008	1.406	1.066	1.153	1.287
Mineral products n.e.c.: Glassware and Tableware	1.309	1.292	1.717	1.288	1.000	2.770	1.517	1.602	1.096
Metal products	1.000	1.487	1.000	1.253	1.042	1.581	1.503	1.291	1.192
Motor vehicles and parts	1.000	1.113	1.000	1.014	1.016	1.002	1.394	1.403	1.157
Electronic equipment	1.064	1.162	1.212	1.066	1.024	1.332	1.073	1.299	1.061
Machinery and equipment n.e.c.	1.159	1.433	1.051	1.239	1.100	1.447	1.313	1.613	1.085
Manufactures n.e.c.	1.052	1.369	1.045	1.206	1.000	1.473	1.376	1.095	1.016
WEIGHTED GEOMETRIC MEANS	**1.147**	**1.315**	**1.078**	**1.184**	**1.116**	**1.581**	**1.312**	**1.377**	**1.087**
WEIGHTED MEANS W/O PETROLEUM, COAL PRODUCTS	**1.102**	**1.224**	**1.078**	**1.131**	**1.083**	**1.528**	**1.222**	**1.284**	**1.087**

These results imply that Canada and the United States have the lowest NTB barriers, averaging less than 10 percent. Australia, Germany, and Italy rank in the middle, ranging from 12 percent to 18 percent. Belgium, the Netherlands, and the UK have average NTB protection in the 30s. Japan's NTBs restrict trade the most, with an average protective impact of 58 percent. Overall, this analysis suggests that there is considerable NTB protection among industrial economies. Also, NTB protection varies fairly widely across rich economies.

Looking at individual sectors, for each country we find evidence of NTB protection in textiles or apparel or both, presumably reflecting the impact of the Agreement on Textiles and Clothing. In food and agriculture, these data show that Japan has huge NTBs. Our results imply that efforts to reduce NTBs should include a focus on Japan's agriculture and food. We find evidence of substantial NTBs for meat in Europe, whose governments have taken actions to restrict imports of meat that most North Americans consider safe.

Interestingly, Japan shows no evidence of protection in automobiles. These numbers appear to support the claim that auto imports into Japan are low because they produce superior cars, not because of hidden barriers. Belgium, the Netherlands, the UK, and the United States, on the other hand, appear to have regulations that restrict auto imports. Pharmaceuticals are a prominent part of the chemicals, rubber, and plastics industry, and here, Japan, the United States, and, to a lesser extent, Germany and the UK have non-trivial NTBs. This result for the United States probably reflects, at least in part, the regulatory power of the U.S. Food and Drug Administration. The Europeans have long complained that the FDA approval process creates longer delays for foreign-produced medicines than for U.S. medicines.[12]

Finally, note the very large numbers for petroleum and coal products for all economies except Canada and the United States. Large taxes on gasoline in these economies complicate these estimates. Canada and the United States have significant but much lower gas taxes. Furthermore, these two economies collect most gasoline taxes from retailers, while the other seven economies collect from producers, before the gas enters the distribution system. Thus, for Canada and the United States, gas taxes get peeled off with the margins, while they do not for the other economies. This means that the inferred producer prices are much higher for these seven: their producer prices include their very high gas taxes, while Canadian and American producer prices do not. The philosophy of our

---

[12] See the EU's Market Access Sectoral and Trade Barriers Database at *http://mkaccdb.eu.int/mkdb/mkdb.pl?METHOD=SECTOR.*

method is that, if producer prices are high for a country, no matter the reason, there must be barriers to trade. And in fact, all of these economies do greatly tax foreign gasoline as part of their high gas tax regime. One can conclude from this that such restrictions constitute NTBs. On the other hand, one may be reluctant to include these taxes with NTBs since the taxes hurt domestic and foreign producers alike and thus do not provide protection per se to domestic producers. We suspect that foreign producers would adapt the former interpretation, while domestic governments and producers would adapt the latter. Given the uncertainty created by the high taxes in this sector, we have reported the weighted averages without petroleum and coal products. Of course, the inferred average NTB protection for the seven economies declines. Italy's inferred NTB average drops below the United States'. Otherwise, the ranking across economies remains the same.

For comparison purposes, we provide tariff data in Table 3. Not surprisingly, tariffs are generally lower and more tightly distributed. Canada, however, actually has a higher average tariff rate than NTB rate. One can use the tariff and NTB numbers to calculate a measure of "protection transparency," which we define as the ratio of NTB protection to total protection (which is simply the sum of NTB and tariff protection). We report transparency measures both with and without our inferred measures for petroleum and coal products. When we include the petroleum data, we see that these data imply that Japan has the most opaque protection regime, while Canada has the most transparent. When we exclude gasoline, Italy's transparency is on par with Canada's. In either case, Australia, Canada, Germany, Italy, and the United States have more transparent protection, while Belgium, Japan, the Netherlands, and the UK have more opaque regimes.

5. Other Evidence on NTBS

Our conclusion that substantial NTBs restrict trade fits with a variety of other evidence. A large number of studies, using a variety of methodologies and asking somewhat different questions, find that international market segmentation is significant. One line of inquiry uses the gravity model that controls for the impact of income and distance in explaining trade volumes. McCallum 1995 found, for example, that, controlling for distance and size, trade between two Canadian provinces was more than 20 times larger than trade between Canadian provinces and US states in 1988-90. Others have replicated these findings

Table 3. Tariffs

	AUS	BEL	CAN	GER	ITA	JAP	NET	UK	US
Vegetables, fruit, nuts	1.009	1.119	1.053	1.119	1.119	1.098	1.119	1.119	1.064
Crops n.e.c.	1.000	1.092	1.054	1.092	1.092	1.003	1.092	1.092	1.020
Live Animals	1.106	1.058	1.097	1.058	1.058	1.074	1.058	1.058	1.043
Other Ag Products	1.000	1.060	1.044	1.060	1.060	1.220	1.060	1.060	1.092
Fishing	1.000	1.122	1.003	1.122	1.122	1.055	1.122	1.122	1.005
Bovine cattle, sheep and goat, horse meat products	1.000	1.000	1.192	1.000	1.000	1.497	1.000	1.000	1.108
Meat products n.e.c.	1.015	1.158	1.079	1.136	1.125	1.128	1.122	1.139	1.060
Vegetable oils and fats	1.052	1.136	1.105	1.127	1.091	1.100	1.174	1.146	1.065
Dairy products	1.006	1.086	1.099	1.088	1.110	1.250	1.086	1.083	1.082
Processed rice	1.000	1.120	1.006	1.120	1.120	1.000	1.120	1.120	1.054
Sugar	1.048	1.150	1.095	1.150	1.150	1.553	1.150	1.150	1.278
Food products n.e.c.	1.038	1.145	1.059	1.132	1.142	1.167	1.136	1.137	1.040
Beverages and tobacco products	1.070	1.384	1.141	1.403	1.507	1.163	1.430	1.317	1.126
Textiles	1.152	1.091	1.151	1.093	1.090	1.050	1.094	1.093	1.072
Wearing apparel	1.107	1.134	1.236	1.134	1.134	1.134	1.134	1.134	1.142
Leather products	1.337	1.116	1.221	1.116	1.116	1.509	1.116	1.116	1.143
Wood products	1.098	1.059	1.139	1.059	1.059	1.005	1.059	1.059	1.045
Paper products, publishing	1.051	1.022	1.034	1.017	1.018	1.003	1.027	1.028	1.008
Petroleum, coal products	1.000	1.045	1.079	1.045	1.045	1.023	1.045	1.045	1.008
Chemical, rubber, plastic products	1.046	1.067	1.085	1.069	1.066	1.028	1.069	1.068	1.049
Mineral products n.e.c.	1.079	1.084	1.092	1.084	1.084	1.027	1.084	1.084	1.087
Metal products	1.100	1.062	1.102	1.062	1.060	1.033	1.060	1.057	1.047
Motor vehicles and parts	1.138	1.099	1.081	1.099	1.100	1.000	1.098	1.099	1.034
Electronic equipment	1.050	1.063	1.045	1.071	1.071	1.001	1.064	1.067	1.042
Machinery and equipment n.e.c.	1.079	1.055	1.061	1.051	1.050	1.004	1.049	1.048	1.040
Manufactures n.e.c.	1.085	1.066	1.088	1.067	1.067	1.061	1.065	1.064	1.065
WEIGHTED GEOMETRIC MEANS	**1.073**	**1.104**	**1.092**	**1.105**	**1.101**	**1.068**	**1.095**	**1.112**	**1.058**
TRANSPARENCY WITH PETROLEUM PRODUCTS	**0.333**	**0.249**	**0.540**	**0.363**	**0.467**	**0.105**	**0.233**	**0.229**	**0.398**
TRANSPARENCY WITHOUT PETROLEUM PRODUCTS	**0.417**	**0.318**	**0.540**	**0.445**	**0.551**	**0.114**	**0.300**	**0.283**	**0.398**

qualitatively, although the size of the effect is sensitive to the period used and the precise specification.[13]

A variety of other studies have generally found large and persistent deviations from the law of one price (LOOP). Isard 1977, the classic study of this question, speculated that nominal exchange rate changes were an important reason for these deviations. Since then his results have been replicated many times. Froot *et al.* 1995 obtained data on eight commodities in England and Holland over a 700 year period and finds that the substantial deviations from the LOOP are no smaller or less persistent than they were in the past.

A related phenomenon is that firms engage in international price discrimination, charging different prices in different markets for the same product. Knetter 1989 looks at 7-digit export unit values from a single source to different destinations and finds large and volatile differentials when similar goods are shipped to different destinations. Haskal and Wolf 2001 explores pricing within a single multinational furniture retailer and find typical deviations across branches in different economies for the same product of between 20 percent to 50 percent. This study also finds that differences in local costs (such as distribution and taxes) do not account for these deviations.

Overall, the literature based on price data supports the idea that border barriers are significant. Obstfeld and Rogoff 2000 concludes that "a recurring theme here is that the markets for most 'traded' goods are not fully integrated, and segmentation due to various trade costs can be quite pervasive. In fact, the spectrum of goods subject to low trade costs may be very narrow."

6. Policies behind the Price Gaps

These NTB estimates may help policy makers in one of two ways. First, for known NTBs, these measures provide estimates of the extent to which those NTBs actually restrict trade. Thus, our results may provide useful information to trade negotiators as they decide how to efficiently focus their efforts on freeing up trade. Second, some sectors that have not reached the trade negotiation agenda may, in fact, enjoy significant disguised NTB protection that is worth negotiating down. This research can help to flag such sectors.

To illustrate how our results can help in the first way mentioned, we have compiled possible barriers for some of the NTB gaps, though much more work along these lines needs to be done. We have drawn on the *EU Market Access Database*, the USTR's 2000 *Report on Foreign Trade Barriers*, and 2000 WTO

[13] See, for example, Wei 1996, Helliwell 1998, and Anderson and Van Win Coop 2001.

Trade Policy Review for the European Union, the United States, and Japan. Table 4 shows the results of an initial survey of these sources. We are sure that a more detailed analysis would reveal more policies behind the NTBs. Also, for any given price gap, the policies we have listed may not be major causes, but they are initial candidates.

Looking back at Table 2, there are a number of NTBs for which we have not listed possible policies. In these cases, more detailed research may reveal particular sources of the gaps, which might then become subject to negotiation. Also, any of these gaps, as well the ones for which we have listed policies, could result from burdensome customs procedures and other administrative friction, as discussed above. Thus, efforts by trade negotiators to remove such widespread sand from the wheels of trade could potentially have large benefits across many sectors and economies.

7. The Welfare Effects of Integration

To provide insights into the importance of NTBs, in this section we simulate their removal. For eight of the nine economies, we seek to compare real incomes in the world as it is with one in which the NTBs are eliminated. (Unfortunately, data problems prevent us from analyzing Belgium separately.) We use an AGE model based on one developed by Harrison, Rutherford, and Tarr (HRT).[14] The model has considerable country and sectoral detail: 16 regions and 33 sectors (See Table 5).[15] The model also allows for both increasing returns to scale and dynamic adjustment of the capital stock. We first describe the model and then report the simulation results.

7.1. *Description of the Model*

7.1.1. *Production Structure*

Production involves the use of intermediate goods and five factors–capital, skilled labor, unskilled labor, land, and natural resources. Only capital can move across national boundaries; all factors can move freely across sectors. Value added in each sector has a CES (constant elasticity of substitution) production

---

[14] The model is based on the computer code provided by Glenn Harrison, Thomas F. Rutherford, and David Tarr. Their code is available for public access at *http://theweb.badm.sc.edu/glenn/ur_pub.htm* and was used in their 1995, 1996, and 1997 articles.

[15] The underlying data come from Version 5 (1997) of the Global Trade Analysis Project (GTAP) database.

Table 4. Potential NTM policies

EU	PANEL A	SOURCE
Vegetables, fruit, nuts	Restrictive banana trade regime	USTR
	Tariff quotas on sweet potatoes and mushrooms	WTO
Crops n.e.c.: Garden Products	Unreasonable water solubility standards for fertilizers	USTR
Live Animals: Pets	Animal products have to be sourced from EU-approved 3rd country establishments	USTR
Other Ag Products: Eggs	Animal products have to be sourced from EU-approved 3rd country establishments	USTR
Fishing	Animal products have to be sourced from EU-approved 3rd country establishments	USTR
	Italy has overly strict interpretation of sanitary requirements	USTR
Bovine cattle, sheep and goat, horse meat prod	Animal products have to be sourced from EU-approved 3rd country establishments	USTR
	Ban on hormone beef	USTR
	Italy has overly strict interpretation of sanitary requirements	USTR
	Beef labeling requirements	WTO
Meat products n.e.c.: Poultry, Pork	Animal products have to be sourced from EU-approved 3rd country establishments	USTR
	Ban on anti-microbial treatments for poultry	USTR
	Tariff quotas	WTO
Dairy products	Animal products have to be sourced from EU-approved 3rd country establishments	USTR
	Tariff quotas	WTO
Sugar	Tariff quotas	WTO
Food products n.e.c.	Modern biotech products face lengthy and unpredictable approval process	USTR
	Standards for flour	WTO
Beverages and tobacco products	Strict standards on wine-making practices for imported wine	USTR
	Alcohol and tobacco labeling requirements	USTR
Textiles	ATC	WTO
Wearing apparel	ATC	WTO
Chemical, rubber, plastic products	Price, volume, and access controls on pharmaceuticals inhibit imports	USTR
	Drug labeling requirements	WTO
	Regulations and standards	WTO
Mineral products n.e.c.	Quotas on tableware and kitchenware from China	WTO

Table 4. Potential NTM policies–Continued

EU	**PANEL A**	**SOURCE**
Motor vehicles and parts	Regulations and standards	WTO
Electronic equipment	Overly restrictive limits on low frequency emissions from electronic equipment	USTR
US	**PANEL B**	
Fishing	Certification requirements for yellowfin tuna	EU
Beverages and tobacco products	Burdensome wine labeling requirements that vary by state	EU
Textiles	Customs requires overly detailed information	EU
	Burdensome labeling requirements	EU
Chemical, rubber, plastic products	Foreign drugs face lengthier approval process	EU
Motor vehicles and parts	Luxury tax, CAFE payments, guzzler tax	EU
	Labeling of proportion of content that is North American	EU
	Must declare which engines and gearboxes are not North American	EU
JAPAN		
Vegetables, fruit, nuts	Overly restrictive sanitary standards	EU
	Complex regulations	EU
Crops n.e.c.: Garden Products	Overly restrictive sanitary standards	EU
Fishing	Quotas	EU
Vegetable oils and fats	Tariff quotas	WTO
Processed rice	Import ban	
Food products n.e.c.	Licensing and distribution barriers for imports	USTR
	Tariff quotas for coffee and tea	WTO
	Quota for chocolate	WTO
Beverages and tobacco products	Burdensome wine testing	EU
	Term "mineral water" not backed by legal obligations in Japan	EU
	High taxes on beer and spirits	USTR
Textiles	Quotas	WTO

Table 4. Potential NTM policies–Continued

JAPAN	PANEL B	SOURCE
Wearing apparel	Quotas	WTO
Leather products: Footwear	Tariff quotas	EU
Chemical, rubber, plastic products	Ban on food supplements in form of capsules	EU
	Burdensome approval and testing procedures for drugs	EU
	Biased government procurement for drugs and other medical supplies	USTR
Metal products	Market barriers	USTR
Electronic equipment	Different standards	EU
Machinery and equipment n.e.c.	Elevator standards	EU
	Regulations on fork lifts and other industrial trucks	EU
	Very costly safety device required for wind turbines	EU
CANADA	**PANEL C**	
Vegetables, fruit, nuts	Overly restrictive sanitary standards	EU
	Packaging requirements	EU
Vegetable oils and fats	Rules on coloring of margarine	EU
Dairy products	Inspection requirements	EU
Food products n.e.c.	Different labeling requirements across provinces	EU
Beverages and tobacco products	Discriminatory price controls, taxes, listing procedures, delivery regulations	EU
AUSTRALIA		
Vegetables, fruit, nuts	Overly strict quarantine laws	EU
Other Ag Products: Eggs	Overly strict quarantine laws	EU
Fishing	Overly strict quarantine laws	EU
Vegetable oils and fats	Overly strict quarantine laws	EU
Dairy products	Overly strict quarantine laws	EU
Food products n.e.c.	Overly strict quarantine laws	EU

Table 5. Sectors and regions in the AGE model

33 SECTORS	16 REGIONS
Fruits, Nuts, Vegetables	Australia
Other Crops	Japan
Other Agriculture	Korea
Live Animals	China
Other Animal Products	Rest of Asia
Fish	Canada
Coal, Gas, Oil	United States
Other Minerals	Brazil
Bovine Cattle, Sheep, Goat, and Horse Products	Rest of Latin America
Other Meat Products	Germany
Vegetable Oils and Fats	Italy
Dairy Products	Netherlands
Processed Rice	United Kingdom
Sugar	Rest of Europe
Other Food Products	Middle East
Beverages and Tobacco Products	Rest of World
Textiles	
Wearing Apparel	
Leather Goods	
Lumber and Wood Products	
Pulp, Paper Products, Publishing	
Coal and Petroleum Products	
Chemicals, Plastics, and Rubber	
Non-metallic Mineral Products	
Primary Ferrous Metals	
Non-ferrous Metals	
Fabricated Metal Products	
Motor Vehicles and Parts	
Electronic Equipment	
Machinery and Equipment	
Other Manufacturing Products	
Trade and Transport Services	
Other Services	
Investment Good	

Sectors in bold are the final goods sectors for which we inserted our protection measures.

Underlined sectors are the ones which are assumed to have increasing returns to scale.

function. This formulation means that, within each sector, the elasticity of substitution between any two of the factors is the same. We use HRT's values for these elasticities, which they estimated econometrically using US time series data from 1947 to 1982 and using the same functional form as is used in this AGE model. In their estimates, however, they used only three factors–capital, labor, and land–instead of five. See Table 6 for these estimates and their standard errors. The production function for intermediates and the value-added composite is Leontief.[16]

Table 6. Substitution elasticities and learner indices

SECTOR	Factor Substitution Elasticities	Lerner Indices* HRT	GATT
Fruits, Nuts, Vegetables	0.945 (0.041)	0	0
Other Agriculture	0.945 (0.041)	0	0
Other Crops	0.945 (0.041)	0	0
Live Animals	0.945 (0.041)	0	0
Other Animal Products	0.945 (0.041)	0	0
Fish	0.945 (0.041)	0.05	0
Coal, Gas, Oil	0.293 (0.102)	0.03	0.05
Other Minerals	0.426 (0.105)	0.08	0.05
Bovine Cattle, Sheep, Goat, and Horse Products	0.945 (0.041)	0.10	0
Other Meat Products	0.945 (0.041)	0.10	0
Vegetable Oils and Fats	0.945 (0.041)	0.03	0
Dairy Products	0.945 (0.041)	0	0
Processed Rice	0.945 (0.041)	0.13	0
Sugar	0.945 (0.041)	0.03	0
Other Food Products	0.945 (0.041)	0.03	0
Beverages and Tobacco Products	0.945 (0.041)	0.03	0
Textiles	0.927 (0.077)	0.06	0.14
Wearing Apparel	0.927 (0.077)	0.13	0.13
Leather Goods	0.927 (0.077)	0.13	0.13
Lumber and Wood Products	0.945 (0.041)	0.05	0
Pulp, Paper Products, Publishing	1.202 (0.090)	0.05	0.15
Coal and Petroleum Products	0.293 (0.102)	0.03	0.05
Chemicals, Plastics, and Rubber	1.009 (0.027)	0.04	0.15
Non-metallic Mineral Products	0.426 (0.105)	0.08	0.05
Primary Ferrous Metals	0.911 (0.241)	0.05	0.13
Non-ferrous Metals	0.958 (0.132)	0.05	0.13
Fabricated Metal Products	1.189 (0.055)	0.05	0.12
Motor Vehicles and Parts	1.202 (0.090)	0.11	0.12
Electronic Equipment	1.202 (0.090)	0.06	0.15
Machinery and Equipment	1.202 (0.090)	0.06	0.15
Other Manufacturing Products	1.202 (0.090)	0.06	0.15
Trade and Transport Services	1.283 (0.525)	0	0
Other Services	3.125 (0.817)	0	0
Investment Good	1.988 (0.477)	0	0
	Standard Errors in Parentheses	*(P-MC)/P	

[16] Relaxing this assumption does not significantly change the results.

Some sectors are assumed to have constant returns to scale. Other sectors, though, are modeled with increasing returns to scale and imperfect competition.[17] In these sectors, there is firm-level product differentiation, with output being a composite of varieties. Firms have fixed costs and constant marginal costs, meaning that reducing the number of firms leads to rationalization gains. These firms compete using quantity conjectures, with entry and exit that drive profits to zero.

Dynamics are incorporated by allowing the capital stock to vary in response to changes in the rate of return caused by liberalization. If the rate of return increases, investment increases the capital stock until its return is driven back down to the long-run equilibrium. The results, therefore, reflect the model's predictions for what happens after the capital stock has changed enough to return the price of capital to its original level. The capital adjustment process is not modeled, and the time horizon implied by these results depends on how long one thinks it takes capital to respond to interest rate differentials. The model ignores the consumption foregone by the increased investment, which may overstate the estimated benefits. On the other hand, the model ignores any impact of growth on productivity and innovation, which leads to an underestimate of the gains.

7.1.2. *Demand Structure*

On the demand side, each region has a representative consumer and a single government agent, each of whom has a nested CES utility function and practices multi-stage budgeting. At the top level, demand across the 33 sectors is Cobb-Douglas. Consumers first decide how much to spend on each of the 33 aggregate goods, given total income and aggregate prices. Each of these goods is a CES composite of domestic output and an import composite, which are imperfect substitutes. In this second level, consumers divide spending between the domestic and import good by maximizing a CES utility function subject to the total spending they have allocated to that sector and given the aggregate prices in that sector. At the third level, the model invokes the Armington assumption in that imports of the same good from different economies are assumed to be imperfect substitutes. Preferences across these different goods from different economies are given by a CES utility function. At this third level, consumers choose quantities of each import subject to the amount they have budgeted for aggregate imports at the second level and subject to the various prices. We

[17] See Table 6 for the sectors and the mark-ups used. This table also presents alternative mark-ups from the GTAP model. The results are robust to the set of mark-ups used.

follow HRT and set the elasticity of substitution across import varieties, σ_{MM}, equal to eight and the elasticity of substitution between the import composite and the domestic good, σ_{DM}, equal to four. These elasticities affect the magnitude of the results. Higher values of these parameters lead to greater substitution in response to price reductions and, in general, higher welfare gains from liberalization. Roughly speaking, cutting these elasticities in half reduces the gains by 10 percent to 50 percent, depending on the region and the simulation. Similarly, doubling these elasticities increases the estimated gains by about 20 percent to 100 percent. Even such wide changes in the calibration, however, do not change any of our main conclusions.

In the sectors with increasing returns, yet another level of constrained choice is introduced. In this set-up, the domestic good and each import good produced in each region, instead of being homogeneous goods, are themselves composites of different varieties produced by the different firms. Consumers have CES preferences over these varieties and allocate spending across them subject to the amount they budgeted for each good at the third level. The elasticity of substitution across these varieties is set at 15. All results are robust to wide changes in this parameter.

7.1.3. *Incorporating Our Data*

7.1.3.1. Protection Data

To simulate the impact of NTBs as we have measured them, we benchmarked the model with our total protection measures–NTBs plus tariffs–instead of the GTAP protection data, which consists almost entirely of tariffs. In the model, all policy distortions enter as *ad valorem* price wedges,[18] which, conveniently, is the form that our protection data takes. So, replacing the GTAP tariff equivalents with our own is fairly straightforward. We did not, however, simply use our measures since they apply only to final goods, while almost all of the sectors of the model contain a combination of final and intermediate goods. Instead, we used a weighted average of our data and the original GTAP data. The weight on our measure was the fraction of output in that sector sold to final demand; the weight on the GTAP measure was one minus our weight. Thus, letting B and GTAP be the two protection measures and α, the final demand fraction, the protection estimate used was $\alpha B + (1-\alpha)GTAP$. Using this method ensures that model sectors with a high proportion of final goods use a protection estimate

[18] Government revenue is held constant throughout all simulations by assuming that lump-sum taxes are used to replace any lost tax revenue.

close to ours, while sectors with a low fraction of final goods use a protection estimate close to the GTAP measure. Put another way, the lower the final demand fraction, the less we deviated from the standard GTAP data. See Table 7 for a comparison of these weighted data and the original GTAP data. As shown in the table, we have not used our NTB estimates for the sector containing gasoline (oil and gas products) in order to avoid any muddying of the waters that gasoline taxes might cause.

7.1.3.2. Distribution Margins Data

The margins data used to derive the protection measures allow us to model distribution more accurately within the AGE framework. Most AGE trade models do not account for margins explicitly. All distribution services are lumped into the trade and transport sector and consumed as a separate good, instead of being linked to the goods that use those distribution services. Since margins vary across sectors, this obscures the role of distribution in the economy and can skew the results of AGE analyses. For instance, simulations of price reductions in other sectors may imply a large substitution out of trade and transport services, even though actual consumption of these will probably increase in order to facilitate commodity flows. Also, not accounting for margins implies that consumers base choices on producer prices instead of the higher consumer prices that include margins.

We attempt to address these problems by incorporating distribution explicitly into each final demand sector for which we have margins data. We do this by treating margins like taxes, since margins create a wedge between consumer and producer prices. For the eight economies involved, therefore, we inserted margin wedges into each of the relevant sectors.[19] We also reduced the value of the trade and transport sector by the total value of these margins. Finally, we reduced inputs into the trade and transport sector and re-distributed them across the final goods sectors in accordance with the amount of distribution used in those sectors.[20]

---

[19] See Gohin 1998 and Komen and Peerlings 1996 for other examples of modeling margins in this way within AGE models. Bradford and Gohin 2002 explicitly model the distribution sector for the United States within an AGE model.

[20] These modifications only apply to final goods. Due to lack of data, we do not modify the model to account for intermediate distribution. It turns out that these intermediate margins are quite a bit smaller than the margins for final goods.

7.2. *Welfare Analysis*

We now seek to estimate the potential gains from including NTBs on the trade negotiation agenda. Since tariffs presumably require much less work to remove, we do not think it likely that negotiators will remove NTBs and not tariffs. So we simulate two sets of scenarios: one in which economies remove all protection – NTBs and tariffs alike – and one in which economies only remove tariffs. For each of these two situations, we conduct three types of simulations: unilateral barrier removal in each of the eight economies; multilateral worldwide opening by all eight at once; and a Preferential Trade Agreement (PTA) in which the eight economies simultaneously remove barriers against each other but not the rest of the world. Analyzing these three scenarios will allow us to see differences among multilateral opening, regional opening, and unilateral opening. We focus on changes in equivalent variation (which, given the model structure, is the same as changes in real consumption) as a percentage of GDP.

Tables 8 and 9 show the main results for total protection and just tariffs. These tables report the permanent, annual effect of trade opening on consumption, as a percentage of GDP, once the capital stock has changed to its new equilibrium. Alternatively, they report the welfare costs, born at home and abroad, of tariff and total protection in the eight economies separately and as a group. Table 10 shows the difference between the two scenarios and thus the predicted extra gains from removing NTBs. For each table, Panel A reports these gains as a percentage of GDP, while Panel B shows them in billions of 1997 US dollars. We find that the efficiency gains from full-fledged integration of goods markets among the economies in our sample would well exceed the gains from eliminating tariffs. In fact, in most cases, the **extra** gains from NTB removal would outweigh the gains from tariff removal, so that the total gains from including NTBs are generally more than twice the gains from just removing tariffs.

Focusing on Panel A of Table 10, each of the economies except Canada and the United States would get an extra annual boost of 0.7 percent or more to GDP from unilateral NTB opening (beyond tariff removal). Multilateral opening from all eight would bring even larger extra gains of at least 2 percent of GDP for all economies except Australia and the United States. Global GDP would rise an additional 1.5 percent with NTB removal.

Two main forces drive the gains for any given country: the amount of protection removed and the share of trade in GDP for that country. The United States' relatively low barriers **and** its low trade/GDP share lead to relatively low predicted gains for the United States. Canada has about the same NTB protection

Table 7. Protection data for the AGI model

	NEW DATA*								GTAP DATA							
SECTOR	AUS	CAN	GER	ITA	JAP	NET	UK	US	AUS	CAN	GER	ITA	JAP	NET	UK	US
Fruits, Nuts, Vegetables	4.6	6.0	35.1	15.3	94.1	13.9	34.0	17.4	2.0	1.9	14.5	14.5	44.9	14.5	14.5	4.7
Other Agriculture									1.0	2.0	3.0	18.0	30.0	4.5	23.0	3.0
Other Crops	2.1	66.8	83.0	6.9	52.5	9.7	89.1	32.2	2.7	2.4	3.1	3.1	22.1	3.1	3.1	21.5
Live Animals	1.0	0.3	36.6	31.4	149.1	34.9	38.2	1.1	0.8	0.2	36.6	36.6	149.1	36.6	36.6	1.1
Other Animal Products	7.2	19.3	6.7	6.4	7.8	7.2	25.6	2.3	0.5	19.8	6.7	6.7	5.0	6.7	6.7	0.6
Fish	8.6	1.2	11.4	11.4	16.2	8.7	7.7	5.1	0.3	0.4	6.8	9.6	4.9	7.5	6.9	0.6
Coal, Gas, Oil									0.0	0.0	0.0	0.0	-0.8	0.0	0.0	0.2
Other Minerals									0.1	0.0	0.0	0.0	0.0	0.0	0.0	0.4
Bovine Cattle, Sheep Goat, Horse Prod.	0.0	18.1	109.7	39.0	265.4	80.6	99.6	8.3	0.1	16.3	88.9	88.9	36.4	88.9	88.9	5.3
Other Meat Products	3.0	29.3	41.8	23.3	119.8	29.6	37.6	5.5	4.1	72.4	30.9	30.9	58.2	30.9	30.9	3.6
Vegetable Oils and Fats	20.2	13.1	27.3	15.4	46.0	13.8	12.2	6.0	2.8	8.6	11.4	11.4	6.6	11.4	11.4	4.3
Dairy Products	19.1	77.8	30.8	33.8	173.7	53.0	43.4	32.0	7.3	214.8	87.7	87.7	287.0	87.7	87.7	42.5
Processed Rice	0.4	0.6	47.9	28.9	224.3	25.4	23.7	13.1	1.0	0.7	87.4	87.4	409.0	87.4	87.4	5.3
Sugar	11.7	8.3	66.3	37.2	111.0	72.4	69.2	46.9	13.9	4.9	76.4	76.4	116.1	76.4	76.4	53.4
Other Food Products	10.9	11.4	21.5	24.8	98.3	23.8	27.1	11.3	5.6	14.1	28.8	28.8	38.3	28.8	28.8	11.4
Beverages and Tobacco Products	54.1	35.6	33.9	37.8	59.6	35.2	45.2	15.4	9.2	62.5	8.3	8.3	16.2	8.3	8.3	3.0
Textiles	24.9	26.3	30.1	9.4	16.6	29.8	29.9	16.8	17.0	15.7	9.7	9.2	8.5	9.8	9.5	11.2
Wearing Apparel	12.7	24.2	23.1	46.1	33.4	33.5	26.0	14.0	29.3	21.2	12.1	12.2	12.5	12.0	11.9	13.3
Leather Goods	27.9	22.8	27.5	12.2	71.4	84.1	20.9	14.1	13.0	15.3	8.4	6.5	15.3	8.7	8.7	13.5

Table 7. Protection data for the AGI model–Continued

	NEW DATA*								GTAP DATA							
SECTOR	**AUS**	**CAN**	**GER**	**ITA**	**JAP**	**NET**	**UK**	**US**	**AUS**	**CAN**	**GER**	**ITA**	**JAP**	**NET**	**UK**	**US**
Lumber and Wood Products	5.7	8.4	4.2	4.4	4.6	6.2	8.8	2.6	4.5	6.8	2.8	2.7	2.7	3.0	2.8	2.2
Pulp, Paper Prod., Pub.	3.9	5.6	3.2	4.2	4.7	12.7	5.7	2.3	3.1	1.9	2.9	2.4	0.5	2.7	2.6	1.0
Coal and Petroleum Products									0.0	6.2	2.7	3.0	3.3	3.1	2.9	2.2
Chemicals, Plastics, and Rubber	4.0	5.4	8.7	5.7	7.6	5.7	7.4	10.4	3.5	4.8	5.1	5.3	2.0	4.8	4.7	3.5
Non-metallic Mineral Products	6.0	13.4	8.6	5.3	10.8	7.3	8.2	6.8	4.7	5.7	5.4	5.2	1.2	5.2	5.1	6.1
Primary Ferrous Metals									4.7	4.7	3.2	3.2	2.5	3.2	3.4	3.4
Non-ferrous Metals									1.4	0.5	2.1	1.2	0.4	2.9	1.5	1.7
Fabricated Metal Products	6.6	6.5	3.7	4.2	3.5	5.6	5.9	4.6	6.4	6.3	3.7	3.9	1.2	4.0	3.8	3.8
Motor Vehicles and Parts	11.4	6.7	11.1	9.7	0.1	20.1	27.9	7.8	9.2	6.1	7.7	8.6	0.0	8.4	8.3	2.4
Electronic Equip.	3.4	10.6	5.7	5.6	5.9	4.9	8.5	2.4	1.6	1.2	4.3	4.5	0.0	4.2	4.2	1.2
Machinery and Equipment	7.2	4.1	4.7	3.7	2.6	4.4	9.7	4.2	4.3	3.3	3.1	3.1	0.3	3.1	3.1	2.7
Other Manufacturing Products	10.3	9.3	10.7	5.1	18.7	21.8	11.9	5.7	3.7	3.8	3.7	3.8	1.9	3.9	2.5	1.7
Other Services									0.0	0.0	0.0	0.0	0.0	0.0	0.0	0.0
Investment Good									0.0	0.0	0.0	0.0	0.0	0.0	0.0	0.0

*A weighted average of our final goods protection data and the GTAP data, with the final demand fraction in each sector used as the weight on our data.

Sectors for which we did not use our protection data are left blank.

Table 8a. Panel A

	REGION IN WHICH PROTECTION IS REMOVED:									8 COUNTRY
IMPACT ON:	AUS	CAN	GER	ITA	JAP	NET	UK	US	ALL 8	PTA
Australia	1.61	0.02	0.11	0.03	1.66	0.01	0.25	0.27	3.95	4.35
Canada	0.04	1.00	0.03	0.10	0.52	0.01	0.07	1.71	3.49	3.66
Germany	0.03	-0.01	1.28	0.25	-0.04	0.29	0.30	0.12	2.26	1.96
Italy	0.05	0.02	0.66	1.97	0.03	0.10	0.37	0.16	3.46	4.61
Japan	0.04	-0.01	-0.01	0.00	3.06	0.01	0.00	0.12	3.27	2.18
Netherlands	0.05	0.01	1.56	0.58	0.14	3.84	1.03	0.33	7.71	9.38
United Kingdom	0.01	0.02	0.27	0.10	0.23	0.21	3.21	0.21	4.29	2.79
United States	-0.01	0.20	0.03	0.01	0.40	0.01	0.06	0.40	1.02	1.35
China	0.04	0.05	0.12	0.04	0.77	0.02	0.05	0.55	1.49	-0.57
South Korea	0.04	0.00	0.03	0.01	0.62	0.00	0.03	0.25	0.96	-0.51
Rest of Asia	0.06	0.02	0.19	0.06	1.03	0.03	0.18	0.49	2.03	-0.81
Brazil	-0.03	0.02	0.18	0.06	0.41	0.03	0.10	0.32	1.05	0.00
Rest of Latin America	0.00	-0.01	0.15	0.07	0.55	0.02	0.09	0.86	1.94	-0.53
Rest of Europe	0.02	0.01	0.59	0.20	0.13	0.18	0.47	0.15	1.69	-0.88
Middle East	0.01	0.03	0.35	0.17	0.55	0.10	0.37	0.41	1.96	-0.05
Rest of the World	-0.01	0.02	0.36	0.16	0.43	0.06	0.21	0.11	1.34	0.03
DEVELOPING ECONOMIES	0.01	0.01	0.21	0.09	0.63	0.04	0.15	0.43	1.60	-0.36
RICH ECONOMIES	0.04	0.10	0.29	0.17	0.90	0.14	0.35	0.29	2.26	1.76
WORLD	0.04	0.09	0.27	0.16	0.84	0.12	0.31	0.33	2.11	1.25

Table 8b. Panel B

	REGION IN WHICH PROTECTION IS REMOVED:									8 COUNTRY
IMPACT ON:	AUS	CAN	GER	ITA	JAP	NET	UK	US	ALL 8	PTA
Australia	5.677	0.071	0.388	0.106	5.853	0.035	0.881	0.952	13.927	15.338
Canada	0.208	5.189	0.156	0.519	2.698	0.052	0.363	8.873	18.109	18.991
Germany	0.543	-0.181	23.182	4.528	-0.724	5.252	5.433	2.173	40.930	35.497
Italy	0.510	0.204	6.727	20.078	0.306	1.019	3.771	1.631	35.264	46.984
Japan	1.761	-0.440	-0.440	0.000	134.732	0.440	0.000	5.284	143.978	95.985
Netherlands	0.153	0.031	4.764	1.771	0.428	11.726	3.145	1.008	23.544	28.643
United Kingdom	0.121	0.242	3.262	1.208	2.779	2.537	38.781	2.537	51.829	33.707
United States	-0.752	15.038	2.256	0.752	30.076	0.752	4.511	30.076	76.694	101.507
China	0.354	0.443	1.063	0.354	6.818	0.177	0.443	4.870	13.194	-5.047
South Korea	0.157	0.000	0.117	0.039	2.426	0.000	0.117	0.978	3.757	-1.996
Rest of Asia	0.783	0.261	2.478	0.783	13.436	0.391	2.348	6.392	26.480	-10.566
Brazil	-0.199	0.133	1.196	0.399	2.723	0.199	0.664	2.125	6.974	0.000
Rest of Latin America	0.000	-0.110	1.646	0.768	6.034	0.219	0.987	9.435	21.284	-5.815
Rest of Europe	0.559	0.280	16.496	5.592	3.635	5.033	13.141	4.194	47.252	-24.604
Middle East	0.057	0.170	1.981	0.962	3.112	0.566	2.094	2.320	11.091	-0.283
Rest of the World	-0.155	0.310	5.572	2.476	6.655	0.929	3.250	1.702	20.739	0.464
DEVELOPING ECONOMIES	0.646	0.646	13.558	5.811	40.674	2.582	9.684	27.762	103.299	-23.242
RICH ECONOMIES	7.973	19.933	57.806	33.886	179.399	27.906	69.766	57.806	450.490	350.824
WORLD	10.556	23.750	71.251	42.223	221.671	31.667	81.807	87.085	556.816	329.867

Table 9a. Panel A

	REGION IN WHICH PROTECTION IS REMOVED:									8 COUNTRY
IMPACT ON:	AUS	CAN	GER	ITA	JAP	NET	UK	US	ALL 8	PTA
Australia	0.91	0.02	0.08	0.02	1.07	0.03	0.15	0.12	2.37	2.79
Canada	0.02	0.63	0.03	0.10	0.49	0.01	0.07	-0.14	1.30	1.41
Germany	0.01	0.01	0.34	-0.08	-0.06	-0.08	-0.10	0.05	0.15	0.12
Italy	0.03	0.04	-0.15	0.78	-0.06	-0.03	-0.08	0.14	0.69	0.69
Japan	0.02	0.01	0.00	0.00	0.99	0.00	0.00	0.08	1.16	0.91
Netherlands	0.02	0.02	-0.49	-0.17	-0.06	1.62	-0.27	0.11	0.61	0.18
United Kingdom	-0.01	0.02	-0.04	-0.02	0.10	-0.03	0.70	0.07	0.81	0.57
United States	-0.01	0.04	0.02	0.01	0.15	0.02	0.04	0.06	0.30	0.48
China	0.06	0.07	0.12	0.03	0.27	0.05	0.08	0.38	1.01	-0.23
South Korea	0.04	0.03	0.07	0.03	0.21	0.01	0.05	0.23	0.68	-0.17
Rest of Asia	0.05	0.05	0.17	0.07	0.31	0.08	0.16	0.47	1.29	-0.37
Brazil	-0.02	0.02	0.10	0.12	0.23	0.08	0.09	0.18	0.79	0.10
Rest of Latin America	0.00	-0.01	0.16	0.10	0.23	0.05	0.09	0.13	0.73	-0.22
Rest of Europe	0.01	0.01	-0.08	-0.04	-0.01	-0.04	-0.08	0.05	-0.16	-0.26
Middle East	0.00	0.02	0.42	0.17	0.23	0.11	0.25	0.27	1.45	0.12
Rest of the World	-0.01	0.02	0.43	0.20	0.23	0.10	0.22	0.10	1.22	0.13
DEVELOPING ECONOMIES	0.01	0.03	0.23	0.11	0.25	0.07	0.14	0.25	1.06	-0.10
RICH ECONOMIES	0.02	0.04	0.01	0.03	0.29	0.01	0.03	0.06	0.52	0.51
WORLD	0.02	0.04	0.07	0.05	0.29	0.03	0.06	0.11	0.66	0.36

Table 9b. Panel B

IMPACT ON:	REGION IN WHICH PROTECTION IS REMOVED: AUS	CAN	GER	ITA	JAP	NET	UK	US	ALL 8	8 COUNTRY PTA
Australia	3.086	0.068	0.271	0.068	3.629	0.102	0.509	0.407	8.037	9.462
Canada	0.100	3.161	0.151	0.502	2.458	0.050	0.351	-0.702	6.522	7.074
Germany	0.170	0.170	5.784	-1.361	-1.021	-1.361	-1.701	0.851	2.552	2.042
Italy	0.288	0.384	-1.441	7.495	-0.577	-0.288	-0.769	1.345	6.630	6.630
Japan	0.812	0.406	0.000	0.000	40.198	0.000	0.000	3.248	47.101	36.950
Netherlands	0.059	0.059	-1.438	-0.499	-0.176	4.754	-0.792	0.323	1.790	0.528
United Kingdom	-0.113	0.225	-0.450	-0.225	1.126	-0.338	7.881	0.788	9.120	6.418
United States	-0.718	2.872	1.436	0.718	10.770	1.436	2.872	4.308	21.539	34.463
China	0.531	0.620	1.063	0.266	2.391	0.443	0.708	3.365	8.944	-2.037
South Korea	0.157	0.117	0.274	0.117	0.822	0.039	0.196	0.900	2.661	-0.665
Rest of Asia	0.652	0.652	2.218	0.913	4.044	1.044	2.087	6.131	16.827	-4.826
Brazil	-0.133	0.133	0.664	0.797	1.528	0.531	0.598	1.196	5.247	0.664
Rest of Latin America	0.000	-0.110	1.755	1.097	2.523	0.549	0.987	1.426	8.009	-2.414
Rest of Europe	0.280	0.280	-2.237	-1.118	-0.280	-1.118	-2.237	1.398	-4.474	-7.269
Middle East	0.000	0.113	2.377	0.962	1.302	0.622	1.415	1.528	8.205	0.679
Rest of the World	-0.155	0.310	6.655	3.095	3.560	1.548	3.405	1.548	18.882	2.012
DEVELOPING ECONOMIES	0.646	1.937	14.849	7.102	16.140	4.519	9.039	16.140	68.436	-6.456
RICH ECONOMIES	3.792	7.583	1.896	5.688	54.980	1.896	5.688	11.375	98.584	96.688
WORLD	5.083	10.166	17.790	12.707	73.703	7.624	15.249	27.956	167.737	91.493

Table 10a. Panel A

IMPACT ON:	REGION IN WHICH PROTECTION IS REMOVED: AUS	CAN	GER	ITA	JAP	NET	UK	US	ALL 8	8 COUNTRY PTA
Australia	0.70	0.00	0.03	0.01	0.59	-0.02	0.10	0.15	1.58	1.56
Canada	0.02	0.37	0.00	0.00	0.03	0.00	0.00	1.85	2.19	2.25
Germany	0.02	-0.02	0.94	0.33	0.02	0.37	0.40	0.07	2.11	1.84
Italy	0.02	-0.02	0.81	1.19	0.09	0.13	0.45	0.02	2.77	3.92
Japan	0.02	-0.02	-0.01	0.00	2.07	0.01	0.00	0.04	2.11	1.27
Netherlands	0.03	-0.01	2.05	0.75	0.20	2.22	1.30	0.22	7.10	9.20
United Kingdom	0.02	0.00	0.31	0.12	0.13	0.24	2.51	0.14	3.48	2.22
United States	0.00	0.16	0.01	0.00	0.25	-0.01	0.02	0.34	0.72	0.87
China	-0.02	-0.02	0.00	0.01	0.50	-0.03	-0.03	0.17	0.48	-0.34
South Korea	0.00	-0.03	-0.04	-0.02	0.41	-0.01	-0.02	0.02	0.28	-0.34
Rest of Asia	0.01	-0.03	0.02	-0.01	0.72	-0.05	0.02	0.02	0.74	-0.44
Brazil	-0.01	0.00	0.08	-0.06	0.18	-0.05	0.01	0.14	0.26	-0.10
Rest of Latin America	0.00	0.00	-0.01	-0.03	0.32	-0.03	0.00	0.73	1.21	-0.31
Rest of Europe	0.01	0.00	0.67	0.24	0.14	0.22	0.55	0.10	1.85	-0.62
Middle East	0.01	0.01	-0.07	0.00	0.32	-0.01	0.12	0.14	0.51	-0.17
Rest of the World	0.00	0.00	-0.07	-0.04	0.20	-0.04	-0.01	0.01	0.12	-0.10
DEVELOPING ECONOMIES	0.00	-0.02	-0.02	-0.02	0.38	-0.03	0.01	0.18	0.54	-0.26
RICH ECONOMIES	0.02	0.06	0.28	0.14	0.61	0.13	0.32	0.23	1.74	1.25
WORLD	0.02	0.05	0.20	0.11	0.55	0.09	0.25	0.22	1.45	0.89

Table 10b. Panel B

IMPACT ON:	REGION IN WHICH PROTECTION IS REMOVED: AUS	CAN	GER	ITA	JAP	NET	UK	US	ALL 8	8 COUNTRY PTA
Australia	2.591	0.003	0.117	0.038	2.224	-0.066	0.373	0.545	5.890	5.876
Canada	0.107	2.028	0.005	0.017	0.240	0.002	0.012	9.575	11.587	11.917
Germany	0.373	-0.351	17.397	5.889	0.296	6.613	7.135	1.323	38.378	33.455
Italy	0.221	-0.181	8.168	12.583	0.882	1.307	4.540	0.285	28.633	40.354
Japan	0.949	-0.846	-0.440	0.000	94.534	0.440	0.000	2.035	96.877	59.036
Netherlands	0.094	-0.028	6.202	2.270	0.604	6.972	3.938	0.685	21.754	28.115
United Kingdom	0.233	0.016	3.712	1.433	1.653	2.875	30.899	1.749	42.709	27.289
United States	-0.034	12.166	0.820	0.034	19.307	-0.684	1.640	25.768	55.155	67.044
China	-0.177	-0.177	0.000	0.089	4.428	-0.266	-0.266	1.505	4.250	-3.011
South Korea	0.000	-0.117	-0.157	-0.078	1.605	-0.039	-0.078	0.078	1.096	-1.331
Rest of Asia	0.130	-0.391	0.261	-0.130	9.392	-0.652	0.261	0.261	9.653	-5.740
Brazil	-0.066	0.000	0.531	-0.399	1.196	-0.332	0.066	0.930	1.727	-0.664
Rest of Latin America	0.000	0.000	-0.110	-0.329	3.511	-0.329	0.000	8.009	13.275	-3.401
Rest of Europe	0.280	0.000	18.733	6.710	3.914	6.151	15.378	2.796	51.725	-17.335
Middle East	0.057	0.057	-0.396	0.000	1.811	-0.057	0.679	0.792	2.886	-0.962
Rest of the World	0.000	0.000	-1.083	-0.619	3.095	-0.619	-0.155	0.155	1.857	-1.548
DEVELOPING ECONOMIES	0.000	-1.291	-1.291	-1.291	24.534	-1.937	0.646	11.621	34.863	-16.786
RICH ECONOMIES	4.182	12.350	55.910	28.199	124.419	26.011	64.079	46.431	351.906	254.136
WORLD	5.473	13.585	53.461	29.516	147.968	24.043	66.558	59.129	389.079	238.374

as the United States but, in relation to GDP, would gain more from its removal because Canada's trade share is much higher. Similarly, the Netherlands' high trade share amplifies its percentage gains. On the other hand, Japan's NTBs are so high that it reaps substantial extra gains from NTB liberalization–2.1 percent of GDP–despite the fact that Japan has the lowest trade share in the sample: only about 10 percent. Another factor at work is changes in the terms of trade, which mute gains for the United States, Japan, and Germany. These economies account for fairly large shares of total world trade so that, when they open, they drive up their import prices and drive down their export prices.

The results also highlight some interesting international linkages and interactions. Canada actually loses from US unilateral tariff opening but would gain significantly from the United States removing all barriers. (See the entry for the Canada row and the United States column in Tables 8 and 9.) In fact, the extra gains from US NTB elimination (1.9 percent of GDP) would far exceed Canada's own NTB opening (0.4 percent). (Canada row in Table 10A) Likewise, the extra gains to the Netherlands from German NTB removal (2.1 percent) rival those that the Netherlands would get from its own unilateral NTB removal (2.2 percent).

It is striking that adding NTB removal to tariff removal in Japan would benefit the United States about as much as the United States itself doing this (about 0.3 percent). The benefits to Japan's neighbors would also be considerable, with extra boosts to GDP in China, South Korea, and the rest of Asia of 0.5 percent, 0.4 percent, and 0.7 percent of GDP, respectively. Overall, developing economies and the world as a whole would see their incomes rise by an additional 0.4 percent. Measured in 1997 dollars, Japanese incomes would rise by an extra 90 billion, while Japan's trading partners would see their incomes rise by 50 billion, of which 24 billion would accrue to developing economies. (Table 10B) Adding Japanese NTBs to the agenda would benefit the world more than twice as much as adding US NTBs would. Indeed, including Japanese NTBs would yield worldwide benefits of $148 billion–more than one third of the global benefits from adding all eight economies' NTBs. Aside from the Japanese NTBs, US NTBs impose the largest costs on developing economies: about 0.2 percent of GDP, or about 12 billion 1997 dollars. As with Japan, US NTBs impose costs on lower-income economies that cancel annual development aid given by the United States.

For all economies except Japan and the UK, the extra gains from multilateral NTB opening are more than twice the extra gains from unilateral opening. These six economies have especially large incentives to engage in multilateral NTB reform, as opposed to going it alone. Also, for each economy except Japan, removing NTBs confer larger extra benefits on the rest of the world than they derive themselves. Indeed, the global benefits that result from Canadian NTB opening are six times larger than the benefits obtained by Canada (Table 10B). For Germany, the Netherlands, and the United States, these ratios are three or more.

Four of the eight economies in the sample actually get larger extra gains from NTB elimination within a PTA than with multilateral worldwide removal. These are Canada, Italy, the Netherlands, and the United States. Apparently, NTBs from within the sample of eight impose greater burdens on these economies than do NTBs outside the sample. Developing economies, however, suffer losses from such an exclusionary arrangement. Instead of the 0.5 percent annual extra gains from multilateral NTB opening by all eight, adding NTBs to a PTA would reduce developing economies GDP by 0.3 percent.

Overall, our results imply that the potential gains to be reaped from deeper integration among the developed economies far exceed the gains from tariff removal alone, although these latter benefits are not trivial. Moreover, the NTB benefits would be widely shared within economies. Of course, such extensive liberalization in these economies is not on the table right now. Complete opening may not be an option because of short run political stresses caused by contraction in protected sectors. Our analysis does not provide a recipe for reform, but it does show that the potential gains from future attempts to integrate markets remain quite large.

While we have estimated the benefits of integration, we have not taken account of certain costs. In particular, differences in national languages, policies, and institutions may well create barriers to price arbitrage, but they may also provide benefits that would be lost if the world economy was to be deeply integrated in the sense we are exploring in this study.

While suppressing diversity could have costs that we have not accounted for, we may also have understated the costs of the barriers by treating them as if they were tariffs. In fact, removing barriers may actually save resources and therefore yield even larger benefits than we estimate here. As Anderson and van Wincoop 2002 emphasizes, trade barriers such as tariffs and quotas generate deadweight losses, but NTBs may consume resources directly. Suppose, for example, that two economies each require drugs to be certified as safe even though their criteria are very similar. Firms that wish to sell in both markets must expend real resources to determine and meet foreign requirements. Drugs approved in one economy cannot simply be sold abroad. Under these circumstances, in addition to the gains from removing the barriers, freeing the resources that are consumed by the (unnecessary) duplicative regulatory processes could produce additional gains. Our estimates are also conservative because they ignore the potential benefits from opening economies outside the sample of eight we have used in the study.

7.3. *Winners and Losers*

Despite overall gains from NTB opening, clearly some groups of people would lose, while others would win. An examination of real factor price changes sheds light on this issue. As mentioned above, the model contains five factors: capital, skilled labor, unskilled labor, land, and natural resources. We can therefore obtain broad results on income distribution among these large groups. Table 11 reports the effects of trade opening on after-tax real factor prices for the different scenarios. Panel A shows the results for total protection and tariffs, and Panel B shows the results for NTBs.

Focusing on the NTB results, we see that, for all economies and all scenarios, both types of labor gain from adding NTBs to the mix, indicating that, for these developed economies at least, NTBs impose burdens on workers as a whole. The more efficient allocation of resources that opening would bring would raise workers' real income overall. Of course, some workers would have to pay the costs of adjusting between sectors in the short run, costs that the model does not capture. Capital would benefit from adding NTB opening as well, except in Canada (for all three scenarios) and in the United States with multilateral opening and with the PTA. Japanese capital owners would gain more than their counterparts in other economies, which reflects the fact that Japan generally has a comparative advantage in capital-intensive goods.

These simulations imply large impacts on landowners in certain economies. In all scenarios involving Japan, the modeling predicts that Japanese landowners' real incomes would decline significantly, 7 to 8 percent. Thus, we predict that they would oppose adding NTBs to the agenda. Landowners in other economies are helped by each scenario and thus should favor including NTBs, with the following exceptions: Italian landowners under unilateral opening and the PTA, Canadian landowners under multilateral opening and the PTA, and Australian landowners with the PTA. Australian landowners would much prefer multilateral NTB opening to a PTA, while Dutch landowners would gain much more from the PTA. As for the other six economies, if NTBs are added to the agenda, Canadian, Italian, and British landowners would prefer multilateral liberalization to a PTA, while landowners in Germany, the Netherlands, and the

Table 11a. Panel A, percentage changes in real after tax factor prices

	TOTAL PROTECTION								TARIFFS							
	Single Country Opening								Single Country Opening							
	Aus	Can	Ger	Ita	Jap	Net	UK	US	Aus	Can	Ger	Ita	Jap	Net	UK	US
Skilled Labor	2.3	3.8	5.2	3.4	7.8	9.1	6.4	1.1	1.3	2.3	1.2	1.2	3.0	2.6	1.4	0.4
Unskilled Labor	2.5	3.8	5.3	3.2	7.0	10.7	6.6	1.1	1.5	2.1	1.2	1.0	2.6	2.9	1.3	0.3
Capital	0.2	1.3	3.4	1.6	6.8	2.5	1.5	0.4	-0.2	2.0	0.7	0.7	2.7	0.8	0.7	0.3
Land	5.5	3.0	-0.4	-14.0	-47.4	8.5	-6.4	-0.6	4.0	-4.0	-6.9	-5.4	-39.3	1.1	-12.4	-1.8
Natural Resources	9.6	7.7	6.6	0.0	-21.6	14.3	18.9	6.6	6.2	4.1	1.6	-0.5	-11.3	3.8	4.4	2.7
	8-Country Worldwide Opening								8-Country Worldwide Opening							
	Aus	Can	Ger	Ita	Jap	Net	UK	US	Aus	Can	Ger	Ita	Jap	Net	UK	US
Skilled Labor	3.2	5.0	5.8	4.0	8.0	11.0	6.9	1.2	1.6	2.1	1.0	1.1	3.2	2.0	1.4	0.4
Unskilled Labor	4.5	5.7	6.1	4.3	7.3	14.2	7.3	1.4	2.8	2.5	1.1	0.9	2.7	2.2	1.3	0.5
Capital	-0.4	1.1	3.4	1.4	6.9	2.0	1.3	0.0	-0.7	1.8	0.6	0.5	2.7	0.6	0.6	0.2
Land	36.5	38.3	7.4	-7.9	-47.2	33.3	-1.0	6.4	4.9	42.5	-8.1	-10.1	-39.3	6.5	-10.8	2.9
Natural Resources	14.5	14.6	10.4	1.8	-21.1	19.7	25.7	11.0	8.3	13.3	3.8	0.3	-11.0	9.5	8.7	6.0
	8-Country PTA								8-COUNTRY PTA							
	Aus	Can	Ger	Ita	Jap	Net	UK	US	Aus	Can	Ger	Ita	Jap	Net	UK	US
Skilled Labor	3.0	4.4	3.6	3.2	6.0	8.8	4.1	1.0	1.5	1.6	0.3	0.5	2.6	0.8	0.6	0.2
Unskilled Labor	4.8	5.7	4.1	4.4	5.4	13.6	4.8	1.3	3.1	2.4	0.4	0.7	2.2	1.0	0.7	0.3
Capital	-0.7	0.5	1.8	0.6	5.0	0.8	0.2	-0.2	-0.9	1.3	0.0	0.1	2.1	0.0	0.1	0.0
Land	49.9	45.0	15.5	2.8	-42.2	74.0	4.5	11.6	51.1	51.8	-0.9	5.3	-35.1	8.6	-3.8	6.6
Natural Resources	-2.5	4.1	4.8	1.5	-13.3	1.8	9.0	1.7	-3.3	7.5	1.3	0.4	-6.0	3.0	2.8	1.3

Table 11b. Panel B, percentage changes in real after tax factor prices

	NTBs							
	Single Country Opening							
	Aus	**Can**	**Ger**	**Ita**	**Jap**	**Net**	**UK**	**US**
Skilled Labor	1.0	1.5	4.0	2.2	4.8	6.5	5.0	0.7
Unskilled Labor	1.0	1.7	4.1	2.2	4.4	7.8	5.3	0.8
Capital	0.4	-0.7	2.7	0.9	4.1	1.7	0.8	0.1
Land	1.5	7.0	6.5	-8.6	-8.1	7.4	6.0	1.2
Natural Resources	3.4	3.6	5.0	0.5	-10.3	10.5	14.5	3.9
	8-Country Worldwide Opening							
	Aus	**Can**	**Ger**	**Ita**	**Jap**	**Net**	**UK**	**US**
Skilled Labor	1.6	2.9	4.8	2.9	4.8	9.0	5.5	0.8
Unskilled Labor	1.7	3.2	5.0	3.4	4.6	12.0	6.0	0.9
Capital	0.3	-0.7	2.8	0.9	4.2	1.4	0.7	-0.2
Land	31.6	-4.2	15.5	2.2	-7.9	26.8	9.8	3.5
Natural Resources	6.2	1.3	6.6	1.5	-10.1	10.2	17.0	5.0
	8-COUNTRY PTA							
	Aus	**Can**	**Ger**	**Ita**	**Jap**	**Net**	**UK**	**US**
Skilled Labor	1.5	2.8	3.3	2.7	3.4	8.0	3.5	0.8
Unskilled Labor	1.7	3.3	3.7	3.7	3.2	12.6	4.1	1.0
Capital	0.2	-0.8	1.8	0.5	2.9	0.8	0.1	-0.2
Land	-1.2	-6.8	16.4	-2.5	-7.1	65.4	8.3	5.0
Natural Resources	0.8	-3.4	3.5	1.1	-7.3	-1.2	6.2	0.4

United States would prefer the PTA.[21] Also, if NTBs are on the agenda, all landowners except those in Canada prefer some kind of multilateral opening to unilateral removal of NTBs and tariffs. The results also indicate that natural resource owners are heavily protected by NTBs in Japan. It should be noted that natural resource factors are the most difficult to measure, making their results the most uncertain.

Overall, these simulations imply that deeper international integration, involving the removal of NTBs as well as tariffs, in developed economies not only will benefit them as a whole but that most factors within each nation will gain. Thus, while opposition to including NTBs will always be strong, we infer from this research that a broad consensus of citizens in these economies would favor keeping them on the table.

[21] It should be kept in mind that small countries' large trade/GDP shares amplify the percentage changes.

8. Conclusion

This paper has presented evidence that rich economies harbor quite a bit more NTB protection than is commonly believed. Our data imply that agriculture and food industries in eight OECD economies enjoy extensive NTB protection, and we also find that NTBs significantly impede trade in manufacturing. Japan has unusually high NTBs, and Europe appears to have more than industrialized North America. AGE simulations imply that negotiating the removal of these barriers, especially in Japan, would bring large benefits to rich and poor economies alike, implying that the extra work required to include NTBs on the agenda would probably pay off. Thus, this research implies that future trade negotiations should build on previous efforts and continue to target NTBs.

Of course, the trade opening devil lurks in the details, and so trade analysts need to determine the actual policies that underlie the protection we have quantified in this paper. It is easy for governments to claim that certain policies in other economies act as trade barriers; the more difficult task is to provide evidence for these claims. We have taken an initial step toward this goal by matching up suspected policies with sectors for which we have evidence of NTB protection. As shown in Table 4, we find that, for agriculture and food products, overly restrictive sanitary requirements, apparently unfounded import bans of certain products, onerous labeling rules, and tariff quotas emerge as potentially damaging trade barriers and worthwhile targets of negotiations. In manufacturing, we have evidence that technical standards, labeling requirements, and regulatory approval procedures in certain sectors may hinder imports.

We hope that the results in this paper have provided useful initial information on the extent of, the effects of, and the policies underlying NTB protection in OECD economies. We also hope this paper will stimulate much-needed future research in this area.

References

1. J.E. Anderson and E. van Wincoop. 2001. Gravity with Gravitas: A Solution to the Border Puzzle. Cambridge, MA: National Bureau of Economic Research Working Paper.
2. J.E. Anderson and E. van Wincoop. 2002. "Borders, Trade and Welfare" in S.M. Collins and D. Rodrik, eds. *Brookings Trade Forum 2001*. Washington DC: Brookings Institution.
3. S.C. Bradford. 2002. "Rejuvenating Japan: Potential Gains from Deregulating International Trade and Domestic Distribution." Under Review.
4. S.C. Bradford. February 2003. "Paying the Price: Final Good Protection in OECD Countries." *Review of Economics and Statistics*. 85(1):24-37.

5. S.C. Bradford and A. Gohin. 2002. "Modeling Distribution Services and Assessing Their Welfare Effects in a General Equilibrium Framework." Under Review.
6. S.C. Bradford and R.Z. Lawrence. February 2004. *Has Globalization Gone Far Enough?* Washington, DC: Institute for International Economics.
7. Eurostat-OECD PPP Programme. 1996. "The Calculation and Aggregation of Parities." Unpublished.
8. J.A. Frankel. 1997. *Regional Trading Blocs in the World Economic System*. Washington DC, Institute for International Economics.
9. K. Froot *et al.* 1995. "The Law of One Price over 700 Years." Cambridge, MA: National Bureau of Economic Research Working Paper.
10. G.W. Harrison, T.F. Rutherford, and D. Tarr. December 1995. "Quantifying the Outcome of the Uruguay Round." *Finance and Development*. 32(4):38-41.
11. G.W. Harrison, T.F. Rutherford, and D. Tarr. 1996. "Quantifying the Uruguay Round" in W. Martin and L.A. Winters, eds. *The Uruguay Round and the Developing Countries*. New York: Cambridge University Press.
12. G.W. Harrison, T.F. Rutherford, and D. Tarr. September 1997. "Quantifying the Uruguay Round." Economic Journal. 107:1405-1430.
13. J. Haskal and G. Wolf. 2001. "The Law Of One Price - A Case Study." Cambridge, MA: National Bureau of Economic Research Working Paper.
14. J. Helliwell. 1998. *How Much Do National Borders Matter?* Washington, DC: Brookings Institution.
15. G.C. Hufbauer *et al.* 2002. *The Benefits of Price Convergence: Speculative Calculations*. Washington, DC: Institute for International Economics.
16. G.C. Hufbauer and K.A. Elliot. 1994. *Measuring the Costs of Protection in the United States*. Washington, DC: Institute for International Economics.
17. P. Isard. 1977. "How Far Can We Push the Law of One Price?" *American Economic Review*. 67:942-948.
18. M.M. Knetter and P.K. Goldberg. 1995. "Measuring the Intensity of Competition in Export Markets." Cambridge, MA: National Bureau of Economic Research Working Paper.
19. J. McCallum. 1995. "National Borders Matter: Regional Trade Patterns in North America." *American Economic Review*. 85(3): 615-23.
20. M. Obstfeld and K. Rogoff. 2000. "The Six Major Puzzles in International Macroeconomics: Is There A Common Cause?" *NBER Macroeconomics Annual 2000*. Cambridge, MA: NBER.
21. Organization for Economic Cooperation and Development (OECD). 1995. *Purchasing Power Parities and Real Expenditure*. Paris: OECD.
22. D.C. Parsley and S.-J. Wei. 1996. "Convergence to the Law of One Price Without Trade Barriers or Currency Fluctuations." *Quarterly Journal of Economics*. 111:1211-36.
23. V. Roningen and A. Yeats. 1976. "Nontariff Distortions of International Trade: Some Preliminary Empirical Evidence." *Weltwirtschaftliches Archiv*. 112(4):613-625.

24. D.J. Rousslang and T. To. 1993. "Domestic Trade and Transportation Costs as Barriers to International Trade." *Canadian Journal of Economics*. 26(1):208-221.
25. United Nations Conference on Trade and Development (UNCTAD). 1992. Analytical Report by the *UNCTAD Secretariat to the Conference*. New York: United Nations.
26. World Bank. 1993. *Purchasing Power of Currencies: Comparing National Incomes Using ICP Data*. Washington, DC: World Bank.

DYNAMIC EFFECTS OF THE "NEW AGE" FREE TRADE AGREEMENT BETWEEN JAPAN AND SINGAPORE

Thomas W. Hertel,[1] Terrie Walmsley,[2] and Ken Itakura[3]

Purdue University

1. Introduction and Overview

In the past decade, there has been a flood of regional trade agreements. Today, more than 130 such agreements are in place (WTO, 2000). The European Union, the North America Free Trade Agreement (NAFTA) and MERCOSUR have been particularly effective at promoting intra-regional trade. This has led other economies to explore options for such regional agreements, and in December, 1999, Japan and Singapore established a Joint Study Group to examine the feasibility and desirability of establishing a FTA. After a favorable report from the Study Group, negotiations on this FTA commenced in early 2001 (Joint Study Group, 2000a).

The main elements of the prospective Japan-Singapore FTA involve bilateral liberalization and facilitation of trade through reduction of tariff and non-tariff barriers as well as the mutual recognition of national standards, streamlining customs procedures, facilitation of increased services trade, as well as establishment of an exemplary framework for foreign investment. This "new age" FTA also envisions increased collaboration on intellectual property, education and training, media and broadcasting and tourism. This trade agreement is particularly significant, since it is viewed by many as providing a possible template for future FTAs in the region. In particular, another working group has been established to explore the potential for a free trade agreement between Japan and Korea (KIEP, 2000). This is expected to have many of the same "new age" elements.

Japan already trades quite intensively with Singapore and Korea. Based on the Brown-Kojima-Drysdale export intensity index, Japan exported about twice as much to these economies as one would expect, solely on the basis of their world import shares in 1998. However, there is some indication that the relative

[1] Professor, and Director of the Center for Global Trade Analysis. The author may be contacted through the Center for Global Trade Analysis, Purdue University, West Lafayette, IN 47907-1145 *via* email at hertel@agecon.purdue.edu, or the Center's website *"http://www.gtap.org.*

[2] Assistant Professor, and Associate Director of the Center for Global Trade Analysis.

[3] Research Assistant at the Center for Global Trade Analysis.

attraction of trading with Korea and Singapore has been diminishing. Figure 1.1 reports Japan's total merchandise trade export *bias* to Korea, Singapore and Rest of World. Drysdale (1982) uses this measure to capture the determinants of export shares, once the size, openness and product composition of the importing market have been taken into account. Anderson and Norheim (1983) argue that this bias component offers a proxy for the kind of transactions costs that FTAs are intended to lower. The higher this bias, the more attractive the export destination, relative to alternative markets.

As can be seen from Figure 1.1, the relative attractiveness of exporting from Japan to Korea and Singapore has been cut in half over the past 30 years. Figure 1.2 reports the export bias from Korea and Singapore to Japan. These, too, have been falling. Thus, while trading costs between Japan and these partners may have fallen significantly over the past 30 years, there is some evidence that trading costs with other partners have fallen more rapidly. In light of this observation, it is perhaps not surprising that these three economies have initiated discussions aimed at lowering trading costs among their respective economies. The goal of this paper is to provide a quantitative assessment of the dynamic effects of one of these "new age" FTAs – namely that between Japan and Singapore.

The paper is organized as follows. In the next section, we outline the key elements of the Japan-Singapore FTA and discuss our approach to quantifying them. Given the relatively low level of industrial tariffs on most trade between these two economies, we devote considerable effort to quantifying the non-tariff elements of this agreement. In Section 3, we outline the dynamic modeling approach taken in this paper. It is aimed explicitly at capturing the impact of these "new age" FTAs, not only on trade, but also on international investment flows. In order to analyze the potential impact of these FTAs, it is important to have a view of the evolution of regional trade and growth in the absence of the agreements. This baseline is established in Section 4 of the paper. Section 5 reports the results and analysis based on a comparison of the baseline with the counterfactual, FTA simulations, and this is followed by the conclusions.

2. Quantifying the New Age Agreement

2.1. *Trade and Tariffs*

As with other such regional trade agreements, the FTA between Japan and Singapore envisions bilateral elimination of tariffs (Joint Study Group, 2000a, 2000b). Table 1 reports estimated average bilateral tariffs levied by Singapore and Japan on one another's exports. The tariff estimates for Singapore are based

Figure 1.1 Japanese export bias: Total merchandise trade

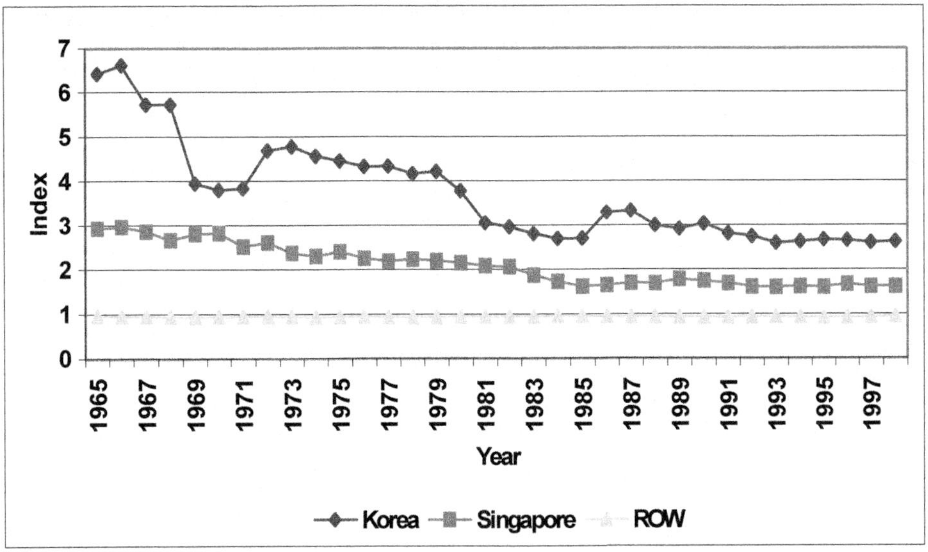

Source: Authors' Computations.

Figure 1.2 Korea and Singapore export biases to Japan

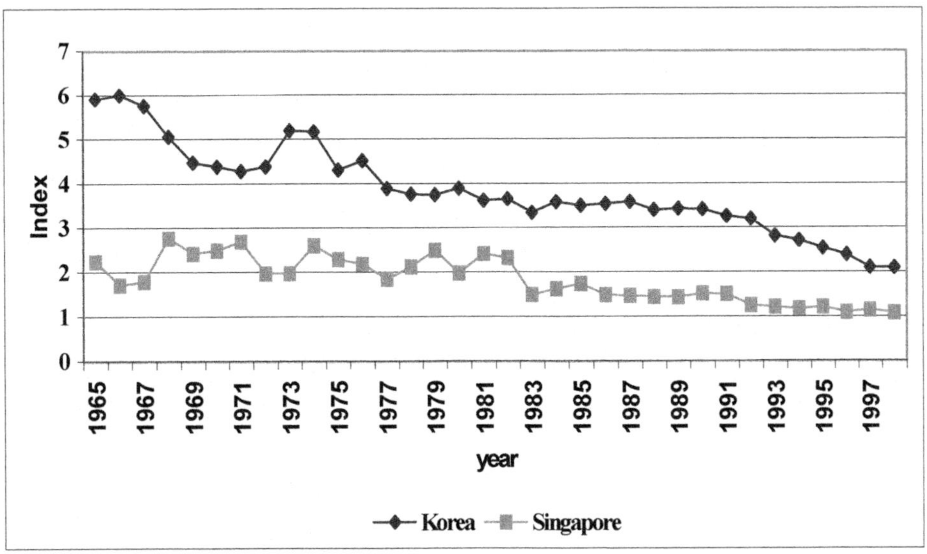

Source: Authors' Computations

Table 1. Bilateral and Composition of Imports
(Post-Uruguay Round, *ad valorem* tariff and projected share of total imports, 2005)

	Imports from Japan		Imports from Singapore	
Commodity	**Trade share**	**Tariff rate**	**Trade share**	**Tariff rate**
		Percent		
rice	0.0	0.0	n.t.	n.t.
other grains	0.0	0.0	n.t.	n.t.
other crops	0.1	0.0	0.5	1.8
meat	0.0	0.0	0.1	473.7
other food	0.6	1.7	1.8	21.3
fish	0.1	0.0	0.1	1.3
texwap	0.6	0.0	0.2	6.6
leather	0.0	0.0	0.1	6.1
extract	7.4	0.0	1.0	0.2
pchemineral	8.2	0.0	6.6	1.2
omnfcs	5.9	0.0	2.7	0.1
autos	4.5	0.0	0.02	0.0
machiequip	59.5	0.0	32.8	0.1
utilities	0.1	0.0	0.1	0.0
construction	0.0	0.0	0.0	0.0
tradetrans	1.3	0.0	48.9	0.0
busfinance	11.7	0.0	5.1	0.0
Total (million US$)	$33,731		$18,066	

on applied rates for 1999, as reported in the WTO Singapore Trade Policy Review (2000). Applied tariffs in Singapore are now zero for all goods outside of alcoholic beverages (other food products in Table 1). This reflects some liberalization from the 1995 applied rates in the version 4, GTAP data base, and these tariff cuts in Singapore are implemented as part of the baseline described in Section 4 below. Based on the non-agricultural tariffs in Table 1, implementation of the FTA will have no direct impact on Singapore's imports of merchandise commodities from Japan – hence the calls for a "new age" FTA.

The tariff estimates for Japan in Table 1 reflect the lower of 1995 applied rates, as obtained from the GTAP version 4 database, and WTO bindings under the Uruguay Round. In cases where the bindings are below 1995 tariffs, we reduce them to the level of the post-Uruguay Round bindings as part of the baseline experiment. Note from the trade share entries in Table 1 that Japan does not import any grains from Singapore. Bilateral imports of meats and other food products are modest, but face a very high average tariff. It is clear from this table why food and agriculture represent a very sensitive part of this agreement. Given the very high tariffs facing these products imported from other destinations, the incentive for trans-shipment through Singapore is likely to be substantial under an FTA. This raises the prospect of significant enforcement costs associated with the rules of origin for this FTA. For this reason, it is quite likely that agriculture will be left out of the final FTA agreement – or perhaps it will be implemented in a delayed fashion. Of course, textiles and apparel products and leather goods also face non-negligible tariffs so that substantial expansion of imports from Singapore is expected under the FTA.

In our study we assume that implementation of the FTA is undertaken in 2005. At the time this work was undertaken, it was unclear how fast Japan and Singapore would move on this agreement. By placing it after completion of the Uruguay Round we also simplified our experimental design. For this reason, we focus on the projected, 2005 trade shares in Table 1 in evaluating the potential impact of this FTA (see Section 4 for details behind the baseline projections). Based on the figures in Table 1, it is clear that this trade relationship is highly concentrated, with the bulk of Japanese exports to Singapore involving machinery and equipment. This is followed in importance by business and financial services, petroleum/chemical and mineral products, extractive products and other manufactures. Singapore's exports to Japan are concentrated in the services sector, followed by machinery and equipment and petroleum/chemical and mineral products. Clearly this trading relationship involves a great deal of intra-industry trade that should receive a substantial boost from any reduction in non-tariff trade costs.

2.2. *Customs Automization*

This brings us to a second aspect of the Japan-Singapore FTA that lends itself to quantification, namely the reduction of customs costs for bilateral trade between these two partners. In building the case for efforts to streamline customs procedures, the Joint Study Group (2000b) cites UNCTAD research indicating that customs paperwork and procedures costs add up to about 7 percent of the global value of trade. This is likely a considerable overstatement of these costs in the case of Japan-Singapore trade. Nevertheless in an era of increasing regional integration and vertical specialization in production, small trade costs can have a significant impact on intra-industry trade. Furthermore, any costs above 1 to 2 percent will represent a more substantial barrier to trade than industrial tariffs. The Joint Study Group (2000b) has focused on a proposal to reduce customs clearance costs by implementing an Electronic Trade Document Exchange System (ETDS) that will increase the speed of customs clearance, reduce the cost of dispatching information and documents and ensure security of associated documents. Singapore currently has such a system in place, so the emphasis is on extending this technology to Japan's customs procedures.

At the heart of the ETDS proposal resides commercially operated electronic document exchange servers that will facilitate the exchange of customs documents between importers, exporters and the Japanese customs authorities. Introduction of an electronically harmonized custom system will reduce the time and cost spent on custom paperwork, processing and shipments. Customs automization will also improve efficiency in shipments of products by eliminating the time spent waiting for custom clearance at ports.

Our estimates of the savings in time and direct costs due to customs automization are based on research conducted in conjunction with the Ministry of Economy, Trade and Industry (METI) and Mitsubishi Research Institute (MRI) in Japan. Through a careful study of the direct costs associated with current customs procedures, as well as the costs of connecting to the ETDS system, the MRI estimates that introduction of custom's automization in Japan would lower the effective merchandise prices for all trading partners by 0.201 percent for exports and by 0.203 percent for imports. Additional reductions in direct costs arise when a trading partner of Japan also implements the electronic custom system to synchronize the custom clearance. For the case of the Japan-Singapore FTA, the effect of linking the two systems is expected to generate additional reductions in effective prices amounting to 0.065 percent in Japanese imports from Singapore and 0.013 percent in Singaporean imports from Japan. It should be noted that these cost saving refer solely to the cost of reduced paperwork, storage and transit expenses.

However, in addition to the direct cost savings of ETDS, there are indirect savings associated with the elimination of customs-related delays in merchandise flows between these two economies. Hummels (2000) emphasizes that such time savings can have a profound effect on international trade by reducing both "spoilage" and inventory holding costs. He argues that spoilage can occur for many types of reasons. The most obvious might be agricultural and horticultural products that physically deteriorate with the passage of time. However, products with information content (newspapers), as well as highly seasonable (fashion) goods may also experience spoilage. Hummels points out that inventory costs include not only the capital costs of the goods while they are in transit, but also the need to hold larger inventories to accommodate variation in arrival time. The latter has become increasingly important due to the use of "just in time" production techniques.

In order to estimate the value of time savings in international trade, Hummels utilizes a detailed data set which he has assembled that includes information on modal choice (air *vs*. sea), modal prices (shipping rates), and modal shipping times at the 10-digit, HS level for US imports. This results in approximately one million observations *per* year over the entire 1974-98 period. Hummels (2000) estimates a discrete choice model, wherein the probability of choosing air over sea transport depends on relative freight rates and the associated time savings. He finds that the average value of firms' willingness to pay for one day saved in trade is estimated to be 0.5 percent *ad valorem* (*i.e.*, one-half percent of the value of the good itself). However, this value of time savings varies widely by product category, with the low values for bulk commodities and the highest values for intermediate goods. The first column of Table 2 below (value of one day saved) reports the percentage *ad valorem* value of a day saved in trade at the level of commodity aggregation used in the present study. The smallest value is 0.13 percent/day for leather, while the value of a one day reduction in transit reaches nearly one percent (0.94 percent) *per* day for petrochemical and mineral products. This value is also quite high for machinery and equipment (0.51 percent/day). Hummels' estimates for agricultural products are not significantly different from zero and are therefore omitted.

Table 2. Time saving per day and price reduction by customs automization (Percent *ad valorem*)

Opportunity costs of a day in trade		No linking effect Exports (a)	Imports (b)	With linking effect Exports (a)	Imports (b)
Rice	0	0.201	0.203	0.214	0.268
other grains	0	0.201	0.203	0.214	0.268
other crops	0	0.201	0.203	0.214	0.268
meat	0	0.201	0.203	0.214	0.268
other food	0	0.201	0.203	0.214	0.268
fish	0.14	0.431	0.406	0.619	0.741
texwap	0.14	0.435	0.409	0.627	0.749
leather	0.13	0.422	0.398	0.604	0.723
extract	0.30	0.707	0.649	1.107	1.309
pchemineral	0.94	1.795	1.609	30287	3.549
omnfcs	0.29	0.686	0.631	1.069	1.266
autos	0.16	0.465	0.436	0.679	0.811
machiequip	0.51	1.072	0.971	1.750	2.061

The MRI estimates that the amount of time that would be saved by the custom automization would be 1.7 days for exports and 1.5 days for imports. These translate into effective price reductions of 0.85 percent and 0.75 percent respectively, based on the average valuation of 0.5 percent *ad valorem* per day. Additional time savings are likely if the economies at both ends of the transaction (this is the case with Japan and Singapore) adopt the same EDTS system. The further saving on lead-time is estimated to be an additional 1.3 days for exports and 2 days for imports, or 0.65 percent and 1 percent reductions in the average effective prices of exports and imports, respectively. By applying these time savings associated with ETDS to Hummels' estimates of the value of time savings, by commodity, we obtain the price reductions associated with customs automization shown in columns (a) to (d) in Table 2. The estimated price reductions in Table 2 vary depending on whether or not the linking effect is present. Columns (a) and (b) apply to trade between Japan and ROW, whereas columns (c) and (d) apply to trade between Japan and Singapore. The full set of bilateral shocks associated with customs automization are summarized in Table 3. Note from this table that Singapore's trade with ROW is unaffected by the implementation of ETDS in Japan.

Table 3. Reductions in bilateral prices due to customs automization (Percent *ad valorem*)

		Imports		
		Japan	**Singapore**	**ROW**
	Japan	n.a.	(c)	(a)
Exports	**Singapore**	(d)	n.a.	0
	ROW	(b)	0	0

Note: See Table 2 for the values of (a), *b), (c) and (d), by sector.

2.3. *E-Commerce*

Another important element of the proposed FTA is the section aimed at improving security and harmonizing standards governing B-to-B and B-to-C e-commerce between Japan and Singapore. The goal of this part of the agreement is to make e-commerce between the two economies as safe and acceptable to customers as is domestic e-commerce presently. Accordingly, we have taken estimates of the extent of B-to-B e-commerce penetration in the domestic Japanese market (column one of Table 4), along with the MRI estimated reduction in wholesale-retail margins (projected to be reduced from 19.6 percent to 4.9 percent of prices in the presence of e-commerce) and computed the potential reduction in average effective price across all transactions that might be attained on products traded between Singapore and Japan (column two of Table 4). This varies by sector, depending on the degree of e-commerce penetration. It is highest for auto parts, which show a 1.39 percent reduction in average price.

Table 4. Reduction in price due to E-commerce.

	E-Commerce penetration rate	Potential in average price (%)
Rice	0.95	0.09
other grains	0.95	0.09
other crops	0.95	0.09
meat	0.95	0.09
other food	0.95	0.09
Fish	0.95	0.09
texwap	2.80	0.27
leather	2.80	0.27
extract	0.82	0.08
pchemineral	0.20	0.02
omnfcs	0.80	0.08
autos	14.20	1.39
machiequip	6.59	0.65
utilities	0.10	0.01
construction	0.04	0.00
tradetrans	0.20	0.02
busfinance	0.20	0.02

Note: Price reduction = e-commerce penetration rate* reduction in margin as a percentage of final price.

Source: Author's computation based on estimates from MRI.

2.4. *Services Trade*

The previously discussed aspects of the FTA – tariff reductions, customs automization and e-commerce – largely affect the cost of merchandise trade between Japan and Singapore. However, the FTA also proposes liberalization of services trade. Here, quantification is quite difficult, as data on services trade and potential barriers are rather scarce. For purposes of this study, we follow the recent work of Joseph Francois (1999) who has estimated two gravity models of trade – one for business services and one for construction services – using bilateral services export data from the United States (BEA, 1999).

Francois' gravity models permit him to predict what trade would be in the absence of barriers to trade – using Hong Kong and Singapore as "free trade" benchmarks. By positing an import demand function he is then able to obtain tariff equivalents for the unobserved trade barriers for services trade in business and finance and construction. Estimation results are reported in Table 5. As can be seen, Japan's estimated tariff equivalent of 20.6 percent is relatively high for business and financial services. The tariff equivalent for construction imports into Japan is even higher (29.9 percent), although other economies have much more restrictive trade barriers in this sector.

Table 5. Estimated tariff equivalent for services

Regions	Business Services	Construction
North America	9.0	9.9
Western Europe	9.4	18.5
Australia and New Zealand	7.2	24.5
Japan	20.6	29.9
China	19.5	41.1
Chinese Taipei	7.1	28.5
Korea	8.1	28.8
Indonesia	6.9	9.6
Other South East Asia	5.2	17.8
India	13.5	61.7
Brazil	36.8	57.5
Other Latin America	5.6	26.3
Other Middle East and North America	4.4	9.6
CEECs and Russia	19.1	52.1
South Africa	15.4	41.9
Other Sub-Saharan Africa	0.4	11.1
Rest of World	19.2	29.1

Note: Price reduction = e-commerce penetration rate* reduction in margin as a percentage of final price.

Source: Author's computation based on estimates from MRI.

We seek to quantify the services trade liberalization portion of the Japan-Singapore FTA by eliminating – on a bilateral basis – these services trade barriers. Since all of the barriers in Table 5 are measured relative to Singapore and Hong Kong, this liberalization once again does not affect Singapore. On the other hand, it lowers the effective price of business and financial services exported from Singapore to Japan by 20.6 percent, and for constructions services the price drop is 29.9 percent. Of course it should be noted that most of the biggest barriers to trade in services arise in the trade and transport sector (Hoekman, 1995), and we have ignored this altogether due to a lack of protection estimates. We also ignore prospective liberalization of investment and the movement of persons providing services – which are major vehicles for delivering services to foreign markets. In short, this quantification is quite limited and should be seen as providing a lower bound on potential impacts of the services component of the FTA between Japan and Singapore.

3. Analytical Framework

It has now become standard practice to use applied general equilibrium (AGE) models to analyze the likely impact of free trade agreements (Francois and Shiells, 1994). Due to the economywide nature of FTAs, it hardly makes sense to examine any given sector in partial equilibrium isolation; the interplay between sectors becomes a key aspect of such regional trade agreements. Their explicit incorporation of bilateral trade flows also makes AGE models well-suited to analyzing the consequences of preferential trade arrangements. Finally, their neoclassical theoretical foundations lend AGE models nicely to analysis of the trade-off between greater openness on the one hand, and potential trade diversion on the other. Accordingly, we use the AGE approach in this study.

In order to capture the dynamic effects of the "new age" FTA between Japan and Singapore, as well as the potential impacts on international investment flows and wealth, we utilize the newly developed, dynamic GTAP model (Ianchovichina and McDougall, 2000). It is a recursive-dynamic extension of the standard GTAP model (Hertel, 1997). The Dynamic GTAP model (GTAP-Dyn) preserves all the standard features of the GTAP model – perfect competition, Armington trade flows, disaggregated import usage by activity, non-homothetic consumer demands and explicit modeling of international trade and transport – while enhancing the investment theory to incorporate international capital mobility and ownership. GTAP-Dyn uses the standard GTAP data base supplemented with foreign income data from the IMF Balance of Payments statistics in order to track international capital mobility and foreign wealth. In this paper we use a 17 region, 17 commodity aggregation of the GTAP database, version 4. The regions and commodities are listed in Appendix 1.

3.1. *Investment Theory*

The dynamic GTAP model uses a disequilibrium approach for modeling international capital mobility. This disequilibrium approach is necessary in order to reconcile the theory of investment with observed reality. Economic theory states that saving is allocated across regions to those investments with the highest rate of return. With perfect capital mobility, rates of return must be equalized across regions. However, empirical evidence indicates that this is not the case (*e.g.*, Feldstein and Horioka, 1980). In the dynamic GTAP model, perfect capital mobility occurs only in the very long run. Investment is the result of the *gradual* movement of rates of return to equality across regions. This is the first use of the disequilibrium approach.

A corollary of the capital mobility theory is that if rates of return in a particular economy are very low, investment will fall and vice versa. Implementation of this theory, however, leads to a dilemma. In many cases actual investment, as reported in the national statistics, does not correspond to that predicted by capital mobility. In particular, observed rates of return are low in some regions, while observed investment is high and *vice versa*. These discrepancies between observation and theory can be rectified in one of two ways: firstly, the data can be altered so that theory and data become consistent; or alternatively, the theory can be modified to more accurately reflect the world. In the dynamic GTAP model the latter method has been used. This has been achieved by incorporating errors in expectations about the actual rate of return. These errors are gradually eliminated over time. This is the second use of disequilibrium in the modeling of international capital mobility. Those interested in further details about the Dynamic GTAP model are referred to Ianchovichina and McDougall (2000).

3.2. *Foreign Capital Ownership*

With the incorporation of international capital mobility it becomes necessary to take account of foreign capital ownership. This is especially important in East Asia, where international investment has boomed in recent decades with the outsourcing of production from Japan and other high wage economies. In the dynamic GTAP model, regional capital is owned either by domestic households or by foreign households – with the latter's ownership mediated via a global trust. (We do not have data on bilateral patterns of foreign ownership.) The saving of each regional household is then allocated either to domestic investment or to foreign investment. The allocation of savings in the model respects the observed home bias in equity portfolios (*e.g.*, French and Poterba, 1991). Specifically, it is assumed that the initial shares of domestic and foreign investments are held constant, subject to the adding-up conditions required to ensure regional saving and investment accounting constraints.

Explicit modeling of the ownership of regional investment in Japan and other Asian economies allows the accumulation of Japanese wealth by foreigners to be determined. In addition Japan's ownership of domestic and foreign assets can also be tracked. Income accruing from the ownership of these foreign and domestic assets can then be appropriately incorporated into total regional income, and hence the computation of welfare for Japan, Singapore and the rest of the world.

3.3. *Treatment of Unobserved Trade Costs*

As we saw above, a key feature of the proposed "new age" FTA between Japan and Singapore involves a series of measures intended to lower non-tariff trade costs between the FTA members. Yet many of these trade costs (*e.g.*, the costs of customs clearance) are not explicitly in the data base. How can we introduce these non-tariff shocks and analyze their likely impact on trade flows? The approach we have taken is to introduce the notion of an "effective price" of commodity *i*, imported from economy *r* at domestic prices in destination market *s*: PMS^*_{irs}. This is related to the observed price, PMS_{irs}, as follows: $PMS^* = PMS / AMS$. The technical coefficient *AMS* is unobserved, and equal to one in initial equilibrium. Changes in its value capture the impact of non-tariff measures on the price of imports from a particular exporter. Thus an increase in AMS_{irs} ensures a fall in the effective domestic price of good *i* exported from *r* to *s*. In order to ensure a balanced data set, a compensating quantity adjustment is required, so we define the "effective quantity" of exports associated with this price: $QXS^* = QXS \cdot AMS$. Therefore, the product of observed price and quantity, equal the product of effective price and quantity. And trade balance is maintained.

When this theory is incorporated into the GTAP model, and the import price and demand equations are totally differentiated and placed in percentage change form (denoted by lower case variables), we obtain the revised equations (1) and (2) reported below.

Import Demand Equation

$$qxs_{irs} = -ams_{irs} + qim_{is} - \sigma^i_m \cdot [pms_{irs} - ams_{irs} - pim_{is}] \quad (1)$$

Composite Import Price Equation

$$pim_{is} = \sum_k \theta_{iks} \cdot [pms_{iks} - ams_{iks}] \quad (2)$$

where:

σ^i_m: elasticity of substitution among imports of *i*

qxs_{irs}: percentage change in bilateral exports of *i* from *r* to *s*

qim_{is}: percentage change in total imports of *i* into *s*

pms_{irs}: percentage change in price of imports of *i* from *r* in *s*

pim_{is}: percentage change in average import price of *i* in *s*

ams_{irs}: percentage change in effective price of *i* from *r* in *s* due to change in unobserved trade costs

From equations (1) and (2), we can see that the impact of a shock to the new variable can be seen to have three distinct effects. Firstly, from the import demand equation, we see that a one percent shock to ams_{irs} will lower the effective price of imports of good *i* from exporter *r* imported into economy *s*, thereby inducing substitution towards this exporter and away from other exporters, as governed by the elasticity of substitution: σ^i_m. However, there is a second effect in the same equation, which works in the opposite direction. Since the effective quantity of the good has also increased, less is required to meet the needs of the importer. Finally, from the composite import price equation, we can see that a one percent shock to ams_{irs} will lower the average import price, thereby encouraging an expansion of imports at the expense of domestic purchases. While the total impact on imports is uncertain in theory, given the values of the trade elasticities in GTAP, we expect a reduction in trade costs to increase both observed expenditures on imports and the share of imports from the FTA partner to which this reduction in trade costs is applied.

4. Baseline

In order to establish the impact of the prospective Japan-Singapore FTA, we must begin by developing a baseline to show what the world economy would look like without the FTA imposed. This gives us two time paths for each variable of interest: firstly, a path which shows how the variable would change over time without the free trade agreement; and secondly, a path which shows how the variable would change with the free trade agreement. The difference between the two paths shows the effect of the free trade agreement. Typically these differences are cumulated and then plotted against time to illustrate the impact of the FTA on a given variable.

The baseline scenario used in this paper is based on the baseline developed by Walmsley, Dimaranan and McDougall (2000) at the Center for Global Trade Analysis, based on input from the World Bank and several other international organizations. It contains information on macroeconomic variables as well as expected policy changes over the 1995- 2020 period. The macroeconomic variables in the baseline include observations or projections for real gross domestic product, gross investment, capital stocks, population, skilled and unskilled labor and total labor (see Appendix 2). By way of illustration, Figure 2 shows the growth rates in real GDP over the 1995-2007 period, for Japan, Singapore, Korea and China. Higher GDP growth tends to translate into higher growth in trade – both for imports and exports, *ceteris paribus*. In the baseline, post-crisis growth rates are positive but quite low for Japan, relative to Korea and Singapore. China's growth remains very strong out to 2007 under this baseline.

The specification of policies in the baseline is very important for our FTA analysis. For example, as tariffs come down worldwide, under the implementation of the Uruguay Round Agreements, the potential for trade diversion is reduced. This is because the remaining preference margin is smaller in the wake of lower MFN tariffs. The policies included in the baseline are those

Figure 2. Growth in real GDP: Baseline

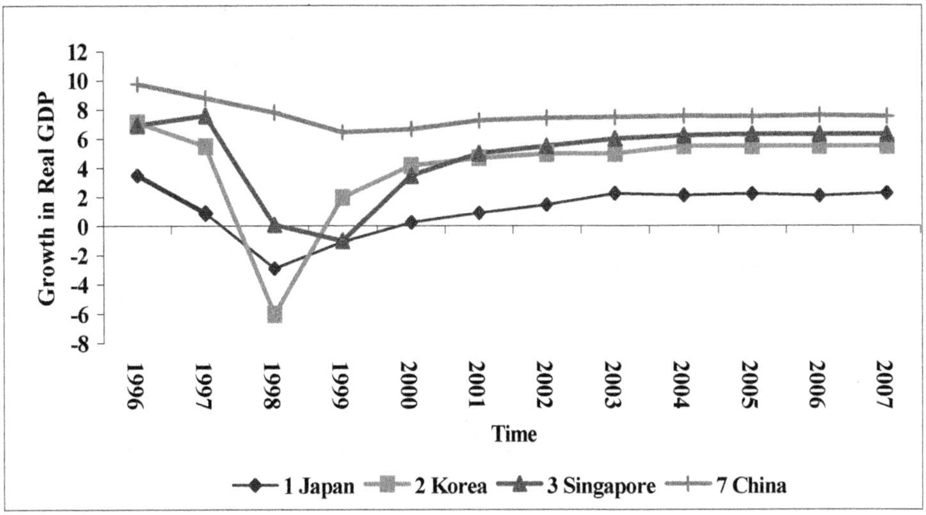

which are expected to occur within the region. They are summarized in Table 6. The aim here is to develop a realistic policy scenario for the free trade experiments undertaken here.

Uruguay Round tariff commitments are assumed to be honored by all economies. However, due to the presence of dirty tariffication in agriculture (Ingco, 1996), it is assumed that there would be no further effective liberalization in agriculture from measured levels of protection in 1995. China and Chinese Taipei are assumed to join the WTO, with their accession offers phased in over the 2000-2005 period. This accession also gives them quota free access to the North American and European textile and apparel markets by 2005. However, the liberalization of these quotas is assumed to be heavily back-loaded with most of the liberalization occurring after 2002 (Francois and Spinanger, 2001).

5. Results

It is the aim of this paper to examine the relative importance of the various components of the Japan-Singapore FTA, as well as their combined effect on international trade, investment flows and growth in these two economies. Towards this end, four FTA simulations were undertaken. Each one adds another dimension of the FTA, thereby permitting an assessment of each part of this prospective agreement. The first simulation simply involves the removal of tariffs between these two trading partners. The next three simulations

Table 6. Baseline policies

	Imports	Exports
1995-2000	1. Uruguay Round tariff reduction for all regions except China and Chinese Taipei (no shocks to agriculture). 2. Singapore reduces tariffs to zero on all commodities except beverages and tobacco. 3. Pre-WTO tariff reductions undertaken by China prior to 2000.	USA and EU quotas increased on exports of textiles and wearing apparel for all regions except Chinese Taipei and China.
2000-2005	Uruguay Round tariff reductions for all regions. China and Chinese Taipei's WTO agreement included (no shocks to agriculture, except for China and Chinese Taipei).	USA and EU quotas increased on exports of textiles and wearing apparel for all regions including Chinese Taipei and China).
2005-2020	None	None

Note: Price reduction = e-commerce penetration rate* reduction in margin as a percentage of final price.

Source: Author's computation based on estimates from MRI.

successively add further "new age" features of the Japan-Singapore FTA, including: the liberalization of direct trade in business services and construction, the implementation of improved security and common standards for e-commerce between Japan and Singapore, and finally, modern, web-based, customs clearance procedures designed to automate this aspect of international trade in Japan.

5.1. *Impacts on Singapore*

Figure 3 shows that all four of these components of the Japan-Singapore FTA lead to higher rates of return on investment in Singapore. The tariff cuts (largely in Japan) boost the demand for Singaporean products, thereby raising returns to capital in that economy. The time profile of this effect is shown by the shaded area at the bottom of the bars in Figure 3 (tariff only). The rise in rate of return encourages additional investment – both domestically and by foreigners – and the additional investment eventually brings the rate of return back down to that attained in the baseline simulation. Indeed, the FTA rate of return actually falls slightly below its baseline level, before rebounding after 2015. Eventually all rates of return are equalized due to perfect capital mobility. But this is only attained in the very long run.

Figure 3. Effect of Japan-Singapore Free Trade Agreement on the rate of return in Singapore

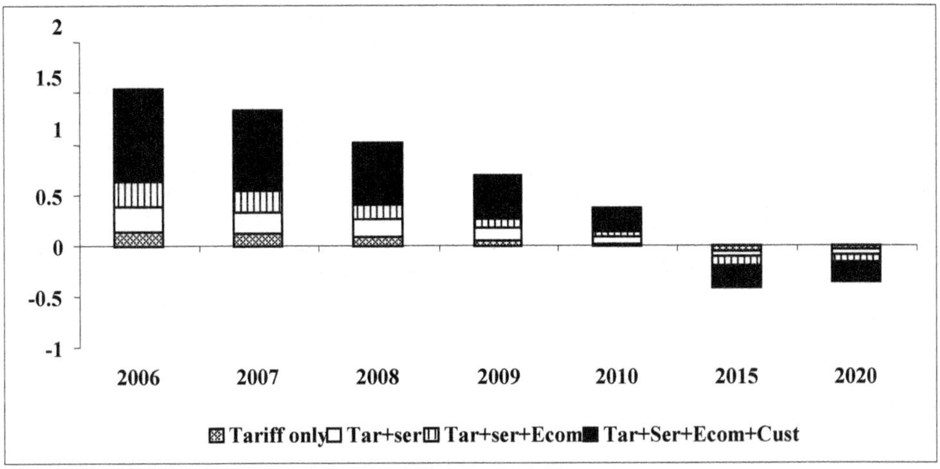

The reduction in barriers to Singapore's direct exports of services to Japan has a similar effect to that of tariffs on the rate of return. This may be seen by considering the incremental effect shown by the second set of bars in Figure 3 (tariffs plus services). Judging from the gap between rate of return effect under the tariffs-only simulation and that under the tariffs and services simulation, services liberalization is somewhat more important for the rate of return.

Unlike the one-sided trade liberalization measures, the e-commerce and customs automization shocks affect both the demand for Singaporean products in Japan, as well as the cost of Japanese imports in Singapore. By lowering the cost of investment goods in Singapore, there is an added boost to the rate of return. Not only has the rental rate on capital risen – due to increased demand for Singaporean products in Japan – but the cost of investing in Singapore has fallen. This is particularly true of customs automization which lowers the effective price of Japanese machinery and equipment in Singapore. As a consequence, these "new age" features of the FTA contribute the majority of the change in rate of return in Singapore.

The increased investment in Singapore, due to the higher rates of return over the 2006-2010 period, dominates the increase in national savings as a result of higher incomes. Therefore Singapore's trade balance deteriorates, relative to the baseline simulation. This is shown in Figure 4. The deterioration reaches its peak in 2008, after which it begins to improve. This reflects the fact that rates of return fall back to their baseline levels and the increase in foreign wealth invested in Singapore gives rise to larger foreign income payments – thereby requiring higher levels of exports, relative to the baseline.

Figure 4. Effect of Japan-Singapore Free Trade Agreement on Singapore's trade balance

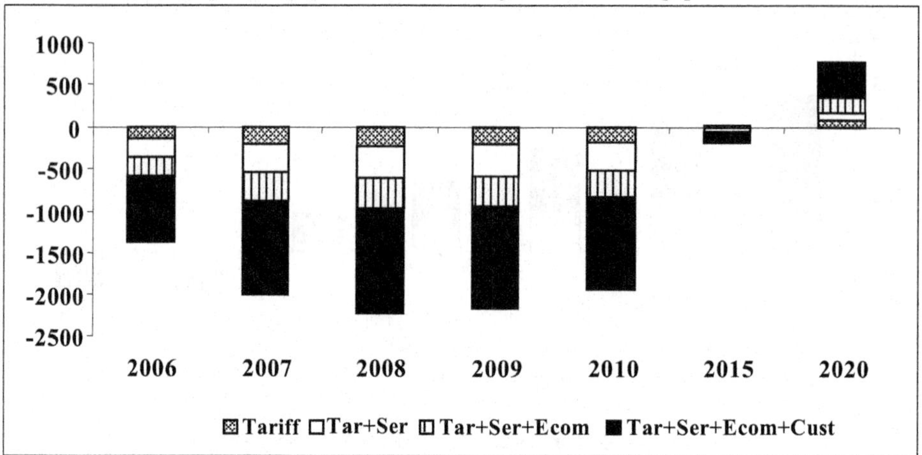

Figure 5 summarizes the long run impact of the Japan-Singapore FTA by reporting the cumulative difference between the FTA and baseline simulations in 2020, for a variety of macro-economic variables of interest. These include: real GDP, capital stock, exports, imports and foreign ownership. The higher rates of return due to the FTA give rise to a large increase in foreign ownership (2.7 percent by 2020), as well as higher capital stocks and GDP. The increase in GDP is larger than the share-weighted increase in capital stock due to the efficiency improvements generated by the "new-age" elements of the FTA. Not surprisingly, both exports and imports are also higher in 2020, although their rates of increase are much smaller than for FDI. This indicates the importance of this "new age" FTA for foreign investment – as well as trade.

Given the importance of this FTA for investment and capital stocks, it is interesting to focus specifically on the resulting changes in the wealth of Singaporean households. This is highlighted in Figure 6. The line connecting the triangular dots in this figure illustrates the cumulative percentage difference between the base case and FTA simulation for the total wealth of Singaporean households. This shows that total wealth rises due to the FTA, and all four elements of the FTA contribute to this increase. However, Singaporean wealth is divided amongst domestic equity and foreign equity. Not surprisingly, Singaporean households choose to invest more in their own economy and less in foreign economies as the domestic rate of return rises.

Figure 5. Effect of Japan-Singapore Free Trade Agreement on Singapore's real GDP, capital, exports and imports and foreign ownership in Japan

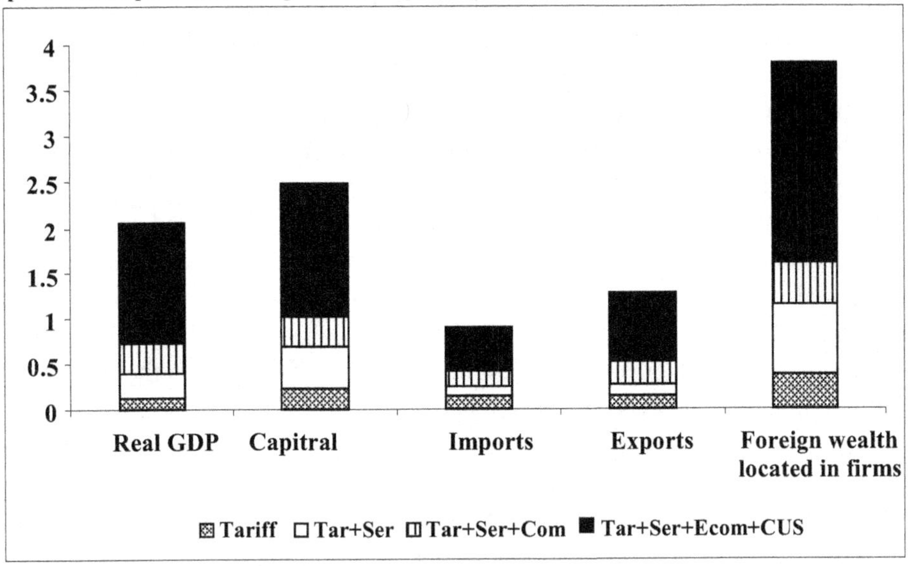

Figure 6. Effect of Japan-Singapore Free Trade Agreement on the wealth of Singaporean households[1]

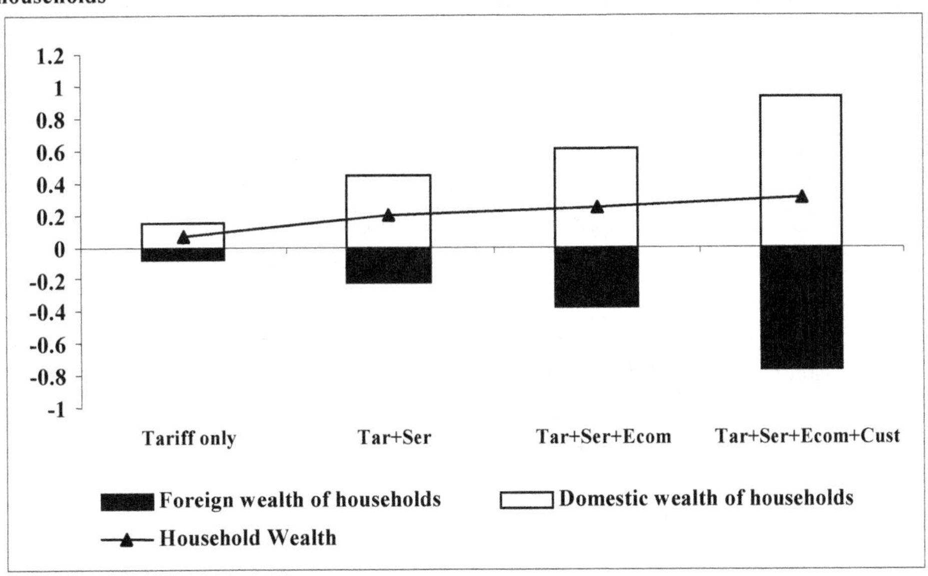

[1] Unlike the previous graph this shows the total (not the additional) cumulative percentage difference between the base case and the policy resulting from the simulation. Thus by adding customs automization (Tar + Ser + Ecom + Cust) benefits are positive overall and higher when compared with the e-commerce simulation (Tar + Ser + Ecom). This is shown by the larger positive numbers under Tar + Ser + Ecom + Cust than under Tar + Ser + Ecom.

Table 7 reports the impacts of the FTA on Singapore's trade with Japan as well as with ROW (all other economies combined). The figures in the table represent cumulative changes in 2020 trade volumes in millions of US$. Percentage changes are reported in parentheses. The biggest volume changes in Singapore's exports to Japan are in machinery and equipment ($1,514 million), followed by business and finance services and other food products. There are large percentage changes in meat products (418 percent), leather, and textiles and apparel, but the initial trade flows are small for these products and so the volume change is also small. However, these large percentage changes indicate a very substantial preference margin for Singaporean goods exported to Japan. This, in turn, signals the potential for trade being routed from third countries, through Singapore to Japan. Hence the interest in strong rules of origin on the part of food and light manufactures producers in Japan.

In contrast, the percentage changes in Singapore's imports from Japan are much more uniform, with the largest changes stimulated by the combined benefits of e-commerce and customs automization for auto imports from Japan (12.6 percent increase in bilateral imports) and imports of machinery and equipment. Due to its predominant role in Japanese exports to Singapore, the increased volume in the latter sector ($2,905 million) is by far the largest change in Singapore's bilateral imports from Japan. Finally, Singapore's imports from the rest of the world rise across the board – indicating this FTA package is not leading to diversion of trade.

Table 8 reports the changes in 2020 volume of output (US$ millions) in Singapore across the four, cumulative simulations. While individual components of the FTA lead to output declines in a few cases, when combined with customs automization, almost all sectors increase their output levels in 2020. (Other crops experience a very small decline in output.) Typically in the case of such FTAs one sees winners and losers – so it is surprising that there is no significant contraction of output across the sectors shown in Table 9. This is due to the growth effects of the FTA. The increase in capital stock available in Singapore, coupled with the relative balanced import effects, permits the simultaneous expansion of nearly all sectors of the economy.

Table 7. Effect of Japan-Singapore Free Trade Agreement on imports in 2020
(import volume change in millions of US$, percent change in parentheses)

	Japan's imports from		Singapore's imports from		ROW's imports from		
	Singapore	ROW	Japan	ROW	Japan	Singapore	ROW
rice	n.t.	0.06	0.0	10.5	-0.04	0.0	-2.0
		(1.12)	(1.72)	(2.04)	(-0.77)	(0.12)	(-0.02)
othgrains		-5.3	0.0	2.3	-0.1	0.0	17.8
	n.t.	(-0.09)	(0.78)	(1.11)	(-0.75)	(0.08)	(0.02)
othcrops	10.8	75.2	0.4	40.9	-7.5	-37.3	120.0
	(7.88)	(0.45)	(0.44)	(0.74)	(-0.78)	(-1.05)	(0.05)
meat	95.7	46.5	0.3	40.8	-2.6	-26.9	166.3
	(417.74)	(0.27)	(1.90)	(1.89)	(-0.41)	(-1.94)	(0.14)
othfood	688.2	42.7	29.2	151.6	-22.5	12.6	758.8
	(124.82)	(0.11)	(9.08)	(1.81)	(-0.64)	(0.13)	(0.20)
fish	2.2	27.3	1.0	1.7	6.8	-2.1	13.0
	(10.58)	(1.38)	(2.46)	(0.86)	(0.61)	(-0.68)	(0.07)
texwap	38.1	1001.9	8.9	81.9	-4.4	-38.7	216.1
	(58.89)	(1.71)	(3.35)	(0.89)	(-0.04)	(-0.74)	(0.04)
leather	54.4	295.8	0.8	31.2	4.7	0.2	101.0
	(79.58)	(1.57)	(5.81)	(1.32)	(0.92)	(0.02)	(0.06)
extract	21.7	1672.0	164.8	336.7	723.8	13.5	-1595.5
	(6.25)	(1.24)	(3.85)	(0.61)	(1.12)	(0.08)	(-0.10)
pchemineral	294.8	1167.9	400.5	341.0	3417.3	-159.5	-3219.4
	(14.40)	(1.83)	(7.91)	(0.68)	(3.63)	(-0.27)	(-0.22)
omnfcs	48.1	950.8	95.5	219.8	235.3	-3.0	-213.6
	(4.87)	(1.59)	(2.98)	(0.82)	(0.78)	(-0.01)	(-0.03)

Table 7. Effect of Japan-Singapore Free Trade Agreement on imports in 2020–Continued
(import volume change in millions of US$, percent change in parentheses)

	Japan's imports from		Singapore's imports from		ROW's imports from		
	Singapore	**ROW**	**Japan**	**ROW**	**Japan**	**Singapore**	**ROW**
autos	1.9	745.0	284.6	66.5	342.3	92.8	-760.3
	(23.99)	(2.83)	(12.60)	(1.08)	(0.42)	(1.97)	(-0.10)
machiequip	1513.6	3839.4	2905.3	1610.7	9509.3	747.5	-10050.2
	(13.45)	(2.72)	(9.12)	(0.72)	(2.49)	(0.31)	(-0.33)
utilities	0.2	16.3	-0.2	30.8	-14.8	-12.4	35.9
	(0.91)	(1.19)	(-1.10)	(0.78)	(-1.86)	(-0.27)	(0.01)
construction	0.2	0.5	0.0	0.4	-0.1	0.3	26.4
	(110.04)	(0.65)	(-0.84)	(0.77)	(-1.53)	(0.29)	(0.04)
tradetrans	160.7	1395.3	-5.0	55.6	-656.3	23.0	647.8
	(0.87)	(0.85)	(-0.82)	(0.85)	(-1.06)	(0.05)	(0.07)
busfinance	1300.1	-386.3	5.7	558.9	-377.8	-14.5	1608.7
	(65.57)	(-0.73)	(0.09)	(1.64)	(-1.46)	(-0.13)	(0.27)

Source: Author's simulation,

Table 8. Effect of Japan-Singapore Free Trade Agreement on outputs in 2020
(volume change in millions of US$, percent change in parentheses)

	Japan				Singapore			
	sim1	sim2	sim3	sim4	sim1	sim2	sim3	sim4
rice	-8.0	-6.0	-6.5	-2.1	0.1	0.1	0.1	0.1
	(-0.01)	(-0.01)	(-0.01)	(-0.00)	(0.50)	(0.46)	(0.56)	(0.95)
othgrains	-0.3	-0.1	-0.6	-18.6	0.0	0.0	0.0	0.1
	(-0.02)	(-0.01)	(-0.03)	(-1.02)	(0.59)	(0.54)	(0.66)	(1.05)
othcrops	-4.3	-3.1	-4.3	-35.3	-9.8	-10.9	-11.4	-12.3
	(-0.01)	(-0.01)	(-0.01)	(0.09)	(-0.50)	(-0.55)	(-0.58)	(-0.63)
meat	-33.8	-26.4	-32.5	-204.8	46.4	44.1	44.3	45.7
	(-0.03)	(-0.02)	(-0.03)	(-0.16)	(2.20)	(2.09)	(2.10)	(2.16)
othfood	-192.3	-169.4	-175.7	-234.6	590.3	575.9	586.5	635.4
	(-0.04)	(-0.03)	(-0.03)	(-0.04)	(4.80)	(4.69)	(4.77)	(5.17)
fish	-6.8	-5.4	-6.2	-21.6	0.0	0.0	0.1	0.2
	(-0.02)	(-0.02)	(-0.02)	(-0.06)	(0.02)	(0.01)	(0.02)	(0.06)
texwap	6.0	23.8	-0.2	-745.7	19.9	3.0	2.3	3.5
	(0.00)	(0.01)	(-0.00)	(-0.36)	(0.36)	(0.05)	(0.04)	(0.06)
leather	-0.5	2.6	-1.3	-161.5	36.5	34.8	37.4	45.5
	(-0.00)	(0.01)	(-0.01)	(-0.74)	(4.11)	(3.92)	(4.20)	(5.12)
extract	49.5	127.5	130.6	458.5	46.2	16.2	66.0	173.1
	(0.01)	(0.02)	(0.03)	(0.09)	(0.17)	(0.06)	(0.25)	(0.65)
pchemineral	-9.2	67.9	60.8	2242.2	111.7	93.4	147.2	203.2
	(-0.00)	(0.01)	(0.01)	(0.27)	(0.17)	(0.14)	(0.22)	(0.31)
Omnfcs	10.5	38.1	32.6	163.6	7.1	-18.1	8.1	108.5
	(0.00)	(0.01)	(0.01)	(0.03)	(0.03)	(-0.07)	(0.03)	(0.40)

Table 8. Effect of Japan-Singapore Free Trade Agreement on outputs in 2020–Continued
(volume change in millions of US$, percent change in parentheses)

	Japan				Singapore			
	sim1	sim2	sim3	sim4	sim1	sim2	sim3	sim4
Autos	38.2	82.1	146.5	312.6	-3.9	-10.9	38.0	86.4
	(0.02)	(0.04)	(0.07)	(0.16)	(-0.05)	(-0.13)	(0.47)	(1.07)
machiequip	101.8	295.6	527.4	6054.3	-78.1	-381.9	540.9	2029.3
	(0.01)	(0.03)	(0.05)	(0.63)	(-0.03)	(-0.16)	(0.23)	(0.86)
Utilities	-7.1	6.9	12.7	355.2	15.7	37.3	60.4	131.0
	(-0.00)	(0.00)	(0.00)	(0.09)	(0.07)	(0.16)	(0.26)	(0.56)
construction	-14.7	17.4	98.6	2777.5	55.1	188.2	246.9	455.7
	(-0.00)	(0.00)	(0.01)	(0.30)	(0.14)	(0.46)	(0.61)	(1.12)
tradetrans	6.3	85.4	87.5	716.8	8.3	-23.6	98.5	491.7
	(0.00)	(0.01)	(0.01)	(0.06)	(0.01)	(-0.02)	(0.10)	(0.50)
busfinance	-5.5	-186.8	-155.5	1124.3	29.6	1155.2	1234.8	1484.5
	(-0.00)	(-0.02)	(-0.01)	(0.10)	(0.05)	(2.11)	(2.26)	(2.71)

Note: sim1-4 differ in components of the simulation as follows, sim1-Tariff only; sim2-Tariff and Service; sim3-Tariff, Service and E-commerce; sim4-Tariff, Service, E-commerce and Customs Automization.

Source: Author's simulation,

Table 9. Welfare Effects of FTA: Equivalent Variation in 2020 in millions of US$

	Tariffs	Services	E-commerce	Customs Automization	Full FTA	Full FTA (% Change in Welfare)
Japan	-85.0	236.7	170.6	6597.5	6919.7	0.146
Korea	-4.9	-6.0	-10.6	258.6	237.1	0.058
Singapore	55.0	115.3	55.5	171.0	396.8	0.668
Malaysia	2.6	-4.0	1.1	135.9	135.6	0.162
Thailand	-1.8	0.3	-15.7	263.6	246.3	0.168
IndPhlViet	-1.9	-8.1	1.9	232.8	224.7	0.088
China	-4.1	-5.9	-12.3	288.4	266.1	0.040
Hong Kong	-0.2	-2.6	3.5	79.3	80.1	0.092
Chinese Taipei	-2.3	-2.1	-3.3	207.1	199.5	0.078
SoAsia	-2.7	-3.2	0.6	45.0	39.7	0.010
AusNZL	-1.7	-4.1	1.4	70.2	65.8	0.019
Canada	-2.4	-5.9	0.6	20.4	12.7	0.002
USA	-20.2	-33.8	-11.0	588.2	523.1	0.008
Mexico	-0.6	-1.0	-0.9	7.9	5.5	0.002
Chile	-1.4	-2.7	0.3	15.4	11.7	0.021
WEurope	-21.2	-39.2	-21.2	212.9	131.3	0.001
Remainder	-12.5	-27.5	6.8	36.8	3.6	0.000
World	-105.3	206.1	167.3	9231.2	9499.2	

Source: Authors' simulation.

5.2. *Results for Japan*

The impacts of the FTA on Japan have a distinctly different character than those for Singapore. Japan's exports to Singapore represent only 3.2 percent of total trade. Therefore, the strictly bilateral measures, including: tariff cuts, reduced services trade barriers and e-commerce regulations, have a relatively minor impact on aggregate output, trade, investment and GDP. Rather, the impacts of the FTA on Japan are driven largely by the customs automization process, which affects the cost of trading with all partners. This may be seen in Figure 7 which reports the impact of individual components of the FTA on the rate of return on investment in Japan. The cumulative effects of the first three (bilateral) elements of the agreement are negligible when compared to the impact of customs automization. The latter reform boosts rates of return in Japan, by increasing efficiency in the economy, and this gives rise to a capital inflow (recall that this was also the case in Singapore). As a result, Japan's trade balance deteriorates, relative to the baseline (Figure 8). However, in the long run, increased foreign

Figure 7. Effect of Japan-Singapore Free Trade Agreement on the rate of return in Japan

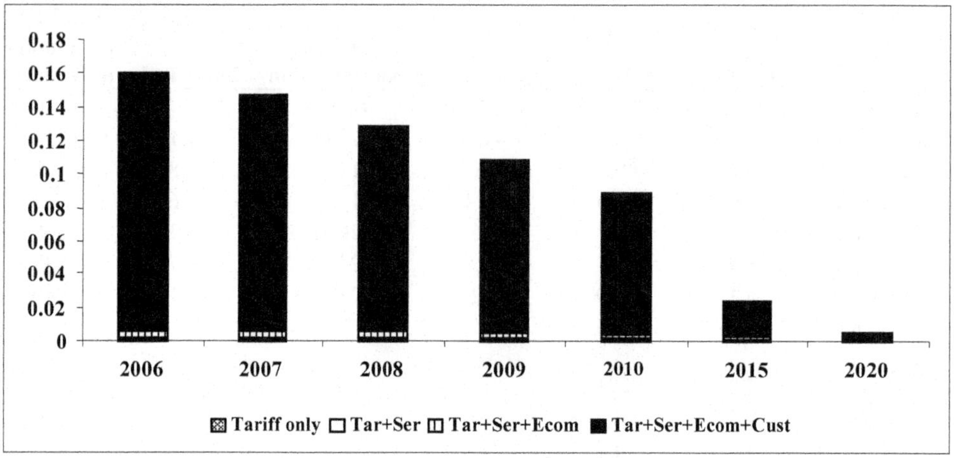

Figure 8. Effect of Japan-Singapore Free Trade Agreement on Japan's trade balance

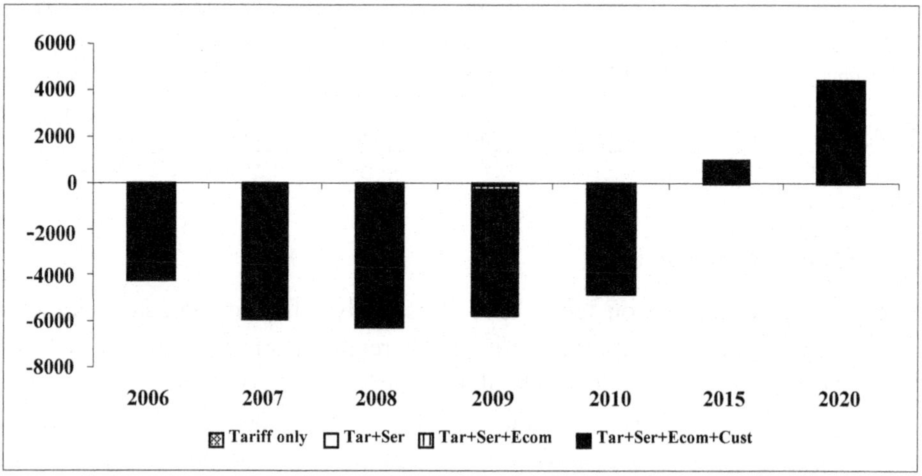

income payments dictate an increase in exports, so that we observe the same U-shaped pattern for the trade balance change, relative to the baseline, as we saw for Singapore.

The long run impacts of the Japan-Singapore FTA on other macro-economic variables in the Japanese economy are reported in the second row of Table 10.

Whereas the investment and GDP results dominated the aggregated trade volume effects in Singapore, in Japan, where customs automization lowers the cost of trade with *all* partners and the trade/GDP ratio is much smaller, the trade

Table 10. Effect of Japan-Singapore Free Trade Agreement on capital, real GDP, exports and imports and equity ownership in 2020
(cumulative percent differences from baseline simulation)

	Capital Stocks	Real GDP	Real Exports	Real Imports	Wealth	Overseas Holdings	Equity held by foreigners
Singapore	1.81	1.67	1.00	0.64	0.31	-0.77	2.66
Japan	0.33	0.20	1.93	1.82	0.34	-0.27	1.45
Korea	0.10	0.11	0.08	-0.05	-0.03	-0.08	0.06
Malaysia	0.27	0.31	0.15	0.01	0.00	-0.10	0.37
Thailand	0.32	0.33	0.30	0.11	-0.04	-1.53	1.72
IndPhlViet	0.17	0.13	0.09	0.00	-0.01	-0.18	0.33
China	-0.01	0.04	0.10	0.00	-0.04	0.20	-0.40
Hong Kong	0.23	0.27	0.08	0.01	-0.26	-0.66	0.15
Chinese Taipei	0.20	0.18	0.10	-0.08	-0.05	-0.16	0.21
SoAsia	-0.02	0.01	-0.02	-0.04	-0.06	0.07	-0.19
AusNZL	0.02	0.03	0.01	-0.02	-0.04	-0.06	-0.02
Canada	-0.04	-0.01	-0.07	-0.07	-0.06	0.07	-0.24
USA	-0.03	0.01	-0.03	-0.01	-0.07	0.08	-0.25
Mexico	-0.02	0.00	-0.08	-0.10	-0.08	0.10	-0.28
Chile	0.03	0.03	0.03	-0.01	-0.04	-0.06	-0.01
WEurope	-0.07	-0.01	-0.09	-0.04	-0.06	0.01	-0.19
Remainder	-0.05	-0.01	-0.04	-0.02	-0.05	0.06	-0.17

Note: Price reduction = e-commerce penetration rate* reduction in margin as a percentage of final price.

Source: Author's computation based on estimates from MRI.

volume changes dominate. Specifically, Japan's exports are projected to be nearly two percent higher, relative to baseline, in 2020. Capital stocks and wealth are about one-third of a percent higher in the wake of the FTA, while Japan's GDP gets a modest 0.2 percent cumulative boost by the year 2020.

The modest macro-economic effects are mirrored at the sector level. While bilateral imports from Singapore receive a considerable boost – particularly for primary products and light manufactures (recall Table 7), the subsequent changes in Japanese output are quite small and reflect a shift towards Japan's comparative advantage in durable goods production (Table 8). The largest output volume declines in Japan are for textiles and apparel (-$746 million), other food and meat products. However, the only decline in excess of one percent, relative to baseline, is for other grains (-1.02 percent). As was the case with Singapore, trade with ROW increases, with the only declines in Japanese imports from ROW coming in other grains and in business and finance services (Table 7).

5.3. *Results for Rest of World*

The remaining rows of Table 10 report the impact of the Japan-Singapore FTA on the macro-economic performance of countries outside the FTA. The automization of custom's procedures increases trade throughout the Asia-Pacific region and the rest of the world, thus boosting real GDP in all regions excepting for Canada, Western Europe and the residual region in the final row of this table. All of the Asian economies gain in terms of real GDP – with the largest impact felt in Thailand and Malaysia – two economies that trade a great deal with Singapore and Japan. These increases in real GDP also fuel increased foreign investment, with the stock of foreign-owned equity in Thailand rising by 1.7 percent as a result of the FTA. The increase in foreign ownership in Singapore, Japan and Thailand is financed by a modest increase in outward FDI by the US, Canada, Mexico, China and South Asia, as reported in the final column of Table 10. Many of the other Asian economies reduce their foreign ownership in order to increase investment in their domestic economies.

5.4. *Welfare Effects*

A natural question to ask in the face of any Free Trade Agreement is the following: Does it leave the world as a whole better off? Given the multi-region, multi-period nature of this study, we face the challenging problem of aggregating benefits over countries and over time periods. To keep things simple, we focus on welfare at a particular point in time – in this case we choose 2020 – at which point the investment story has played itself out. We then compute the static equivalent variation, for the representative household in each region, associated with the cumulative changes that have occurred between the baseline and the FTA simulations. These dollar values represent the annual increase (or decrease) in real income stemming from the presence of the FTA. The simple sum of these EV measures is our annual measure of the change in world welfare.

Equivalent variations for each region and for the world as a whole are reported in Table 9. Here, each of the first four columns corresponds to one of the four components of the FTA. (The final column reports the *per capita* percentage changes in welfare due to the FTA. This will be discussed below.) The traditional, bilateral tariff elimination associated with most FTAs generates global welfare losses, as the only significant bilateral tariffs remaining are Japan's tariffs on primary products and light manufactures. Taken on their own, elimination of these tariffs creates costly trade diversion, with increased imports coming from Singapore at the expense of lower cost suppliers elsewhere.

Singapore's welfare rises as a result of the terms of trade gain that they experience. However, Japan's welfare falls, as does that for all other economies.

As one moves from this traditional tariff-based FTA to the "new age" elements that focus less on commercial policy and more on improving efficiency, the prevalence of regional benefits increases. In the case of services trade liberalization, both Japan and Singapore gain and the overall benefits outweigh the costs, generating a global welfare gain of $206 million. In the case of e-commerce, the gains are spread across more than half of the trading partners. Finally, in the case of the customs automization component of the FTA, all regions gain. In fact, the latter component dominates all of the others, and consequently, all regions benefit from the FTA.

The very favorable outcome from customs automization has several explanations. Firstly, this is the only FTA measure that is non-discriminatory. Customs automization benefits all trading partners. Of course, the "linking benefit" derived from two economies synchronizing their systems gives an additional margin of preference to Japan –Singapore trade. However, eventually other economies that implement this system will also obtain this linking effect. Secondly, unlike tariff cuts which lead to lost revenue, customs automization saves time and hence lowers the effective price of the product. There is no lost revenue – apart from the cost of implementation – so the liberalizing economy is unlikely to experience a loss in welfare.

This raises the question: if customs automization is such a windfall, why hasn't it already been implemented? One answer is that, like many administrative reforms, the barriers to reform are not merely economic. A second, more interesting, answer is that the direct benefits of customs automization are quite small, and the costs are non-negligible. The Mitsubishi Research Institute (MRI) estimates that the cost of running the new system will be $36.7 million *per* year. It is only when the indirect benefits – specifically the opportunity costs of time in trade – are taken into account, that this becomes an important feature of the FTA. To date, this particular barrier to trade has received scant attention. Hence the importance of Hummels' (2000) work in quantifying the *ad valorem* value of time savings in trade.

The final column of Table 9 reports the percentage changes in *per capita* welfare in each region of the world as a result of the FTA. Unlike the EV measure, this controls for economic size when making comparisons across regions. Not surprisingly, Singapore is the largest *per capita* winner from the FTA. Singapore is a very open economy, trade with Japan is quite important, and Singapore receives a substantial preference margin on tariffs, services trade, and e-commerce, as well as a linking benefit associated with Japan's customs automization measures. More surprising is the fact that Thailand and Malaysia gain relatively more from the FTA than does Japan. This, despite the fact that they are not directly included in the FTA. The reason for these large gains is their relatively high trade dependence on Japan and Singapore, both of which are importing more from all destinations as a result of the agreement. Japan's imports rise as a result of customs automization. Singapore's imports rise in response to the increased demand for its own products in the Japanese markets, as well as due to higher incomes. The subsequent increase in demand for products from Thailand and Malaysia give rise to substantial terms of trade gains for both economies.

6. Summary and Conclusions

This study has sought to quantify the dynamic benefits of Japan's "new age" Free Trade Agreement currently under negotiation with Singapore. We find that the impact of the FTA on investment, capital accumulation and economic growth is significant – particularly in Singapore. Furthermore, global benefits from the proposed FTA are substantial – on the order of $9.5 billion *per* year by 2020. All regions of the world gain from this agreement, although 70 percent of the gains are captured by Japan – which is the region undertaking most of the reforms.

It is interesting to note that if the FTA were implemented as a traditional trade agreement with tariff cuts being the centerpiece – perhaps adding some liberalization of rules governing direct trade in services – none of this would be true. The global welfare gains would be uncertain, trade diversion would be significant, and most non-participating regions would lose from the agreement. It is only when the "new age" features – e-commerce and customs automization – are added that benefits to the other regions begin to appear and the global gains become pronounced.

In closing, it is important to note the limitations of this study. Firstly, since this work was begun, a number of aspects of the agreement have become clearer. In particular, it is likely that agriculture will be left out of the agreement – due to the problem of enforcing rules of origin on these heavily protected products. Also, the timetable for implementation has been moved up to begin in spring 2002, if all goes as planned. Since agriculture generates relatively few of the gains in our study, its omission unlikely to have a substantial impact on our results. Similarly, we have found that the results are quite robust with respect to the baseline. The main developments between 2002 and 2005 in our baseline are China's accession to the WTO and elimination of the textiles and apparel export quotas. Neither of these has direct bearing on the Japan-Singapore trade relationship and results not reported here show that China's accession makes little difference for the direct impacts of this FTA on the member economies.

Despite our best attempts to quantify "new-age" features of the Japan-Singapore FTA, there remain a number of important elements of this agreement that we have omitted. Specifically, we have not incorporated the effects of liberalization of direct trade in transport and telecommunications services where barriers are potentially quite large. We have also failed to quantify the impact of liberalizing rules governing investment and the movement of natural persons. These are central modes of delivery for the rapidly growing services sector, and their omission surely leads to an understatement of the impacts of the FTA on efficiency, investment and growth.

Finally, while there are many potential benefits of the proposed FTA between Japan and Singapore, there are also some costs that have been neglected. Several elements of the FTA will involve implementation costs. Also, customs automization will involve recurring costs of about $37 million *per* year (MRI estimate). However, these are small when compared with the potential gains. Perhaps of greater concern are the costs associated with verifying that the products granted preferential treatment under the FTA in question are indeed produced in the partner economy. This issue is of particular concern in the case of food products, textiles, apparel, and leather products under the Japan-Singapore FTA. Japan's tariffs in these sectors are still high and, given the high volume of re-exports from Singapore, the potential incentive for other economies to export foodstuffs and light manufactures through Singapore to Japan would be substantial. Very tight rules of origin that would prevent such transshipment could also prove costly to the businesses involved, thereby frustrating trade.

References

1. Ahuja, V. and D. Filmer. (1995). "Educational Attainment in Developing Countries; New Estimates and Projections Disaggregated by Gender," World Bank Policy Research Working Paper 1489, Washington, DC, July.
2. Anderson, K. and H. Norheim. (1993). "Is World Trade Becoming More Regionalized?" *Review of International Economics* 1(2):91-109.
3. Brown, A.J. (1949). *Applied Economics: Aspects of the World Economy in War and Peace*, London: George Allen-Unwin.
4. Bureau of Economic Analysis. (1999) *International Accounts Data U.S. International Services: Cross-Border Trade & Sales Through Affiliates, 1986-99*, (*http://www.bea.doc.gov/bea/di/1000serv/intlserv.htm*)
5. Central Intelligence Agency. (1997). *The World Factbook 1997-1998*. Brassey's: Washington.

6. CPB. (1999). "WorldScan: the Core Version," CPB Netherlands Bureau for Economic Policy Analysis, December.
7. Dee, P. and K. Hanslow. (2000) "Multilateral Liberalisation of Services Trade," Staff Research Paper, Productivity Commission, Australia.
8. Drysdale, P. (1967). *Japanese-Australian Trade*, Ph.D. Dissertation. Australian National University, Canberra.
9. Drysdale, P. and R. Garnaut. (1982). "Trade Intensities and the Analysis of Bilateral Trade Flows in a Many-Country World," *Hitsubashi Journal of Economics* 22(2):62-84.
10. Fan, M. and Y. Zheng. (2000). "China's Trade Liberalisation for WTO Accession and Its Effects on China - A Computable General Equilibrium Analysis," mimeo.
11. Feldstein, M. and C. Horioka (1980). "Domestic Saving and International Capital Flows," *The Economic Journal*, Vol.90, June: 314-329.
12. Francois, J. (1998). "Scale Economies and Imperfect Competition in the GTAP Model," GTAP Technical Paper No. 14, Center for Global Trade Analysis, September.
13. Francois, J. (1999). "A Gravity Approach to Measuring Services Protection." Unpublished manuscript, Erasmus University, Rotterdam.
14. Francois, J. and C. Shiells. (1994). *Modeling Trade Policy: Applied General Equilibrium Assessments of North American Free Trade*. Cambridge University Press.
15. Francois, J. and D. Spinanger. (2001). "With Rags to Riches But Then What?" paper presented at the Fourth Annual Conference on Global Economic Analysis, West Lafayette, June 27-29, 2001.
16. Francois, J. and A. Strutt. (1999). "Post Uruguay Round Tariff Vectors for GTAP v.4," memo, June.
17. French, K. and J. Poterbe. (1991). "Investor Diversification and International Equity Markets," *American Economic Review* 81:222-26.
18. Harrison, W J and K. R. Pearson. (1996). "Computing Solutions For Large General Equilibrium Models Using GEMPACK," *Computational Economics* 9:83-127.
19. Harrison, J., M. Horridge, and K. Pearson (1999) "Decomposing Simulation Results with Respect to Exogenous Shocks," paper presented at the Second Annual Conference on Global Economic Analysis, Denmark, June 20-22, 1999.
20. Hertel, T. W. (1992). "Introducing Imperfect Competition into the SALTER Model," Purdue University, Department of Agricultural Economics Staff paper No. 93-3.
21. Hertel, T. W. (1997). *Global Trade Analysis: Modeling and Applications,* Cambridge University Press, Cambridge.
22. Hoekman, B. (1995). "Assessing the General Agreement on Trade in Services," in Martin, W. and Winters, L. A. eds. *The Uruguay Round and the Developing Economies,* World Bank Discussion Paper 307, World Bank, Washington DC.
23. Hummels, D. (2000). "Time as a Trade Barrier," unpublished manuscript, Purdue University, W. Lafayette, IN.
24. Ianchovichina, E. I. (1998). "International Capital Linkages: Theory and Applications in A Dynamic Computable General Equilibrium Model," Ph.D. Dissertation, Purdue University.
25. Ianchovichina, E. I., and R. A. McDougall. (2001). "Theoretical Structure of Dynamic GTAP" GTAP Technical Paper No. 17, Center for Global Trade Analysis, Purdue University, West Lafayette, IN, 47906-1145, USA.
26. IDE-JETRO. (2000). "Toward Closer Japan-Korea Economic Relations in the 21st Century."

27. (*http://www.ide.go.jp/English/Lecture/pressmenu/pressE000606.html*)
28. Ingco, M. (1996). "Tariffication in the Uruguay Round: How Much Liberalization?" *The World Economy*, 19(4): 425-47, July.
29. Joint Study Group (2000). *Report on the Free Trade Agreement between Japan and Singapore,* Ministry of Foreign Affairs, Japan and Singapore.
30. Joint Study Group (2000) "Japan-Singapore Economic Agreement for a New Age Partnership," Japan Study Group Report
31. (*http://www.mofa.go.jp/region/asia-paci/singapore/econo_b.html*)
32. Kawasaki, K. (1999) *Foundations and Applications of Applied General Equilibrium Analysis: A Simulation Analysis on Economic Structural Reform*, Nihonhyohronsya.
33. Kojima, K. (1964). "The Pattern of International Trade among Advanced Countries," *Hitsubashi Journal of Economics 5*(1).
34. Korea Institute for International Economic Policy (KIEP). (2000). "Economic Effects of and Policy Directions for Korea-Japan FTA."
35. Martin, W., B. Dimaranan and T. Hertel, (1999): "Trade Policy, Structural Change and China's Trade Growth," mimeo.
36. McDougall, R.A., A. Elbehri, and T.P. Truong. (1998). *Global Trade Assistance and Protection: The GTAP 4 Data Base*, Center for Global Trade Analysis, Purdue University.
37. Nakajima, T. and Kwon, O. (2001). "An Analysis of the Economic Effects of Japan-Korea FTA," Economic Research Institute for Northeast Asia (ERINA).
38. Tsutsumi, M. (2000) "Regional Economic Integration an China's Participation to WTO," JCER Discussion Paper No. 60.
39. Walmsley, T. L., B. Dimaranan and R. A. McDougall, (2000) "A Base Case Scenario for the Dynamic GTAP Model." Paper prepared for the Dynamic GTAP Short Course, Purdue University, West Lafayette, IN, October.
40. WTO (2000) Trade Policy Review: Singapore, Geneva.

Appendix Table A1. Sector Aggregation

Aggregation of GTAP Database from GTAP(v.4) Full Scale Data (50 sectors)

50 Sectors	GTAP code	This study
1 Paddy rice	pdr	rice
2 Wheat	wht	othgrains
3 Cereal grains nec	gro	othgrains
4 Vegetables, fruit, nuts	v_f	othcrops
5 Oil seeds	osd	othcrops
6 Sugar cane, sugar beet	c_b	othcrops
7 Plant-based fibers	pfb	othcrops
8 Crops nec	ocr	othcrops
9 Bovine cattle, sheep and goats, horses	ctl	meat
10 Animal products nec	oap	meat
11 Raw milk	rmk	othfood
12 Wool, silk-worm cocoons	wol	othcrops
13 Forestry	for	extract

Appendix Table A1. Sector Aggregation–Continued

Aggregation of GTAP Database from GTAP(v.4) Full Scale Data (50 sectors)		
50 Sectors	**GTAP code**	**This study**
14 Fishing	fsh	fish
15 Coal	col	extract
16 Oil	oil	extract
17 Gas	gas	extract
18 Minerals nec	omn	extract
19 Bovine cattle, sheep and goat, horse meat prods	cmt	meat
20 Meat products nec	omt	meat
21 Vegetable oils and fats	vol	othfood
22 Dairy products	mil	othfood
23 Processed rice	pcr	rice
24 Sugar	sgr	othfood
25 Food products nec	ofd	othfood
26 Beverages and tobacco products	b_t	othfood
27 Textiles	tex	texwap
28 Wearing apparel	wap	texwap
29 Leather products	lea	leather
30 Wood products	lum	omnfcs
31 Paper products, publishing	ppp	omnfcs
32 Petroleum, coal products	p_c	pchemineral
33 Chemical, rubber, plastic products	crp	pchemineral
34 Mineral products nec	nmm	pchemineral
35 Ferrous metals	i_s	extract
36 Metals nec	nfm	extract
37 Metal products	fmp	extract
38 Motor vehicles and parts	mvh	autos
39 Transport equipment nec	otn	machequip
40 Electronic equipment	ele	machequip
41 Machinery and equipment nec	ome	machequip
42 Manufactures nec	omf	omnfcs
43 Electricity	ely	utilities
44 Gas manufacture, distribution	gdt	utilities
45 Water	wtr	utilities
46 Construction	cns	construction
47 Trade, transport	t_t	tradetrans
48 Financial, business, recreational services	osp	busfinance
49 Public admin and defense, education, health	osg	utilities
50 Dwellings	dwe	utilities

Appendix Table A2. Regional Aggregation

Aggregation of GTAP Database from GTAP(v.4) Full Scale Data (45 regions)

45 Regions	GTAP code	This study
1 Australia	aus	AusNZL
2 New Zealand	nzl	AusNZL
3 Japan	jpn	Japan
4 Korea	kor	Korea
5 Indonesia	idn	Indphlviet
6 Malaysia	mys	Malaysia
7 Philippines	phl	Indphlviet
8 Singapore	sgp	Singapore
9 Thailand	tha	Thailand
10 Viet Nam	vnm	Indphlviet
11 China	chn	China
12 Hong Kong	hkg	HongKong
13 Chinese Taipei	twn	Chinese Taipei
14 India	ind	SoAsia
15 Sri Lanka	lka	SoAsia
16 Rest of South Asia	ras	SoAsia
17 Canada	can	Canada
18 United States of America	usa	USA
19 Mexico	mex	Mexico
20 Central America and the Caribbean	cam	ROW
21 Venezuela	ven	ROW
22 Colombia	col	ROW
23 Rest of the Andean Pact	rap	ROW
24 Argentina	arg	ROW
25 Brazil	bra	ROW
26 Chile	chl	Chile
27 Uruguay	ury	ROW
28 Rest of South America	rsm	ROW
29 United Kingdom	gbr	WEurope
30 Germany	deu	WEurope
31 Denmark	dnk	WEurope
32 Sweden	swe	WEurope
33 Finland	fin	WEurope
34 Rest of European Union	reu	WEurope
35 EFTA	eft	WEurope
36 Central European Associates	cea	ROW
37 Former Soviet Union	fsu	ROW
38 Turkey	tur	ROW

Appendix Table A2. Regional Aggregation–Continued

Aggregation of GTAP Database from GTAP(v.4) Full Scale Data (45 regions)

45 Regions	GTAP code	This study
39 Rest of Middle East	rme	ROW
40 Morocco	mar	ROW
41 Rest of North Africa	rnf	ROW
42 South African Customs Union	saf	ROW
43 Rest of southern Africa	rsa	ROW
44 Rest of sub-Saharan Africa	rss	ROW
45 Rest of World	row	ROW

Appendix 2. Construction of the Baseline

The baseline scenario should reflect as closely as possible the changes expected to occur, in the world economy, over the period of interest. The baseline scenario contains macroeconomic forecasts of each country. The baseline scenario used in this report is based on a baseline developed by Walmsley, Dimaranan and McDougall (2000) for the Dynamic GTAP model (Ianchovichina, 1998 and Ianchovichina, and McDougall, 2001). The aim here was to obtain yearly macroeconomic data/projections for 211 countries, over the period 1995 to 2020. The macroeconomic variables of interest included: real gross domestic product, gross investment, capital stocks, population, skilled and unskilled labor and total labor. Not all of the data could be collected and estimates had to be made. Once projections are obtained or estimated for all 211 countries and years (1995-2020), the projections are aggregated and growth rates calculated to obtain the macro shocks for the base case scenario. The following sections describe this process and show the final baseline scenario used in this report.

Projections were obtained for gross domestic product, gross domestic investment, population, labor force and skilled labor. The source of these projections and a description are given below:

- Gross domestic product, gross domestic investment and population data and projections were available for 133 countries/regions for the period 1992 to 2007 (projections 1998 to 2007). These projections were obtained by combining historical and forecast data provided by the World Bank (Global Economic Perspectives Data Base, 1999).
- Labor force projections in the form of number of male and female workers were available for 205 countries/regions. Projections were provided on a five yearly basis from 1990 to 2020. These projections were obtained from the

World Bank. Before proceeding data on male and female workers were added together to obtain projections for the total labor force.

- Skilled labor projections were obtained from two sources.
  - For the less developed countries projections of the share of secondary and tertiary educated labor as a proportion of the population were obtained for 71 developing countries. These were five yearly projections from 1990 to 2020. These projections were obtained from Ahuja and Filmer (1995).
  - For the developed economies skilled labor projections were based on projected skilled labor shares for 12 developed/developing regions over the period 1994 to 2050. These were obtained from the CPB (1999).

In addition to projections, macro data for the base or initial year (1995) was also collected for all 211 standard countries. For GDP and population, data was obtained for each of the countries from either from the World Bank or from the CIA World Factbook. Other macro variables, including gross domestic investment and capital stocks, were either obtained directly from the World Bank or GDP shares were used to estimate their value. This base year data was used to scale data, fill in missing values and obtain capital stock projections.

Undoubtedly, the projections obtained from the various sources listed above will be incomplete and in some cases incompatible. Some processing is required to get them into a common format and ensure that there are values for all 211 countries and for all years of interest (1995-2000). The methods used, including extrapolation and using GDP shares to fill in missing countries, to obtain the complete projections data set are outlined in greater details in Walmsley, Dimaranan and McDougall (2000).

Once estimates are obtained for the 211 countries over the period 1995 to 2020, these estimates are then aggregated to obtain the estimates of real GDP, investment, capital stocks, population, and skilled and unskilled labor for the 17 regions and 13 periods used in this paper. The yearly growth rates of real GDP, investment, capital stocks, population, and skilled and unskilled labor for the 17 regions are depicted in Figures A1-A6. Note that in the baseline, the 2007 growth rates are extrapolated out to 2020 for GDP, investment, and population.

In the baseline capital stocks are the accumulation of investment over time. Figures A1-A3 illustrate the growth rates in real GDP, gross and capital investment. Capital is equal to the capital stocks from the previous period plus gross investment less depreciation of 4 percent. 1995 to 1997 are taken from historical data and 1998 to 2007 are projections. The decline in real GDP, gross investment and capital stocks in 1997 and 1998 is the result of the Asian crisis, which affected most of the countries examined in this report. Growth in Real GDP of Japan is projected to be low relative to the newly industrialized countries – Singapore and Korea – and significantly lower than China, where very high growth rates are projected.

Growth rates of unskilled labor were obtained from taking skilled labor from total labor projected. The growth rate of unskilled and skilled labor decline slowly over time as the population gets older in many of these countries. Although declining over time, skilled labor growth is much stronger than unskilled labor growth due to the emphasis on education and increasing the skill levels of the workforce. In Japan, the population growth rate is very low reflecting the general trend towards very low even negative population growth in the Industrialized countries. In Japan skilled and unskilled labor is also expected to decline.

Not all of these macroeconomic variables are shocked in the baseline scenario. Firstly, the projected changes in population, and skilled and unskilled labor were incorporated into the baseline as shocks to the growth rates of these endowments. Shocks to capital stocks were not incorporated, but were determined endogenously as the accumulation of projected investment. Secondly, it is assumed that any changes in real GDP, which were not explained by the changes in endowments, are the result of changes in technology. Forecasts in real

Figure A1. Growth in real GDP

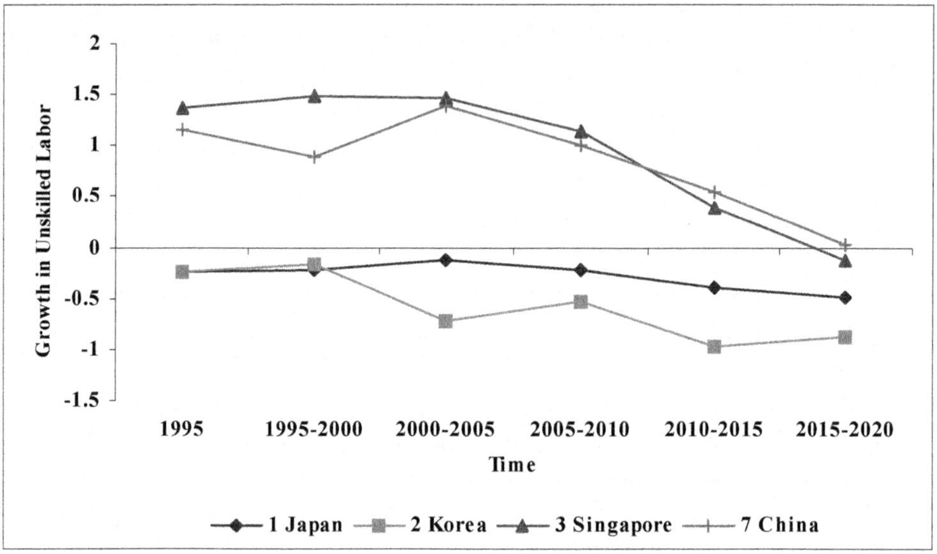

Figure A2. Growth in gross investment

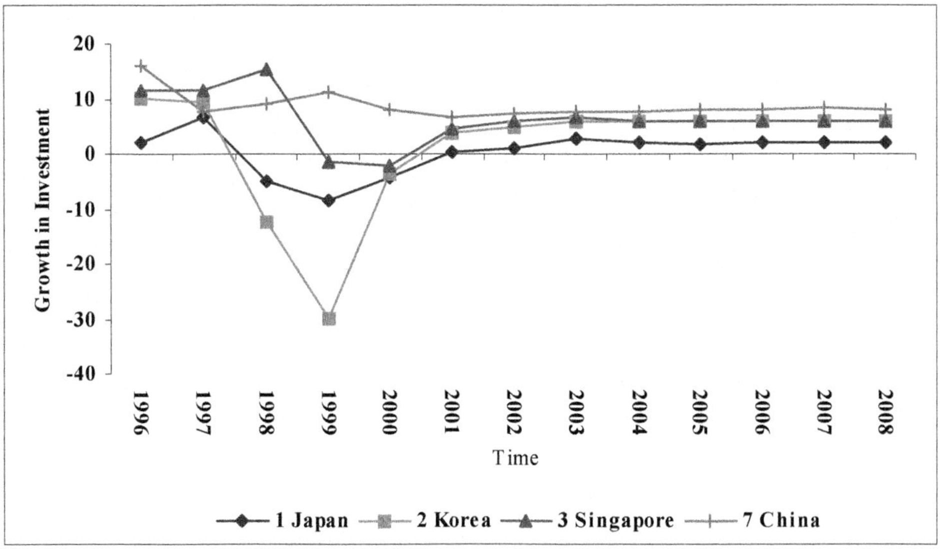

Figure A3. Growth in capital stocks

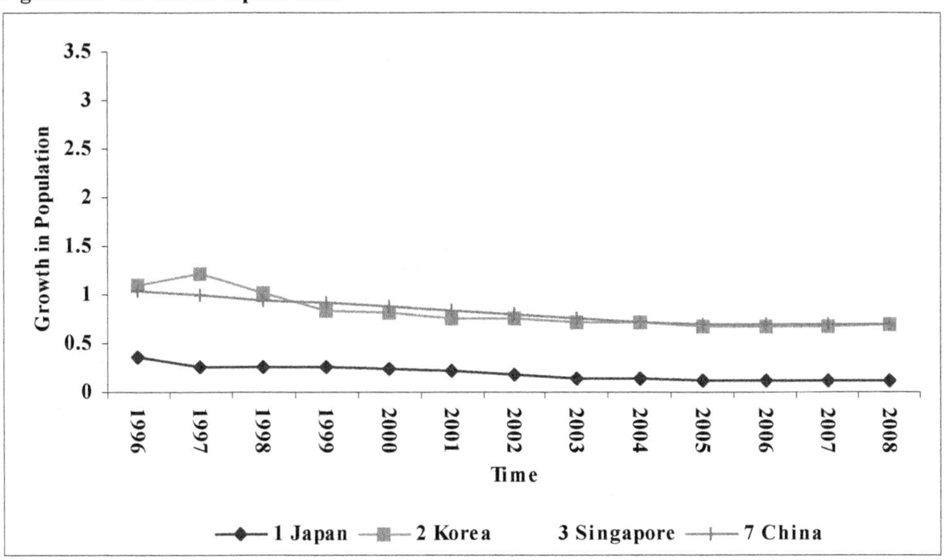

Figure A4. Growth in population

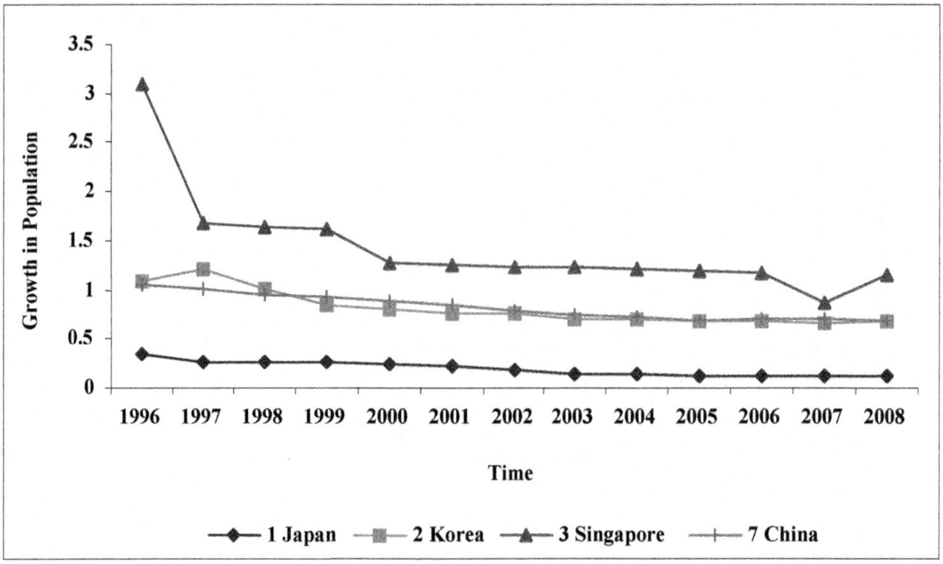

Figure A5. Growth in skilled labor

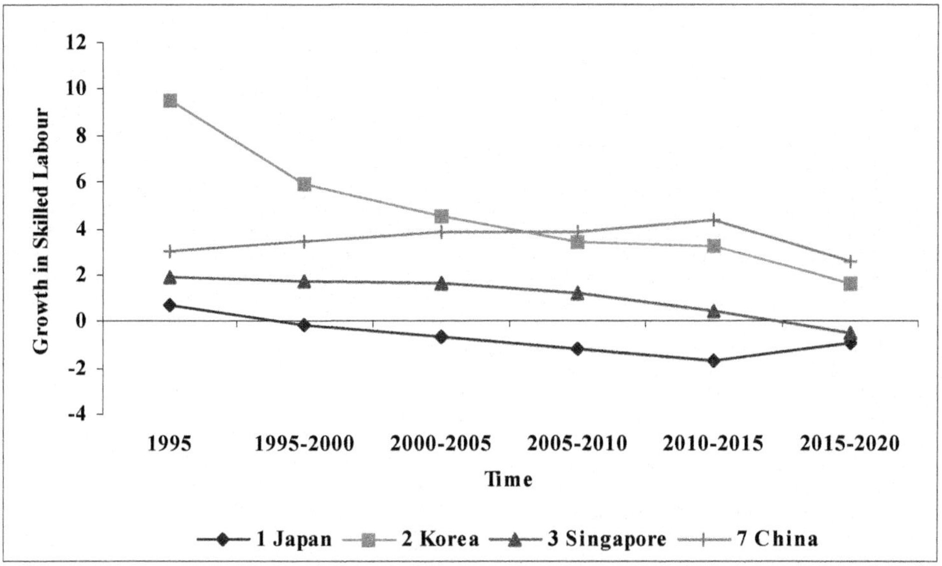

Figure A6. Growth in unskilled labor

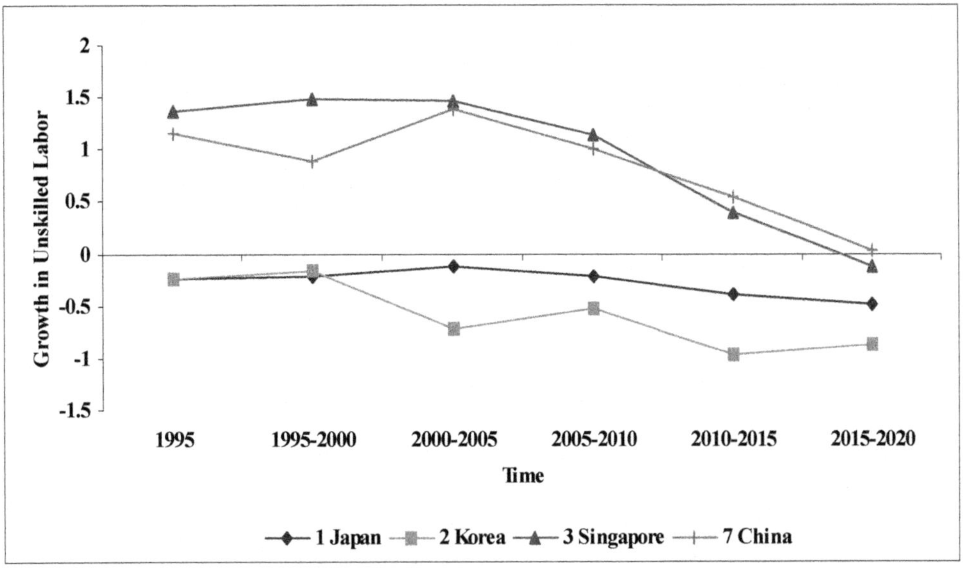

ALTERNATIVE APPROACHES IN ESTIMATING THE ECONOMIC EFFECTS OF NON-TARIFF MEASURES

RESULTS FROM NEWLY QUANTIFIED MEASURES

Soamiely Andriamananjara, Michael Ferrantino, and Marinos Tsigas
U.S. International Trade Commission[1]

1. Introduction

Through successive multilateral as well as bilateral trade negotiations, the general level of tariffs has declined significantly during the past few decades. Concurrently, non-tariff measures (NTMs) have become more visible and their relative importance has considerably grown. Indeed, it has been argued that the use of tariffs by governments has gradually been replaced by the use of NTMs in order to attain the policy goals formerly achieved with tariffs (see *e.g.*, Baldwin, 1984).

A large literature has now emerged that aims at studying the different existing types of NTMs. Generally, one can distinguish three main types of contributions. The first type attempts to define and to provide an organized classification of the different non-tariff measures affecting international trade.[2] Another substantial part of this literature concerns itself with the quantification of the degree of restrictiveness of NTMs.[3] A final branch consists of the use of economic simulation models to estimate the economic effects of the removal of NTMs, based on quantitative estimates of their economic effects. This paper is a part of a larger research program that is currently being undertaken by economists at the U.S. International Trade Commission and which attempts to cover all the three branches of research. It falls into the last category–introducing newly estimated measures of NTM restrictiveness in a simulation model.

---

[1] The authors are affiliated with the Research Division of the Office of Economics, U.S. International Trade Commission. The views expressed in this article are those of the author. They are not the views of the U.S. International Trade Commission (USITC) as a whole nor any of its individual Commissioners. The authors may be contacted *via* email at soamiely.andriamananjara@usitc.gov, michael.ferrantino@usitc.gov, marinos.tsigas@usitc.gov, respectively.

[2] See for instance, Laird and Vossenaar (1991).

[3] For a thorough review of the main contributions in this literature, see Bora, Kuwahara, and Laird (2002).

An important feature of the current research is that it attempts to assess the effects of NTMs globally, combining data at a product-specific level with more aggregated data in the simulation model in a manner which permits in principle comparisons across product sectors and regions.[4] This approach differs from that of much previous work on NTMs. For many purposes, the heterogeneous nature of both NTM policies and the products they are applied to indicates a "handcrafted" approach in which the effects of policies are estimated on narrow product categories bringing a large amount of specific institutional information to bear (Deardorff and Stern, 1997). The present work represents an attempt to "mass-produce" estimates of NTM effects which have previously been "handcrafted," a process which inevitably introduces a certain amount of noise into the estimates. It is hoped that the ability of the mass-produced estimates to provide a survey of the landscape of NTM effects compensates at least partly for the loss of handicraft precision in estimating the effects of particular policies in particular economies.[5]

Section 2 provides a conceptual framework and discusses different techniques regarding the implementation of NTM price wedges in a model. The techniques discussed in this section attempt to restore at least some of the "handicraft" tradition of NTM policy estimation by giving consideration to the manner in which policies in particular sectors are usually implemented. Section 3 characterizes a new set of estimated NTM price wedges as well as the computable general equilibrium (CGE) as well as that is used to simulate the likely economic effects of their removal. Section 4 presents the results of the simulation exercises for three sectors – footwear, apparel and miscellaneous processed foods. The fourth section concludes.

2. Conceptual and Analytical Framework

To the extent that they are designed to limit trade, NTMs create an artificial scarcity and an artificially high price. In general, the degree of restrictiveness of an NTM is measured by the price differential that it drives between the price of imported goods and the producer price of the domestic substitutes, or

[4] The most comparable work in this respect is that of Lawrence and Bradford (2003).

[5] In the historical merchandise economy, consumers have frequently rejected mass-produced merchandise products such as cake mixes and cigarettes on their first introduction, because of concerns regarding quality. Subsequent improvements in quality caused the products to enter into widespread household use. It is to be hoped that a similar learning curve operated with respect to mass-produced estimates of NTM effects.

alternatively, between the domestic and the world price.[6] The "wedge" between the distorted and the non-distorted prices is the key input used in studying the potential economic effects of the removal of a given NTM. This section discusses alternative ways to implement a given price wedge into standard simulation models.

Because NTMs create a wedge between the world price and the domestic one, the most straightforward way to model them is as a "tariff equivalent" above and beyond the actual tariffs. This is generally appropriate, especially when the studied policy is implemented to directly affect the domestic price of the imported good. For this type of policy, economic rents that results from the higher import prices are captured by the importing economy. From the viewpoint of the liberalizing economy, the NTM removal is in this case expected to deteriorate the terms of trade (*i.e.*, pre-tariff prices of the imported good increase as demand for it increases) but to improve resource allocation. Estimates of the effects NTMs for footwear and for apparel (except for apparel importers imposing quotas under the Agreement on Textiles and Clothing) have been implemented as tariff equivalents in this exercise.

Alternatively, NTMs can be modeled as export tax equivalents, since they restrict the ability of exporters to ship their products. This approach hade been widely adopted in the study of "voluntary export restraints" (VERs), which are administered by means of the exporting economy granting licenses to particular firms to sell in the importing economy. For this type of policy, the exporter earns the economic (quota) rents that result from being granted the right to export. In contrast to the tariff-equivalent approach, the liberalizing economy is in this case expected to experience an improvement in its terms of trade (*i.e.*, availability of cheaper untaxed imports) as well as a better allocation of resources. Estimates of the effects of NTMs for apparel importers whose policies fall under the Agreement on Textiles and Clothing have been implemented as export tax equivalents in this exercise.

Another way to model NTMs is to introduce them as institutional frictions or "sand in the wheels" of trade – *i.e.*, policies that do not really create economic rents, only efficiency losses. For instance, burdensome customs and administrative procedures, technical regulations, sanitary and phytosanitary (SPS) regulations, or other red tapes tend to produce an harassment effect and to discourage imports into an economy. Removing this type of NTMs can be

[6] Note that when foreign and domestic goods are not perfectly substitutes for each other, their price may diverge even in the absence of any trade restraints. The introduction of a NTM will further increase such divergence.

modeled as an import-enhancing technological shock. The liberalizing economy in this case is expected experience deterioration in its terms of trade (*i.e.*, world price of the imported good increases as demand for it increases) combined with an improved resource allocation. The estimated effects of NTMs affecting the miscellaneous food processing sectors have been modeled in this manner.

For the study of any given NTM, the choice of the most appropriate approach should be made on a case by case basis. In the next section, we provide an illustration for each of those three approaches using a widely used general equilibrium model, in order to determine the potential economic effects of liberalizing newly estimated NTM price wedges.

3. Estimating the Effects of NTM Price Wedges - Methodology

As part of a large project on the quantification of NTMs, Dean, Feinberg and Ferrantino (2003) provide ranges of new estimates of the NTM price-wedge in three selected sectors (footwear, wearing apparel, and processed food)[7] for a number of economies or regional aggregates. They report different estimates for different model specifications (depending on which database or combination of database they use). In this exercise, we pick the estimates from the specification labeled "Composite."[8] These estimates are presented in Table 1.[9] The absence of an estimated wedge means one of three things: (a) the region had no NTMs on these products, (b) the policy data contained no information on NTMs, or (c) the policy data did contain such information, but the NTMs were not statistically associated with above-average prices given the characteristics of the economy in question.

The caveats presented in Dean *et al.* (2003) regarding these estimates should be borne in mind when looking at the simulation results. For instance, these wedges in general were estimated for relatively specific products but have been assigned to broader product categories for the purposes of CGE modeling. Similarly, in some cases the existence of the measures analyzed may have only

---

[7] "Processed food" here refers to GTAP sector 25, "Food products n.e.c." This sector refers to miscellaneous processed foods – in particular, it excludes meat and dairy products, processed rice and sugar, and vegetable oils and fats. See Dean, Feinberg and Ferrantino (2003) for a list of the products used. to estimate the wedges.

[8] This specification introduces a composite dummy which takes a value of 1 if either TRAINS or Manifold-Donnelly (2004) records the presence of an NTM.

[9] At the time of writing, work is underway to provide similar estimates for approximately 15-18 additional GTAP sectors, which exhaust the available data and span the set of traded goods, though they exclude some for which price data are not at present available.

Table 1. Estimated NTM price wedges for three selected sectors (percent)

	Footwear	Apparel	Processed Food
Australia and New Zealand			
China			
Japan		71	
East Asia		43	
South Asia			
Southeast Asia			
Canada		34	
United States		24	
Mexico, Central America and Caribbean	38	146	
Mercosur	95	31	
Rest of Latin America		65	20
EU15		34	
EFTA			
Eastern Europe and Former Soviet Union		25	
Middle East and North Africa		37	
Sub Saharan Africa			58
Rest of the World			

Source: Dean, Feinberg and Ferrantino (2003).

been documented for one member of a regional grouping, but are applied to the import policies of the entire regions. These mappings in principle mean that the estimated effects are upper bounds. A computationally more expensive procedure, which would have provided lower bounds, would have been to weight the measures so that they applied only to the narrow product definitions of the price data used in the econometrics and only for the economies for which NTMs have been documented. The choice to present upper-bound estimates reflects the judgment that missing data for both product prices and NTM policies are extensive, and that the error involved in treating the missing data like the available data may be smaller than that involved in treating the missing data as if it represented situations that were completely free of NTM distortions.

In general, greater weight should be placed on the global effects and on the differences among sectors than on the differences among economies at this stage of research. Changes in the functional form, underlying data, or other details of the econometric exercise might redistribute the estimated price-increasing effects of NTMs across economies, but are less likely to change the estimated global amount of distortion by a substantial amount.

The estimates presented here are in the nature of sectoral liberalization initiatives – it is assumed that all NTMs in a given sector are abolished worldwide on an MFN or "open regionalism" basis. Estimating effects for three sectors on a simultaneous basis would not add much additional information to that already presented. This method of presenting the results not only allows a (small) computational savings, it can be considered to be in the broader tradition of APEC initiatives. The Information Technology Agreement, which was a sectoral tariff initiative, began through discussions in APEC which were generalized to the WTO, and the APEC Automotive Dialogue and Chemicals Dialogue can be considered as examples of sectoral initiatives which cover a wide variety of topics.

To estimate the economic impact of removing the NTMs, we use the Global Trade Analysis Project (GTAP) framework which allows for the assessment and the decomposition of the welfare effects of various trade agreements.[10] GTAP has been widely used to study the likely effects of different trade agreements and other trade policy issues, it is readily available to the public and, the results reported in this paper can be easily replicated. [11]

The GTAP modeling framework consists of a comparative static CGE model and a global database. The CGE model is based on commonly applied assumptions of constant returns to scale, perfect competition and product differentiation by economy of origin (*i.e.*, the Armington assumption). The database contains information on international and domestic markets and primary factors, as well as tariffs and other taxes. An additional component of the data is the set of parameters which, in the context of the model's equations, determines responses to changes in relative prices, among other things. The latest version of the standard GTAP database (base year 1997) is used to study the likely effects of removing the estimated price wedges.

The welfare impact of the removal of the studied NTMs is measured using the money metric equivalent variation (EV), which can be broken down into component parts in order to enable us to decompose the liberalization. The equivalent variation measures the welfare impact of a policy change in monetary terms and it is defined as the amount of income that would have to be given to (or taken away from) the economy before the policy change to leave the economy as well off as the economy would be after the policy change. A positive figure for equivalent variation implies that the policy change would improve economic welfare.[12] The equivalent variation of a policy change consists mainly of two components: allocative efficiency and terms-of-trade. Allocative efficiency contributions arise when the allocation of productive resources

---

[10] For additional information about the GTAP model and data, see Hertel and Tsigas (1997).
[11] Several analytical works conducted using GTAP can be accessed at "http://www.gtap.agecon.purdue.edu/".
[12] For more on the concept, see Varian (1999, pp. 252-253).

changes relative to pre-existing policies; terms-of-trade contributions arise from changes in the prices received from an economy's exports relative to the prices paid for its imports.[13]

4. Results

In this section, we introduce the estimated NTM policy measures into the GTAP modeling framework and discuss the effects of their removal on trade, production, and welfare of different regional aggregates.

4.1. *Overall Characteristics*

Four general equilibrium experiments are presented here – liberalizing respectively footwear, apparel among the economies applying ATC policies, apparel among all economies applying NTM policies, and miscellaneous processed foods. Of these, three of the experiments are similar in that the estimated NTMs are concentrated in only two or three regions. These three experiments share some common features. All of the liberalizing economies experience welfare gains, which represent the gains to consumers from lower prices. All of the liberalizing economies experience increases in both gross and net imports and decreases in production of the products previously covered by NTMs. While most of the global welfare gains accrue to the liberalizing economies, most other regions in the world economy experience at least some welfare gains due to increased market access, with estimated welfare losses unusual geographically and negligible in value when they do occur. Global production of the covered product falls, indicating that the NTMs led to overproduction in general.

The case of generalized apparel liberalization, in which 10 of the 17 regions are assumed to change policies, is more complex. In this case, at least some of the liberalizing regions experience increases in apparel production and net exports in the context of a more general liberalization. Total global production increases, and the distributional effects of the policy are more problematic. While aggregate global welfare as measured on an equivalent-variation basis increases,

---

[13] The standard GTAP simulations conducted here represent only the static impacts of a policy change, while dynamic effects due to increased investment, increased competition, and economies of scale might be important. It should also be pointed out that, under one of the central assumptions of the GTAP model, each region has large enough market power to be able to affect world price by changing its policies.

welfare declines by a non-trivial amount in some liberalizing economies and some non-liberalizing economies, due to adverse terms-of-trade effects associated with increased global production.

4.2. *Footwear*

Dean, Feinberg and Ferrantino (2003) report price gaps for the footwear sector in Mexico, Central America, and Caribbean (38 percent) and in Mercosur (95 percent). An inspection of the underlying data reveals that the policy measures behind these wedges are mainly in the form of quantitative import restrictions. In the GTAP model, these are treated as equivalent to *ad valorem* tariffs, *i.e.*, the quota rents are captured by the importing region in the form of government revenues.[14] Using a model closure which holds trade shares constant, the wedges are introduced *on top* of the existing GTAP protection data. Thus if the initial GTAP price wedge (consisting entirely of *ad valorem* tariffs) for Mexico, Central America, and Caribbean is around 20 percent, the adjusted wedge is will be 58 percent (38 percent plus 20 percent) once the NTMs are included.

The policy experiment conducted is the removal of the part of the price wedge which relates to the NTMs. The results are reported in Table 2. According to our simulations, shoes imports in Mexico, Central America, and Caribbean and in Mercosur would jump by 118 percent ($1.7 billion) and 258 percent ($2.6 billion), respectively. Footwear exports would increase in many regions, especially those in the Western Hemisphere (including those that are liberalizing) and in Asia. Global trade in shoes is estimated to increase by almost 6 percent ($5 billion), while global shoes output decreases by 0.6 percent (1.3 billion).

The removal of footwear NTMs in Mexico, Central America, and Caribbean and in Mercosur would lead to deterioration in those regions' terms of trade, in the sense that their increased demand for foreign shoes leads to an increase in the pre-tariff import prices. The welfare losses from the decline in the terms of trade ($227 million and $265 million, respectively), however, are more than offset by a large improvement in resource allocation ($425 million and $1.4 billion, respectively). Most regions in the model stand to gain from the NTM liberalization–welfare in China and the United States rise by $121 million and $252 million, respectively. Global welfare increases by $1.9 billion.

[14] The GTAP database does not have a broken out "footwear" sector. In our analysis, it is assumed that the quantified NTMs apply uniformly to the much more aggregated "leather products" sector, which contains footwear and other products.

Table 2. Effects of the removal of footwear NTMs on trade, production, and welfare

	Percent Changes			Value Changes ($ millions)			Welfare effects (Equivalent Variation: $ millions)		
Region/Economy	**Footwear Imports**	**Footwear Exports**	**Footwear Production**	**Footwear Imports**	**Footwear Exports**	**Footwear Production**	**Allocative Efficiency**	**Terms of Trade**	**Total EV**
Australia and New Zealand	0.55	4.32	1.79	6	26	26	2	5	7
China	2.14	3.01	2.03	64	631	771	20	102	121
Japan	0.08	1.75	0.01	5	5	1	-5	5	0
East Asia	0.64	1.42	0.68	23	72	66	-4	10	5
South Asia	1.95	0.26	0.04	5	5	2	-4	-3	-7
Southeast Asia	2.35	2.44	1.84	41	178	167	-1	30	29
Canada	0.82	0.13	-0.73	15	0	-8	-1	-1	-2
United States	1.48	28.74	4.72	364	610	566	-15	267	252
Mexico, Central America and Caribbean	118.17	16.23	-18.96	1746	221	-1350	425	-227	198
Mercosur	258.11	37.85	-7.71	2606	1313	-1438	1444	-265	1179
Rest of Latin America	3.82	26.00	1.22	37	74	54	13	26	38
EU15	0.33	-0.16	-0.28	104	-44	-143	19	46	65
EFTA	0.10	-0.31	-0.31	2	-1	-2	1	4	5
Eastern Europe and Former Soviet Union	0.16	-0.56	-0.29	8	-16	-28	-1	4	3
Middle East and North Africa	0.22	0.11	-0.02	6	1	-5	0	1	1
Sub Saharan Africa	0.30	-0.17	-0.19	4	-1	-3	-1	-1	-2
Rest of the World	0.12	-0.56	-0.20	1	-4	-6	-2	-2	-4
Total	5.64	4.05	-0.65	5036	3071	-1331	1889	-1	1888

Regions with NTM wedges: Mexico, Central America, and Caribbean (38) and Mercosur (95)

Source: Authors' simulations using GTAP and NTM price wedges from Dean, Feinberg and Ferrantino (2003).

4.3. *Wearing Apparel*

In the wearing apparel sector, Dean, Feinberg and Ferrantino (2003) estimate NTM wedges for a number of regions: Canada (34 percent), United States (24 percent), EU15 (34 percent), Japan (71 percent), East Asia (43 percent), Mexico, Central America, and Caribbean (146 percent) and Mercosur (31 percent), Rest of Latin America (65 percent), Eastern Europe and the Former Soviet Union (25 percent), Middle East and North Africa (37 percent). The actual policy behind these wedges can be categorized into policies under the Agreement on Textiles and Clothing (ATC), which take the form of Voluntary Export Restrictions (VERs) for the first three regions, and general quantitative import restrictions (QRs) for the others. In the GTAP framework, the formers are treated as equivalent to export taxes that are uniformly applied in *all* source regions (*i.e.*, the quota rents are captured by the exporting region), while the QRs are modeled as non-discriminatory *ad valorem* tariffs (*i.e.*, the quota rents are captured by the importing region). The new export tax numbers are used *instead of* the existing ones in the GTAP protection data. On the other hand, the new QR wedges are introduced *on top* of the existing GTAP tariff data.

To analyze the apparel NTMs, we conduct two policy experiments. The first experiment is the removal of only the ATC quotas for Canada, United States, and EU15.[15] The second experiment studies the removal of all quantified apparel NTMs. The results of each experiment are reported in Table 3 and Table 4.

The removal of the ATC quotas is estimated to lead to large changes in the patterns of world trade. Global clothing import increases by more than 53 percent ($88 billion), with the imports of Canada, United States, and EU15 increasing by 173 percent, 84 percent, and 70 percent respectively. With the exception of the EU15, all regions in the model experience large increases in their clothing exports.[16] The lifting of the ATC quotas is expected to lead to a terms-of-trade improvement (cheaper import prices) and a better resource allocation (less distortion) in the three liberalizing regions, so that total welfare in Canada, the

---

[15] As part of the Agreement on Textiles and Clothing (ATC), the MFA quotas are scheduled to be lifted by 2005. For a recent review of the literature on the MFA quotas, see OECD (2003).

[16] Our approach makes a very strong assumption that the ATC quotas are uniformly restrictive across all exporting regions – that is we assume that they are non-discriminatory. In reality, there is a great deal of discrimination and the restrictiveness of the quotas varies greatly from exporter to exporter. For instance, it is widely recognized that the quota is much more binding in Asia than in other regions. While interpreting our results (especially regarding the export pattern), this drawback should be kept in mind.

Table 3. Effects of the removal of wearing apparel quotas on trade, production, and welfare – ATC policies only

	Percent Changes			Value Changes ($ millions)			Welfare effects (Equivalent Variation: $ millions)		
Region/Economy	Apparel Imports	Apparel Exports	Apparel Production	Apparel Imports	Apparel Exports	Apparel Production	Allocative Efficiency	Terms of Trade	Total EV
Australia and New Zealand	0.06	49.10	3.49	1	185	153	26	21	47
China	0.73	27.48	10.04	18	5915	4337	1336	-3782	-2446
Japan	0.58	64.36	0.82	82	621	502	56	-793	-738
East Asia	3.98	101.03	35.75	325	12086	8941	1729	-2644	-915
South Asia	42.29	105.36	56.60	71	10362	7794	1924	-2866	-942
Southeast Asia	7.90	100.49	41.60	81	9994	7773	1567	-2461	-894
Canada	173.58	122.09	-27.44	4749	1436	-1918	769	955	1724
United States	84.30	106.08	-28.41	35800	4322	-24476	3455	6777	10232
Mexico, Central America and Caribbean	8.89	96.21	39.46	546	9180	6602	1657	-2088	-431
Mercosur	0.91	80.74	0.74	9	350	256	65	-89	-24
Rest of Latin America	2.27	94.86	5.04	24	754	543	128	-116	12
EU15	70.64	-46.23	-46.71	44814	-15954	-45138	143	14297	14440
EFTA	2.90	195.22	54.66	111	1092	741	176	47	223
Eastern Europe and Former Soviet Union	9.56	185.24	55.61	688	14577	10132	2709	-2833	-124
Middle East and North Africa	9.81	160.55	51.88	551	16567	11504	3644	-3008	636
Sub Saharan Africa	1.68	137.89	37.76	20	1556	1120	282	-324	-42
Rest of the World	16.51	137.29	46.89	187	4395	3249	816	-926	-111
Total	53.76	60.40	-1.68	88078	77438	-7886	20481	167	20648

Regions with NTM wedges modeled as export tax equivalent in ALL partner countries: Canada (34), United States (24), EU15 (34).

Source: Authors' simulations using GTAP and NTM price wedges from Dean, Feinberg and Ferrantino (2003).

Table 4. Effects of the removal of wearing apparel NTMs on trade, production, and welfare – policies in all economies

	Percent Changes			Value Changes ($ millions)			Welfare effects (Equivalent Variation: $ millions)		
Region/Economy	**Apparel Imports**	**Apparel Exports**	**Apparel Production**	**Apparel Imports**	**Apparel Exports**	**Apparel Production**	**Allocative Efficiency**	**Terms of Trade**	**Total EV**
Australia and New Zealand	-2.93	104.01	9.62	-56	391	420	-3	18	15
China	22.89	215.82	99.29	580	46452	42899	2794	4568	7362
Japan	986.87	145.60	-85.53	140276	1405	-52303	2393	-12209	-9816
East Asia	222.16	155.07	15.75	18155	18550	3939	3361	-2615	746
South Asia	33.89	80.31	45.51	57	7898	6267	1202	-2495	-1293
Southeast Asia	12.29	160.97	75.14	126	16009	14040	1348	-36	1313
Canada	175.51	131.31	-26.15	4802	1544	-1828	706	479	1184
United States	99.86	860.04	5.96	42408	35042	5133	3781	13632	17413
Mexico, Central America and Caribbean	1320.15	211.79	36.04	81066	20208	6030	-11840	-6916	-18756
Mercosur	351.31	326.80	-4.70	3651	1415	-1615	681	-553	127
Rest of Latin America	1506.44	384.51	-51.26	16011	3055	-5521	504	-1378	-874
EU15	113.03	204.63	13.77	71706	70620	13304	10922	16680	27602
EFTA	2.78	157.71	47.65	106	882	646	8	-162	-154
Eastern Europe and Former Soviet Union	95.61	121.93	7.55	6878	9596	1375	2584	-3794	-1210
Middle East and North Africa	194.17	126.77	8.78	10901	13081	1948	3213	-4463	-1251
Sub Saharan Africa	0.30	85.98	24.68	4	970	732	73	-449	-376
Rest of the World	13.61	105.36	38.43	154	3373	2663	411	-767	-355
Total	242.20	195.37	8.12	396826	250491	38126	22137	-460	21677

Regions with NTM wedges modeled as tariff equivalent: Japan (71), East Asia (43), Mexico, Central America, and Caribbean (146) and Mercosure (31), Rest of Latin America, and Caribbean (146) and Mercosur (31), Rest of Latin America (65), RussiaEE (25), Middle East and North Africa (37). Regions with NTM wedges modeled as export tax equivalent in ALL partner countries: Canada (34), United States (24), EU15 (34).

Source: Authors' simulations using GTAP and NTM price wedges from Dean, Feinberg and Ferrantino (2003).

United States, and the EU15 is expected to rise by $1.7 billion, $10 billion, and $14 billion, respectively. Total world welfare increases by $21 billion.[17]

The removal of all quantified NTMs (inclusive of the MFA quotas) leads to even larger changes in global clothing trade, with total import increasing by more than 242 percent ($297 billion). Simulation results suggest very large increases in the clothing imports of the Rest of Latin America (1506 percent), Japan (986 percent), Mexico, Central America, and Caribbean (1320 percent). These changes are much larger than the effects of the removal of the MFA quotas. The welfare impacts are also much larger with the biggest gainers being the EU15 ($27 billion), The United States ($17 billion) and China (7 billion). While some regions like Japan and Mexico, Central America, and Caribbean experience some welfare losses, global aggregate welfare increases by almost $21 billion.

4.4. *Miscellaneous Processed Foods*

The Dean, Feinberg and Ferrantino (2003) study reports price gaps for miscellaneous processed foods in Sub Saharan Africa (58 percent) and the rest of Latin America (20 percent). The policies policy measures behind these wedges are generally categorized as "non-automatic licensing" (or "prior authorization" needed to import for various health or safety reason). While not directly affecting the price or the amount of the imported good, these policies have a dampening or a harassment effect because they require some type of burdensome customs procedures, or in some case necessitate cost-increasing production improvements. In this analysis, they are consider as "sand in the wheels" of trade and their removal is modeled as an "import augmenting technical change" for which a parameter is readily available in the GTAP framework.[18] The shock applied to technological parameter is calibrated in such a way that the difference between

---

[17] It should be noted that the (non-discriminatory) ATC quota wedges here are different from those existing in the base GTAP model. For the United States, the wedge used here lies within the range of the discriminatory default wedges in GTAP, with wedges for imports from China higher on an *ad valorem* basis and the rest lower. For the EU15 and Canada, the estimated wedges are uniformly higher than those in base GTAP. The net effect of these changes is that the estimated effects from using the current wedges are larger than those in base GTAP. Estimated global welfare increases from eliminating the base GTAP wedges are about $7.6 billion as compared to the current $21 billion, and estimated global imports increase by $23.9 billion as compared to $88 billion in the experiment presented here.

[18] For the reader familiar with the GTAP framework, the technical parameter used here is "ams." This procedure is similar to that used in Hertel, Walmsley and Itakura (2001), and can be used to model the effects of trade facilitation more generally.

the import and the domestic prices declines by the quantified NTM price wedge.[19]

The simulation results are reported in Table 5. The removal of the food NTMs in the rest of Latin America and the SSA region would increase global trade in food by about 1 percent ($1.5 billion). Food imports of the two regions would increase by 19 percent ($307 million) and 48 percent ($1.1 billion) respectively. Given their small size, changes in other economies' trade and production are relatively small. Food exports by Mercosur increase by 1.56 percent ($54 million). Although, they experience deteriorations in their terms of trade, the efficiency gains (both in terms of resource allocation and import technological efficiency) lead to large welfare gains for the rest of Latin America ($368 million) and Sub Saharan Africa ($1.7 billion). Almost all regions in the world would gain from the trade liberalization, and global welfare would increase by almost $2.3 billion.

5. Conclusion

This paper introduces a set of new estimates of NTM price gaps in a simulation model, and studies the economic effects of their removal. Although its ambitions are modest, its contributions could be useful for both policymakers and economic researchers.

One main contribution is methodological in nature. We characterize and illustrate three different techniques to implement measures of NTM restrictiveness into a CGE modeling framework. NTMs could be modeled as tariff equivalent, as export tax equivalent, or as sand-in-the-wheels-of-trade. The choice of the most appropriate approach depends on the nature of the NTM that is being studied. Each technique is implemented for a specific sector.

The economic impact of removing the quantified NTMs on footwear, wearing apparel, and processed foods are discussed. For all of the considered sectors, NTM liberalization leads to a substantial jump in world trade, and an improved global welfare. Contrary to the frequently expressed neomercantilist view that the goal of trade policy should be to increase the merchandise trade surplus of a particular economy (*i.e.*, increased exports are good, and increase imports are bad), most of the gains from the elimination of NTMs accrue to the liberalizing

[19] As noted before when foreign and domestic goods are not perfectly substitutes for each other, their price may diverge even in the absence of any trade restraints. The introduction of a NTM will further increase such divergence.

Table 5. Effects of removal of food processing NTMs on trade, production, and welfare

	Percent Changes			Value Changes ($ millions)			Welfare effects ($ millions)			
Region/Economy	Food Imports	Food Exports	Food Prod.	Food Imports	Food Exports	Food Prod.	Allocative Efficiency	Tech. gains	Terms of Trade	Total EV
Australia and New Zealand	0.04	0.23	0.04	1	6	5	0	0	-1	0
China	0.1	0.04	0	3	2	0	0	0	2	2
Japan	0.05	0.35	0	12	7	-4	5	0	18	23
East Asia	0.04	0.08	0	3	3	1	0	0	4	4
South Asia	0.05	0.31	0.12	0	8	8	2	0	2	5
Southeast Asia	0.03	0.06	0.01	1	6	5	0	0	2	2
Canada	0.01	0.03	0	0	1	0	0	0	-1	-1
United States	0.07	0.56	0.02	11	61	55	6	0	30	36
Mexico, Central America and Caribbean	0.04	0.4	0.04	1	13	14	0	0	2	2
Mercosur	0.09	1.53	0.07	2	54	56	5	0	9	14
Rest of Latin America	19.27	2.7	-1.56	307	156	-461	77	317	-26	368
EU15	0.06	0.64	0.11	32	313	315	44	0	93	136
EFTA	0.07	0.3	0.11	4	15	15	4	0	3	6
Eastern Europe and Former Soviet Union	0.01	-0.03	-0.01	1	-1	-3	1	0	2	3
Middle East and North Africa	0.04	0.65	0.04	3	19	18	3	0	3	6
Sub Saharan Africa	47.83	6.72	-10.24	1113	190	-2209	577	1311	-143	1745
Rest of the World	0.01	0.03	0	0	0	0	0	0	0	0
Total	1.00	0.72	-0.20	1495	854	-2184	723	1629	0	2352

Regions with NTM wedges: Rest of Latin America (20) and Sub Saharan Africa (58)

Source: Authors' simulations using GTAP and NTM price wedges from Dean, Feinberg and Ferrantino (2003).

regions–suggesting that those barriers to trade are higher than their "optimal-tariff" level.

Bibliography

1. Baldwin, Robert E. (1984), "Trade Policies in Developed Countries," in R. Jones and P. Kenen (eds), Handbook of International Economics, Vol 1, Amsterdam: North Holland.
2. Bora, Bijit, Aki Kuwahara and Sam Laird (2002), "Quantification Of Non-Tariff Measures," Policy Issues In International Trade And Commodities, Study Series No. 18, United Nations Conference On Trade And Development (UNCTAD).
3. Dean, Judith M., Robert Feinberg and Michael Ferrantino (2003), "Estimating the Tariff-Equivalent of NTMs," manuscript.
4. Deardorff, Alan V., and Robert M. Stern (1997), "Measurement of Non-Tariff Barriers," OECD Economics Department Working Papers No. 179 (OCDE/GD(97)/129), Paris: Organization for Economic Cooperation and Development.
5. Hertel, Thomas and Marinos Tsigas (1997) "Structure of the GTAP Model," chapter 2 in *Global Trade Analysis: Modeling and Applications*, T. Hertel, editor, Cambridge Univ. Press, January.
6. Hertel, Thomas, Terrie Walmsley and Ken Itakura (2001), "Dynamic Effects of the 'New Age' Trade Agreement Between Japan and Singapore," working paper, Purdue University (GTAP).
7. Laird, Sam and René Vossenaar (1991), "Porqué Nos Preocupan Las Bareras No Arancelarias?," Informacion Comercial Española, Special Issue on Non-tariff Barriers, November, pp. 31-54.
8. Robert Z. Lawrence and Scott Bradford (2003), *Paying the Price: The Cost of Fragmented International Markets* (forthcoming October, Washington, D.C., Institute for International Economics
9. Manifold, D., and W. Donnelly (2004), "A Compilation from Multiple Sources of Measures which May Affect Trade," this volume, Chapter 2.1.
10. OECD(2003), Liberalizing Trade in Textiles and Clothing: A Survey of Quantitative Studies. Working Party of the Trade Committee, TD/TC/WP(2003)2, January 2003.
11. Varian, Hal (1999) Intermediate Microeconomics: A Modern Approach, Fifth Edition, W. W. Norton & Company, New York.

WITS – WORLD INTEGRATED TRADE SOLUTION

Vlad Manole

World Bank [1]

The **World Integrated Trade Solution**[2] (WITS) is a software program developed by the World Bank, in close collaboration with the United Nations Conference on Trade and Development (UNCTAD). WITS provides access to the major trade and tariffs data compilations:

- The **COMTRADE** database maintained by the UNSD;
- The **TRAINS** maintained by the UNCTAD;
- The **IDB** and **CTS** databases maintained by the WTO.

1. What is WITS?

WITS is a data consultation and extraction software with analytical capabilities.

WITS accesses and retrieves information on trade and tariffs which is compiled by the following international organizations:

- **The United Nation Statistical Division** (UNSD) **Commodity Trade** (COMTRADE) Data Base that contains Exports and Imports by Commodity and Partner Country. Values are recorded in US Dollars along with a variety of quantity measures. The Data Base includes information for over 130 countries, some of which have been reporting these types of statistics to the United Nations since 1962. The data are recorded according to six internationally recognized trade and tariff classifications.
- **The United Nations Conference on Trade and Development** (UNCTAD) **Trade Analysis Information System** (TRAINS) that contains information on Imports, Tariffs, Para-Tariffs and Non-Tariff Measures for 119 countries. The data on tariffs, para-tariffs and non-tariff measures are available at the most

---

[1] The World Bank, 1818 H Street, NW, Washington, DC. The views expressed here are those of the authors and should not be attributed to the World Bank.

[2] The presentation material was prepared with the help of Will Martin, Marc Bacchetta, Olivier Jammes, Phillip Schuler and Azita Amjadi. Many thanks to the technical development team of Jerzy Rozanski, Ganeshkumar Sathiyamoorthy and Butch V. S. Satuluri.

detailed commodity level of the national tariffs (*i.e.*, at the tariff line level). The data are recorded according to three internationally recognized trade and tariff classifications.

- **The World Trade Organization** (WTO) **Integrated Data Base** (IDB) that contain Imports by Commodity and Partner Country and MFN Applied Tariffs for over 80 countries at the most detailed commodity level of the national tariffs; and, the **Consolidated Tariff Schedule** Data Base (CTS) that contains WTO Bound Tariffs, Initial Negotiating Rights (INR) and other indicators. The CTS is the official source for bound tariffs which are the concessions made by countries during a negotiation (*i.e.*, the Uruguay Round of Multilateral Trade Negotiations). The data are recorded according to two internationally recognized trade and tariff classifications.

As an analytical tool, WITS offers:

- Analysis of extracted data
- Built-in analytical modules to simulate trade policy changes
  - Multilateral (WTO) tariff cuts
  - Preferential trade liberalization
  - *Ad hoc* tariff reductions
- Tariff aggregators[3]

2. The Cost of WITS

WITS software is free of charge. The analytical part is a component of the software and, in consequence, is free of charge.

However, databases have different contractual arrangements, therefore access rights and fees may vary depending on the user's status:

- Access to COMTRADE data can be purchased through UNSD;
- Access to UNCTAD TRAINS can be purchased through UNCTAD;
- Developing country governments have free access to WTO IDB and CTS data at tariff-line level. WTO 6 digit data are generally available.

[3] WITS constructs TRI (Anderson and Neary, 1992), Revenue Tariff Aggregator and Expenditure Tariff Aggregator (the last two aggregators were defined in Martin and Bach, 2001, they were used in Martin, Van der Mensbrugghe & Manole, 2003 and the versions that are implemented in WITS are described in Martin and Manole, 2004).

For more detailed information, check *http://wits.worldbank.org/witsweb/FAQ/Basics.aspx#Price* or send an e-mail to *wits@worldbank.org*.

3. How to Install WITS?

To use WITS it is necessary to have:

- Internet connection, ideally broadband;
- Microsoft Windows operating system either Windows 98, NT4 (SP4), 2000, XP;
- MS Internet Explorer 4.0 or higher.

3.1. *To Obtain WITS software*:

- WITS uses MS Internet Explorer, but certain support software must be installed on your computer 4
- Log on to *http://wits.worldbank.org*
- If WITS client software is not installed, then a dialog box will ask for registration details
- Complete the form and apply for registration and a password

3.2. *To Install WITS*:

- Download the client software and install it on your Windows PC
- This will require administrative rights to the machine if there are controls on what users can do. The administrative rights are necessary just for the installation of WITS and not for the use of the program.
- Log on and enjoy online WITS!!!
- Give feedback & suggestions to *wits@worldbank.org*

3.3. *To Access WITS*:

- Open Internet Explorer and type the URL *http://wits.worldbank.org*

---

[4] For more detailed technical information, check *http://wits.worldbank.org/witsweb/FAQ/Installation.aspx#TechReq*. For most configurations, WITS may be installed directly. In certain situations, some components must be downloaded (for free) from Microsoft site and installed before WITS installation. To pre-check if your system meets WITS requirements, you can download the WITS Check System software (31 Kb) and run it.

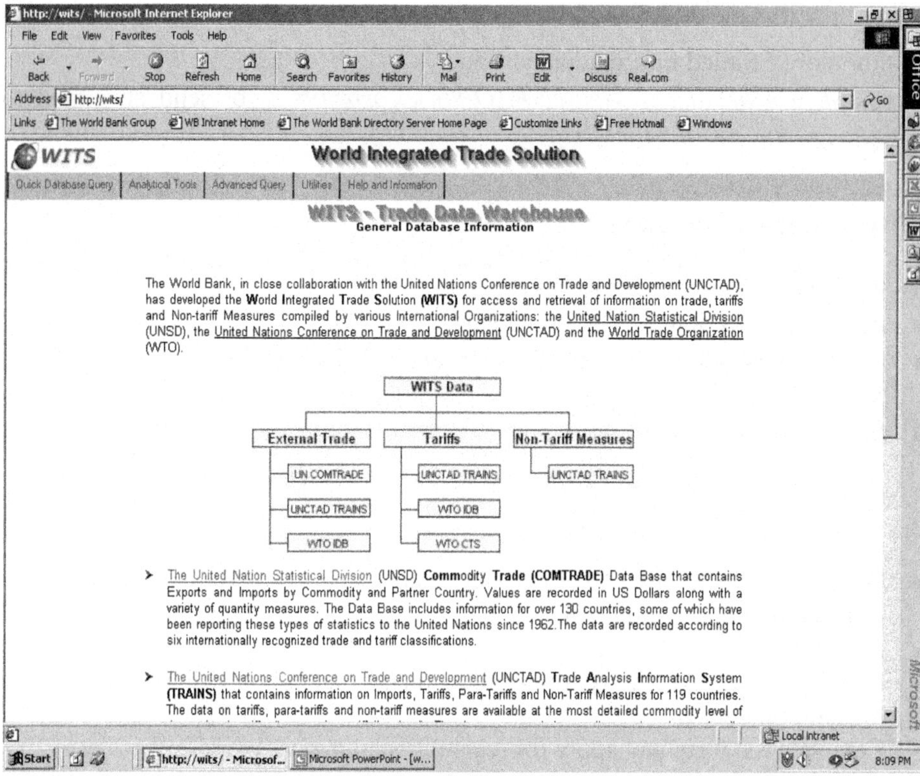

- The start page (next image) will help you to find the data that you need. Look for what kind of data you are interested (external trade, tariffs or non-tariffs measures) and find the database that contains your data.

4. Data Extraction

There are two ways to extract data using WITS. A "Quick Query" module may be used to view and download basic information. An "Advanced Query" module may be used to extract any possible combination of countries, product groups and years. It is useful first to understand some technical issues concerning data. The "Help" section contains tables with the available data for any country and year for each database. There are also product classifications (nomenclatures) and concordances to map products from one classification to another. WITS has the following product classifications:

– Commodity

- Standard International Trade Classification (SITC)

- Harmonized System (HS)

– Industry

- International Standard Industrial Classification (ISIC)

– Others

- WTO Multilateral Trade Negotiations
- GTAP (for general equilibrium modeling)

For efficient data extraction WITS allows aggregation into country groups (like NAFTA or APEC) and commodity groups (like agricultural goods). Many standard groups are available, *i.e.*,

- Manufactured *vs.* Agriculture
- WTO's stage of processing classification

To create a new country group or product group, users should go to "Utilities," choose the appropriate section, then select new group, choose the elements of the new group and save it with a suitable name.

4.1. *Quick Database Query*

Quick Database Query allows one to view trade values, tariffs, and non-tariff barriers for one product at a time for many countries and years, or many products at a time for one country and one year. Quick Database Query offers the following options:

1. COMTRADE by Product
2. COMTRADE by Country/Period
3. TRAINS -Trade, Tariffs, NTBS
4. TRAINS -View and Export Raw Data
5. TRAINS -User Criteria
6. WTO Integrated Database
7. WTO -View and Export Raw Data
8. WTO CTS - View and Export Raw Data

We consider an example of Quick Database Query for COMTRADE by Product. We may follow the algorithm:

- Select the desired nomenclature (product classification). These include two versions of Harmonized System (HS) and three versions of Standard International Trade Classification (SITC).
- Select the level (tier) of the products. In other words, how you would like the system to display the product codes and names based on different digits depending on the selected nomenclatures (from one-digit codes in SITC to 6-digit codes in HS).
- Select the trade flow (imports, exports, or re-exports).
- Select the product from the drop-down list.
- Select years, reporter countries, and partner countries.
- Click on View data.

For other options, the queries are similar. It is useful to know some characteristics of databases or options.

4.2. *UN COMTRADE Database*

- Bilateral commodity trade for 1962–present
- Countries report their imports and exports to the UN Statistical Division
- Some countries also report "re-exports"

4.3. *Quick Database Query by Country/Period*

- Displays data for all or one partner, products, years, and for only one reporting country at a time.
- Results can be saved as an ASCII or Excel file by clicking on "Save" button.

4.4. *Quick Query: TRAINS*

- TRAINS contains non-tariff measures, tariffs, "para tariffs," and import data.
- In this option, users have access to **tariff line** information given by each country. Normally, trade and tariff data are aggregated to at least the 6-digit level.

4.5. *TRAINS -View and Export Raw Data*

- This option allows one to view and save data at the most detailed level available
- Countries define tariff lines at levels more disaggregated than 6 digits of HS

- This option allows you to extract full collection of data on a country's non-tariff measures

4.6. *WTO Integrated Database*

- Tariff and trade data reported to Geneva by WTO members
- A Quick Query on the WTO IDB database returns information on import values or tariffs.
- A Quick Query can be used to view imports at the tariff line level and the tariffs for that level by type.
- IDB includes MFN **applied** and **bound** duties, with some countries also notifying **preferential** tariffs on an optional basis.

4.7. *Advanced Query*

Advanced query lets user select the data from any of the databases according to hers own criteria. It allows the use of country groups or product groups (as an example, the export of agricultural products from one country to a group of countries). It can be used for simulation analysis or tariff aggregation.

4.8. *Query Procedure*

- Create new query definition (products, markets, *etc.*)…
- …Or open previously defined query
- Submit query
- [wait]
- View and save results

To create your own query, click on Query Definition and select from all listed dimensions.

- Click on "Markets" and select desired countries from selection boxes by placing a checkmark next to each country or country group
- Click on "Products," select the desired nomenclature and products.
- Products can be selected by list of items, clusters, or aggregates.
- Products are selected by "Clusters" in the displayed screen.
- Click on "Partner countries" and select desired countries from selection boxes.
- Click on "Years" and select desired years from the selection box.

- Click on "Trade flow" and select from the selection box.
- Finally, click on "Data sources" and select from the selection box.

Once that all selections are made, click on "Save" icon, enter a name and description for your query, and click on OK.

Click on "Submit" to run your query. Click on "Status." Once the job is completed, click on "View" to display the results.

Results are displayed. Click on "Alter View" to change the data format or click on Save to save the data as an ASCII or Excel file.

5. What is the next step for WITS?

I conclude here our short introduction to WITS. For more detailed information about WITS and how to use WITS, check *http://wits.worldbank.org/witsweb/default.aspx* or e-mail to *wits@worldbank.org*. I wish to mention that we work to add new capabilities to WITS all the time. We just added the tariff aggregators feature and we are looking to add a new database. We appreciate the feedback from WITS' users and we consider that their suggestions really help us to improve the product.

References

1. Anderson, J. and Neary, P. (1992), 'Trade reform with quotas, partial rent retention, and tariffs' *Econometrica* 60:57-62.
2. Bach, C. and Martin, W. (2001), 'Will the right tariff aggregator for policy analysis please stand up?' *Journal of Policy Modeling* 23:611-35.
3. Martin W., van der Mensbrugghe, D. and Manole V., 2003, "Is the Devil in the Details? Assessing the Welfare Implications of Agricultural and Non Agricultural Trade Reforms," presented at the International Conference on "*Agricultural policy reform and the WTO: where are we heading*?," Capri, Italy; June 23-26, 2003.
4. Martin W. and Manole V., 2004, "Optimal Indexes of Protection," Mimeo, World Bank.

EMPIRICAL ANALYSIS OF BARRIERS TO INTERNATIONAL SERVICES TRANSACTIONS AND THE CONSEQUENCES OF LIBERALIZATION

Alan V. Deardorff [1] and Robert M. Stern[2]

University of Michigan

Executive Summary

This module provides an overview of the methods that can be used to identify and quantify barriers to international trade in services. Trade in services is customarily classified into four "modes of supply": Mode 1 – services that are traded internationally across borders; Mode 2 – services that require the consumer to be in the location of the producer; Mode 3 – services that require commercial presence in the form of foreign direct investment; and Mode 4 – services that require the temporary cross-border movement of workers. Barriers to any of these forms of trade typically take the form of regulations that either restrict supply or make it more costly. In either case, the economic impact of such a barrier can in principle be quantified as a "tariff equivalent," defined as the percentage tax on foreign suppliers that would have the same effect on the domestic market for the service as is caused by the barrier.

Barriers to trade in services are extremely diverse, making it difficult to classify them in any simple yet detailed way. Broadly, they may be separated on the one hand into those that restrict entry of firms *versus* those that affect firms' operations, and on the other hand into those that discriminate against foreign service providers *versus* those that do not. Within these broad categories, barriers have been classified much more finely in terms of characteristics that are appropriate to particular service industries.

Measurement of service barriers can be either direct or indirect. Direct measurement involves documenting barriers that are known to exist, either by extracting information about them from government documents or by questioning those market participants who confront them. Ideally, both of these methods should be based on detailed knowledge of the industries involved, since services differ greatly among themselves in the kinds of regulations that apply to them and in the rationales and effects of these regulations.

Indirect measurement attempts to infer the presence of barriers from their market effects, much as nontariff barriers on trade in goods are often inferred from price differences across borders. Unfortunately, most services do not cross a border in this way, and even those that do are often differentiated sufficiently

[1] The University of Michigan, Department of Economics, Ann Arbor, MI 48109-1220.

[2] The author may be contacted through the University of Michigan, Department of Economics, Ann Arbor, MI 48109-1220 *via* email at *rmstern@umich.edu*, and website at *www.umich.edu/~rmstern/*.

that comparable prices do not exist inside and outside of economies. Thus indirect measurement has to be even more indirect, drawing heavily on theoretical models of activity in the absence of barriers.

We illustrate these various approaches by citing in some detail a number of studies that have been carried out, some for broad categories of service trade and others for particular sectors. We also, in an appendix, summarize a much larger number of studies. Procedures differ somewhat across studies, but most employ one or more of the following steps:

- Collect the details of regulations and other policies affecting service firms in the economies and/or sectors being examined. Ideally, this information should be collected by systematic surveys of governments and/or firms. However, it may also be possible to infer it less directly from documents prepared for other purposes.
- For each type of regulation or policy, define degrees of restrictiveness and assign scores to each.
- Construct an index of restrictiveness by: weighting the above scores based on subjective judgments; using a statistical methodology; or designing proxy measures.
- Convert these indices of restrictiveness into a set of tariff equivalents by one or more of the following methods.
    - Assign judgmental tariff-equivalent values to each component of the index.
    - Use data on prices and their determinants in a regression model to estimate the effect on prices.
    - Use data on quantities produced or traded in a regression model to estimates the effect on quantities, and convert to tariff equivalents.
- Use the above measures as inputs into a model of production and trade in order to ascertain the economic effects of the presence of changes in the services barriers involved.

1. Introduction

Issues to be Addressed:

- Modes of supply of services
- Direct *versus* indirect measurement of barriers
- Overview of the module

Barriers to trade interfere with the ability of firms from one economy to compete with firms from another. This is true of trade in goods, where a tariff or nontariff barrier (NTB) typically drives a wedge between the price of the good on the world market and its domestic price. This wedge, or "tariff equivalent," provides a convenient and often observable measurement of the size of the impediment. In the case of services, however, no such simple measurement is often observable. It remains true, though, that the concept of a tariff equivalent – now thought of as the equivalent tax on foreign suppliers in their competition with domestic suppliers – is a useful way of quantifying a barrier to trade even though it may be much harder to observe. Both the role of barriers to trade in services and the possible meaning of a tariff equivalent can be better understood in the context of each of the standard four "modes of supply" that arise for traded services and are shown in Table 1 for 1997. The four modes of supply are:

- Mode 1 – services that are traded internationally across borders
- Mode 2 – services that require the consumer to be in the location of the producer
- Mode 3 – services that require commercial presence in the form of foreign direct investment
- Mode 4 – services that require the temporary cross-border movement of workers

Table 1. International services transactions by modes of supply, 1997

Mode of Supply[a]	Category	Value ($bn)	Cumulative share (%)
Mode 1	Commercial services (excl. travel)	890	41.0
Mode 2	Travel/Tourism	430	19.8
Mode 3	Gross output of foreign affiliates	820	37.8
Mode 4	Compensation of Employees	30	1.4
Total		2,170	100.0

[a] Modes 1, 2, and 4 are derived from balance-of-payments accounts. Mode 3 is derived from data on the operations of foreign affiliates in host economies.

Source: Karsenty (2000).

To clarify further, Mode 1 refers to "separated" services such as telecommunications, which are traded internationally across borders in a manner similar to cross-border trade in goods. Here, foreign suppliers of a service provide it to domestic buyers through international means of communication and perhaps transportation, with a unit of the service itself often unobservable as it crosses national borders. A French telecoms company, for example, may provide telephone services to a customer in Mexico, in competition with a Mexican-based provider. A trade barrier in this case might consist of Mexican restrictions on the French firm's access to phone lines in Mexico, discriminatory taxes on its operations, or regulations on the ways that Mexican consumers are allowed to access the foreign firm's services. A tariff equivalent of all such impediments would be defined as the tax on the French firm's operations in Mexico that, if it replaced all other impediments, would cause it to operate at the same level and have the same effects on the domestic telecoms providers and consumers within Mexico. As in the case of traded goods, a single tariff equivalent may not capture all of these effects simultaneously, especially if competition is imperfect. And even with perfect competition, such a tariff equivalent is unlikely to be observable as a simple price difference. There is no world price of Mexican telephone services, for example, with which to compare what Mexican firms are charging, since the nature and cost of a service depend in part on the location of the consumer. Nonetheless, a tariff equivalent is a conceptually useful way of quantifying barriers to trade in services as well as goods, and many studies have sought to express their results in this form.

Mode 2 of services trade refers to services that require the consumer to be in the location of the producer, as in the cases of tourism and education. Here again, the service provided is likely to be differentiated by the location or identity of the provider, so that a world price of the service may not be meaningful. It would be meaningless, for example, to try to compare the "world price" of a visit to the Taj Mahal or an MBA degree from the Wharton School with the prices of these services within, say, Brazil. But it remains the case that Brazilian restrictions on their citizens' travel to India or the U.S. to consume these services will alter the markets for other tourist attractions and educational institutions within Brazil. Such restrictions again can in principle be quantified as equivalent to a tax on Brazilians' visits abroad for these purposes.

Mode 3 of international services provision is arguably the most general and the most important: provision through a commercial presence that is the result of foreign direct investment (FDI). Almost any service can be provided by firms from one economy to consumers in another if the firms are allowed to establish a physical presence there. This is true even of tourism – think of Euro-Disney. In this case there may well be a foreign price with which one could easily compare, but the comparison is unlikely to be meaningful. It would be a mistake to infer a trade barrier from the higher price of admission to Euro-Disney in Paris as compared to Florida, or the absence of a trade barrier from the lower price of a McDonald's hamburger in Argentina than in New York. In all such cases, prices depend on local costs of labor and raw materials as much as they do on trade barriers. However, and once again, foreign service providers may well face impediments, both to their establishment and to their ongoing operations, the effects of which would be similar to a tax if only we could infer what it is.

The final mode of supply, Mode 4, refers to the temporary cross-border movement of workers. Examples are the movement of computer programmers, engineers, management personnel, and lesser skilled construction workers who are granted temporary visas to work in a host economy. Most movement that is actually permitted consists of workers within industries that produce traded goods or that produce services that are primarily thought of as traded through other modes. Thus we do not think of many industries as producing services that are primarily traded through Mode 4. On the other hand, labor itself is a service that could be traded in this way, and occasionally it has been, in the form of guest-worker programs and the like. The fact that Mode 4 service-provision figures appear to be relatively small in the data on services trade in Table 1 is therefore symptomatic of the very high barriers that exist for Mode 4, except within industries where it facilitates other kinds of trade. Mode 4 is the one mode in which the tariff equivalent of barriers could most easily be measured, as simply the differences across economies in the real wages of particular kinds of labor.

For all of the modes, then, one objective of empirical measurement is to deduce some sort of tariff equivalent of the barrier to trade in particular services. Since direct price comparisons seldom serve that purpose, however, researchers have pursued other means of inferring the presence and size of barriers to trade. Some of these methods have been quite direct: they simply ask governments or participants in markets what barriers they impose or face. The answers are usually only qualitative, indicating the presence or absence of a particular type of barrier, but not its quantitative size or effect. Such qualitative information takes on a quantitative dimension, however, when it is tabulated by sector, perhaps with subjective weights to indicate severity. The result is a set of "frequency measures" of barriers to trade, recording what the barriers are and where, and perhaps also the fraction of trade within a sector or economy that is subject to them. Frequency measures do not directly imply anything like the tariff equivalents of trade barriers, but in order to use them for quantitative analysis, analysts have often converted them to that form in rather *ad hoc* ways that we will indicate below.

Other, more indirect, measurements of trade barriers in service industries have also been used, alone or in combination with frequency measures. These may be divided into two types: measurements that use information about prices and/or costs; and measurements that observe quantities of trade or production and attempt to infer how trade barriers have affected these quantities. In both cases, as we will discuss, if one can also measure or assume an appropriate elasticity reflecting the response of quantity to price, a measured effect on either can be translated into an effect on the other. Thus both price and quantity measurements are also often converted into, and reported as, tariff equivalents.

In what follows, we begin in Section II with a conceptual framework for understanding international services transactions and the barriers that may affect them. We then turn in Section III to a discussion of the characteristics of services barriers, and we provide some examples of barriers for the banking sector and for foreign direct investment in services sectors. This is followed in Section IV with a discussion of methods of measurement of services barriers, including frequency measures and indexes of restrictiveness, price-effect and quantity-effect measurements, gravity-model estimates, and financial-based measurements. In each case, we provide information and examples of how the measurements are constructed and an evaluation of their merits and limitations. We also provide in Appendix A brief summaries of studies that have used these methods. In Section V, we consider how the various measurements can be used in assessing the economic consequences of the liberalization of services barriers. Since this module is designed for instructional purposes, we conclude in Section VI with a presentation of guideline principles and recommended procedures for measuring services barriers and assessing the consequences of their liberalization. Finally, we include an appendix containing discussion of selected technical issues and summaries of literature pertinent to methods of measurement of services barriers.

2. Conceptual Framework

Issues to be Addressed:

- Service market equilibrium
- Differentiated services
- Imperfect competition

In this section, we use demand-and-supply analysis to show how the introduction of a services barrier will affect the domestic price of a service, the quantity demanded, and the quantity supplied by domestic and foreign firms. We show, using diagrammatic analysis, how the service barrier can be measured as a tariff equivalent. Three cases are presented:

- Figure 1 – domestic and foreign firms are highly competitive and their services are highly substitutable.
- Figure 2 – the services of the domestic and foreign firms are not readily substitutable and have distinctive prices.
- Figure 3 – there is a single domestic firm with monopoly power and the entry of foreign firms is restricted.

The effects of a service barrier, and thus the tariff equivalent, in these various cases will depend on the competitiveness of domestic and foreign firms and the degree of substitution between the services that they provide.

Figure 1 illustrates the functioning of a domestic market for a service when there are domestic and foreign suppliers present. It is assumed here that the suppliers are highly competitive and that their services are readily substitutable. Other cases will be considered below. The foreign suppliers may be serving the domestic market through any of the four modes of supply already discussed, although the degree of substitution between the foreign and domestic services may vary for the different modes.

The horizontal axis in Figure 1 measures the quantity of the service supplied to and demanded by domestic purchasers. This could include amounts purchased abroad, as in the case of Mode 2, which are nonetheless regarded here as competing with domestic supplies. The demand schedule for the service is downward sloping with respect to the price, P, which is the same for all suppliers. The supply schedules for the two sets of suppliers, domestic and foreign, are upward sloping and shown by S_D for domestic firms and S_F for foreign firms.[3] In the absence of any impediments to trade, the relevant total supply schedule in this market is the horizontal sum, labeled S_D+S_F. Price is determined where the total supply schedule intersects the demand schedule at P^0, with the quantity Q^0 divided between domestic firms, Q_D^0, and foreign firms, Q_F^0.

Let us suppose now that a barrier is introduced that inhibits the ability of the foreign firms to serve this market. This may raise foreign firms' costs, shifting their supply schedule upward, or it may reduce or constrain the quantity that they supply, shifting the schedule to the left. Either way, S_F is shifted up and to the left, as is the total supply schedule, S_D+S_F, to the positions shown as S_F' and S_D+S_F'. The effect is to raise the price of the service to P^1, reduce the total quantity purchased, and increase the quantity sold by domestic firms. Sales by the foreign firms fall from Q_F^0 to Q_F^1, which is the decline in imports of the service due to the barrier.

The tariff equivalent of this barrier may be defined as the *ad valorem* tax on foreign service providers that would have caused the same effects as this barrier. Such a tax, by increasing the cost of sales by foreign firms, would cause their supply schedule to shift up by the amount of the tax. Therefore, a tax that shifts S_F up so as to pass through point A is the tariff equivalent. That is, the tariff

[3] Domestic supply is shown as further to the right (larger quantity for given price) than foreign supply, but this is not needed for any of the implications of the analysis.

Figure 1. Perfect Competition and Perfect Substitution Between Domestic and Foreign Services Firms

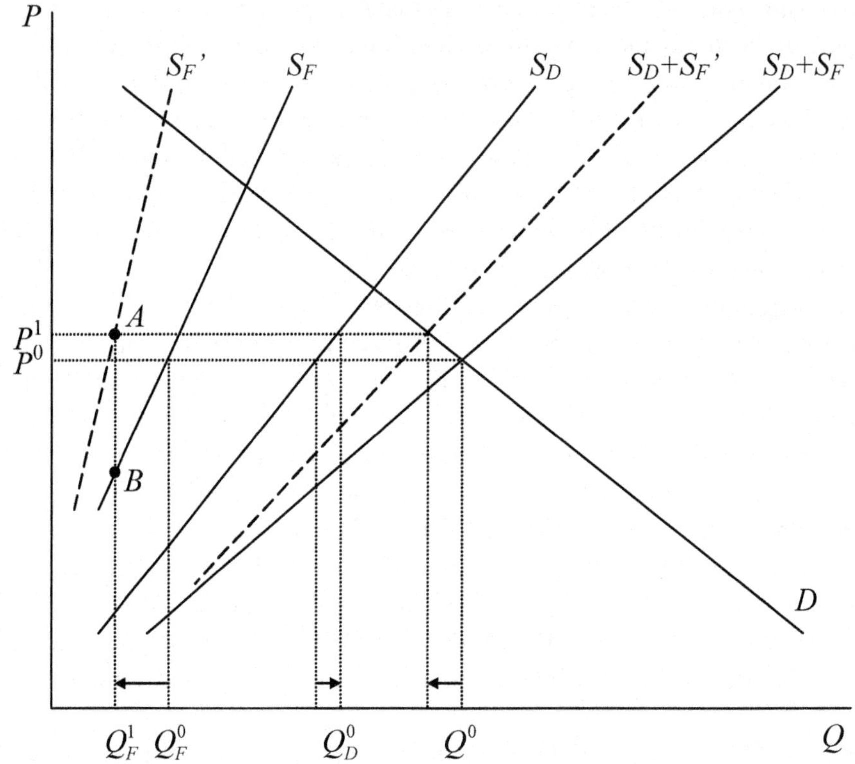

equivalent is the percentage by which point *A* lies above point *B*. What should be noted in the case of Figure 1 is that the tariff equivalent is not measurable from any observable price or price change. That is, the increase in the price of the service on the domestic market is considerably smaller than the tariff equivalent of the barrier that caused it.

There is, however, one special case in which the tariff equivalent would equal the price change. This occurs when the foreign supply schedule is horizontal (*i.e.*, infinitely elastic) at some price P^0 so that the effect of the barrier is to raise foreign firms' cost to P^1. Then the two foreign supply schedules are horizontal at these prices, and the tariff equivalent would be just the amount by which they are shifted upward. To the extent that empirical measurements of tariff equivalents are based on observed prices, a horizontal foreign supply schedule will represent a special case that may exist for a small economy that faces a given world price for the service.

Figure 2 shows a case in which the services provided by domestic and foreign firms are not readily substitutable and can therefore have different prices. In this case we must consider markets for the two services separately, as is done in the two panels of Figure 2, and we must also allow for the two services being imperfect substitutes. This is done by having each of the two demand schedules depend on the price in the other market, as indicated. Once again, the figure shows supply and demand schedules, quantities, and prices without any trade barrier with superscript 0, and those in the presence of a trade barrier with superscript 1. The introduction of a barrier shifts the foreign supply schedule to the left and up, as before, to S_F^1 and leads to higher prices in both markets, P_F^1 and P_D^1, which now cause both demand schedules to shift somewhat to the right. As in the case of Figure 1, with close substitution of the services, the domestic quantity supplied increases while the foreign quantity supplied declines. And here again, the tariff equivalent can be observed in the figure as the percentage by which S_F^1 lies above S_F^0, that is, the percentage by which point *A* is above point *B*.

So far we have assumed that markets are highly competitive. But this is clearly inappropriate in many service markets where an incumbent domestic firm may have a monopoly or only a very limited number of competitors. In such markets, a barrier to service trade may be a limit on entry by new firms that, though not explicitly discriminatory, favors the domestic incumbent firm and implicitly limits trade more than domestic supply. We therefore now consider, in Figure 3, the case in which there is a single domestic incumbent firm together with competing foreign suppliers. If there is unimpeded entry of firms, the market price will be P^0. In this case, the single domestic firm whose costs are increasing along *MC* will produce Q_D^0. Total sales are Q^0, and the foreign firms will sell $Q_F^0 = Q^0 - Q_D^0$ in the domestic market. Let us now suppose that a barrier is introduced that raises the cost of the foreign firms when they sell in the domestic market. This would cause the domestic firm's sales to rise along *MC* and foreign sales to decline. If the foreign cost rises above P^a (the intersection of domestic *MC* and demand), however, then foreign sales will fall to zero. The domestic firm can thus charge a price that just barely undercuts the foreign cost, so that the domestic firm will be able to monopolize the market. The tariff equivalent of the barrier in the case of Figure 3 is therefore the amount by which it increases foreign cost, up to the limit of $P^m - P^0$. However, if the foreign supply schedule were instead upward sloping rather than horizontal, then both the analysis and the identification of the tariff equivalent would be accordingly more difficult to measure. But the general conclusion is that the tariff equivalent of an

Figure 2. Imperfect Competition and Substitution Between Domestic and Foreign Services Firms

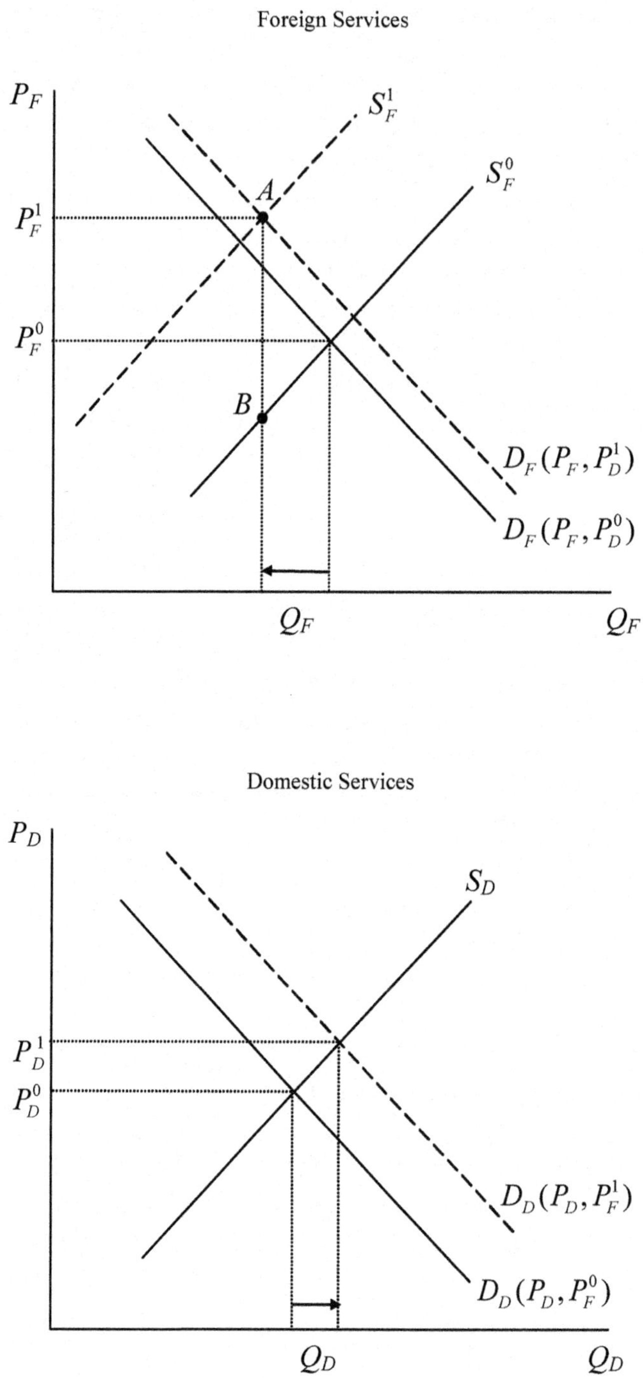

Figure 3. Domestic Services Firm with Monopoly Power and Restrictions on Foreign Firms

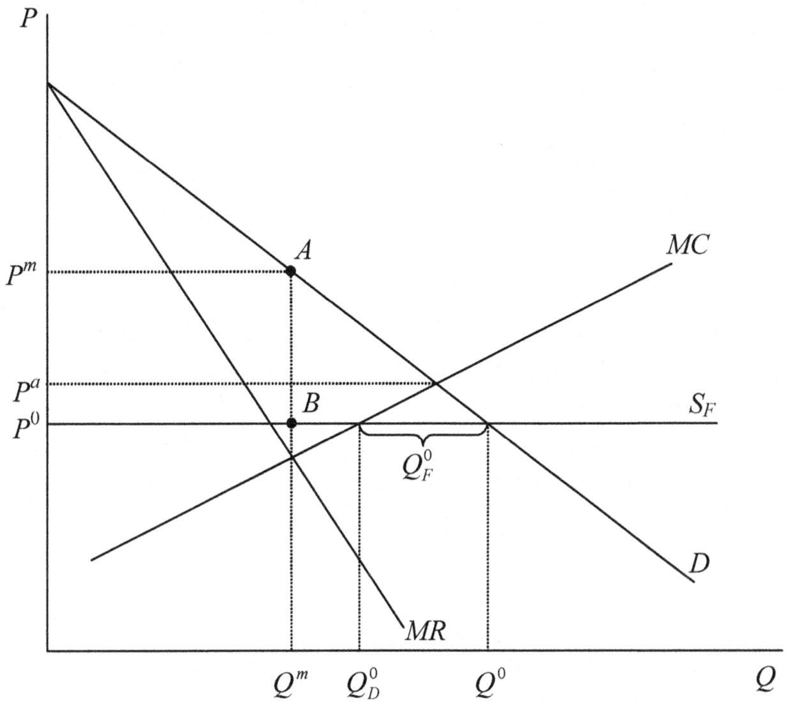

entry restriction will be measured by the excess of the monopoly price over the competitive price that would have obtained if both trade and entry were free.

Figures 1-3 clearly do not exhaust all of the possible cases. The real world is bound to involve further mixtures of imperfect substitution between the products of domestic and foreign services firms and the degree of competition between these firms that have not been considered here. Also, many service industries have numerous special features, both in the ways that they operate and in their amenability to measurement, and simple theoretical models do not take these factors into account. Empirical work is therefore essential to address the measurement of the various services barriers that impede international services transactions. In what follows, we review and summarize many of the studies that have been done.

3. Characteristics of Services Barriers

Issues to be addressed:

- Broad classifications of service barriers
- Detailed classifications: example
- Barriers on foreign direct investment
- Legitimate *versus* illegitimate regulations

As noted by Hoekman and Primo Braga (1997, p. 288), border measures such as tariffs are generally difficult to apply to services because customs agents cannot readily observe services as they cross the border. It is also the case, as discussed above, that many services are provided in the economy of consumption rather than cross-border. Typically, therefore, services restrictions are designed in the form of government regulations applied to the different modes of services transactions. Thus, for example, regulations may affect the entry and operations of both domestic and foreign suppliers of services and in turn increase the price or the cost of the services involved. Services barriers are therefore more akin to NTBs than to tariffs, and their impact will depend on how the government regulation is designed and administered.

These regulations can take many forms, and are usually specific to the type of service being regulated. Therefore, since services themselves are so diverse, services barriers are also diverse, making them somewhat difficult to classify in general terms. There are, however, two distinctions that that tend to apply across many types of services and service barriers: regulations that apply to entry or establishment of firms *versus* their operations; and regulations that are nondiscriminatory *versus* discriminatory[4] That is, most barriers to trade in services can be placed in one of the four cells of the following simple 2×2 classification:

[4] These distinctions are suggested by the Australian Productivity Commission, whose website can be consulted for more details, (*www.pc.gov.au/research/memoranda/servicesrestriction/index.html*). See also Hoekman and Braga (1997, p. 288), who classify and provide examples of services barriers as follows: (1) quotas, local content, and prohibitions; (2) price-based instruments; (3) standards, licensing, and procurement; and (4) discriminatory access to distribution networks.

	Entry/establishment	Operations
Non-discriminatory		
Discriminatory		

For example, a limit on the number of firms that may be licensed without regard to their nationality would fall into the upper left cell, while such a limit that favors domestically owned firms would be in the lower left. Likewise, a regulation that all service providers in an industry to perform certain extra tasks would raise cost or operations in a nondiscriminatory fashion and lie in the upper right cell, while a regulation that requires special performance by foreign providers that is not expected of domestic firms would be in the lower right. Of course a policy could in principle be discriminatory in favor of foreign firms rather than against them, but that would not be typical.

In terms of the conceptual framework in Section II, the entry vs. operations distinction may be thought of as determining whether the regulation shifts the supply schedules of services to the left or up. That is, regulations that restrict or impede the establishment of service providers within a market will usually reduce their numbers and therefore the quantity supplied at any given price. Regulations of ongoing operations, on the other hand, may not reduce the number of suppliers, but they will increase their costs, causing them to supply a given quantity only at a higher price. This distinction is not perfect, however, and in any case it does not need to be, since as long as the supply schedules are upward sloping, shifts to the left and up have the same qualitative effects, as we have seen. The distinction is useful mainly for classifying different types of barriers.

Likewise, the nondiscriminatory vs. discriminatory distinction above determines whether a regulation shifts the supply curve of only foreign service providers (when it is discriminatory), or instead raises costs and shifts supply for both foreign and domestic suppliers. As we saw in Section II, however, a regulation that impedes establishment of all new service providers, in spite of being nondiscriminatory, can nonetheless limit trade and competition by favoring a domestic incumbent. It is also important to note that some regulations may be designed to achieve certain social objectives, such as health and safety or environmental requirements, and may not be protectionist in intent.

Of course, actual regulations differ greatly across service industries and are often based on characteristics of the particular service being provided. Thus, within each cell of the table above we may think of additional distinctions being made, usually distinctions that are peculiar to the service sector under consideration.

To illustrate, we use the case of banking services based on a study by McGuire and Schuele (2000) done under the auspices of the Australian Productivity Commission. Table 2 lists groupings of restrictions that apply especially to Modes 3 and 4 of international banking services transactions. These restrictions relate to commercial presence and "other restrictions" applied to banking services, together with a brief indication of what these restrictions represent and how an index of them has been constructed.[5] As McGuire and Schuele note (p. 206): "The commercial presence grouping covers restrictions on licensing, direct investment, joint venture arrangements, and the movement of people. The 'other restrictions' grouping covers restrictions on raising funds, lending funds, providing other lines of business (insurance and securities services), expanding banking outlets, the composition of the board of directors and the temporary movement of people." Thus the top half of Table 2 corresponds roughly to regulations of entry/establishment in the small table above, while the bottom half corresponds to roughly to regulations of operations. For each type of restriction, separate columns also indicate whether they apply to foreign and domestic firms, hence being discriminatory if they apply only to the former. An indication of the restrictiveness of these regulations is also provided in Table 2 and will be discussed below.

Just as different sub-classifications may be needed for different types of services, so too may the appropriate classification depend on the purpose for which the classification will be used. This point is made especially by Hardin and Holmes (1997) in their discussion of barriers affecting FDI (Mode 3). Focusing, in effect, on the lower left cell of our table above – the establishment of a commercial presence in many sectors in host economies – they define (p. 24) an FDI barrier as "...any government policy measure which distorts decisions about where to invest and in what form." In considering ways of classifying such FDI barriers, they note (pp. 33-34):[6]

> "The appropriate classification system may vary, depending on the purpose of the exercise. For example, if the purpose is to check and monitor compliance with some policy commitment, then the categories should reflect the key element of the commitment.... If the primary interest is instead the resource allocation implications of the barriers, some additional or different information may be useful.

---

[5] See the Productivity Commission website for detailed listings by economy of the categories of domestic and foreign restrictions on establishment and ongoing operations for some selected services sectors, including: accountancy, architectural, and engineering services; banking; distribution; and maritime services.

[6] See also Holmes and Hardin (2000).

Table 2. Restriction categories for banking services

Restriction category	**Relevant for foreign index**	**Total weight**	**Relevant for domestic index**	**Total weight**
Restrictions on commercial presence				
Licensing of banks	Yes	0.200	Yes	0.190
Based inversely on the maximum number of new banking licenses issued with only prudential requirements				
Direct investment	Yes	0.200	Yes	0.190
Based inversely on the maximum equity participation permitted in an existing domestic bank				
Joint venture arrangements	Yes	0.100	No	n.a.
New bank entry only through joint venture with a domestic bank				
Movement of people	Yes	0.020	No	n.a.
Based inversely on years that executives, specialists and/or senior managers can stay				
Other restrictions				
Raising funds by banks	Yes	0.100	Yes	0.143
Banks are restricted from accepting deposits from the public and/or raising funds from domestic capital markets				
Lending funds by banks	Yes	0.100	Yes	0.143
Banks are restricted in types or sizes of loans and/or are directed to lend to housing and small business				
Other business of banks – insurance and securities services	Yes	0.200	Yes	0.095
Banks are excluded from insurance and/or securities services				
Expanding the number of banking outlets	Yes	0.050	Yes	0.048
Based inversely on the number of outlets permitted.				
Composition of the board of directors	Yes	0.020	No	n.a.
Based inversely on the percentage of the board that can comprise foreigners				
Temporary movement of people	Yes	0.010	No	n.a.
Based inversely on the number of days temporary entry permitted to executives, specialists and/or senior managers				
Total weighting or highest possible score		1.000		0.808

Source: McGuire and Schuele (2000), Tables 12.1 and 12.3, pp. 204-05, 208.

> Barriers to FDI may distort international patterns and modes of...trade. They may also distort allocation of capital between different economies, between foreign and domestic investment, between different sectors, and between portfolio and direct investment. ...the classification system...should highlight the key characteristics of the barriers that will determine their size and impact. Market access and national treatment are...relevant categories from a resource allocation perspective. ...national treatment is generally taken to refer to measures affecting firms after establishment. A...way to classify barriers is therefore...according to what aspect of the investment they most affect: establishment, ownership and control; or operations. In addition..., some further information may be useful...on distinctions...between direct *versus* indirect restrictions on foreign controlled firms; and rules *versus* case-by-case decisions."[7]

The main types of FDI barriers that have been identified by UNCTAD (1996) are noted in Table 3, which divides barriers into three groups, the first of which concerns entry and the last operations. The middle group – ownership and control restrictions – illustrates the weakness of any simple classification system since it seems to include elements of both. Further information on the barriers most commonly used to restrict FDI especially in the APEC economies is provided in Hardin and Holmes (1997, esp. pp. 37-40 and 45-55). As they note (p. 40), some common characteristics appear to be:[8]

> "application of some form of screening or registration process involving various degrees of burden for the foreign investor; restrictions on the level or share of foreign ownership, particularly in some service sectors, and often in the context of privatisations; widespread use of case-by-case judgments, often based on national interest criteria; widespread use of restrictions on ownership and control (*e.g.*, restrictions on board membership), particularly in sectors such as telecommunications, broadcasting, banking; and relatively limited use of performance requirements on input controls in services sectors."

It is evident from the foregoing discussion that services barriers exist in a variety of forms, depending on the types of services involved, the economy imposing the barriers, and the sectors to which the barriers are applied. To help further the understanding of the different services barriers, it would be useful

---

[7] Direct restrictions include limitations on the total size or share of investment in a sector and requirements on inputs used (*e.g.*, local content). Indirect restrictions include net benefit or national interest criteria and limitations on membership of company boards. The distinction between rules and case-by-case decisions relates to issues of clarity in specification and transparency as compared to the exercise of administrative discretion.

[8] Hardin and Holmes (pp. 40-43) also provide information on investment incentives, which are widely used and for the most part are not subject to multilateral disciplines.

Table 3. Barriers to FDI

Restrictions on market entry	Bans on foreign investment in certain sectors Quantitative restrictions (*e.g.*, limit of 25 percent foreign ownership in a sector) Screening and approval (sometimes involving national interest or net economic benefits tests) Restrictions on the legal form of the foreign entity Minimum capital requirements Conditions on subsequent investment Conditions on location Admission taxes
Ownership and control restrictions	Compulsory joint ventures with domestic investors Limits on the number of foreign board members Government appointed board members Government approval required for certain decisions Restrictions on foreign shareholders' rights Mandatory transfer of some ownership to locals within a specified time (*e.g.*, 15 years)
Operational restrictions	Performance requirements (*e.g.*, export requirements) Local content restrictions Restrictions on imports of labor, capital and raw materials Operational permits or licences Ceilings on royalties Restrictions on repatriation of capital and profits

Source: UNCTAD (1996).

accordingly to organize the available information by economy and sector, according to the four modes of international services transactions and whether or not they are protectionist in intent. As already noted, these modes cover: cross-border services (Mode 1); consumption abroad (Mode 2); FDI (Mode 3); and the temporary movement of workers (Mode 4). Using this information, the next and difficult step will be to devise methods of measurement of the various barriers and to integrate these measures within a framework designed to assess their economic effects.

It should be emphasized, finally, that not all regulations of services should be viewed as protectionist, even when they do serve to reduce service imports. Many regulations serve legitimate purposes, such as protecting health and safety or preventing fraud and other misconduct. Such a regulation, if applied in a nondiscriminatory manner, is not protectionist and should not be viewed as a barrier to service trade, even though it may maintain a higher standard than prevails abroad and thus reduce imports compared to what they would be without the regulation. On the other hand, nondiscrimination is not by itself enough to absolve a regulation from being protectionist if it, say, enforces a standard that has no legitimate purpose but happens to be met by domestic providers and not by foreign ones. Distinguishing legitimate from illegitimate regulations may not be easy, especially since it usually requires the sort of detailed knowledge of the industry that can only be gotten from industry insiders who are unlikely to be disinterested.

4. Methods of Measurement of Services Barriers

Issues to be Addressed:

- Direct and indirect measurement
- Frequency studies
- Indexes of restrictiveness
- Price-impact measurements
- Quantity-impact measurements
- Gravity-model estimates
- Financial-based measurements

Measurements of trade barriers, in markets for both goods and services, can be either direct or indirect. Direct measurements start from the observation of an explicit policy or practice, such as an import quota or a regulation of a foreign provider of services, and then attempt in some fashion to measure its economic importance. Indirect measurements try instead to infer the existence of barriers using observed discrepancies between actual economic performance and what would be expected if trade were free. Direct measurements have the advantage that one knows what one is measuring, and the disadvantage that they can only include those barriers that are in fact explicit and recognized. Indirect measurements have the advantage that their quantitative importance is known, at least in the dimension used to identify them, but the disadvantage that they may incorporate unrecognized frictions other than the policy impediments that one seeks to identify.

In the case of trade in goods, direct measurements of NTBs typically take the form of inventories of identified trade restrictions, such as those compiled in the United Nations Conference on Trade and Development (UNCTAD) Trade Analysis and Information System (TRAINS).[9] Since NTBs usually cover only some industries or products, a first step in quantifying them is often to measure the fraction of trade that they cover in different sectors and economies. These

[9] TRAINS is available on-line at *http://www.unctad.org*.

fractions may then be used directly in empirical work, even though they do not themselves say anything about how effective the NTBs have been in restricting trade.[10] Indirect measurements, on the other hand, can be fairly straightforward in the case of goods, based either on their observed prices before and after they cross an international border or on the quantities that cross it. For example, one can often infer both the presence of an import barrier and its effect on price by simply comparing the price of a good inside an economy to that outside, since in the absence of any barrier one would expect competitive market forces to cause these prices to be the same. Indirect measurements based on quantities are more difficult, since they depend on a theoretical benchmark for comparability that is likely to be much less certain. Nonetheless, as we note in our discussion below, such quantity-based measurements of NTBs have been used with some success.

For trade in services, direct measurements must be carefully done, since regulation in service industries is so common that merely to document its presence would not be informative. A common approach is therefore to complement the documentation of regulations by incorporating information about the restrictiveness of the regulations, and then use this information to construct an index of restrictiveness that can be compared across economies. We will provide further detail of how this may be done below, together with examples from the literature.

Indirect measurements of restrictiveness are also possible with traded services, although simple price comparisons are seldom of much use. This is because many services are differentiated by location in a way that renders comparison of their prices inside and outside of an economy meaningless. For example, the cost of providing telephone service to consumers on the Texas side of the U.S.-Mexican border need bear no particular relationship to the cost, for the same firm, of providing it across the border in Mexico, where wages are much lower but costs of infrastructure may be much higher. So even if trade in the service were completely unimpeded, we would not expect these prices to be the same, and we therefore cannot infer a trade barrier in either direction from the fact that they are not. Similar arguments can be made about most traded services.

Indirect measurements of barriers to trade in services are therefore less common than for trade in goods, although they do exist. As we will discuss below, there has been some success using the so-called gravity model as a benchmark for quantities of trade in services, and the results of these models have therefore been the basis for indirect measurement of barriers in the quantity

---

[10] In fact, they are somewhat perverse for this purpose, since the more restrictive is a NTB, the less will be the trade that it permits.

dimension. Financial data have also been the basis for inferring barriers from differences in the markups of price over cost, as we will also discuss.

With indirect measurements of the presence of services barriers less common, however, there is therefore the need for some other approach to quantifying the effects of barriers that have been identified. In this connection, indexes of restrictiveness can be constructed that are typically measured on a scale of zero to one, and they do not purport to say how much a barrier either raises price or reduces quantity. To get such information, another step is needed. Commonly, this step involves using econometric analysis to relate an index of restrictiveness to observed prices or quantities, thus translating the measures of the presence of barriers into an estimate of their economic effect in particular services markets.

In what follows, then, we first discuss the construction of measures of the presence of barriers, commonly referred to as frequency-based measurements, and the use of these measurements to construct indexes of restrictiveness. This is followed by a discussion of how the effects on prices and quantities can be derived. We then turn to methods that attempt to infer the presence of services barriers indirectly, first from a gravity model of the quantities of trade, and second from financial data within service firms.

4.1. *Frequency Studies and Indexes of Restrictiveness*

Studies of frequency-based measures start by identifying the kinds of restriction that apply to a particular service industry or to services in general. For particular industries, this requires considerable industry-specific knowledge, since each industry has, at a minimum, its own terminology, and often also its own distinctive reasons for regulatory concern. Regulations often serve an ostensibly valid purpose – protecting health and safety, for example – and knowledge of the industry is also necessary to distinguish such valid regulations from those that primarily offer protection. Thus, a frequency study is best carried out by an industry specialist, or it must draw upon documents that have been prepared by such specialists. Industry studies therefore often build upon the documentation provided by industry trade groups, such as the International Telecommunications Union in the case of telecoms, bilateral air service arrangements in the case of passenger air travel, or the TradePort website in the case of maritime services.

For broader studies of restrictions in services, covering multiple industries, some source must be found that incorporates such expertise across sectors. An early approach to doing this was in the studies by PECC (1995) and Hoekman (1995,1996) that we discuss below. These studies used information that economies had submitted to the General Agreement on Trade in Services

(GATS), to be used as the basis for commitments to be made for services liberalization in the Uruguay Round negotiations. Such measures are therefore not ideally suited for documenting trade barriers. Better information requires that someone deliberately collect the details of actual barriers and regulatory practices, as in the data collected by Asia Pacific Economic Cooperation (APEC) and used by Hardin and Holmes (1997), whose study we also discuss below. In all cases, the goal is not just to assemble a complete list of barriers, but also to know the restrictiveness of these barriers in terms such as the numbers of firms or economies to which they apply and other characteristics. This latter information is then used to construct an Index of Restrictiveness. Typically, each barrier is assigned a score between zero and one, with a score of one being the most restrictive and a score of zero being the least restrictive. These scores are then averaged, using weights that are intended to reflect the relative importance of each type of barrier.

There are several ways in which the weights on different barriers in a restrictiveness index may be assigned. Most commonly, these reflect the judgments of knowledgeable investigators as to the importance of each type of barrier. This may well be the best approach if the investigator really is knowledgeable, as in the case when an index is being constructed for a specific, narrowly defined industry.

An alternative that has been used by Nicoletti *et al.* (2000) and subsequently by Doove *et al.* (2001) is to apply factor analysis to the data once they are assembled. This enables them to distinguish those barriers that vary most independently among their data, and then to apply the largest weights to them. This is a purely statistical technique that is not, in our view, necessarily an improvement on the use of judgmental weights.

A third approach is not to construct an index at all, but rather to use the scores or proxy measures for each barrier separately in an empirical analysis. The difficulty here is that these scores may be interrelated, so that their independent influence on any variable of interest may be impossible to ascertain using standard statistical methods. If this can be done, however, the advantage is that it allows for the fact that barriers may differ in their importance for different aspects of economic performance, and this approach allows these differences to make themselves known. Ideally, one would prefer an approach that allows the weights in an index of restrictiveness to be estimated simultaneously with the importance of that index for a particular economic outcome. Thus the construction of the index would be interlinked with its use for estimating effects on prices and quantities, for example, which we will discuss below.

First, however, we discuss a few of the main studies that have constructed frequency measurements and indexes of restrictiveness.

4.1.1. *PECC and Hoekman*

PECC (1995) and Hoekman (1995,1996) use information contained in the member schedules of the GATS, referring to all four modes of supply of services, to construct frequency ratios that measure the extent of liberalization promised by economies in their commitments to the GATS, as part of the Uruguay Round negotiations completed in 1993-94. The frequency ratios are constructed based on the number of commitments that were scheduled by individual economies designating sectors or sub-sectors as unrestricted or partially restricted. The ratios that are calculated equal the number of actual commitments in relation to the maximum possible number of commitments.[11] Hoekman focused on commitments relating to market access and national treatment. As he notes (1996, p. 101), there were 155 sectors and sub-sectors and four modes of supply specified in the GATS. This yields $620 \times 2 = 1{,}440$ total commitments on market access and national treatment for each of 97 economies.[12] The frequency ratio for an economy or a sector is then defined as the fraction of these possible commitments that were in fact made, implying an index of trade restrictiveness equal to one minus this fraction.

There are some important limitations to these calculations that are worth mentioning. Thus, as Holmes and Hardin (2000, pp. 58-59) note, Hoekman's method may be misleading or biased because it assumes that the absence of positive member commitments in the GATS schedules can be interpreted as indicating the presence of restrictions, which may not be the case in fact. Also, the different types of restrictions are given equal weight.[13]

[11] In counting commitments, the commitment for a sector or sub-sector to be unrestricted is counted as one, whereas a listing of the restrictions that will continue to apply, so that the commitment to liberalization is only partial, is counted as one-half.

[12] As noted in Hardin and Holmes (1997, p. 70), the GATS commitments are based on a "positive list" approach and therefore do not take into account sectors and restrictions that are unscheduled. In PECC (1995), it is assumed that all unscheduled sectors and commitments are unrestricted, which will then significantly raise the calculated frequency ratios compared to Hoekman (1996), who treats unscheduled sectors as fully restricted.

[13] More information is needed accordingly on the restrictions that may apply to both scheduled and unscheduled services sectors in order to obtain a comprehensive measure of all existing restrictions.

4.1.2. *Hardin and Holmes*

Hardin and Holmes (1997) and Holmes and Hardin (2000) have attempted to build on and improve Hoekman's methodology, though focusing only on restrictions on FDI in services (Mode 3). In particular, they use information on the actual FDI restrictions taken from Asia Pacific Economic Cooperation (APEC), rather than just the GATS commitments. Rather than treating all restrictions equally, they devise a judgmental system of weighting that is designed, as in the case of the banking restrictions noted in Table 2, to reflect the efficiency costs of the different barriers. The components of their index and the weights assigned to the different sub-categories are given in Table 4. It can be seen, for example, that foreign equity limits are given greater weights than the other barriers noted. Their results for 15 APEC economies for the period 1996-98 are summarized in Table 5.[14] It is evident that communications and financial services are most subject to FDI restrictions, while business, distribution, environmental, and recreational services are the least restricted. Korea, Indonesia, China, Thailand, and the Philippines have relatively high restrictiveness indexes, while the United States and Hong Kong have the lowest indexes.

Table 4. Components of an index of FDI restrictions

Type of restriction	Weight
Foreign equity limits on all firms	
No foreign equity permitted	1.000
Less than 50 percent foreign equity permitted	0.500
More than 50 percent and less than 100 percent foreign equity permitted	0.250
Foreign equity limits on existing firms, none on greenfield	
No foreign equity permitted	0.500
Less than 50 percent foreign equity permitted	0.250
More than 50 percent and less than 100 percent foreign equity permitted	0.125
Screening and approval	
Investor required to demonstrate net economic benefits	0.100
Approval unless contrary to national interest	0.075
Notification (pre or post)	0.050
Control and management restrictions	
All firms	0.200
Existing firms, none for greenfield	0.100
Input and operational restrictions	
All firms	0.200
Existing firms, none for greenfield	0.100

Source: Holmes and Hardin (2000, p. 62).

[14] Details on the construction of the indexes and their sensitivity to variations in the restrictiveness weights are discussed in Hardin and Holmes (1997, esp. 103-11).

Table 5. FDI restrictiveness indexes for selected APEC economies and selected sectors, 1996-98 (Percentage)

Sectors	Australia	Canada	China	Hong Kong	Indonesia	Japan	Korea	Malaysia
Business	0.183	0.225	0.360	0.015	0.560	0.062	0.565	0.316
Communications	0.443	0.514	0.819	0.350	0.644	0.350	0.685	0.416
Postal	1.000	1.000	1.000	1.000	1.000	1.000	1.000	1.000
Courier	0.175	0.200	0.275	0.000	0.525	0.050	0.550	0.075
Telecommunications	0.300	0.325	1.000	0.200	0.525	0.100	0.550	0.375
Audiovisual	0.295	0.530	1.000	0.200	0.525	0.250	0.640	0.215
Construction	0.175	0.200	0.400	0.000	0.525	0.050	0.750	0.775
Distribution	0.175	0.200	0.275	0.050	0.525	0.050	0.625	0.075
Education	0.175	0.200	0.525	0.000	0.525	0.200	0.550	0.075
Environmental	0.175	0.200	0.275	0.000	0.525	0.117	0.700	0.075
Financial	0.450	0.375	0.450	0.233	0.550	0.358	0.875	0.608
Insurance and related	0.275	0.425	0.475	0.400	0.575	0.450	0.838	0.600
Banking and other	0.625	0.325	0.425	0.067	0.525	0.267	0.913	0.617
Health	0.175	0.200	0.275	0.000	0.525	0.050	0.550	0.317
Tourism	0.175	0.200	0.283	0.000	0.525	0.050	0.617	0.542
Recreation	0.175	0.200	0.275	0.000	0.525	0.050	0.550	0.175
Transport	0.204	0.235	0.455	0.093	0.525	0.114	0.573	0.122

	Mexico	New Zealand	Papua New Guinea	Philippines	Singapore	Thailand	United States
Business	0.289	0.086	0.300	0.479	0.261	0.775	0.005
Communications	0.739	0.434	0.475	0.758	0.518	0.838	0.345
Postal	1.000	1.000	1.000	1.000	1.000	1.000	1.000
Courier	0.775	0.075	0.300	0.475	0.250	0.775	0.000
Telecommunications	0.705	0.425	0.300	0.975	0.571	0.804	0.200
Audiovisual	0.475	0.235	0.300	0.580	0.250	0.775	0.180

Table 5. FDI restrictiveness indexes for selected APEC economies and selected sectors, 1996-98 (Percentage)–Continued

Sectors	Australia	Canada	China	Hong Kong	Indonesia	Japan	Korea	Malaysia
Construction	0.450	0.075	0.300	0.475	0.250	0.775	0.000	
Distribution	0.325	0.075	0.300	0.475	0.250	0.775	0.000	
Education	0.450	0.075	0.300	0.475	0.250	0.775	0.000	
Environmental	0.075	0.075	0.300	0.475	0.250	0.775	0.000	
Financial	0.554	0.200	0.300	0.954	0.378	0.875	0.200	
Insurance and related	0.575	0.125	0.300	0.975	0.250	0.775	0.000	
Banking and other	0.533	0.275	0.300	0.933	0.506	0.975	0.400	
Health	0.408	0.075	0.300	0.475	0.250	0.775	0.000	
Tourism	0.275	0.075	0.300	0.808	0.317	0.775	0.000	
Recreational	0.075	0.075	0.300	0.475	0.250	0.775	0.000	
Transport	0.283	0.131	0.300	0.975	0.250	0.780	0.025	

Note: The higher the score, the greater the degree to which an industry is restricted. The maximum score is 100 percent. Because of data constraints on the value of output by sector, the indexes shown are based on simple averages of the sub-sectors involved in the individual economies.

Source: Adapted from Holmes and Hardin (2000, pp. 63-64).

4.1.3. *McGuire and Schuele*

Table 2 indicated the restriction categories and weights applied to banking services in the study by McGuire and Schuele (2000), which is based on a variety of data sources (pp. 202-03), including the GATS schedules of commitments and a number of other reports and documentation pertaining to actual financial-sector restrictions in 38 economies for the period 1995-98. McGuire and Schuele (pp. 204-05) have assigned scores for different degrees of restriction, ranging between 0 (least restrictive) and 1 (most restrictive). The various categories are weighted judgmentally in terms of how great the costs involved are assumed to be with respect to the effect on economic efficiency. Thus, it can be seen in Table 2 that restrictions on the licensing of banks are taken to be more burdensome than restrictions on the movement of people. Also, the scores are given separately for the restrictions applicable only to foreign banks and the "domestic" restrictions applicable to all banks. The differences between the foreign and domestic measures can then be interpreted as indicating the discrimination imposed on foreign banks. Finally, it will be noted that the foreign scores sum to a maximum of 1 and the domestic scores to a maximum of 0.808, because some of the restrictions noted apply only to foreign banks and not to domestic banks.

Based on detailed information available, the scores for banking restrictions in individual economies can be constructed. Using the category weights in Table 2, it is then possible to calculate "indexes of restrictiveness" of the foreign and domestic regulations by economy. These indexes are depicted graphically for selected Asia-Pacific economies, South Africa, and Turkey in Figure 4 and for Western Hemisphere economies in Figure 5. India, Indonesia, Malaysia, and the Philippines can be seen to have relatively high foreign index scores, Korea, Singapore, Thailand, and Turkey have moderate foreign index scores, and Australia, Hong Kong, Japan, New Zealand, and South Africa have the lowest foreign index scores. The domestic index scores are indicative of the restrictions applied both to domestic and foreign banks, and it appears that the domestic index scores are highest for Japan, Korea, Malaysia, and the Philippines.

While the absolute values of the foreign and domestic index scores are not reported, the differences in the scores can be interpreted visually as a measurement of the discrimination applied to foreign banks. Thus, in Figure 4, India, Indonesia, Korea, Malaysia, the Philippines, Singapore, Thailand, and Turkey appear to have the highest discrimination against foreign banks. In Figure 5, Brazil, Chile, and Uruguay have the highest foreign index scores, Colombia, Mexico, and Venezuela have moderate scores, and Argentina, Canada, and the

Figure 4 Restrictiveness Indexes for Selected Asia-Pacific Economies, South Africa, and Turkey

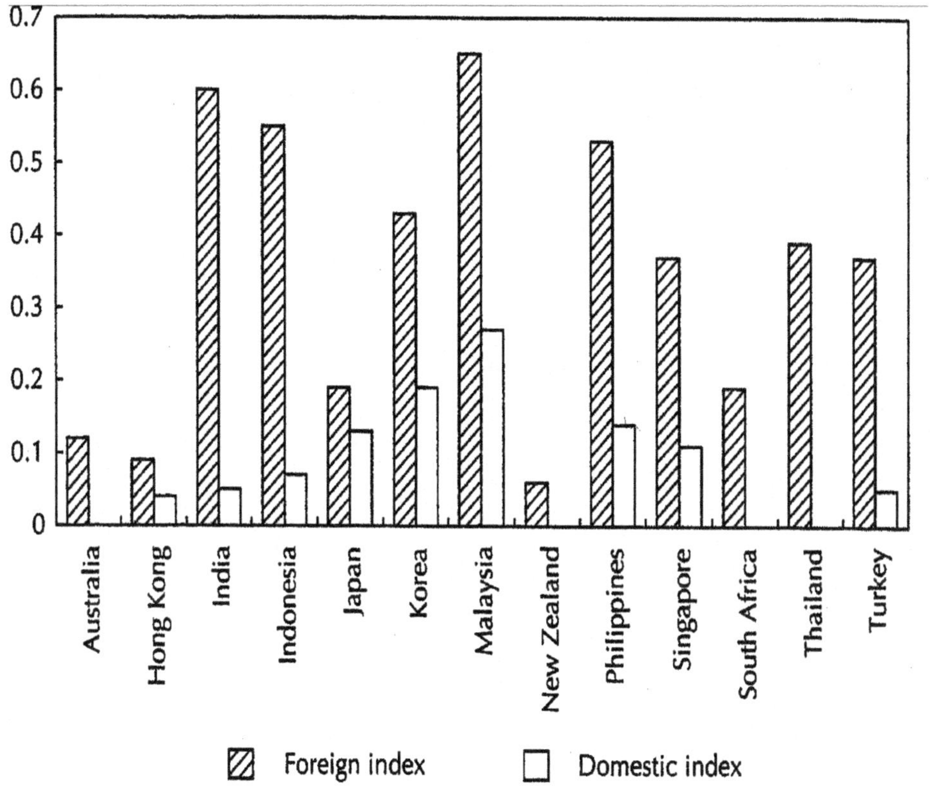

Note: The higher the score the more restrictive an economy; scores range from 0 to 1.

Source: McGuire and Schuele (2000, p. 211)

Figure 5 Restrictiveness Indexes for Selected Western Hemisphere Economies

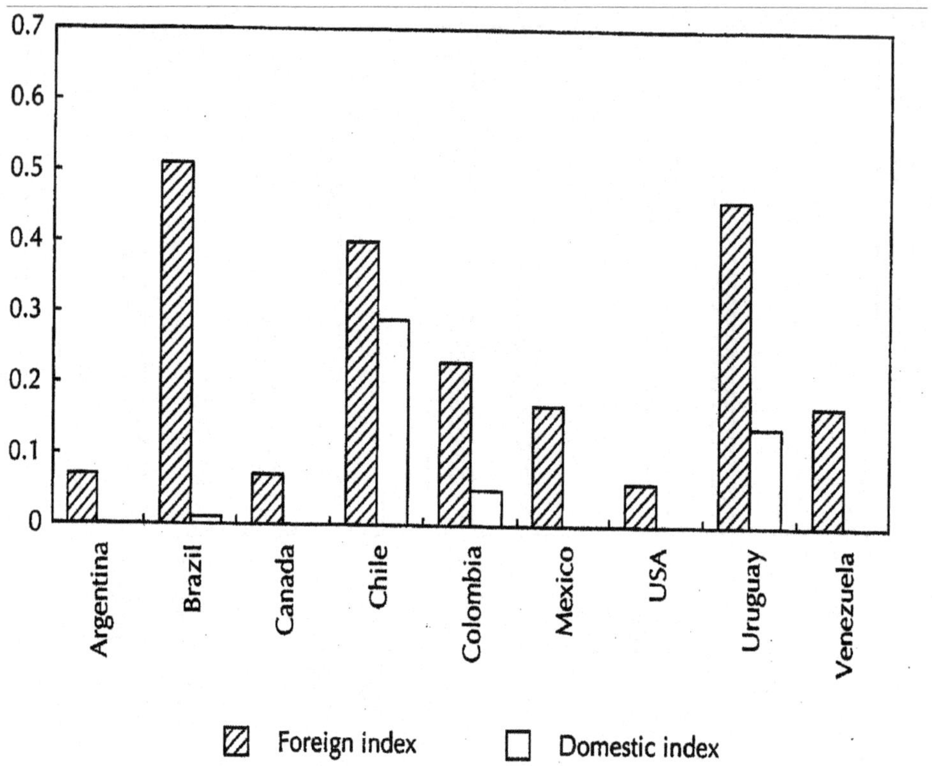

Note: The higher the score the more restrictive an economy; scores range from 0 to 1.

Source: McGuire and Schuele (2000, p. 211).

United States have the lowest scores. Chile and Uruguay have the highest domestic index scores, while Argentina, Canada, Mexico, the United States, and Venezuela have domestic index scores of zero. Brazil, Colombia, and Uruguay have the most discriminatory regimes against foreign banks.[15] McGuire and Schuele (2000, pp. 212-13) further found that economies with less restricted banking sectors tended to have higher GNP *per capita*.

The frequency measures and indexes of restriction that we have discussed thus far are especially useful in identifying the types of barriers and the relative degrees of protection afforded to particular services sectors across economies. In

[15] The detailed scores for the components of the domestic and foreign banking restrictions are broken down by individual economies and are available on the Productivity Commission website.

Appendix A below, we review briefly some other studies that are based on measurements of this type. It is evident accordingly that there exists a considerable amount of information on barriers covering a wide variety of services sectors, including financial services, telecommunications, accountancy, distribution, air transport, and electricity supply. As such, the compilation of such measurements and construction of such indexes are important first steps that can provide the basis for the next step, which involves using available methodologies to assess the economic effects of maintaining or eliminating the barriers.

4.2. *Price-Impact Measurements*[16]

As discussed above, the nature of services tends to prevent the use of price and quantity differences across borders to measure their presence or size. Therefore, in order to construct measurements of the price and/or quantity effects of barriers to trade in services, some other approach is needed.

The simplest is just to make an informed guess. For example, having constructed a frequency ratio for offers to liberalize services trade in the GATS as discussed above, Hoekman (1995,1996) then assumed that failure to liberalize in a sector would be equivalent to some particular tariff level that he selected using knowledge of the sector. These maximum tariff equivalents ranged from a high of 200 percent for sectors in which market access was essentially prohibited in most economies (*e.g.*, maritime cabotage, air transport, postal services, voice telecommunications, and life insurance) to 20-50 percent for sectors in which market access was less constrained. He then applied his frequency-ratio measurements of liberalization to these maximum tariffs to construct tariff equivalents that differed by economy based on their offers in the GATS. Thus, for example, assuming a benchmark tariff equivalent of, say, 200 percent for postal services, and a frequency ratio of 40 percent to reflect an economy's scheduled market access commitments, the tariff equivalent for that sector and economy is set at $200 - 0.4(200) = 120$ percent.

Using the value of output by sector for a representative industrialized economy, it is then possible to construct weighted average measurements by sector and economy. The resulting weighted-average tariff equivalent "guesstimates" for 1-digit International Standard Industrial Classification (ISIC) sectors for selected economies are indicated in Table 6. It can be seen that the tariff equivalents are highest for ISIC 7, Transportation, Storage &

[16] See Bosworth, Findlay, Trewin, and Warren (2000) for a useful methodological discussion of the construction and interpretation of price-impact measurements of impediments to services trade.

Table 6. Constructed Ad Valorem tariff equivalent "guesstimates" by 1-digit ISIC services sectors for selected economies (Percentage)

Economy	ISIC 5 Construction	ISIC 6 Wholesale & Retail Distr.	ISIC 7 Transp., Storage & Communic.	ISIC 8 Business & Fin. Services	ISIC 9 Social & Personal Services
Australia	12.0	7.4	183.4	24.8	25.4
Austria	5.0	4.6	98.7	20.1	13.9
Canada	6.0	9.0	117.7	25.9	40.2
Chile	40.0	34.4	182.2	45.2	42.9
European Union	10.0	10.0	182.0	27.2	23.6
Finland	19.0	14.6	181.0	23.8	31.7
Hong Kong	32.0	31.5	149.8	39.0	42.9
Japan	5.0	4.6	142.0	28.9	32.3
Korea	16.0	21.4	164.9	36.3	40.7
Mexico	24.0	21.3	152.3	40.9	29.8
New Zealand	5.0	13.4	181.5	30.5	36.1
Norway	5.0	13.4	122.2	25.7	24.0
Singapore	12.0	34.4	138.8	35.9	33.7
Sweden	12.0	13.4	184.2	22.5	26.9
Switzerland	5.0	8.0	178.1	27.7	32.3
Turkey	5.0	34.4	31.6	35.4	35.9
United States	5.0	4.6	111.4	21.7	31.7

Source: Hoekman (1995, pp. 355-56).

Communication, reflecting the significant constraints applied within this sector. There is also considerable variation within the individual sectors for the relatively highly industrialized economies listed in Table 6.

It should be emphasized that Hoekman's measurements are designed to indicate only the *relative* degree of restriction. We refer to them as "guesstimates," which are not to be taken literally as indicators of absolute ad valorem tariff equivalents. That is, the tariff equivalent benchmarks are just judgmental and are not distinguished according to their economic impact. Further, the benchmarks include only market access restrictions and cover all of the different modes of service delivery.

An improved approach that has been used in more recent studies is to combine other data together with an index or proxy measures of restrictiveness in order to estimate econometrically the effects of barriers. For example, suppose that an index of restrictiveness has been constructed for a group of economies, and that price data are also available for the services involved in this same group. Using knowledge and data on the economic determinants of these prices, an econometric model can be formulated to explain them. Then, if the restrictiveness index and/or proxy measures of restrictiveness are included in this equation as additional explanatory variables, the estimated coefficient(s) will measure the effect of the trade restrictions on prices, controlling for the other determinants of prices that have been included in the model.

Use of this method of course requires data on more than just the barriers themselves, including prices and other relevant determinants of prices. However, these additional data may be needed for only a subset of the economies for which the restrictiveness measures have been constructed, so long as one can assume that the effects of restrictions may be common across economies. The coefficients relating restrictiveness to prices can be estimated for a subset of economies for which the requisite data are available, and the estimated coefficients can then be applied to the other economies as well.

An example of this approach may be found in the study of the international air passenger transport industry by Doove *et al.* (2001, Chapter 2), which is summarized in Appendix A. They built on work by Gonenc and Nicoletti (2001), who had constructed an index of restrictiveness for this industry in the manner already discussed, and who had also used an econometric model to estimate the effects of restrictiveness for a group of 13 OECD economies. Doove *et al.* extended the index of restrictiveness to a larger set of 35 OECD and non-OECD economies and applied this estimated coefficient to calculate price effects.

The estimating equation used for this was the following:

$$\dot{p} = \alpha + \beta BRI + \gamma E + \varepsilon \tag{1}$$

where $\dot{p}$ represents the price of air travel over a particular route, BRI is the index of restrictiveness for that route, and E is a vector of variables for the determinants of prices, including indexes of market structure both for the route and at the route ends, measurements of airport conditions, government control, and propensity for air travel. The coefficients, α, β, and γ, are to be estimated econometrically, while ε is the disturbance term. The price variable $\dot{p}$ in this equation is of some interest, since it demonstrates the not uncommon need to model particular features of a service industry. It is based on a separate analysis of international airfares, relating them to distance and to other route-specific variables. The price that is entered in equation (1) is then the percentage that the actual airfare lies above the price predicted from this analysis.

Thus, holding this predicted price constant as unaffected by a particular trade restriction, the estimated coefficient β measures the percentage by which the price – air fare in this case – is increased by a restrictiveness of one, compared to the price at a restrictiveness of zero. Applying this estimated coefficient to the values of the index of restrictiveness for the larger set of economies, Doove *et al.*

produced the price-effect estimates reported in Table 7. As can be seen, these tend to be largest for developing economies and for business travel.

Other studies have been done using variations on this technique. These variations include the use of separate indexes of restrictiveness or proxy measures for different types of trade barriers, including individual modes of supply. A number of these other studies of price impacts of services restrictions are summarized in Appendix A below. These studies cover several sectors, including international air services, wholesale and retail food distributors, banks, maritime services, engineering services, telecommunications, and industrial electricity supply in both developed and developing economies. These various sectors are evidently distinctive in terms of their economic characteristics and the regulatory measures that affect their operations. Specialized knowledge of the sectors is thus essential in designing the conceptual framework and adapting the available data to calculate the price impacts of the regulatory measures involved.

4.3. *Quantity-Impact Measurements*

Another approach, appropriate for some service industries, is to model the determination of quantity rather than price, and then to include the trade restrictiveness index in a quantity equation. The result, analogous to that for prices above, is an estimate of effects of trade barriers on quantities. This can in turn be converted into an effect on prices by use of an assumed or an estimated price elasticity of demand.[17]

For example, Warren (2000b) has assessed the quantitative impact of barriers in telecommunications services, chiefly mobile telephony and fixed network services, for 136 economies. For this purpose he estimated equations such as the following, which was for mobile telephony:

$$Q_i^m = \alpha + \beta_1 Y_i + \beta_2 Y_i^2 + \beta_3 PD_i + \beta_4 [P_i^m] + \varepsilon_i \qquad (2)$$

Here, for each economy *i*, Q_i^m is the number of cellular telephone subscribers *per* 100 inhabitants, Y_i is GDP *per capita*, and PD_i is population density. $[P_i^m]$ is a policy variable, which for mobile telephony took two forms: an index of market access for investment in the industry based on number of competitors, privatization, and policies towards competition; and a broader average of several trade and investment-related indexes.

---

[17] That is, having estimated that barriers reduce the quantity of a service by some percentage, this is divided by the elasticity of demand to obtain the percentage price increase to which it corresponds.

Table 7. International air passenger transport: Bilateral restriction indexes and price impacts

	Number of Agreements/Routes	Bilateral Restriction Index[a]	Price Impacts[b]		
			Business	Economy	Discount
		Asia Pacific economies			
Australia	24	0.62	146.0	54.8	14.6
India	20	0.77	164.4	81.3	21.8
Indonesia	16	0.73	139.7	53.0	20.4
Japan	29	0.73	121.1	41.4	18.1
Korea	18	0.72	181.5	89.9	20.4
Malaysia	22	0.71	199.1	95.6	18.4
New Zealand	15	0.39	82.1	66.8	11.7
Philippines	20	0.79	207.5	70.1	20.9
Singapore	30	0.70	141.5	57.5	16.8
Thailand	25	0.68	124.5	71.3	16.2
Americas economies					
Argentina	12	0.74	161.7	62.0	17.5
Brazil	19	0.70	195.5	63.9	15.5
Canada	29	0.60	114.5	56.9	11.4
Chile	17	0.61	125.2	49.5	12.9
Mexico	19	0.82	224.7	92.2	18.4
Uruguay	32	0.52	96.9	38.5	12.3
USA	32	0.40	52.9	33.2	8.9
		European economies			
Austria	28	0.32	47.2	20.6	6.1
Belgium	31	0.36	63.3	22.0	6.9
Denmark	30	0.34	53.1	21.1	7.0
Finland	22	0.23	33.6	11.5	3.8
France	32	0.35	57.0	20.8	8.3
Germany	32	0.37	56.5	20.3	8.1
Greece	26	0.31	72.1	24.9	7.2
Ireland	23	0.21	32.2	20.1	4.5
Italy	25	0.29	49.9	18.5	6.4
Luxembourg	23	0.24	36.9	15.0	4.2
Netherlands	31	0.39	104.0	20.0	10.0
Norway	28	0.32	62.1	16.4	4.4
Portugal	21	0.14	45.5	20.3	6.1
Spain	31	0.36	68.0	25.4	8.9
Sweden	29	0.32	45.5	20.3	6.1
Switzerland	32	0.75	102.5	42.6	13.8
Turkey	20	0.56	98.8	32.2	10.7
United Kingdom	32	0.30	46.3	21.5	7.6

[a] Unweighted average of the route-level bilateral restriction indexes for each economy based on the number of agreements/routes shown in the preceding column. Ranges from 0 to 0.97, with a higher score indicating more restrictions.

[b] Percentage increase in airfares compared to the benchmark regime.

Source: Doove *et al.* (2001, p. 39).

Combining these quantitative estimates of the effects of removing existing barriers with an estimate of the price elasticity of demand for the telecommunications services involved, tariff equivalents in the form of price wedges were calculated. The tariff equivalents for domestic and for foreign providers of telecommunication services in the major nations are shown in Table 8. The estimates for the advanced industrialized economies are relatively low in comparison to the much higher estimates for the newly industrializing economies shown. There are cases of developing economies (not shown) that in some cases have very large tariff equivalents, including some with several hundred percent, *e.g.*, China (804 and 1,000 percent), Colombia (11 percent and 24 percent), India (861 and 1,000 percent), Indonesia (71 and 128 percent), South Africa (14 and 21 percent), and Venezuela (10 and 15 percent).

Table 8. Tariff equivalents of barriers to telecommunication services in major nations (Percentage)

	Domestic	Foreign
Australia	0.31	0.31
Austria	0.85	0.85
Belgium	0.65	1.31
Brazil	3.81	5.68
Canada	1.07	3.37
Chile	1.68	1.68
Hong Kong	1.26	1.26
Colombia	10.55	24.27
Denmark	0.20	0.20
Finland	0.00	0.00
France	0.34	1.43
Germany	0.32	0.32
Ireland	1.46	2.67
Italy	1.00	1.00
Japan	0.26	0.26
Korea	4.30	8.43
Mexico	6.24	14.43
Netherlands	0.20	0.20
New Zealand	0.27	0.27
Singapore	2.10	2.72
Spain	2.03	3.93
Sweden	0.65	0.65
Switzerland	1.23	1.23
Turkey	19.59	33.53
United Kingdom	0.00	0.00
United States	0.20	0.20

Source: Adapted from Warren (2000b).

4.4. *Gravity-Model Estimates*

Because the modeling of prices that is needed to estimate a price effect above is necessarily very sector specific, the techniques described so far have limited use for quantifying barriers across sectors. Likewise, they are not useful for comparing the overall levels of service trade barriers across economies. For that, one needs a more general model of trade to use as a benchmark, and the natural choice is the so-called gravity model. This model relates bilateral trade volumes positively to the incomes of both trading partners, and also negatively to the distance between them.[18] It has become a very popular tool in recent years for eliciting the effects of a wide variety of policy and structural influences on trade in a manner that controls for the obvious importance of income and distance.

Francois (1999) has fit a gravity model to bilateral services trade for the United States and its major trading partners, taking Hong Kong and Singapore to be free trade benchmarks. The independent variables, in addition to distance between trading partners, included *per capita* income, gross domestic product (GDP), and a Western Hemisphere dummy variable. The differences between actual and predicted imports were taken to be indicative of trade barriers and were then normalized relative to the free trade benchmarks for Hong Kong and Singapore. Combining this with an assumed demand elasticity of 4, tariff equivalents can be estimated. The results for business/financial services and for construction are indicated in Table 9. Brazil has the highest estimated tariff equivalent for business/financial services (35.7 percent), followed by Japan, China, Other South Asia, and Turkey at about 20 percent. The estimated tariff equivalents are considerably higher for construction services, in the 40-60 percent range for China, South Asia, Brazil, Turkey, Central Europe, Russia, and South Africa, and in the 10-30 percent range for the industrialized economies. Further details are given in Appendix A on the limitations of the use and interpretation of gravity models.

4.5. *Financial-Based Measurements*

Hoekman (2000) has suggested that financial data on gross operating margins calculated by sector and economy may provide information about the effects of

[18] Typically, the log of the volume of total bilateral trade between two economies is regressed on the logs of their national incomes, the log of distance between them, and other variables such as *per capita* income and dummy variables to reflect a common border, common language, *etc.*

Table 9. Estimated tariff equivalents in traded services: gravity-model based regression method

(Percentage)

Economies/regions	**Business/financial services**	**Construction**
North America+	8.2	9.8
Western Europe	8.5	18.3
Australia and New Zealand	6.9	24.4
Japan	19.7	29.7
China	18.8	40.9
Chinese Taipei	2.6	5.3
Other Newly Industrialized Economies	2.1	10.3
Indonesia	6.8	9.6
Other South East Asia	5.0	17.7
India	13.1	61.6
Other South Asia*	20.4	46.3
Brazil	35.7	57.2
Other Latin America	4.7	26.0
Turkey*	20.4	46.3
Other Middle East and North Africa	4.0	9.5
CEECs & Russia	18.4	51.9
South Africa	15.7	42.1
Other Sub-Saharan Africa	0.3	11.1
Rest of World (ROW)	20.4	46.3

* Turkey and Other South Asia are not available, separately, in the U.S. data, and have been assigned estimated ROW values.

\+ North America values involve assigning Canada/Mexico numbers to the United States.

Source: Francois (1999).

government policies on firm entry and conditions of competition.[19] As he notes (p. 36):

> "In general, a large number of factors will determine the ability of firms to generate high margins, including market size (number of firms), the business cycle, the state of competition, policy enforcement, the substitutability of products, fixed costs, *etc.* Notwithstanding the impossibility of inferring that high margins are due to high barriers, there should be a correlation between the two across economies for any given sector. Data on operating margins provide some sense of the relative profitability of activities, and therefore, the relative magnitude (restrictiveness) of barriers to entry/exit that may exist."

[19] Gross operating margins are defined as total sales revenue minus total average costs divided by total average costs.

The economy-region results of Hoekman's analysis, averaged over firms and sectors for 1994-96, are indicated for agriculture, manufacturing, and services in Table 10. Sectoral results for services only are given in Table 11. Services margins are generally higher than manufacturing margins by 10-15 percentage points, and the services margins vary considerably across economies. Australia, Hong Kong, and Singapore have the lowest services margins – in the neighborhood of 20 percent – while Chile, China, Indonesia, Philippines, Chinese Taipei, Thailand, and the United States have services margins in excess of 40 percent. The sectoral results indicate that the margins for hotels and financial services are relatively high, and the margins for wholesale and retail trade are lower. The margins for several developing economies appear to be relatively high in a number of sectors. Overall, as Hoekman suggests (p. 39):

> "...business services, consultancy, and distribution do not appear to be among the most protected sectors. ...barriers to competition are higher in transportation, finance, and telecommunications. These are also basic 'backbone' imports that are crucial for the ability of enterprises to compete internationally."

Table 10. Average gross operating margins of firms listed on national stock exchanges, 1994-96 by economy/region

(Percentage)

Economy/Region	Agriculture	Manufacturing	Services
Australia	8.4	15.5	16.6
Canada	32.1	22.6	32.9
Chile	39.1	40.8	44.0
China	30.6	28.1	49.5
European Union	22.9	23.8	31.6
Hong Kong	25.9	12.8	18.1
Indonesia	41.8	34.3	41.3
Japan	38.4	26.4	28.7
Republic of Korea	11.2	25.7	25.8
Malaysia	22.6	6.0	21.6
Mexico	38.4	39.3	37.2
New Zealand	33.3	16.6	26.8
Philippines	18.1	28.6	42.3
Singapore	0.0	11.1	22.0
Chinese Taipei	19.6	25.1	41.3
Thailand	38.2	27.3	52.6
United States	36.6	21.2	42.3
Rest of Cairns Group[a]	36.3	31.1	39.0

[a] Includes Argentina, Brazil, and Colombia.

Source: Hoekman (2000). Based on calculations using Disclosure, Worldscope (1998) data.

Table 11. Average gross operating margins of services firms listed on national stock exchanges, 1994-96, by economy/region and by sector (Percentage)

Economy/Region	Recreation	Business Services	Construction	Consulting	Finance	Health	Hotels	Retail Trade	Wholesale	Transport/ Utilities
Australia	17.9	13.8	15.3	7.0	41.0	b	27.3	7.9	9.1	c
Canada	60.1	51.7	14.4	19.2	44.5	2.3	67.8	12.0	16.0	36.5
Chile	b	b	68.7	b	55.2	b	b	21.3	27.9	46.8
China	b	b	45.9	67.1	34.0	b	77.5	24.4	25.5	46.9
European Union	42.5	32.1	19.3	22.1	51.6	22.3	23.7	23.6	19.9	32.6
Hong Kong	b	6.5	12.9	11.5	25.4	b	31.3	10.1	6.9	31.0
Indonesia	b	81.1	22.9	25.3	53.6	b	68.2	26.4	24.8	45.3
Japan	28.1	31.6	14.2	28.6	40.5	40.1	27.2	32.9	15.6	20.6
Republic of Korea	b	41.2	15.3	b	b	b	b	26.7	14.9	31.2
Malaysia	13.3	c	18.3	14.7	28.3	24.3	38.7	11.2	10.8	30.7
Mexico	19.6	b	25.7	37.3	33.3	b	49.6	28.4	25.0	51.0
New Zealand	b	b	13.8	b	57.6	b	26.9	6.6	19.7	35.6
Philippines	19.9	b	40.2	b	53.9	b	55.8	43.9	40.3	42.3
Singapore	46.7	8.6	10.6	7.7	46.3	29.2	28.2	5.4	7.9	28.0
Chinese Taipei	79.9	36.3	21.6	11.1	64.8	b	74.5	21.5	23.2	38.9
Thailand	85.4	35.8	38.1	c	60.3	40.6	55.5	44.2	25.6	56.7
United States	46.8	56.2	20.2	c	56.3	37.0	48.5	34.6	27.0	43.4
Other Cairns[a]	b	B	28.9	26.2	69.8	29.3	64.6	24.2	22.9	52.4

[a] Includes Argentina, Brazil, and Colombia.

[b] Data not available.

[c] Reflects negative gross operating margin.

Source: Hoekman (2000). Based on calculations using Disclosure, Worldscope (1998) data.

4.6. *Diversity of Methods*

As should be clear from the foregoing, studies of services barriers have used a wide variety of approaches. This is not surprising given the wide variety of the service industries themselves and the variation across them in the data that may be available. In our concluding section, below, we will outline the steps that seem to have been most commonly used and/or successful in the largest number of studies, as a guide to those who intend to replicate their work in other industries and economies. However, it will often be the case that one or more of these steps cannot be followed in particular cases. Research on services barriers must therefore often make do with whatever information may be available. As illustrated by the studies discussed here, this may require creative exploitation of seemingly heroic assumptions in order to extract any information at all.

5. Measuring the Economic Consequences of Liberalizing Services Barriers

Issues to be Addressed:
- Sectoral modeling
- CGE modeling

While the various measurements of services barriers that we have reviewed are of interest in themselves, they need to be incorporated into an explicit economic modeling framework in order to determine how the existence or removal of the barriers will affect conditions of competition, productivity, the allocation of resources, and economic welfare within or between sectors and economies. In this regard, a modeling framework can be devised for individual sectors or on an economy-wide basis using computable general equilibrium (CGE) modeling.

5.1. *Sectoral Modeling*

An example of sectoral modeling is provided by Fink, Mattoo, and Rathindram (2003), who analyze the impact of policy reform on sectoral performance in basic telecommunications. Their data cover 86 developing economies globally for the period, 1985-1999. They address three questions, covering the impact of: (1) policy changes relating to ownership, competition, and regulation; (2) any one policy reform coupled with the implementation of complementary reforms; and (3) the sequencing of reforms.

Their findings are: (1) privatization and the introduction of competition significantly increase labor productivity and the density of telecommunication mainlines; (2) privatization and competition work best through their interactions; and (3) there are more favorable effects from introducing competition before privatization. They further conclude that autonomous technological progress outweighs the effects of policy reforms in increasing the growth of teledensity.

What is especially noteworthy about this type of study is its focus on both the policy and market structure of the sector and the econometric framework that is designed to measure the determinants of teledensity and telecommunications productivity. The assessment of particular services barriers may therefore be most effectively addressed when incorporated into a sectoral modeling framework.[20]

5.2. *CGE Modeling*

In contrast to sectoral modeling, CGE modeling provides a framework for multi-sectoral and multi-economy analysis of the economic effects of services barriers and related policies. Most CGE modeling research to date has been focused on barriers to international trade in goods rather than trade in services and FDI. The reasons for this stem in large part from the lack of comprehensive data on cross-border services trade and FDI and the associated barriers, together with the difficult conceptual problems of modeling that are encountered. Some indication of pertinent CGE modeling work relating to services is provided in Hardin and Holmes (1996, p. 85), Brown and Stern (2001, pp. 272-74), and Stern (2002, pp. 254-56). The approaches to modeling can be divided as follows: (1) analysis of cross-border services trade liberalization in response to reductions in services barriers; (2) modeling in which FDI is assumed to result from trade liberalization or other exogenous changes that generate international capital flows in the form of FDI in response to changes in rates of return; and (3) modeling of links between multinational corporations' (MNCs) parents and affiliates and distinctions between foreign and domestic firms in a given economy/region.

The third type of CGE modeling study just noted comes closest to capturing the important role played especially by MNCs and their foreign affiliates in providing Mode 3-type services. This, for example, is the focus of the study by Brown and Stern (2001), some details of which are presented in Appendix A below. Brown and Stern analyze the effects of removal of services barriers under alternative conditions of international capital mobility and changes in the world

---

[20] See also Fink, Mattoo, and Neagu (2002) and Appendix A below for a summary of their study of the importance of restrictive trade policies and private anti-competitive practices relating to international maritime services.

capital stock due to increased investment. Their results, presented in Table A-7, suggest that the welfare effects of removing services barriers are sizable and vary across economies depending on how international capital movements and changes in domestic investment respond to changes in rates of return. The largest potential benefits are realized for all of the major developed and developing economies when allowance is made for changes in investment that augment the stock of capital.

6. Guideline Principles and Recommended Procedures for Measuring Services Barriers and for Assessing the Consequences of Their Liberalization

As a summary of what we have reported in detail here about the methodologies for measuring services barriers and using these measurements to assess the consequences of liberalization in services, we conclude first with several principles to be kept in mind during this process and then with more detailed procedural steps that we recommend should be followed:

Principles:

1. Most barriers to trade and investment in services take the form of domestic regulations, rather than measures at the border.
2. No single methodology is sufficient for documenting and measuring barriers to trade in services. Instead, investigators need to draw upon all available information, including both direct observation of particular barriers and indirect inference of barriers using data on prices and quantities.
3. Because of the special role of incumbent firms in many service industries, regulations do not need to be explicitly discriminatory against foreign firms in order to have discriminatory effects.

Procedures:

1. Collect the details of domestic regulations and related policies affecting services firms in the economies and/or sectors being examined, including the manner in which they apply to foreign *versus* domestic firms, plus quantitative details of their application, such as any percentage or dollar limits that they impose.
2. Ideally, this information should be collected by systematic surveys of governments and/or firms. However, it may also be possible to infer it less

directly from documents prepared for other purposes, such as the commitments that governments made to the GATS in the Uruguay Round and subsequent negotiations.

3. For each type of regulation or policy, define degrees of restrictiveness and assign scores to each, ranging from zero for least restrictive to one for most restrictive.
4. Construct a measure of restrictiveness by: weighting the scores from step 3 based on judgments of the relative importance of each policy; using a statistical methodology such as factor analysis that will serve to identify the weights; or designing proxy measures, such as dummy variables, to represent particular restrictions. The resulting measures can then be used directly for reporting the presence and importance of barriers across industries and economies, as well as for providing an input to subsequent analysis.
5. Convert the measures of restrictiveness from step 4 into a set of tariff equivalents by one or more of the following methods. Depending on the quality of information that goes into their construction, these tariff equivalents may be superior to the measures themselves for reporting about barriers and analyzing their effects.

   a. Assign judgmental tariff-equivalent values to each of the component measures, representing the percentage taxes on foreign suppliers to which each component is thought to correspond at their most restrictive levels (index = 1).

   b. Use data on prices and their determinants as the basis for a regression model that includes an index or other measures of restrictiveness and that estimates the effect on prices.

   c. Use data on quantities produced or traded as the basis for a regression model that includes an index or other measures of restrictiveness and that estimates the effect on quantities. This estimate can then be converted to tariff equivalents using an assumed or estimated price elasticity of demand.
6. Use an index or other measures of restrictiveness or the tariff equivalents constructed above as inputs into a model of production and trade in order to ascertain the effects of changes in the barriers to which they correspond. The appropriate model for this purpose depends on whether sectoral or economy-wide policy changes are to be analyzed. For economy-wide policy changes, the model should be a general equilibrium one, incorporating the full effects of barriers across sectors and economies. Ideally, too, the model should be designed to capture the effects of service regulations in the form that they have been observed and quantified as above.

References

1. Anderson, James E. 1979 "A Theoretical Foundation for the Gravity Equation," *American Economic Review* 69, (March), pp. 106-116.
2. Bosworth, Malcolm, Christopher Findlay, Ray Trewin, and Tony Warren. 2000. "Price-impact Measures of Impediments to Services Trade," in Christopher Findlay and Tony Warren (eds.), *Impediments to Trade in Services: Measurement and Policy Implications*. London and New York: Routledge.
3. Boylaud, O. and G. Nicoletti. 2000. "Regulation, Market Structure and Performance in Telecommunications," Working Paper No. 237ECO/WKP (2000), 10, Economics Department, OECD, Paris, 12 April.
4. Brown, Drusilla and Robert M. Stern. 2001. "Measurement and Modeling of the Economic Effects of Trade and Investment Barriers in Services," *Review of International Economics* 9:262-86
5. Colecchia, Alessandra. 2000. "Measuring Barriers to Market Access for Services: A Pilot Study on Accountancy Services," in Christopher Findlay and Tony Warren (eds.), *Impediments to Trade in Services: Measurement and Policy Implications*. London and New York: Routledge.
6. Deardorff, Alan V. "Determinants of Bilateral Trade: Does Gravity Work in a Neoclassical World?" in Jeffrey A. Frankel, ed., *The Regionalization of the World Economy*, Chicago: University of Chicago Press, 1998.
7. Deardorff, Alan V. and Robert M. Stern. 1998. *Measurement of Nontariff Barriers*. Ann Arbor: University of Michigan Press.
8. Dee, Philippa and Kevin Hanslow. 2001. "Multilateral Liberalization of Services Trade," in Robert M. Stern (ed.), *Services in the International Economy*. Ann Arbor: University of Michigan Press.
9. Dee, Philippa, Alexis Hardin, and Leanne Holmes. 2000. "Issues in the Application of CGE Models to Services Trade Liberalization," in Christopher Findlay and Tony Warren (eds.), Impediments to Trade in Services: Measurement and Policy Implications. London and New York: Routledge.
10. Disclosure. 1998. *Global Researcher – Worldschope Database*. Bethesda, Maryland: Disclosure.
11. Doove, Samantha, Owen Gaabbitas, Duc Nguyen-Hong, and Joe Owen. 2001. "Price Effects of Regulation: Telecommunications, Air Passenger Transport and Electricity Supply," Productivity Commission Staff Research Paper, AusInfo, Canberra (October).
12. Findlay, Christopher and Tony Warren (eds.). 2000. *Impediments to Trade in Services: Measurement and Policy Implications*. London and New York: Routledge.
13. Fink, Carsten, Aaditya Mattoo, and Ileana Cristina Neagu. 2002. "Trade in International Maritime Services: How Much Does Policy Matter?" *World Bank Economic Review* 16:81-108.
14. Fink, Carsten, Aaditya Mattoo, and Randeep Rathindran. 2003. "An Assessment of Telecommunications Reform in Developing Countries," *Information Economics and Policy* 15:443-66.
15. Francois, Joseph. 1999. "Estimates of Barriers to Trade in Services," Erasmus University, unpublished manuscript.

16. Gonenc, R. and G. Nicoletti. 2001. "Regulation, Market Structure and Performance in Air Passenger Transportation," OECD Economic Studies, No. 32, OECD, Paris.
17. Hardin, Alexis and Leanne Holmes. 1997. *Services Trade and Foreign Direct Investment.* Staff Research Paper, Industry Commission. Canberra: Australian Government Publishing Services.
18. Hoekman, Bernard. 1995. "Assessing the General Agreement on Trade in Services," in Will Martin and L. Alan Winters (eds.), *The Uruguay Round and the Developing Countries*, World Bank Discussion Paper No. 307. Washington, D.C.: The World Bank. Revised version published in Will Martin and L. Alan Winters (eds.), Cambridge University Press, 1996.
19. Hoekman, Bernard. 2000. "The Next Round of Services Negotiations: Identifying Priorities and Options," *Federal Reserve Bank of St. Louis Review* 82:31-47.
20. Hoekman, Bernard and Carlos A. Primo Braga. 1997. "Protection and Trade in Services: A Survey," *Open Economies Review* 8:285-308.
21. Holmes, Leanne and Alexis Hardin. 2000. "Assessing Barriers to Services Sector Investment," in Christopher Findlay and Tony Warren (eds.), *Impediments to Trade in Services: Measurement and Policy Implications*. London and New York: Routledge.
22. Johnson, Martin, Tendar Gregan, Geraldine Gentle, and Paul Belin. 2000. "Modeling the Benefits of Increasing Competition in International Air Services," in Christopher Findlay and Tony Warren (eds.), *Impediments to Trade in Services: Measurement and Policy Implications*. London and New York: Routledge
23. Kalirajan, Kaleeswaran. 2000. "Restrictions on Trade in Distribution Services," Productivity Commission Staff Research Paper, AusInfo, Canberra (August).
24. Kalirajan, Kaleeswaran, Greg McGuire, Duc Nguyen-Hong, and Michael Schuele. 2000. "The Price Impact of Restrictions on Banking Services," in Christopher Findlay and Tony Warren (eds.), *Impediments to Trade in Services: Measurement and Policy Implications*. London and New York: Routledge.
25. Kang, Jong-Soon. 2000. "Price Impact of Restrictions on Maritime Transport Services," in Christopher Findlay and Tony Warren (eds.), *Impediments to Trade in Services: Measurement and Policy Implications*. London and New York: Routledge.
26. Karsenty, Guy. 2000. "Just How Big Are the Stakes? An Assessment of Trade in Services by Mode of Supply," in Pierre Sauvé and Robert M. Stern (eds.), Services 2000: *New Directions in Services Trade Liberalization*. Washington, D.C.: Brookings Institution.
27. Kemp, Steven. 2000. "Trade in Education Services and the Impacts of Barriers on Trade," in Christopher Findlay and Tony Warren (eds.), *Impediments to Trade in Services: Measurement and Policy Implications*. London and New York: Routledge.
28. Marko, M. 1998. "An Evaluation of the Basic Telecommunications Services Agreement, CIES Policy Discussion Paper 98/09, Centre for International Economic Studies, University of Adelaide.
29. Mattoo, Aaditya. 1998. "Financial Services and the WTO: Liberalization in the Developing and Transition Economies," for presentation at the Workshop, "Measuring Impediments to Trade in Services," Productivity Commission, Canberra, April 30 – May 1, 1998.
30. McGuire, Greg. 1998. *Australia's Restrictions on Trade in Financial Services*. Staff Research Paper, Productivity Commission, Canberra.

31. McGuire, Greg and Michael Schuele. 2000. "Restrictiveness of International Trade in Banking Services," in Christopher Findlay and Tony Warren (eds.), *Impediments to Trade in Services: Measurement and Policy Implications*. London
32. McGuire, Greg, Michael Schuele, and Tina Smith. 2000.. "Restrictiveness of International Trade in Maritime Services," in Christopher Findlay and Tony Warren (eds.), Impediments to Trade in Services: Measurement and Policy Implication. London and New York: Routledge.
33. Nguyen-Hong, Duc. 2000. "Restrictions on Trade in Professional Services," Productivity Commission, Staff Research Paper, Ausinfo, Canberra, August.
34. Nicoletti, G., S. Scarpetta, ad O. Boylaud. 2000. "Summary Indicators of Product Market Regulation with an Extension to Employment Protection Legislation," Working Paper No. 226, Economics Department, ECO/WKP(99)18, OECD, Paris, 13 April (revised).
35. Pacific Economic Cooperation Council (PECC). 1995. *Survey of Impediments to Trade and Investment in the APEC Region*. Singapore: PECC.
36. Steiner, F. 2000. "Regulation, Industry Structure and Performance in the Electricity Supply Industry," Working Paper No. 238, ECO/WKP (2000), Economics Department, OECD, Paris, 12 April.
37. Stern, Robert M. 2002. "Quantifying Barriers to Trade in Services," in Bernard Hoekman, Aaditya Mattoo, and Philip English (eds.) *Development, Trade, and the WTO: A Handbook*. Washington, D.C: The World Bank.
38. Trewin, Ray. 2000. "A Price-Impact Measure of Impediments to Trade in Telecommunications Services," in Christopher Findlay and Tony Warren (eds.), *Impediments to Trade in Services: Measurement and Policy Implications*. London and New York: Routledge.
39. United Nations Conference on Trade and Development (UNCTAD). 1996. *World Investment Report 1996: Investment, Trade and International Policy Arrangements*. New York and Geneva: UNCTAD.
40. Verikios, George and Xiao-guang Zhang. 2001. "Global Gains from Liberalising Trade in Telecommunications and Financial Services," Productivity Commission Staff Research Paper, AusInfo, Canberra (October).
41. Warren, Tony. 2000a. The Identification of Impediments to Trade and Investment in Telecommunications Services," in Christopher Findlay and Tony Warren (eds.), *Impediments to Trade in Services: Measurement and Policy Implications*. London and New York: Routledge.
42. Warren, Tony. 2000b. "The Impact on Output of Impediments t Trade and Investment in Telecommunications Services," in Christopher Findlay and Tony Warren (eds.), *Impediments to Trade in Services: Measurement and Policy Implications*. London and New York: Routledge.
43. Warren, Tony and Christopher Findlay. 2000. "How Significant Are the Barriers? Measuring Impediments to Trade in Services," in Pierre Sauvé and Robert M. Stern (eds.), *Services 2000: New Directions in Services Trade Liberalization*. Washington, D.C.: Brookings Institution.

Appendix A
Literature Summaries of Methods of Measurement

In this appendix, we provide a somewhat more technical discussion of the various methods of measurement of services barriers, focusing especially on available studies that have been completed and that can be consulted for more information on methodology and data and possible adaptation in further research.

A-1: Frequency Studies and Indexes of Restrictiveness

In what follows, we summarize several studies that complement our discussion in the main text:

- Mattoo (1998) analyzed market access commitments in **financial services**, covering direct insurance and banking. His results indicated that Latin America was the most restricted in direct insurance and Asia the most restricted in banking services.
- Marko (1998) constructed frequency measures for the basic **telecommunications** markets, using Hoekman's (1995) methodology. Marko found that 58 percent of the basic telecommunications services market for the 69 signatories of the February 1997 Agreement on Basic Telecommunications was covered by partial or full GATS commitments.
- McGuire (1998) showed that Australia's impediments in **financial services**, including banking, securities, and insurance, were much lower as compared to other economies in Asia.
- Colecchia (2000) provided a methodological, pilot study of the barriers on **accountancy services** for Australia, France, the United Kingdom, and the United States, using OECD information on regulatory regimes for 1997. The United Kingdom was found to be the most liberal, the United States the least liberal.
- Kalirajan (2000) constructed restrictiveness indexes for 38 economies, using GATS schedules and a variety of other information on barriers to **distribution services** as of June 1999. The indexes covered the services of commission agents, wholesalers, retailers, and franchisers. The findings were that: (1) Belgium, India, Indonesia, France, Korea, Malaysia, the Philippines, Switzerland, and Thailand were the most restrictive economies and Singapore and Hong Kong the most open; and (2) the economies that were the most discriminatory against foreign firms included Malaysia, the Philippines, Venezuela, Brazil, the United States, and Greece. The detailed domestic and

foreign restrictiveness indexes were broken down by economy and are available on the Productivity Commission website.

- Kemp (2000) constructed restrictiveness indexes for the four modes of providing **educational services**, using GATS data on commitments for market access and national treatment for the five sub-sectors of educational services and covering 29 economies. While only a quarter of GATS member economies scheduled commitments, the evidence suggested that consumption abroad, which is the major mode of educational trade in terms of foreign-student tuition, fees, and expenditures, was comparatively the least restricted mode.
- McGuire, Schuele, and Smith (2000) developed indexes for restrictions on foreign **maritime service** suppliers and all maritime service suppliers covering 35 economies during the period 1994-98, using a variety of GATS and other data sources. They found that: (1) Brazil, Chile, India, Indonesia, Korea, Malaysia, the Philippines, and the United States had the most restricted markets against foreign maritime suppliers; and (2) Chile, the Philippines, Thailand, Turkey, and the United States were the most discriminatory in favoring domestic suppliers. The detailed domestic and foreign indexes of restrictiveness were broken down by economy and are available on the Productivity Commission website.
- Nguyen-Hong (2000) constructed restrictiveness indexes for **accountancy, architectural, and engineering services** for 34 economies and legal services for 29 economies. The indexes were compiled from WTO, OECD, APEC, and a variety of other sources. The findings were that: (1) legal and accounting were the most highly restricted services; (2) Indonesia, Malaysia, Austria, Mexico, and Turkey were the most restrictive for the four professions, and Finland and the Netherlands the most open; (3) nationality requirements were the most extensive in legal and accountancy services; (4) residency requirements were common in accountancy services; (5) partnerships and practices between accountants and lawyers were commonly restricted; and (6) recognition of foreign qualifications and licenses was subject to a variety of restrictions among economies. The detailed domestic and foreign restrictiveness indexes were broken down and are available on the Productivity Commission website.
- Warren (2000a) used data for 136 economies from the International Telecommunications Union (ITU) to construct five indexes for the regulation of **telecommunications** policies that discriminate against: (1) all potential providers of cross-border telecommunications services; (2) foreign providers of cross-border services; (3) all potential providers of fixed network services;

(4) all potential providers of cellular services via FDI; and (5) foreign providers of mobile services via FDI. He found: (1) significant variation across economies in all five indexes; (2) most economies relied only on foreign carriers to provide competition in mobile markets; (3) economies were less prepared to use majority-owned foreign carriers in their fixed network markets; (4) economies that liberalized their mobile networks were more likely to liberalize their fixed networks; (5) economies that limited commercial presence via FDI were more liberal in permitting cross-border entry; and (6) GATS-based indexes that tended to reflect legal conditions, as calculated by Marko (1998), were not altogether well correlated with ITU-based indexes that were designed to reflect economic conditions. The detailed domestic and foreign indexes by economy are available on the Productivity Commission website.

- Doove, Gabbitas, Nguyen-Hong, and Owen (2001) constructed restrictiveness indexes for international air passenger transport, telecommunications, and electricity supply. The index for air **transport** was an average of the bilateral restrictiveness indexes applicable to pairs of economies. The data covered 875 airline routes for 35 economies and refered to the late 1990s. The bilateral restrictions included designation, capacity, fares, and charter services, with weights derived using factor analysis in an OECD study by Gonenc and Nicoletti (2001). The bilateral restrictions were generally not covered under the GATS, so that discriminatory restrictions on third economies may have been applied. The results are shown in column (2) of Table 7 and indicate substantial variation across economies as a consequence of the agreement-specific bilateral restrictions.
- The restrictiveness index for **telecommunications** covered 24 OECD member economies and 23 non-OECD economies, using data for 1997. The telecommunications industry has been undergoing rapid technological change in recent decades, and there has been widespread regulatory reform and structural reform undertaken in many economies. Doove *et al.* built upon the OECD study by Boylaud and Nicoletti (2000), who focused on the four major telecommunications sectors: trunk (domestic long distance); international (international long distance); mobile (cellular); and leased-line services. The regulatory measures covered include: market share of new entrants; index of governmental control of the public telecommunications operators (PTOs); degree of internationalization of domestic markets; time to liberalization; and time to privatization. These measurements were incorporated into an econometric framework for the individual sectors in order to estimate the price impacts involved that are noted in Table A-1.

Table A-1. Price impact of regulation on telecommunications prices, 1997 (Percent of Notional Price Existing under Benchmark Regulatory Regime)

Economy	Trunk	International	Mobile	Leasing	Industry-wide
OECD					
Australia	21	33	23	4	19
Austria	10	51	17	11	20
Belgium	41	207	18	5	52
Canada	33	95	8	0	27
Denmark	63	12	16	3	39
Finland	5	34	50	17	22
France	41	95	16	9	34
Germany	40	176	17	8	38
Greece	37	35	10	19	27
Iceland	31	199	96	11	54
Ireland	17	56	16	10	22
Italy	32	41	10	3	21
Japan	39	34	14	5	23
Luxembourg	17	108	105	22	59
Netherlands	32	30	13	5	23
New Zealand	30	24	15	1	21
Norway	26	67	42	14	31
Portugal	22	15	8	6	15
Spain	28	30	7	4	18
Sweden	53	[b]	54	15	[b]
Switzerland	13	165	49	16	40
Turkey	35	[b]	17	24	[b]
United Kingdom	78	63	6	2	47
United States	61	32	8	1	38
Unweighted mean	34	73	26	9	31
Standard deviation	17	61	27	7	13
Additional OECD[a]					
Czech Republic	36	20	6	ne	22
Hungary	69	44	2	ne	38
Korea	18	16	9	ne	14
Mexico	54	16	7	ne	40
Poland	18	30	9	ne	17
Unweighted mean	39	25	7	na	26
Standard deviation	23	12	3	na	12
NON-OECD					
Argentina	64	21	6	ne	45
Brazil	27	15	16	ne	23
Chile	41	35	7	ne	32
China	[b]	[b]	[b]	ne	[b]
Colombia	28	22	20	ne	25
Hong Kong	49	47	24	ne	43

Table A-1. Price impact of regulation on telecommunications prices, 1997–Continued (Percent of Notional Price Existing under Benchmark Regulatory Regime)

Economy	Trunk	International	Mobile	Leasing	Industry-wide
India	68	41	b	ne	b
Indonesia	41	52	56	ne	46
Malaysia	23	34	23	ne	24
Peru	32	12	7	ne	24
Philippines	30	23	8	ne	23
Russia	63	b	b	ne	b
Singapore	25	196	35	ne	44
South Africa	35	26	b	ne	b
Chinese Taipei	25	54	40	ne	32
Thailand	41	111	18	ne	42
Uruguay	42	37	8	ne	33
Vietnam	b	b	b	ne	b
Unweighted mean	40	48	21	na	34
Standard deviation	15	47	15	na	9
All 47 Economies					
Minimum	5	12	2	0	14
Maximum	78	207	105	24	59
Unweighted mean	36	58	22	9	31
Standard deviation	17	54	22	7	12

ne: not estimated.
na: not applicable.

[a] OECD economies not included in Boylaud and Nicoletti (2000).
[b] Excluded.

Source: Doove *et al.* (2001, pp. 72-73).

Electricity supply has also been undergoing significant deregulation and structural reform. Building upon OECD work by Steiner (2000), Doove *et al.* assembled data for 50 economies for 1996. The regulatory measures covered were: unbundling of electricity generation from transmission; third party access; presence of a wholesale electricity market; degree of private/public ownership; time to liberalization; and time to privatization. The price impacts of regulation were estimated and are indicated in Table A-2.

Table A-2. price impacts of regulation on industrial electricity prices, 1996[a]

Economies in Original Study	Percent	Extended Coverage	Percent
Australia	0.0	Argentina	0.0
Belgium	15.4	Austria	13.2
Canada	8.8	Bolivia	16.5
Denmark	8.5	Brazil	15.6
Finland	0.0	Chile	0.0
France	16.0	China	17.2
Germany	8.3	Colombia	0.0
Greece	16.6	Czech Republic	13.6
Ireland	13.9	Hong Kong	15.6
Italy	17.1	Hungary	13.3
Japan	10.2	Iceland	35.3
Netherlands	15.5	India	17.2
New Zealand	0.0	Indonesia	16.8
Norway	0.0	Korea	15.4
Portugal	17.9	Luxembourg	13.8
Spain	9.5	Malaysia	16.6
Sweden	0.0	Mexico	17.3
United Kingdom	0.0	Peru	0.0
United States	7.5	Philippines	17.6
		Poland	13.6
		Russia	17.1
		Slovak-Republic	14.8
		Singapore	15.6
		South Africa	15.6
		Switzerland	21.9
		Chinese-Taipei	16.1
		Thailand	16.3
		Turkey	20.7
		Uruguay	32.2
		Venezuela	27.2
		Vietnam	32.0

[a] Percentage increase in pre-tax industrial electricity prices relative to the estimated price under the benchmark regulatory regime.

Source: Doove *et al.* (2001, p. 105).

A-2: Price-Impact Studies

We summarize below a number of other pertinent studies of price-impacts that may be consulted for further technical details and results:

- Johnson, Gregan, Gentle, and Belin (2000) noted that **international air services** are regulated by means of bilateral agreements and are largely excluded from the GATS. They developed a partial-equilibrium, spatial econometric model that was used to analyze the effects on prices, quantities, and economic welfare, in Australia and foreign economy, of the entry of a new airline (Ansett) into the Australian market, as well as plurilateral reform for an "open club" for airlines among Australia, China, Hong Kong, and Japan. They showed that there were significant benefits realized from the entry of new competitors into the airline markets. Also, members of an open club gained, but at the expense of non-members.

- Kalirajan (2000) used firm-level accounting data for wholesale and retail **food distributors** in 18 economies to indicate the relationship between trade restrictiveness and distributors' price-cost margins. The results suggested that the restrictions were primarily cost creating rather than rent creating and were accounted for mainly by restrictions on establishment. Using the restrictiveness indexes, coefficient estimates, and sample means, the estimated cost impacts noted in Table A-3 range between 0 and 8 percent.

Table A-3 Estimated Cost Impacts of Foreign and Domestic Barriers to Establishment in Wholesale and Retail Food Distributors (Percent)

Economy	Cost Impact of Foreign Barriers to Establishment	Cost Impact of Domestic Barriers to Establishment
Australia	0.57	-
Belgium	4.87	6.69
Canada	3.09	0.98
Chile	1.32	1.92
France	5.16	7.10
Greece	0.25	-
Hong Kong	0.06	-
Indonesia	3.66	-
Ireland	2.70	-
Japan	2.26	6.79
Malaysia	8.23	3.97
Netherlands	2.73	-
New Zealand	0.77	-
Singapore	0.03	-
South Africa	0.47	-
Switzerland	5.24	8.32
United Kingdom	2.76	-
United States	2.26	-

- = Zero.

Source: Kalirajan (2000, p. 52).

- Kalirajan, McGuire, Nguyen-Hong, and Schuele (2000) developed and estimated a model applied to 694 banks in 27 economies for 1996-97 to assess the impact of non-prudential restrictions on the interest margins of **banks**. The net interest margin is the difference between a bank's lending and deposit rates. A two-stage procedure was used for estimation purposes. In the first stage, bank-specific variables were used to explain the interest margins in all the economies, and, in a second stage, cross-economy estimation was used to take economy-wide variables into account. The foreign and domestic restrictiveness indexes calculated in McGuire and Schuele (2000) entered into the second-stage estimation. The foreign restrictiveness index was found to be a significant determinant of interest rate spreads, while the domestic restrictiveness index was not significant. The price impacts of the restrictions were calculated from the second-stage results and are presented in Table A-4. Chile, Indonesia, Malaysia, the Philippines, Singapore, South Korea, and Thailand have the highest price impacts due to the restrictions on foreign banks.

Table A-4. estimated price impacts of foreign and domestic trade restrictiveness indexes (TRI) on net interest margins of banks (Percent)

Economy	Price Effect Using the Foreign TRI_i	Price Effect Using the Domestic TRI_i[b]
Argentina	5.34	0.00
Australia	9.30	0.00
Canada	5.34	0.00
Chile	34.00	23.67
Colombia	18.35	3.73
European Union[a]	5.32	0.00
Hong Kong	6.91	2.97
Indonesia	49.32	5.26
Japan	15.26	9.99
Malaysia	60.61	21.86
Philippines	47.36	10.79
Singapore	31.45	8.39
South Korea	36.72	14.93
Switzerland	5.95	0.00
Thailand	33.06	0.00
United States	4.75	0.00

[a] The European Union grouping excludes Finland, Ireland and Luxembourg.

[b] Uses the coefficient estimate for the foreign trade restrictiveness index as a proxy.

Source: Kalirajan *et al.* (2000, p. 229).

- Kang (2000) investigated the impact of restrictions on **maritime services**, using a partial-equilibrium econometric model that incorporated cross-economy and bilateral trade data as determinants of demand for these services. Shipping margins for manufactured goods were derived from F.O.B./C.I.F. value differentials and were used as a proxy for price. The shipping margins were to be explained by bilateral restrictions, distance, and the scale of bilateral trade. Indexes for 23 economies were adapted from

McGuire, Schuele, and Smith (2000), and the remaining data were from the 1995 database of the Global Trade Analysis Project (GTAP). The foreign index of restrictiveness was decomposed into measures affecting commercial presence and into other restrictions such as on cabotage and port services. Allowance was also made for different bilateral relationships as between industrialized and developing economies. The most important conclusion reached was that a low degree of restrictions in any trading partner was necessary in order to have low shipping charges. Further, low-income economies stood to gain the most from eliminating restrictions on shipping services.

- Nguyen-Hong (2000) estimated the influences of restrictions on the price-cost margins of 84 **engineering service** firms in 20 economies, using 1996 company accounting data compiled from a variety of private and official sources. A model of firm behavior was developed to include the determinants of the observed price-cost margins, and a linear version using ordinary least squares was implemented with cross-section data. The index of foreign barriers to establishment was highly significant and had a positive and statistically significant impact on price-cost margins. The index of domestic barriers to establishment had a negative and significant impact. The price and cost impacts of the restrictions were calculated, using the actual indexes of restrictiveness, estimated coefficients, and the sample means of the independent variables. The price impacts, which are summarized by economy in Table A-5, exceed 10 percent for Austria, Mexico, Malaysia, Indonesia, and Germany. The cost impacts are relatively small, ranging between 0.7 and 6.8 percent. The price and cost impacts were also calculated by types of barriers.
- Trewin (2000) used time-series data on the total costs of providing **telecommunications services** for 37 economies obtained from the International Telecommunications Union (ITU) for the period 1982-92. He used a frontier cost method as a means of estimating the minimum possible costs that are expended from a given combination of inputs. The distance of an observation above the cost frontier is a measurement of the degree of technical inefficiency. The measurements of restrictiveness calculated by Marko (1998) and Warren (2000a) were used in the estimation process. The results suggested that economies that provide higher levels of FDI face lower costs. Making allowance for the quality-cost aspects of telecommunication services reinforced the importance of the cost impacts of restrictions. When the sample was divided between low and high income economies, the average efficiency of the high income set was more than three times better than the

Table A-5. Estimated price and cost impacts of restrictions on engineering services (Percent)

	Price Impact			Cost Impact
	Foreign Barriers to Establishment	Foreign Barriers to Ongoing Operations	All Foreign Barriers	Domestic Barriers to Establishment
Austria	11.1	3.5	14.5	6.8
Mexico	13.9	0.2	14.2	1.9
Malaysia	11.3	0.7	12.0	5.3
Indonesia	9.9	0.3	10.2	3.2
Germany	4.7	5.5	10.2	2.9
Spain	5.1	3.7	8.7	3.9
United States	5.1	2.2	7.4	3.8
Sweden	5.9	0.9	6.8	0.7
Japan	3.1	3.4	6.6	2.2
Canada	3.1	2.2	5.3	2.7
Singapore	4.9	0.2	5.0	0.8
Hong Kong	3.6	1.5	5.1	2.3
South Africa	3.5	0.2	3.7	0.7
Netherlands	3.5	0.2	3.7	5.2
Australia	2.1	0.7	2.8	2.1
United Kingdom	2.3	0.2	2.5	1.4
Finland	1.8	0.5	2.3	0.7
Denmark	0.3	0.8	1.1	0.7
France	0.3	0.6	0.9	0.7
Belgium	0.3	0.2	0.5	0.7

[a] The price impact for all foreign barriers is the sum of the price impacts for foreign barriers to establishment and ongoing operations, respectively.

Source: Nguyen-Hong (2000, p. 63).

low income set. The results are listed in Table A-6. It can be seen, in the high income set, that Luxembourg is close to the efficiency frontier whereas Portugal and Korea are relatively high cost economies.

- Doove, Gabbitas, Nguyen-Hong, and Owen (2001) constructed restrictiveness indexes and estimates of price impacts for international air passenger transport, telecommunications, and electricity supply. Their indexes of bilateral restrictions on **international air passenger transport** referred to 35 economies in the Asia-Pacific, Americas, and European regions. Focusing on the discount segment of the air passenger market, they implement a procedure for estimating the price effects of the applicable restrictions, using fare data primarily for the end years of the 1990s. The results, which are shown above

Table A-6. Coefficient estimates of technical efficiency in telecommunications services

Low Income	Technical Efficiency	High Income	Technical Efficiency
Chile	3.82	Australia	1.67
China	6.31	Austria	1.31
Hungary	2.61	Belgium	1.55
Iceland	1.16	Canada	1.34
Indonesia	11.96	Denmark	1.43
Ireland	3.22	Finland	1.24
Malaysia	4.31	France	1.74
Mexico	15.41	Germany	1.66
PNG	7.75	Greece	1.11
Philippines	3.06	Hong Kong	1.44
Poland	2.30	Italy	1.71
Thailand	5.25	Japan	1.21
Turkey	4.07	Korea	1.98
		Luxembourg	1.03
		Netherlands	1.43
		New Zealand	1.83
		Norway	1.75
		Portugal	2.08
		Singapore	1.57
		Spain	1.75
		Sweden	1.40
		Switzerland	1.42
		United Kingdom	1.67
		United States	1.48
Mean	5.48	Mean	1.54

Note: A coefficient estimate equal to 1.00 indicates full technical efficiency in relation to the minimum-cost frontier.

Source: Trewin (2000, p. 112).

in Table 7, indicated that the higher price effects range from 12 to 22 percent in the Asia-Pacific economies, 9 to 18 percent in the Americas, and generally below 10 percent in the European economies. The price impacts for business and economy airfares were considerably higher but should be interpreted tentatively due to data constraints.

- Measurements of the impact of **telecommunications** regulations were derived for 24 OECD and 23 other economies, using data for 1997. Price-impact measurements of regulation were calculated for four major sectors of telecommunications, including trunk, international, mobile, and leasing services and are listed by economy and type of service in Table A-1. While the results suggested that economies with more stringent regulatory regimes tended to have higher telecommunications prices, the authors noted that there were several cases in which the results appeared to be counter intuitive and sensitive to small changes in the data. The reported results should therefore be treated with caution, pending further clarification and improvement of the model and data that were used.

- Measurements of regulation and impacts on **industrial electricity** prices for 50 economies, using 1996 data, were developed. The estimated price impacts are listed by economy in Table A-2. The impacts ranged from 0 to 35 percent, with a mean of 13 percent and a standard deviation of 13 percent. The authors noted, however, that the estimated price impacts were quite sensitive to the methodology and data used and therefore should be treated as ordinal rankings rather than absolute values.
- Fink, Mattoo, and Neagu (2002) analyzed the importance of restrictive trade policies and private anti-competitive practices for **international maritime services**. For this purpose, they used data on U.S. imports carried by liners from 59 economies that accounted for about 65 percent of the total value of U.S. maritime imports in 1998. While restrictions on the provision of port services were found to be significant, private anti-competitive practices involving collusion among international maritime cartels were shown to have a considerably greater influence on maritime transport prices.

A-3: Gravity-Model Estimates

Deardorff and Stern (1998, p. 24) have noted that measurements based on the gravity model are useful mainly in identifying *relative* levels of protection across sectors and economies. But gravity models have some important drawbacks. That is, by attributing to trade barriers all departures of trade from what the included variables can explain, there is a great burden on the model being used. Thus, the worse the model, the more likely it is that trade barrier estimates will have an upward bias.

An additional problem exists when this technique is used to infer barriers for separate industries. The theoretical basis for the gravity equation, as in Anderson (1979) and Deardorff (1998), applies to total trade, not to trade in individual sectors. The gravity equation makes sense at the sectoral level only if all economies are equal in their capacity to produce in a sector, which of course would be a denial of the role of comparative advantage. Thus, if an economy were in fact to have a comparative advantage in a particular service sector, so that its output would be high and its cost of serving its domestic market itself would be low, then it will import less from abroad than would be expected based on income and distance alone. Thus comparative advantage may show up as an implicit barrier to trade, when in fact none exists.

A-4: Computable General Equilibrium (CGE) Modeling

In the study by Brown and Stern (2001), each MNC is assumed to produce a differentiated product and to allocate production to its various host-economy locations. The monopolistically competitive firms employ capital, labor, and intermediate inputs in their production, and they set prices as an optimal mark-up of price over marginal cost. The number of firms is permitted to vary to hold MNC profits at zero. Consumers are assumed to allocate their expenditure between goods and services that are produced by firms domestically and varieties that are imported from each national source. Labor is taken to be freely mobile among domestic sectors but not across borders. Capital, however, is mobile internationally, although not perfectly so, because there is a risk premium that will vary depending on the size of an economy's capital stock.

Barriers to FDI are assumed to take the form of an increased cost of locating investment in a host economy. For this purpose, Brown and Stern use the cost-price margins estimated by Hoekman (2000), which have been discussed above and are listed in Tables 10 and 11, as indicative of barriers to FDI. Since the cost-price gap is smallest in most sectors in Hong Kong, an economy thought to be freely open to foreign firms, the excess in any other economy above the Hong Kong figure is taken to be due to barriers to the establishment of foreign firms.

Using the aforementioned modeling structure with three sectors (agriculture, manufactures, and services) and 18 economies/regions, Brown and Stern calculate the economic effects of removal of services barriers according to the following three scenarios:[21]

Scenario A: Removal of services barriers, with perfect international capital mobility and fixed world capital stock.

Scenario B: Removal of services barriers, with risk-premium elasticity = 0.1 to allow for imperfect capital mobility, and fixed world capital stock.

Scenario C: Removal of services barriers, with risk-premium elasticity = 0.1 to allow for imperfect capital mobility, and world capital stock increased by 3 percent.

When barriers are lowered, international capital in the form of FDI will then be attracted to economies with the relatively highest rates of return and away from other economies.

---

[21] See also studies undertaken at the Australian Productivity Commission by Dee and Hanslow (2001) and Verikios and Zhang (2001) for computational results based on a related modeling framework and with estimates of services barriers taken from Kalirajan *et al.* (2000) and Warren (2000 a,b).

The welfare effects, as a percentage of GNP and in billions of dollars, resulting from the assumed removal of the services barriers for each of the three scenarios are listed in Table A-7 for the economies/regions covered by the model.[22] When services barriers are lowered, international capital in the form of FDI will then be attracted to economies with the highest rates of return and away from other economies.

It is evident in Table A-7 that the welfare effects of removing the services barriers are sizable and that they vary markedly across economies. For the industrialized economies in Scenario A with perfect international capital mobility, the largest increases are for Canada, $84.0 billion (14.8 percent of GNP), the European Union (EU), $42.4 billion (0.5 percent of GNP), and the United States, $35.0 billion (0.5 percent of GNP). Because it loses capital, Japan has a decline of $103.7 billion (2.0 percent of GNP). Among the developing economies, the largest increases are for Indonesia, $30.8 billion (15.6 percent of GNP), China, $26.9 billion (3.8 percent of GNP), and Chinese Taipei, $20.7 billion, $7.6 percent of GNP). It is also evident that there are declines in welfare for a number of developing economies, in particular, Korea, Thailand, Chile, Mexico, and the Rest of Cairns Group. What is reflected in the results is that welfare is affected by whether or not an economy attracts or loses capital as a result of services liberalization. Economies that lose capital become "smaller" in the economic sense of the word. As the economy contracts, surviving firms produce less than before. The fall in firm output generally occurs in order to avoid a large loss in variety of domestically produced goods. The subsequent economy-wide reduction in scale economies is usually the source of the welfare loss.

The results in Scenario A are sensitive to the assumption of perfect capital mobility. As noted above, economies that import capital are assumed to pay a risk premium that is a function of capital imports. The elasticity of the risk premium with respect to the volume of capital imports can be set exogenously in

---

[22] See Brown and Stern (2001, pp. 277-78) for the results for the absolute changes in imports and exports, the percentage change in the terms of trade, and the percentage change in the real wage. The sectoral results for the three aggregated sectors for Scenario C are reported in Brown and Stern (pp. 281-82). They show that output increases economy-wide in just about every sector in all economies/regions, and there is a wide prevalence of the realization of economies of scale. There are also generally significant increases in activity by foreign-owned affiliates, especially in the economies that record large increases in output.

Table A-7. Welfare effects of elimination of services (Percent and billions of dollars)

Economy	Scenario A Perfect Int'l Capital Mobility and Fixed World Capital Stock		Scenario B Risk-Premium Elasticity=0.1 and Fixed World Capital Stock		Scenario C Risk-Premium Elasticity=0.1 and World Capital Stock Increased by 3%	
Industrialized Economies	**% GNP**	**$Bill.**	**% GNP**	**$Bill.**	**% GNP**	**$Bill.**
Australia	1.8	6.0	1.5	5.0	4.9	16.8
Canada	14.8	84.0	12.9	73.7	14.9	85.0
European Union	0.5	42.4	0.5	38.0	2.5	202.4
Japan	-2.0	-103.7	-1.7	-88.4	0.5	25.7
New Zealand	9.1	5.2	7.5	4.3	10.5	6.0
United States	0.5	35.0	0.3	23.2	3.1	222.5
Developing Economies						
Asia						
China	3.8	26.9	3.2	22.9	6.0	42.8
Hong Kong	6.6	6.6	5.4	5.5	13.4	13.5
Indonesia	15.6	30.8	13.1	25.8	16.9	33.3
Korea	-2.8	-12.3	-2.3	-10.1	1.4	6.4
Malaysia	2.3	2.1	1.9	1.8	4.7	4.4
Philippines	2.3	1.6	1.9	1.3	8.3	5.7
Singapore	1.7	1.0	1.3	0.7	4.3	2.5
Chinese Taipei	7.6	20.7	6.8	18.5	7.7	21.2
Thailand	-2.2	-3.6	-1.8	-2.9	4.4	7.1
Other						
Chile	-2.0	-1.3	-1.6	-1.0	2.7	1.7
Mexico	-4.3	-11.7	-3.2	-8.8	0.2	0.5
Rest of Cairns	-3.7	-39.6	-3.2	-34.1	0.6	6.2
Total		**90.3**		**75.6**		**703.7**

Source: Brown and Stern (2001, pp. 277-78).

the model. Thus, in Scenario B, Brown and Stern assume that capital imports that result in a 1 percent increase in the capital stock generate an interest-rate risk premium of 0.1 percent. That is, the risk-premium elasticity is 0.1 percent. It is apparent from the results for Scenario B in Table A-7 that the introduction of a risk premium that reflects a decrease in international capital mobility has the effect of reducing the welfare effects of services liberalization as compared to Scenario A, in which there was perfect capital mobility.

In both Scenarios A and B, there is a rise in the real return to capital. Therefore, it is likely that, over time, there will be an increase in the world's capital stock as savers and investors respond to the increased incentive to accumulate capital. To take this into account, in Scenario C, with the risk premium elasticity remaining at 0.1 percent, Brown and Stern allow for an increase in the world's capital stock by 3 percent. This is the amount necessary to hold the real return to capital equal to the level in the base period. As can be seen in Table A-7, the welfare effects of services liberalization are now positive for all of the economies shown. For the world as a whole, welfare rises by $703.7 billion. Canada's welfare increases by $85.0 billion (14.9 percent of GNP), the EU by $202.4 billion (2.5 percent of GNP), and the United States, $222.5 billion (3.1 percent of GNP). There are also sizable absolute and percentage increases for the developing economies, in particular China, Indonesia, Chinese Taipei, and Hong Kong. It is further noteworthy that welfare increases for all of the economies/regions shown.

It is evident accordingly that these welfare effects associated with an increase in the world's capital stock in response to an increase in the rate of return to capital are considerably larger than what is commonly seen in CGE models in which capital is assumed to be internationally immobile.[23] This may not be surprising because it has been apparent from previous CGE analyses of trade liberalization that have made allowance for international capital flows that the largest welfare gains stem from these flows rather than from the removal of tariffs and other trade barriers that distort consumer choice in goods trade.[24]

The understanding of the consequences of liberalizing services barriers thus is enhanced when allowance is made for the behavior of multinational firms whose foreign affiliates are already located in or attracted to host economies. When services liberalization occurs and the real return to capital is increased, so that there are FDI (Mode 3) international capital flows and the world capital stock expands, most economies stand to gain significantly in terms of economic welfare.

---

[23] Compare, for example, the results of the Michigan Model reported in Brown, Deardorff, and Stern (2003).

[24] See Brown, Deardorff, and Stern (1992).

TECHNIQUES FOR ESTIMATING SERVICES BARRIERS

Duc Nguyen-Hong
Australian Productivity Commission[1]

1. Introduction

In a collaborative project, researchers from the Productivity Commission and the Australian National University have developed a methodology to measure restrictions on trade in services. The results from this work have produced trade restrictiveness index and price measures of service barriers in several sectors for a number of economies in Europe, Asia, and North and South America.

Services barriers take the form of government regulatory restrictions that affect the entry and operations of firms. Restrictions apply not only to foreign service suppliers, but also to domestic service suppliers. Service barriers have the effect of raising the price of services, but this effect on trade is not directly observable like a tariff on goods trade and would need to be quantified.

The methodology for measuring services barriers generally involves two steps:

- *Step 1*: Calculate a trade restrictiveness index to convert qualitative information about regulations into a quantitative measure.
- *Step 2*: Use econometric techniques to estimate the direct effect of restrictions, on the economic performance of firms in that sector.

1.2. *Trade Restrictiveness Index*

Restrictions on trade in services can be measured using a trade restrictiveness index. An index is simply a frequency measure based on the number of restrictions and how stringent they are across economies. A service sector in an economy with fewer or less severe restrictions is more liberal than an economy with a greater number of stringent restrictions.

Developing an index involves the following procedures:

[1] The views expressed in this paper are those of the author and do not necessarily reflect those of the Productivity Commission.

- Collect detailed information on restrictions. The information on restrictions is drawn from various sources such as the WTO, OECD and APEC, or may already be available from the General Agreement on Trade in Services (GATS) schedules.
- Classify and compare restrictions across economies to define their relative restrictiveness.
- Assign scores to the restrictions to get an indication of how a restriction is more stringent across economies. The scores range from 0 to 1 according to the degree of restrictiveness.
- Calculate the index by weighting the scores based on a judgment of the relative importance of the restriction. Two separate indexes are calculated. A foreign index is calculated to measure all discriminatory and non-discriminatory restrictions on foreign suppliers. The domestic index is calculated to measure (typically non-discriminatory) restrictions applying to domestic providers. The foreign index includes the domestic index.

1.2.1. *Case Study: Banking Services*

McGuire and Schuele (2000) constructed a trade restrictiveness index for banking services. Tables 1 and 2 provide an illustrative example of the index calculation for just two types of restriction – the number of bank licences and limits on direct investment in banks. The information sources indicate that economy A and B apply different restrictive requirements on bank licenses and investment. An economy which does not provide any new licence is defined to be more restrictive than an economy which issues new licences with only prudential requirements. Index scores between 0 and 1 are assigned to reflect different bank licensing requirements in the economies studied.

In the same manner, the restriction on direct investment receives scores based on the stated limits on the proportion of equity investment in domestic banks. For example, economy A allows investment in domestic banks up to 75 percent of equity, and a score of 0.25 is given as a measure of the extent to which bank investment remains restricted.

The foreign and domestic indexes are then calculated for banking services. Since the information sources indicate that the restriction on bank licensing and direct investment applies to both foreigners and domestic providers, their scores are used to compute a foreign index and a domestic index separately. Each restriction would also receive a weight which reflects a judgment on the relative importance of the restrictions. In this example, banking licences and direct investment restriction are given an equal weight, but minor measures in banking services such as a restriction on the temporary movement of people can be assigned a lower weight.

Table 1. Banking services – assigning scores

Restriction	Index score	Economy A	Economy B
1 Number of bank licences issued			
- no new licences are available	1.00	1	
- up to 3 licences issued	0.75		
- up to 6 licences issued	0.50		
- up to 10 licences	0.25		
- issue new licences subject on to prudential requirements	0.00		0
2 Direct investment in banks			
- % ownership prohibited	%	0.25	0.33

Table 2. Banking services – calculating foreign and domestic indexes

		Economy A		
Restriction	**Score**	**Foreign index**	**Domestic index**	**Weights**
1 No. of bank licences issued		Yes	Yes	0.20
- no new licences	1.00			
- up to 3	0.75			
- up to 6	0.50			
- up to 10	0.25			
- new licences issued	0.00			
2 Direct investment		Yes	Yes	0.20
- % ownership limits	%			

1.2.2. *Extensions*

In recent work, researchers have developed an index measure by extending the existing studies on services barriers to cover additional markets and economies. For some service sectors, index measures of service barriers may already be available in previous research, and by extending the index methodology, only information for additional economies is generally required. An example of this approach is Doove *et al.* (2001) who built on an OECD study (Gonenc and Nicoletti 2000) to construct index measures for international air passenger transport.

Table 3 provides an example of calculating an index measure of bilateral restrictions in international air services and extending existing works to cover new economies. In international air passenger transport, most economies have bilateral agreements with one another that maintain restrictions on the number of airlines, airline capacity, air fares and charter services. Restrictions that are of a bilateral or regional nature can also be captured in the index methodology.

In the example (table 3), the OECD study assigns index scores to the types of restrictions identified in the bilateral agreement between economy A and economy B. This OECD methodology is then applied to the bilateral agreement between economy A and economy C, which has some lesser restrictive requirements on the number of airlines. This process is repeated for each bilateral agreement. An index measure of the bilateral restrictions for economy A can then be obtained by computing an average of the bilateral restriction scores.

Table 3. International aviation

		Bilateral agreement	
Bilateral restriction	**Index score**	**Economy A-Economy B (OECD study)**	**Economy A-Economy C (Extension)**
1 Number of designated airlines			
- Single airline	1.00	1	
- Multiple airlines with route limitations	0.67		
- Multiple airlines with no route limitations	0.33		0.33
- No restrictions	0.00		
2 Airline capacity limits			
- Predetermined airline capacity	1.00		
- Mixed (hybrid) arrangement	0.67	0.67	0.67
- *Ex post* government review (Bermuda 1)	0.33		
- Free airline determination	0.00		
3 Airfare controls	1.00	1	1
4 Charter services not allowed	1.00	1	1

1.3. *Price Impact Measures*

While the trade restrictiveness index conveys useful information about restrictions, it is not linked to prices or economic performance. Economic estimation provides a method to measure the direct price effect of services barriers and correct for other economic influences.

For econometric estimation, the methodology is to enter the restrictiveness index into an econometric model of economic performance in the sector in question (where Y is some measure of performance, such as prices), along with industry-specific or economy-wide factors (X) that economic theory suggests might be important determinants of performance.

$$Y = \alpha + \beta R + \gamma X + \varepsilon$$

Once an estimate of β is made, the model can be used to give a price impact measure of restrictions – as the percentage increase in services price resulting from restrictions relative to the price in free trade.

Computing a price measure requires mathematical manipulation of the functional form to convert the econometric results into a percentage price formula. The price measure can then be computed based on the information on the coefficient estimate (β) and the restrictiveness index (R). The appropriate mathematical manipulation depends on the particular measure of performance and the particular functional form for the estimating equation.

1.3.1. *Case Study: Banking Price Measure*

An example of deriving price impacts is provided in Kalirajan *et al.* (2000)'s study on banking services. The estimated model is equation 1, where P is the observed price for bank financial intermediation service (bank interest margin); R is the trade restrictiveness index; and X includes all the environmental variables. By rearranging the functional form of the model, the estimation gives a formula for calculating the price impact in equation 5 – as the increase in price compared to the price is in the absence of restrictions (P_o).

$$\text{Ln } P = \alpha + \beta R + \gamma X \qquad (1)$$

$$P = P_o{*}e^{\beta R} \qquad (2)$$

$$P / P_o = e^{\beta R} \qquad (3)$$

$$(P / P_o) - 1 = e^{\beta R} - 1 \qquad (4)$$

Price impact:

$$(P - P_o) / P_o = e^{\beta R} - 1 \qquad (5)$$

The calculation of price impacts is shown in table 4.

Table 4. Banking price measure

	R	β	Price impact
Economy A	0.1	0.7	9%
Economy B	0.6	0.7	61%
Economy C	0.4	0.7	37%

This methodology can also be generalised to include additional economies. Once an estimate of β has been obtained from a particular sample, a price impact measure can be calculated for additional economies by deriving an index score R to characterise their services trade restrictions without redoing the econometrics.

This technique generally requires data on the regulatory regimes for the additional economies only, under the assumption that the effect of restrictions is common across economies studied. In the econometric estimation, the original sample needs to be fairly representative of the economies of the world. The samples could at least include the APEC economies, the members of the European Union, and key economies from the rest of the world (preferably at least Switzerland, Turkey, India, and South Africa).

Since services barriers apply to both foreign and domestic service suppliers and there are different restrictions, individual price effects of restrictions are also of interests. In the econometric estimation, the scores of individual restrictions or components of the restrictiveness index can be entered separately into the estimated equation. This also helps to minimise the judgments on the weight about the relative importance of restrictions.

Separate price effects for foreign and domestic providers can be estimated in the following functional form:

$$P = \alpha + \beta_F R_F + \beta_D R_D + \gamma X + \varepsilon \tag{1}$$

or

$$P = \alpha + \beta_F R_F + \gamma X + \varepsilon \tag{2}$$

Where it is not possible to enter the restriction scores separately or when there is multicollinearity or lack of in sample variation, the total foreign index can just be entered in the econometric estimation (equation 2). The econometric results of the foreign index can then be used to obtain the results for the domestic providers. This is because the domestic index is a subset of the foreign index (figure 1).

1.3.2. *Additional examples*

The attached tables provide additional details of the trade restrictiveness index compiled for the following sectors:

- banking services (McGuire and Schuele 2000);
- maritime services (McGuire, Schuele and Smith 2000);
- distribution services (Kalirajan 2000);
- professional services (Nguyen-Hong 2000);

- international air passenger transport (Doove *et al.* 2001); and
- education services (Nguyen-Hong and Wells 2003).

These publications are available at the Productivity Commission's website (at *www.pc.gov.au/work/trade/index.html*).

Figure 1. A trade restrictiveness index

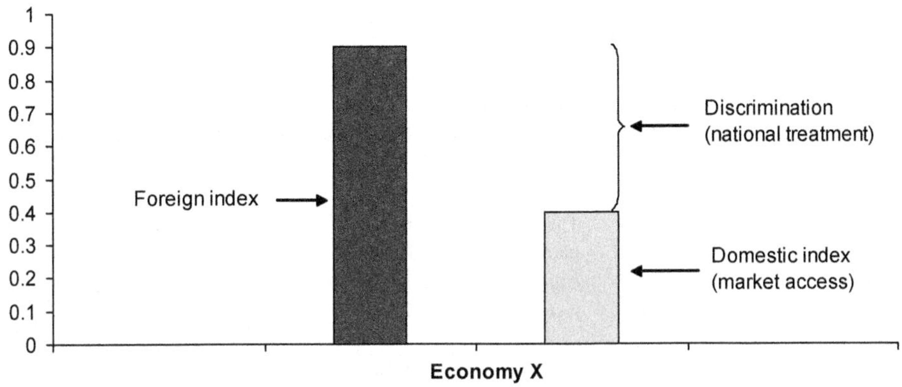

BANKING SERVICES

Table 5. Restrictiveness index for banking services

Category weightings[a]				
R[b]	**MFN[c]**	**Total[d]**	**Score**	**Restriction category**
				Restrictions on commercial presence
0.190	0.010	0.20		**Licensing of banks**
			1.00	Issues no new banking licences.
			0.75	Issues up to 3 new banking licences with only prudential requirements.
			0.50	Issues up to 6 new banking licences with only prudential requirements.
			0.25	Issues up to 10 new banking licences with only prudential requirements.
			0.00	Issues new banking licences with only prudential requirements.
0.190	0.010	0.20		**Direct investment**
				The score is inversely proportional to the maximum equity participation permitted in an existing domestic bank. For example, equity participation to a maximum of 75 percent of a bank would receive a score of 0.25.
0.095	0.005	0.10		**Joint venture arrangements**
			1.00	Issues no new banking licences and no entry is allowed through a joint venture with a domestic bank.
			0.50	Bank entry is only through a joint venture with a domestic bank.
			0.00	No requirement for a bank to enter through a joint venture with a domestic bank.
0.019	0.001	0.02		**Permanent movement of people**
			1.00	No entry of executives, senior managers and/or specialists.
			0.80	Executives, specialists and/or senior managers can stay up to 1 year.
			0.60	Executives, specialists and/or senior managers can stay up to 2 years.
			0.40	Executives, specialists and/or senior managers can stay up to 3 years.
			0.20	Executives, specialists and/or senior managers can stay up to 4 years.
			0.00	Executives, specialists and/or senior managers can stay a period of 5 years or more.
				Other Restrictions
0.143	0.007	0.15		**Raising funds by banks**
			1.00	Banks are not permitted to raise funds in the domestic market.
			0.75	Banks are restricted from raising funds from domestic capital markets.
			0.50	Banks are restricted in accepting deposits from the public.
			0.00	Banks can raise funds from any source with only prudential requirements.
0.143	0.007	0.15		**Lending funds by banks**
			1.00	Banks are not permitted to lend to domestic clients.

Table 5. Restrictiveness index for banking services

Category weightings[a]				
R[b]	**MFN[c]**	**Total[d]**	**Score**	**Restriction category**
			0.75	Banks are restricted to a specified lending size or lending to government projects.
			0.50	Banks are restricted in providing certain services such as credit cards, leasing and consumer finance.
			0.25	Banks are directed to lend to housing and small business.
			0.00	Banks can lend to any source with only prudential restrictions.
0.095	0.005	0.10		**Other business of banks – insurance and securities services**
			1.00	Banks can only provide banking services.
			0.50	Banks can provide banking services plus one other line of business – insurance or securities services.
			0.00	Banks have no restrictions on conducting other lines of business.
0.048	0.003	0.05		**Expanding the number of banking outlets**
			1.00	One banking outlet with no new banking outlets permitted.
			0.75	Number of banking outlets is limited in number and location.
			0.25	Expansion of banking outlets is subject to non-prudential regulatory approval.
			0.00	No restrictions on banks expanding operations.
0.019	0.001	0.02		**Composition of the board of directors**
				The score is inversely proportionately to the percentage of the Board that can comprise foreigners. For example, a score of 0.80 is allocated where 20 percent of the board of directors of a bank can comprise foreigners.
0.010	0.001	0.01		**Temporary movement of people**
			1.00	No temporary entry of executives, senior managers and/or specialists.
			0.75	Temporary entry of executives, senior managers and/or specialists up to 30 days.
			0.50	Temporary entry of executives, senior managers and/or specialists up to 60 days.
			0.25	Temporary entry of executives, senior managers and/or specialists up to 90 days.
			0.00	Temporary entry of executives, senior managers and/or specialists over 90 days.
0.950	0.050	1.00		**Total**

a Totals may not add due to rounding.
b R is the restriction category weighting.
c MFN is the most-favoured-nation category weighting.
d Total of the restriction category and most-favoured-nation category weightings.

Table 6. Scores for MFN exemptions – banking services and movement of people

Score	Type of MFN exemption
1.00	No MFN exemption
0.50	MFN exemption with reciprocity with selected or all economies
0.00	MFN exemption with preferential treatment with selected or all economies

Table 7. Relevance of restriction categories for foreign and domestic index

Restriction category	Relevant for foreign index	Total weight	Relevant for domestic index	Total weight
Restrictions on commercial presence				
Licensing of banks	Yes	0.200	Yes	0.190
Direct investment	Yes	0.200	Yes	0.190
Joint venture arrangements	Yes	0.100	No	na
Permanent movement of people	Yes	0.020	No	na
Other restrictions				
Raising funds by banks	Yes	0.100	Yes	0.143
Lending funds by banks	Yes	0.100	Yes	0.143
Other business of banks – insurance and securities services	Yes	0.200	Yes	0.095
Expanding the number of banking outlets	Yes	0.050	Yes	0.048
Composition of the board of directors	Yes	0.020	No	na
Temporary movement of people	Yes	0.010	No	na
Total weighting or highest possible score		1.000		0.808

The term "na" indicates not applicable.

a Totals may not add due to rounding.

MARITIME SERVICES

Table 8. Examples of restrictions on maritime services

Restriction	Description of restriction
Right to fly the national flag	Requires ships to be registered or licensed to provide maritime services on domestic and international routes. The conditions on registration may include having a commercial presence in the domestic economy, the ship being built and owned domestically, and meeting seaworthiness and safety requirements.
Cabotage	Restricts shipping services on domestic or coastal routes to licensed vessels that meet certain conditions. Shipping services between domestic ports may be required to be carried out by domestically owned, operated, built and crewed ships.
Cargo sharing	Stipulates the allocation of cargo on particular routes between parties to bilateral and multilateral agreements.

Table 8. Examples of restrictions on maritime services–Continued

Restriction	Description of restriction
Bilateral agreements	Agreements between two economies that primarily restrict the supply of shipping services and the allocation of cargo. Some bilateral agreements also restrict the use of port facilities.
United Nations Convention on a Code of Conduct for Liner Conferences (UN Liner Code)	Stipulates that conference trade between two economies can allocate cargo according to 40:40:20 principle. Forty percent of tonnage is reserved for the national flag lines of each economy and the remaining 20 percent is to be allocated to liner ships from a third economy. The Code also entitles any national flag shipping line to be a member of a conference and to fix freight rates.
Conferences	Restricts the free and open participation of maritime service suppliers. Conference members set freight rates and schedules. Conferences may be open or closed. Open conferences have unrestricted entry and exit, and freight rates are set on a route. Closed conferences set freight rates, allocate cargo and restrict membership. Governments usually permit the existence of conferences though exemptions from price setting and collusion provisions of domestic competition legislation.
Port services	Requires ships to use a designated supply of port services. These services include pilotage, towing, tug assistance, navigation aids, berthing, waste disposal, anchorage and casting off.

Sources: Kang, Findlay and Choi (1998), White (1988) and WTO (1998).

Table 9. Restrictiveness index for maritime services

Category weightings[a]				
R[b]	MFN[c]	Total[d]	Score	Restriction category
				Restrictions on commercial presence
0.143	0.008	0.15		Conditions on the right to fly the national flag
			0.40	Commercial presence is required in the domestic economy.
			0.30	50 percent or more of equity participation must be domestic.
			0.20	50 percent or more of the crew are required to be domestic.
			0.10	Ship must be registered.
0.095	0.005	0.10		**Form of commercial presence**
			1.00	Measures which restrict or require a specific type of legal entity or joint venture arrangement.
			0.50	Shipping service suppliers must be represented by an agent.
			0.00	No restrictions on establishment.
0.095	0.005	0.10		**Direct investment in shipping service suppliers**
				The score is inversely proportional to the maximum equity participation permitted in an existing shipping service supplier. For example, equity participation to a maximum of 75 percent of an existing shipping service supplier would receive a score of 0.25.

Table 9. Restrictiveness index for maritime services

Category weightings[a]				
R[b]	MFN[c]	Total[d]	Score	Restriction category
0.095	0.005	0.10		**Direct investment in onshore maritime service suppliers**
				The score is inversely proportional to the maximum equity participation permitted in an existing onshore maritime service supplier. For example, equity participation to a maximum of 75 percent of an existing onshore service supplier receives a score of 0.25.
0.019	0.001	0.02		**Permanent movement of people**
			1.00	No entry of executives, senior managers and/or specialists.
			0.80	Executives, specialists and/or senior managers can stay a period of up to 1 year.
			0.60	Executives, specialists and/or senior managers can stay a period of up to 2 years.
			0.40	Executives, specialists and/or senior managers can stay a period of up to 3 years.
			0.20	Executives, specialists and/or senior managers can stay a period of up to 4 years.
			0.00	Executives, specialists and/or senior managers can stay a period of 5 years or more.
				Other Restrictions
0.095	0.005	0.10		**Cabotage**
			1.00	Foreigners generally cannot provide domestic maritime services.
			0.75	Foreigners that fly the national flag can provide domestic maritime services.
			0.50	Restrictions on type and length of time cargoes can be carried.
			0.00	No cabotage restrictions.
0.095	0.005	0.10		**Transportation of non-commercial cargoes**
			1.00	Private shipping service suppliers cannot carry non-commercial cargoes.
			0.50	National flag shipping service suppliers can carry non-commercial cargoes.
			0.00	No restrictions on access to non-commercial cargoes.
0.095	0.005	0.10		**Port services**
			0.30	Some restrictions on access to ports.
			0.20	Mandatory use of pilotage.
			0.15	Mandatory use of towing.
			0.10	Mandatory use of tug assistance.
			0.05	Mandatory use of navigation aids.
			0.05	Mandatory use of berthing services.
			0.05	Mandatory use of waste disposal.
			0.05	Mandatory use of anchorage.

Table 9. Restrictiveness index for maritime services

Category weightings[a]				
R[b]	**MFN[c]**	**Total[d]**	**Score**	**Restriction category**
			0.05	Mandatory use of casting off.
0.048	0.003	0.05		**Discretionary imposition of restrictions including for retaliatory purposes**
			1.00	Governments are able to impose selective restrictions.
			0.00	Governments are unable to impose selective restrictions.
0.048	0.003	0.05		**United Nations Liner Code**
			1.00	Economy is party to the Code and applies Article 2 of the Code.
			0.75	Economy is party to the Code but does not apply Article 2 of the Code.
			0.00	Economy is not party to the Code.
0.048	0.003	0.05		**Government permits conferences**
			1.00	Government permits the operation of conferences.
			0.00	Conferences are subject to effective competition.
0.050	na	0.05		**Bilateral maritime services agreements on cargo sharing** The score for an economy is taken from the 35 by 35 matrix of bilateral agreements on cargo sharing.
0.019	0.001	0.02		**Composition of the board of directors** The score is inversely proportionately to the percentage of the Board that can comprise foreigners. For example, a score of 0.80 is allocated where 20 percent of the board of directors of a maritime service supplier can comprise foreigners.
0.010	0.001	0.01		**Temporary movement of people**
			1.00	No temporary entry of executives, senior managers and/or specialists.
			0.75	Temporary entry of executives, senior managers and/or specialists up to 30 days.
			0.50	Temporary entry of executives, senior managers and/or specialists up to 60 days.
			0.25	Temporary entry of executives, senior managers and/or specialists up to 90 days.
			0.00	Temporary entry of executives, senior managers and/or specialists over 90 days.
0.952	0.048	1.00		**Total**

The term "na" indicates not applicable.

a Totals may not add due to rounding.
b R is the restriction category weighting.
c MFN is the most-favoured-nation category weighting.
d Total of the restriction category and most-favoured-nation category weightings.

DISTRIBUTION SERVICES

Table 10. Restrictiveness index for distribution services

Category weightings[a]				
R[b]	MFN[c]	Total[d]	Score	Restriction category
				Restrictions on establishment
0.2000	na	0.2000		**Restrictions on commercial land**
			1.00	Acquisition of commercial land is not permitted.
			0.50	Acquisition of commercial land is permitted, but is restricted to a certain size.
			0.00	No restrictions on the acquisition of land.
0.2000	na	0.2000		**Direct investment in distribution firms**
				The score will be inversely proportional to the maximum foreign equity participation permitted in a domestic distribution firm. For example, equity participation to a maximum of 75 percent of an existing distribution firm receives a score of 0.25.
0.0500	na	0.0.500		**Restrictions on large-scale stores**
			1.00	National legislation prohibits large-scale stores.
			0.50	Regional and local authorities restrict large-scale stores.
			0.00	No restrictions on large scale stores.
0.0750	na	0.0750		**Factors affecting investment**
			0.30	Takeovers are hindered by regulation.
			0.30	Investors must meet performance requirements.
			0.20	Establishment subject to an economic needs test.
			0.20	Government screening of investment.
0.0750	na	0.0750		**Local government requirements**
			0.40	Establishment subject to a local environmental impact assessment or zoning requirements.
			0.40	Local employment requirements.
			0.20	Restrictions on operating hours.
0.0475	0.0025	0.0500		**Movement of People – Permanent**
			1.00	No entry of executives, senior managers or staff.
			0.80	Executives, senior managers or staff can stay a period of up to 1 year.
			0.60	Executives, senior managers or staff can stay a period of up to 2 years.
			0.40	Executives, senior managers or staff can stay a period of up to 3 years.
			0.20	Executives, senior managers or staff can stay a period of up to 4 years.
			0.00	Executives, senior managers or staff can stay a period of more than 4 years.

Table 10. Restrictiveness index for distribution services–Continued

Category weightings[a]				
R[b]	MFN[c]	Total[d]	Score	Restriction category
0.0750	Na	0.0750		**Wholesale import licensing**
			1.00	No new import licences are available for wholesalers.
			0.50	A limited number of new import licences are available for wholesalers.
			0.00	There are no limits on the issue of import licences.
0.0500	Na	0.0500		**Limits on the promotion of retail products**
			1.00	Distribution firms are prohibited from using advertising and promotion to market retail products.
			0.50	Distribution firms are limited in their use of advertising and promotion to market retail products.
			0.00	No restrictions on advertising/promotion of retail products.
0.1000	Na	0.1000		**Statutory government monopolies**
				The score for an economy is taken from a table of 16 product categories, in which distribution occurs through statutory government monopolies (see text).
0.0500	Na	0.0500		**Protection of intellectual property rights**
			1.00	An economy is on the USTR priority 301 watch list.
			0.50	An economy is on the USTR priority watch list.
			0.00	Intellectual property rights are not on USTR watch lists.
0.0475	0.0025	0.0500		**Licensing requirements on management**
			1.00	All directors or managers or at least a majority of them must be nationals or residents.
			0.75	At least 1 director/manager must be a national or resident.
			0.50	Directors and managers must be locally licensed.
			0.25	Directors and managers must be domiciled in the foreign economy.
0.0237	0.0013	0.0250		**Movement of people – Temporary**
			1.00	No temporary entry of executives, senior managers or staff.
			0.75	Temporary entry of executives, senior managers or staff up to 30 days.
			0.50	Temporary entry of executives, senior managers or staff up to 60 days.
			0.25	Temporary entry of executives, senior managers or staff up to 90 days.
			0.00	Temporary entry of executives, senior managers or staff over 90 days.
0.9937	0.0063	1.00		**Total**

The term "na" indicates not applicable.

a Totals may not add due to rounding. b R is the restriction category weighting. c MFN is the most-favoured-nation category weighting. d Total of the restriction category and MFN category weightings.

Table 11. Restriction categories in the foreign and domestic indexes

Restriction category	Relevant for foreign index	Total weight	Relevant for domestic index	Total weight
Restrictions on commercial presence				
Restrictions on commercial land	Yes	0.200	Yes	0.200
Direct investment	Yes	0.200	Yes	0.200
Restrictions on large-scale stores	Yes	0.050	Yes	0.050
Factors affecting investment	Yes	0.075	Yes	0.075
Local government requirements	Yes	0.075	Yes	0.075
Movement of people – Permanent	Yes	0.050	No	na
Other restrictions				
Wholesale import licensing	Yes	0.075	Yes	0.075
Limits on promotion of retail products	Yes	0.050	Yes	0.050
Statutory government monopolies	Yes	0.100	Yes	0.100
Protection of intellectual property rights	Yes	0.050	Yes	0.050
Licensing requirements on management	Yes	0.050	No	na
Movement of people – Temporary	Yes	0.025	No	na
Total weighting or highest possible score		**1.00**		**0.875**

The term "na" indicates not applicable.

PROFESSIONAL SERVICES

Table 12. Restrictiveness index for professional services

Category weights	Specific score	Restriction category
		BARRIERS TO ESTABLISHMENT
0.08		**Form of establishment**
	1.00	Prohibition on incorporation
	0.50	Some form of incorporation permitted
	0.00	No restrictions
0.08		**Foreign partnership or joint venture**
	1.00	Prohibition on partnership with foreign professionals
	0.50	Partnership or joint venture with local professionals required
	0.00	No restrictions
0.05		**Investment and ownership by foreign professionals**
		Firms must be owned or controlled by local professionals. The score is inversely proportional to the maximum foreign equity participation permitted in a professional firm. For example, equity participation to a maximum of 75 percent in an existing firm receives a score of 0.25.

Table 12. Restrictiveness index for professional services–Continued

Category weights	Specific score	Restriction category
		BARRIERS TO ESTABLISHMENT
		Investment and ownership by non-professional investors
0.05		Firms must be owned or controlled by professionals. The score is proportional to the non-professional equity participation permitted in a professional firm. For example, equity participation to a maximum of 75 percent in an existing firm receives a score of 0.25.
0.135		**Nationality or citizenship requirements**
	1.00	Nationality required to qualify or to practice
	0.25	Nationality required for use of professional title, but practice is relatively free
	0.00	No restrictions
0.135		**Residency and local presence**
	1.00	Permanent or prior residency (more than 12 months)
	0.75	Less than 12 months prior residency
	0.50	Prior residency required for local training
	0.25	Domicile or representative office only
	0.00	No restrictions
0.10		**Quotas or economic needs tests on the number of foreign professionals and firms**
	1.00	Quotas or economic needs tests
	0.50	Some restrictions apply
	0.00	No restrictions
	0.25	Aptitude tests
	0.00	Foreign licence and qualifications sufficient to practice
0.05		Licensing and accreditation of local professionalsa
	0.25	Compulsory membership of professional association
	0.25	Professional examination
	0.25	Practical experience
	0.25	Higher education
0.02		Permanent movement of people
	1.00	No entry of executives, senior managers or specialists
	0.80	Entry of up to 1 year
	0.60	Entry of up to 2 years
	0.40	Entry of up to 3 years
	0.20	Entry of up to 4 years
	0.00	Entry of up to 5 years or more
0.05		Activities reserved by law to the profession
	1.00	4 core activities and over
	0.75	3 core activities
	0.50	2 core activities
	0.25	1 core activity
	0.00	None

Table 12. Restrictiveness index for professional services–Continued

Category weights	Specific score	Restriction category
		BARRIERS TO ONGOING OPERATIONS
0.05		**Multi-disciplinary practices**
	1.00	Prohibition on partnership or association with other professions
	0.50	Majority partnership required
	0.00	No restrictions
0.05		**Advertising, marketing and solicitation**
	1.00	Prohibition of advertising, marketing and solicitation
	0.50	Restrictions apply to some groups or activities
	0.00	General legal requirements
	0.50	Restrictions apply to some groups or activities
	0.00	Setting fee freely
0.02		**Licensing requirements on management**
	1.00	At least a majority of managers must be nationals or residents
	0.50	Directors and managers must be locally licensed
	0.25	Directors and managers must be domiciled
	0.00	No restrictions
0.02		**Other restrictions**[a]
	0.33	Restrictions on hiring local professionals
	0.33	Restrictions on the use of firm's international names
	0.33	Government procurement – restrictions towards foreign suppliers
	0.00	No restrictions
0.01		**Temporary movement of people**
	1.00	No temporary entry
	0.75	Temporary entry of up to 30 days
	0.50	Temporary entry of up to 60 days
	0.25	Temporary entry of up to 90 days
	0.00	Temporary entry over 90 days
1.00		**FOREIGN INDEX**[b]
0.38		**DOMESTIC INDEX**[b]

a Addition categories.

b Sum of individual weights for foreign and domestic restrictions. See also table 6.

Table 13. Restriction categories for foreign and domestic index

Restriction categories	Relevant to foreign index	Weight	Relevant to domestic index	Weight
Barriers to establishment				
Form of establishment	Yes	0.080	Yes	0.080
Foreign partnership or joint venture	Yes	0.080	No	na
Investment and ownership by foreign professionals	Yes	0.050	No	na
Investment and ownership by non-professional investors	Yes	0.050	Yes	0.050
Nationality requirements	Yes	0.135	No	na
Residency and local presence requirements	Yes	0.135	No	na
Quotas/economic needs test	Yes	0.100	No	na
Licensing and accreditation of foreign professionals	Yes	0.100	No	na
Licensing and accreditation of local professionals	No	na	Yes	0.05
Permanent movement of people	Yes	0.020	No	na
Barriers to ongoing operations				
Activities reserved by law to the profession	Yes	0.050	Yes	0.050
Multi-disciplinary practices	Yes	0.050	Yes	0.050
Advertising, marketing and solicitation	Yes	0.050	Yes	0.050
Fee setting	Yes	0.050	Yes	0.050
Licensing requirements on management	Yes	0.020	No	na
Other restrictions	Yes	0.020	No	na
Temporary movement of people	Yes	0.010	No	na
Total weight		**1.000**		**0.380**

The term "na" indicates not applicable.

INTERNATIONAL AIR PASSENGER TRANSPORT

Table 14. Bilateral index for international air passenger transport

Restriction category		Specific score	Weights[a]
Designation requirements			0.24
Single destination	Each economy permits only one airline to provide the service between it and other destinations	1.00	
Multiple destination with route limitations	The bilateral partners permit more than one airline to provide the service, but on specific routes only one airline is allowed to operate	0.67	
Multiple destination	Each economy may designate more than one airline to operate the service (without specific route limitations)	0.33	
No requirements		0.00	

Table 14. Bilateral index for international air passenger transport–Continued

Restriction category		Specific score	Weights[a]
Capacity regulation			0.24
Predetermination	Agreement on capacity reached by both economies before airline operations begin. Predetermination can involve a specified capacity share between airlines, maximum (or minimum) frequencies of flights, or geographic allocation of capacity	1.00	
Hybrid	Provisions which cannot be classified under any of the above categories, or combinations of the above categories.	0.67	
Bermuda 1	Capacity regulations similar to those in the 1946 agreement between the United Kingdom and the United States. Under this arrangement, airlines act separately to determine capacity with *ex post* government monitoring and review (if an airline contests the capacity provided by an another airline)	0.33	
Free determination	Liberal provisions in which both economies agree not to impose unilateral restrictions, except for general safety and technical reasons.	0.00	
Price regulation			0.27
Double approval	Proposed airfares require the approval of both economies before they can take effect	1.00	
Country of origin approval	A country may disapprove airfares only for flights from its own territory	0.67	
Double disapproval	Airfares would be allowed unless they are disapproved by both economies, reducing government involvement and providing airlines the flexibility to set fares	0.33	
No requirements		0.00	
Non-scheduled services			0.22
No formal traffic rights for charter services		1.00	
Explicit traffic rights for charter services		0.00	
Total score			**0.97**

a Weights derived by factor analysis (Gonenc and Nicoletti 2000).

Source: Gonenc and Nicoletti (2000).

EDUCATION SERVICES

Table 15. Restrictiveness index for education services, consumption abroad

Restriction category	Specific score	Maximum index score
DOMESTIC INDEX – INWARD MOVEMENT OF FOREIGN STUDENTS		
Numbers of foreign students		1.00
Quotas on foreign students	1.00	

Table 15. Restrictiveness index for education services, consumption abroad–Continued

Restriction category	Specific score	Maximum index score
DOMESTIC INDEX – INWARD MOVEMENT OF FOREIGN STUDENTS		
Number of foreign students are restricted for particular foreign countries, or educational institutions/sub-sectors	0.50	
No restrictions	0.00	
Visa entry requirements – addition categories		1.00
Length/class of visa	0.20	
Requirements for admission to educational institutions	0.20	
Proof of financial support	0.20	
Language skills	0.20	
Cost of visa and other requirements	0.20	
Recognition of overseas qualifications		1.00
Reported non-recognition of foreign qualifications for admission to domestic educational institutions	1.00	
Overseas qualifications are recognised in part or on a case-by-case basis	0.50	
Full recognition of overseas qualifications	0.00	
Registration requirements specific to export of education services – addition categories		1.00
Compulsory registration	0.33	
Financial viability/assurance/prepayment of course fees requirement	0.33	
Charges/levies	0.33	
Other restrictions – addition categories		1.00
Limits on foreign student access to employment	0.50	
Limits on foreign student access to public concessions	0.50	
Transparency of regulations		1.00
Reported difficulties in obtaining information on regulations and lack of consistency and clarity in regulatory implementation	1.00	
Regulations are stated in legislation, but inconsistency in implementation is reported	0.50	
Lack of transparency is not reported	0.00	
TOTAL		6.00
FOREIGN INDEX – OUTWARD MOVEMENT OF DOMESTIC STUDENTS		
Number of domestic students studying abroad		1.00
Quotas on domestic student numbers	1.00	
No restrictions	0.00	
Visa exit requirements – addition categories		1.00
Requirement to have licensed travel agents	0.50	
Age restrictions	0.50	

Table 15. Restrictiveness index for education services, consumption abroad–Continued

Restriction category	Specific score	Maximum index score
Recognition of overseas qualifications		1.00
Reported non-recognition of overseas qualifications obtained by domestic students	1.00	
Overseas qualifications are recognised in part or on a case-by-case basis	0.50	
Full recognition of overseas qualifications	0.00	
Other restrictions – addition categories		1.00
Limits on foreign exchange, payment transfers or use of credit cards by students	0.33	
Limits on access to public concessions for domestic students to study abroad	0.33	
Restrictions on student recruitment for study in overseas institutions	0.33	
Transparency of regulations		1.00
Reported difficulties in obtaining information on regulations and lack of consistency and clarity in regulatory implementation	1.00	
Regulations are stated in legislations, but inconsistency in implementation is reported	0.50	
Lack of transparency is not reported	0.00	
TOTAL		5.00

Table 16. Restrictiveness index for education services, commercial presence

Restriction category	Specific score	Maximum index score
BARRIERS TO ESTABLISHMENT		
Number of foreign providers		1.00
Quotas on the number of foreign providers permitted to establish a campus	1.00	
Registration and authorisation required for establishment, including different approval requirements at the sub-national level	0.50	
No restrictions	0.00	
Foreign direct investment		1.00
The score is inversely proportional to the maximum equity participation permitted in domestic businesses. For example, equity participation to a maximum of 75 percent in an existing firm receives a score of 0.25.		
Joint venture or partnership		1.00
Entry is only allowed through joint venture or partnership with local institutions	1.00	
No restrictions	0.00	
Local enrolment in international schools		1.00
Quotas/restrictions on domestic student enrolments in international schools	1.00	

Table 16. Restrictiveness index for education services, commercial presence–Continued

Restriction category	Specific score	Maximum index score
No restrictions	0.00	
Recognition of qualifications		1.00
Reported non-recognition of qualifications provided by foreign institutions established domestically	1.00	
Qualifications are recognised in part or on a case-by-case basis	0.50	
Full recognition of qualifications	0.00	
ONGOING OPERATIONS		
Other restrictions – addition categories		1.00
Legal use of names or university title	0.10	
Quotas for employment of local staff	0.10	
Curriculum content	0.10	
Fee setting	0.10	
Repatriation of earnings, foreign exchange and capital transfers	0.10	
Advertising and marketing of education services	0.10	
Licensing requirements on management	0.10	
Local language requirement for teaching	0.10	
Limited measures to protect intellectual property	0.10	
Limits on access to public subsidies for foreign providers of education services	0.10	
TRANSPARENCY OF REGULATIONS		
Lack of transparency		1.00
Reported difficulties in obtaining information on regulations and lack of consistency and clarity in regulatory implementation	1.00	
Regulations are stated in legislations, but inconsistency in implementation is reported	0.50	
Lack of transparency is not reported	0.00	
TOTAL		7.00

Table 17. Restrictiveness index for education services, cross-border supply

Restriction category	Specific score	Maximum index score
Local presence and partnership		1.00
A local presence and/or partnership is required in order to provide distance education	1.00	
No restrictions	0.00	
Recognition of overseas qualifications		1.00
Reported non-recognition of overseas qualifications obtained via distance education	1.00	
Overseas qualifications are recognised in part or on a case-by-case basis	0.50	
Full recognition of qualifications	0.00	

Table 17. Restrictiveness index for education services, cross-border supply–Continued

Restriction category	Specific score	Maximum index score
Other restrictions – addition categories		1.00
Import of educational material	0.25	
Access to internet services	0.25	
Repatriation of earnings, foreign exchange and payment transfers	0.25	
Advertising of distance education services	0.25	
Transparency of regulations		1.00
Reported difficulties in obtaining information on regulations and lack of consistency and clarity in regulatory implementation	1.00	
Regulations are stated in legislations, but inconsistency in implementation is reported	0.50	
Lack of transparency is not reported	0.00	
TOTAL		4.00

Table 18. Restrictiveness index for education services, presence of natural persons

Restriction category	Specific score	Maximum index score
Number of (temporary) staff and working permits		1.00
Limits on the number of temporary foreign staff and working permits or visas	1.00	
Grant of working permits or visas is subject to recognition of professional qualifications	0.50	
Limits on the length of working permits	0.25	
No restrictions	0.00	
Other restrictions		1.00
Repatriation of earnings, foreign exchange and capital transfers	1.00	
No restrictions	0.00	
Transparency of regulations		1.00
Reported difficulties in obtaining information on regulations and lack of consistency and clarity in regulatory implementation	1.00	
Regulations are stated in legislations, but inconsistency in implementation is reported	0.50	
Lack of transparency is not reported	0.00	
TOTAL		3.00

References

1. Boylaud, O. and Nicoletti, G. 2000, *Regulation, Market Structure and Performance in Telecommunications*, Working Paper No. 237, ECO/WKP(2000)10, Economics Department, OECD, Paris, 12 April.

2. Dee, P. 2001, 'Trade in services', paper presented at conference on Impacts of Trade Liberalisation Agreements on Latin America and the Caribbean, Inter-American Development Bank, Washington DC, 5-6 November.
3. Doove, S., Gabbitas, O., Nguyen-Hong, D. and Owen, J. 2001, *Price Effects of Regulation: International Air Passenger Transport, Telecommunications and Electricity Supply*, Productivity Commission Staff Research Paper, Ausinfo, Canberra.
4. Findlay, C. and Warren, T. (eds) 2000, *Impediments to Trade in Services: Measurement and Policy Implications*, Routledge, London and New York.
5. Gonenc, R. and Nicoletti, G. 2000, *Regulation, Market Structure and Performance in Air Passenger Transport*, Working Paper No. 254, ECO/WKP(2000)27, Economics Department, OECD, Paris, 3 August.
6. Hardin, A. and Holmes, L. 2000, 'Assessing barriers to services sector investment', in Findlay, C. and Warren, T. (eds) 2000, *Impediments to Trade in Services: Measurement and Policy Implications*, Routledge, London and New York, pp. 52–70.
7. Johnson, M., Gregan, T., Gentle, G. and Belin, P. 2000, 'Modelling the benefits of increasing competition in international air services', in Findlay, C. and Warren, T. (eds) 2000, *Impediments to Trade in Services: Measurement and Policy Implications*, Routledge, London and New York, pp. 119–51.
8. Kalirajan, K. 2000, Restrictions on Trade in Distribution Services, Productivity Commission Staff Research Paper, Ausinfo, Canberra.
9. ———, McGuire, G., Nguyen-Hong, D. and Schuele, M. 2000, 'The price impact of restrictions on banking services', in Findlay, C. and Warren, T. (eds) 2000, *Impediments to Trade in Services: Measurement and Policy Implications*, Routledge, London and New York, pp. 215–30.
10. Kang, J. 2000, 'Price impact of restrictions on maritime transport services', in Findlay, C. and Warren, T. (eds) 2000, *Impediments to Trade in Services: Measurement and Policy Implications*, Routledge, London and New York, pp. 189–200.
11. Kemp, S. 2000, 'Trade in education services and the impacts of barriers to trade', in Findlay, C. and Warren, T. (eds) 2000, *Impediments to Trade in Services: Measurement and Policy Implications*, Routledge, London and New York, pp. 231–44.
12. McGuire, G. 1998, *Australia's Restrictions on Trade in Financial Services*, Productivity Commission Staff Research Paper, Ausinfo, Canberra.
13. and Schuele, M. 2000, 'Restrictiveness of international trade in banking services', in Findlay, C. and Warren, T. (eds) 2000, *Impediments to Trade in Services: Measurement and Policy Implications*, Routledge, London and New York, pp. 201–14.
14. ———, Schuele, M., and Smith, T. 2000, 'Restrictiveness of international trade in maritime services', in Findlay, C. and Warren, T. (eds) 2000, *Impediments to Trade in Services: Measurement and Policy Implications*, Routledge, London and New York, pp. 172–88.
15. Nguyen-Hong, D. 2000, *Restrictions on Trade in Professional Services*, Productivity Commission Staff Research Paper, Ausinfo, Canberra.
16. and Wells, R. (2003), *Restrictions on Trade in Education Services*, Productivity Commission Staff Working Paper, Canberra.

17. Steiner, F. 2000, *Regulation, Industry Structure and Performance in the Electricity Supply Industry*, Working Paper No. 238, ECO/WKP(2000)11, Economics Department, OECD, Paris, 12 April.
18. Trewin, R. 2000, 'A price-impact measure of impediments to trade in telecommunications services', in Findlay, C. and Warren, T. (eds) 2000, *Impediments to Trade in Services: Measurement and Policy Implications*, Routledge, London and New York, pp. 101–18.
19. Verikios, G. and Zhang, X-G. 2001, *Global Gains from Liberalising Trade in Telecommunications and Financial Services*, Productivity Commission Staff Research Paper, Ausinfo, Canberra.
20. Warren, T. 2000a, 'The identification of impediments to trade and investment in telecommunications services', in Findlay, C. and Warren, T. (eds) 2000, *Impediments to Trade in Services: Measurement and Policy Implications*, Routledge, London and New York, pp. 71–84.
21. 2000b, 'The impact on output of impediments to trade and investment in telecommunications services', in Findlay, C. and Warren, T. (eds) 2000, *Impediments to Trade in Services: Measurement and Policy Implications*, Routledge, London and New York, pp. 85–100.

DEVELOPING GOVERNMENTAL ANALYTICAL CAPACITIES IN THE TRADE POLICY AREA

Robert Koopman

U.S. International Trade Commission[1]

1. Introduction - The Role of Analysis as Conducted at the United States International Trade Commission

Within the United States trade policy formulation process economic analysis is but one part of the process. The ITC and other government analytical groups provide economic analysis for policymakers (such as USTR, the President, and Congress) as input to their deliberations. Many others provide input including advisors, Congress, special interest groups, think tanks, *etc.*

2. The Role of Analytics

Understanding the role of analytics in the policy process is important. But one can also not take for granted that customers understand what the analysis is able to show. Economics predicts that reducing or removing restrictive trade policies increases economic efficiency and enhances economic growth through: expanding trade volumes; Resources move from less productive sectors of the economy to more productive sectors; prices for imported goods fall, consumers benefit; prices for exported goods may rise, firms benefit; increased investment in growing sectors brings longer term economic growth.

The analyst needs tools and data to try and measure these effects. Typically the analyst will use economic models to simulate impacts on economy and up-to-date, comprehensive data bases for use policy formulation and in models. A critical factor is the need for the analyst to provide the information generated from models and databases to policymakers in a useful format to decision makers.

Careful analytics can help identify who benefits and who may suffer losses, and by how much. This helps the policymakers weigh the benefits and costs of the policy change. A good, independent analysis, with high quality tools will therefore position the policy maker with objective advice on benefits and losses, early

---

[1] Robert Koopman is Director of the Office of Economics, U.S. International Trade Commission. The views expressed in this article are those of the author. They are not the views of the U.S. International Trade Commission (USITC) as a whole nor any of its individual Commissioners. The author may be contacted *via* email at *robert.koopman@usitc.gov*.

warning on which sectors will have the greatest interests – positive or negative, and a comprehensive assessment of complicated economic interactions.

For the analysis to be most useful to policymakers the trade policy analyst must understand the frame of reference of the policymaker, rather than academic colleagues. Thus the analyst must get the question the policy maker wants answered defined in an understandable way, and also a way that can be answered reasonably well, decide what kind of framework is appropriate to answer the question, and realize that the policymaker may know very little about how the analyst will answer the question – and is mainly interested in a defensible answer.

To do this work well the analyst must organize their thinking, must devise a plan of attack that produces a timely, understandable, sensible, and defensible answer.

Economists often use economic models to organize their thinking. All models, applied and theoretical, are incomplete by definition. They are deliberately simple representations of a complex world, designed to let us focus on possible interactions in a subset of important elements. As a result – the answers we generate are often narrowly focuses and sensitive to how we chose to simplify the world in our model. Our answers are often in the "neighborhood" of what could actually happen. Sometimes we provide a range of outcomes. It is important for policymakers to understand how we use models, their strengths and limitations.

Quite frankly, applied models simply help organize our thinking. Applied modeling allows us to use real world data in combination with a specific representation of how we think these variables are related to one another. We state clearly, for others to see, both the data and the nature of the relationship – they may agree or not – and can specify their own thinking.

It is important to keep in mind that institutions like the ITC studies seldom rely solely on modeling. Most ITC studies include extensive industry by industry discussions on the potential impact of the proposed policy change on that industry. These describe specific trends occurring in the industry, and what industry representatives think about the proposed changes. In addition the Commission collects, synthesizes, and analyzes/interprets large amounts of data.

What kinds of analytical simulation tools does the ITC use? All are "supply" and "demand" market equilibrium models. We use both partial equilibrium models and general equilibrium models.

In addition to simulation models we often use econometric models to provide insights on parameter values and to test the existence and size of specific economic relationships.

Most of the partial equilibrium models used at the ITC describe a single sector, in a multi-country setting, and can be very industry detailed – by tariff line. We also have a single country CGE model that is multi-sector model that describes all economic activity in the economy, and captures intersectoral relationships. This model is much more aggregate than the partial equilibrium models, breaking the economy into hundreds of sectors that reflect large groups of similar tariff lines. The ITC also uses a multi-country CGE model called GTAP (Global Trade Analysis Project), which is a multi-sector, multi-country model that describes all economic activity in each economy, and captures intersectoral relationships, is highly aggregated – perhaps breaking economies into around 60 sectors

3. The ITC's Partial Equilibrium Models

The ITC primarily uses "COMPAS", which uses an Armington specification (that is goods are distinguished by country of origin.). COMPAS is a multi-country, single sector, imperfect substitutes, perfect competition model. It focuses on equilibrium demand and supply within a single industry. COMPAS has the advantages that it is highly focused on one sector, easy to run, has very small data requirements, is highly flexible in applications, and is spreadsheet based.

COMPAS' disadvantages are that it does not capture interactions between focus industry and other markets, and the analyst often must guess at values for economic relationships. The model also does not provide for highly specialized market specifications.

The skills required to use most partial equilibrium models include a good knowledge of economics (Masters degree or better), knowledge of spreadsheets or simple modeling software, and trade databases. Models like COMPAS are relative low cost to use and maintain.

There are many partial equilibrium models other than COMPAS. Many partial equilibrium models are used to link up and downstream sectors *i.e.*, sugar, cocoa, and the chocolate market. Other models will model a subsector of the economy – such as agriculture, some examples include E-SIM and SWOPSIM. Where to find some useful partial equilibrium models? Contact me at rkoopman@usitc.gov or see Joe Francois' site
http://www.intereconomics.com/handbook/Models/Index.htm. You can also find downloads or links to major applied modeling tools UNCTAD, WTO International Trade Centers' PC-TAS: THE WORLD'S LARGEST TRADE DATABASE ON CD-ROM can be found at *http://www.intracen.org/* then click on PC-TAS.

4. The ITC's Single Country CGE Models

The ITC currently uses two large single country models, the USITC CGE and USAGE-ITC models. These are multi-sector (500 sectors), imperfect substitutes, perfect competition models with a 1999 base year. The ITC also uses a smaller single country model called TSCAPE model, which has 42 sectors, and a database covering 1978-2001.

These models focus on simultaneous changes in all product and factor markets within the U.S. economy, and on the "real" side of the economy, *i.e.*, economywide versus macro model. Their main advantage is the simultaneous tracking of interactions between all product and factor sectors. Their main disadvantages include: a high level of complexity, they are very resource intensive, have a single country focus, their data is relatively inflexible, and they have a relatively high level of aggregation.

The skills required to use these detailed single country CGE models include a high level of economic expertise (PhD), preferably with extensive experience in CGE work (*i.e.*, dissertation.) They also require an excellent knowledge of relevant software, excellent knowledge of national income accounts, various trade databases, tariff and NTM databases.

5. The ITC's Multi-Country CGE models

The ITC uses the Global Trade Analysis Project (GTAP) multi-country/regional (around 60 regions), multi-sector (about 50 sectors), imperfect substitutes, perfect or imperfect competition, "real" economy model. GTAP focuses on simultaneous changes in all product and factor markets across economies.

GTAP's advantages include a global GE structure, a standard database, exceptional technical support, a user friendly interface, and an extensive user community. GTAP's

Disadvantages include high level of complexity, resource intensive, inflexible data base (currently 1997 base year), a high level of aggregation, and the need to check and confirm existing data.

The skills required to use these multi country CGE models include a high level of economic expertise (PhD), preferably with extensive experience in CGE work (ie dissertation.) They also require an excellent knowledge of relevant software, excellent knowledge of national income accounts, various trade databases, tariff and NTM databases.

Where can you find some useful general equilibrium models? See Joe Francois' site *http://www.intereconomics.com/handbook/Models/Index.htm*, or downloads or links to major applied modeling tools see the International Food Policy Research Institute site *http://www.ifpri.org/* - click on Research, then Research Division, then Trade and Macroeconomics, then look under Methodologies. Finally see the Global Trade Analysis Project site *http://www.gtapage.com.purdue.edu/* or see Deardorff and Stern's "Michigan Model" site *http://www.umich.edu/~fschool/rsie/model/*

6. Econometric Estimation at the USITC

Econometrics is the study of the application of statistical techniques to the analysis of economic relationships. Many of the statistical techniques were developed specifically to deal with situations typically encountered in empirical work in economics. Econometrics is often used to combine economic theory and statistical inference to modify, refine, possibly refute conclusions drawn from economic theory. Usually used to examine ex post relationships. Econometrics uses historical data to assess historical relationships between economic factors. It can look at microeconomic or macroeconomic relationships.

In trade policy, econometric estimation can be used to examine a very wide variety of topics: measuring the effect of certain variables or policies on one industry, assessing whether trade liberalization improves economic performance, testing the validity of policy tools (*e.g.* simulation models), determining signs, specific values, and the reliability of variable coefficients in economic relationships (this often includes determining parameter values for simulation models.) Econometrics is frequently very data intensive, and it is often hard to distinguish the separate effect of different factors.

The skills needed to conduct econometric analysis include generally a PhD in economics, with emphasis on econometrics, excellent understanding of economic theory and statistical properties, and excellent knowledge of databases and data handling software.

7. Data Collection and Presentation at the USITC

The ITC is a major source of data on trade and trade policy. The ITC is responsible for keeping the Official Tariff Schedule of the United States – the HTS. The ITC collects data on trade from US Government statistical agencies, and integrates the data into an easily accessible data base – DATAWEB – see *http://dataweb.usitc.gov/*. In addition the ITC uses World Bank, WTO, and UNCTAD Trains databases, which can be found at *http://www.worldbank.org/data/*, *http://www.wto.org/english/res_e/statis_e/statis_e.htm* *http://r0.unctad.org/trains/*. We also collect data through questionnaires and other sources I have provided a CD that contains copies of some recent USITC publications that utilize some or all of the topics we have covered – all of these can be found on our website, *www.usitc.gov*.

TECHNIQUES FOR ESTIMATING TRADE FACILITATION EFFECTS

Tsunehiro Otsuki

World Bank [1]

Three Challenges in Measuring Effect

- Measuring trade facilitation
  - Not just about transport cost, or customs clearance, or inventory, or communications, or standards, but all of these.
- Choosing a methodology
  - Needs to be broad-based for many economies
  - CGE vs. econometric
- Designing a scenario to gauge benefits
  - One-size fits all vs. scaled changes for different economies

What to Consider in Measuring Trade Facilitation?

- Coverage – More than Transport
- Consistency – Economy-specific information on a consistent basis from multiple sources for each indicator
- Reliability – Can be increased by "oversampling" multiple sources for each indicator reduces dependence on any one source

Trade Facilitation: Areas of Focus in Existing Empirical Works

- Transports
  - UNCTAD (2001), APEC (1999), Fink, Mattoo, Neagu (2002)
- Customs
  - Hummels (2001)
- Information technology infrastructure
  - Freund and Weinhold (2000), Hertel, Walmsley and Itakura (2001)
- Multi-dimensional approach
  - Wilson, Mann, Otsuki (2003)

---

[1] Development Research Group (DECRG), the World Bank, 1818 H Street, NW, Washington, DC. The author may be contracted *via* email at tsuki@worldbank.org. The views expressed here are those of the author and should not be attributed to the World Bank.

Measuring Trade Facilitation: Definition

- Simplification & harmonization of trade procedures through:
  - Reduced transport costs
  - Improved ports facilities
  - Efficient and modern customs regimes
  - Transparent and harmonized regulations
  - Improved information technology infrastructure

Measuring Trade Facilitation: Four Areas of Focus

- Port efficiency
- Customs environment
- Regulatory environment
- Service sector infrastructure

Building Indicator–Step 1: Defining Inputs to Indicator

- Cross-economy survey data- 75 economies
  - Global Competitiveness Report (GCR)
  - World Competitiveness Yearbook (WCY)
  - Kaufmann, Kraay and Zoido-Lobaton (KKZ)
- "Port efficiency" for each economy J is the average of two indexed inputs from GCR:
  - Port facilities and inland waterways
  - Air transport
- "Customs environment" for each economy J is the average of two indexed inputs from GCR:
  - Hidden import barriers
  - Irregular extra payments and bribes
- "Regulatory environment" for each economy J is constructed as the average of indexed inputs from WCY and KKZ:
  - Transparency of government policy is satisfactory (WCY)
  - Control of corruption (KKZ)
- "Service-sector infrastructures" for each economy J is from GCR:
  - Speed and cost of internet access
  - Effect of internet on business

Building Indicator–Step 2: Normalization

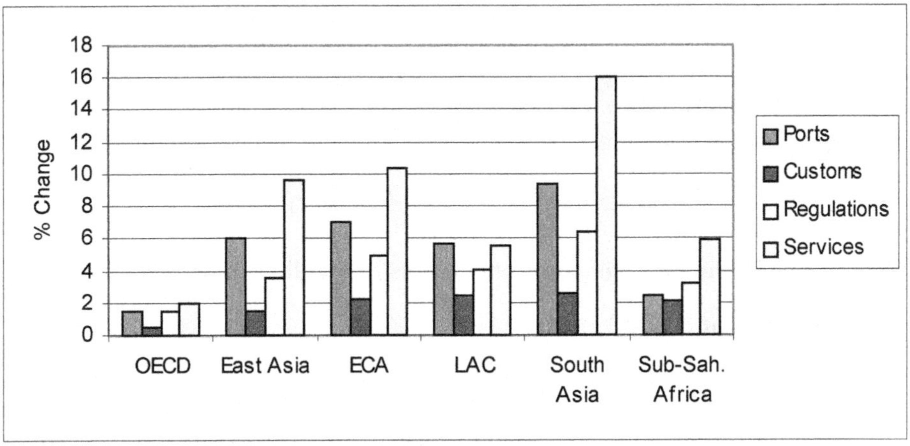

Figure 1. Two indexed inputs to port efficiency

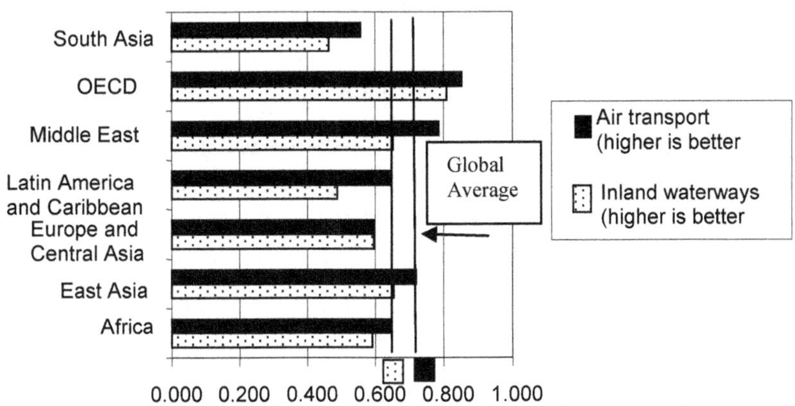

Building Indicator–Step 3: Aggregation

- Averaging inputs
  - Arithmetic average
  - Geometric average
- More advanced approach
  - Weighted average
  - Factor analysis

Method of Measuring: Computable General Equilibrium

- Trade gains and GDP gains:
  - UNCTAD: 1 percent cost reduction yields $3.3 billion in Asia
  - APEC: 1 percent (ICs) 2 percent (LDCs) reduction in import prices yields 3.3 percent increase in exports

Measuring Effect: Choice of Methods

- Impact assessment w.r.t. welfare, GDP, wage income, returns to capital, *etc.* → CGE
- Impact assessment w.r.t. import/export, market prices→ Econometrics

Measuring Effect: CGE Model Approach

- UNCTAD (2001) & APEC (1999)–Results for trade and GDP gains
  - UNCTAD: 1 percent cost reduction yields $3.3 billion in Asia
  - APEC: 1 percent (ICs) 2 percent (LDCs) shock to import prices yields 3.3 percent increase in exports

Method of Measuring: Econometrics

- Hummels: Customs clearance
  - One day equals 0.5 reduction in tariffs
- Freund and Weinhold: E-commerce
  - 10 percent increase web-hosts increase trade 1 percent
- Fink, Mattoo, Neagu: Communications costs
  - 10 percent fall in telecom costs increase trade 8 percent
- Wilson, Mann and Otsuki (2003)
  - Four indicators of trade facilitation in APEC trade

Measuring Effect: Gravity Model

Gravity model-Accounting trade by

- ❖ Gravity factors- GNP, population, distance
- ❖ Trade promoting factors-FTA, facilitation
- ❖ Trade limiting factors- regulations, frictions

Characteristics

- ❖ Statistical approach
- ❖ Essentially based on partial equilibrium

Model Specification

Tariff

$$\ln(V_{JI}^{t}) = b_1 \ln(100+TARIFF_{JI}^{t})$$

Exporter's TF Indicator

$$+ b_2 \ln PE_J + b_3 \ln RE_J + b_4 \ln SI_J$$

$$+ b_5 \ln PE_I + b_6 \ln CE_I + b_7 \ln REI_I + b_8 \ln SI_I$$

Importer's TF Indicator

$$+ b_9 \ln(GNP_I^{t}) + b_{10} \ln(GNP_J^{t}) + b_{11} \ln(GNPPC_I^{t})$$

$$+ b_{12} \ln(GNPPC_J^{t}) + b_{13} \ln(DIST_{IJ})$$

Gravity Variables

$$+ b_{14} D_{ADJ} + b_{15} D_{ASEAN} + b_{16} D_{NAFTA} + b_{17} D_{LAIA}$$

$$+ b_{18} D_{AUNZ} + b_{19} D_{MERCOSUR} + b_{20} D_{EU}$$

FTA Dummies

$$+ b_{21} D_{ENG} + b_{22} D_{FRC} + b_{23} D_{SPN} + b_{24} D_{ARB} + b_{25} D_{CHN}$$

$$+ b_{26} D_{GMN} + b_{27} D_{POR} + b_{28} D_{RUS} + b_{29} D_{2000}$$

Language Dummies

$$+ e_{JI}^{t}$$

Error Term

Gravity Model Result

Port Efficiency	Importer	0.307*
	Exporter	0.924***
Customs Environment	Importer	0.472**
	Exporter	n.a.
Regulatory Environment	Importer	0.281*
	Exporter	0.620***
Service-sector infrastructures	Importer	0.729***
	Exporter	1.943***
GNP	Importer	0.915***
	Exporter	1.246***
Per capita GNP	Importer	-0.182***
	Exporter	-0.226***
Geographical Distance	Importer	-1.258***
	Exporter	0.307*

Simulation

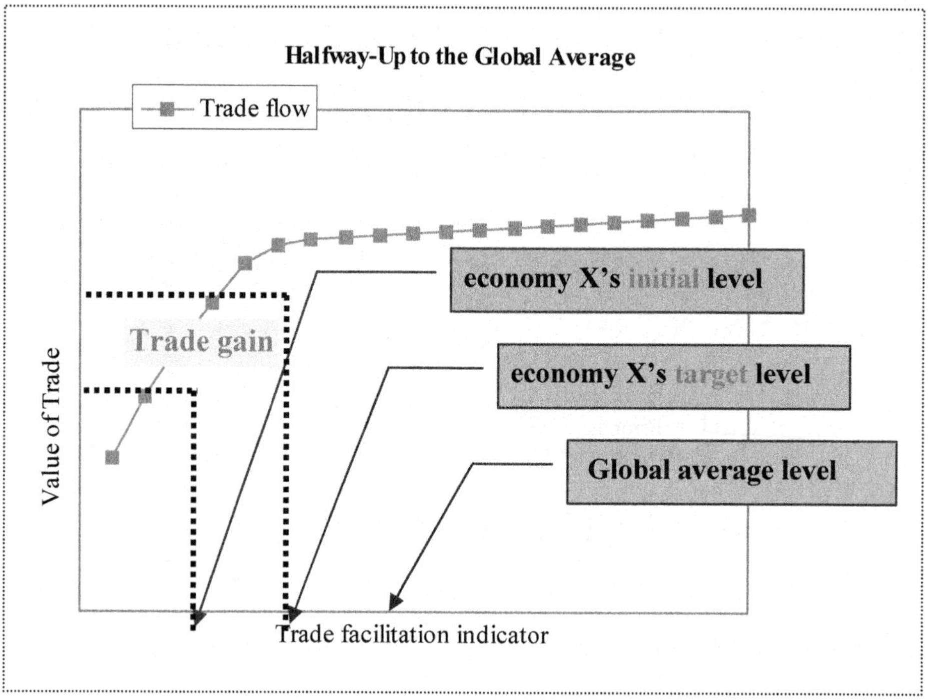

Raising Capacity Half-Way to Global Average
$377 billion increase in 75 economies

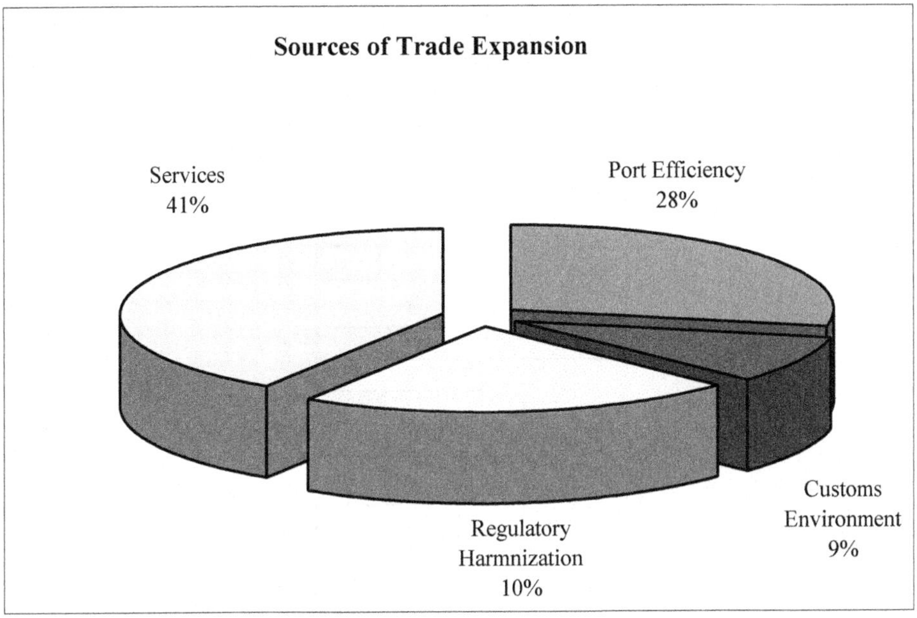

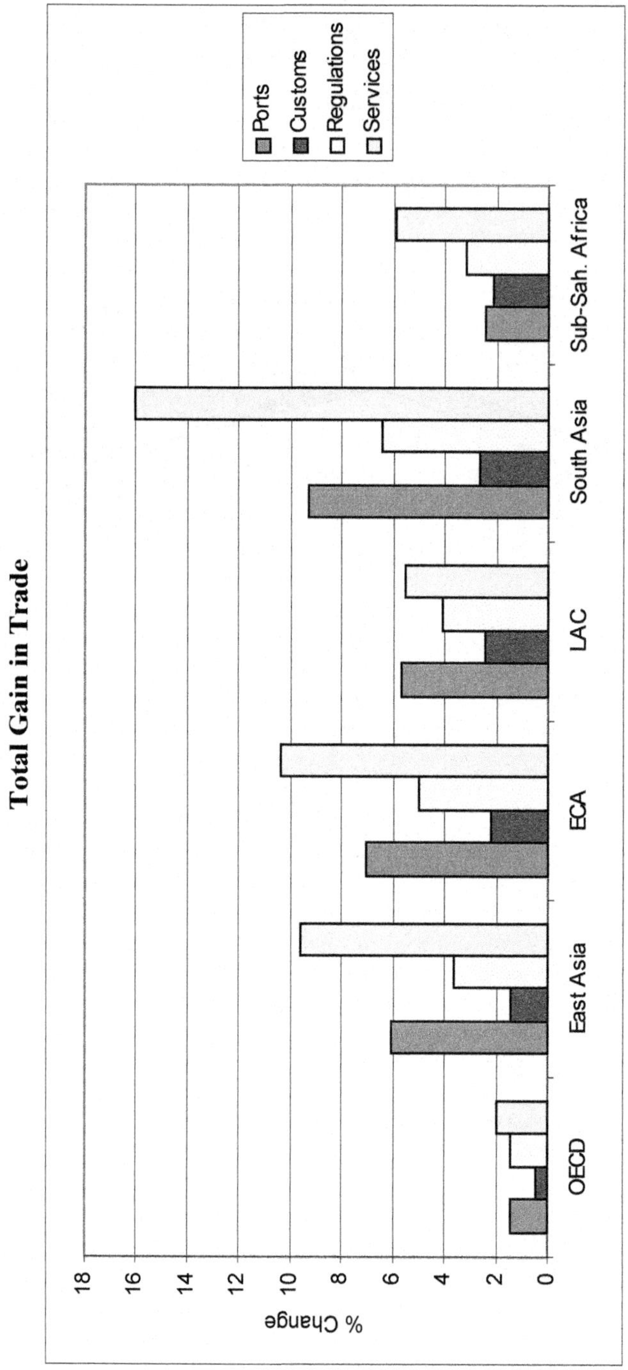
Total Gain in Trade
Ports
Customs
Regulations
Services
% Change
18
16
14
12
10
8
6
4
2
0
OECD
East Asia
ECA
LAC
South Asia
Sub-Sah. Africa

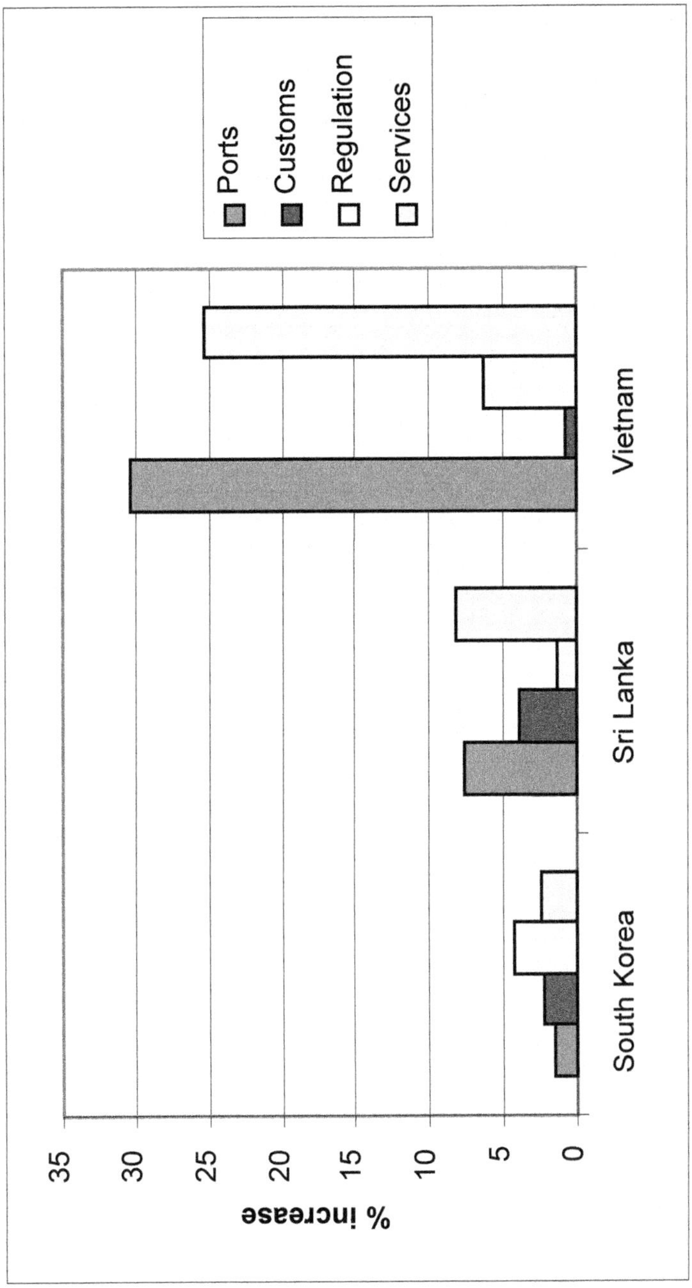
Trade Gain from Domestic & Partner's Reform
% increase
35
30
25
20
15
10
5
0
South Korea
Sri Lanka
Vietnam
Ports
Customs
Regulation
Services

Trade Gain from Domestic Reforms

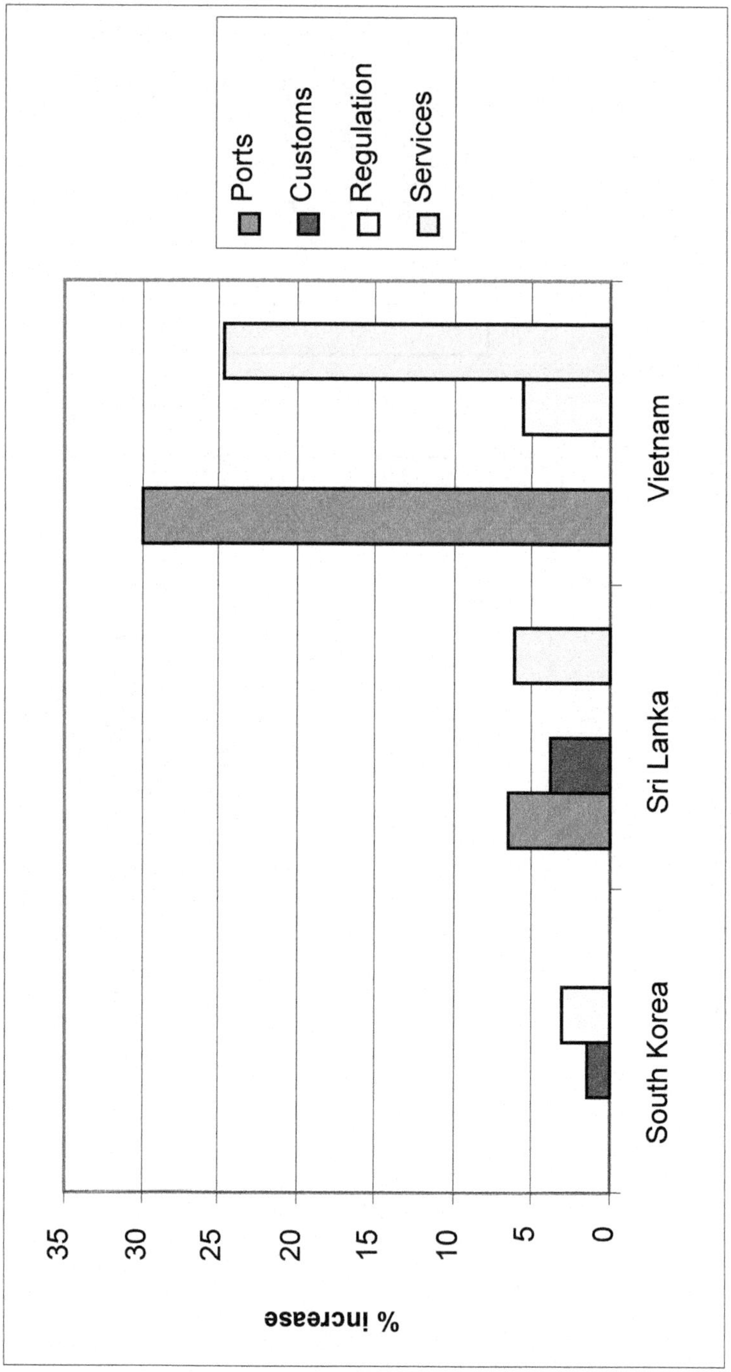

INDEX

O

P

Q

R

S

CPSIA information can be obtained at www.ICGtesting.com
Printed in the USA
BVOW07*0026240216

437781BV00005B/11/P